Reader's Digest
Treasury of
HUMOROUS
WRITING

Reader's Digest
Treasury of

HUMOROUS WRITING

Selected by the Editors of
Reader's Digest Condensed Books

The Reader's Digest Association, Inc.
Pleasantville, New York
Cape Town, Hong Kong, London, Montreal, Sydney

READER'S DIGEST CONDENSED BOOKS

Editor-in-Chief: Barbara J. Morgan
Executive Editor: Tanis H. Erdmann
Senior Managing Editor: Marjorie Palmer
Managing Editors: Jean E. Aptakin, Thomas Froncek, Herbert H. Lieberman
Senior Staff Editors: Anne H. Atwater, Joseph P. McGrath, James J. Menick,
Angela H. Plowden-Wardlaw, Virginia Rice (Rights), Ray Sipherd
Senior Editors: Dana Adkins, M. Tracy Brigden,
Catherine T. Brown, Linn Carl, John R. Roberson
Senior Associate Editors: Thomas S. Clemmons, Maureen A. Mackey
Associate Editors: Emily Easton, Catharine L. Edmonds, Alice Jones-Miller
Senior Copy Editors: Claire A. Bedolis, Jeane Garment, Jane F. Neighbors
Senior Associate Copy Editors: Maxine Bartow, Rosalind H. Campbell, Jean S. Friedman
Associate Copy Editors: Ainslie Gilligan, Jeanette Gingold,
Tatiana Ivanow, Marilyn J. Knowlton
Editorial Administrator: Ann M. Dougher
Art Director: William Gregory
Executive Art Editors: Soren Noring, Angelo Perrone
Associate Art Editors, Research: George Calas, Jr., Katherine Kelleher

CB INTERNATIONAL EDITIONS
Senior Staff Editor: Gary Q. Arpin
Associate Editors: Bonnie Grande, Eva C. Jaunzems, Antonius L. Koster

The credits and acknowledgments that appear on page 640
are hereby made part of this copyright page.
Library of Congress Cataloging-in-Publication Data
Main entry under title: Reader's digest treasury of humorous writing.
1.American prose literature—20th century.   2.Humorous stories, American.
3.American wit and humor.   I.Reader's Digest Association.
II.Reader's digest condensed books (Pleasantville, N.Y.)
PS648.H84R43   1988   817'.5'08   85-19636
ISBN 0-89577-224-8

Printed in the United States of America

CONTENTS

Pioneer, Go Home!

A CONDENSATION OF THE NOVEL BY

Richard Powell

ILLUSTRATED BY SANFORD KOSSIN

Stranded on the Gulf Coast, on a scenic
but lonely stretch of highway, the Kwimpers
do what any red-blooded American
family would do: they set up camp beside
the road and then claim squatters'
rights to the land. The authorities, of
course, try to oust them. How the Kwimpers
withstand the onslaught, of angry officials
and blustering bureaucrats, is a rollicking romp
through the larger theme of Little
Man versus Big Government. It is also
rib-tickling proof that the true pioneering
spirit still burns brightly in America.

  Richard Powell, author of many short
stories and novels, including *The Philadelphian*,
actually watched a little community of
"squatters" in Florida prosper and grow. The
people were eventually granted title to their land
and that gave Powell the inspiration
for *Pioneer, Go Home!*

CHAPTER ONE

NONE OF THIS WOULD have happened if Pop had minded what the sign told him. The sign was on a barrier across a new road that angled off the one we was driving on, and it said POSITIVELY CLOSED TO THE PUBLIC. But after all his years of being on Relief, or getting Unemployment Compensation and Aid to Dependent Children and things like that, Pop didn't think of himself as The Public. He figured he was just about part of the government on account of he worked with it so close. The government helped Pop, and Pop done his best to keep the government busy and happy. To tell the truth, I reckon if it hadn't been for Pop, a lot of the government would have had to pack up and go home.

The five of us—Pop and the twins and the baby-sitter, Holly, and me—had been taking a vacation trip down South. Pop had needed a rest. He had finished a spell of Compensation and had wore himself to a nub trying to figure should he go on Relief or should he work long enough to take another crack at Compensation. He wanted to go on Social Security at sixty-five, but he hadn't put in enough time at work to make out good on Security. So it was a matter of balancing Relief on one side against a job and Compensation and Security on the other, and it was so upsetting a thing for Pop that he had needed a vacation.

The trip had picked him up a lot, so now we was starting back to New Jersey and Pop figured he would do a little work there so he could pick up credit on his Social Security and line up another round of Compensation.

It was a nice warm day in April. Pop's old car was running good and there warn't much traffic on the Gulf Coast Highway and everything was fine until we come to the new road. Just before we reached it there was a big sign that said:

ANOTHER BETTERMENT PROJECT
FOR HIGHWAY UTILIZATION

GOV. GEORGE K. SHAW

STATE OF COLUMBIANA

I read the sign and wished I knowed what it meant. Beyond it was the new road with the barrier across it and the little sign saying POSITIVELY CLOSED TO THE PUBLIC. Pop swung the wheel of the car and snaked by the barrier and onto the new road.

"Didn't you see that sign, Pop?" I asked.

"Yep," he said.

"You didn't do much about it."

"I went around her ruther than knocking her over, didn't I?"

"I don't think they meant for you to go around it, Pop. I think they meant for you to stay on the old road."

"This is headed the way we want, ain't it, Toby Kwimper? It can't swing west without going into the Gulf of Mexico."

"It could end in a mangrove swamp."

"I'm willing to trust the government not to send me into no mangrove swamp. I been trusting the government a long time and it never let me down yet."

Well, I didn't argue, because when Pop gets set on something you can't budge him with a bulldozer. So I set back and enjoyed the ride. The new road was a two-lane blacktop that ran through some mighty empty country. What I mean is, it might seem like nice plumped-out country to a gator or pelican but it run a little lean on people. It put me in mind of the Jersey pine barrens, except there warn't no palm trees in the barrens. Now and then we passed patches of mangroves and hopscotched over some islands before getting back to the mainland again. We drove mile after mile and I didn't see a living thing but a couple of herons in the shallows, standing around waiting for a minnow to make a false move. They put me in mind of the way them doctors at the Veterans Administration hospital stood around looking at me when I come in to see about Disability. I kept telling them my back was all right, that it was as good as new. But the more I told them, the more they shook their heads and said no, it was easy to see I warn't all right at all, and not just in the back, either, and they would have to put me down for Total Disability.

"Pop," I said, "I think this vacation done my back a lot of good."

"Turn around and let me give her a poke and see."

"I'd ruther you didn't poke it, Pop. 'Specially as you're driving."

"Turn around, Toby."

There warn't nothing else to do, so I turned and got set and Pop began poking. Anybody who ever got poked by an axe handle would know how Pop's finger felt, jabbing into my back. "Couldn't you poke easier, Pop?" I asked.

"I got to prove to you it still hurts."

"It hurts, all right."

"Well then, Toby, your pop just saved you sixty-six dollars and fifteen cents a month. How many young fellers only twenty-two years old can count on sixty-six dollars and fifteen cents coming in every month, rain or shine, Republicans or Democrats?"

"I reckon not many. Only I don't know as I feel right about it."

"The Army takes a man's son and lets him pull his back all out of kilter lifting a six-by-six truck out of a mud hole, and the least they can do is—"

"It warn't no six-by-six. It was just a little old jeep."

When he wants to, Pop could give an old hound that don't want to be kicked away from the fire lessons on looking sad. He give me one of them looks and said, "I reckon a man shouldn't hope for no thanks from his boy no matter how much he does for him. If I hadn't come to Fort Dix that time to see how you was doing, you would of had a bad back all your life and never knowed it. So don't let me hear no more about that back of yours feeling good."

We rode on a piece and I began wondering how the twins and the baby-sitter was getting on in the back seat. The twins are seven years old. They been living with Pop and me since they was real little, after their folks tried to beat a train across a grade crossing and only come out tied. I don't know just what kin they are to me. Some say they're my cousins and some say my uncles. All us Kwimpers are related to each other half a dozen ways, what with living in Cranberry County, New Jersey, since the year one and getting married to each other when there warn't nothing much else to do. Matter of fact you would have trouble finding anybody in our part of the county who isn't a Kwimper. Except of course the baby-sitter, Holly Jones. She come to Cranberry County a few years back, a thin little kid with stringy hair and big scared eyes, and asked one of my aunts and uncles could she stay awhile. Nobody ever got out of her where she come from or why, but she was a nice kid, and pretty soon folks stopped looking down on her because she warn't a Kwimper and decided it was good and democratic to have a Jones around.

I turned and took a look at them in the back seat. The baby-sitter was in the middle. Eddy was on her right and Teddy on her left, or maybe it was the other way around. It's not easy to keep track of which is which. Both them twins have corn-tassel hair and blue eyes like all us Kwimpers, and of course they look alike, but that's not the big problem. The trouble is they don't want nobody to tell them apart on account of that way you dassent blame Eddy for doing something bad because maybe he isn't Eddy. Anyhow, the twins and the baby-sitter was sleeping. That is, it looked like the twins was sleeping, but there was something funny about the way Eddy had his eyes squinched shut. I watched, and sure enough he was awake and sliding his left arm slow and quiet along the back of the seat, clean past the baby-sitter and toward Teddy's head. Then he cocked his middle finger against his thumb and let fly at Teddy's ear.

Teddy must have thought he just lost an ear, but all he did was tighten up and not even open his eyes. Nothing happened for maybe five minutes, and I could see Eddy getting set to snake his arm out again. But just then Teddy moved. In a blink he had a rubber band out of his pocket and let fly a paper wad at Eddy's nose and then was back in his corner all peaceful with his eyes closed. The wad hit Eddy's nose but he didn't even squeak. His face seemed to curl up, though, like it was sorry for the nose. I should have stepped in right there but it looked to me like they was even and might quit. I should have knowed better. Without any warning Eddy leaned forward and bounced a punch off Teddy's eye, and Teddy grabbed Eddy's arm and bit into it, and all of a sudden they was down on the floor of the car going at it like a couple of buzz saws.

12

The baby-sitter come to with a jerk and said, "Boys! Boys!"

You might think nothing but dynamite would have busted them two apart, but like magic they was sitting back in their places. "Yes'm?" Eddy said. "Yes'm?" Teddy said.

"I'm ashamed of you," Holly said.

Eddy said, "We fell on the floor."

"On account of," Teddy said, "the car stopped too quick."

"Holly, don't let 'em get away with that," Pop called from the front seat. "This car didn't stop."

Eddy said, "Well, we would have fell if the car *had* stopped quick."

Teddy said, "We was dreaming the car stopped quick."

"All right," the baby-sitter piped in. "If that's the way you're going to act, we'll practice our lessons. Eddy, you begin the alphabet."

Eddy said all in one breath, "A-c-e-g-i-k-m-o-q-s-u-w-y."

Like a flash Teddy chimed in, "B-d-f-h-j-l-n-p-r-t-v-x-z."

Then they both looked at her so proud and happy you would think there hadn't been no alphabet before and they had just invented it.

"No, that isn't the way we do it," Holly said. "Each of you has to learn the *whole* alphabet, not just every other letter. All right, Eddy. Start again."

"Why can't we split it up like any chore?" Eddy said.

"Lookit the work it saves," Teddy said.

"We're going to learn it the way everybody learns it," she said. "Now, Eddy, you start and do the whole thing this time."

Eddy let out a groan a couple sizes too big for him and said, "A . . . um . . . um . . ."

"B," Teddy offered.

"Oh shut up," Eddy said.

"Who you telling to shut up?"

"Boys!" the baby-sitter said.

"Yes'm?" Eddy said. "Yes'm?" Teddy said.

This sounded like it could go on for an hour, so I turned back to watching the road. "Pop," I said after a spell, "did you take notice we haven't passed a house or a gas station or an orange juice stand the whole time we been on this road?"

"It's a new road through country that ain't been built up yet, Toby. It takes time to get them things."

"It don't take time for a new road to get cars on it. You don't think there would be a reason why we haven't seen another car, Pop? Like maybe the road ending in a mangrove swamp like I said?"

"Why would a road want to end in a mangrove swamp?"

"They could have run out of money."

"Toby, the government don't run out of money. It's only folks that run out of money."

I looked at the gas needle and seen it was hovering over EMPTY. "What do you figure the gas tank says, Pop?"

He looked and said cheerfully, "I figure she says empty, but them gauges is built to try to scare folks. When she says empty, she's got two, three gallons left in the tank."

Just then the car give a polite burp. Pop stiffened. It burped a couple of more times. "Dirt in the line," he said, and tromped on the gas pedal.

The car went into a fit of hiccups. It give a few shakes and stopped cold. "Damn!" Pop said. "Wouldn't you think a gas tank would warn a man before it quits on him?"

I knew it wouldn't make Pop any easier to live with if I said he was wrong. So I didn't say nothing. And anyway, Pop had a point. When you trust a thing to be lying to you, it isn't fair of it to turn honest all of a sudden.

WHERE WE RUN OUT of gas, the road had just come around a bend off the mainland and was going along a strip of landfill that must have been dredged up from the bay because it was mostly crushed shell. A little ways on, there was a wooden bridge about a hundred feet long that crossed a deep-water channel, and then a bunch of mangroves tiptoeing into the water on their long roots. Beyond that was an island. When you looked around, you got the feeling nobody had ever been there before, except of course they must have been to have left the road.

The twins come out of the car like wads from a double-barreled shotgun and went chasing up the road. The baby-sitter kited along after them to make sure they didn't try biting it out with no panthers. After a while she brung them back and Pop and I got out a map and tried to figure where we was. It warn't easy on account of the map didn't show the new road at all, but Pop reckoned we had come forty miles on it. "There ain't no need to worry, though," he said. "I look for one of them state highway patrol cars to come along any moment."

It began to get dark and all of us remembered lunch had been a long time back. The baby-sitter poked around in the car and come up with a carton of soda pop and some chocolate bars. We had those and then I pushed the car off the road and onto the shoulder just to get it out of the way. Then we settled down for the night, the twins in the back seat and the baby-sitter in the front, and Pop and me out on the fill with some old clothes under us. Pop complained about the shell, but it didn't seem bad to me. Most of it was crushed, and the few big pieces that stuck up warn't really sharp enough to cut. So I slept pretty good. The first thing Pop asked next morning was had any cars passed in the night. Nobody had heard nothing.

I got into my bathing trunks and took a swim off the bridge and come back feeling real good. "Things always look better in the morning, don't they?" I said.

Eddy said, "I'm hungry." Teddy said, "I'm thirsty."

Pop said, "One thing they don't need in this here state is another ray of sunshine, so you can just quit trying to make things look bright, Toby. I'm hungry *and* thirsty. I can't figure why no highway patrol cars went by. Why, a man could starve to death here."

"I think I know how we can get some water," Holly said, "but it would take a lot of work."

Pop said, "Can't you think of a way that don't take a lot of work?"

Pop hasn't never been nothing like as big as I am, but they tell me that years ago he could whomp down a thirty-foot pine with four, five swings of an axe and then drag it off by himself. But when he found out the government would ruther give you a cord of wood than have you chopping it up, he started taking things easier. Now it would run Pop out of puff to try to whomp down a sapling.

"The only way to get fresh water here is to dig for it," Holly said. "When it rains, the water sinks into the ground, but it doesn't mix with the salt water. So if you go back a little way and dig far enough, there's sure to be fresh water."

"I'm willing to give it a try," I told her.

"Toby," Pop said, "you lay off straining that back of yours."

"I won't put my back into it. I'll just put my arms."

"Well, all right, then," Pop said.

Across the wooden bridge and up the road the mangroves stopped and there was sand instead of muck. I looked around for something to dig with and couldn't find nothing. There was too many shells in the sand for me to scoop fast with my hands. I went back to the car and poked around and was getting nowhere. Finally I took a little poke at one of the front fenders.

Pop thinks the world of that car, old as it is. "If you put a dent in that fender . . ." he said.

I got down and looked underneath. On Pop's old car the fender and the body is not all one piece. Each fender is a separate piece bolted onto the body, and it was easy to get at the bolts. "Pop," I said, "I got to borrow this fender."

"You're not taking my fender. You'd get her all scratched up and dented."

"Pop," I said, "would you ruther have a scratched fender and a nice smooth throat with cold water running down it, or a nice smooth fender and a dry scratchy throat?"

Pop ran his tongue over his lips. "Well," he said, "I reckon you got to do it. But I can't bring myself to watch." He walked off a ways down the road.

I got the fender off the car, but it screeched as it come loose, and down the road I seen Pop wince like he had been stabbed. I carried the fender back to where I wanted to dig, and it worked good. In twenty minutes I had a deep hole six feet around and I clumb out. Then we all watched. It was like magic to see the water come in. I got down and took a swig and it was as nice and fresh as you would want. The baby-sitter passed me the empty pop bottles from the night before and I kept filling them and passing them on until everybody had enough.

"Well, I got to hand it to you, Toby," Pop said. "You . . . damn! Look at that fender."

It was lying beside the hole, and I had to admit it had got a might rumpled.

"Now when do we eat?" one of the twins asked.

"I reckon we wait for a car to come along," Pop said.

I hadn't been real hungry before, but what with the exercise, I could have gone through a few steaks without even waiting for them to stop mooing. After a while the baby-sitter and the twins had a whispered talk, and the twins got their fishing outfits from the car and they all went off to the bridge.

"Do you figure they'll catch anything, Pop?" I said.

"They never caught nothing in their lives. And on top of that they don't have no bait."

I walked over to them just as one of the twins yanked back hard and brung up his line and cussed a little at the bare hook. "Maybe if you put a bit of cloth on that hook," I said, "it might fool something."

"Ho," the twin said, "we got something better than that. Holly, can I have another bait?"

Holly dug into a pocket of her blue jeans and brung out a small black thing no bigger than the end of her thumb. It had one big claw that it kept waving around like a batter getting set to knock one over the fence. "They're fiddler crabs," she said. "I found some on the other side of the bridge in the mangroves. They make good bait for some kinds of fish, and the twins have been getting bites."

"You never done any fishing," I said. "For that matter you never dug no wells that I know about. Where did you pick up all this about fiddler crabs and digging for fresh water?"

"I read a lot, Toby."

"Oh, well, that explains it," I said. For a moment I had wondered if she was a lot smarter than you would think, but it warn't nothing but reading after all.

Just then one of them twins let out a yell. There was a great big bend in his rod, and he had something. The twins was both screaming at once and you couldn't tell which was saying what. "I got him I got him, don't you lose him you dope, who's a dope, he's taking you under the bridge, who's fish is this, it ain't gonna be yours very long, you're losing him. . . ."

All of a sudden it got too much for the twin that hadn't got the bite. He went right off the bridge after that fish. I was scared, because this was deep water and he couldn't swim. So I kicked off my shoes and dove after him and seen a swirl in the water by a piling and went under. That twin was down there hanging onto the piling with one hand and holding the fish by the gills with the other. I grabbed him by the pants and brung him up and towed him to shore, with him hanging onto that fish like it couldn't swim neither. "What's the idea of jumping off the bridge? You can't swim. Don't you try that again until I can give you some lessons," I said and set him down.

The fish was a fat one, maybe four or five pounds, and looked like good eating. "How are we going to cook him?" Pop asked.

"Well," Holly said, "let's see. I guess we'll have to use a pan."

Pop said, "But we haven't got no pan."

"Umm." The baby-sitter walked to the car and studied it.

"Quit looking at my car," Pop said. "I already lost one fender."

"A fender would be too big, but those hubcaps are just right."

She couldn't have asked for nothing Pop set more store by. He couldn't get a new car every year but he could get new hubcaps, and he always got the biggest ones he could figure out how to fit on the wheels. Pop said, "I'd ruther give up my teeth than a hubcap."

I said, "You better not give up those teeth, Pop. Because you sure as fate will need them to eat this fish raw."

"I might think about letting you have a hubcap," Pop said, thinking he saw a way out, "but you couldn't use it for a pan because it has a hole in it for the tire valve."

But we'll use two hubcaps and make sure the holes don't line up."

"Durn it!" Pop said. "Now I lost two hubcaps instead of one."

"Could we have three?" Holly asked. "I'll need a third for a cover."

Pop gulped a few times. "Once you start giving in to a woman," he said, "there ain't no end to it. Go ahead, but this fish will choke me."

I levered off the hubcaps. The twins took them down to the water to scrub them off, and the baby-sitter began cleaning the fish. I got some dead pine and built us a fire. The baby-sitter worked out a cute trick to keep the fish from burning. She put the fender I had used to dig the well into the fire and poured in a couple inches of water. Then she put the fish in the hubcaps, using one for a cover, and let them rest over the fender like a sort of double boiler. It didn't take long before we had the best steamed fish I ever thrun a lip over.

After we ate, Pop clumb in the back of the car to catch a little sleep. The twins began fishing again, and Holly and I cleaned up. Then she said, "I thought I might do some crabbing in the shallows."

"You won't get no crabs without a net," I said.

"I can make one," she said. "The twins have a big ball of string for that kite your pop bought them. I can tie that into a net. I can get a long smooth branch for a pole. All I need is a hoop to hold open the net. Can you think of anything we could use as a hoop?"

Pop warn't very lucky that day because I saw a nice chromium strip on the car, running below the doors. It was a good five feet long. I snuck up and worked it off, and in the back seat Pop squirmed but didn't wake up. The baby-sitter said it would do fine.

"Now what are you planning to do, Toby?" she asked.

"I might catch a little nap in the front seat," I said.

"You could get a much better nap in a bed. Wouldn't it be nice to have a big lean-to for you and your pop, and one for the twins and me? You could cut pine branches for the framework, and thatch it with palm fronds. And you could make beds inside from little thin pine branches. Would you like to do that, Toby?"

It sounded like fun so I said I would do it. I got a Scout axe one of the twins owned, but before I went off into the woods I had a thought and said to the baby-sitter, "Do you recollect Pop saying that once you start giving in to a woman, there ain't no end to it?"

She looked flustered for some reason. "Yes. What about it?"

"What woman was Pop talking about?"

"What woman? Why, me, Toby."

I grinned, and warn't going to say anything, because if Pop meant that, he sure needed glasses.

"What's so funny about it?" the baby-sitter said.

"Well," I said, "I never seen a nicer kid than you, Holly, but I wouldn't call you no woman yet. What are you, fifteen now?"

"Why, Toby Kwimper, I'm nineteen! I finished high school two years ago."

Well, she wouldn't lie about it, so it looked like I was wrong. "I reckon maybe I warn't paying attention," I said.

"You certainly weren't! You might take a look at me now, just to see how wrong you were. Go ahead, look."

I reckon I hadn't give her no real look before, but it warn't a case of having missed much. She was wearing an old pair of blue jeans and a man's white shirt, and she looked like she would have to take a deep breath before she could cast much of a shadow. There warn't nothing wrong with her face and maybe another girl could have done something with it, but I reckon all Holly figured you ever did with a face was just scrub it. She had yanked her brown hair back and tied it in a pony tail, and maybe on a pony it would have looked real cute. I wanted to be fair, but I can't say I knowed much about women. "Holly," I said finally, "all I know about women is what I seen in the pinup pictures the fellers had at Fort Dix, and it wouldn't be fair to judge you by them because when nature poured them pinups into their skin I reckon somebody forgot to say when."

"Did you like the pictures, Toby?"

"Well, yes and no. I would have to admit they bothered me."

"That's encouraging," she said.

I couldn't follow what she meant by that, and I knowed I shouldn't have started thinking about them pinups because it was bothering me. When I get bothered like that I go over the times table to myself. So I started going through it kind of under my breath. "Two times two is four. Two times three is six. Two times four is seven—"

"What are you mumbling about?" Holly said.

"I was practicing the times table. If I don't keep working at it I forget how it goes."

"Toby Kwimper," she said with a giggle, "you're fibbing."

"Well, then, the truth is I go over the times table when I get bothered about girls."

She giggled again. "How high have you ever had to count?"

"The worst was the time some girls come to Fort Dix for a dance, and this one girl had red hair and green eyes and I reckon she was afraid she would fall down in them high heels she was wearing, so she hung on tight when we danced. I counted up to four times seven."

"Didn't you get worried having to count that high?"

"Oh, it warn't really bad," I said. "I can take the times table up to five times eight if I have to, so that still gives me a lot of leeway."

"Oh, Toby," she said. "You're funny. But look at me now. Do I look like a woman to you?"

I don't like telling whoppers, but this time I was going to tell a good one. "Holly," I said, "I got to apologize. You could take a man's breath away."

She looked at me for a moment and then give me a funny smile. "I guess I could," she said. "Especially if I poked him in the stomach. Thank you, Toby. You tried hard."

"What makes you think I tried hard?"

"Toby," she said, "maybe I don't seem to have much else that goes with being a woman, but I'm well equipped with what they call woman's intuition."

That was a little deep for me, so all I done was say, "It looks right good on you, too, Holly." Then I went on about the job of building the lean-tos and the beds.

They come out pretty good. I cut branches with crotches in them for uprights, and laid poles across the crotches. I found some palm trees that have a kind of burlap stuff they wrap around themselves where the branches start, and that made a binding to lash the poles to the crotches. All I had to do was just lay palm fronds on top for the roof. I cut little pine branches and stuck them point down in the crushed shell, close together, and come up with beds you'd be proud to have in your home. While doing the lean-tos and beds I seen some coconut palms, and I swarmed up one and cut off a clump of the nuts. Holly thought they might come in handy, and I hatcheted off the husks for her.

That night Holly fixed us a mighty good dinner. The twins had caught more fish and Holly had snagged a mess of crabs, and she had cooked them all together in coconut milk and bits of chopped coconut. A man couldn't ask for nothing better. Holly had figured out how to get a set of spoons and dishes, too. Some of the palm trees have foot-long seed pods, and after they open and dry out they make good bowls. And on the shore she had found mussel shells, which made good spoons.

That evening little puffs of cool air was coming off the water and mixing with the warm land air, and the stars was so thick and close you could have reached up with a broom and swept yourself down a bucketful. What with one thing and another we didn't have a worry in the world, and so it come as a shock when Pop all of a sudden looked startled and said, "Ain't there been no cars along today?"

"Come to think of it," I said, "I reckon not."

"What are we going to do about it?" Pop asked. "A person can't just set here and not get ahead in the world. I can't get back on Compensation, and what's going to happen to your checks for Disability?"

"Well," I said, "I could jog along back to where we turned onto this road. I don't reckon them forty miles would take me more than six, seven hours."

"It would look mighty queer for a man who is on Total Disability to go running forty miles. It might upset the government. No, I reckon we just set here and wait, and hope we don't starve."

"We won't starve, Pop. At least we won't as long as this car of yours holds out. It turns out that folks can live pretty good off a car."

"Toby, you let that car be—"

Holly broke in and said in a dreamy way, "I think this is just wonderful. It's . . . it's like being pioneers."

"You take it easy," Pop said. "I wouldn't want it said we run out on the government to go off and be pioneers. If everybody done that, where would the government be?"

CHAPTER TWO

NOT A SINGLE CAR come along the road the next day. Or the next. By the fourth day we had got pretty well settled in. Like with the fishing, for example. Anybody knows you can't count on fish every time you want them, and there was times Holly and the twins caught more than we could use and times when they didn't catch none. Holly had me cut branches and make a framework about five feet by three by three, using that burlap stuff from the palm trees to bind the corners, and then she took long palm fronds and made a basket-weave bottom and sides and a lid. Then we put the extra fish, or the crabs we caught, in the box and anchored it in the shallows. It was better than a boughten refrigerator because them fish was alive.

There was a lot of other food around, too. Within a quarter mile I would say there was fifty coconut palms, and Holly and me scouted the island beyond our bridge and found what was left of an orange grove somebody had planted years ago. Most of the trees was old and dying, but some had nice little oranges even if they was on the tart side. Holly found other trees she said was mango and avocado trees, with fruit that would be ripe in a couple months.

Like I said, it warn't that Holly was so smart or anything but just that she had read a lot, and I reckon if a person isn't too bright it is real helpful to count on books. The time I found us some food didn't come from books but from doing some good hard thinking. The more I looked at the shell they had used for landfill, the more I figured there had to be clams and oysters around. So I scouted the shore and I sure did find me a nice bed of clams.

As time went on, even Pop got interested in things. I come back from clamming one day and there he was putting up a little rail fence around our lean-tos. He was using long thin poles with a bark something like birch that Holly said was called cajeput. Pop claimed he was just killing time, but the next day he was planting a couple of little coconut palms in the front yard and watering them. I couldn't recollect Pop doing nothing like that to fix up our place at home.

The twins was doing good, too. Back home they hadn't been much use around the place, but here Holly kept them at chores. Only the twins didn't look at it like it was work. They was happier and not scrapping as much and I was learning them to swim and Holly was learning them schoolwork.

One morning, maybe the fifth we was there, Pop put words to something I reckon all of us had been thinking about. "What if," he said slowly, "there ain't never no cars along this road?"

"We can get along!" Holly said. She got it out so fast you might think she had been waiting for somebody to ask that question.

"I say we could, too," I told Pop.

"Well, all right then," Pop said. "I just want to make sure I don't have to worry if there ain't going to be no more cars."

And dog me if there warn't just then the sound of a big old six-by-six truck coming down the road. You might think all of us would have been out on the road yelling and waving. Instead we just set there and listened to the truck like it was a big change coming into our lives and none of us ready for it. It rumbled over the plank bridge and started by, and then somebody in the cab yelled at the driver and the brakes jammed on and it come to a stop a little ways past us. There was some lettering on the cab of the truck that said DEPARTMENT OF PUBLIC IMPROVEMENTS, STATE OF COLUMBIANA.

A young feller riding beside the driver jumped out and walked back to us. He had a tanned face and a crew cut, and at Fort Dix this would have been a feller you jumped up for and saluted. He put his hands on his hips and barked, "What's going on here?"

"We run out of gas," Pop said, "and—"

"Don't give me that stuff. You've been camping here, and on our right-of-way, too."

I was proud of the way Pop kept his temper, because he warn't used to the government treating him like this. He said, "We near about had to camp—it was five days ago we run out of gas, and—"

The feller said, "How did you get on this road, anyway? It's not open yet. Where are you people from?"

"We're the Kwimpers of Cranberry County, New Jersey," Pop said, trying not to take on big about it.

Well, this was an ignorant feller because the name Kwimper didn't mean nothing to him. "My name is King, H. Arthur King," he said. "You don't have to remember that, but you'd better remember I'm District Director of Public Improvements and I'm telling you to load all your junk in that jalopy and get going. Here the department builds a new road through completely unspoiled country, and you come along and mess up the best view. You folks don't appreciate what the government does for you."

Pop was getting riled. "I know what the government done for me," he said, "but I reckon you don't know what I done for the government. I helped it out on everything it wanted to do, Relief and Compensation and Disability—"

"Somebody's nuts around here and it isn't me," Mr. King said. "You claim you're out of gas, do you?"

Pop said, "I am out of gas and mighty near out of patience, and—"

This feller had a trick of cutting you off before you done talking. He swung around and called back to the truck, "Hey, Joe! Bring that spare can of gas and slop enough in their tank to get them to Gulf City." He turned back to Pop and said, "I don't know why I should try to explain anything to you, but this road is part of the biggest planned betterment project this state has ever seen. The state owns the land and it's all programmed right down to the last acre. The island on the other side of the bridge will be a bird sanctuary. Back on the mainland we'll have a wildlife preserve. We— "

"Don't you have no place for people?" Pop asked.

"People? Certainly we have. There's going to be a model farm to show people how to grow things, and a model housing facility to show them how to live."

Pop said, "I guess you're going to let 'em figure out how to die on their very own, though, ain't you?"

"We'll get around to whatever—say, you think that's smart, don't you? I knew it was no use trying to give you the big picture." He dug in his pocket and brung out a pad and pencil, and scribbled a note and handed it to Pop. "This will get you across the drawbridge into

Gulf City. It's about twelve miles ahead of you across the island. And don't let me catch you camping on this road again. Why, the governor himself will be along three days from now to dedicate the road, and this view isn't going to be messed up by any campers. Joe, did you slop in enough gas?"

The truck driver screwed the cap back on our gas tank and said, "Yes sir, Mr. King. She's all set."

"Okay," he said. Then he told Pop, "Don't waste time clearing out." He clumb in the truck and it moved off down the road.

Pop said, "Well, I got to admit I am mad clear through. I am near about ready to be agin the government."

I said, "Why didn't you rattle off some regulations at him, Pop?" The way Pop handles anybody from Relief or Compensation or Aid to Dependent Children who gives him trouble is to rattle off regulations, and if he don't know of none he makes them up as he goes along. Pop says the government has so many regulations that if you throw in a few extra nobody knows the difference.

"You got to get the feel of things," Pop said, "before you can fire regulations at the government. Like that time the government come bothering me about why did I have this here car. Well, I had the *feel* of Relief, so I told the government I reckon you forgot that regulation that says it ain't right to go around upsetting folks on Relief by poking into their private life. Well, I had the feel of Relief so good it turned out they *did* have that regulation. I didn't have no feel of this today, so I couldn't make nothing up. Well, looks like we pack and clear out, don't it?"

We didn't have the heart to do much packing. We dumped the fish and crabs out of their box, and Pop rounded up his hubcaps and throwed them in the trunk of the car, and that was that. We drove away leaving the lean-tos and everything else in place. The twins was blubbering in the back seat and Holly was crying and Pop was clearing his throat so it sounded like the car was stripping gears. It was a pretty miserable drive. We gave Mr. King's note to the guard at the drawbridge into Gulf City, drove across and stopped at the first gas station. The feller looked at our car and asked if somebody had tried to strip it when we warn't around.

"No," Pop said, "they kind of come off while we was on that new cutoff road from the south."

"You don't say?" the feller said. "It's that bumpy, is it? Well, I read about it in the papers. Two lanes and a little space to pull off on each side. Anybody that builds a road these days on a measly fifty-foot right-of-way is not building much of a road is what I say. It ain't like they couldn't get enough land, either. They own it all from hell to breakfast. What I hear is they don't want a lot of cars using that road and pulling off to stop at bridges to fish and things like that."

"Well," Pop said, "thank you kindly, and is there a grocery around here?"

The feller told him where to find a grocery, and we drove there and Pop began stocking up on food. We stowed it in the car and pulled away from the curb and all of a sudden Pop made a U-turn.

"North is the other way, Pop," I said.

"You mean I'm heading south, Toby?" Pop said. "That certainly is good because south is where I'm planning to head."

"All you will find this way is the drawbridge to the new road."

"I hope you are right, Toby. It certainly would upset me to find they had taken away the drawbridge in the last hour, because I got my mind set on going back. There ain't no use letting the government get away with what it done to us, Toby, because it will get the government in bad habits."

The twins caught what he said and started yelling, "We're going back! We're going back! Hooray!"

"Are we really?" Holly cried. "I would just love it. But won't they arrest us?"

"Not now they won't," Pop said. "Because now I have got the feel of this. Toby, how wide was the blacktop part of the road, where we was camped?"

"About twenty-five feet."

"And the fill on each side, where we was camping?"

"Well, across the road there might have been thirty feet of fill, Pop. And on our side maybe thirty-five feet. I figure they dredged out a channel where the bridge was to go, and had to put the extra spoil somewheres and just dropped her right there."

Pop said, "Maybe you call to mind the feller at the gas station saying the right-of-way was only fifty feet? That's twenty-five feet for the blacktop, and twelve and a half feet of shoulder each side. Toby, we warn't camped on state land or on nobody's land. They put in extra fill at that wooden bridge and it goes beyond their right-of-way, and it's just as much ours as anybody's. So we're going back and teach the government a lesson."

All of us was real proud of Pop, and Holly said it made her think of the embattled farmers at Concord and Lexington. But I don't know where she finds towns called Concord and Lexington in Jersey, or why them farmers would be embattled. Anyway, we drove back to the drawbridge and the guard wouldn't leave us across, but Pop told him to look at that note again and he would see it said to pass this car over the bridge and it didn't say nothing about only passing it over once. There is something about listening to Pop that makes folks dizzy, and the feller got sort of glassy-eyed and let us cross.

Things was just the way we had left them at our camp, and we all felt it was sort of like coming home. Holly and the twins got right to work to stock up on fish and crabs again, and I went after firewood. I had figured Pop would be taking a nice long nap to celebrate, but when I come back to camp, dog me if he warn't working. He had built a fence all down the line of our land and had made a sign:

ANOTHER BETTERMENT PROJECT
THE KWIMPERS

I couldn't offhand think of any times before that any Kwimpers had done a betterment project, but Pop said the sign meant that the government had done a betterment project and now we had done one, too. It was a nice sign and I was proud to have it, but I couldn't help thinking that maybe the government warn't going to like having just anybody stepping out and bettering things.

WELL, WE HAD A high old time for the next two days working on our betterment project. We laid out some walks with coconuts for markers, and I built a big lean-to that we could have our meals in. Pop wanted some pots and pans and things from town, so I drove to the drawbridge. This time the guard wouldn't let the car through, but he couldn't stop me from walking. One thing I brung back was a big American flag. I cut us a nice flagpole and run up the flag while Pop and Holly and the twins stood at attention.

The afternoon of the third day we were back, we heard a siren off in the distance, and pretty soon we heard a bunch of cars coming

across the island. We reckoned it might be Governor George K. Shaw opening up the new road, so we all lined up to watch. First a state highway patrol car come across our bridge and the fellers in it jerked their heads around and stared at us as they went by. Then come the Department of Public Improvements car and those fellers was staring. Then come a long shiny car with state flags flying on its fenders, and the governor stared at us, too. Well, we had a mighty nice betterment project, but it didn't hardly seem worth all that staring, so I looked around to see if we had got the flag upside down or something. But it warn't that at all. It was Pop and the twins. They was at attention and saluting. Only they warn't saluting the regular way. Each one of them had his thumb up at his nose, wiggling his fingers at the government.

A line of ten cars went by with everybody staring at us. For a minute I thought Pop might get away with it, but just before the bend of the road horns tooted and brakes screeched and the cars all come to a stop. Then there was a lot of folks running up and down, and finally two cars pulled out of line and headed back while the others went on. The first was a state highway patrol car, the other was a Department of Public Improvements car. They skidded to a halt and a couple of troopers jumped out, looking like they was ready to shoot if we made a false move. Mr. King jumped out looking like he was ready to shoot even if we didn't.

"Mighty funny!" Mr. King yelled. "Well, we'll see who ends up laughing. I warned you. Now we're going to have some action. Sergeant," he said, turning to one of the troopers, "you can arrest these people for trespass and half a dozen other things that I'll think of when I'm not so upset."

The trooper started toward us, but Pop said, "Speaking of trespass, this is private property back of this here fence, and the regulations is the police can't come on no private property unless they got a warrant or they seen a crime. This is a free country and there ain't no law that says it's a crime to thumb your nose at the government."

Mr. King said to the trooper, "I tell you these people are crazy. This fill is state land."

"Not all of it," Pop said. "You only got a fifty-foot legal right-of-way. Twenty-five for the blacktop and twelve and a half each side. Our fence don't start till fourteen feet from the blacktop, and our land runs from there to the water."

Mr. King was sputtering like a rocket ready to take off. "I never heard of anything so crazy. It's state land and you're trespassing on it. Sergeant—"

"The last time I looked at that state law they passed in eighteen-o-two," Pop said mildly, "it said any land that hadn't been titled was free land anybody could settle on up to a quarter section. All you got to do is show me this land was titled before we settled down on it and we'll move off."

Mr. King was getting that glassy look in his eyes that folks sometimes get when they argue with Pop. "How could it be titled before? This land was just made! Sergeant, come here." They went back to their cars, got out a map and studied it. Then they paced off the width of the blacktop and went back to the map again, giving us some mean looks they had to spare.

I sidled over to Pop and whispered, "You don't know nothing about any eighteen-o-two law."

"Oh, I ain't worried," Pop said. "I have got the feel of this now, and that is a law they ought to have even if they don't."

"Pop," I said, "you are the smartest man I ever seen. It probably takes the government months to whomp up a law, and you toss one off without even taking a deep breath."

"I wouldn't want to take too much credit," Pop said. "Back in the year one, when the Kwimpers first settled in Cranberry County, there warn't nobody bought land. I call to mind my Pop telling me how the Kwimpers had a big row with the government about titles, and some state senator that knowed the Kwimpers swung a lot of votes dug out a law like that one I just made up. If they had a law like that in Jersey they ought to have one down here, and if they don't, it is about time they did."

Mr. King finished with the map and the measuring and walked over to us. "What did you say the date of that law was?" he asked.

"Eighteen-o-two," Pop said.

"I hope for your sake you're right," Mr. King said. "Meanwhile, if you know what's good for you, you'll take mighty good care of this land."

"Why wouldn't I take good care of my own land?"

Mr. King stood there a moment, and then turned and clumb in his car. I reckon he was a little upset, because he shoved her in gear and banged into the back of the patrol car, and the patrol car got into reverse by mistake and backed into him, and they done quite a lot of talking back and forth but finally got together on when to start and what direction to go in, and took off down the road to Gulf City.

Two, three days went by and we didn't hear nothing from Mr. King. What we figured was he probably got bogged down going through old laws, because them things must get piled up pretty high. Finally Pop and Holly drove to Gulf City to see what was happening.

They come back with Pop looking as happy as a clam. "Toby," he said, "I only missed her by eighteen years. That law, Toby, they got one like it, only it was eighteen-twenty ruther than eighteen-o-two. It says you got to keep a building up on unclaimed land and live on that land for six months and then you can file for a title, and if you live on it eighteen more months you can get your title for good and all. But you got to live on that land and keep a building on it all that time. One of the fellers at the county courthouse had me swear out a paper that we are starting our six months."

"Pop," I said, "I think you are getting carried away. You are a

Jerseyman, and this is the end of April and we was going to head back home as soon as you taught the government a lesson."

"I know that," Pop said. "It's just that I ain't going to let the government get in bad habits. All it has to do is come around and say nice and polite it would like this land back, and we will be heading home before you can say 'betterment project.' "

"Then I am with you, Pop," I said.

We figured Mr. King would be around soon to say the government was sorry, but a couple more days went by and he didn't come. Then one day I was out on the bridge neatening it up. Some cars had come by and tracked dirt onto the bridge, so I was out with a broom and shovel cleaning up. I had just finished and was leaning on the shovel when five big Public Improvement dump trucks loaded with shell come across from the island and stopped by me. The driver of the first truck leaned out and said Hi Mac, and I said Hi Mac, and he said, "You must work for the department so I guess you can steer us right. Is this what they call Bridge Number Four?"

"This is her," I said. "There's a little metal plate on the bridge that says Bridge Number Four."

"Good," he said. "We got some shell that Mr. King sent. Prolly you know all about it."

"No," I said. "Mr. King didn't say nothing to me about it, but then it's been four, five days since I seen him. How is he these days?"

"High and mighty as ever. He said to dump the shell just beyond this bridge, right in front of some shacks. Are those the shacks?"

"They are really lean-tos," I said, "but I reckon Mr. King don't know that is their name and thinks they are shacks."

"Maybe you wouldn't mind hopping up here with me and riding across the bridge to make sure we get it right?"

I said I wouldn't mind, and clumb up with him and we drove across and stopped in front of our land. "Well," the driver said, "I guess we back up and dump the loads here. But it sure is going to leave a big heap of shell in front of these lean-tos."

"Do you think that's what Mr. King had in mind?" I asked. "Anybody can see that would block off them lean-tos from the road. And it sure won't do no good to have more shell right there."

"There's something in that," the feller said.

"But on the other side of the lean-tos there is a real narrow beach,"

I said. "At high tide the water comes near about up to the lean-tos, so if you dumped shell there it would help keep out the tide."

"What about that fence?" the feller said. "Would they mind us taking down a section so we could get to the beach?"

"Oh, Pop won't mind," I said.

"Pop, you call him?"

"Most everybody calls him Pop," I said. "Hey, Pop!" I called. "Some fellers want to dump shell on the beach and part of the fence has to come down."

Pop said we sure could use more shell, and we took down a section of fence and the trucks took turns backing onto the beach and dumping the loads. While they done it, Holly and the twins come back from crabbing, and Holly told the men she'd be glad to heat up some coffee for them. They allowed as that was right nice of her, and one of them said he didn't like leaving no untidy piles of shell around and why didn't they smooth it out some. So we all grabbed shovels and in fifteen minutes we had the nicest shell beach you ever seen. Then we all had coffee and the trucks left.

I made a note to thank Mr. King as soon as he showed up, and have a good laugh with him about how them fellers in the trucks almost made a mistake about where to dump the shell. It turned out I didn't have long to wait. Not more than ten minutes later a Department of Public Improvements car screeched to a stop and Mr. King jumped out. "What the hell is going on!" he shouted, before I could start thanking him. "I passed those trucks on my way here and they waved as if everything was fine."

"Oh, everything is fine," I said. "That beach you sent—"

"Beach! Beach! Oh no!" He jumped over our fence and run down to the beach and found Pop there, tamping down the new shell with the butt end of a log. "You stole that shell!" Mr. King yelled. "I don't know how you stole forty tons of shell in fifteen minutes, but you're going to put every piece back or I'll have you in jail."

About then I seen it warn't that Mr. King had made a mistake but that I had, so I give him the whole story and said we would be glad to put his shell back but there warn't no way to tell it from ours.

Mr. King stood there breathing like an old steam engine trying to start up a string of freight cars. Finally he said, like he was talking to himself, "It's not that he's too smart for me. The trouble is he's too dumb for me." Then he stopped talking to himself and said to Pop and me, "By tomorrow morning there are going to be ten trucks out here, dumping shell between your shacks and the road, with me watching to make sure it goes in the right place."

"I wouldn't do that if I was you," Pop said. "There is all kinds of regulations agin things like that. A pile of shell would be a health hazard to me and my family, on account of the little stuff would blow in my eyes, and it would cut off sun and air. You would be blocking folks from going lawfully into and out of their home. I would have to claim trespass if even one bit of shell tumbled down from the pile onto our land. Them piles would fill the shoulder of the road and be a danger to traffic. And I reckon I would have to ask to see your dumping permit."

Mr. King sort of quivered, like the lid on a pot coming to a boil. "I know when I'm licked," he said. "You win. No hard feelings?" He shook Pop's hand and then mine. His handshake felt like it had been shucked out of them clam shells.

"I'm glad we got together on this," Pop said, "because I never had no trouble working with the government before."

"Ah yes, you mentioned something about that the first time we met," Mr. King said. "What exactly was it?"

"I have helped the government out on near about everything it wanted to do," Pop said. "Relief and Compensation and Aid to Dependent Children and Total Disability."

"You don't mean you're getting all those things now? How can you be getting Aid to Dependent Children from New Jersey while you're in Columbiana?"

Pop said, "All us Kwimpers stick together good, and I fixed things so my cousin Lon would pick up any check and get it cashed at the store and send me a money order."

"What's this Total Disability you mentioned?"

"That's my son Toby here," Pop said. "He was in the Army at Fort Dix and near about kilt his back lifting a six-by-six truck out of a mud hole. The doctors at the V.A. give him Total Disability for it."

Mr. King walked around me the way a feller might walk around a tree he is thinking of chopping down. "I wish I were half as disabled," he said. "Now let me give you some advice."

"That's mighty nice of you," Pop said. "But now that things is friendly and I am sure the government ain't getting into bad habits, I got something to tell you."

"I'll do the telling," Mr. King said, and he was looking grim. "My advice to you is to pack up and head back to New Jersey just as fast as you can. If you're still here tomorrow, I'm going to notify the Jersey authorities that you've changed residence and don't qualify any longer for aid. And if you think you can get any kind of state aid from Columbiana, just try, that's all I ask, just try."

"Toby," Pop said, "it turns out the government is getting into worse habits all the time. Do you think it would bother your back to pitch this feller off our land?"

I figured Mr. King wouldn't weigh more than a hundred seventy pounds, and I said, "If I swang him around by the heels I could get him out in the water, Pop. And it won't bother my back none."

"I dare you, I dare you!" Mr. King said, but by then he'd skimmed over our fence and was on the government's right-of-way.

Pop said, "You can leave him be, Toby. I don't think you could have thrun him farther than he went on his own."

"And let me warn you," Mr. King said. "You've been cutting down trees and taking coconuts and God knows what from the department's land. I can't stop you from picking up deadwood or fallen coconuts or from fishing, but if you take so much as one living branch from a tree I'll have you arrested. I'm going to have men looking in here all the time to make sure you don't break the law anymore." He clumb into his car, started the motor and drove off.

Pop said, "Toby, the funny thing is I was just getting ready to give him back the land when he turned nasty on us. But now, if you're with me, I am bent on fighting it out."

"I am with you, Pop," I said.

CHAPTER THREE

IN THE NEXT few weeks Mr. King was real active. We had been picking up our mail at general delivery in Gulf City, and first we got a letter from the government in Jersey saying they heard we had moved to Columbiana and so of course Columbiana would have to come up with the Aid to Dependent Children from now on. Then I got a letter from the V.A. saying to report to the nearest V.A. hospital on account of they heard my back was getting along pretty good now. While it is nice to get mail, I would ruther the government had just wrote saying everything is fine here hope you are the same.

Pop and me had counted up our money. All told we had about eighty dollars. But that warn't going to last forever. We still had all the fish you would want, but now I dassent go climbing for coconuts or cut down cabbage palms or pick oranges, so we had to buy some food in Gulf City, and gas to get there and back. Then there was the worry about the lean-tos. We was starting to get rain, because in Columbiana instead of having four seasons like any sensible state they only have two, wet and dry, and the wet season was coming on now that it was near the end of May. We could fix the roof of a lean-to so it would shed rain, but there warn't no way to make a lean-to so it would shed the skeeters that began to visit us. What we needed was a shack built on pilings with a screen door and screened windows. I'd have liked to whomp down some big old cabbage palms and use the trunks for pilings. But Mr. King had fellers keeping an eye on us now, and we dassent take any stuff off the government's land.

There warn't much else to do so I done a lot of fishing. We kept a mess of pinfish and little crabs around for bait, and even some shrimp. Our bridge crossed a deep-water pass between two big bays, and all kinds of fish come through that pass. I began to find out when the different kinds was likely to come, and what they ate and how to catch them.

This one afternoon there was a school of big tarpon hanging around the pass and I was on the bridge giving them a little exercise. Them fish run eighty, ninety pounds and I didn't want to land none that big but that was all right because they didn't plan on being landed with that little rod and light line I had borrowed from one of the twins. Well, I had this tarpon that was better than a hundred pounds, and I heard a car come across the bridge and the brakes slam on. I couldn't look because that tarpon was spending more time in the air than in the water and it was pretty to watch. But I heard the car door thrun open and a bald-headed feller in fancy sports clothes jumped out beside me. He was right excited. "That's a beauty," he said. "Do you think you can land him?"

"Oh, I'm just playing with him," I said.

"I've been spending sixty-five bucks a day for charter boats," the feller said. "When I hook a big tarpon, I've usually got him on a rod I could beat him to death with, and still the charter boat captain is scared I'll lose the fish and mess up his record. So he starts his boat and drags the tarpon around and half drowns him. I'd give ten dollars to play that tarpon on your light rod."

"Well," I said, "you're welcome to him."

The feller took the rod. He warn't too good of a fisherman but he was real willing. He barked his knuckles on the reel and burned his thumb on the spool when the tarpon made a run, and near about sprained his left wrist, and all in all I never seen a feller have a better time. Holly come out to watch, and I told her how I happened to lend the feller my tarpon, and we admired his car which was one of them Imperials you could have set up housekeeping in.

Well, him and that tarpon went at it for twenty minutes, and I would say if the tarpon had gone at it serious he could have caught that feller in another ten minutes, but the tarpon put on a little too much pressure and straightened the hook and that was that. "Gee, that was wonderful," the feller said. He handed me back the rod and dug in his pocket and pulled out a twenty-dollar bill. "Here's the ten bucks," he said, "and another ten for some new hooks."

"Oh, I couldn't take that," I said. "It was fun for me, too."

Before the feller could do anything, Holly gave him a real nice smile. "I'll be glad to take the twenty dollars for him, because at the moment I think he has exactly thirty-five cents to his name."

The feller grinned at Holly. "Sister, I'm for you. Here's the twenty. Buy a few steaks with it for this man mountain of yours and keep him in condition. Next year I may want to borrow a few more tarpon from him." He clumb in his car and waved and drove off.

Holly said, "I hated to do that, Toby, but we do need the money. Of course that man must be feebleminded. Nobody sensible would pay money like that to go fishing."

"That's where you're wrong, Holly," I said. "Some folks will pay anything."

"Toby," she said thoughtfully, "may I keep this money?"

"Why, sure. Maybe you would like to buy some dresses, which I understand girls like to wear when they get tired of blue jeans."

She smiled at me and blinked, and dog me if for some reason she didn't start crying. Then she run back to the lean-tos and got the car key from Pop, and in five minutes she was on her way to Gulf City.

I reckon she couldn't find nothing she liked to wear better than blue jeans, on account of she didn't buy no dresses in Gulf City. She went to every tackle store in town and bought hooks and lines and things, and at each place she told folks that at our pass we had the biggest run of the biggest tarpon that ever swum. And when she got back, she got busy collecting pinfish and crabs and shrimp for bait.

The next day was Saturday, and a feller drove up before breakfast and wanted to buy some bait and catch a tarpon. The twins warn't happy about it. They said they didn't want nobody coming to catch their fish. They had learnt to swim fine and liked to dive under the bridge and be neighborly with the snook and sheepshead, and now you might think they was being asked to give up their best friends.

The feller hadn't been fishing ten minutes before two more come along. When we got them fixed up, four more cars was pulling off the road. Well, by nine in the morning thirty fellers was lined up on that bridge, and we was doing real fine selling bait and coffee and sandwiches and soda pop. The only trouble was them fellers warn't doing fine. Way off down the pass I seen tarpon rolling lazily on top of the water, but not a one of them come around to take a bait, and the fellers was starting to say this was a place where the fish didn't get hooked, only the fishermen did. I scooped up a bucketful of little shrimp and went out on the bridge and said, "Fellers, there are plenty of tarpon out there but they are just not in the mood yet. Maybe you'd like to try fishing with these shrimp under the bridge where we got all kinds of snook and sheepshead."

They all thought that sounded good, and I fixed them up with shrimp and it warn't long before they started getting action. The only trouble was they was getting action but no fish. I would see a line jerk and the feller would give her a yank and up would come a bare hook. Well, that made me start thinking of the twins. I run back to the lean-to and put on my trunks and swam out under the bridge and there them little imps was, happy as eels, yanking shrimp off hooks and making sure nobody caught nothing. I drug them ashore and give them a talking to and marched them out onto the bridge and called all them fellers together.

"Fellers," I said, "this is Eddy and this is Teddy, or maybe the other way around because they are twins. They got something to tell you."

One of the twins said, "Toby says to tell you we been under the bridge stealing bait off the hooks."

"On account of," the other said, "we didn't want people catching our fish under our bridge. Toby says to tell you we're sorry and I guess we ought to be even if we aren't."

I thought them fellers would be mad, but instead they carried on like it was the best joke ever. I offered them back all the money they paid but they wouldn't take it. They went back to fishing under the bridge and I never seen snook and sheepshead go at it like they done.

For an hour there was a lot of fish caught, and just as we was running out of shrimp, I seen the tarpon moving in. You never know about fish, and maybe the bits of shrimp floating out with the tide and all the lively doings under the bridge got them tarpon excited. I had the fellers change back to pinfish and crabs, and you never seen such fun. There was tarpon flying through the air and fellers on the bridge tumbling over each other and lines getting tangled. And one time it looked like them tarpon was coming out ahead, because two fellers fell off the bridge and one tarpon jumped on the bridge. But them fellers couldn't have had more fun.

That school of tarpon hung around one more day and we done a lot more business, and by the time everyone left, Holly figured we

had made nearly a hundred dollars selling the bait, coffee, sand-wiches and soda pop. And even after the tarpon left, we had people stopping by every day to try the fishing and to buy bait.

We was setting around after dinner one night, with Pop and me talking about how things was going real nice, when Holly spoke up and said, "We ought to stop kidding ourselves."

She sounded like she does when she is making them twins do lessons, and when you heard that tone you knowed why the twins always done their lessons. "We're all feeling good about making that money," she went on, "but is it getting a home built for us? No. And we need to put in a line of pilings that reach out maybe fifty feet from shore."

"What do you want the pilings for?" Pop asked.

"So we can build a dock on them."

"Yes," Pop said, "but what do you want the dock for, Holly?"

"So we can tie up our rowboats."

"Pop," I said, "don't ask no more questions, because it will turn out she wants the rowboats to take folks out to our forty-five-foot charter boat, and she wants the charter boat so we can take folks to our hotel out on one of them islands."

"Right now I just want rowboats," Holly said. "Two or three row-boats that we can rent and maybe a couple of outboard motors for them, too. What I'm getting at is this. If we're going to stay here, we have to go into business, and go into it in the right way. I've been all over Gulf City getting prices on secondhand lumber and used boats and things, and I think we can do everything for about two thousand dollars."

Pop said, "My cousin Billy had eight hundred dollars once from a load of logs falling on him at the sawmill, but he warn't used to handling money and it run through his fingers in a couple years. So we couldn't borrow it off him."

Holly said, "How do business people get money when they need it? They go to a bank and borrow it."

"I never been in a bank," I said. "What is it like?"

Holly said, "A bank is really no different than a supermarket, Toby, except that it deals in money instead of groceries. And all you hand over is a promise to pay the bank back."

"I don't think it's as easy as you let on."

"I don't think it's easy," she said, "but they can't shoot you for trying, Toby. Will you do it?"

Well, I said I would, but the fact of the matter is, when you go to a bank to get money, they *can* shoot you for trying.

THE NEXT MORNING I drove to Gulf City and parked near a bank. I went in and looked around for the feller that had the money. It was a real fancy place, with marble as good as any you will see in washrooms at the railway station in Trenton, New Jersey, and along one side of the room they had three fellers in little cages with bars to keep them from getting out. Maybe they was on display as a warning to folks not to get caught breaking no laws. It looked like visiting hours because two or three folks was waiting in line at each cage to talk to them.

I stood around taking things in for a while so I wouldn't make no mistakes, and a feller in uniform come up and asked could he help, and I said no, I was just seeing what was what. A girl went by me and walked up to a little door that was mostly glass and waited there a moment, and the door give a buzz and she walked through to where most of the bank people was setting. Well, I went to that door and stood, but it didn't buzz at me, and when I give it a little push it didn't open. I didn't want to pound on the door and bother folks who was working inside, so I waited for somebody who would know how to make the door buzz open. Pretty soon along come a thin feller who looked like he had been growed in a cellar, and he gave me a frown and shoved by and went to the glass door. It buzzed at him and opened, and he started through and I slipped right in behind him.

The feller swung around quick and said in a squeaky voice, "What do you want?"

"Oh," I said, "I just come for some money, and I reckon I will have to trouble you to show me where to get it."

That had been a real dark cellar he had been growed in, because I mean he was pale. He opened his mouth and looked like he was trying to yell, only nothing come out. I asked him to try again and leaned close so I could catch what he said. It turned out he was saying, "Help, help," and it was lucky I was there or nobody would have heard him. There warn't no question he needed help fast so I took a big breath and yelled "Help, help!" for him. Well, you might think them people in the bank didn't have the sense they was born with, because they started diving under desks and screaming, and a big bell started clanging, and that feller looked like he would die right there.

He seemed about ready to fall, so I picked him up and started carrying him out to where somebody could do some good for him. Them people finally caught on that something was wrong, and half a dozen fellers run up to us and milled around. The feller in uniform, who had asked me earlier could he help, warn't offering no help at all now. He was just getting in the way waving a gun around.

Somebody was going to get hurt, with him as excitable as that, so when he warn't expecting it, I snaffled that gun away from him. Well, I shouldn't have done that, because two other fellers in uniform had come in and they got all confused and started waving guns and yelling at everybody to stand back and they would shoot it out with me.

But them two couldn't shoot it out with me while I was carrying that sick feller, and for a while not a soul could figure out what to do. Finally an older feller with white hair come across the clear space around me and said, "I think you're making a big mistake. Why don't you give me that gun and let this man go? Then we'll sit down and talk things over. Don't you remember me from that tarpon fishing last weekend?"

"I reckon I do remember you," I said. "And I am glad to see you because I never seen folks get so excited. But it is other people making the mistake because I got a sick man here who needs help."

The feller I was carrying piped up and said, "Mr. Endicott, I hate to say it, but I think everybody has been making a mistake."

"Why, the man tried to hold up the bank and you bravely yelled for help," Mr. Endicott said. "I never thought you had it in you, George."

My feller give a weak smile and said, "Mr. Endicott, as far as a yell for help is concerned I still have it in me, because I tried to yell and couldn't. This man did the yelling. He heard me get out a little squeak for help and must have thought I was sick, so he let out that bellow that scared everybody. If you could quiet things somewhat, I'm sure I can convince him to put me down."

I begun to see that things was even more mixed up than I had thought, so I put the feller down. "I'm sorry I been such a bother. Here is that gun I took off a feller so nobody would get hurt."

Mr. Endicott took the gun and called out to everybody that it had been a big mistake and they should calm down and go about their business. He turned to George and me and said, "Come on in my office so I can get the story straight."

It turned out that Mr. Endicott was the president of the bank and a right nice feller. We hashed over what had happened, and it turned out George had thought I was trying to rob the bank, which was why he had that spell. "Now all we have to find out," Mr. Endicott said, "is what you did come in for, Mr. Kwimper."

I told him how we needed money to build a shack on pilings and to build a dock and get us a few rowboats and maybe outboard motors, and that it would take two thousand dollars for everything.

Mr. Endicott looked at George and grinned. "You certainly came to the right person, because George here is our loan officer. But this is the first time anybody ever acted as if he wanted to borrow a loan officer instead of a loan. Go ahead, George, take over."

George put the tips of his fingers together in a little tent and peeked inside, and you might think he seen bad news in his little tent because he looked unhappy. "Now then, Mr. Kwimper," he said, "let us start by—"

I said, "You could call me Toby. I think you are a brave feller and I would like to be friends with you."

George's pale face turned pink. He looked sort of helplessly at Mr. Endicott and said, "We're not starting in a very businesslike way."

Mr. Endicott said, "Go on, George. Throw away your principles and call him Toby."

George took a deep breath. "Now then, Toby, a bank has to have some kind of security for a loan. In other words, we have to be sure we will get our money back."

"You can count on us paying it back, if nothing goes wrong."

"Umm. Yes. I see. But by security we mean something more than a mere promise. Take the land you're living on, for example. That might be acceptable, if your title is good."

"Oh, we don't have no title," I said. "We're just squatting on it. We can't even put in a claim for a title for about five more months."

George looked in that little tent again that he made with his fingers, and seen the news getting worse. "What," he said in a weak voice, "are the chances that you *will* get a title?"

"Pretty bad," I said. "Mr. King, who is District Director of Public Improvements, is real unhappy about us, and if he can find a way to get us off that land he will do it before you can say betterment project."

There must have been a draft where George was setting because he shivered some. Mr. Endicott said to him, "George, I'll bet not a loan officer in the country has ever had an experience like this. Don't back away from it too quickly."

George said, "I don't suppose it's any use, but let's explore another field. Do you own any stocks or bonds?"

"George," I said, "if you will tell me what they are, I'll give a look when I get back to the lean-to."

"Let's forget stocks and bonds. We might consider a chattel mortgage on your household goods, auto and other personal property, if the valuation is high enough."

"Well," I said, "Pop sets a lot of store by that car of his. It would bring fifty dollars, anyway. It's outside if you'd like to look."

"I think we can pass that up. Do you or your father have any income aside from what you earn selling bait at the bridge?"

"Pop had Aid to Dependent Children for the twins," I said. "And I had Total Disability from the V.A. But Mr. King fixed it so them payments all stopped."

"Is there any chance you could get them started up again?"

George was looking so sad I wanted to cheer him up. I said, "The way Mr. King works, we won't never get nothing more. But it don't bother us none."

"Mr. Endicott," George said in almost a whisper, "do you have anything to add to all this?"

"Only one thing. When I was fishing off his bridge last weekend, those Kwimper twins didn't want anybody catching what they look on as their private fish. So they were swimming under the bridge swiping everybody's bait. Toby caught them at it and made them tell us they were sorry, and he offered to give us back all our money. Those twins were so cute we almost died laughing."

"Mr. Endicott," George said, and you couldn't hardly hear his voice now, "I don't see that what you said is very helpful. If a man came in to *prove* he didn't have any tangible security for a loan, he couldn't have done a better job than our visitor has done."

"Spoken like a true loan officer, George. Now let's just forget tangible security and deal with intangibles. I want to find out if you really knew what you were doing when you thought Toby was a bank robber and you tried to yell for help. Do you have it in you or don't you?"

George looked at him for a moment and all of a sudden his jaw set hard and he banged his fist on the desk and turned to Toby. "Toby, this bank is about to lend you two thousand dollars." Then he swung around to Mr. Endicott again and snapped, "And at the prime rate, too. Like it or lump it!"

Mr. Endicott grinned and said, "George, I like it."

"I'm mighty grateful, Mr. Endicott," I said, "but I don't want to fool nobody. If we don't pay back that money, you got nothing to take off us but Pop's car, and you might have trouble shifting that from low into second because you got to know just the notch to put her in."

"That's all right, Toby," Mr. Endicott said. "We're making what is called a character loan. We do that now and then, although probably not often enough for the good of our souls."

So everything ended up fine, and Holly and Pop couldn't get over the way I handled things. But it warn't nothing much. When you want to get money from a bank all you need is either real good character or real bad character, and I reckon most folks have trouble because they come sort of in between.

CHAPTER FOUR

FOR THE NEXT FEW weeks we was as busy as a dog with three cats to chase. We got some pilings off a feller in Gulf City and put in our dock. We bought four old rowboats and fixed them up and got some secondhand outboards. Then we built a twenty by fifteen-foot shack on pilings and tacked on a front porch where we could eat, and a back porch for a kitchen, with wooden flaps you could let down to keep rain out but let air in. The pilings for the shack was on the thin side, on account of Pop swiped the four biggest ones for his rest room. One of the finest things about traveling, Pop said, was the rest rooms in the filling stations you stopped at. Back home none of us Kwimpers had rest rooms, just one- or two-holers back in the woods, and when the skeeters was around you would not call them rest rooms but maybe unrest rooms. So Pop wanted the finest rest room a person ever had, and he took them four big pilings for it because he said the first thing a man wants in a rest room is the feel of something solid.

It is not often Pop gets wound up about something he has to sweat over, so we give him a free hand, and he built a two-room place you would want to show off to your friends. He picked up secondhand four of them johns that flush automatically when you get up off the seat. He got a big cypress water tank that somebody in Gulf City had used to catch rainwater, and Pop put that up next to the rest room and hooked it into them johns.

But there was one thing about the rest room that you might say was unusual. Pop warn't too good of a plumber and he got them pipes from the water tank sort of scrambled. I don't mean they didn't work good. You might say they worked too good. When a person got up off one seat, all them johns flushed at once, and I mean there was a lot of water flying around, and a person who didn't jump up at the same time as the first person might get up sooner than he expected. It was all right when just two people was in one side, because one of them could say "Ready" and the other could say "Go" and they could both leap off at once. But you couldn't do that when folks was in different sides of the rest room with the wall between, and now and then somebody would get caught short and come off there like a partridge scared up out of a bush. Afterward you knowed why folks talk about a dog flushing a partridge.

EARLY IN JULY two cars come along from Gulf City and pulled off the road in front of our place. One was a Department of Public Improvements car, and Mr. King got out of it. The other was a two-tone coupe and a girl got out of it. At first look you would say she was a plain girl that taught fourth grade somewhere. She had on a dark skirt and a white blouse that buttoned up to the neck, and she had pulled her yellow hair straight back like it better not give her no nonsense. She wore glasses with more tortoiseshell on the rims than you would think even a tortoise would want to carry around. Well, you give her a second look and you would still say she was a plain girl. You give her a third and fourth look and come out the same. Then you begin to wonder why you are giving this plain girl so many looks.

I had been taking a swim off the bridge and was setting on the bridge rail to dry off. Mr. King and the girl was so close I could hear what they was saying. "Look at that mess, Alicia," Mr. King said. "There's a perfect example of slum formation in full swing."

"Well, Arthur," the girl said, "I assume that you're hoping I'll do something." She had a low voice, with the purr in it a cat has when it comes up to your ankles and wonders should it wind around them or hone its claws on them.

"You're the county welfare supervisor, aren't you? You must know a dozen ways to stop this sort of thing."

"On the surface, it doesn't look too dirty."

"I thought you welfare people looked below the surface. Where are these people getting drinking water? What about sewage and sanitation? They just let it go right out into the bay."

"At Gulf City I believe we're still using the Gulf."

"Yes, but we're building a treatment plant. Alicia, I hate to say it, but this isn't the sort of coordination that Public Improvements expects from Public Welfare. Look at those two little brats running around almost bare."

"Cute, aren't they?"

"What has cute to do with it? I'll bet they're not going to school, either."

"You're probably right, Arthur. After all, it is summer."

"You're just playing with me, Alicia. You know perfectly well you can find things wrong here."

"You always try to rush me," she said. "I like to go at things in my own way. To start with, I'd like to meet these people."

Mr. King jerked a thumb over his shoulder. "One of them is sitting on that bridge rail right back of us, listening to every word we say."

"That wasn't very diplomatic of us, Arthur."

"The hell with diplomacy. His IQ can't be more than seventy and I'd be surprised if he understands more than every other word."

The girl turned and looked me up and down. "His IQ may only be seventy but that body of his ought to get a genius rating," she said.

"Oh, I admit he's a big brute. Want to meet him?"

"Yes, I think I do."

Mr. King brung her up to me and said, "Kwimper, this is Miss Alicia Claypoole, the county welfare supervisor."

Miss Claypoole said, "How do you do. Did Arthur say your name is Kwimper?"

"Yes ma'am. Toby Kwimper."

"There's something familiar about that name," she said.

"What on earth," Mr. King said, "can be familiar about the name of a bunch of pineys from the backwoods of South Jersey?"

"Did you say the pinewood of South Jersey?" Miss Claypoole asked, starting to get excited. "Are you really one of the Kwimpers of Cranberry County?"

I got down off the rail and scuffled around a bit and said, "Well, ma'am, I don't want to take on big about it, but that's us all right."

Mr. King said, "What the hell is all this about?"

"Oh, Arthur!" she said, grabbing him by the arm. "You don't know what you've done for me! This is the answer to a social scientist's prayer! Haven't you ever heard of families that settled in one place and intermarried and had nothing to do with the outside world? Well, the Kwimpers of Cranberry County are legendary! They never used to leave the pine barrens and they never let anybody study them, and this is the perfect opportunity for me to do that. Here I am with just a piddling little M.A. to my name and I get a fascinating subject for a Ph.D. thesis handed to me!"

"Now wait," Mr. King said, looking nervous. "You couldn't do a thesis like that overnight."

"Of course not. It might take months of in-depth interviews and tests with Rorschach inkblots and such. Then I'd have to do—you know, word-association tests, sentence completion. We *can't* let these Kwimpers leave."

If you ever seen a person start finding out he has been setting on a nest of fire ants, you would know how Mr. King looked. "Alicia," he said, "you can't do this to me!"

"Arthur, you can't show me a map of buried treasure and then ask me to light a fire with it."

"Alicia, I'm going to get rid of this bunch somehow."

"Oh, Arthur, try to be calm. I may find a way to keep both of us happy. But in the meanwhile, if you persecute these wonderful people, I'll get them every kind of state aid I can. I simply won't have them chased away."

"All right. You've got me over a barrel. All I hope is you have half the trouble with them that I've had." He clumb into his car and turned it around and only bent one fender on a bridge piling as he took off.

Miss Claypoole shrugged and turned toward me. "Well, Toby," she said, "I hope we're going to be good friends. Can we sit down somewhere and talk? We could sit in my car if you don't mind."

I told her I warn't really dressed to sit around in a car, what with just swimming trunks on, but she said it didn't matter and we clumb in. It was hot and she loosened up the top of her white blouse and took off them tortoiseshell glasses, and when she done that you wouldn't say she was a plain girl after all.

"Toby," she said, "did you know what Mr. King meant when he said you probably had an IQ of seventy?"

"I reckon he meant I am not very smart. And maybe I'm not smart in Mr. King's way, but I am smart in my own way."

"I'd like to give you an IQ test. Have you ever had one?"

"Oh, a few. But the fellers that give me them tests went off looking confused. One of them said right out the test proved either I was an idiot or he was, and he warn't too sure which it was."

"Toby, you used the word idiot. Have outsiders ever applied that name to you or any of the other Kwimpers?"

"Well," I said, "some folks call us crazy, only not usually when a Kwimper is listening on account of some Kwimpers can get riled. Like once when a feller on another football team kept shouting 'Cwazy Kwimper' at me. The joke didn't wear good, so I run a play through him and he warn't saying much of anything when they drug him off the field. What I think is that us Kwimpers are not crazy, just different."

"So you played football, did you?"

"Yes ma'am. Pop give me a football when I was a kid, but there warn't nobody to play it with. So I would go out and throw that football up and run to catch it. I got so good I could throw that football up and out pretty far and run and catch it."

"You must have been magnificent. If only you could have gone to college!"

"Oh, I went to college," I said, trying not to take on big about it. "I went to Princeton."

"You . . . went . . . to . . . Princeton?"

"Yes ma'am. For a while. I had always wanted to go there and play football for them Tigers. So one fall when I was nineteen I hiked up there from home and found the team practicing and got talking with the coach. One thing led to another and they let me play. I throwed myself five or six passes and made a few touchdowns. Well, the coach took me to a couple of them professors. One taught what they called psychology, and he took me to some of his classes. Then that professor and the coaches had a big session with me, and it ended up they sure wished I could stay at Princeton and play football but they had a rule you had to finish high school first and I hadn't done that so I couldn't stay. They all looked right sorry about it."

Miss Claypoole said, "This is going to be the most fascinating experience of my life. I want to talk to you about your dreams and your friends and your parents and relatives and—"

"Well, ma'am," I said, "I don't mind talking about me, but when it comes to the rest you'll have to talk to Pop, and you'll find he don't like to talk to outsiders about the Kwimpers."

"We'll just talk about you, then. Toby, did anyone ever tell you that you're a very handsome young man?"

"No ma'am. Not unless you would count girls."

"I think I would. Both you and the two little boys I saw have blond hair. Is that true of all the Kwimpers?"

"Yes ma'am."

"You even have little silky golden hairs on those tanned legs of yours." She reached out a hand and run her fingertips along my leg and I give a jump on account of she hit a real ticklish spot. She laughed, then all of a sudden stopped, and I took notice there warn't no sunlight coming in the car window beside me no more on account of somebody was standing there. I looked up and seen Holly. Most times Holly is a right pleasant kid to have around, but it looked like things warn't going well for her today.

"If you have finished tickling Toby's leg," Holly said, "I'd like to borrow him for a chore."

"Who would this be?" Miss Claypoole said, yanking back her hand like it had touched a hot stove.

I said, "This is Holly, our baby-sitter. Holly is a Jones, but we don't hold it agin her. Holly, this is Miss Claypoole who is the county welfare supervisor."

"How lucky," Holly said. "Because it's plain to me that somebody's welfare needs a lot of supervising. We're all out of fresh water, Toby. Could you make some trips to the well?"

"I filled that water barrel last night, Holly."

"The twins were playing around it and they pushed it over."

"Well," I said, "I'll go, but them twins is getting mighty strong to push over a barrel of water that weighs two hundred pounds."

"Maybe they had help," Miss Claypoole said. "I'll tell you what, Toby, you introduce me to your father, and I'll talk to him while you do your chores."

I took her to the shack and met her up with Pop, and went to look at that barrel. I seen where a length of two-by-four had been used for a lever to get under the barrel and tip her over, and I reckon even them twins can tip over a heavy barrel if they use a big enough lever. I spent more than an hour getting it full up again. By then it was too late for Miss Claypoole to have another talk with me.

I don't think she did too good talking with Pop, because what little I heard, all Pop was doing was bragging on that rest room he had built. She said good-bye to me and said we would have a lot of nice talks later on, and that before she left she would try out that wonderful rest room. Pop and me was on the porch when we heard the rumble the tank gives when you leap up off the seat, and all of a sudden there was a screech and Miss Claypoole come flying out of there. She was real upset because she clumb right in her car and took off.

"Well," I said, "them twins is across the road and there isn't nobody else around, so I reckon this is just a day when water is doing things by itself." Just then Holly come around the side of the shack and set down on the porch with us. And she was sure looking a lot more smoothed down than she was earlier.

WE DIDN'T HAVE NO business at the bridge that night so I was out there by myself with a cane pole trying for snook when a girl come toward me. She had on a white dress that looked nice in the moon-

light. But when she got up close I saw it warn't a girl at all but Holly.

"Well," I said, "I near about didn't know you in that dress."

"I got it a few days ago. Do you like it, Toby?"

"It looks good," I said. "But of course it could be just the moon which has a tricky light and can fool you. I see you got a ribbon around your hair, too. That is a handy thing to keep the hair out of your eyes."

"Would you like my hair better if it were blond, Toby?"

"Well, I reckon I'm partial to blond hair. But a person has to take the hair they are born with, so it don't do no good to wish for blond."

"Oh, Toby, what you don't know! That Miss Claypoole of yours doesn't have natural blond hair. She dyes it."

"How did you work that out?"

"Because nobody has dark eyebrows and blond hair naturally. Did you like her, Toby?"

"Oh, I could take her or leave her."

"I didn't like to see her tickling your leg that way."

"It didn't tickle much. All it done was get a little jump out of me."

"That's not the point, Toby. The point is one thing can lead to another. I'll bet you've never even kissed a girl."

"When I was a kid there was a couple I pecked on the cheek."

"You've never kissed a girl on the lips?"

"Well, no," I said. "It don't really seem too sanitary to me."

"Toby Kwimper! I think you ought to learn what it's like."

"Well, all right," I said. "But I don't know where we will find no girl."

"How about me, Toby?" she said in a voice so small you near about had to listen for it twice. "I could give you a lesson."

I give her a careful look. She had put on some of them high heels, and while she warn't what I would really call a girl, that moon worked some tricks with light and shadow so if you didn't know it was just Holly you might be fooled. Her hair had took on the deep shiny color you get in cedar water pools in Cranberry County. "I'll give it a try and do the best I can, Holly," I said. "But you'll have to tell me how to start."

"You start by putting your arms around my waist."

"I couldn't hardly do that on account of I am holding this cane pole and skittering for snook, and the fastest way to lose a snook is not to hang onto your pole."

"Well, then, you could hold the pole in one hand and put just one arm around my waist."

"All right," I said, and done it, and it was kind of a new feeling to have an arm around Holly's waist.

"Now you draw me up close against you."

I give her a little tug and she come in against me. Then she put her arms around my neck and all hell busted loose. It warn't exactly what Holly thought, though, because what happened was a big old snook whomped the bait and the pole near about jumped out of my hand. When a girl is hanging onto you on one side and a snook is hanging onto you on the other, you have your hands full and are going to lose one or the other of them. It was a real job getting loose of Holly but I done it finally and went to work on that snook. In a couple minutes I yanked in a nice eight-pounder.

"Well, Holly," I said, "you brung some luck." I put my arm around her waist again and hauled her in close, and dog me if that warn't right about it bringing me luck. I had another real good strike, but Holly got kind of tangled in the pole and the fish shook himself off. I got Holly in close again. Her lips was real close and when you come to study on it they looked sanitary after all, so I begun kissing her. Ten or fifteen seconds went by, and I could see how a feller could get to like this if he practiced on it. When another big old snook hit, I tried to shake him loose.

Holly pushed herself away from me and said, "You're catching another one of those darn fish."

"No," I said. "I am trying to get rid of this one."

"I don't believe it," she said, backing away from me. "Good night, Toby. Have fun with your fish."

"But Holly, what about the lesson?" But she walked off, and I stood there a moment watching her and suddenly recollected that big old snook. I gave the pole a yank, but by then he had found something better to do. He would have gone fifteen pounds easy, and I wish he had picked a time when I was more interested in him.

CHAPTER FIVE

ALL DURING JULY we seen a lot of Miss Claypoole. She talked to Pop or the twins, but mostly she spent her time asking me questions and giving me tests, and she must have filled up a couple of notebooks with things about us. I couldn't help feeling real proud that science wanted to know everything I thought and said and done. The only trouble was things kept happening to bust up our talks. One time it would be the water barrel leaking so it had to be filled again. Or one of our rowboats would start drifting off, or Holly would lose track of the twins and ask me to see where they was, or something Holly was cooking would blaze up and I would have to put it out. You might almost have thought Miss Claypoole brung bad luck, but anybody with brains knows things like that is just the result of chance.

Then one afternoon Miss Claypoole brung out a real important test that she didn't want anything to bust in on, so we drove to a quiet little place on the beach with nobody around. Miss Claypoole brung out a blanket from the car and some pillows and one of them little pocket radios to pick up music. It was a warm afternoon and right nice setting there on the beach. She got out a notebook and pencil and said, "I have some sandwiches in case we get hungry, but let's get the test out of the way first, shall we?"

"Well, I hope this is not one of them inkblot tests where I am supposed to see all kinds of things but don't see nothing but inkblots."

"Those tests were disappointing. But this is different. It's a word-association test. I'll say a word, and then you say the first word that pops into your head."

"It don't sound very scientific to me. I would ruther give it some thought."

"But answering quickly is the whole point, Toby. This is a test to probe your motivations. Everybody has three levels of motivations. One is the conscious-outer level. We all know our motivations on this level, and we don't mind telling other people about them."

I hauled one of the pillows over so I could lean on it and said, "Like me asking why you brung this pillow and you telling me you brung it so we could have a comfortable thing to lean on."

She give me a funny smile and said, "That's right, Toby. Now, the second level is the conscious-inner level. We know our motivations on this level, too, but for one reason or another we won't tell people about them."

"That would be like you brung this pillow for some other reason than to lean on."

Miss Claypoole got took with a little coughing fit, and it reddened her face some. "I don't know what you're talking about," she said.

"Well," I said, "you might be feeling lazy and not really like doing no work. But you wouldn't want to let on you felt lazy, so you wouldn't tell nobody why you really brung the pillow."

She laughed and said, "Oh, Toby, you're so refreshing. Let me tell you about the third level, the unconscious-unrecognized level. It makes us do things, but we don't know that it's making us do them."

"A person like that don't know his own mind. There is never a time I don't know my own mind."

"I wonder," she said in a soft voice. "Anyway, the word-association test makes people reveal unverbalized attitudes that are on the second and third levels of motivation. So remember, when I give you a word, you say the first word that pops into your mind. Here's your first word, Toby. Hurt."

"Ow," I said.

"I'm not sure we can count that as a word, but it will have to do. Yes, as a matter of fact, it indicates a simple, uncomplicated reaction. So that's all right. The next word is king."

Naturally I thought right off of Mr. King, so I said, "Mister."

"What an odd combination! Perhaps when your ancestors left England, they disliked royalty and felt they were as good as anybody. So they would equate a king with a mister. That would come down to you as a family tradition. Now the next word is friend."

"Can't."

"Did you say can't, Toby?"

"Yes ma'am. The reason I said it was—"

"Oh no, Toby, you mustn't tell me. You would only give me your conscious-outer level reason for saying can't. It's up to me to figure out the conscious-inner level, or the unconscious-unrecognized level motivation. So don't try to explain anything, please."

"Yes ma'am," I said, but I warn't sure she could figure out I said can't on account of I always liked that song "Can't We Be Friends."

She said, "The next word is government."

"Pop."

"Oh yes, of course. You look on government as the provider, the head of the family, the father, or 'Pop.' "

"Well," I said, wanting to tell her I was thinking of my Pop, "what I had in mind was—"

"Toby!"

"Yes ma'am. I'm sorry. I won't do it no more."

"The next word is life."

Her little radio had a feller on it telling you to drive careful on account of the life you save may be your own, so I said, "Death."

She studied on me and then said right quick, like she wanted to catch me off balance, "What do you think of first when I say death?"

All I had to do was turn them words around. "Life," I said.

"That's very interesting. You have real depths in you, Toby. You have the concept that the Chinese call yin and yang—the pairing of good and evil, light and dark, life and death. Fascinating! Now let's take the word kiss."

"Snook."

"How intriguing! To snook a kiss, I suppose, is another way of saying snuck a kiss or sneaked a kiss."

That warn't it, because what I had thought of was kissing Holly and having that big old snook on the cane pole.

"Toby, here's the next. Steal."

"Home," I said, like you would steal home in baseball.

"Kill," she said.

"Empire," I said, because when you're thinking about stealing home in baseball and somebody says kill, you think about killing the empire who has maybe called your feller out stealing home.

"Honest," Miss Claypoole said.

"Try," I said, on account of I try to be honest even if I do slip now and then.

"The next word is kidnap."

"Them twins," I said, thinking of how them kids take naps.

"Oh dear," she said, "I'm afraid there's what we call wish fulfillment in that response, Toby. You don't like the twins much, and sometimes you think it would be a relief if they were kidnapped."

"Well," I said, "I am mighty sorry to hear that. I already like them little imps pretty good, but I will try to like them even better."

"I'm afraid you can't help any of your deep-down feelings, Toby. Now here's the last word on my list. Sex."

"One times one is one," I said. "One times two is two. One—"

"What a fascinating concept! Simple and primitive, but really quite beautiful. You're expressing the realization that when there is only one person or one of any species, sex is sterile. But as soon as there are two, sex becomes productive."

"And that is something a person has to watch out for," I said.

"Oh, Toby, don't spoil the poetry of it. Well, that's the end of my list, and I've never had such remarkable pairing of words. Do you mind if I read them over and make some notes now?"

"You go right ahead," I said, and watched as she went to work on them words. I never seen anybody work harder. She made notes and scratched them out, and chewed on the end of her pencil, and tried to fit them words together different ways.

Finally she said, "I think I have it, although it's just a preliminary diagnosis." She looked at me and gave my hand a pat. "Poor Toby.

We have some upsetting things here about you. I hope you won't take them too hard. Most of them are the result of heredity, and you can't do anything about that. For example, when I said steal you said home, and I'm afraid that means some of the Kwimpers aren't very honest. But you want to be different, because when I said honest you said try. Now we have some nice things, too. We have those delightful and surprisingly poetic depths that I uncovered in you. The yin and yang concept we find in life-death and death-life. And then the simple but perfect philosophy of sex embodied in the one times one is one thought. I'm really quite pleased with you, Toby."

"Miss Claypoole," I said, "that is real nice of you because some folks wouldn't want nothing to do with a feller that turns out the way I done."

"I'd like you to call me Alicia."

"Yes ma'am. I'll practice on it and see if it comes out easy."

"Are you tired after that long test, Toby? Why don't you stretch out on the blanket, with your head on this pillow, and relax."

I told her I warn't really tired, but she had it that I was, so I stretched out and she sat beside me and run her hand over my forehead to make me feel better. Then she thought she would relax a little, too, and reached up and unfastened her hair. It was real pretty hair and it come down all bright and sunny past her shoulders. She took off her tortoiseshell glasses and bent over me and said, "Do you like me this way, Toby?"

"Yes ma'am," I said. "Only now I wouldn't take you for no county welfare supervisor but more like one of them close-ups in the movies where the girl comes floating at you all misty and soft." I reached up and ran my fingers through her hair, and it was real nice and silky, and all of a sudden there we both was together in a kind of bright silky cave that her hair made around our faces. Before either of us knowed what was happening I reckon you would have to admit we was kissing each other. It's a good thing I can hold my breath two, three minutes underwater because it come in handy.

After a while she raised her head a little and said, "Oh, Toby, isn't it nice to be here together and not be one times one is one?"

She couldn't have done anything handier than start me off on the times table, on account of I had been getting so bothered I hadn't even been able to think of it. I started through them tables and got up to four times five is twenty, but then I clean forgot what came after that.

"Toby," she said, "are you sick or anything?"

"Six!" I said. "That's the one! Four times six is twenty-four!"

I felt so good about getting it that I jumped up and run down into the water for a good swim. When I come ashore, she had her glasses back on and her hair up and was acting pretty cool, and we drove back home without nothing more happening.

ALL THROUGH AUGUST Miss Claypoole come to see us two, three times a week, but she didn't get much out of it. Pop wouldn't gossip about the Kwimpers, and I didn't want to go off on no more trips with her to take tests.

"The trouble is," Miss Claypoole said, when me and her was setting on the porch one day, "as far as my research is concerned, this is a hostile environment. The whole spirit here is one of noncooperation with any and all representatives of the government. I have an idea I want to propose to your father. Can you find him for me?"

I found Pop building a walkway to the rest room. I told him Miss Claypoole wanted to talk to him and he said it won't do no good for her to ask him again if many Kwimper girls has babies before they get married, because he looked on that as a private thing between the girl and the feller. I told him this was about something else, so he left off work and come around to the porch. Miss Claypoole give him one of them smiles that looks like she is getting ready to brush her teeth, and said, "Mr. Kwimper, it worries me to see a fine family like yours living here from hand to mouth and working your hearts out."

Pop said, "Four months ago I would have worried right along with you, but it has turned out to be more fun than you'd think and pretty good on the pay. How much did we make last week, Toby?"

"Near about forty dollars, Pop. And we got more than a hundred in the bank and we been making payments right along on that loan the bank give us."

"But suppose a hurricane comes along and wipes you out?" Miss Claypoole asked. "Or suppose you have a long spell of sickness? I'm prepared to offer you reinstatement of Aid to Dependent Children, what you call Relief, and Toby's Disability payments as well. But for me to do all this, you will have to move into Gulf City."

"Why would we have to move?" Pop said.

"Because things are so mixed up that nobody is sure whether this is state or even county land, and I can only help people who are legal residents of the county. Now, the Department of Public Welfare operates a housing facility in Gulf City, a lovely place called Sunset Gardens, and I can get you in one of the units. General assistance payments would cover the rent."

Pop looked at me and said, "What do you think, Toby?"

I studied on Pop, but there is times when he is pretty deep and you can't tell what he is thinking. I warn't going to come right out and say what I liked was living here, because maybe Pop was hankering to live in an honest-to-goodness facility, which I reckon is a lot finer than just a plain old building. "Pop," I said, "it will take me awhile to find out what I think, so you tell me what you think."

"I asked you first, Toby."

"There's a fine school for the twins," Miss Claypoole said. "You ought to think of their welfare, too."

"Toby," Pop said, "if I said I liked the idea, what would you say?"

"I would say I liked it, too, Pop."

"Wonderful!" Miss Claypoole said. "Then it's all settled."

"Hold on a moment." Pop turned to me again. "Now, Toby, if I said I didn't like the idea, what would you say?"

"I would say I didn't like it neither, Pop."

"That's what I was feared of."

"Why don't both of you take your car and follow me into Gulf City?" Miss Claypoole offered. "I'll show you Sunset Gardens and introduce you to a nice couple who live there. Once you see how lovely it is, you won't have any trouble deciding."

"That's a good idea," Pop said. "But I would ruther Toby went. He's more used to big towns and facilities."

"You're putting this off on me again, Pop. I don't know if you are being ornery or just plain lazy."

"If a man can't trust his own son to run an errand, I don't know what he's got a son for."

"Well, I'll go," I said. "But after I tell you what it's like, you're still going to have to say first what you want to do."

I got Pop's car and drove into Gulf City following Miss Claypoole. Sunset Gardens was a real nice setup that covered a whole block. There was half a dozen one-story buildings of cement blocks, and each building had maybe ten units where folks lived. Every unit had its own little porch out front, with a hibiscus bush at each side and a walk going down to the street. Back of every unit was a place to park a car and one of them umbrella things to hang wash onto.

"I can't take you into the unit that you will have because it's still occupied," Miss Claypoole explained, "but I'm going to introduce you to a fine couple, Mr. and Mrs. Brown, and leave you with them. They'll be glad to tell you anything you want to know."

She met me up with Mr. and Mrs. Brown and then went off. Mr. Brown had been setting on the porch reading a newspaper. He was a thin feller with a habit of peeking at you sideways, like a hound might look at you around a corner to see if you wanted him in the room or not. Mrs. Brown was a friendly lady, plump as a cupcake. She had been setting there knitting. Mr. Brown brung out a chair for me, and Mrs. Brown brung out a glass of milk and some cookies.

"So you're going to live here, are you?" she said. "You and your folks are very lucky to get a unit here, aren't they, Will?"

"They're lucky for sure. There's a waiting list as long as my arm."

I said, "Have you folks been here awhile?"

"We came south four years ago from Minneapolis," Mr. Brown said. "I did all right as a carpenter there, but I was getting onto sixty-five and the winters started feeling pretty cold. A man can really live down here. Ellie, is it time for one of my pills yet?"

Mrs. Brown looked at her watch. "Just about, Will."

"Did I have a green one or a yellow one last time, Ellie?"

"A green one. Now it's time for a red one."

Mr. Brown dug out a bottle with different colored pills in it, and shook a red pill into his hand and and swallowed it down with some water. "Man has to watch his health when he gets my age," he said.

"I reckon Pop ought to watch his health, too," I said. "But he works so hard he don't have time."

"What sort of work does he do here?" Mr. Brown asked.

"Well," I said, "we squatted on some land a few miles from here, and Pop got interested in helping to put our place together. You can't hardly get him to put down his hammer and saw lately."

Mr. Brown said, "When we came down here I thought I might hire out as a carpenter, just to keep my hand in, but it isn't easy for a northerner to pick up jobs like that. Anyway, when I thought it over, I knew my health wouldn't stand it."

"Oh, but Will," Mrs. Brown said, "you still keep your hand in. Show the young man some of those lovely things you make."

"Maybe he wouldn't want to be bothered, Ellie."

"I'd be right happy to see them," I said.

Mr. Brown jumped up. "I'll bring them right out."

Mrs. Brown said, "It's wonderful for him to have his carpentry. People need a little something to do, don't they? Like my knitting."

"That's mighty nice knitting," I said. "I reckon a sweater can come in handy down here in winter."

"Oh, I'm not going to wear it. I already have two. It's just something to keep my hands busy. When I finish it I'll unravel the yarn and start all over on something else."

"I would think you could sell them things."

"Well, I really don't know where. So many other women here knit that you can't even give them away."

Mr. Brown come out just then with an armful of things and lined them up for me to look at. He had some of the best-made little birdhouses you ever seen. Then he had a batch of wooden signs for the lawn with his name carved in different ways, like MR. AND MRS. WILLIAM BROWN and THE BROWNS. He had polished the wood until it shone, and I mean you could have sold them signs in a jewelry store.

"These are mighty fine," I said. "Which one will you be using?"

"Oh, we're not going to use any of them," Mr. Brown said. "We have rules here. We don't allow signs out front. If we did, first thing you know folks would have a lot of junky ones, like Bide-a-Wee and Dew-Drop-In, and it would look pretty bad."

I said, "Them birdhouses are going to look nice outside with birds flying in and out of them."

"We can't put them up, either. If we did, folks in the next unit would want a TV antenna, and folks on the other side would want a flagpole, and you can see how it would get out of hand. It's kind of nice having birdhouses on the mantel, though. Except I haven't room for any more. Maybe you'd like one for your place?"

Mrs. Brown said, "Will, you're forgetting the young man and his folks are moving here."

"I forgot that," Mr. Brown said. "What's this place like, where you're living now?"

I told them about the shack and Pop's rest room and how we didn't have no electricity or gas or any water except what we carried or pumped ourselves. "I reckon it's like camping out," I said.

"Think of that," Mrs. Brown said. "You'll be so much better off here. Did you say that girl who lives with you and takes care of the twins sells sandwiches to the fishermen?"

"Yes ma'am," I said. "She makes out real good at it, too."

"I make wonderful pecan pies," Mrs. Brown said. "The only trouble is, not many people around here have good enough teeth to eat them. I'm going to wrap up a couple for you to take back with you. I make good Key lime pie, too, and that's easy to eat, but all our neighbors are tired of it so I kind of gave it up."

Mr. Brown said, "Did you say your pop built a fence around your place?"

"I reckon you wouldn't think much of it," I said. "It's just thrun together from little thin trees called cajeputs."

"I used to like making fences," Mr. Brown said. "But after we got settled in the unit and couldn't build a fence, I began to see that they are really kind of selfish. What I mean is, a fence is to keep folks out. In Sunset Gardens, everybody's lawn is open and friendly."

Mrs. Brown added, "And you don't have any of that keeping-up-with-the-Joneses about gardening, either. They don't allow gardens, and this way, everybody has two hibiscus bushes and the whole facility looks very neat. Oh, now I want to remember to get those pecan pies for you."

She went off to pack the pies, and Mr. Brown asked more questions about our fishing business. Then Mrs. Brown come back with a big package. "I've put in three pies and six jars of kumquat marmalade and guava jelly. Now you folks use all these up, because I'll have more for you when you move in."

"That's mighty nice of you, ma'am," I said. "And if we do move in, we'll be right happy to have some more."

"Did you say *if* you move in?" Mr. Brown asked. "I thought they had offered you a unit."

"Oh, they done that," I said. "But it's up to Pop to decide if we move in or not."

"Why, I should think you'd talk him into it," Mrs. Brown said. "I'm sure you see all the advantages."

"Yes ma'am. I seen them all, but I am not much used to advantages and I would just as soon stay where we are at. But if Pop wants them advantages, I will try to want them, too."

"Well, I never!" Mrs. Brown said.

Mr. Brown said, "Remember, Ellie, he's young, and young folks don't worry much about hardships. Toby, you tell your Pop that this is the finest place folks would want to live. Is it time for my next pill, Ellie?"

"Not yet, Will. Well, good-bye, young man, and I hope you'll be sensible."

I left Sunset Gardens and drove partway home and then pulled off the road and parked, so I could think about what to tell Pop. I was afraid if I told him about all the fine things at Sunset Gardens, you couldn't hold him back.

It got a little late and time for dinner, so I broke out one of them pecan pies and ate it. That was near about the best pie I ever tasted. After Pop sunk a tooth in one of these and heard he could get more whenever he wanted at Sunset Gardens, that would be a good reason for him to want to move. I thought about eating up them other two reasons, but I told myself it wouldn't be right. So I drove home and turned in the pies and the marmalade and jelly, and told Pop and Holly all about Sunset Gardens, not leaving out anything. When I got through, Holly said right quick, "I vote no."

Pop said, "I reckon me and Toby both knowed that before you spoke up. Now we got to get a vote from Toby and one from me."

"I done the work of finding out about Sunset Gardens," I said. "The least you could do is vote first, Pop."

"Well, I ain't going to do the least I could do."

"Why don't you both admit you want to stay here?" Holly said.

"Pop's the head of the family—he ought to say what we should do."

Pop said, "I'm an old man that hasn't got longer to live than thirty or forty years the way us Kwimpers die off, so whatever we do will be more Toby's worry than mine and he ought to speak up."

We warn't getting anywhere that way, and we all set down and tried to figure what to do when a knock come on the screen door and who was there but Mr. and Mrs. Brown from Sunset Gardens. I brung them in and met them up with Pop and Holly.

Mr. Brown said, "Ellie and I thought we'd take a run out here and see if we could tell you folks anything more about Sunset Gardens. Did this young man here tell you all about the advantages?"

"He made it sound pretty good," Pop said. "And you folks sound like mighty fine neighbors to have. That pecan pie is the best I ever had."

Holly said, "But we hadn't decided what to do yet."

Mr. Brown looked at his wife, who nodded at him, and then he said, "Folks, don't do it. Stay right here."

"This is a surprise," Pop said. "What makes you say that?"

"I don't know I can really explain it." Mr. Brown paused. "All I can say is, once you've lived in a house, you won't like living in a thing called a unit. What I mean is, you folks wanted a fence and you have one. We wanted a fence and we're not allowed to have one."

"Oh, I get it," Pop said. "The government is telling you folks what to do, instead of you telling the government what to do."

"That's it exactly," Mrs. Brown said.

"Toby didn't tell us none of this," Pop said. "I reckon either he didn't see it or he held it back on account of wanting to live there."

"Oh, he didn't like it," Mr. Brown said. "He said he would just as soon stay where you are."

Pop looked at me and worked his face into a kind of putty grin and said, "We could of saved a lot of time if you'd spoke up, Toby. On account of I'd ruther stay here, too."

"Well, thank heaven!" Holly exclaimed.

"The only thing I'm going to miss about Sunset Gardens," Pop said, "is having you folks for neighbors."

Mr. Brown cleared his throat and said, "If you really mean that, you wouldn't even have to miss us. Would there be a little piece of land here that we could settle down on?"

Well, the three of us started letting out whoops and cheers and talking so loud we routed out the twins, and they started running around like fire sirens with legs on, and we had a high old time. Mr. Brown said he had a lot of good years as a carpenter ahead of him, and Mrs. Brown said she would set up a little stand to sell the things Mr. Brown made and her pies and jams and jellies. Then we worked out that the Browns would build a place across the road from us and we would all have birdhouses and fences and signs with our names on them in front of our places.

When it was getting pretty late, Mrs. Brown give a jump and said, "Will, it's past the hour for your green pill."

"Thanks, Ellie," he said. He dug out the bottle of pills and walked onto the porch and opened the screen door and gave that bottle a real good throw.

"Oh, Will!" Mrs. Brown said. "You have the bursitis and might have wrecked your shoulder doing that."

Mr. Brown looked a mite worried and give his arm a test by moving it around. Then he grinned. "What do you know? Throwing away that bottle loosened up my shoulder. So those pills finally did me some good."

Well, that was how we got to stay at the bridge and got us a pair of nice new neighbors. When Miss Claypoole heard what had happened, she was real mad and said we would end up sorry we had crossed her. And from the look on her face you could get the idea that when we did end up sorry it wouldn't be by no accident.

CHAPTER SIX

IN SEPTEMBER WE PICKED up another set of neighbors. They warn't as nice as the Browns, and we could have done without them. But mostly you don't have much say about who you get as neighbors, and we got these new ones like you might get the mumps.

The day they showed up it was near about sunset. We had a run of snook at the bridge and a pretty good crowd of fishermen, and Pop and Holly and me was busy baiting them up and running soft drinks and sandwiches. A station wagon come along dragging the biggest, shiniest trailer you ever seen. There was two fellers in the wagon and they backed the trailer onto the shell fill a little past our fence and parked it parallel to the road but maybe 15 feet off the blacktop. Then they got out and unhitched the station wagon.

About that time the snook went crazy and kept us hopping for a couple hours. It was ten at night before the fishermen left and we could look over our new neighbors. By then, four cars had pulled in next to the station wagon and lights was on in the trailer and you could hear the mumble of voices.

"Pop," I said, "maybe we should pay them a call."

"What for?" Pop said. "Maybe they is furriners."

"What is your notion of a furriner, Pop?"

"It's somebody I don't know and don't want to know."

"Pop, if you don't know them, how do you work it out that you don't want to know them?"

"I just use my head, Toby. Them people come in next to us without a by-your-leave, so they ain't neighbors of mine. And if they ain't neighbors, they is most likely furriners."

Pop is always like that about new people, so I asked Holly if she wanted to pay a call with me. "I don't think I'd better," she said. "I have to get the twins ready to start school."

"I thought they warn't starting until two days from now."

"They've never been to school, so it will take a lot of getting ready."

"I reckon you don't want to visit them new neighbors."

"To tell the truth, I feel the way your Pop does. All the cars and lights are sort of disturbing. But you go if you want to."

I heated up a pot of coffee in case the new neighbors wanted some, and filled a carton with cups and spoons and a can opener and canned milk and sugar, and headed for the trailer.

When I was a couple steps away, two fellers jumped out of the station wagon and grabbed me by the arms. "Where do you think you're going, punk?" one of them said, reaching for the coffeepot.

"Yeah, and what the hell you got there?" the other said, reaching into the carton.

It was dark and them fellers couldn't see, and I didn't have time to tell them that the coffeepot was hot and that the can opener was setting point up in one of the cups.

"He got me!" the feller that burnt his hand yelled.

"Watch out for his knife!" the one that jabbed himself yelled.

"Fellers," I said, "if you had only give me a little time—"

The door of the trailer slid back and a third feller come skidding out like a cat. "What is it? What's up?"

"Watch it, Blackie!" one of them yelled. "He slashed me with a knife!"

"We grabbed a punk and he must have thrown acid on my hand," the other called. "It's burning like fire!"

Against the light from the trailer I seen the feller called Blackie crouch and grab something from inside his coat. "Don't make a move," he said to me in a soft voice. "All right, you two. Put a flashlight on him and let's see what gives."

Someone put a flashlight beam on me, and Blackie said, "If he can throw acid and pull a knife while he's carrying all that stuff, maybe we better fire you two creeps and take him on. Gimme that light and let me see." He took the flashlight and walked up to me and looked at what I was carrying. "Well, Al," he said, "your acid turns out to be a pot of hot coffee, and Carmine, the only thing he could have pulled on you is a can opener."

The two fellers come up to me and took a look. One of them said, "Why didn't you tell us what you was carrying, punk?"

"You never give me a chance," I said. "I'm from next door and just trying to act neighborly. I am real sorry you got hurt."

"Listen to him," Al said. "A wise guy."

"Ah, relax," Blackie said. "The guy's only trying to be friendly. What's your name, buddy?"

"Toby Kwimper. Pop and Holly and me and the twins live in that shack the other side of the fence."

"Hiya, Toby," he said. "I'm Blackie Zotta. Al, you and Carmine let this guy alone. Toby, come on in and meet the boss."

I followed him into the trailer. He was a nice-looking feller only two or three inches shorter than me, but he had hair that looked like he used black shoe polish on it, and a little strip of mustache and a lot of white teeth he wore out in the open. One thing he didn't wear out in the open was a bulge under his suit jacket where I reckon he carried a gun.

"Nice setup, huh, Toby?" he said. "Generator for electricity and everything. Look it over while I get the boss out here to meet you."

Where we come in was a little kitchen that was mostly stainless steel, and off to the right a bedroom with a couple beds in it. On the left was a door and I heard fellers talking back of it. First there was some mumbling, and then somebody said to stay away from snake eyes, which I wouldn't think you would want to get close to anyways. Blackie rapped on the door, and it slid open about an inch and a feller's eye looked out at us. "Yeah?" he said.

"Want some coffee in there?" Blackie said. "Little Red Riding Hood just came calling with a basketful of goodies."

"What the hell you talking about? I don't know any hoods named Red. Who's that clown with you?"

"Our next-door neighbor. Come on out and meet him."

The door slid open all the way and a short, fat bald feller come out. "Hello," he said. "I'm Nick Poulos. You're from that woodpile next to us, huh? Look, is it right what they told us in Gulf City, that this is a kind of no-man's-land? What I mean is, nobody owns it? No cops come around?"

I said, "The highway patrol come around once, but that was before they found out this warn't state land. It isn't county land neither."

"Blackie, get the full story from him, will you?" Nick said. "I want to get on with the game." He went back into the other room and shut the door.

"He didn't take no coffee," I said.

"Little Nick don't want coffee," Blackie said. "He's on Scotch. Let's us two have a cup, and you can tell me about the setup here."

We set around real neighborly drinking coffee, and I told him all about how we come to settle down at the bridge and how the government turned agin us. When I ended, Blackie said softly, "What a gold mine you got here! Me and Little Nick and the boys might stick around awhile. You see, Toby, the government sort of turned against us, too. What I mean is, the heat's on. We had a nice little operation on the East Coast, but the cops started pulling raids and we headed out here to get a little peace and quiet. What sort of racket do you run, Toby? Numbers? A little moonshining, maybe?"

"Is that like jacklighting a deer when you hope the game warden don't see you?"

"Nah. What I mean is, what do you do to make a living?"

"We mostly sell bait and rent boats to fellers that want to fish."

"Toby, looks like nobody's given you the word. Of course, maybe that's just the kind of front we need to run some games here."

"There is nothing I like better than a good game. What kinds do you fellers play? Football?"

"Little Nick might run a book on a big football game. But mostly it's roulette or poker or blackjack or craps. For real action give me craps, the way they're playing it in there."

"The fellers in my outfit at Fort Dix was always opening up a blanket on the floor and playing craps. But they was gambling and I warn't sure gambling was right."

Blackie looked at me kind of queer and said, "I see. Well, it's going to be interesting, setting up in business here. Thanks for the coffee, Toby. I'll see you sometime."

I said I would see him, too, and left.

FOR THE NEXT WEEK we didn't see much of them new neighbors. Mostly they slept during the day, and we were busy helping the Browns get their place finished across the road from us. But then one day some trucks showed up with loads of pilings and lumber. Then a bulldozer. Then a crew of carpenters that began to put up the framing for a building on the pilings. Then out in the pass a dredge come in, to dig a channel to the place. Then come a barge with a pile driver on it, to put in pilings for a dock. In three, four days we hardly knowed the spot.

Pop done a lot of grumbling about all that. He was riled because the first day the bulldozer was working, the feller running it knocked down Pop's fence. Blackie come around to say how sorry he was, and for us not to worry on account of he would see we got an even better fence. Well, in a way he done that. But it warn't a cajeput fence. It was one of them heavy wire fences like they put around factories, and it ended up more their fence than ours. It run between us and them, and then across the front of their place and down the other side right to the water. And when you took a good look, you seen they had moved ten feet closer to us in putting up the fence. I started telling Blackie how they come onto our land, but it begun to make him feel bad from getting the idea we didn't like our new fence, so I didn't push it with him.

After I got him cheered up by saying we liked the fence pretty good, he took me into the trailer and showed me the plans of their new place. It would have a bar, a big room to play games in, an office and a kitchen, and a place to sleep. "We're not putting in a lot of dough this season," Blackie said. "We'll see how it works out first. If we make out all right with the winter visitors we might add a restaurant and night club and a marina for yachts next year."

"Them games you're going to have," I said. "Are you fellers fixing to have bets and all?"

"Sure. People like to have a little flutter with their dough."

"But Blackie, that's gambling, and there is laws agin it."

"Don't worry. This isn't state or county land, is it?"

"Well, no, but—"

"If it isn't state or county land, the laws don't apply. And that makes it all right to have a little friendly gambling, don't it?"

"I got to hand it to you for working it out real smart," I said. "But there is just one thing, Blackie. Around the end of October, we will have been here six months with a building up on our land, and then we can file a claim. Maybe that will make this county land, and the county laws agin gambling will take hold."

Blackie give a jump and said, "What's that again?"

"When we first come here," I said, "the government was trying to run us off, but there's a law that says if you keep a building up on unclaimed land and live there for six months, then you can file for a title. Back at the end of last April we started our six months. So around the end of next month, Pop will file our claim."

"Wow!" Blackie said. "I got to let Nick hear this."

He went into the bedroom and got Little Nick, and had me go over the whole thing again. "Puts a new light on things, don't it, Nick?" Blackie said.

"This is the sweetest setup a guy ever run into," Little Nick said, "and nobody is gonna mess it up. Let's go see the kid's old man now."

We went over to our place and set down. Then Little Nick said to Pop, "The kid here says you're gonna put in a claim for this land the end of October."

"That's the way of it," Pop said.

"You're making a big mistake," Little Nick said. "That's likely to bring this land under county control. We'll have cops and everything."

"I got nothing agin cops," Pop said.

"I got nothing against them either," Little Nick said. "But sometimes cops get in your hair. So don't let's ask for trouble."

"It's right nice of you to warn us," Pop said. "But I reckon we'll be putting in a claim anyways. I want Toby to have a place he can call his own and he can't hardly call it his own if he don't have a regular claim on it."

Nick reached into his pocket and brung out a big wad of money and started to count off bills. "I like to do things nice if I can. Here's two thousand bucks," he said. He put a pile of bills on the table. "Blackie and me want to buy your place."

Pop said, "We already got two thousand dollars in this place, which Toby borrowed off the bank."

Little Nick counted off some more bills and dropped them on the pile. "I'll make it five grand."

"I like it here," Pop said. "I'm not fixing to sell. And I ain't going to change my mind so there's no use talking."

Blackie scratched at an itch he found inside his suit jacket and said, "Nick, we're way off base."

"Yeah, it looks as if we are." Little Nick picked up his money and stared at it like it had let him down. "Well," he said, "I gave it a try."

Nick and Blackie's place opened the next week and folks was coming from Gulf City and even the East Coast to get down their bets. And that's when our troubles started. I went down to check our dock and found all our rowboats gone. They had been tied up good and I knowed they hadn't untied themselves. It was lucky I went down when I did, because the tide hadn't had time to take them far and I swum out and got them all back. But I couldn't set on the dock every night watching that it didn't happen again, so I took to mooring the rowboats a ways out in the water and swimming back. That stopped the boat trouble. But it turned out we had traded in boat trouble for other kinds, because one night somebody opened up the live bait boxes that was floating beside the dock with our crabs and shrimp and minnows in them and all the bait got away. So I took to mooring them bait boxes out by the rowboats.

Then a few nights later a car drove past our shack and somebody heaved a jar of green paint in through the window. The jar broke and spattered our place some. Well, that warn't so bad, on account of we had been trying to fix on a color to paint the inside of the shack and that green was a nice cool shade and looked pretty good. But the next night somebody come by in a car and thrun a rock through the window and fired a shot in after it. The green paint had turned out handy, but there is nothing much you can do with a rock and a used bullet.

There was a paper wrapped around the rock, and it said, "If you're smart you'll get out before they have to carry you out." Pop and Holly got the idea Little Nick and Blackie had something to do with what was happening, so I decided to go around and talk to Blackie about it.

"Toby," he said, "it hurts me to have you think we'd pull stuff like that."

"Well," I said, "if it's not you folks, who is it?"

"In about three weeks you're gonna put in a legal claim for that property of yours, aren't you?"

"That's right, Blackie. And maybe you and Little Nick might want to run us off our place before the time is up."

"Maybe you ought to think about other guys who don't want you to put in a legal claim."

"What other guys, Blackie?"

"The way I get it, the government is down on you. Maybe the Department of Public Welfare figures you need more ventilation in your shack and drilled a hole with a forty-five slug."

"That's a real interesting idea, Blackie. And it's smart of you to guess it was a forty-five slug on account of that's what it was. But I still don't know what we ought to do about it."

"You can always sell out to Little Nick and me."

"But then you might get them bullets."

"Anything for a friend, Toby."

"Well," I said, "I don't reckon we will be selling out, but I'm glad to know you and me are still friends."

I told Pop and Holly about our talk, but they still warn't satisfied.

And them troubles kept on. One night it would be a stink bomb thrun into our rest room, and the next it would be a dead fish dropped in our barrel of drinking water. Like Blackie said, maybe them things was done by the government, but there was other things going wrong that you had to blame on Little Nick and Blackie. Some pretty rough fellers was coming out with their women to play them gambling games, and they done a lot of drinking at Little Nick's bar, and whooped and hollered at all hours. Near about every night there was a scrap of some kind, and once the Browns got an empty whiskey bottle through their window. I seen we had to do something, and I drove into Gulf City one morning and told the sheriff what was going on.

"Well," he said, giving a little yawn but covering it real polite with his hand, "I'd like to help, but you folks aren't on county land so I can't do a thing. You might talk to the state highway patrol, but they can't operate off the road, and anyway, they're kind of down on you people for squatting on land the state forgot to claim. Looks to me like you have a little law problem of your own out there."

I said, "What do folks do when they got a law problem like this and can't count on no law officers?"

"I guess you elect your own. It won't be legal, but as far as I can see, nothing's legal out there."

Well, that give me an idea. I talked to Pop and Holly and then to the Browns, and we called a town meeting for that afternoon to elect a law officer. To be fair about it, I told Nick and Blackie and invited them to come and vote. Little Nick give a grunt. "You clowns have gone nuts!" He turned to Blackie. "We been too easygoing. I told you last week we oughtta quit foolin' around."

"Now wait," Blackie said. "I got an idea. I think we ought to give that meeting a whirl. Count us in, Toby."

We set the meeting for three that afternoon on our porch. When the time come, Little Nick and Blackie warn't there but we started off anyways. Holly knowed how to run a meeting from going to them in high school, so we elected her to what they call the chair, which is a person who sets at a table and bangs on it when folks talk too much. Holly asked if we had any old business, and then said that we had no old business because we hadn't had no meetings before. We got to new business finally and I brung up the bullet I had dug out of our wall and the rock somebody had thrun into the shack. I had no more than started on the other troubles when eight fellers come crowding onto our porch. There was Little Nick and Blackie, Al and Carmine, and four of the fellers that run the games. We told them what we had done so far.

Blackie said, "All of us have a lot of work to do so let's get on with the voting."

Holly said, "The chair rules you're out of order."

Blackie said, "I know something about meetings, too, sister. I move that the chair is out of order. All in favor say aye."

Every one of them fellers that had just come in yelled "Aye!"

"Opposed?" Blackie said.

The Browns and Pop and me yelled "No," but we couldn't make as much noise as them eight.

"Motion carried," Blackie said. "I move we elect a new chairman and that it's Carmine. All in favor?" There was another yell that drowned out the rest of us, and Carmine shoved up to the table and kind of nudged Holly out of the way and set down.

"Now hold on, Carmine," I said. "This don't look right to me and—"

"You're out of order," Carmine said, giving me a shove. "Are there any motions?"

"Yes," Blackie said. "I move we elect Nick mayor of this town."

They all yelled "Aye" again and Little Nick bowed and smiled and said he would try to be a good mayor.

From then on things got too fast to follow, and Pop was mumbling, the Browns was looking scared, and Holly was crying. Among the things them fellers done was pass a tax of two hundred dollars on every property owner and it had to be paid in two days or you would lose your furniture. And them fellers was all laughing and carrying on, and I was getting worried.

Then Holly edged up to me and gulped and said, "Toby, everything they're doing is out of order. It's out of order because only Little Nick and Blackie live here and have the right to vote. Al and Carmine and those four other men can't vote because they don't live here."

"I am real glad you brung that up," I said, "because now we will get things straightened out." All this time I had been holding the rock that had been thrun into our shack. It was as big as my two fists and must have weighed five pounds. I banged on the table with that rock

and yelled "Order! Order!" I am not sure them fellers would have listened, but I am sorry to say that I warn't watching where I banged that rock and it come down on Carmine's little finger. He let out a howl and everybody shut up and stared at him jumping up and down and sucking his finger.

"Fellers, fellers!" I said. "I'm real sorry I mashed Carmine's finger, but if he hadn't been up here in the chair where he hadn't ought to be, it wouldn't have happened. I have got to tell you that nothing you have done is in order, because only folks that live in this here town can vote. That means Nick and Blackie. You other fellers live in Gulf City and just come out here to work. So I move we put Holly back in the chair and forget everything that's been done. All in favor?"

A big yell of "Ayes" and "Noes" went up. I said, "The ayes have it by five to two, so now we will—"

"Toby!" Holly screamed. "Watch it!"

What had happened while I took that vote was that Carmine dug some brass knuckles out of his pocket and put them on the hand which hadn't been mashed. When I swung around after Holly yelled, I seen Carmine starting to throw a punch at me and I thrun up a hand to block it. Well, I am sorry to say that the hand I thrun up was the one with the rock in it, and Carmine's brass knuckles come whamming into that rock and I reckon he felt the jar clear up his arm and over his shoulder and down to his heels. He howled, but I didn't have no time to listen because Al come at me with a blackjack. I wanted to get out of the way and didn't want to be carrying no extra weight so I dropped that rock and it come down on Al's right foot. He yelled and began jumping up and down on one foot. I didn't want him getting in trouble with that blackjack and anyways I needed something to rap on that table with, so I reached over, took his blackjack and rapped on the table. That place quieted down nice as you please but for a little moaning from Carmine and Al.

"Folks," I said, "I reckon we will go back to where we was before this meeting got out of order. Holly, you take over the chair again."

Holly whispered to Pop, and Pop said, "I move we elect Toby sergeant at arms to keep order." Mr. Brown said he would second that motion and even third it on account of it sounded so good to him. Holly called for a vote and I got elected. I felt mighty good about that, because at Fort Dix I never got to be nothing but a private. Then Mr. Brown moved we adopt some law around town and there was a lot of talk about what laws we should have, and nobody was getting nowhere what with all the laws to pick from.

Finally I said, "Why don't we just pass one law? I move it is agin the law in this town to do things you ought to be ashamed of doing."

Blackie laughed and said, "Who's gonna decide what I ought to be ashamed of doing?"

"Well," I said, "you ought to be the one to decide that. But if you can't, I reckon the rest of us could help you out on it."

"What a law!" Blackie said. "You don't spell out what's wrong and you don't spell out the penalty."

Mrs. Brown said, "I think it's a wonderful law. From what I hear, a lot of trouble comes from trying to put everything you can think of in a law, because then other folks try to find something you forgot to put in. If you don't mind my saying so, it's kinda like a three-way-stretch girdle that you can fit to things. I second Toby's law."

Holly called for a vote, and my law got passed. I felt real good about that, because not everybody gets his first law passed. Then Mrs. Brown moved I be elected law officer and I got that, too. After that we closed the meeting and folks come up to shake my hand. Nick and Blackie come up to me, too, and Blackie brung out a badge from his pocket and pinned it on my shirt.

"There you are, Toby," he said. "Now you have a star like a real live deputy, and I only hope you stay that way. Alive, I mean."

"I'm real obliged," I said. "But I hope you didn't take this off no deputy sheriff when he warn't looking."

"The sheriff of Palm County gave it to me," Blackie said. "You'd be surprised how many cops get along good with me."

Little Nick said, "I think you're making a big mistake, Blackie."

"Can't a guy have a little fun?"

Little Nick said, "I ain't sure who the joke will be on."

"Well, I am," Blackie said. "I'm gonna call up a few pals of mine and get them to run over, in case of trouble. I want to be sure they know Toby when they see him."

"I get it," Little Nick said. "You're talking sense after all." He turned to me and said, "Keep that star shined up good, Toby. I wouldn't want these pals of Blackie's to miss you."

"Yes sir," I said. "I will do that little thing."

That night I spent an hour shining up that badge. Then after supper I took off for a little jog down the road. I always liked doing a little run of four, five miles, and now that I was law officer and had to keep in shape I was going to be sure to jog every night.

When I come back I visited around at the Browns' to see if they had all the law and order they needed, and they said things was fine, but would I just make sure the noise quieted down at Little Nick's after midnight so folks could sleep. I said I would. I had been hoping Little Nick and Blackie would run things nicer at their place now that we had law and order, but that night they was making more noise than ever and I went around to ask them to be quiet.

Little Nick and Blackie came to the door. "You want things quiet?" Little Nick said. "Go ahead and quiet them."

It was right nice of Little Nick to say that, and I went into the room where they was gambling and walked around whispering to folks to make a little less noise, but they didn't pay what you would call any real attention. I went back to the doorway where Little Nick and Al and Carmine was standing and told them I warn't making out very good. I looked around and seen a switch box on the wall, and I recollected from having watched the place being built that a switch in that box connected up their generator with all the lights. I thought if I flashed the lights a few times I could get folks to listen to me. So I opened the box and took hold of the switch.

"Take your hand off that!" Little Nick shouted.

"All I am going to do is flick these here lights a few times."

Little Nick turned to Al and Carmine. "If he don't beat it, take him."

I seen I was getting into trouble, because Al had got himself another blackjack and Carmine had put on his brass knuckles. But there warn't no way I could back out. I flipped the light switch on and off twice and yelled, "Everybody quiet!" Either that yell or the lights going off and on done the trick, and folks turned to look at me. I reckon everybody saw that star of mine because they got real quiet.

"Folks," I said, "as the law officer around here I got to—"

From the back of the room a feller yelled, "It's a raid!"

That turned out to be the wrong thing for him to say. Women started screaming and fellers started running and Al and Carmine come at me. All I could think of was that the switch box would be a handy thing to have between me and the blackjack and the brass knuckles. So I wrenched it out of the wall and all them lights went out. Al and Carmine jumped somebody but it warn't me, and there was an awful fuss, and I didn't have no idea what was happening on account of all the yells and screams and noise of tables busting and folks going out through windows taking the screens along with them. Outside, things was real active in the parking lot, and not many fenders got out of there whole. For about ten minutes you would have said I done a poor job in quieting things down. But after all them folks was gone, there warn't a sound. That is, not unless you counted Little Nick saying to Blackie, "You and your damn star."

AFTER SUPPER THE next night, Little Nick and Blackie stopped by our shack and said they heard a good way to relax and forget your troubles was to go fishing, and they would like to try fishing off the bridge if we would show them how. I was all set to do that but they said no, they didn't want to stop me from running my four, five miles and for me to go ahead, they would let Pop and Holly and the twins show them about fishing. So I started off.

It was a middling dark night with no moon, but I don't have no trouble seeing in the dark and I ran along the road at a good clip. After maybe a couple miles I heard a car coming up behind me, and swung over to the side of the road to give it plenty of room. The scrub pine and palmettos lit up ahead of me from his lights and I reckoned he must see me and would watch out where he drove. Well, it was good I was listening to the sound of that feller's car because at the last moment his tires give a screech like he had twisted the wheel. I didn't waste no time. I dove off that road and so his left front fender only dusted off my pants as he went roaring by.

As I picked myself up, I heard his brakes clamp on. The car slued around and I see four fellers was in the car and they was yelling at each other. Likely they was drunk and going to get hurt if they kept on. Sure enough, they didn't see the drainage ditch by the road and got a couple of wheels stuck in it. They was still yelling at each other and didn't hear me when I run up.

My first look in the car showed me them fellers was on a hunting trip. Lucky for them I warn't a game warden because the deer and turkey season hadn't opened yet, and anyways, it is agin the law to hunt with a repeating shotgun and a burp gun like they had. I wanted to keep them fellers out of trouble, and before they knowed I was there I reached in beside the driver, switched off the ignition and yanked out the key. "Fellers," I said, "you are all drunk and I'm not giving this key back until you sleep it off."

For a moment they just stared at me. Then the one with the shotgun tried to swing it around on me, but if there is one thing I am not, it is stupid, and I had knowed all along that a bunch of likkered-up hunters was not going to like me taking their car key. By the time that feller had his shotgun ready to use on me, I had run around back of the car and jumped into the woods.

They come piling out of the car, mad as fire ants when you kick their nest, and let off some shots at the wrong side of the road. From the sound of it, they had pistols as well as the shotgun and the burp gun. I figured I hadn't ought to leave them fellers because they was too drunk for their own good. There is nothing like a long walk to sober a feller up, and that is what I thought I had better give them. So I moved back into the scrub pine and palmettos and called, "Here I am, fellers." Then I hit the ground.

The next minute was kind of like wriggling along the combat course at Fort Dix. Of course, being drunk they couldn't shoot straight, but it turned out they was lucky and a pattern of shot clipped the twigs right over me. Then they come in after me. The way they moved, crashing along like bulldozers, I could tell they was city fellers and I had nothing to worry about. The only thing was a couple of them had flashlights, and I had to make sure I didn't get caught in no flashlight beam.

I kept calling to them, leading them deeper into the woods and away from the road. Then I dropped off to the side and after they had plowed by, I come up behind the one that had a flashlight and the shotgun. At the last moment he heard me and give a jump. "Jack?" he whispered. "That you, Jack?"

"Yep, it's me," I whispered back. "I just seen him hiding over there. I'll hold the flashlight and you shoot him."

"Swell," he said, and he let me take the flashlight. "Where is he?"

I yanked the shotgun off him. "He's right here," I said, and switched off the flashlight and snuck away.

The way that feller begun carrying on you might have thought I took his scalp along with his gun and light. He started running and falling and running again, yelling for Jack and Red and Izzy, and howling about how the guy had nearly got him. In all that noise it warn't no trouble to move up beside the next feller. "Nice shooting," I said.

"Yeah, but did I get him?"

"I reckon not," I said, and reached over and snagged the burp gun off him. Well, he went off faster than you would think a man could, and headed toward them others. Then all four kind of huddled together like they was getting cold. What they had left now was one flashlight and two pistols.

There is a way of yelling in the woods that don't give away where you are. You cup your hands and yell through them, sending the sound up in the air and off to one side. So I done that and called, "Fellers, you are in a bad way." One of them took a shot, but he was way off. "Fellers," I called, "I have got a burp gun and a shotgun, and these here woods is just like home to me. So if you and me do some more shooting, I give you one guess who gets hurt."

"Look, Mac, it was all a mistake."

"It's always a mistake to act like you done."

"You quit and we'll quit, Mac."

I said, "I am not going to quit until I get that flashlight and them pistols. Switch on the light, put it down and put the pistols where the light shines on them, and move about twenty feet away from them."

"The hell with you, Mac."

"That is not very nice talk, fellers." And I give them a real low burst from the burp gun that kicked some pine needles over them.

"Lay off, lay off!" one of them yelled. "You can have the hardware."

"Thank you, fellers," I said, and before long I seen the flashlight start glowing on the ground and some metal shining in the beam. Then I heard them fellers move away.

I took my time creeping up behind the light. I wormed out of my shirt and reached out and dropped it over the flashlight. That made it dark again. I figured if anybody wanted to shoot up my shirt, I would ruther not be inside it. Nothing happened, so I squirmed forward, snuck a hand under the shirt, turned off the flashlight, gathered up the two pistols and crept away.

When I had put enough trees between me and them I yelled, "Fellers, I will leave your key in the ignition, and I hope you will not do no more drunken driving."

"Hey," one of them called in a weak voice. "You're not going to leave us in this jungle, are you?"

"This isn't a jungle," I said. "This is just a plain old piney wood. The road is east of you. If you wait till morning and head for the sun you can't miss it."

"Yeah, but what about swamps and alligators and rattlers?"

I said, "There is a swamp about a mile southwest of here, and I give you my word it won't sneak up on you if you stay put. The alligators will stay pretty close to the swamp, too. I reckon you can find some real big rattlers in here if you try hard, so if you do not want rattlers you had better stay right there till it's light. . . . Well, good night, fellers."

I headed back to their car and left the flashlight there and put the key in the ignition. I took the guns because I felt better having them with me ruther than with those fellers, and I started home.

When I got there I could see a couple lanterns on the bridge where Pop and Holly and the twins was teaching Little Nick and Blackie how to fish. As I come to the steps of our shack I spotted a shadow ducking behind one of the pilings. I was a little jumpy and all I could think was that one of them fellers had managed to get out of the piney wood and get back here to lay for me. I put the burp gun on automatic and said, "Who's that?"

Nobody answered, so I run under the shack and come up on one side of that piling while the feller behind it was peeking around the other side. I jabbed the muzzle of the burp gun in his ribs and said, "I gotcha."

He turned and I seen I had made a mistake. It was only Carmine. He warn't laying for me, neither, on account of he had a wrapped package in one hand and a gallon jug in the other, ruther than his brass knuckles. But I didn't have time to say I was sorry because Carmine took one look at that burp gun, dropped the package and the jug and run like mad down the road.

I picked up the jug and unscrewed the top and gave a sniff. It was kerosene. Likely Carmine had asked Pop if he could borrow some for a lantern, on account of me leaving them with no lights the night before. I didn't know what was in the package, but it could have been a lantern, even if it was a mite small for one. I knowed Little Nick and Blackie would need light in their place, so I took the jug and the package over there and stuck them inside the front door. Then I headed for the bridge. Blackie had an interest in guns and I took the burp gun along to show him.

When I come onto the bridge I called, "Hello, folks. How is the fishing?"

I must have startled Little Nick because he was leaning over the rail when I called and he almost fell in the water. Blackie was on edge, too, because he whirled around and went into a crouch. Little Nick said to him, "If he's carrying what I think he's carrying, don't make no wrong moves."

Pop asked, "What you got there, Toby?"

"A little old burp gun I picked up in the woods, Pop."

Holly held up a lantern so the light shown on me. "Toby Kwimper!" she said. "What is that awful thing?"

Little Nick said, "I think I'm getting ready to be sick."

Just then Eddy and Teddy saw the gun. Eddy said, "It's real! It's real!" He wheeled around on Blackie, aimed his arms like a gun and said, "Ba-da-da-da-da!" Blackie shrunk back.

"How'd you go about picking up a little old burp gun in the woods?" Pop asked.

"A feller had it that was shooting at me," I said. "I left him in the woods with the other three fellers to sober up till morning."

Blackie said, "The . . . other . . . three?"

"Oh, there was four of them. I reckon they was all drunk because they almost hit me coming along in their car. So I snuck up and took their ignition key and led them about a mile west of the road and got their guns. Then I left them there to sober up. Them guns is not legal for hunting."

"The guy's driving me nuts," Blackie said to Little Nick. Then he turned to me. "Why don't you say right out what you come here for?"

"Why, I did. The first thing I said when I come out was how's the fishing?"

"Is he kidding?" Little Nick said to Blackie.

"I'm getting to the point where I just don't know."

"Oh, and by the way," I said to them, "I put that jug of kerosene and the package in your place."

"You what!" Little Nick yelled.

Blackie gasped, "You put them in *our place?*"

"Right inside the door where you can find them easy."

"Jeez!" Blackie said to Little Nick. "Let's go!"

Little Nick grabbed his arm. "Wait!" He looked at his wristwatch. "It's too late," he said. "Five. Four. Three. Two. One . . . There she goes."

Boom!

The roof of Little Nick's and Blackie's place lifted a couple feet and the front wall bugged out and squirts of flame splashed around.

"Fire!" I yelled. "Fire!"

"Is he kidding?" Little Nick said to Blackie.

"I still don't know."

"I'm through here," Little Nick said. "Every pass with the dice I been crapping out. Let's go."

They started running toward their place and I run after them to help put out the fire, and you never seen two fellers move faster than they done. Their car was parked in front of their place and first thing, they jumped in and started getting it out of the way, which was a smart thing to do. But then they didn't stop. They swung the car toward the mainland and kept going. I guessed they had lost their heads, and I let off a burst from the gun to try to get their attention but they just went faster.

Well, we had us a real fire on our hands. The Browns and Pop and Holly and me had to work hard to save our places, which we done by getting buckets of water and wetting down the walls and roofs. We couldn't do nothing to save Little Nick's and Blackie's.

We never seen Little Nick or Blackie or any of them fellers afterward. I done a lot of thinking about that jug of kerosene and the package, and finally I worked it all out. Carmine had come to our place to swipe the kerosene. And the package didn't have no lantern in it. It was a time bomb, and that fire warn't no accident. They had planned to burn down their own place for the insurance! I hate to say it, but Little Nick and Blackie warn't honest.

CHAPTER SEVEN

FOR THE NEXT WEEK things went real good for all of us. It was getting on to the end of October, and tourists was starting to come from up north. They bought pies and birdhouses and things off the Browns, and some of them liked to fish, too, so along with our steady fishermen from Gulf City we done pretty fair. If things had stayed that way we would all have got fat and sassy, but we begun having more trouble about law and order. Only this time it was a matter of getting more law and order than we wanted. Late one afternoon a car come up the road and the feller driving it yelled, "Is Mr. Elias Kwimper there?"

Pop poked his head out the door and asked him in, but the feller said he had a bad ankle and did Pop mind coming out to the car. While that was going on, I took notice there was a woman beside the driver. It was Miss Claypoole, who hadn't been around since she got mad over the Browns leaving Sunset Gardens.

"You're Elias Kwimper?" the feller asked when Pop come up beside the car.

Pop said, "I reckon I am if I stop to think about it."

"All right, Mr. Kwimper," the feller said. "Here's something for you." He handed over a paper, and as soon as Pop took it the feller turned to Miss Claypoole and said, "You're my witness that service took place legally and on state land."

Pop was studying the paper, kind of spelling words out to himself. "I'll get around to reading this when I get a little help," he said.

"Better not waste time," the feller said. "You just got a summons."

Pop said, "Up to now I never heard of nobody getting a summons except from the Almighty."

"Well," the feller said, "Judge Robert Lee Waterman is kind of almighty in his way but he don't rate quite that high. Miss Claypoole, maybe you better explain."

Pop leaned down and looked in the car. "Why, hello, Miss Claypoole. Nice of you to come see us."

"This was a real pleasure trip for me," she said. "That summons orders you to attend a hearing tomorrow at two p.m. in the county courthouse in Gulf City. As county welfare supervisor, I am asking for a court order placing the twins, Edward and Theodore, under the control and guardianship of the Department of Public Welfare."

"I ain't too sure what that means," Pop said.

"It means we don't think you're fit people to raise those children. We're going to take them away from you if the judge agrees with us."

Pop started swelling up like a turkey gobbler getting a mad on. "I just want to see somebody try that," he said. "I just want to take a good look at them over the sights of a shotgun and—"

"Make a note of that," Miss Claypoole said to the driver. "This man is threatening us."

"Hang on a minute," I said. "What brung all this up?"

"A great many things," Miss Claypoole said. "But what forces me to act is the way those children have been behaving since they began school in September."

I said, "If them twins done wrong in school, they'll get their hides tanned."

"Make another note," Miss Claypoole said to the driver. "Cruelty to children."

Pop and me looked at each other, and Pop said, "You still got that burp gun, Toby?"

"Look, friend, I'm just a process server," the driver said. He put the car in gear, made a real brisk turn and got out of there.

Pop and me looked at each other again. "We are not going to get far shooting it out with the government," I said. "What we got to do is outthink the government. Because where the government is weak is in thinking, and you have proved it lots of times."

"You're right, Toby. Maybe we better find out if them twins been burning down the school or just scarring it up a little."

We got Holly and the twins, and Pop showed the summons to Holly and told her what happened. "I don't understand it!" she said.

"I've been driving them to the school bus stop every morning and meeting them every afternoon. Everything seemed to be fine. Boys, what have you been doing in school?"

They was both standing there with their hands folded in front of them and their eyes rolled up like they was ready to bust into a hymn.

"We have been doing fine in school," Teddy said.

"We read real fast and get our work done better than any of those other clucks," Eddy said.

"But what have you been doing to cause trouble?" Holly asked.

"Well," Teddy said, "the teacher told us we each had to be in different rooms, and said I would stay in her room and Eddy would have to be in another one."

"We were not having any of that," Eddy said. "If Teddy got in another room, he'd start letting on that he knew more than me."

"I got to keep my eye on him, too," Teddy put in.

"When the teacher wanted to send me to the other room," Eddy said, "she got mixed up and sent Teddy instead. The teacher in the other room didn't know I was supposed to be there, so Teddy didn't go. He just went outside and played."

"But that wasn't fair," Teddy said. "So we worked out a deal. Eddy would go to class one period and I'd go the next. And we each told the other what we had learned. The teacher didn't know the difference."

"But one of the kids squealed on us yesterday and we got caught," Eddy said. "That's all there is to it."

"What it comes down to," Pop said, "is that you two have been skipping school and you know good and well it was wrong. Now they're blaming us for it. They want to scare us back to Jersey, so they're calling us into court to try to take you two away from us."

Teddy said, "We'd head out of here if they did that, one at a time, so they wouldn't know who to look for."

Pop told them to run along while the rest of us talked things over. Holly said she didn't see how Miss Claypoole could take the twins off us just because they had been taking turns skipping class. But I warn't too sure. Anyway, we all said nobody was going to run us off our land when there was only three days before we could put in a legal claim for it. So we reckoned we would all go to that hearing and see what was what.

The next morning we spent a lot of time hauling up our rowboats and shutting up our place good, because a hurricane was working itself into a swivet out in the Gulf, and we was starting to get gusts of wind and rain. At 2:00 p.m. Pop and Holly and the twins and me got to the county courthouse and were sent to the judge's chambers. Miss Claypoole was there, and one of the teachers from the twins' school, and Mr. King. Judge Waterman was a feller that had done a little fishing off our bridge, and I hoped he knowed more about the law than he did about fishing. He asked if we had a lawyer and Pop said no, we didn't need nobody to do our fighting for us.

The judge said, "Well, suit yourself. This is a hearing on a request by the Department of Public Welfare for a court order giving the department control and guardianship of these two children I see here. Miss Claypoole, why don't you start off?"

Miss Claypoole begun by allowing that the Department of Public Welfare had a warm spot in its heart for everybody but most of all for children. The department had been worrying about Edward and Theodore Kwimper for a long time, but couldn't do nothing while they spent all their time on land that wasn't part of the county. But now they was at school on county land, the department could step in. Miss Claypoole said there was a teacher in the room who would tell the judge what had been happening in school.

The teacher told the judge how the twins had taken turns attending class while the other one played truant. Then Miss Claypoole got up again and said, "It is a clear case, Your Honor, of a split personality, aggravated by a bad home environment."

The judge rubbed his chin and said, "I thought a split personality was one person having two personalities."

"This is even worse," Miss Claypoole said. "This is two people having only one personality between them. Psychiatric care is needed to enable these children to make a successful life adjustment."

"Let's have these two boys up here," the judge said.

I nudged Eddy and Teddy, and they got up and edged toward the judge. He asked, "Which one of you is Edward?"

"He is," one of them said, pointing at the other.

"He is," the other said, pointing at the first one.

The judge looked at the teacher. "Which one is which?"

She frowned and said, "I think the one on the right is Theodore. Or . . . or is it the one on the left?"

"Miss Claypoole?" the judge said.

"Oh, I can't tell them apart," she admitted.

One of them twins looked up at the judge with big wide eyes and said, "I could have been in that schoolroom all along doing my work. You want to hear the reading lesson we had yesterday? 'Oh. Oh. Come. Come. See the car. It—' "

"I could have been the one in that schoolroom," the other twin said. "I know that lesson, too. 'See the car. It is a red car. Come, Jane. Come, Jack. See the red car.' "

The judge looked at Miss Claypoole. "Somebody had better do some identifying here pretty soon, or I don't know what happens to your case. You're accusing both of them of being truants. But one of them could have been attending school properly. If you can't tell which is which, you can't prove any truancy."

I seen the twins grinning a bit and I warn't going to let them get away with it. "Judge," I said, "them twins know perfectly well which of them is which." I pointed at one of them and said, "You quit this game and tell the judge which one you are."

"I'm Eddy," he said. And the other allowed as how he was Teddy.

"That's good," I said. "Now tell the judge what you done."

They scuffled around a bit but finally come across with the story.

"There now, Judge," I said. "That fixes things, don't it?"

The judge said, "Young man, you need a lawyer. You just gave the department back its case. All right, Miss Claypoole, you have a pair of truants. So far, all I'd be inclined to do is warn the family not to let this happen again."

Miss Claypoole opened up a big envelope and took out a stack of papers. "Your Honor," she said, "truancy is just one tiny angle. To prove the Kwimpers unfit to raise children, I would like to ask Mr. H. Arthur King, District Director of Public Improvements, to report his dealings with them."

Mr. King got up and told how his department had built a fine new road to give folks a look at unspoiled nature and how by a tiny little mistake they forgot to claim land that they had filled in on a causeway leading to Bridge Number Four. The Kwimpers had come along and squatted on that land and spoiled the view, and there was some old law that kept the department from throwing them out on their ears.

On top of that, those Kwimpers had thumbed their noses at the governor himself, and then to make things worse, they had what you might call stolen five truckloads of shell. "These are the most shiftless people I ever saw, Your Honor," Mr. King said. "Before they squatted on that land, they lived by exploiting the government. The one they call Pop boasted to me that he had been getting Relief and Unemployment Compensation and Aid to Dependent Children. The one they call Toby tricked the doctors into discharging him from the Army with a disability pension. I sent an inquiry to the Veterans Administration about this Toby Kwimper, and they ordered him to report for a checkup. He never reported."

Mr. King set down, and the judge looked at me and said, "May I repeat that I think you need a lawyer?"

"You sure may repeat it, Judge," I said. "But I hadn't forgot you said it before."

"Don't say I didn't warn you," the judge said. "All right, Miss Claypoole. Anything more?"

"Oh, a great deal more," she said. "At one time the department tried to help this family by offering them a unit in our lovely housing facility, Sunset Gardens. Not only did they reject this opportunity, they even managed to coax one of our couples, Mr. and Mrs. William Brown, to go live with them at the bridge. I suppose they succeeded in breaking down the moral fiber of the Browns, perhaps by hinting at all the illicit pleasures that could be found there."

"Aren't you doing a lot of supposing and perhapsing?" the judge said. "What illicit pleasures are you talking about?"

"Your Honor," Miss Claypoole said, "the department can prove that there was uncontrolled drinking and gambling at Bridge Number Four. The Kwimpers allowed two notorious gangsters to set up a roadhouse on the land they had squatted on. Then, after some kind of quarrel, the Kwimpers burned down the roadhouse and drove out these gangsters at gunpoint."

"I did hear something like that," the judge said. "Anything more?"

"Yes indeed, Your Honor. These people are part of the antisocial Kwimper family of Cranberry County, New Jersey. They have been inbreeding for generations, and no doubt have all the quirks and vices that inbreeding can produce. And now, Your Honor, I have one final piece of evidence. At one time I gave Toby Kwimper a word-association test. I have analyzed his answers carefully, and the results are shocking. I submit a copy of my report herewith."

She handed some sheets of paper to the judge, who give them a look and then whistled. "Quite a thing," he said. "Quite a thing. Well, do you Kwimpers have anything to say to all this?"

Pop said, "Judge, we'd kind of like to hash this over among ourselves for a couple minutes, if that would be all right."

The judge said he didn't mind, and the three of us got off in a corner. "Pop," I said, "we are not looking real good."

"It's ridiculous!" Holly said. "She's twisted every single fact!"

"Somebody has got to stand up and untwist things," Pop said. "Who's it going to be?"

"You are the head of the family, Pop," I said.

"No," Pop said. "I'll get mad and that won't help. You do it, Toby."

"My trouble is I am not thinking as good as usual. Look how I helped Miss Claypoole by making them twins tell which is which."

"Go ahead anyway, Toby," Pop said. "We can't be worse off than we are now."

Well, I didn't like the idea but said I would, so I got up and told the judge we had settled on what to do. He said kind of hopefully, "A lawyer?"

"No, I am going to talk for us, Judge," I said. "I will try to take up all the points that has been made agin us. First is that them twins is charged with getting in trouble in school, and I got to admit they done that, but I reckon it is our fault. Pop and Holly and me have seen them work tricks like that before, and might have knowed they was doing it. All I can say is that they won't do it again. Then there was the points Mr. King made. They was real good points, Judge. There isn't no question we squatted on that land. The only excuse I can give is we didn't mean to do it at the start. Our car run out of gas, and we was stuck there for days with no other folks coming along."

The judge said, "Did you have food with you?"

"All we had was some soda pop and chocolate bars. We dug us a well for fresh water, and we caught fish and found clams and coconuts and even a little fruit from an old farm. Then we cut branches and palm fronds and made a couple of lean-tos. Mr. King come along finally and was real upset at how we was camping there and spoiling the view. He ordered us off that land, and I got to admit we turned ornery and stubborn. Pop said he warn't going to let the government push us around because it would just get the government in bad habits. And about our thumbing our noses at the governor, well, that was just part of us being ornery."

"Pardon me," the judge said. "Are you defending yourself or making a confession?"

"I am just telling you what happened, Judge. Is that all right?"

"Yes, but it's a bit unusual. How about those five loads of shell?"

"I was just plain dumb about that," I said. "It turned out Mr. King had meant them loads to be dumped in front of our lean-tos, to shut us off from the road. But I thought he was being friendly and sending us a beach, so that is where I had the trucks dump it."

"I see. How about that business of getting Relief and all the rest of it?"

"I am sorry you brung that up, Judge, because we don't feel very good about that. Back in the thirties, when Pop had to scratch to make ends meet, the government come around and give him some money and food. Things went on that way, with Pop taking the money and food the government wanted to get rid of, until Pop and the government come to depend on each other. Then when I was at Fort Dix I strained my back. I told them doctors it warn't from nothing but lifting a little old jeep out of a manhole, but they said no, I had to go on Total Disability.

"Well, Mr. King fixed it so I got over my disability. We couldn't get Relief or Aid to Dependent Children from Jersey while we was living down here, so we had to start scratching to make ends meet. I reckon we have been letting the government down by not taking Relief or nothing, but there is times when folks has to think of themselves and not of the government."

"Umm," the judge said. Then he asked me, "How did you lure the Browns from Sunset Gardens?"

"I never rightly understood how I done that, Judge. I thought them Browns was real happy at Sunset Gardens. But dog me if they didn't come out and ask could they build a shack at the bridge, and Mr. Will Brown thrun away his pills and he sure hasn't had no time to let himself get sick since then."

"Let's get on to some other points," the judge said.

"Well," I said, "there was that point about them gamblers. When they first moved in next to us, Little Nick and Blackie said gambling couldn't be agin the law at our bridge because it warn't state or county land, but after a while, the gambling and the drinking and the fights at their place got a mite loud for the rest of us—"

"Did you or did you not," the judge interrupted, "burn down their place?"

"Judge, I did, and all I can say is I didn't mean to."

"Tell me about it."

"Well, I come home from the woods where I had taken some guns off four fellers who nearly shot me, and I seen a shadow under the shack and thought one of them fellers was laying for me. But it was just one of Little Nick's fellers with a jug of kerosene and a package. He lit out of there, and I thought the package and the kerosene were for Little Nick and Blackie, so I took them over to their place. I am afraid that package had a bomb in it, because it went off and their place burned down. I think that feller really wanted to burn it down for the insurance. Anyway, maybe Little Nick and Blackie got a mite discouraged, because they jumped in their car and drove off and that was the last we seen of them."

Miss Claypoole said, "Your Honor, either these are just plain lies or else what he says proves that the Kwimpers are crazy."

"Judge," I said, "I give in on every point made agin us, but this here point I don't give in on. Us Kwimpers is a little different from some folks, but for them to call us crazy is like a feller that is six feet tall saying everybody shorter than him is a freak. Maybe it is the feller six feet tall that is the freak, and maybe it is them other folks that is not all there in the head. Maybe it will turn out you are six feet tall, so don't take none of this personal."

"I'll try not to," the judge said. "Fortunately I'm five eleven and three-quarters. Now let's see. The only point you didn't comment on was that word-association test Miss Claypoole gave you. Would you care to see her report?"

"Well, no, Judge. I reckon I would just get embarrassed, like I done the time she give it to me."

"Then if nobody has anything else to say—yes, young lady?"

Holly had jumped up and was waiting to talk. She said, "Can I come up and ask you something privately, Judge?"

The judge said it was all right, and Holly went up and whispered to him. Finally he looked at Miss Claypoole. "This young lady brought up an interesting matter. She points out that much of the testimony has dealt with Toby Kwimper, whereas actually his father has been responsible for the twins. The young lady suggests that you give a word-association test right now to Elias Kwimper, and interpret it for me. How do you feel about that, Miss Claypoole?"

"I'd be delighted, Your Honor."

"Good," the judge said. "Now we need a few ground rules. The young lady pointed out that your tone of voice, Miss Claypoole, might influence the answers that Mr. Kwimper gives. So I suggest that you write down your list of words and give it to me. I'll take Mr. Kwimper into my clerk's office and go through the list with him and write down his answers. Then you can have the whole thing back to study and give us your analysis."

Well, everybody in the room thought that was fine. Miss Claypoole set there writing out her list, and the judge took it and went off with Pop. After a while they come back and the judge give Miss Claypoole the material. She studied it and made notes, and now and then shook her head like a doctor getting ready to tell you things has gone too far. In about ten minutes she got up and said, "Your Honor, I don't know when I've seen a more revealing collection of word associations. Would you like me to consult with you privately?"

"No, let's have it right out in the open."

"Very well, Your Honor. As you know, the words on the list were carefully selected to bring out hidden levels of motivation. The first word was court, and Mr. Kwimper associated that with the word crime. This of course shows a fear of legal processes."

The judge said, "Just out of curiosity, what would have been your reaction to the word court?"

"Perhaps the word justice, Your Honor."

"Thank you, Miss Claypoole. Please go on."

"The second word was girl, and the reaction was boy. If the overall pattern of responses had been different, this might look like an innocent association. As it is, however, I'm inclined to say that it shows an unhealthy sex fixation. The third word was election, and Mr. Kwimper was reminded of the word fight. This falls into the pattern of a lawless nature. He thinks of an election as something to be settled by physical violence. The next word was law. His reaction was the word books. This shows a belief that law is not a real living thing but something dead that is embalmed in books."

"There were some law books in the clerk's office, Miss Claypoole. Maybe a look at them gave him the answer."

"It's possible, Your Honor, but it doesn't fit the overall pattern. Then we have the word child, and he responded with labor. Obviously he thinks of children in terms of exploiting their labor."

"Could he have merely been thinking of the child labor laws?"

"I doubt it, Your Honor. The next word was wife, and his reaction was cousin. This links up with the inbreeding among Kwimpers."

"I don't suppose his wife could have a cousin who might be coming to visit them, or something like that?"

"Your Honor, if he has a wife, his wife *is* his cousin. Now the next word was moon, and he replied with the word shine. Moonshine is of course liquor made illegally, and once again this shows his preoccupation with lawlessness. The next word was trick, and he came up with the word treat. In other words, tricking a person is a real treat."

The judge said, "This is almost the end of October, and trick-or-treat night is coming along. Do you think—"

"No, I don't, Your Honor."

"No, I guess not. Please go on."

"Well, Your Honor, that's the analysis. I hope you find it helpful."

"As a matter of fact," the judge said, "I didn't really need it at all, but the young lady asked for it and I wanted to be fair. Well, now. You Kwimpers haven't had a lawyer. I wish you'd had one, because he'd be summing up your case now, and I'd be interested to see how he'd handle it. Let's see. Probably he'd get up and put a fatherly look on his face, and come up and lean one hand right there on the desk in front of me. Like this." The judge got up from back of his desk and went around in front and leaned one hand on it and looked in a real solemn way at the empty chair. "Your Honor," he said, "today you have heard a very remarkable thing. You have heard my client come right out and agree with almost every charge that has been made against himself and his family. Today, Your Honor, we have been privileged to listen to an honest man." He stopped and turned to me and said, "How does that sound?"

"It sounds right good, Judge," I said. "Who is this honest feller?"

"That's you, young man."

Miss Claypoole jumped up and said, "Your Honor, isn't this quite irregular?"

"This isn't a trial, Miss Claypoole. It is just an informal hearing. At this moment I am merely allowing myself a little intellectual exercise. Now let's see." He leaned on the desk and looked at the empty chair again and said, "We have heard today the story of a little family that found itself alone in the wilderness. With their hands they carved out a homestead, standing up bravely to thirst and hunger, just as did their forebears two and three hundred years ago. They stood off the attacks of hostile natives—"

"Your Honor!" Miss Claypoole cried. "There weren't any hostile natives."

The judge cleared his throat and said in a kind of embarrassed way, "I have to get hostile natives in here somehow. I hope you don't mind, Miss Claypoole and Mr. King, but as the lawyer for the Kwimpers I am looking on the Department of Public Welfare and the Department of Public Improvements as the hostile natives."

Mr. King said, "This is ridiculous."

The judge said, "A lawyer has a right to be ridiculous if he chooses, and I must say that they often do so choose. But let me get back to my hostile natives. Your Honor, the little settlement met the attacks of the hostile natives with true American courage, and it survived. Others came to join the settlement. Then, just as happened so many times along the frontier, the lawless element came in—the gambler, the gunfighter, the saloon keeper. To what law could the little settlement turn for aid? There was no law, Your Honor. The tiny settlement must stand or fall on its own. And it stood! Yes, it stood, Your Honor! The good people of the settlement rose up in their just anger, and swept out the men of evil." The judge walked up and down a couple of times, and then turned back to the empty chair behind the desk. "Your Honor," he said, "the frontier may have vanished from America, but its spirit lives on. It lives on in these good people who have told you their story today. These, Your Honor, are the last pioneers. The young man whose honesty has so enthralled us is a far cry from today's youth. His exploits are the stuff of legend. His strength is as the strength of ten because his heart is pure. This is not merely Toby Kwimper, this is Dan'l Boone, Davy Crockett, Johnny Appleseed and Paul Bunyan. Your Honor, I do not ask you to rule today in favor of my clients. I ask you to rule in favor of America! Thank you."

He mopped his face some, pulled himself around the desk like he was wore out, and set down in his chair. "Well," he said, "I don't think I ever heard a better closing argument."

Miss Claypoole said, "Now that you have had your—what did you call it, intellectual exercise?—I hope we can get back to business."

"Oh yes," the judge said. "Thank you for reminding me, Miss Claypoole. Your request for a court order is denied."

"But Your Honor! After all our testimony! And after I analyzed the word-association test right in front of you and proved how shocking a character that man has!"

"Oh, that reminds me," the judge said. "Mr. Kwimper didn't take the test. I took it."

CHAPTER EIGHT

EVERYBODY WAS HAPPY about the way that hearing came out except maybe Miss Claypoole and Mr. King, and they didn't stay around to say if they was happy or not. The rest of us talked to the judge awhile. He was a real nice feller even if he hadn't showed up very good in that word-association test. It turned out Holly had give him the idea of taking that test instead of Pop on account of I hadn't done too good talking up for us. But the judge said he would of been on our side, test or no test. I reckon nobody could say us Kwimpers was crazy, now that a real live judge said we warn't.

When we started for home it was late afternoon and the wind had picked up. There would be a gust like the clouds had let out a heavy sigh, the palm fronds would lay out like smoke, and a little rain would hiss through them. Then the wind would suck in its breath getting ready for the next time. At the drawbridge we stopped. The red lights was on and the bridge was tipped up a little. A feller come out of the bridge tender's house and it was Mr. King. "Hello there," he said. "No hard feelings about the hearing, I hope?"

"No sir," I said. "If the government is big about it, we will try to be big about it, too."

"Yes, there's no use carrying on a feud. Let's see, now, you people can put in your claim in a day or so, can't you?"

"Day after tomorrow."

"Lucky for you this hurricane isn't going to hit us head on. Might lose your place if that happened."

"I reckon that wouldn't be good," I said. "Do you think we can get across this bridge pretty soon, Mr. King?"

"I don't know. The machinery's not working. We've sent for a mechanic. May not get it working until tomorrow morning."

"Looks to me like there's only a little gap between the two halves of your bridge. I could lay down a few boards and drive the car over."

"I couldn't allow that," Mr. King said. "We have orders not to let anybody cross this bridge from Gulf City until it's fixed."

"What about the Browns out there? The storm might worry them."

"I already thought of that. One of my trucks was on the other side, and I sent it to pick them up. Not that I think the hurricane is going to hit us, but just to be safe."

"That is right thoughtful of you," I said. "I reckon we will get us a motel down the road, and I'd take it kindly if you would pass the word to the Browns where we are staying."

"I'll do that," Mr. King said.

We drove down the road to a motel where they was real glad to have us because they needed help putting up shutters on the windows. By the time we finished helping, the Browns had showed up. Mr. King and the highway patrol had brung them across the drawbridge real careful with ropes and all, which was mighty nice of Mr. King. The Browns said the wind was starting to pile up water in our pass, and if it kept on it might come clear over the road. We was worried about our place and got out maps to see if we could drive there in a roundabout way, but that meant a lot of miles with maybe some roads underwater and trees down, so all we could do was wait.

The next morning things had got worse. The palm fronds was tattered from laying out in the gusts, and there was a roaring like you might hear listening at the bottom of a chimney in a gale. We left the twins with the Browns and drove to the drawbridge. It hadn't been fixed yet. At the gate I told the two fellers from the state highway patrol who was on duty that we was real worried about our place. They was right sorry, but said they had orders not to let nobody cross until the bridge was fixed. It was raining hard and I went inside the bridge tender's house to talk with them. While I was looking around at all them big gears and things, I seen a big greasy nut lying on the floor and picked it up. "I wonder where this belongs," I said.

One of the patrolmen said, "You better leave things alone, Mac."

I said, "I don't know of an easier way to lose a nut than to leave it lay on the floor. If I don't miss my guess, over there is some bare threads that look like they is meant to take this nut. Let me see if it fits." I started screwing it on the threads at the end of a shaft, but it come up against a gear wheel. I had to push the gear wheel back on the shaft so it meshed with another wheel before I could get room to screw the nut on all the way.

"I hope you're not doing anything wrong," the feller said.

"It looks all right to me," I said. "But just to make sure, I will pull this lever and show you that the gears work good."

"I don't think you better," he said, but by that time I had already give the lever a little pull. There warn't nothing but a little hum, and them gears started turning real nice.

Just then Pop come busting in. "The bridge is down! The bridge is down!" he yelled. "It's fixed! Come out and see."

Well, we went out, and that bridge was down as nice as you please. "Imagine," one of the patrolmen said, "being able to figure that out."

"It warn't nothing," I said. "It is just that a nut is meant to go on threads, and that gears is meant to mesh with each other. Do you reckon we could drive across now?"

"You sure can, Mac," he said.

"And I'll run and find Mr. King," the other feller said. "He'll be glad to get this news." So he run off to find Mr. King, and we drove across the drawbridge and headed back toward our place.

It was the kind of drive where you would be happier with a bulldozer than with a car, on account of it is not easy to blow a bulldozer over and they come in handy for moving trees. In open spaces, where the wind come from the side, it tipped the car like a sailboat, and we had to crowd over to windward to hold her down. Every little while I had to stop for a tree that was down across the road, and hitch up our towing chain and drag it aside so we could get by. It took us nearly three hours to make the twelve miles, and when we got to our little bridge you might have thought it warn't there, with half a foot of water running over it.

We had a real busy afternoon. The Browns' shack was lower than ours, and so we got all their furniture and stuff and stowed it in one side of the rest room. I strung a rope between the rest room and the Browns' place so I could get across and back if the water come higher. Holly cooked food for us ahead of time, and I brung in fresh water from the water barrel, and by the time night come, we was ready.

There was two feet of water under our shack by then, and the way the wind was working on things, it sounded like we was setting inside a big old violin with somebody running wet fingers up and down the strings. After a while we thought we better move into the rest room ourselves, and we carried all our stuff across the walkway. A little later I thought I would see how the Browns' place was getting along, and took hold of the rope I had strung over to it. But that rope seemed loose, so I got a flashlight and aimed it across the road. Well, there just warn't nothing there.

"Pop," I called, "the Browns' place has gone."

Pop and Holly come to the door of the rest room and looked out.

"What is that big thing drifting by, right in front of us?" Pop said. "Could that be the Browns' place?"

"I don't reckon so."

"It looks like a real nice little shack."

"It is, Pop," I said. "In fact I think it is ours."

"Oh. It come off the pilings, did it? Well, we are a foot higher here in the rest room, and on bigger pilings, too."

Something was nuzzling around at my feet and I turned the flashlight on it and seen it was one of our rowboats come up to the door. "I think I will bring this rowboat inside," I said.

The rowboat was pretty full of water, but I bailed it out and got it through the doorway. We closed the door to help keep out the water, and piled heavy things against it to keep it shut. Then we fixed cushions in the rowboat and clumb in, and it was real cozy with the kerosene lamps going. Now and then I went to the window and looked out. All you could see in the flashlight beam was water going by, and you could hear the gusts of wind passing overhead, roaring like an express train, and sometimes the place would shake.

"You did build this real good, Pop," I said, after one of those looks out the window. "That water outside is up a foot above our floor level, and we haven't got hardly a drop in here."

"It's lucky we didn't stay in Gulf City," Pop said, "or everything out here would have gone. And that there law said we had to keep a building up on our land for six months before we could claim it."

Holly said, "I hope we don't end up needing a periscope."

"That's a woman for you," Pop said. "Always wanting something she don't have, whatever a periscope is."

We set in the boat and waited. The wind kept howling and outside the water kept creeping up little by little until our floor began to bulge up. "That's water pressure," Holly said, "and it's going to lift this place right off its pilings."

"Pop, I think Holly is right." I jumped out of the boat, grabbed a crowbar and levered up a floorboard. In come a jet of water that hit the ceiling. Gradually I felt the bulge in the floor settle down. Then the water give one more spurt and dog me if a big snook didn't come in with it. I waded back to the boat and clumb in, and the snook went off to sulk in a corner.

In a couple of hours the water was lapping within six inches of the windowsills, and I began to wonder if I could bust a hole in the wall and get the rowboat out if the water lifted much higher. But finally the water began going down. After a while you could see by the wet marks on the wall that the level had dropped a couple of inches. In another hour the wind had quieted and there was moonlight outside the window. The hurricane had gone.

I opened the door. Pretty soon the snook found the doorway and went out with a swish of his tail. All of us had come through that hurricane all right.

The next morning there was still a lot of puddles, and plenty of mud and trash lying around, but nothing you couldn't clean up. Our shack had come to rest right at the bridge and partway across the road, and it wouldn't be no trouble to get it on rollers and move it back where it belonged. On account of Mr. Brown was a good carpenter his place held together when it drifted away, and it had grounded on a beach nearby. One nice thing the hurricane had done was clean off the fill where Little Nick's and Blackie's place had burned down. But the big dock they built had come through and we could use the planking from it to repair things, so we was in real good shape.

We worked all morning cleaning up, and in the afternoon I heard some kind of engine over on the island and went to the bridge to see what was coming. A bulldozer waddled around the bend pushing a couple trees out of the way. Then a jeep cut around the bulldozer and zipped down to where I was waiting on the bridge.

Mr. King jumped out. "All of you get through?" he asked.

"Yes sir," I said. "It is right neighborly of you to come out and ask."

"I should have known it wasn't any use to try to keep you in Gulf City." He turned back to the jeep and said, "Benny, start taking photos. I want a complete set showing exactly what happened here." A feller with a camera got out of the jeep, and Mr. King peered along the bridge at our shack, which was kind of blocking his view of our land. "That's your shack," he said. "You do admit it's no longer on the land you squatted on, don't you?"

"Yes sir."

"You admit the law says you had to keep a building *up* on the land six months before you could put in a claim?"

"You got it right, Mr. King."

"You admit that building can hardly be called *up?*"

"It is what I would call down," I said.

"Take a picture of it," he said to Benny.

"Okay. Do you also want one of the building beyond it?"

"What building?" Mr. King said. He give me a kind of hunted look and run over to where Benny was standing and looked past the shack. I walked down after him and heard Mr. King saying, "Oh no! They can't do this to me!" He was staring at Pop's rest room.

Benny said, "Did you want a photo of that, Mr. King?"

"No," Mr. King said. "But maybe you can get a shot of me cutting my throat." He looked at me and shrugged and said, "All right. I give up. It's your land. But get this damn shack off my road, you hear?"

"Yes sir," I said. "Now if you could lend us that feller in the bulldozer, I could have the shack out of your way in no time."

Mr. King done some deep breathing and said, "Gee, it's nice of you to be so helpful, Kwimper. Anything else you want?"

"Well, if you are going back to Gulf City now, I'd take it kindly if you would give Pop a lift. Our car is underwater and Pop would like to get to the courthouse and put in a claim for the land."

Mr. King kicked some shell around for a few moments. "What was it that judge said?" he muttered to himself. "Oh yes, 'His strength is as the strength of ten because his heart is pure.' Yeah, his heart is pure and his head is empty, and I don't know how you can beat that combination." He stopped muttering to himself and said, "Take the bulldozer. Call your father and I'll give him a lift. What do I care?" He turned and stomped back to his jeep.

It was real handy having that bulldozer around. The feller running it helped me yank out a couple pilings where our shack had stood and we used them for rollers, and in a couple hours had our place back where it wouldn't take nothing but jacks to lift it up again and put it on pilings. After the bulldozer left, Holly and me fixed dinner and then set around outside feeling good.

Holly said, "I don't suppose your pop will get back tonight."

"No," I said, "he was fixing to stay in town and come back tomorrow. And them twins are still with the Browns."

"Toby, this is sort of like being married and alone together in our own place, isn't it?"

"It is real restful, if that is what you mean."

"Oh, you make me tired!" she said, and went in the shack.

I set there watching the moon come up, and in a while Holly come back out. She had put on her high heels and a right pretty dress that buttoned down the front and nipped in at her waist. "You look real nice," I said. "It is too bad there is nobody around to see."

She leaned against the doorway and wriggled a little against it like a cat scratching its back. Then she said, "You haven't kissed me since that night on the bridge when I gave you that lesson."

"That was a right good lesson," I said. "I bet it will come in handy when I run up against a girl."

She said in a funny tone, "Isn't it lucky I'm not a girl."

"Well," I said, "you are getting kind of close to it." The moonlight come through her hair and made her face real pale and pretty, like one of them lilies floating in a cedar water pool.

After a minute she left the doorway and come right up close to me. I got a little bit dizzy, so I went to work real quick on the times table.

"Toby Kwimper," Holly whispered, "you're doing that damn times table."

"Yes ma'am," I said. "And I am running out of numbers, too."

"How far are you?"

"I just done five times five."

Holly said real fast, "Five times six is thirty. Five times seven is thirty-five. Five times eight is forty."

"Holly! That is as far as I can go!"

"I know it, Toby."

I took a deep breath, hoping it would steady me some, and said, "Holly, what comes after five times eight?"

She wriggled closer and said in a kind of pleased way, "Me, Toby."

It turned out she was right about that.

THINGS STARTED LOOKING real good for us after we come through the hurricane. Pop had put our claim in at the courthouse and brought the twins back with him. The Browns moved back, and we helped them get fixed up. We used some of the lumber from the big dock to build a little place right by the bridge where Holly could serve coffee, sandwiches and the Key lime and pecan pies that Mrs. Brown made. By the end of November, the tourists was coming along steady and we was starting to make a hundred dollars clear every week, which was better than we had done living off the government. It was more fun, too.

I had done some worrying about what happened that night on the porch with Holly, but I couldn't rightly say I didn't want it to happen again. So I talked it over with Holly, and she said things like that was fine if the two people was married. I said I didn't have nothing agin getting married as long as it was to her, and if she warn't doing anything some day maybe we could run into Gulf City and see how you went about it. Well, it turned out she didn't have much she was planning for that day, so we went into Gulf City and got things rolling and in a few more days we was married as nice as you please. Being married worked out so good it was a wonder I hadn't thought of it before, or that Holly hadn't, for that matter.

So things was fine until the end of November, when Mr. Smith from the county tax collector's office come around to Holly's little place and started in telling us about taxes.

"Oh yes," I said. "I heard about them things. But I reckon we have not come up agin them before."

"So I understand," Mr. Smith said. "We didn't feel we could visit you to talk about tax matters before your claim was recognized. But now I'm happy to say we fully recognize it."

"That is real nice of you," I said.

"Now," Mr. Smith went on, "there is the little matter of the occupational tax for this diner your good wife has here. At the moment you're under fifteen chairs, so the state and county tax is only seven dollars and seventy-five cents."

"We want to do what's right," I said, "so we will bring around the seven dollars and seventy-five cents."

"Good. Tomorrow will be soon enough. We're open till five on weekdays. Now there is the tax on boat rentals. I see that you have four rowboats for rent. That is four seventy-five per boat, plus three dollars for each person employed. Let's be friendly about this and say that you are the only one employed on the boats. The total is, I believe, twenty-two dollars."

"Well," I said, "it is not a real big lot of money, and the way things is going we'll make it up selling bait to the fellers that fish here."

"I'm glad you brought up the subject of bait," he said. "Bait is handled by the state's Fish Conservation Department, and you will need a permit. It doesn't cost much. The department has a man in Gulf City, and when you stop by my office tomorrow I'll give you his name."

"It isn't a lot of trouble for you?"

"No, no. It's my pleasure to help. Now of course there is the personal property tax. And then there is the real estate tax. I'll work it out and have a bill ready for you to pick up tomorrow. And you mustn't forget to collect state sales tax from customers."

"Is . . . is that all?" I said.

Mr. Smith frowned and lowered his voice. "No," he said. "There's federal income tax. Don't ask me to give any advice on it. They're very rigid people. They don't allow a man a bit of leeway, the way we do. Well, nice to have met you folks, and I'll see you tomorrow." He smiled and waved and went out to his car and drove away.

Pop and Holly and me looked at each other. "Holly," I said, "what is all this going to cost us?"

"I—I don't know, Toby. I'll have to study up on it."

"We have been making a hundred dollars clear a week," I said. "That's better than we done living off the government. How much do we make now that the government is starting to live off us?"

Holly give a sigh. "Less, I suppose."

"What do we do about it? Go back to living off the government?"

Pop drew himself up tall and said, "We do not! They have tried everything they could think of, from trying to run us off the land to trying to coax us off, and from trying to take them twins away to sending a hurricane that I don't doubt they stirred up with one of them atom bombs. Now they are trying taxes. We are going to stay right here and pay them taxes and fight it out! Holly is with me. Are you with me, Toby?"

I took a deep breath and said, "Yes, Pop, I am with you. But I reckon us Kwimpers are crazy, after all."

The Education of
H∗Y∗M∗A∗N K∗A∗P∗L∗A∗N

The Education of

H*Y*M*A*N

K*A*P*L*A*N

A CONDENSATION OF THE NOVEL BY
Leonard Q. Ross

ILLUSTRATED BY TED MICHENER

Fractured spelling, improbable
pronunciation, and grammar gone
wild confront patient Mr. Parkhill each
evening as he faces his beginners'
night-school class in citizenship.
For his students, all recent immigrants
from Europe, inevitably rampage
through the King's English in their struggle
to master it. But no one in the class
wrestles with the language more valiantly—
or more vainly—than the irrepressible
Mr. Hyman Kaplan. To him the great Roman
general will always be "Julius Scissor,"
our first president "Judge Vashington." And
as his lovable, laughable efforts innocently
pull the language out of shape (isn't the
plural of cat "Katz"?), we find that there is
an enduring, and endearing, lesson in
it for all of us.

Leonard Q. Ross is really Leo Rosten,
best-selling author of *The Joys of Yiddish*.
A former university teacher, a screenwriter,
and a collector of jokes and puns, he is perhaps best known for his creation of the
plump, smiling, and quite unforgettable
Mr. Hyman Kaplan.

The Rather Difficult Case of
Mr. K★A★P★L★A★N

I N THE THIRD WEEK of the new term, Mr. Parkhill was forced to the conclusion that Mr. Kaplan's case was rather difficult. Mr. Kaplan first came to his special attention, out of the thirty-odd adults in the beginners' grade of the American Night Preparatory School for Adults ("English—Americanization—Civics—Preparation for Naturalization"), through an exercise the class had submitted. The exercise was entitled "Fifteen Common Nouns and Their Plural Forms." Mr. Parkhill came to one paper which included the following:

house..................	makes	....................houses
dog	''	....................dogies
libary..................	''	....................Public libary
cat	''	....................Katz

Mr. Parkhill read this over several times, very thoughtfully. He decided that here was a student who might, unchecked, develop into a "problem case." It was clearly a case that called for special attention. He turned the page over and read the name. It was printed in large, firm letters with red crayon. Each letter was outlined in blue, and between every letter was a star, carefully drawn, in green. The multicolored whole spelled, unmistakably, H★Y★M★A★N K★A★P★L★A★N.

This Mr. Kaplan was in his forties, a plump, red-faced gentleman, with wavy blond hair, *two* fountain pens in his outer pocket, and a perpetual smile. It was a strange smile, Mr. Parkhill remarked,

vague, bland, and consistent in its monotony. The thing that emphasized it for Mr. Parkhill was that it never seemed to leave the face of
Mr. Kaplan, even during Recitation and Speech period. This disturbed Mr. Parkhill considerably, because Mr. Kaplan was particularly
bad in Recitation and Speech.

Mr. Parkhill decided he had not applied himself as conscientiously
as he might to Mr. Kaplan's case. That very night he called on Mr.
Kaplan first.

"Won't *you* take advantage of Recitation and Speech practice, Mr.
Kaplan?" he asked with an encouraging smile.

Mr. Kaplan smiled back. "Vell, I'll tell abot Prazidents United
States. Fife Prazidents United States is Abram Lincohen, Hodding,
Coolitch, Judge Vashington, an' Banjamin Frenklin."

Further encouragement revealed that in Mr. Kaplan's literary
Valhalla the "most famous tree American wriders" were Jeck
Laundon, Valt Viterman, and the author of "Hawk L. Barry-Feen,"
one Mock-tvain. Mr. Kaplan took pains to point out that he did
not mention Relfvaldo Amerson because "He is a poyet, an' I'm
talkink abot wriders."

Mr. Parkhill diagnosed the case as—among other things—an in-
ability to distinguish between *a* and *e*. He concluded that Mr. Kaplan
would need special attention.

Mr. Kaplan's English showed no improvement during the next
weeks. Indeed the originality of his spelling and pronunciation flourished—like a sturdy flower in the rich earth. A man to whom Katz is the
plural of cat soon soars into higher and more ambitious endeavor. As a
one-paragraph "Exercise in Composition," Mr. Kaplan wrote:

> When people is meating on the boulvard, on going away one is saying,
> "I am glad I mat you," and the other is giving answer, "Mutual."

Mr. Parkhill felt that perhaps Mr. Kaplan should be confined to
simpler exercises.

Mr. Kaplan was an earnest student. He worked hard, knit his
brows regularly (albeit with that smile), did all his homework, and
never missed a class. Only once did Mr. Parkhill feel that Mr. Kaplan
might, perhaps, be a little more *serious* about his work. That was
when he asked Mr. Kaplan to give an example of a noun.

"Door," said Mr. Kaplan, smiling.

It seemed to Mr. Parkhill that "door" had been given only a moment earlier, by Miss Mitnick.

"Y-es," said Mr. Parkhill. "Er—and another noun?"

"Another door," Mr. Kaplan replied promptly.

Mr. Parkhill put him down as a doubtful *C*. Everything pointed to the fact that Mr. Kaplan might have to be kept on for an extra three months before he was ready for promotion to Composition, Grammar, and Civics, with Miss Higby.

One night Mrs. Moskowitz read a sentence from *English for Beginners*, referring to "the vast deserts of America." Mr. Parkhill soon discovered that poor Mrs. Moskowitz did not know the meaning of vast. "Who can tell us the meaning of vast?" asked Mr. Parkhill.

Mr. Kaplan's hand shot up, volunteering wisdom. He rose, radiant with joy. "Vast! It's commink from *diraction*. Ve have four diractions: de naut, de sot, de heast, and de vast."

Mr. Parkhill shook his head. "Er—that is *west*, Mr. Kaplan." He wrote VAST and WEST on the blackboard. To the class he added, tolerantly, that Mr. Kaplan was apparently thinking of west, whereas it was vast that was under discussion.

This seemed to bring a great light into Mr. Kaplan's inner world. "So is vast vat you eskink?"

Mr. Parkhill admitted that it was vast for which he was asking.

"Aha!" cried Mr. Kaplan. "You minn *vast*, not"—with scorn—"*vast*."

"Yes," said Mr. Parkhill faintly.

"Hau Kay!" said Mr. Kaplan, essaying the vernacular. "Ven I'm buyink a suit clothes, I'm gattink de coat, de pents, an' de vast!"

Stunned, Mr. Parkhill shook his head, very sadly. "I'm afraid that you've used still another word, Mr. Kaplan."

Oddly enough, this seemed to give Mr. Kaplan great pleasure.

Several nights later Mr. Kaplan took advantage of Open Questions period. This ten-minute period was Mr. Parkhill's special innovation in the American Night Preparatory School for Adults. It was devoted to answering any questions which the students might care to raise about any difficulties they might have encountered in the course of their adventures with the language. Mr. Parkhill enjoyed Open Questions. He liked to clear up *practical* problems. He felt he was being ever so much more constructive that way. Miss Higby had once told him that he was a born Open Questions teacher.

"Plizz, Mr. Pockheel," asked Mr. Kaplan as soon as the period opened. "Vat's de minnink from___" What followed sounded, in Mr. Kaplan's rendition, like "a big department."

"A big department, Mr. Kaplan?" asked Mr. Parkhill, just to make sure.

"Yassir!" Mr. Kaplan's smile was beauteous to behold. "In de stritt, ven I'm valkink, I'm hearink like 'I big de pottment.' "

It was definitely a pedagogical opportunity.

"Well, class," Mr. Parkhill began. "I'm sure that you have all . . ."

He told them that they had all probably done some shopping in the large downtown stores. (Mr. Kaplan nodded.) In these large stores, he said, if they wanted to buy a pair of shoes, for example, they went to a special *part* of the store, where only shoes were sold—a *shoe* department. (Mr. Kaplan nodded.) If they wanted a table, they went to a different *part* of the store, where *tables* were sold. (Mr. Kaplan nodded.)

"Well, then," Mr. Parkhill summed up hastily, "each article is sold in a different *place*. These different and special places are called *departments*." He printed DEPARTMENT on the board in large, clear capitals. "And a *big* department, Mr. Kaplan, is merely such a department which is large—*big!*"

He put the chalk down and wiped his fingers.

"Is that clear now, class?" he asked with a little smile. (It was rather an ingenious explanation, he thought; it might be worth repeating to Miss Higby during the recess.)

It *was* clear. There were thirty nods of approval. But Mr. Kaplan looked uncertain. It was obvious that Mr. Kaplan, a man who would not compromise with truth, did *not* find it clear.

"Isn't that clear *now*, Mr. Kaplan?" asked Mr. Parkhill anxiously.

Mr. Kaplan pursed his lips in thought. "It's a *fine* haxplination, Titcher," he said generously, "but I don' unnistand vy I'm hearink de voids de vay I do. Simms to me it's used in annodder minnink."

"There's really only one meaning for 'a big department,' " Mr. Parkhill said, but he was definitely worried by this time. "*If* that's the phrase you mean."

Mr. Kaplan nodded gravely. "Oh, dat's de phrase—ufcawss! It sonds like dat—or maybe a leetle more like 'I big de pottment.' "

Mr. Parkhill took up the chalk. (*I big department* was obviously a case of Mr. Kaplan's own curious audition.) He repeated the explanation carefully, this time embellishing the illustrations with a shirt department.

Mr. Kaplan followed it all politely, smiling throughout with consummate reassurance.

Mr. Parkhill was relieved, assuming in his folly that Mr. Kaplan's smiles were a testimony to his exposition. But when he had finished, Mr. Kaplan shook his head once more, this time with a new firmness.

"Is the explanation *still* not clear?" Mr. Parkhill was genuinely concerned by this time.

"Is de haxplination clear!" cried Mr. Kaplan with enthusiasm. "Ha! I should live so! Soitinly! Clear like *gold!* But Mr. Pockheel—"

"Go on, Mr. Kaplan," said Mr. Parkhill, studying the white dust on his fingers. There was, after all, nothing more to be done.

"Vell! I tink it's more like 'I big de pottment.'"

"Go on, Mr. Kaplan, go on."

Mr. Kaplan rose; his smile was transcendent, his manner was regal.

"I'm hearink it in de stritt. Somtimes I'm stendink in de stritt, talkink to a frand, or mine vife, mine brodder—or maybe only stendink. An' somvun is pessink arond me. An' by hexident he's givink me a bump, you know, a *poosh!* Vell, he says, 'Axcuse me!' But somtimes, an' *dis* is vat I minn, he's sayink, '*I big de pottment!*'"

Mr. Parkhill studied the picture of "Abram Lincohen" on the back wall, as if reluctant to face reality. He wondered whether he could reconcile it with his conscience if he were to promote Mr. Kaplan to Composition, Grammar, and Civics—at once!

Mr. K★A★P★L★A★N,
The Comparative, and the Superlative

FOR TWO WEEKS Mr. Parkhill had been delaying the inescapable: Mr. Kaplan, like the other students in the beginners' grade of the American Night Preparatory School for Adults, would have to present a composition for class analysis. All the students had had their turn writing the assignment on the board, a composition of one hundred words, entitled "My Job." Now only Mr. Kaplan's rendition remained.

It would be more accurate to say Mr. K★A★P★L★A★N's rendition of the assignment remained, for even in thinking of that distinguished student, Mr. Parkhill saw the image of his unmistakable signature, in all its colorful glory. That signature was more than a trademark; it was an assertion of individuality, a proud expression of Mr. Kaplan's Inner Self. To Mr. Parkhill, the signature took on added meaning because it was associated with the man who had said his youthful ambition had been to become "a physician and sergeant," the Titan who had conjugated the verb *to fail*: "fail, failed, bankrupt."

One night, after the two weeks' procrastination, Mr. Parkhill decided to face the worst. "Mr. Kaplan, I think it's your turn to—er—write your composition on the board."

Mr. Kaplan's great, buoyant smile grew more great and more buoyant. "My!" he exclaimed. He rose, looked around at the class proudly as if surveying the blessed who were to witness a linguistic tour de force, stumbled over Mrs. Moskowitz's feet with a polite "Vould you be so kindly?" and took his place at the blackboard. There he rejected several pieces of chalk critically, nodded to Mr. Parkhill, and then printed in firm letters:

> My Job A Cotter in Dress Faktory
> Comp. by
> H★Y★

"You need not write your name on the board," interrupted Mr. Parkhill quickly. "Er—to save time . . ."

Mr. Kaplan's face expressed astonishment. "Podden me, Mr. Pockheel. But de name is by me *pot* of mine composition."

"Your name is *part* of the composition?" asked Mr. Parkhill in an anxious tone.

"Yas*sir!*" said Mr. Kaplan with dignity. He printed the rest of H★Y★M★A★N K★A★P★L★A★N for all to see and admire. You could tell it was a disappointment for him not to have colored chalk for this performance. Indeed, in pale white the elegance of his work was dissipated. The name seemed unreal, the letters stark, anemic, almost denuded.

His brow wrinkled and perspiring, Mr. Kaplan wrote the saga of "A Cotter in Dress Faktory" on the board, with much scratching of the chalk and an undertone of sound. Mr. Kaplan repeated each word to himself softly, as if trying to give to its spelling some of the flavor and originality of his pronunciation. The smile on the face of Mr. Kaplan was beatific: it was his first experience at the blackboard; it was his moment of glory. He seemed to be writing more slowly than necessary as if to prolong the ecstasy. When he had finished he said "Hau Kay" with distinct regret in his voice, and sat down. Mr. Parkhill observed the composition in all its strange beauty:

My Job A Cotter In Dress Faktory
Comp. by
H★Y★M★A★N K★A★P★L★A★N

Shakspere is saying what fulls man is and I am feeling just the same way when I am thinking about mine job a cotter in Dress Faktory on 38 st. by 7 av. For why should we slafing in dark place by laktric lights and all kinds hot for $30 or maybe $36 with overtime, for Boss who is fat and driving in fency automobil? I ask! Because we are the deprassed workers of world. And are being exployted. By Bosses. In mine shop is no difference. Oh how bad is laktric light, oh how is all kinds hot. And when I am telling Foreman should be better conditions he hollers, Kaplan you redical!!

So I keep still and work by bad light and always hot. But someday will the workers making Bosses work! And then Kaplan will give to them bad laktric and positively no windows for the air should come in! So they can know what it means to slafe! Kaplan will make Foreman a cotter like he is. And give the most bad dezigns to cot out. Justice.

Mine job is cotting Dress dezigns.

THE END

Mr. Parkhill read the amazing document over again. His eyes, glazed but a moment before, were haunted now. It was true: spelling, diction, sentence structure, punctuation, capitalization, the use of the present perfect for the present—all true.

"Is plenty mistakes, I s'pose," suggested Mr. Kaplan modestly.

"Y-yes . . . yes, there are many mistakes."

"Dat's because I'm tryink to give *dip ideas*," said Mr. Kaplan with the sigh of those who storm heaven.

Mr. Parkhill girded his mental loins. "Mr. Kaplan—er—your composition doesn't really meet the assignment. You haven't described your *job*, what you *do*, what work is."

"Vell, it's not soch a interastink jop," said Mr. Kaplan.

"Your composition is not a simple exposition. It's more of a—well, an *essay* on your *attitude*."

"Oh, fine!" cried Mr. Kaplan with enthusiasm.

"No, no," said Mr. Parkhill hastily. "The assignment was *meant* to be a composition. You see, we must begin with simple exercises before we try—er—more philosophical essays."

Mr. Kaplan nodded with resignation. "So naxt time should be no ideas? Should be only *fects?*"

"Y-yes. No ideas, only—er—facts."

You could see by Mr. Kaplan's martyred smile that his wings, like those of an eagle, were being clipped.

"And Mr. Kaplan, why do you use 'Kaplan' in the body of your composition? Why don't you say *'I* will make the foreman a cutter' instead of *'Kaplan* will make the foreman a cutter'?"

Mr. Kaplan's response was instantaneous. "I'm so glad you eskink me dis! Ha! I'm usink 'Keplen' becawss I didn't vant de reader should tink I am *prajudiced* against de foreman, so I said it more like abot a strenger: *'Keplen* vill make de foreman a cotter!' "

In the face of this subtle passion for objectivity, Mr. Parkhill was silent. He called for corrections. A forest of hands went up.

Miss Rose Mitnick pointed out errors in spelling, in the use of capital letters, in punctuation; Mr. Norman Bloom corrected several more words, rearranged sentences, and said, "Woikers is exploited with an *i*, not *y* as Kaplan makes"; Miss Carmen Caravello changed *fulls* to *fools*, and declared herself uncertain as to the validity of the word Justice standing by itself in "da smalla da sentence"; Mr. Sam Pinsky said he was sure Mr. Kaplan meant *"opprassed* voikers of de voild, not *deprassed,* aldough dey are deprassed *too,*" to which Mr. Kaplan replied, "So ve bote got right, no? Don' *chenge* deprassed, only *add* opprassed."

Then Mr. Parkhill went ahead with his own corrections, changing tenses, substituting prepositions, adding the definite article. Through the whole barrage Mr. Kaplan kept shaking his head, murmuring "Mine gootness!" each time a correction was made. But he smiled all the while. He seemed to be proud of the very number of errors he had made; of the labor to which the class was being forced in his service; of the fact that his *ideas,* his creation, could survive so concerted an onslaught. And as the composition took more respectable form, Mr. Kaplan's smile grew more expansive.

"Now, class," said Mr. Parkhill, "I want to spend a few minutes explaining something about adjectives. Mr. Kaplan uses the phrase—er—'most bad.' That's wrong. There is a word for 'most bad.' It is what we call the superlative form of bad." Mr. Parkhill explained the use of the positive, comparative, and superlative forms of the adjective. "Tall, taller, tallest. Rich, richer, richest. Is that clear? Well then, let us try a few others."

The class took up the game with enthusiasm. Miss Mitnick submitted "dark, darker, darkest"; Mr. Scymzak, "fat, fatter, fattest."

"But there are certain exceptions to this general form," Mr. Parkhill went on. The class, which had long ago learned to respect The Exception to the Rule, nodded solemnly. "For instance, we don't say good, gooder, goodest, do we?"

"No, sir!" cried Mr. Kaplan impetuously. "Good, gooder, good*est*? Ha! It's to leff!"

"We say that X, for example, is good. Y, however, is . . . ?" Mr. Parkhill arched an eyebrow interrogatively.

"Batter!" said Mr. Kaplan.

"Right! And Z is . . . ?"

"High-cless!"

Mr. Parkhill's eyebrow dropped. "No," he said sadly.

"*Not* high-cless?" asked Mr. Kaplan incredulously. For him there was no word more superlative.

"No, Mr. Kaplan, the word is best. And the word bad . . . It isn't bad, badder, baddest. What's the comparative form of bad? Anyone?"

"Worse," volunteered Mr. Bloom.

"Correct! And the superlative?"

"Worse also?" asked Mr. Bloom hesitantly.

"No, Mr. Bloom. It's not the same word, although it—er—sounds a good deal like it. Anyone? Come, come. It isn't hard. X is bad, Y is worse, and Z is the . . . ?"

An embarrassed silence fell upon the class. Miss Mitnick, who was the best student in the class, but also the shyest, blushed and played with her pencil. Mr. Bloom shrugged, conscious that he'd given his all. Mr. Kaplan stared at the board, his mouth open, a look of desperate concentration on his face.

"Bad—worse. . . . What is the word you use when you mean most bad?"

"Aha!" cried Mr. Kaplan suddenly. When Mr. Kaplan cried "Aha!" it signified that a great light had fallen on him. "I know! De exect void! So easy! *Ach!* I should know dat ven I vas wridink! Bad—voise—"

"Yes, Mr. Kaplan?" Mr. Parkhill was definitely excited.

"Rotten!"

Mr. Parkhill's eyes glazed once more, unmistakably. He shook his head dolorously, as if he had suffered a personal hurt. And as he wrote WORST on the blackboard there ran through his head, like a sad refrain, this latest manifestation of Mr. Kaplan's peculiar genius: bad—worse—rotten; bad—worse . . .

Mr. K★A★P★L★A★N's
Hobo

PERHAPS MR. PARKHILL should have known better. Perhaps he should have known Mr. Kaplan better. And yet, in Mr. Parkhill's conscientious concern for every student in the beginners' grade, there could be no discrimination. Despite Mr. Kaplan's distressing class record, despite his amazing renditions of the English language, Mr. Parkhill insisted on treating him as any other student. Just because Mr. Kaplan referred to rubber heels as "robber hills," or called a pencil sharpener a "pantsil chopner," was no reason he should not participate in the regular exercises of the class on an equal footing. (Mr. Parkhill had weakened a bit in this resolution when Mr. Kaplan had given the opposite of new as "secondhand.")

And now Mr. Kaplan stood at the front of the room before the class, ready to speak for five minutes during the Recitation and Speech period.

"Speak slowly, Mr. Kaplan," said Mr. Parkhill. "Watch your pronunciation. Remember it isn't how—er—*fast* you talk, or how *much* you say. Try to be accurate. Speak distinctly."

Mr. Kaplan nodded with a great and confident smile.

"And do watch your *e*'s and *a*'s. You always confuse them."

Mr. Kaplan nodded again, beaming. "I'll be so careful, Mr. Pockheel, you'll be soprize," he said gallantly.

"And the class will feel free to interrupt with corrections at any time." Mr. Parkhill finished his instructions with an encouraging nod to the class. Allowing the students to interrupt with corrections had proved very successful. It kept them alert, and it made the student who was reciting particularly careful, since there was a certain stigma attached to being corrected by a fellow student—much greater than if Mr. Parkhill did the correcting. It was natural for *him* to catch errors.

"Very well, Mr. Kaplan." Mr. Parkhill sighed, aware that he could do no more. Now it was in the hands of God. He took Mr. Kaplan's seat. (He always took the seat of the student reciting during Recitation and Speech period. It seemed to establish a comradely rapport in the class; besides, it was easier to hear and watch the student speaking.)

Mr. Kaplan took a deep breath. For a suspended moment he surveyed the class. There was pride in his glance. Mr. Kaplan loved to recite. He loved to write on the blackboard. In fact, he loved any activity in which he was the center of attention. He laughed a strange, soft, rather meaningless laugh. Then he began:

"Ladies an' gantleman—I s'pose dat's how I should beginnink—an' also Mr. Pockheel an' faller students—"

He cleared his throat, almost with a flourish.

"I'm spikking tonight becawss it's Rasitation an' Spitch time an'—"

"Sp*ee*ch, Mr. Kaplan," Mr. Parkhill said gently. "Watch your *e*'s."

"Becawss it's Rasitation an' Sp*eeee*ch time, so I'll talkink abot mine vaca—no—*my* vacation." Mr. Kaplan corrected himself, smiling, as he saw Mr. Parkhill frown. "So is de name from my leetle spi—sp*eeee*ch: My Vacation!"

Mr. Kaplan stopped sententiously. He had a keen sense of structure.

"Foist, I must tell abot my hobo."

The class, with the fervent intensity with which it listened to students reciting, looked puzzled. So did Mr. Parkhill.

"My hobo is—"

"Your—er—*what?*" asked Mr. Parkhill anxiously.

"My hobo."

"No soch woid!" cried Mr. Norman Bloom. Whenever Mr. Bloom suspected an error in vocabulary, he jumped to the conclusion that there was "no soch woid." It was the safest tactic.

"Oh, no?" asked Mr. Kaplan, smiling. "Maybe you *positif?*"

"Well, there is such a word," said Mr. Parkhill quickly. "But—er—are you sure you *mean* hobo?"

"Aha!" Mr. Kaplan cried triumphantly, looking at Mr. Bloom. "So *is* soch a void! Vell, I tink I minn hobo. My hobo is hiking—hiking in de voods or op de mountains—all kinds hiking. Venever is a fine day, mit sonshinink, I go hiking in—"

"He means hobby," hissed Miss Rose Mitnick to Mrs. Rodriguez. Because Miss Mitnick was a shy girl, she ordinarily did not volunteer corrections. But between Miss Mitnick and Mr. Kaplan something of a feud was developing. Mr. Kaplan heard Miss Mitnick's hiss. So did everyone else.

"So I'm corrected by Mitnick," said Mr. Kaplan generously. "Is not my *hobo.* My *hobby*—Hau Kay! But Bloom shouldn't say dere's no void hobo. It's only *annoder* void, dat's all."

Mr. Kaplan smiled graciously at both Miss Mitnick and Mr. Bloom, with the faintest suggestion of irony. Suddenly he straightened up and an exalted look came into his eyes. With a sudden motion he stretched both hands outward and cried, "De sky! De son! De stoss! De clods. De frash air in de longs. All—all is pot from Netcher!"

A reverent hush fell over the class as Mr. Kaplan depicted the glories of Nature.

"An' do ve human fools taking edwantage? No!"

Miss Mitnick blushed as if she were personally responsible for man's indifference to the out-of-doors.

"But in hiking is all enjoymint from soch Netcher. Dat's vy I'm makink a hobby from hiking. Ladies an' gantleman, have you one an' all falt *in de soul* de trees, de boids, de gress, de bloomers—all de scinnery?"

A swift titter from the ladies made Mr. Kaplan pause, his hands arrested in midair.

"Yas, de trees, de boids, de gress, de bloomers—"

"Er—pardon me," said Mr. Parkhill, clearly embarrassed. "But what word *are* you using, Mr. Kaplan?"

"All kinds," Mr. Kaplan said with sublime simplicity.

"But—er—you used one word—"

"Bloomers ain't natural hobjects!" blurted Mrs. Moskowitz firmly. Mrs. Moskowitz, a large woman, was a straightforward, earthy soul.

And, as a married woman, she felt she could speak out where Mr. Parkhill or the class might hesitate. "You mean flowers, Mr. Kaplan," she said emphatically, "so don't mix op two languages!"

Mr. Parkhill, who had thought that Mr. Kaplan's use of bloomers came from a misconstruction of the verb *to bloom*, naïvely transformed into a noun, suddenly recalled that *Blumen* meant flowers in Mr. Kaplan's native tongue.

"Hau Kay!" said Mr. Kaplan promptly. "So podden me an' denk you! Is de void batter flower? So I love to smallink de flowers, like Moskovitz said. And I love to breed-

Miss Mitnick

ink de frash air. But mostly, I love to hear de boids sinking."

"You *must* watch your *k*'s and *g*'s," said Mr. Parkhill earnestly. "*Singing,* not *sinking.*"

Mr. Kaplan lifted his eyebrows with a responsive "Ah!"

"An' ven de boids is *singing,* den is Netcher commink ot in all kinds gorgeous."

Mr. Parkhill looked at the floor; there was no point in his being picayune.

"Vell, lest veek I took my vife ot to de contry. I told my vife, 'Sarah, you should have an absolute vacation. Slip—eat—valk aron' in Netcher. Stay in de bad how late you vant in de mornink!' But my vife! *Ach!* Did she slapt late? No! Not my Sarah. Avery mornink she got op six o'clock, no matter vat time it vas!"

For a moment there was a stunned silence. Then Miss Mitnick interrupted with shy but firm determination. She did not look at Mr. Kaplan at all. She addressed her words to Mr. Parkhill—rather, to Mr. Parkhill's tie. "How can Mr. Kaplan say she got up every morning at six o'clock no matter what time it was? A mistake."

The class nodded, the full meaning of Mr. Kaplan's paradox sinking in.

"Yes," said Mr. Parkhill. "I'm sure you didn't mean that, Mr. Kaplan."

Mr. Kaplan's great smile did not leave his face for a moment. He looked at Miss Mitnick through half-closed eyes and, with infinite superiority, said, "I have a foist-class idea vat I'm minnink, Mitnick. My vife gats op so oily in de mornink dat *you* couldn't tell vat time it vas, *I* couldn't tell vat time it vas, even Mr. Pockheel couldn't tell. Avery day in de contry she vas gattink op six o'clock, *no matter vat time it vas.*"

Miss Mitnick's blush was heartrending.

"Don' be like that, Kaplan!" exclaimed Mr. Bloom, jumping into the gap chivalrously. "If it's six o'clock, so you *do* know what time it was, no? So how you can say—"

"Aha!" Mr. Kaplan cried defiantly. "Dat's exactel de mistake you makink just like Mitnick. If I'm *slippink* an' it's six o'clock, so do *I* know vat time it is? Vould *you* know it vas six o'clock if *you* vas slippink?"

It was a dazzling stroke. It silenced Mr. Kaplan's critics with instant and deadly accuracy. Mr. Bloom pursed his lips miserably. Miss Mitnick frowned and flushed, such reasoning quite beyond her. Mrs. Moskowitz's eyes held awe for Mr. Kaplan's devastating logic. It remained for Mr. Parkhill to break through the impasse.

"But—er—Mr. Kaplan, if one *states* the time as six o'clock, then it's incorrect to add 'no matter what time it was.' That's a contradiction."

The class sat breathless. Mr. Kaplan's smile seemed ossified for one long moment as he looked at Mr. Parkhill. Then it flowed into life and peace again. "Oh, vell. If it's a *conterdiction*"—he looked haughtily at Miss Mitnick and Mr. Bloom—"dat's difference!"

Mr. Bloom nodded in acquiescence, as if he understood this masterful denouement; he tried to achieve a profound expression. A bewildered look crept into Miss Mitnick's eyes.

Mr. Kaplan beamed. He put his hands out dramatically and exclaimed, "How many you fine city pipple ever saw de son commink op? How many you children from Netcher smalled de gress in de mornink all vet mit dues? How many—"

Just then the bell rang in the corridors of the American Night Preparatory School for Adults. Mr. Kaplan stopped, his hand in midair, like a gull coasting. The class seemed suspended, like the hand.

"I'm afraid the period's up," said Mr. Parkhill.

Mr. Kaplan sighed philosophically, took his handkerchief from his pocket, and wiped the perspiration from his brow. "Vell, denks Gott dat's de end from de spi-sp*ee*ch of"—he drew himself erect— "Hymen Keplen."

As Mr. Kaplan uttered his own name, as if he were referring to some celebrity known to them all, Mr. Parkhill, by some visual conditioned reflex, *saw* the name. He saw it just as Mr. Kaplan always wrote it—in color, with a star between each letter. It seemed impossible, fantastic, yet Mr. Kaplan had *pronounced* his name H★Y★M★A★N K★A★P★L★A★N.

Mr. K★A★P★L★A★N
and Vocabulary

"VOCABULARY!" SAID MR. PARKHILL to the class. "Above all, we must work on vocabulary."

He was probably right. For the students in the beginners' grade, vocabulary was a dire and pressing need. Spelling, after all, was not of such immediate importance to people who did little writing during their daily lives. Grammar? They needed the substance—words, phrases, idioms—to which grammar might be applied. Pronunciation? Mr. Parkhill had come to the reluctant conclusion that for some of them accurate pronunciation was a near impossibility. Take Mr. Kaplan, for example. Mr. Kaplan was a willing, an earnest, aye! an enthusiastic pupil. And yet, despite Mr. Parkhill's tireless tutelage, Mr. Kaplan referred to the most celebrated of movie lovers as "Clock Gebble," who, it appeared, showed a fine set of teeth "venever he greens." Mr. Kaplan, when asked to use heaven in a sentence, had replied promptly, "In sommer, ve all heaven a fine time."

Yes, vocabulary—that, Mr. Parkhill thought, was the greatest need.

". . . And so tonight I shall write a list of new, useful words on the blackboard. To each student I shall assign three words. Write a sentence in your notebooks using each word. Make sure you have no mistakes. You may use your dictionaries, if you wish. Then go to the board and copy your three sentences for class analysis."

The class was impressed and pleased. Miss Mitnick's ordinarily shy expression changed to one of eager expectancy. Mrs. Moskowitz, simple soul that she was, prepared her notebook with stolid solemnity. And Mr. Kaplan, in the middle of the front row, took out his box of crayons, smiled more broadly than ever (a chance to use his crayons always intensified Mr. Kaplan's natural euphoria), turned to a fresh page in his notebook and printed, slowly and with great love:

VOCAPULERY
(Prectice in Book. Then Going to Blackb. and putting on.)

For the title he chose purple crayon; for the part in parenthesis, orange. His name he printed, fondly, as always in flamboyant colors:

H★Y★M★A★N K★A★P★L★A★N

As he handled the crayons Mr. Kaplan smiled with the sweet serenity of one in direct communication with his Muse.

Mr. Parkhill assigned three words to each student and the beginners' grade went into action. Lips were pursed, brows wrinkled, distant looks appeared in thoughtful eyes; heads were scratched, chins stroked, dictionaries fluttered. Mr. Kaplan tackled his three words with gusto: *pitcher, fascinate, university*. Mr. Parkhill noticed that Mr. Kaplan's cerebration was accompanied by strange sounds: he pronounced each word, and tried fitting it into a sentence, in a whisper which could be heard halfway across the room. He muttered the entire process of his reasoning. Mr. Kaplan, it seemed, thought only in dialogue with his other self. There was something uncanny about it.

"Pitcher . . . pitcher," Mr. Kaplan whispered. "Is maybe a pitcher for milk? Is maybe a pitcher on de vall—*art!* Aha! Two minninks! 'Plizz take milk from de pitcher.' Fine! 'De pitcher hengs cockeye.' Also fine! Pitcher . . . pitcher."

This private colloquy was not indulged in without a subtle design, for Mr. Kaplan watched Mr. Parkhill's facial expressions carefully out of the corner of his eye as he whispered to himself. Mr. Kaplan hoped to discover which interpretation of pitcher was acceptable. But Mr. Parkhill had long ago learned to beware of Mr. Kaplan's strategies, and so he preserved a stern facial immobility as Mr. Kaplan's stage whispers floated through the classroom.

When Mr. Kaplan had finished writing his three sentences in his notebook, he reread them proudly, nodded happily to Mr. Parkhill (who, though pretending to be watching the blackboard, was watching Mr. Kaplan out of the corner of *his* eye), and went to the blackboard. He whispered the sentences aloud as he copied them off. Ecstasy illuminated his face.

"Well," said Mr. Parkhill after all the students had transcribed their work, "let's start at this end. Mr. Bloom, I think?"

Mr. Bloom read his sentences quickly:

She *declined* the money.
In her red hat she falt *conspicuous.*
Last Saturday, I saw a *remarkable* show.

"Excellent!" said Mr. Parkhill. "Are there any questions?" There were no questions. Mr. Parkhill corrected "falt" and the exercise continued. On the whole the sentences were quite good. All went surprisingly well and Mr. Parkhill was delighted. The experiment in vocabulary-building was proving a decided success. At last Mr. Kaplan's three sentences came up.

"Mr. Kaplan is next, I believe." There was a note of caution in Mr. Parkhill's voice.

Mr. Kaplan went to the board. "Mine foist void, ladies an' gantleman," he announced, smiling (Mr. Kaplan always did things with a certain bravado), "is pitcher. So de santence is: Oh, how beauriful is dis *pitcher.*"

Mr. Parkhill saw that Mr. Kaplan had neatly straddled two words by a deliberately noncommittal usage. "Er—Mr. Kaplan. The word is p-i-t-c-h-e-r, not p-i-c-t-u-r-e."

Too late did Mr. Parkhill realize that he had given Mr. Kaplan the clue he had been seeking.

"Mr. Pockheel," Mr. Kaplan replied with consummate simplicity, "dis void *is* p-i-t-c-h-e-r."

"But when you say, 'Oh, how *beautiful* this pitcher is,' " said Mr. Parkhill, determined to force Mr. Kaplan to the wall, "you suggest—"

"Ah!" Mr. Kaplan murmured with a tolerant smile. "In som houses even de *pitchers* is beauriful."

"Read your next sentence, Mr. Kaplan."

Mr. Kaplan went on, smiling. "De sacond void, ladies an' gantleman, is fescinate—an' believe me is a plenty hod void! So is mine santence: In India is all kinds snake fescinators."

"You are thinking of snake *charmers.*" (Mr. Kaplan seemed to have taken the dictionary's description of fascinate too literally.) "Try fascinate in another sentence, please."

Mr. Kaplan gazed ceilingward, one eye half closed. Then he ventured, "You fescinate me."

Mr. Parkhill hurried Mr. Kaplan on to his last word.

"Toid void, faller students, is univoisity. De santence usink dis void: Eleven yiss is married mine vife an' minesalf, so is time commink for our tvalft *univoisity.*"

It was the opportunity for which Miss Mitnick had been waiting. "Mr. Kaplan mixes up two words," she said. "He means anniversary. University is a high college—the *highest* college."

Mr. Kaplan listened to this unwelcome correction with a fine sufferance. Then he arched his eyebrows and said, "You got right, Mitnick. Hau Kay! So I'll givink anodder santence: Som pipple didn't have aducation in a *univoisity*"—he glanced meaningfully at Miss Mitnick—"but just de same, dey havink efter eleven yiss de tvalft *annivoisery.*"

With this retort Mr. Kaplan took his seat. Through the next few recitations he was strangely silent. He did not bother to offer a correction of Miss Kowalski's spectacular misuse of *guess*. ("Turn out the guess.") He did not as much as volunteer an opinion on Miss Hirschfield's "The cat omits a cry." For all his proud smile it was clear that Mr. Kaplan had suffered a deep hurt: like a smoldering cinder in his soul lay the thought of his humiliation at the mundane hands of one Rose Mitnick. He smiled as bravely as ever, but his silence was ominous. He seemed to be waiting, waiting. . . .

"Miss Mitnick, please," said Mr. Parkhill. A flame leaped into Mr. Kaplan's eyes.

Miss Mitnick's first sentence was *"Enamel* is used for painting chairs." Before she could read it Mr. Kaplan's voice rang out in triumph.

"Mistake by Mitnick! Ha! Mit *enimals* she is painting chairs? Ha!"

"The word is *enamel,*" said Mr. Parkhill coldly. "Not *animal.*"

Rebuffed, Mr. Kaplan allowed Miss Mitnick's reading of that sentence, and her next, go unchallenged. But the flame burned in his eyes again when she read her final effort: "The prisoner stood in the *dock.*"

"Well," suggested Mr. Parkhill, before Mr. Kaplan, squirming with excitement in his chair, could offer a rash correction, "that's one way to use the word. The English use it that way. But there is a—er— more common usage. Can you use dock in a more familiar meaning, Miss Mitnick?"

Miss Mitnick was silent.

"Anyone?"

"I like roast *duck!*" cried Mr. Kaplan promptly.

"*Dock!*" Mr. Parkhill said severely. "Not *duck!*" Once again Mr. Kaplan bowed to a cruel fate.

"Dock isn't hard," said Mr. Parkhill encouragingly. "I'll give you a hint, class. Each of you, in coming to America, has had *direct experience with a dock.*" He smiled almost gaily, and waited.

The class went into that coma which signified thought, searching its collective memory of coming to America. Mrs. Moskowitz closed her eyes as the recollection of her seasickness surged over her like a wave, and searched her memory no more. Mr. Kaplan, desperate to make the kill, whispered his associations tensely: "Dock . . . commink to America . . . boat . . . feesh . . . big vaves."

It was clear they were getting nowhere.

"Well, I'll make it even easier," said Mr. Parkhill lightly. "Where did your boats land?"

"New York!" cried Mr. Kaplan eagerly.

Mr. Parkhill cleared his throat. "Yes—of course. But I mean—"

A cry of joy came from the lips of Hyman Kaplan. "I got him! Ufcawss! *Dock!* Plain an' tsimple! Ha!" He shot a look of triumph toward Miss Mitnick. "I'm soprize so high-cless a student like Mitnick—she knows all abot fency voids like univoisities and annivoiseries—she shouldn't know a leetle void like dock!"

Something in Mr. Parkhill warned him. Not for a moment could he believe that Mr. Kaplan's confidence and enthusiasm were authentic indications of a correct answer. Mr. Parkhill would have preferred that some other student try a sentence with dock. But no one volunteered.

"Very well, Mr. Kaplan," he said, staring at his fingers.

Mr. Kaplan rose, inspiration in his eyes. His smile was so wide that his face seemed to be one ecstatic cavern. He cast majestic glances to both sides, as if reading the tribute in the faces of his fellow students. Then he said, in one triumphant breath, "Hollo, Doc!"

Peace fell upon the room. The features of Abraham Lincoln in the picture on the wall took on, somehow, a softer understanding. But Mr. Parkhill was aware only of a strange and unaccountable ringing in his ears (Hello, Doc! . . . Hello, Doc!) and, while shaking his head sadly to show Mr. Kaplan that he was wrong, he thought to himself with feverish persistence, Vocabulary. Above all, vocabulary.

Mr. K★A★P★L★A★N
the Magnificent

MR. PARKHILL HAD decided that perhaps it might be wise for the class to attempt more *practical* exercises. On a happy thought, he had taken up the subject of letter-writing. He had lectured the students on the general structure of the personal letter: shown them where to put the address, city, date; explained the salutation; talked about the body of the letter; described the closing. And now the fruits of Mr. Parkhill's labors were being demonstrated. Five students had written the assignment, "A Letter to a Friend," on the blackboard.

On the whole Mr. Parkhill was satisfied. Miss Mitnick had a straightforward and accurate letter—as might be expected—inviting her friend Sylvia to a surprise party. Mr. Norman Bloom had written to someone named Fishbein, describing an exciting day at Coney Island. Miss Rochelle Goldberg had told "Molly" about a "bos ride on a bos on 5 av." Mrs. Moskowitz, simple soul, had indulged her fantasies by pretending she was on vacation in "Miame, Floridal," and had written her husband, Oscar, to be sure "the pussy should get each morning milk." (Apparently Mrs. Moskowitz was deeply attached to the pussy, for she merely repeated the admonition in several ways all through her epistle, leaving no room for comment on the beauties of "Miame, Floridal.") And Mr. Hyman Kaplan—Mr. Parkhill frowned as he examined the last letter on the blackboard.

"It's to mine brodder in Varsaw," said Mr. Kaplan, smiling in happy anticipation.

Mr. Parkhill nodded rather absently; his eyes were fixed on the board.

"Maybe it vould be easier I should readink de ladder alod," suggested Mr. Kaplan delicately.

"*Letter,* Mr. Kaplan," said Mr. Parkhill, ever the pedagogue. "Not *ladder.*"

"Maybe I should readink de *lat*ter?" repeated Mr. Kaplan.

"Er—no—no," said Mr. Parkhill hastily. "We—er—we haven't much time left this evening. It *is* getting late." He tried to put it as gently as possible, knowing what this harsh deprivation might mean to Mr. Kaplan's soul.

Mr. Kaplan sighed philosophically, bowing to the tyranny of time.

"The class will study the letter for a few minutes, please," said Mr. Parkhill. "Then I shall call for corrections."

The class fell into that half stupor which indicated concentration. Miss Mitnick studied the blackboard with a determined glint in her eye. Mr. Pinsky stared at Mr. Kaplan's letter with a critical air, saying "Tchk! Tchk!" several times, quite professionally. Poor Mrs. Moskowitz stared ceilingward with an exhausted expression. Apparently the vicarious excitements of the class session had been too much for her; an invitation to a surprise party, a thrilling day at Coney Island, a Fifth Avenue bus ride, and her own trip to Florida. That was quite a night for Mrs. Moskowitz.

Mr. Kaplan sat with his joyous smile unmarred, a study in obvious pride and simulated modesty, like a god to whom mortals were paying homage. First he watched the faces of the students as they wrestled with his handiwork, and found them pleasing. Then he concentrated his gaze on Mr. Parkhill. He saw anxious little lines creep around Mr. Parkhill's eyes as he read that letter; then a frown—a strange frown, bewildered and incredulous; then a nervous clearing of the throat. Any other student might have been plunged into melancholy by these dark omens, but they only added a transcendental quality to Mr. Kaplan's smile.

This was the letter Mr. Kaplan had written:

> 459 E 3 Str
> N.Y.
> New York
> Octo. 10

HELLO MAX!!!

I should telling about mine progriss. In school I am fine. Making som mistakes, netcheral. Also however doing the hardest xrcises, like the best students the same. Som students is Mitnick, Blum, Moskowitz—no relation Moskowitz in Warsaw. Max! You should absolutel coming to N.Y. and belonging in mine school!

Do you feeling fine? I suppose. Is all ok? You should begin right now learning about ok. Here you got to say ok. all the time. ok the wether, ok the potatos, ok the prazident Roosevelt.

How is darling Fanny? Long should she leave. So long.

With all kinds entusiasm

> Your animated brother
> H★Y★M★I★E

Mr. Kaplan simply could not resist the aesthetic impulse to embellish his signature with those stars; they had almost become an integral part of the name itself.

It was at this point that Mr. Parkhill had nervously cleared his throat. He felt vaguely distressed. He asked, "Has everyone finished reading?" Heads nodded in halfhearted assent. "Well, let us begin. Corrections, please."

Mrs. Tomasic's hand went up. "Should be N.Y. after New York and New York should be on top of."

"Correct," said Mr. Parkhill, explaining the difference and making the change on the board.

"In all places is *mine* wrong," said Mr. Feigenbaum. "It should be *my*."

Mr. Parkhill nodded, happy that someone had caught that most common of Mr. Kaplan's errors.

The onslaught went on: the spelling of words, the abbreviation of October and street, the tenses of the verbs.

"Mr. Kaplan got so many mistakes," began Mr. Bloom with hauteur. Mr. Bloom was still annoyed because Mr. Kaplan had rashly offered to correct the spelling of Coney Island, in Mr. Bloom's letter, to "Corney Island, like is pernonced." Mr. Bloom said, "He spelled wrong *progress, some, natural*. He means long should she *live*—not long should she *leave*. That means going away. He even spelled wrong my name! Is double *o*, not *u*. I ain't like *som* Blooms!" It was clear from Mr. Bloom's indignant tone that this was by far the most serious of Mr. Kaplan's many errors.

With this jealous defense of the honor of the house of Bloom, Mr. Bloom looked at Mr. Kaplan coolly. If he had thought to see Mr. Kaplan chagrined by the barrage of corrections, he did not know the real mettle of the man. Mr. Kaplan was beaming with delight.

"Honist to Gott, Bloom," said Mr. Kaplan with admiration, "you soitinly improvink in your English to seeink all dese mistakes!"

There was a fine charity in this accolade. It had, however, the subtle purpose of shifting attention from Mr. Kaplan's errors to Mr. Bloom's progress.

Mr. Bloom did not know whether to be pleased or suspicious, whether this was a glowing tribute or the most insidious irony.

"Thenks, Kaplan," he said finally, acknowledging the compliment with a nod, and considered the injuries of "Corney Island" and "Blum" expiated.

"I see more mistakes," said Miss Mitnick, intruding an unwelcome note into the happy Kaplan-Bloom rapport. Mr. Kaplan's eyes gleamed when he heard Miss Mitnick's voice. Here was a foe of a different caliber. "Absolutel should be absolute*ly*. Potatos has an *e*. Prazident is wrong; it should be *e* and *s* and a capital." Miss Mitnick went on and on making corrections. Mr. Parkhill transcribed them to the board as swiftly as he could, until his wrists began to ache. "The

ok is wrong, should be O.K.—with *capitals* and *periods*—because it's abbreviation."

All through the Mitnick attack Mr. Kaplan sat quietly, alert but smiling. There was a supreme confidence in that smile, as if he were waiting for some secret opportunity to bring the whole structure that Miss Mitnick was rearing so carefully crashing down upon her head.

Miss Mitnick rushed on to the abyss. "Last," she said, slowing up to emphasize the blow, "*three* exclamation points after Max is wrong. Too many."

"Aha!" cried Mr. Kaplan. It was The Opportunity. "Podden me, Mitnick. De odder corractinks you makink is foist-cless—even Hau Kay, an' I minn Hau Kay mit *capitals* an' *periods*," he added sententiously. "But batter takink back abot de tree haxclimation points!"

Miss Mitnick blushed, looking to Mr. Parkhill for succor.

"Mr. Kaplan," said Mr. Parkhill with caution, sensing some hidden logic in Mr. Kaplan's tone. "A colon is the proper punctuation for the salutation, or a comma. If you *must* use an exclamation point, then, as Miss Mitnick says, *three* are too many."

"For de vay *I'm* fillink abot mine *brodder?*" asked Mr. Kaplan promptly. In that question, sublime in its simplicity, he inferentially accused his detractor of (1) familial ingratitude, (2) trying to come between the strong love of two brothers.

"But, Kaplan," broke in Mr. Bloom, jumping into the fray on the side of Miss Mitnick, "three exclama—"

"Also he's mine *faworite* brodder!" said Mr. Kaplan. "For mine *faworite* brodder you eskink *vun—leetle—haxclimation point?*" It was an invincible position. "Ha! Dat I give to *strengers!*"

Mr. Bloom retired from the field, annihilated. One could hardly expect a man of Mr. Kaplan's exquisite sensitivity to give equal deference and love to *strangers* and his favorite brother.

"How's about entusiasm?" said Miss Mitnick, determined to recover face. "Is spelled wrong—should be *th*. And 'With all kinds enthusiasm' is bad for ending a letter."

"Aha!" Mr. Kaplan gave his battle call again. "Maybe *is* de spallink wronk. But not de vay I'm *usink* antusiasm, becawss"—he injected a trenchant quality into his voice to let the class get the deepest meaning of his next remark—"becawss *I* write to *mine* brodder in Varsaw *mit real antusiasm!*"

The implication was clear: Miss Mitnick was one of those who, corrupted by the gaudy whirl of the New World, let her brothers starve, indifferently, overseas. Miss Mitnick bit her lip. Mr. Parkhill, trying to look judicious, avoided her eyes.

"Well," began Miss Mitnick yet a third time desperately, "animated is wrong. Your *animated* brother, Hymie? *That's* wrong."

She looked at Mr. Parkhill with a plea that was poignant.

"Yes," said Mr. Parkhill. "Animated is quite out of place in the final greeting."

Mr. Kaplan sighed. "I looked op de void enimated *spacial*. It's minnink 'full of life,' no? Vell, I falt plenty full of life ven I vas wridink de ladder."

Miss Mitnick dropped her eyes, the rout complete.

"Mr. Kaplan!" Mr. Parkhill was left to fight the good fight alone. "You may say 'She had an animated expression,' or 'The music has an animated refrain.' But one doesn't say animated about one's self."

The appeal to propriety proved successful. Mr. Kaplan confessed that perhaps he had overreached himself here.

"Suppose we try another word," suggested Mr. Parkhill. "How about fond? Your *fond* brother—er—Hyman?" (He couldn't quite essay "Hymie.")

Mr. Kaplan half closed his eyes, gazed into space, and meditated on this moot point. "Fond, fond," he whispered to himself. He was like a man who had retreated into a secret world, searching for his Muse. "Your fond brodder, Hymie." He shook his head. "Podden me," he said apologetically. "It don' have de *fill*ink."

"What about dear?" offered Mr. Parkhill quickly. "Your *dear* brother, and so on?"

Once more Mr. Kaplan went through the process of testing. "Dear, dear, Your dear brodder, Hymie. Also no." He sighed. "Dear, it's too *common.*"

"What about—"

"Aha!" cried Mr. Kaplan suddenly, as the Muse kissed him. His smile was as the sun. "I got him! Fine! Poifick! Such a void!"

The class, to whom Mr. Kaplan had communicated some of his own excitement, waited breathlessly. Mr. Parkhill himself, it might be said, was possessed of a queer eagerness.

"Yes, Mr. Kaplan. What word would you suggest?"

"Megnificent!" cried Mr. Kaplan.

Admiration and silence fell upon the class like a benediction. "Your magnificent brother, Hymie." It was a *coup de maître*, a masterstroke. Mr. K★A★P★L★A★N the Magnificent.

As if in a trance, the beginners' grade waited for Mr. Parkhill's verdict.

And when Mr. Parkhill spoke, it was slowly, sadly, aware that he was breaking a magic spell. "N-no, Mr. Kaplan. I'm afraid not. Magnificent isn't really—er—appropriate."

The bell rang in the corridors, as if it had withheld its signal until the last possible moment. The class moved into life and toward the door. Mr. Norman Bloom went out with Mr. Kaplan. Mr. Parkhill could hear the last words of their conversation.

"Kaplan," said Mr. Bloom enviously, "*how* you fond soch a beautiful woid?"

"Megnificent, megnificent," Mr. Kaplan murmured to himself wistfully. "Ach! Dat *vas* a beauriful void, ha, Bloom?"

"Believe me!" said Mr. Bloom. "*How* you fond soch a woid?"

"By *dip* tinking," said Mr. Kaplan.

He strode out like a hero.

Mr. K★A★P★L★A★N
Almost Comes Through

It was painfully clear to Mr. Parkhill that Mr. Kaplan's English was long to remain a source of surprise in the beginners' grade. Promotion to Composition, Grammar, and Civics with Miss Higby was, Mr. Parkhill concluded, quite out of the question.

Every assignment that bore that strange and unmistakable signature, H★Y★M★A★N K★A★P★L★A★N, contained some remarkable version of the English language that Mr. Kaplan had determined to master. For Mr. Kaplan was no ordinary student. He was no ordinary mortal, for that matter. In his peculiar linguistic universe there was the germ of a new lexicography. To Mr. Kaplan, an instrument for the repair of plumbing was "a monkey ranch"; verbal indiscretions were caused by "a sleeping of the tongue"; and, in the sphere of romance, the most attractive women were "female ladies with blondie hairs and blue or maybe gray ice—like Molly Dietritch." Mr. Parkhill sometimes wondered whether Mr. Kaplan might not be some sort of genius. Isaac Newton, after all, had been considered dull-witted by his teachers.

One night a composition of Miss Mitnick's was up for class analysis. Miss Mitnick had written the assignment on the blackboard. Blushing, with pointer in hand, she read it aloud in a small voice:

My Work—A Waitress

My job is, a waitress in a cafeteria restaurant. I am working nine hours a day. From 7½ in morning to 4½ by night. We are serving there meals, breakfast, lunch, and supper—or dinner as Americans say. My work is, standing behind counter and giving Coffee, Tea, Milk, as customers ask for one. It is not so hard. But I get tired with standing all day and have often headackes. The pay is not so good. But I am happy for having any job. We should be happy for having any job. Because all over the world is a depression.

Miss Mitnick stopped. Public performances of any type were an ordeal to her.

"That's very good." Mr. Parkhill smiled. It *was* very good. Miss Mitnick was easily the best student in the class. "There are some mistakes, naturally—in punctuation or in the use of certain prepositions, for example—but on the whole that is excellent."

Miss Mitnick blushed and looked at her pointer. Mr. Kaplan, in his seat in the front row, center, nodded in tolerant agreement with Mr. Parkhill's praises.

Mr. Parkhill adjusted his glasses. "Now then, corrections. Please examine the composition carefully, class, and make a note of any mistakes you see, in your notebooks. In five minutes I shall call for volunteers."

Mr. Parkhill thought this pedagogical technique very effective; it forced the students to concentrate; it challenged them. In his chats with Miss Higby, Mr. Parkhill sometimes told her, with a modest smile, of "the method of direct participation."

The class became a sea of stares and furrowed brows as the students applied themselves to Miss Mitnick's composition. Mrs. Moskowitz lowered her head and examined the floor. Mr. Norman Bloom jotted several words down swiftly. And Mr. Kaplan, serene and smiling as always, took one careless look at the blackboard and began writing in his notebook.

Mr. Parkhill sauntered down the aisle, glancing at the students' desks. "I'll give the class a hint," he said lightly. "There's *one word* spelled wrong."

All looked up except Mr. Kaplan. He was still preoccupied with the original error he seemed to have caught. His brow was knit, his pencil clutched in hand. He paid no attention to Mr. Parkhill's suggestion. Mr. Kaplan wrote on.

"Don't spend too much time on any *one* mistake," said Mr. Parkhill uneasily. "Just make note of the error."

Miss Caravello smiled at him knowingly. Still Mr. Kaplan wrote on.

"All right," said Mr. Parkhill. "I think we've had enough time now. Who will be the first volunteer? Corrections?"

Mrs. Moskowitz, who simply had no ear for sounds, raised her hand. "Shouldn't be by Miss Mitnick a *d* on de end 'restaurant'?"

"I'm afraid not," Mr. Parkhill said gently. "Restaur*ant* is correct."

The class, made timid by Mrs. Moskowitz's disastrous effort, was silent.

"Corrections?" asked Mr. Parkhill again. "Come, come. Please don't be so—er—shy. Mr. Kaplan? No corrections?"

Mr. Kaplan smiled happily. "I'm positif is plenty mistakes by Mitnick, but"—he grinned—"I'm still figgerink."

"Well, just give us the mistakes you jotted down." Mr. Parkhill nodded toward Mr. Kaplan's open notebook.

Mr. Kaplan shook his head pleasantly. "Not a tsingle mistake did I jotted don."

"But—" Mr. Parkhill smiled and walked over to Mr. Kaplan's desk. Mr. Kaplan held the notebook up. It was clear now what had taken so much of Mr. Kaplan's time and concentration. On the page he had printed in fine, strong letters:

Mistakes By Mitnick

by

H★Y★M★A★N K★A★P★L★A★N

The rest of the page was blank.

Suddenly, Mr. Norman Bloom raised his hand. "It shouldn't be ½ after 7 and after 4," he said. "Like that is the figgers for size, like hats, or fractions—like 12½ ponds meat."

"Good!" said Mr. Parkhill. "That's a very good point. How should half past seven and half past four be written?"

"Saven-three-zero and four-three-zero," Mr. Bloom called off.

Mr. Parkhill erased the 7 and the 4. He wrote 730 and 430 in their places. "Like *this*, Mr. Bloom?" he asked, raising an eyebrow.

Mr. Kaplan had learned that whenever Mr. Parkhill raised an eyebrow the answer was no. Mr. Kaplan shook his head vigorously, trying to catch Mr. Parkhill's eye.

"N-no," said Mr. Bloom cautiously.

"Like *this*?" Mr. Parkhill made it 7-30 and 4-30.

Mr. Kaplan, watching Mr. Parkhill's eyebrow like a hawk, cried "Ha!" and shook his head again.

"It still don' *look* good," said Mr. Bloom.

"Of course not!" cried Mr. Parkhill happily. "Well, like *this*?" He made it 7/30 and 4/30. His eyebrow was arched with absolute delight at the method he was using. ("The gradual elimination of incorrect alternatives.")

Mr. Bloom was silent.

"Wronk!" cried Mr. Kaplan with enthusiasm. "Plain wronk!"

The class looked up, impressed. Mr. Parkhill, let it be said, was impressed too. "Yes, Mr. Kaplan. That *is* wrong." He had been keenly aware of the decision and accuracy of Mr. Kaplan's successive negations. "Tell the class which is the correct form." It was *splendid* to feel that Mr. Kaplan was making progress.

Mr. Kaplan's smile congealed into vacuity.

"I dunno," he said, the victim of his own strategy.

Mr. Parkhill felt distinctly let down. A case of knowing what was wrong, he thought, but not knowing what was *right*. A common failing. Without looking at Mr. Kaplan he inserted colons, making the numerals read 7:30 and 4:30.

"Now?" he asked. His tone was the same, but a practiced eye would have seen that Mr. Parkhill's eyebrow was inert.

"Aha!" cried Mr. Kaplan. "Fine! Poifick! Dat's Hau Kay!"

It was, in its way, a minor redemption. Mr. Parkhill was glad, for Mr. Kaplan's sake.

"Correct, Mr. Kaplan. This mark is used in figures, to indicate time, and in many other ways—as, for instance, to introduce a long quotation, or after Dear Sir in a letter."

Mr. Kaplan nodded, a study in pride, agreement, and noblesse oblige. Mr. Parkhill placed a large, clear colon on the board.

"What do we call this mark?"

A nonplussed silence gripped the class.

"Semicolon?" asked Miss Mitnick tentatively.

"N-no, not quite. But that's close. Anyone?"

Up shot the hand of Hyman Kaplan.

"Again?" Mr. Parkhill said gaily. "Well, good for you! What *do* we call this mark of punctuation?"

"Two periods," said Mr. Kaplan simply.

In a soft voice, and with his eyes on the blackboard, Mr. Parkhill spoke. "No, Mr. Kaplan, I'm afraid not. . . . It's called the *colon.*"

Then Mr. Parkhill went on, changing tenses, prepositions, dependent clauses; removing superfluous commas and adding necessary articles; making every correction, indeed, except the spelling of "headackes."

"I have left one mistake," he said at last. "A mistake in spelling. One word is obviously spelled incorrectly, and I should like someone in the class to correct it."

Eyes glazed, brows knit, foreheads became damp with perspiration, as the beginners' grade of the American Night Preparatory School for Adults searched for truth. Miss Mitnick stared with an anxious look, as if wanting to wipe out her disgrace by being the first to locate the error. Mr. Bloom studied the composition on the board with feverish intensity. Mr. Kaplan smiled and murmured each word aloud to himself, to strengthen his analytic powers: "My—jop—is—a—vaitress—in—a—"

"Aha! Vaitress!" he cried out. "Should be a *v* in vaitress!"

Mr. Parkhill shook his head severely. "No, Mr. Kaplan, decidedly not. The word is *wait*ress, not—er—*vait*ress. Just put the word wait, from which waitress comes, in front. Wait is the first syllable; we spell it just as if it stood alone."

"Oh."

Mr. Parkhill wasn't sure whether Mr. Kaplan looked sheepish or was just smiling less energetically.

"I think the word headackes is in my composition wrong," said Miss Mitnick with dignity. "I wasn't sure about the spelling when I was writing it."

"Ufcawss!" Mr. Kaplan cried. "Hadakes is wronk! Plain an' tsimple wronk!"

"That's what Miss Mitnick said," commented Mr. Parkhill caustically.

"Becawss she didn't spallink de void *just like as if it should be alone!*" Mr. Kaplan rushed on, exploiting the great principle he had just learned. "Had-akes—two voids! Spall like separate, den put togadder. Like in vaitress you puttink de vait in front, so now you puttink de ackes in back—an' de void must comm ot all right!"

This unexpected tour de force of analysis made Mr. Parkhill rather ashamed of his sarcasm of a moment earlier. "Exactly!" he said. "The rule applies here in the same way. Spell the word as if it were two separate words; combine head and aches and you have headaches!"

Mr. Kaplan beamed with joy. "Exactel vat I'm sayink, Mr. Pockheel! Hadakes mit *k* in de middle? Ha!" There was deep scorn in that Ha! "Is no *k* in ackes alone, so can't be a *k* in hadakes!"

By this time Mr. Parkhill was genuinely delighted with the inexorable logic that Mr. Kaplan was following.

"That's precisely the point. Come to the board and make the change, Mr. Kaplan."

Mr. Kaplan, ebullient, overjoyed, went to the board, took a piece of chalk, and scratched a firm line through the word Miss Mitnick had so lucklessly misspelled.

"No *k!* Only two voids—had and akes."

Then, as the class watched with bated breath (Miss Mitnick lost in the torments of embarrassment), Mr. Kaplan printed, in letters three inches high, "HEADAXE."

For a long moment Mr. Parkhill was as silent as the class, speechless before this orthographic triumph. Then he shook his head, slowly, with absolute finality. He felt that once again Mr. Kaplan had failed to fulfill an expectation which he had clearly aroused.

Mr. K★A★P★L★A★N
and the Magi

WHEN MR. PARKHILL saw that Miss Mitnick, Mr. Bloom, and Mr. Hyman Kaplan were absent, and that a strange excitement pervaded the beginners' grade, he realized that it was indeed the last night before the holidays and that Christmas was only a few days off. Each Christmas the classes in the American Night Preparatory School for Adults gave presents to their teachers. Mr. Parkhill, a veteran of many sentimental Yuletides, had come to know the procedure. That night, before the class session had begun, there must have been a hurried collection; a Gift Committee of three had been chosen; at this moment the Committee was probably in Mickey Goldstein's Arcade, bargaining feverishly, arguing about the appropriateness of a pair of pajamas or the color of a dozen linen handkerchiefs, debating whether Mr. Parkhill would prefer a pair of fleece-lined slippers to a set of mother-of-pearl cuff links.

"We shall concentrate on—er—spelling drill tonight," Mr. Parkhill announced.

The students smiled wisely, glanced at the three empty seats, exchanged knowing nods, and prepared for spelling drill.

Mr. Parkhill always chose a spelling drill for the night before the Christmas vacation: it kept all the students busy simultaneously; it dampened the excitement of the occasion; above all, it kept him from having to resort to elaborate pedagogical efforts in order to hide his own embarrassment.

Mr. Parkhill called off the first words. Pens and pencils scratched, smiles died away, eyes grew serious, preoccupied, as the beginners' grade assaulted the spelling of "banana . . . romance . . . groaning." Mr. Parkhill sighed. The class seemed incomplete without its star student, Miss Mitnick, and barren without its most remarkable one, Mr. Hyman Kaplan.

"Charming . . . horses . . . float," Mr. Parkhill called off.

Mr. Parkhill's mind was not really on "charming . . . horses . . . float." He could not help thinking of the momentous event to take place that night. After the recess the students would come in with flushed faces and shining eyes. The Committee would be with them, and one member of the Committee would be carrying an elaborately bound Christmas package, which they would try to hide from Mr. Parkhill's eyes. Then, just as Mr. Parkhill resumed the lesson, that student would rise, apologize nervously for interrupting, place the package on Mr. Parkhill's desk, utter a few half-swallowed words, and rush back to his or her seat. Mr. Parkhill would say a few halting phrases of gratitude and surprise, everyone would smile and fidget uneasily, and the lesson would drag on, somehow, to the final and distant bell.

As the students filed out after the bell they would cry, "Merry Christmas, Happy New Year!" in joyous voices. The Committee would crowd around Mr. Parkhill with tremendous smiles to explain that if the present wasn't *just right* in size or color (if it was something to wear) or in design (if it was something to use), Mr. Parkhill could exchange it. He didn't *have* to abide by the Committee's choice. He could exchange the present for *any*thing. They would have arranged all that carefully with the store manager himself.

That was the ritual, fixed and unchanging, of the last night of school before Christmas.

"Cucumber . . . goose . . . violets."

The hands on the clock crawled around to eight. Mr. Parkhill could not keep his eyes off the three seats, so eloquent in their vacancy, which Miss Mitnick, Mr. Bloom, and Mr. Kaplan ordinarily graced with their presences. He could almost see these three in the last throes of decision, harassed by the competitive attractions of gloves, neckties, an electric clock, a cane, spats, a "lifetime" fountain pen. Mr. Parkhill grew cold as he thought of a fountain pen. Three times already he had been presented with "lifetime" fountain pens, twice with "lifetime" pencils to match. Mr. Parkhill hoped it wouldn't be another fountain pen. Or a smoking jacket. He had never been able to understand how the Committee in 1932 had decided upon a smoking jacket. Mr. Parkhill did not smoke. He had exchanged it for fur-lined gloves.

Just as Mr. Parkhill called off "Sardine . . . exquisite . . . palace," the recess bell rang. The heads of the students bobbed up as if propelled by a single spring. There was a rush to the door, Mr. Sam Pinsky well in the lead. Then, from the corridor, their voices rose. Mr. Parkhill began to print BANANA on the blackboard, so that the students could correct their own papers after recess. He tried not to listen, but the voices in the corridor were like the chatter of a flock of birds.

"Hollo, Mitnick!"

"Bloom, Bloom, vat is it?"

"So vat did you gat, Keplen? Tell!"

Mr. Parkhill could hear Miss Mitnick's shy "We bought—" interrupted by Mr. Kaplan's stern cry, "Mitnick! Don' say! Plizz, faller students! Com *don* mit de voices! Titcher vill awreddy hearink, you hollerink so lod! Still! Order! Plizz!" There was no question about it: Mr. Kaplan was born to command.

"Did you bought a Tsheaffer's Fontain Pan Sat, guarantee for de whole life, like *I* said?" one voice came through the door. A Sheaffer Fountain Pen Set, Guaranteed for Life. That would be Mrs. Moskowitz. Mrs. Moskowitz, who showed so little imagination even in her homework.

"Moskovitz! Mein Gott!" The stentorian whisper of Mr. Kaplan soared through the air. "Vy you don' open op de door Titcher should *positivel* hear? Ha! Let's goink to odder end from de hall!"

The voices of the beginners' grade died away as they moved to the "odder end" of the corridor, like the chorus of *Aïda* vanishing into Egyptian wings.

Mr. Parkhill printed CHARMING and HORSES on the board, repeating to himself, "Thank you, all of you. It's *just* what I wanted," again and again. One Christmas he hadn't said, "It's just what I wanted," and poor Mrs. Oppenheimer, chairman of the Committee that year, had been hounded by the students' recriminations for a month.

It seemed an eternity before the recess bell rang again. The class came in en masse and hastened to their seats to view the impending spectacle. The air hummed with silence.

Mr. Parkhill was printing CUCUMBER. He did not turn from the board as he said, "Er—please begin correcting your own spelling. I have printed most of the words on the board."

There was a low and heated whispering. "Stend op, Mitnick!" he heard Mr. Kaplan hiss. "You should stend op *too!*"

"The *whole* Committee," Mr. Bloom whispered. "Stand op!"

Apparently Miss Mitnick, a gazelle choked with embarrassment, did not have the fortitude to "stend op" with her colleagues.

"A fine reprezantitif *you'll* gonna make!" Mr. Kaplan hissed scornfully. "Isn't for *mine* sek I'm eskink, Mitnick. Plizz *stend op!*"

There was a confused, half-muted murmur, and the anguished voice of Miss Mitnick saying, "I *can't.*" Mr. Parkhill printed VIOLETS on the board. There was a tense silence. And then the voice of Mr. Kaplan rose, firmly, clearly, with a decision and dignity that left no doubt as to its purpose.

"Podden me, Mr. Pockheel!"

It had come.

"Yes?" Mr. Parkhill turned to face the class.

Messrs. Bloom and Kaplan were standing side by side in front of Miss Mitnick's chair, holding between them a large, long package, wrapped in cellophane and tied with huge red ribbons. A pair of small hands touched the bottom of the box. The owner of the hands, seated in the front row, was hidden by the box.

"De hends is Mitnick," Mr. Kaplan said apologetically.

Mr. Parkhill gazed at the tableau. It was touching.

"Er—yes?" he said again feebly, as if he had forgotten his lines and was repeating his cue.

"Hau Kay!" Mr. Kaplan whispered to his confreres. The hands disappeared behind the package. Mr. Kaplan and Mr. Bloom strode to the front of the room with the box. Mr. Kaplan was beaming, his smile rapturous, exalted. They placed the package on Mr. Parkhill's desk, Mr. Bloom dropped back a few paces, and Mr. Kaplan said, "Mr. Pockheel! Is mine beeg honor, becawss I'm Chairman from de Buyink an' Deliverink to You a Prazent Committee, to givink to you dis fine peckitch."

Mr. Parkhill was about to stammer a thank you when Mr. Kaplan added hastily, "Also I'll sayink a few voids."

Mr. Kaplan took an envelope out of his pocket. He whispered loudly, "Mitnick, *you still got time to comm op mit de Committee.*" Miss Mitnick stood up. She blushed furiously and lowered her eyes. Mr. Kaplan sighed, straightened the envelope, smiled proudly at Mr. Parkhill, and began to read.

"Dear Titcher—dat's de beginnink. Ve stendink on de adge from a beeg holiday." He cleared his throat. "Ufcawss is all kinds holidays in U.S.A. Holidays for politic, for religious, an' *plain* holidays. In Fabrary, ve got Judge Vashington's boitday, a *fine* holiday. Also Abram

Lincohen's. In May ve got Memorable Day, for dad soldiers. In July is commink, netcheral, Fort July. Also ve have Labor Day, Denksgivink, for de Peelgrims, an' for de feenish from de Voild Var, *Armistress* Day."

Mr. Parkhill played with a piece of chalk nervously.

"But arond dis time year ve have a *difference* kind holiday, a spacial, movvellous time. Dat's called—Chrissmas."

Mr. Parkhill put the chalk down.

"All hover de voild," Mr. Kaplan mused, "is pipple celebraking dis vunderful time. Becawss for som pipple is Chrissmas like for *odder* pipple is Passover. Or Chanukah, batter. De most fine, de most beauriful, de most *secret* holiday from de whole bunch!"

(Sacred, Mr. Kaplan, sacred, Mr. Parkhill thought.)

"Ven ve valkink don de stritt an' is snow on de floor an' all kinds tarrible cold!" Mr. Kaplan's hand leaped up dramatically, like a flame. "Ven ve see in de vindows trees mit rad an' grin laktric lights boinink! Ven is de time for tellink de fancy-tales abot Sandy Claws commink from Naut Pole on rain-enimals, an' climbink don de jiminies mit *stockings* for all de leetle kits! Ven ve hearink abot de beauriful toughts of de Tree Vise Guys who vere follerink a star from de dasert! Ven pipple sayink, 'Oh, Mary Chrissmas! Oh, Heppy Noo Yiss!' Den ve *all* got a varm fillink in de heart for all humanity vhich should be brodders!"

From his seat Mr. Feigenbaum nodded philosophically at this profound thought; Mr. Kaplan, pleased, nodded back.

"*You* got de fillink, Mr. Pockheel. *I* got de fillink, dat's no qvastion abot! Bloom, Caravello, Moskowitz, even Mitnick"—Mr. Kaplan was punishing Miss Mitnick tenfold for her perfidy—"got de fillink! An' vat is it?" There was a momentous pause. "De Chrissmas Spirits!"

(Spirit, Mr. Kaplan, spirit, the voice of Mr. Parkhill's conscience was saying.)

"Now I'll givink de prazent," Mr. Kaplan announced subtly. "Becawss you a foist-less titcher, Mr. Pockheel, an' learn abot gremmer an' spallink an' de hoddest pots pernonciation—ve know is a plenty hod jop mit soch students—so ve fill you should havink a sample from our—from our . . ." Mr. Kaplan turned the envelope over hastily. "Aha! From our santimental!"

Mr. Parkhill stared at the long package and the huge red ribbons.

"From de cless, to our lovely Mr. Pockheel!"

Mr. Parkhill started. "What?" he asked involuntarily.

"From de cless, to our lovely Mr. Pockheel!" Mr. Kaplan repeated with pride.

(*Beloved*, Mr. Kaplan, *beloved*.)

A hush had fallen over the room. Mr. Kaplan, his eyes bright with joy, waited for Mr. Parkhill to take up the ritual. Mr. Parkhill tried to say, "Thank you, Mr. Kaplan," but the phrase seemed meaningless, so big, so ungainly, that it could not get through his throat. Without a word Mr. Parkhill began to open the package. He slid the big red ribbons off. He broke the tissue paper inside. For some reason his vision was blurred and it took him a moment to identify the present. It was a smoking jacket. It was black and gold, and a dragon with a green tongue was embroidered on the front.

"Horyantal style," Mr. Kaplan whispered delicately.

Mr. Parkhill nodded. The air trembled with the tension. Miss Mitnick looked as if she were ready to cry. Mr. Bloom peered intently over Mr. Kaplan's shoulder. Mrs. Moskowitz sat entranced, sighing with behemothian gasps. She looked as if she were at her daughter's wedding.

"Thank you," Mr. Parkhill stammered at last. "Thank you. . . . All of you."

Mr. Bloom said, "Hold it op everyone should see."

Mr. Kaplan turned on Mr. Bloom with an icy look. *"I'm* de chairman!" he hissed.

"I—er—I can't tell you how much I appreciate your kindness," Mr. Parkhill said without lifting his eyes.

Mr. Kaplan smiled. "So now you'll plizz hold op de prazent. Plizz."

Mr. Parkhill took the smoking jacket out of the box and held it up for all to see. There were gasps—oh's and ah's and Mr. Kaplan's own ecstatic "My! Is beauriful!" The green tongue on the dragon seemed alive.

"Maybe ve made a mistake," Mr. Kaplan said hastily. "Maybe you don' smoke—dat's how *Mitnick* tought." The scorn dripped. "But I said, 'Ufcawss is Titcher smokink! Not in de cless, netcheral. At home! At least a *pipe!*' "

"No, no, you didn't make a mistake. It's *just* what I wanted!"

The great smile on Mr. Kaplan's face became dazzling. "Hooray!

Vear in de bast of helt!" he cried impetuously. "Mary Chrissmas! Heppy Noo Yiss! You should have a *hondert* more!"

This was the signal for a chorus of acclaim. "Mary Chrissmas!" "Wear in best of health!" "Happy New Year!" Miss Schneiderman burst into applause, followed by Mr. Scymzak and Mr. Weinstein. Miss Caravello, carried away by all the excitement, uttered some felicitations in rapid Italian. Mrs. Moskowitz sighed once more and Miss Mitnick smiled feebly.

The ceremony was over. Mr. Parkhill began to put the smoking jacket back into the box with fumbling hands. Mr. Bloom marched back to his seat. But Mr. Kaplan stepped a little closer to the desk. The smile on Mr. Kaplan's face was poignant and profoundly earnest.

"Er—thank you, Mr. Kaplan," Mr. Parkhill said gently.

Mr. Kaplan shuffled his feet, looking at the floor. For the first time since Mr. Parkhill had known him, Mr. Kaplan seemed to be embarrassed. Then, just as he turned to rush back to his seat, Mr. Kaplan whispered, so softly that no ears but Mr. Parkhill's heard it, "Maybe de spitch I rad vas too *formmal*. But avery void I said—it came from *below mine heart!*"

Mr. Parkhill felt that, for all his weird, unorthodox English, Mr. Kaplan had spoken with the tongues of the Magi.

Mr. K★A★P★L★A★N's
White Banner

IT WAS ONLY LOGICAL that, having drilled the class before the holidays on the writing of personal letters, Mr. Parkhill should now take up the business form with the beginners' grade. Business letters, indeed, might be even more practical from the students' point of view. They might want to apply for a job or answer an advertisement, or things of that sort.

"The general structure of the business letter follows that of the personal letter," Mr. Parkhill had said. "It, too, requires the address, the date, a salutation, and a final greeting, or complimentary close." Then he had gone on to explain that the business letter was more formal in mood and content; that the address of the person or company to whom you were writing had to be included in the form of the letter itself, on the left-hand side, above the salutation; that both the salutation and final greeting were formalized: Dear Sir, Dear Sirs, or Gentlemen, and Yours truly, Yours very truly, Very truly yours. Mr. Parkhill was a conscientious teacher and, aware of the queer things some of the students had done with previous exercises, he was careful to introduce the beginners' grade to business letters with particular care.

All had gone well—very well. So much had Mr. Parkhill been pleased by his success that, for homework, he had assigned a composition entitled "A Short Business Letter."

And now the students were presenting their homework on the blackboard for class analysis. Mrs. Tomasic, anticipating some halcyon day in the future, was applying for a position as private secretary to the President of the Good English Club. Mr. George Weinstein was ordering "a dozen sox size 12 silk" from a well-known department store. Mr. Bloom, ever the soul of business, was inscribing a polite but firm note reminding "S. Levin—Inc.—Jobbers" that they still owed him $17.75 for merchandise taken on consignment. Miss Schneiderman described a hat, coat, and "pair gloffs" she wished delivered "C.O.T." Mr. Hyman Kaplan was copying his letter on the blackboard in the right-hand corner of the room, near the door. This night there was a luminous serenity on Mr. Kaplan's face as he put the finishing touches to his newest creation. Mr. Parkhill, always uneasy about the form Mr. Kaplan's genius might give to any assignment, found himself reading Mr. Kaplan's letter with unconscious curiosity and quite conscious anxiety. This was the letter Mr. Kaplan had written:

Bus. Let.

459 E. 3. Street
New York
Janu. 8

Joseph Mandelbaum
A-1 Furniture Comp. N.Y.

Dear Sir Mandelbaum—
   Sarah and me want to buy refrigimator. Sarah wants bad. Always she is saying "Hymie, the eyes-box is terrible. Leeking." Is true. So I answer "Sarah, by me is O.K. refrigimator."
   Because you are in furniture so I'm writing about. How much will cost refrigimator? Is axpensif, maybe by you is more cheap a little. But it *must not* have short circus. If your eye falls on a bargain please pick it up.
   Very Truly Your Customer

H★Y★M★A★N K★A★P★L★A★N
(Address on Top)

Best regards Sarah and me.

Affectionately,
H★Y★M★I★E

Mr. Parkhill frowned several times during his reading of this document and sighed when he had finished his examination of it, resigning himself to another tortuous excursion into the strange linguistic universe of his most remarkable student. As for Mr. Kaplan, from his seat he reread his handiwork several times lovingly, his eyes half closed in what was supposed to be a self-critical attitude.

He kept shaking his head happily as he read, as if delighted by the miracle of what he had brought into being. Mr. Kaplan was an appreciative soul.

When the last student had finished, Mr. Parkhill said quickly, "I think we'll take your composition *first,* Mr. Kaplan." He wasn't quite sure why he had said that. Generally he started with the exercise in the *left*-hand corner of the blackboard.

"Me *foist?*" asked Mr. Kaplan.

"Er—yes." Mr. Parkhill almost wavered at the last minute.

Mr. Kaplan smiled widely. "My!" he said, getting up from his seat. "Is awreddy *foist* I'm makink rasitations!" By the time he had reached the blackboard his smile had become positively celestial. He turned and faced the class, as if it were an exercise in Recitation and Speech rather than composition. "Ladies an' gantleman," he began, "in dis lasson I falt a fonny kind problem. A problem abot how—"

"Er—Mr. Kaplan," Mr. Parkhill broke in, "please *read* your letter."

Only Mr. Kaplan's delight in being first carried him over this cruel frustration. "Podden me," he said softly. He began to read the letter. "Dear Sir Mendelbum." He read slowly, with dignity and with feeling. His smile struggled between pride and modesty. When he came to the last words, there was a tinge of melancholy in his voice. "Affectionately, Hymie." Mr. Kaplan sighed. "Dat's de end."

"Mr. Kaplan," began Mr. Parkhill cautiously, "do you think that's strictly a *business* letter?"

Mr. Kaplan considered this challenge by closing his eyes and whispering to himself. "Business ladder? *Streectly* business ladder? Is?"

Mr. Parkhill waited. The years had taught Mr. Parkhill patience.

"It's *abot* business," suggested Mr. Kaplan tentatively.

Mr. Parkhill shook his head. "But the content, Mr. Kaplan. The tone. The final—er—well—" Mr. Parkhill caught himself on the verge of an oration. "I'll let the class begin the corrections. There are *many* mistakes, Mr. Kaplan."

Mr. Kaplan's grave nod indicated that even the wisest of men knew what it was to err.

"Corrections, class. First, let us consider the basic question. Is this a business letter?"

The hand of Miss Rose Mitnick went up with a menacing resolution. When the work of Mr. Kaplan was under consideration, Miss Mitnick functioned with devastating efficiency.

"I think this isn't," she said. "Because in business letter you don't tell your wife's *first* name. And you don't send best regards. All that's for *personal* letters like we had before."

"An' vat if I vanted to wride a *poisonal* business ladder?" asked Mr. Kaplan with diabolic logic.

Miss Mitnick paid no attention to this casuistry. "It's wrong to give family facts in business letter," she insisted. "It's no business of the company what is a wife saying to a husband."

"Aha!" cried Mr. Kaplan. "Mitnick, you too axcited. You forged-dink to *who* is dis ladder!"

Mr. Parkhill cleared his throat. "Mr. Kaplan, Miss Mitnick is quite right. One doesn't discuss personal details, or give one's wife's first name, in a business letter—which is, after all, to a stranger."

Mr. Kaplan waited until the last echo of Mr. Parkhill's voice had died away. Then, when the classroom was very quiet, he spoke. "Mendelbum," he said, "is mine oncle."

There was a collective gasp. Miss Mitnick flushed. Mr. Marcus' eyes opened very wide. Mrs. Moskowitz blinked blankly.

"But, Mr. Kaplan," said Mr. Parkhill quickly, realizing that in such a mood there were no limits to Mr. Kaplan's audacity. "If the letter *is* addressed to your uncle"—he pronounced uncle suspiciously, but Mr. Kaplan's firm nod convinced him that there was no subterfuge here—"then it shouldn't be a business letter in the first place!"

To this Miss Mitnick nodded with hope.

"Dat pozzled me, too," said Mr. Kaplan graciously. "An' dat's vy I vas goink to axplain abot de fonny kind problem I falt, in de few voids before I rad de ladder." His tone was one of righteousness. "I figgered: buyink a refrigima—"

"Refrig*erator*! *R*, not *m*."

"Buyink a refrig*erator* is business. Also de axercise you givink for homevork is abot business. So I must kipp in business atmosvere. So in de foist pot I wrote mine oncle a real business ladder—cold, formmal. You know, stock-op!" Mr. Kaplan wrinkled his nose into a pictorialization of stuck-up. "But den, by de end, I falt is awreddy time to have mit family fillink. Becawss *is*, efeter all, mine oncle. So I put don Affectionately, Hymie."

"And is Affectionately right for a business letter?" asked Miss Mitnick, trying to conceal the triumph in her voice.

"It's *spalled* right!" Mr. Kaplan cried with feeling.

Mr. Parkhill felt old and weary; he began to realize the heights yet to be scaled. "Mr. Kaplan," he said softly, "we are not concerned with the spelling of affectionately at the moment. Affectionately is *not* proper in a business letter." He spent a few minutes analyzing the impasse. "Either you write a business letter *or* a personal letter. You cannot combine the two forms, Mr. Kaplan." He suggested that in the future Mr. Kaplan write personal letters to his uncle, but choose absolute strangers for his business communications. "Now let us go on with the corrections, please."

Mr. Bloom's hand went up.

"Mistakes is terrible," he said. "Where's the address from the company? How is abbreviated Company? Where's colon or comma after Dear Sir? And Dear Sir Mandelbaum! What kind combination is this? Is maybe Mr. Kaplan's uncle in English House Lords?"

Mr. Kaplan smiled bravely through this fusilade. Even the sarcasm about his titled lineage did no perceptible damage to that smile.

"Sarah and me should be Sarah and I," Mr. Bloom went on. "And eyes-box! Phooey! I-c-e means ice; e-y-e-s means eyes. One is for seeing, the other for freezing!"

Mr. Bloom was in faultless form. The class listened breathlessly to his dissection of Mr. Kaplan's business letter and it filled them with confidence. They leaped into the critical fray when he had finished, and a forest of hands went up. It was pointed out that "leaking" was spelled wrong, and "expensive." Mr. Pinsky remarked pointedly that there should be no capitals after "Very" in "Very truly" and cast doubts on the legitimacy of "Very Truly Your Customer." Miss Caravello suggested that Mr. Mandelbaum might be wise enough to read Mr. Kaplan's address without being told where to look for it, in the phrase "Address on Top." Even Mrs. Moskowitz, simple, uninspired Mrs. Moskowitz, added her bit to the autopsy. "I only know vun ting," she said. "I know vat is a circus. Dat's mit hanimals, clons, tricks, horses. An' you ken't put a circus in icebox—even a *short* circus!"

"You don' know abot laktric!" cried Mr. Kaplan, desperate to strike back at this united front. "Ufcawss, you a voman."

"Laktric—gas—even *candles!*" retorted Mrs. Moskowitz. "A circus ken't go in icebox!"

"Maybe de kind *you* minn," said Mr. Kaplan hotly. "But in laktricity is alvays denger havink short coicus."

Mr. Parkhill intervened, conscious that here was the making of a feud to take its place beside the Mitnick-Kaplan *affaire*. "You don't mean short circus, Mr. Kaplan. You mean short cir*cuit!*"

From the expression on Mr. Kaplan's face it was clear that even this approximation to "circus" was a victory for him and a rebuff to Mrs. Moskowitz and the forces she had, for the moment, led into battle.

"Another mistake," said Miss Mitnick suddenly. There was a glow in her cheeks; evidently Miss Mitnick had discovered something very important. Mr. Kaplan's eyes turned to narrow slits. "In the letter is, 'If your eye falls on a bargain please pick it up.' " Miss Mitnick read the sentence slowly. " 'If your *eye* falls on a bargain pick *it* up?' "

The class burst into laughter. It was a masterly stroke. Everyone laughed. Even Mr. Parkhill, feeling a bit sorry for Mr. Kaplan, permitted himself a dignified smile.

And suddenly Mr. Kaplan joined in the merriment. He didn't laugh; he merely smiled. But his smile was grandiose, invincible, cosmic.

"An' vat's wronk dere, plizz?" he asked, his tone the epitome of confidence.

Mr. Bloom should have known that he was treading on ground mined with dynamite. But so complete had been the rout of Hyman Kaplan that Mr. Bloom threw caution to the winds. "Miss Mitnick's right! 'If your *eye* falls on a bargain please pick *it* up?' Som English, Mr. Kaplan!"

Then Mr. Kaplan struck.

"Mine oncle," he said, "has a gless eye."

The effect was incredible. The laughter came to a convulsive stop. Mr. Bloom's mouth fell open. Miss Mitnick dropped her pencil. Mrs. Moskowitz looked at Mr. Kaplan as if she had seen a vision; she wondered how she had dared criticize such a man. And Mr. Kaplan's smile was that of a child, deep in some lovely and imperishable sleep. He was like a man who had redeemed himself, a man whose honor, unsmirched, was before him like a dazzling banner.

O K★A★P★L★A★N! My K★A★P★L★A★N!

MR. PARKHILL WAS NOT surprised when the first three students to participate in Recitation and Speech practice delivered eloquent orations on Abraham Lincoln, Little George and the Sherry Tree, and Wonderful U.S., respectively. For the activities of the month of February had injected a patriot fervor into the beginners' grade that would last well into March. There was a simple enough reason for this phenomenon: Mr. Robinson, principal of the school, did not allow either Lincoln's or Washington's Birthday to pass without appropriate ceremonies. On each occasion the whole student body would crowd into the assembly hall of the school to commemorate the nativity of one of the two great Americans.

At the Lincoln assembly, Mr. Robinson always gave a long eulogy entitled "The Great Emancipator." ("His name is inscribed on the immortal roll of history, in flaming letters of eternal gold!") A prize student from the graduating class delivered a carefully corrected speech on "Lincoln and the Civil War"—a rather short speech. Then Miss Higby recited "O Captain! My Captain!" to an audience which listened with reverently bated breath.

For the Washington convocation Mr. Robinson's address was entitled "The Father of His Country." ("First in war, first in peace, and first in the hearts of his countrymen—his name burns in the hearts of true Americans, each letter a glowing ember, a symbol of his glorious achievement!") The prize student's speech was on "Washington and the American Revolution." And Miss Higby recited "My Country, 'Tis of Thee."

The result of these patriotic rites was that for weeks afterward the faculty would be deluged with compositions on Lincoln, even little poems on Lincoln or Washington. Night after night, the classrooms echoed with the hallowed phrases: 1776, Father of His Country, The Great Emancipator, Honest Abe, Valley Forge. Mr. Parkhill found it a nerve-sapping ordeal. He thought of this annual period as "the Ides of February and March."

"I will spik ona Garibaldi," announced Miss Carmen Caravello, the fourth student to face the class. Mr. Parkhill felt a surge of gratitude within him. It was, however, short-lived.

"Garibaldi—joosta lak Washington!" she went on. "Firsta da war, firsta da peace, firsta da heartsa da countrymens!"

In the middle of the front row, Mr. Hyman Kaplan printed his name aimlessly for the dozenth time on a large sheet of foolscap, and sighed. Mr. Kaplan had been sighing, quite audibly, throughout each of the successive historico-patriotic declamations. Mr. Parkhill felt a distinct sense of comradeship with Mr. Kaplan.

"Hisa name burns, lak Mist' Principal say. Da *g*, da *a*, da *r*, da *i* . . ." Miss Caravello articulated the letters with gusto. Miss Schneiderman stared into space, vacantly. Mrs. Moskowitz rounded out the latest of a lengthy series of yawns. Mr. Parkhill frowned.

Miss Caravello

"Hooray Washington! Viva Garibaldi!"

In a fine Latin flush, Miss Caravello resumed her seat.

"Corrections, please," Mr. Parkhill announced, trying to be as cheery as possible.

The zest of competition animated the class for a few brief moments. Someone commented on Miss Caravello's failure to distinguish between past and present tenses of verbs, and her habit of affixing mellifluous *a*'s to prosaic Anglo-Saxon words. Someone else sugggested, with a certain impatience, that it was "foist *in* war, foist *in* peace, foist *in* the hots his countryman."

"How you can comparink a Judge Vashington mit a Gary Baldy?" Mr. Kaplan remarked with icy scorn. "Ha!"

Mr. Parkhill quickly spread oil on the troubled nationalistic waters. To avoid an open clash (Miss Caravello had long ago allied herself with the Mitnick forces in the Kaplan-Mitnick vendetta) and to introduce a more stimulating note into Recitation and Speech, Mr. Parkhill said, "Er—suppose *you* speak next, Mr. Kaplan." Mr. Parkhill had learned to respect the catalytic effect of Mr. Kaplan's performances, oral or written.

Mr. Kaplan advanced to the front of the room, stuffing crayons into his pocket. Then he buttoned his coat with delicate propriety, made a little bow to Mr. Parkhill, and began. "Ladies an' gantleman, faller students, an' Mr. Pockheel." He paused for the very fraction of a moment, as if permitting the class to steel itself; then in a dramatic voice he cried, "JUDGE VASHINGTON, ABRAM LINCOHEN, AN' JAKE POPPER!"

The class was galvanized out of its lassitude. Other less adventurous students might undertake comments on Lincoln *or* Washington, but only Mr. Kaplan had the vision and the fortitude to encompass Lincoln *and* Washington—to say nothing of "Jake Popper."

"Er—Mr. Kaplan," suggested Mr. Parkhill anxiously. "It's *George*, not Judge, Washington. And Abra*ham* Lin*coln,* not Ab*ram* Lin*cohen.* Please try it again." (Mr. Parkhill could think of nothing relevant to say in regard to Jake Popper.)

"*J*AWDGE VASHINGTON, ABRA*HAM* LIN*COLLEN,* AN' JAKE POPPER!" Mr. Kaplan repeated with renewed ardor. "Right, Mr. Pockheel?" he asked confidently.

Mr. Parkhill decided it might be best to let well enough alone. "It's—er—*better.*"

"Hau Kay! So foist abot Jawdge Vashington. He vas a fine man. Ectually Fodder from His Contry, like dey say. Ve hoid awreddy, from plenty students, all abot his movvellous didds. How, by beink even a leetle boy, he chopped don de cherries so he could enswer, 'I cannot tell lies, Papa. I did it mit mine leetle hatchik!' But ve shouldn't forgat dat Vashington vas a beeg ravolutionist! He was fightink for Friddom, against de Kink Ingland, Kink Jawge Number Tree, dat tarrible autocrap who—"

"Auto*crat!*" Mr. Parkhill put in, but too late.

"—who vas puddink stemps on *tea* even, so it tasted bed, an' Jawdge Vashington trew de tea in Boston Hobber, drassed op like a Hindian. So vas de Ravolution!"

The class, Mr. Parkhill could not help observing, hung on Mr. Kaplan's every word, entranced by his historiography.

"Jawdge Vashington vas a hero. A foist-cless hero! In de meedle de coldest vedder he crossed de ice in a leetle boat, so he should cetch de Bridish an' de missionaries—"

*"Mercen*aries, Mr. Kaplan, *mercen*aries!"

"—foolink around, not mit deir minds on de var!" Mr. Kaplan, having finished the sentence, said, "Podden me, *Moisinaries* I mant!" and, with scarcely a break in his stride, continued. "So efter de Ravolution de pipple said, 'Jawdge Vashington, you our hero an' lidder! Ve elactink you Prazident!' So he vas elected Prazident U.S.— anonymously!"

Mr. Parkhill's "Unanimously!" was lost in Mr. Kaplan's next words.

"An' like Mr. Robinson said, 'In Vashington's name is itch ladder like a coal, boinink ot his gloryous achivmants!' "

Mr. Kaplan ended the peroration with a joyous sweep of the arm.

"Mr. Kaplan!" Mr. Parkhill took the occasion to interrupt firmly. "You *must* speak more slowly, and—er—more carefully. You are making too many mistakes. It is very difficult to correct your English." Mr. Parkhill was aware that "Abraham Lincollen an' Jake Popper" were still to come.

Mr. Kaplan's face fell as he recognized the necessity of smothering the divine fire that flamed within him. "I'll try mine bast," he said. In a gentler mood, he continued. "Vell, I said a lot of fine tings abot Jawdge Vashington. But enyho, is Abraham Lincollen more *close* to me. Dat Abraham Lincollen! Vat a sveet man. Vat a fine cherecter. Vat a hot—like *gold!* Look!" Mr. Kaplan pointed dramatically to the lithograph of the Great Emancipator, which hung on the back wall; the heads of the students turned. "Look on his face! Look his ice, so sad mit fillink. Look his mot, so full goodness. Look de high fore-hat—dat's showink *brains!*" Mr. Kaplan's invidious glance toward Miss Caravello left no doubt that this high quality was missing in Gary Baldy. "Look de honest axpression! I esk, is it a *vunder* dey vas callink him Honest Abie?"

"Honest Abe!" Mr. Parkhill exclaimed with desperation, but Mr.

Kaplan, carried away by the sweep of his passion, had soared on.

"No, it's no vunder. He vas a poor boy, a voodchopper, a rail-splinter like dey say. But he made de Tsivil Var! Oh my, den vas tarrible times! Shoodink, killink, de Naut Side U.S.A. aganst de Sot Side U.S.A. Brodder fightink brodder, de Blues mit de Grays. An' who von? *Who?* Ha! Abraham Lincollen von, netcherally! So he made de blacks should be like vhite. Ufcawss, Lincollen didn't change de *collars,*" Mr. Kaplan footnoted with scholarly discretion. "Dey vas still *black.* But *free* black, not slafe black. Den"—Mr. Kaplan's voice took on a pontifical note—"Lincollen gave ot de Mancipation Prockilmation. Dat vas, dat all men are born an' created *in de same vay!* So he vas killed."

Exhausted by this mighty passage, Mr. Kaplan paused. Mrs. Moskowitz chose the opportunity to force down a yawn.

"Vell, vat's got all dis to do mit Jake Popper?" Mr. Kaplan asked suddenly. He had taken the question out of the very mouths of Miss Mitnick, Mr. Bloom, et al. "Vell, Jake Popper vas also a fine man, mit a hot like gold. Ve called him Honest Jake. Ufcawss, Jake Popper vasn't a beeg soldier; he didn't make Velley Fudges or free slafes. Jake Popper had a dalicatessen store." The modest shrug that accompanied this sentence made it live and breathe. "He had a dalicatessen store, an' in his store could even poor pipple mitout money alvays gat somting to eat—if dey vas honest. Jake Popper did a tremandous beeg business—on cradit. An' averybody loved him.

"Vun day vas Honest Jake fillink bed. He vas hot an' cold by de same time; vat ve call a fivver. So averybody said, 'Jake, lay don in bad, rast.' But did Jake Popper lay don in bad, rast? No! He stayed in store, day an' night. He said, 'I got to tink abot mine *customers!*' Dat's de kind high sanse *duty* he had!"

Whether from throat strain or emotion, a husky tone crept into Mr. Kaplan's voice at this point.

"Den de doctor came an' said, 'Popper, you got bronxitis!' So Jake vent in bad. An' he got voise an' voise. So de doctor insulted odder doctors—"

"*Con*sulted other—"

"—an' dey took him in Mont Sinai Hospital. He had double demonia! So dere vas all kinds maditzins de bast. Even blood confusions dey gave him."

"Transfusions, Mr. Kaplan!" It was no use. Mr. Kaplan, like a spirited steed, was far ahead.

"An' dey shot him in de arm, he should fallink aslip. . . . An' efter a while, Honest Jake Popper pest avay." Mr. Kaplan's face was bathed in reverence, suffused with a lofty dignity. Mrs. Moskowitz yawned no more; she was shaking her head sadly, back and forth.

"So in Jake Popper's honor I made dis leettle spitch. An' I vant also to say for him somting like 'O Ceptin! My Ceptin!'—dat Miss Higby said abot Abraham Lincollen. I got from her de voids." Mr. Kaplan took a piece of paper out of an inner vest pocket, drew his head up high, and, as Mr. Parkhill held his breath, read:

> *"O hot! hot! hot!*
> *O de bliddink drops rad!*
> *Dere on de dack*
> *Jake Popper lies,*
> *Fallink cold an' dad!"*

Celestial wings fluttered over the beginners' grade of the American Night Preparatory School for Adults, whispering of the grandeur that was Popper.

"Isn't dat beauriful?" Mr. Kaplan mused softly, with the detachment of the true artist. "My!"

Mr. Parkhill was just about to call for corrections when Mr. Kaplan said, "Vun ting more I should say, so de cless shouldn't fill *too* bed abot Jake Popper. It's awreddy nine yiss since he pest avay!"

Mrs. Moskowitz shot Mr. Kaplan a furious look; her tender emotions had been cruelly exploited.

"An' *I* didn't go to de funeral!" On this strange note, Mr. Kaplan took his seat.

The class hummed, protesting against this anticlimax which left so much to the imagination.

"Why you didn't?" cried Mr. Bloom.

Mr. Kaplan's face was a study in sufferance. "Becawss de funeral vas in de meedle of de veek," he sighed. "An' I said to minesalf, 'Keplen, you in America, so tink like de *Americans* tink!' So I tought, an' I didn't go. Becawss I tought of dat *dip* American idea, *Business bafore pleasure!"*

Mr. K★A★P★L★A★N's
So-and-so

THE MARCH RAIN slithered across the windows. It was a nasty night of wet feet, drab spirits, and head colds. Mr. Parkhill, indeed, *had* a head cold. He was at home, indisposed, and a young substitute teacher, bubbling with the courage of a year and a half of practice teaching, was at the desk in front of the beginners' grade. The young man could tell, by the way the students received the sad news of Mr. Parkhill's indisposition, that they really liked him and were worried by his absence. This filled the young substitute with pride in his calling.

"Is maybe Mr. Pockheel *seryous* seeck?" asked a pleasant-looking gentleman in the front row, center.

"No, I'm sure not. He'll be back with you Monday night, Mr.—?"

"Hyman Keplen," the man with the pleasant face said. "Denks Gott isn't seryous awreddy." Mr. Kaplan sighed with relief. Many other students sighed with relief, too; the collective sighs were like a choral Amen! "Dat soitinly takes a beeg load off!"

"You mean 'That takes a load off my mind'!" Mr. Parkhill's substitute corrected quickly. Nothing escaped this young man.

"A load off mine *mind?*" Mr. Kaplan repeated softly. He thought this over for a moment, nodded and said, "An' off mine *hot* also."

The young man saw at once that this Mr. Kaplan had a subtle mind. (Had he known that only last week Mr. Kaplan had said, "For eatink smashed potatoes I am usink a knife an' fog!" he would have concluded that Mr. Kaplan had a *remarkable* mind.)

"Well, let us begin tonight's lesson. Mr. Parkhill suggested that we—"

"Podden me, Titcher." It was Mr. Kaplan again, Mr. Kaplan with an apologetic smile. "Can ve know plizz *your* name?"

The young man laughed boyishly. "Well, pardon me! How stupid of me. Of course. My name is Jennings."

From the look on Mr. Kaplan's face, the name might have been Chinese. "Channink?" he asked incredulously.

"No, *Jennings.*" The young man got up from the desk and wrote the characters on the board with undismayed fingers.

"Aha!" Mr. Kaplan beamed. *"Chen*nink!"

Mr. "Chennink" smiled feebly. He was a realist.

"As I was saying, Mr. Parkhill suggested that we spend the first part of the period in what he calls Open Questions. I have been told you keep notes of the questions you may wish to ask. If you will refer to them now, please, for *just* a few minutes . . . Everybody, now!"

The students seemed a little breathtaken by this gust of energetic tutelage. Then there were shrugs, exchanges of glances, and sighs as the beginners' grade girded its scholastic loins for Open Questions. Notebooks, foolscap pages, envelopes, scraps of paper, even chewing-gum wrappers appeared, to be studied for the great event. A fat woman seemed to be reading the wall just above Mr. Jennings' head, seeking inspiration. A man with a conspicuous gold tooth fumbled through his pockets. Mr. Hyman Kaplan, for whom Mr. Jennings already felt a certain respect, merely leaned his head to one side, half closed his eyes, and whispered audibly, "So now is Haupen Qvastions! My! Esk Titcher abot *a room goink arond.*"

"Pardon?" Mr. Jennings asked quickly. "I didn't hear what you were saying."

Mr. Kaplan slowly opened his eyes. "I vasn't sayink," he murmured dreamily. "I vas *tinking.*"

Mr. Kaplan continued thinking. "Esk Titcher," he whispered. "Abot *a room goink arond!*" Mr. Jennings felt a damp sensation on his brow. "Abot *so-an'-so!* Esk Titcher abot . . ."

For some strange reason a quotation flashed through Mr. Jennings' mind: "That way madness lies." Mr. Jennings fought it down.

"Let us begin," he said with calculated briskness. "We shall recite in order, starting with—with the lady in the back row, please."

That would leave Mr. Kaplan and his cryptic "room goink arond," to say nothing of "so-an'-so!" almost to the end. Mr. Jennings caught himself hoping that the recess bell would ring before Mr. Kaplan's turn came. This was contrary to all that Mr. Jennings had been taught in Professor Heppelhauser's Education V and he felt ashamed of himself.

Mr. Kaplan opened his eyes with an injured air. *"Goldboig* foist," he whispered sadly. "Oi!" His expression was that of a man betrayed.

Miss Goldberg wanted to know whether "trumpet" had anything to do with bridge, "like, with my Jeck I trumpet." After this brilliant beginning, Mr. Weinstein sought aid with "Tsintsinnati," where his brother and "fife" children lived. (He hadn't been able to find Tsintsinnati in the dictionary, so he said; he admitted, however, that it was a *cheap* dictionary.) Mrs. Moskowitz asked whether "Specific" was the name of the *other* ocean. (The Atlantic and the Specific.) Miss Mitnick, obviously a superior student, was puzzled by the difference between "beside" and "besides." Miss Caravello ventured to query what the *G* in "G-men" stood for.

Through all these weighty matters Mr. Kaplan sat with heroic resignation, occasionally indulging in wistful and philosophic sighs.

Mr. Jennings treated each of these problems with profound earnestness. He was exhilarated by the challenge of communication. He was tasting, as never before in his year and a half of practice teaching, the simple joys of the schoolman. And before he knew it, with a good ten minutes to spare, it was Mr. Kaplan's turn.

"Mr. Kaplan," he said slowly, and something in him went taut. This was journey's end.

Mr. Kaplan's face took on the luster of ecstasy. "My!" he breathed semipublicly. "Now is comink *mine* time!"

He rose. No other student had risen, but there was something eminently fitting about Mr. Kaplan's rising. A rustle of anticipation, pleasure, and anxiety went through the classroom.

"Ladies an' gantleman," Mr. Kaplan began in his finest oratorical manner. "Mr. Pockheel told us dat if ve vant to *loin*, den avery place ve goink, ve should vatchink for mistakes, for Haupen Qvastions. In de sopvay, on de stritt, day an' night, alvays ve should be *stoodents!* Believe me, dat vas a fine, smot idea!"

To this Mrs. Moskowitz nodded reverently, as if to a reading of the Psalms.

"So like Mr. Pockheel said, avery place I vas goink, I vas vatchink, vatchink—" Mr. Kaplan narrowed his eyes and looked suspicious to lend authenticity to his comment—"all de time vatchink for tings I should esk by Haupen Qvastions time!"

This, Mr. Jennings sensed, was the introduction. It was.

"So de foist qvastion is vat's de minnink from 'A room is goink arond'?"

"A room is going around?" repeated Mr. Jennings, though he knew perfectly well what the words had been.

"A room is goink arond!" Mr. Kaplan repeated firmly, and then sat down.

The beginners' grade was hushed.

"Yes . . . a room is going around." There was no doubt about it. "Well, the meaning of the words is perfectly simple, Mr. Kaplan. As anyone can tell—" Mr. Jennings explained the meaning of the words. He treated them individually, collectively, conceptually. But he admitted that the phrase, as a phrase, seemed strange. "Of course, if one were dizzy, or faint, or *drunk*"—Mr. Jennings was not the type to mince words—"why, then one *would* say, 'I feel as if the room is going around.'"

Mr. Norman Bloom snickered. "I think that's a crazy quastion!"

Mr. Kaplan surveyed Mr. Bloom with a haughty glance. "Mine dear Bloom," he said with dignity. "To *som* pipple is even de *bast* qvastions crazy!"

Mr. Bloom's face collapsed.

"Could you tell us exactly how you heard the phrase?" Mr. Jennings suggested quickly.

Mr. Kaplan nodded. "From mine vife. She vas talkink to Mrs. Skolsky—dats de lady livink opstairs—abot Mrs. Backer—dat's de femily livink donstairs. An' Mrs. Skolsky said, 'You know, I tink Mrs. Backer vill saparate Mr. Backer mit divorce!' So mine vife esked, netcheral, 'So how you know?' So Mrs. Skolsky gave answer: 'Averybody's sayink dat! *A room is goink arond!*'"

"A rumor's going around!" cried Mr. Jennings. Meaning burst within him like a firecracker. "Why, Mr. Kaplan, that's an excellent phrase! A rumor refers to—"

But Mr. Kaplan hardly listened. His smile was phosphorescent. He dropped rays of sweet redemption over his shoulders, right and left. For Mr. Norman Bloom, staring moodily at the floor, Mr. Kaplan had a special and triumphant radiance.

When Mr. Jennings had given his all to "A rumor's going around," Mr. Kaplan murmured, "My! Dat vas som qvastion!" (There was a fine objectivity in the awe with which Mr. Kaplan regarded his brainchildren.) Then he asked his second question.

"I hoid soch an axpression, I can't believe. It sonds fonny. *Fonny,*" Mr. Kaplan repeated with a telling glance at Mr. Norman Bloom, "not crazy. Plizz, vat's de minnink from 'so-an'-so,' a 'so-an'-so'?"

It had come.

"Do you want me to explain so-and-so, or *a* so-and-so? There is a distinction, you know." Mr. Jennings faced the worst bravely.

"Awright, lat be *a* so-an'-so," said Mr. Kaplan with a benign wave of the hand.

Mr. Jennings took a deep breath. Education V and the pedantic wisdom of Professor Heppelhauser seemed very far away now, and totally worthless in dealing with problems of the magnitude of a so-and-so.

"The phrase a so-and-so," he began earnestly, "is heard quite commonly. But it's vulgar. It's used instead of—well, profanity."

Mr. Jennings paused hopefully, ready to go no further. But in the eyes of the class there was no flicker of understanding to the concept "profanity." Mr. Jennings faced the task of explaining profanity without using it.

"Profanity means—well, cursing, swearing, using bad, foul, *not nice* language." Still the faces were blank; still the eyes held no flame of recognition. "Let me put it this way, class. Suppose someone wants to say something bad about someone else, wants to *curse* him, really—but doesn't actually want to use profane language. Well, he'll say, 'He's a so-and-so!' instead of—" Too late did young Mr. Jennings realize that he had gone too far. "Instead of—" The class waited expectantly, Miss Mitnick with a blush.

"Low life! Tremp! Goot-fa-nottink!" cried Mr. Kaplan impetuously.

"Yes! Fine! Exactly!" Never had Mr. Jennings been so grateful. "That's *precisely* how a so-and-so is used."

An "Ah!" of illumination went through the class. But Mr. Bloom glowered. "That's a bad quastion to ask with ladies in room!" he cried.

"Aha!" Mr. Kaplan's war cry resounded against the walls. "Who is sayink mine qvastion is bed? Who? *In aducation is no bed qvastions!*"

And the opposition fell into shamed silence. Mr. Kaplan's face glowed. "De kind so-and-so *I* minn, Mr. Chennink," Mr. Kaplan said in a clarion voice, "*isn't* volgar! I minn altogadder difference."

Mr. Jennings took counsel with his soul. He had done his duty with patience and discretion. And yet, undaunted, Mr. Kaplan pursued some strange, evasive Truth. It was in a voice freighted with caution that Mr. Jennings said, "Perhaps you had better illustrate what you mean, Mr. Kaplan."

Mr. Kaplan rose for the last time that memorable night. The raindrops did an impish dance on the windowpanes, and the room echoed their derision.

"Vell, lest veek I mat in de stritt mine old frand Moe Slavitt," Mr. Kaplan began, sotto voce. " 'Hollo, Moe!' I said. 'How you fillink dis beauriful mornink?' So Moe said, 'I got a hadake.' So I esk, 'A *bed* hadake, Moe?' So he gives enswer, 'Not a tarrible hadake, but also not *not* a hadake.' Dat Moe—alvays he's sayink yas an' no at de same time! So I said, 'Leesen, Moe! Don' talkink all de time in reedles! I esk a tsimple qvastion, so give, plizz, a strong, plain enswer. Do you fill Hau Kay? Yas or no?' Vell, vat Moe did? Ha! He made like dis mit his shouldiss"— Mr. Kaplan shrugged his shoulders with profound expressiveness—"an' said, 'I don' fill rotten. I don't fill A Number Vun. *I'm just so-an'-so!'* "

The recess bell rang. And the raindrops howled on the steamy windows like madmen.

Mr. K★A★P★L★A★N's
Fine Friend

No TRUMPETS BLARED as the fat little man entered the classroom. He was roly-poly and ruddy. He had a tiny nose and a thick reddish mustache that made his nose seem incredibly small. He looked like a fat little Buddha—a Buddha with a mustache. He walked up to Mr. Parkhill's desk and, without a word, handed him a card. It read:

VISITOR'S CARD

AMERICAN NIGHT PREPARATORY SCHOOL FOR ADULTS

PLEASE ADMIT THE BEARER: *Mr. Teitelman* FOR ONE TRIAL LESSON.

Leland Robinson
PRINCIPAL

"Mr.—er—Teitelman?" asked Mr. Parkhill.

The fat little man nodded. He seemed very sad.

"Just take a seat, please, anywhere." Mr. Parkhill smiled reassuringly. He was careful to treat new students and visitors with particular kindliness; he knew how choked with embarrassment most of them were. "And please consider yourself a member of the class for the evening. I hope you will—er—enter into the work just as if you were one of our regular students. I hope you *will* be after tonight."

The fat little man looked at the rows of chairs, then walked to an empty place in the front row without a word. He sat down. Mrs. Tomasic was on his left. Mr. Hyman Kaplan was on his right.

"Valcome!" said Mr. Kaplan to the newcomer with a fine generosity.

The fat little man seemed startled.

Mr. Parkhill smiled encouragingly at the visitor and said, "We shall devote the first half of the class session tonight to finishing the Recitation and Speech exercise of last Thursday. As I recall, we have still to hear from—let me see—Mrs. Moskowitz, Mr. Pinsky, Miss Kowalski, and Mr. Marcus." The four students named stirred uneasily. "Suppose we allow these students a few minutes to prepare themselves. The rest of the class can study the list of spelling words on page ninety-six of *English for Beginners*."

The class began to rustle through *English for Beginners* while three of the four fated to recite went through individual rites of preparation. Mrs. Moskowitz simply heaved a low moan.

Mr. Hyman Kaplan paid no attention to these matters. He was examining the fat little man on his left, curiously, insistently, out of the corner of his left eye. Mr. Kaplan had an independent nervous system for each orb: his left eye scrutinized the fat little man; his right, like a sentry, was trained on Mr. Parkhill. It was uncanny.

For a long moment Mr. Kaplan subjected the visitor to his most critical gaze. It was clear to Mr. Parkhill that Mr. Kaplan was trying to discover whether this newcomer was friend or foe. Finishing the examination Mr. Kaplan leaned his head to the left and whispered, in a tone just loud enough to be heard by everyone in the room, "How's by you de name, plizz?"

The fat little man looked sadly at Mr. Kaplan and said nothing.

Mr. Kaplan cleared his throat. "Eh . . . vat is de *name*—plizz?" Now his whisper was more compelling.

The fat little man took a fountain pen out of his pocket and, without turning his head, laid it on the arm of his chair. A name was stamped in black on the barrel of the pen.

"F. Teitelman," Mr. Kaplan read. "Aha! F—for Philip, ha?"

The fat little man shook his head.

"*Not* for Philip?" Amazement was in Mr. Kaplan's voice. "My!" He closed his eyes, pursed his lips, and pondered this baffling matter. Then he whispered politely, "So vat *is* by you de name, vill you be so kindly?"

"Jerome," said the fat little man.

"Jerome. . . . *Jerome*. . . . Dat's mit a *G!* So vy is on de fontain pan *F*? There was a ring of accusation in his voice and he watched every move the fat little man made, devoting particular attention to the mustache.

The fat little man looked at Mr. Kaplan more sadly than ever and said, "De pan belongs mine vife."

"I think we are ready to start now," Mr. Parkhill announced. He had been fascinated by the little drama in the front row. "Er—Mrs. Moskowitz, will you speak first, please?"

Mrs. Moskowitz sighed. "I s'pose," she said and rose, smoothed her dress, stumbled over Mr. Scymzak's feet, apologized with a quick "Axcusing!" ran her hand across her hair, coughed, almost dropped her purse, and smiled a weak greeting to Miss Mitnick—all in the time it took her to walk from her seat in the second row to the front of the room.

"Sobject—About Arond De House."

Mr. Kaplan shot the fat little man a you-see-what-I-have-to-go-through look. Mrs. Moskowitz generally spoke of those aspects of life which dealt with something "arond de house." She did not lead a very rich existence.

"De men don't know how hard is de life for de ladies," she said. "De men tink—"

"*Men* don't know how hard *life* is for *women*—not ladies, Mrs. Moskowitz," Mr. Parkhill interrupted. "You mean men and women in general."

Mrs. Moskowitz tried to produce an expression of comprehension.

"Soch a fine titcher ve got," Mr. Kaplan whispered to the fat little man, smiling. The face of Buddha was immobile. Mr. Kaplan sighed; he was making no headway on the fraternal road.

Mrs. Moskowitz began all over again. "*Men* don't know how hard is *life* of *women*. Som of the—no—som women work in shop all day, I do, and by night must comming home, clinn op de house, making sopper, take care of children if have children, which I have, fix clothes, and so far."

Mrs. Moskowitz stopped, exhausted. She had overtaxed her imagination in that one great flight. "So vat more I should tell?"

"Tell abot feexing claws!" Mr. Kaplan cried out. He gazed proudly at the fat little man to see whether *this* maneuver would win any response. The fat little man blew his nose. In sheer desperation Mr. Kaplan whispered, "Teitelman, don' be afraid! You should givink ideas too!"

The fat little man looked at Mr. Kaplan for a moment, expressionless. Then, and it was all the more impressive because it was so unexpected, he nodded vigorously three times. A warm, triumphant smile flooded Mr. Kaplan's countenance. Teitelman *was* his friend.

"Awright, so like Mr. Kaplan says," Mrs. Moskowitz announced, "about fixing clothes I'll tell. Vell, for fixing clothes or socks you should have a niddle, a spool trad, and also a little—eh—how you say—"

"Time!" said the fat little man suddenly.

The students reacted with surprise. Visitors never recited. Here was a man of a new order. Mr. Kaplan cried, *"Fine,* Teitelman! Dat's de boy!"

Mrs. Moskowitz stared at the fat little man, dazed. Then she blinked her eyes indignantly. "Vy about *time* all of a sodden? For fixing clothes you should have niddle, trad—but vat's got to do *time?*"

Mr. Teitelman

"You nid time *too,* netcheral," Mr. Kaplan suggested promptly, with a nod to his new bosom friend.

Mrs. Moskowitz turned on Mr. Kaplan with scorn. "And you should have a chair also, for sitting, and laktric lights you should see, and a house for being insite. So do I have to tell *all* about if I'm talking about sewing somting?"

Mr. Parkhill interceded hastily. "I'm sure our visitor didn't mean any harm, Mrs. Moskowitz. He didn't quite understand. Do—er—go on."

Mrs. Moskowitz gave Messrs. Kaplan and Teitelman a smirk, aware that she had gained a prestige point. Mr. Kaplan whispered consolation to the fat little man. "Tsall right, Teitelman. It's Hau Kay! *Give ideas!*"

Mrs. Moskowitz continued with great dignity. "So like I said, you should have a niddle, trad, and somting alse. Maybe you having a tick piece goods, like an overcoat, and you ken't pushing de niddle trough, so you put on de finger a little cop, from tin it's made ot. It's called a—"

"Dumbbell!" said the fat little man.

The class gasped. Miss Mitnick blushed for Mrs. Moskowitz and Mr. Bloom shook his head. Mr. Kaplan squirmed in his seat with delight. Mrs. Moskowitz pressed her lips together and then in one long, uninterrupted breath blurted out, "Mister-I-dunno-who-you-are—"

"De name is Teitelman," said Mr. Kaplan proudly.

"—I don't mean dumbbell! Maybe your vife is using dumbbells. I use a *timble!*" Wrapped in her wrath, Mrs. Moskowitz was like a Valkyrie, spear and all. "Now I'll go farder. So if you have niddle, trad, and *timble,* de rast is easy. You fill op de holes."

Mrs. Moskowitz stopped. She was perspiring. Her eyes clouded now, as she sought inspiration to go on. "I s'pose I should talk som more," she muttered miserably. The class waited for Mrs. Moskowitz to go on; the silence was painful. Suddenly, like a thunderbolt, inspiration came. "Also arond de house is to *cook!*" New vistas opened before Mrs. Moskowitz. "Cooking is to me like painting maybe to artist. I love. Since I'm ten yiss old I'm cooking. I bake brat—rye and pumpernickel—rolls, cookeess, even—"

"Pies!" cried the fat little man.

"Cake!" retorted Mrs. Moskowitz hotly. "*Not* pies, Mister."

Like a falcon Mr. Kaplan swooped to the defense of his protégé. "You makink pies *too*, no?"

"I—bake—CAKE!"

"Moskovitz, don' gat axcited!" Mr. Kaplan exclaimed. "Mine frand Teitelman is tryink to *halp* you. He's trying to say you an A Number Vun cook. You *got* to bakink pies!"

"Batter Mr. New Student should halping you!" shouted Mrs. Moskowitz with fury. "Me he's telling dumbbells for timbles, time all of a sodden, and now he's even trowing in *pies!* Dat's enoff!"

She stalked to her seat, her head high. The classroom roared with excitement. In this dazzling, hectic interchange there was the seed of a great feud.

Mr. Parkhill, overcome by embarrassment, tried to placate Mrs. Moskowitz. He apologized for the new student's excessive eagerness. He assured her that no one had meant to offend her. He urged her to continue. It was of no avail. Where *l'honneur* was concerned, Sadie Moskowitz was not the type to be bought with light phrases. She shook her head stubbornly. The class buzzed with the scandal.

And Messrs. Kaplan and Teitelman sat in the front row oblivious of the tempest that seethed around them. They paid no attention to the speeches that followed. They just sat, these two, united by a mighty bond. They looked like men who had faced death together.

When the recess bell rang, the classroom filled with happy noises. Mr. Kaplan smiled at the fat little man and said, "Lat's goink outside now." The fat little man shook his head sadly. Mr. Kaplan said, "Hau Kay, Teitelman. You *rast.* Tink op som more fine ideas." He went into the corridor, beaming.

The fat little man sat in the room, staring at Mr. Parkhill. He seemed to be thinking. After a few moments he took his hat, said "Goombye," and left.

When Mr. Kaplan returned after recess, he found his comrade in arms gone. "Who seen Teitelman?" he cried in pain.

No one had seen Teitelman. No one seemed to know what had happened to him. Mr. Parkhill called on Miss Caravello and the reading exercise began.

But Mr. Kaplan sat plunged in a moody silence. For the rest of the evening gloom enveloped him like a shroud. He did not participate in the reading drill. He did not call out daring thoughts during the vocabulary exercise. The heart seemed to have gone out of Hyman Kaplan. Lost was the great flair.

Only once did he emerge from the abyss. That was when, staring wistfully at the empty seat beside him, on which the fat little man had left his Visitor's Card as an eloquent souvenir, Mr. Kaplan sighed the sigh of the heavy-laden and murmured, "My! I lost a *fine* frand."

Mr. K★A★P★L★A★N
and Shakespeare

IT WAS MISS HIGBY's idea in the first place. She had suggested to Mr. Parkhill that the students came to her class unaware of the *finer* side of English, of its beauty and, as she put it, "the glorious heritage of our literature." She suggested that perhaps poetry might be worked into the exercises of Mr. Parkhill's class. The beginners' grade had, after all, been subjected to almost a year of English and might be presumed to have achieved some linguistic sophistication. Poetry would make the students conscious of precise enunciation; it would make them read with greater care and an ear for sounds. Miss Higby *loved* poetry and she argued her cause with considerable logic. Poetry *would* be excellent for the enunciation of the students, thought Mr. Parkhill.

So it was that when he faced the class the following Tuesday night, Mr. Parkhill had a volume of Shakespeare on his desk and an eager, almost an expectant, look in his eye. The love that Miss Higby bore for poetry in general was as nothing compared to the love that Mr. Parkhill bore for Shakespeare in particular. To Mr. Parkhill, poetry meant Shakespeare.

"Tonight, class," said Mr. Parkhill, "I am going to try an experiment. I am going to introduce you to poetry—great poetry."

Mr. Parkhill then delivered a modest lecture on the beauty of poetry, its expression of the loftier thoughts of men, its economy of statement. He hoped it would be a relief from spelling and composition exercises to use poetry as the subject matter of the Recitation and Speech period. "I shall write a passage on the board and read it for you. Then you will each give a short address, telling us what thoughts the passage has brought to your minds."

The class seemed pleased by the announcement and Mr. Hyman Kaplan, looking at Mr. Parkhill with admiration, whispered to himself, "Now is poyetry! My! Mus' be progriss ve makink awreddy!"

"The passage will be from Shakespeare," Mr. Parkhill announced, opening the volume.

An excited buzz ran through the class as the magic of that name fell upon them.

"Imachine!" murmured Mr. Kaplan. "Jakesbeer!"

"*Shakespeare*, Mr. Kaplan!"

Mr. Parkhill took a piece of chalk and, with care and evident love, wrote the following passage on the board in large, clear letters:

> *Tomorrow, and tomorrow, and tomorrow,*
> *Creeps in this petty pace from day to day,*
> *To the last syllable of recorded time;*
> *And all our yesterdays have lighted fools*
> *The way to dusty death. Out, out, brief candle!*
> *Life's but a walking shadow, a poor player*
> *That struts and frets his hour upon the stage*
> *And then is heard no more: it is a tale*
> *Told by an idiot, full of sound and fury,*
> *Signifying nothing.*

A reverent hush filled the classroom as eyes gazed with wonder on this passage from the Bard. Mr. Parkhill was pleased at this.

"I shall read the passage first," he said. "Listen carefully to my enunciation and let Shakespeare's thoughts sink into your minds."

"Tomorrow, and tomorrow, and tomorrow . . ." Mr. Parkhill read very well and this night, as if some special fire burned in him, he read with rare eloquence. "Out, out, brief candle!" In Miss Mitnick's eyes there was inspiration and wonder. "Life's but a walking shadow . . ." Mrs. Moskowitz sat with a heavy frown, indicating cerebration. "It is a tale told by an idiot . . ." Mr. Kaplan's smile was luminous, but his eyes were closed; it was not clear whether Mr. Kaplan had surrendered to the spell of the Immortal Bard or to that of Morpheus.

"I shall—er—read the passage again," said Mr. Parkhill, clearing his throat vociferously until he saw Mr. Kaplan's eyes open. "Tomorrow, and tomorrow, and tomorrow . . ."

When Mr. Parkhill had read the passage for the second time he said, "That should be quite clear now. Are there any questions?"

There were a few questions. Mr. Scymzak wanted to know what "frets" was. Miss Schneiderman asked about "struts." Mr. Kaplan wasn't sure about "cripps." Mr. Parkhill explained the words carefully, with several illustrative uses of each.

"No more questions? Well, I shall allow a few minutes for you to think over the meaning of the passage. Then we shall begin Recitation and Speech."

Mr. Kaplan promptly closed his eyes again, his smile beatific. The students sank into that reverie miscalled thought, searching their souls for the symbols evoked by Shakespeare's immortal words.

"Miss Caravello, will you begin?" asked Mr. Parkhill at last.

Miss Caravello went to the front of the room. "Da poem isa gooda," she said slowly. "Itsa have—"

"It *has.*"

"It hasa beautiful wordsa. Itsa lak Dante, Italian poet—"

"Ha!" cried Mr. Kaplan scornfully. "Shaksbeer you metchink mit Tante? *Shaksbeer?* Mein Gott!"

It was obvious that Mr. Kaplan had identified himself with Shakespeare and would tolerate no disparagement of his alter ego.

"Miss Caravello is merely expressing her own ideas," said Mr. Parkhill pacifically. (Actually, he felt completely sympathetic to Mr. Kaplan's point of view.)

"Hau Kay," agreed Mr. Kaplan with a generous wave of the hand. "But to me is no comparink a high-cless man like Shaksbeer mit a Tante, dat's all."

Miss Caravello, her poise shattered, said a few more words and then sat down.

Mrs. Yampolsky's contribution was brief. "This is full deep meanings," she said, her eyes on the floor. "Is hard for a person not so good in English to unnistand. But I like."

"Like!" cried Mr. Kaplan with a fine impatience. *"Like?* Batter *love,* Yampolsky. Mit Shaksbeer mus' be *love!"*

Mr. Parkhill had to suggest that Mr. Kaplan control his aesthetic passions. He did understand how Mr. Kaplan felt, however, and he sensed a new bond between them. Mrs. Yampolsky staggered through several more nervous comments and retired.

Mr. Bloom was next. He gave a long declamation, ending, "So is passimistic ideas in the poem, and I am optimist. Life should be happy—so we should remember this is only a poem. Maybe is Shakespeare too passimistic."

"You wronk, Bloom!" cried Mr. Kaplan with prompt indignation. "Shaksbeer is passimist because is de *life* passimist also!"

Mr. Parkhill, impressed by this philosophical stroke, realized that Mr. Kaplan, afire with the glory of the Bard of Avon, could not be suppressed. The only solution was to call on Mr. Kaplan for his recitation at once. Mr. Parkhill was indeed curious about what fresh thoughts Mr. Kaplan would utter after his passionate defenses of the Bard. After correcting certain parts of Mr. Bloom's speech he said, "Mr. Kaplan, will *you* speak next?"

Mr. Kaplan's face broke into a glow; his smile was like a rainbow. "Soitinly," he said, walking to the front of the room. Never had he seemed so dignified, so eager, so conscious of a great destiny.

"Er—Mr. Kaplan," added Mr. Parkhill, suddenly aware of the possibilities of the situation, "speak *carefully.*"

"*Spacially* careful vill I be," Mr. Kaplan reassured him. He cleared his throat, adjusted his tie and began. "Ladies an' gantleman, you hoid all kinds minninks abot dis piece poyetry, an'—"

"*Po*etry."

"—abot dis piece *po*etry. But to me is a difference minnink altogadder. Ve mus' tink abot Julius Scissor an' how *he* falt! In dese exact voids is Julius Scissor sayink—"

"Er—Mr. Kaplan," said Mr. Parkhill, "the passage is taken from *Macbeth.*"

Mr. Kaplan looked at Mr. Parkhill with injured surprise. "*Not* from *Julius Scissor?*" There was pain in his voice.

"No. And it's—er—*Julius Caesar.*"

Mr. Kaplan waited until the last echo of the name had permeated his soul. "Podden me, Mr. Pockheel. Isn't *see*zor vat you cottink somting op mit?"

"That," said Mr. Parkhill quickly, "is scissor. You have used Caesar for scissor and scissor for Caesar."

Mr. Kaplan nodded, marveling at his own virtuosity.

"But go on with your speech, please." Mr. Parkhill, to tell the truth, felt a little guilty that he had not announced at the very beginning that the passage was from *Macbeth*. "Tell us *why* you thought the lines were from *Julius Caesar*."

"Vell," said Mr. Kaplan to the class, his smile assuming its normal serenity, "I vas positif, becawss I can *see* de whole scinn." His eyes filled with a strange enchantment. "It's in a tant, on de night bafore dey makink Julius de Kink from Rome. So he is axcited an' ken't slip. He is layink in bad, tinking, 'Tomorrow an' tomorrow an' tomorrow. How slow dey movink! Almost cripps! Soch a pity de pace!'"

Before Mr. Parkhill could explain that "petty pace" did not mean "Soch a pity de pace!" Mr. Kaplan had soared on.

"De days go slow, from day to day, like leetle tsyllables on phonograph racords from time."

Anxiety and bewilderment invaded Mr. Parkhill's eyes.

"An' vat abot yestidday? tinks Julius Scissor. Ha! All our yestiddays are only makink a good light for fools to die in de dost!"

"Dusty death doesn't mean—" There was no interrupting Mr. Kaplan.

"An' Julius Scissor is so tired, an' he vants to fallink aslip. So he hollers, mit fillink, 'Go ot! Go ot! Short candle!' So it goes ot."

Mr. Kaplan's voice dropped to a whisper. "But he ken't slip. Now is bodderink him de idea from life. Vat is de life altogadder? tinks Julius Scissor. An' he gives enswer, de pot I like de bast. Life is like a bum actor, strottink an' hollerink arond de stage for only vun hour bafore he's kicked ot. Life is a tale told by idjots, dat's all, full of fonny sonds an' phooey!"

Mr. Parkhill could be silent no longer. " 'Full of sound and fury!' " he cried desperately. But inspiration, like an irresistible force, swept Mr. Kaplan on.

"Life is monkey business! It don' minn a ting. It signifies nottink! An' den Julius Scissor closes his ice fest"— Mr. Kaplan demonstrated the Consul's closing his eyes—"an' falls dad!"

The class was hushed as Mr. Kaplan stopped. In the silence, a tribute to the fertility of Mr. Kaplan's imagination and the power of his oratory, Mr. Kaplan went to his seat. But just before he sat down, as if adding a postscript, he sighed. "Dat vas mine idea. But ufcawss is all wronk, becawss de voids ain't abot Julius Scissor altogadder. It's all abot an Irishman by de name Macbat."

Then Mr. Kaplan sat down.

It was some time before Mr. Parkhill could bring himself to criticize Mr. Kaplan's pronunciation, enunciation, diction, grammar, idiom, and sentence structure. For Mr. Parkhill discovered that he could not easily tear himself away from that tent outside Rome, where "Julius Scissor," cursed with insomnia, had thought of time and life—and philosophized himself to a strange and sudden death.

Mr. Parkhill was distinctly annoyed with Miss Higby.

The Terrible Vengeance of
H★Y★M★A★N K★A★P★L★A★N

MR. PARKHILL WONDERED whether he had not been a little rash in taking up idioms with the beginners' grade. Idioms were, of course, of primary importance to those who sought an understanding of English; they were the very essence of the language. At the last session of the class, Mr. Parkhill had spent a careful hour explaining what idioms were, how they grew, how they took on meaning. He had illustrated his lecture with many examples, drawn from *English for Beginners*. He had answered questions. And for homework, he had assigned what seemed a simple enough exercise: three short sentences, using an idiom in each sentence. But now Mr. Parkhill realized that he had been too optimistic. The assignment was not proving a success. In truth it was incredible.

Mr. Marcus, for example, had used the expression, "It will cost you free." That, to Mr. Marcus, was an idiom. Mrs. Tomasic had submitted only one sentence, as much as confessing that her imagination quailed before the magnitude of the assignment. The sentence was "Honestly is the best policy." Mr. Jacob Rubin was groping in the right direction, at least; he seemed to suspect what an idiom *was;* and yet, for one of his efforts, he had given, "By twelve a.m. the job will be as good as down."

And now, a full half hour before the end of the period, it was time for the contribution of Mr. Hyman Kaplan. There on the board were three sentences—under a heading like an illuminated marquee:

3 SENT. (&ID.)

by

H★Y★M★A★N K★A★P★L★A★N

(Mr. Parkhill had learned that trying to dissuade Mr. Kaplan from printing his name in all its starry splendor, on the slightest provocation, was just a waste of time.)

"Mr. Kaplan, read your sentences, please," said Mr. Parkhill briskly.

The briskness was intentional; it buttressed Mr. Parkhill's morale. The class had snickered several times while reading Mr. Kaplan's sentences; now, with Mr. Kaplan to read them, there was no telling to what heights their emotions might ascend.

Mr. Kaplan rose, his smile that of an angel in flight. "Ladies an' gantleman an' Mr. Pockheel. Tree santences I vas wridink on de board, mit idyoms. An' mine idea vas dat—"

"Please *read* the sentences," Mr. Parkhill broke in. Mr. Kaplan was congenitally incapable of resisting the urge to orate.

"I back you podden. De foist santence . . ." Mr. Kaplan read it. He read it distinctly, and with pride.

1. He's nots.

Mr. Parkhill took a long, deep breath. "That's *not* an idiom, Mr. Kaplan," he said emphatically. "That's—er—*slang*. No one who used English correctly, with taste, would ever use an expression like 'He's—er—nuts.' "

Dismay crept into Mr. Kaplan's face. "Is *not* a good axprassion, 'He's nots'?" he asked with a certain hurt. It was apparent that Mr. Kaplan had put his heart and soul into "He's nots."

"No, Mr. Kaplan. It's *very* bad."

Mrs. Moskowitz, large, serene, behemothian, shot Mr. Kaplan a pitying glance. "He's nots!" she crowed. It wasn't clear whether Mrs. Moskowitz was merely repeating Mr. Kaplan's words or was indulging in a little commentary of her own.

"But so many pipple are usink dese voids," Mr. Kaplan protested, shooting Mrs. Moskowitz an injured look. "Honist, avery place I'm goink I hear, 'He's nots!' "

Mr. Parkhill shook his head, adamant. "It doesn't matter how many people say it, Mr. Kaplan. It's an incorrect phrase. It has no place in good English. Besides, you spelled the word—er—nuts wrong. It's n-*u*-t-s."

Mr. Parkhill printed NUTS on the board. He explained what nut really meant, distinguishing it from not with care. With much feeling, he drove home the point that "He's nuts" was outlawed by the canons of good usage. Mr. Kaplan bowed to the purist view, but he seemed a little saddened. Something in him had died with the death of "He's nots."

"Mine sacond santence." The second sentence was, if anything, more astonishing than the first.

2. Get the pearls. By hook or cook!

"By hook or cook," Mr. Parkhill repeated, very softly. "Mr. Kaplan, I'm afraid you've made another serious mistake."

This was too much for Mr. Kaplan to believe. *"Also* tarrible?" he asked, his voice charged with pain. "I tought dis one vould be a real high-cless idyom."

Mr. Parkhill shook his head. "You seem to have an idea of what an idiom is, in this sentence." (Mr. Kaplan shot Mrs. Moskowitz a triumphant smile.) "But you've ruined the idea by your spelling." (Mr. Kaplan's smile scurried into limbo.) "You have confused two entirely different words. Can anyone tell me what's wrong with Mr. Kaplan's sentence?"

Mr. Sam Pinsky answered first. "Should be 'by hook *and* cook!' "

"No!" Mr. Parkhill exclaimed severely. "That would only make it worse."

"I think it should better be, 'By hook or *crook,*' " suggested Miss Mitnick.

"Exactly! *Crook,* not *cook,* Mr. Kaplan."

Miss Mitnick lowered her eyes and smiled modestly. This had a depressing effect on Mr. Kaplan.

"I tought dat crook is like a boiglar or a robber or a chitter," he objected.

"It does mean that," said Mr. Parkhill. "But the phrase 'by hook or by crook' is something altogether different. It refers to . . ."

Mr. Kaplan was wrapped in gloom. To be both scorned by Mrs. Moskowitz, whom he regarded with condescension, and bested by Miss Mitnick—these were blows that a man like Mr. Kaplan did not take lightly. He sighed. It was the sigh of one who has just seen justice fail.

"Your third sentence, please."

Mr. Kaplan seemed a little shorter, a little more rotund, a little less euphoric than usual. The disaster of his sentences had left its mark. "I s'pose," he said, "dat mine toid santence vill be awful also."

It was a touching admission. Mr. Parkhill felt sorry for Mr. Kaplan. He felt worse when Mr. Kaplan read the third sentence.

3. Hang yourself in reseption hall, please.

There was a burst of laughter from Mr. Bloom, followed by peals of hilarity from Messrs. Rabinowitz and Weinstein, and reinforced by an unmaidenly guffaw from Mrs. Moskowitz. Miss Mitnick, a creature of more delicate habits, smiled shyly.

"Heng—yoursalf—in—resaption—hall—plizz!" Mr. Kaplan repeated stubbornly, clinging to the words with the love of a father for his own flesh and blood.

Mr. Parkhill waited for order to filter back into the noisy classroom. "Mr. Kaplan, you have made a rather amusing error." He said it as gently as he could. "If you will merely read the sentence carefully, and pay attention to the word order especially, I'm sure you will see why the sentence struck the class as being—er—funny."

Mr. Kaplan nodded dutifully and read the sentence again, aloud. "Heng—yoursalf—in—resaption—hall—plizz!" He pursed his lips, wrinkled his brow, closed one eye wisely, and stared at the ceiling while everyone waited.

"Aha!" It was Mr. Kaplan's first "Aha!" of the evening, and it rang with his old courage. "I got him!" This was more like the real Hyman Kaplan, valiant, audacious. "Ufcawss! Should be *kepital ladders* on resaption hall! Tsimple!"

The Mitnick-Bloom-Moskowitz entente was swept to new peaks of rapture. This was a rare opportunity: at last Mr. Kaplan seemed to have lost his magic talent for emerging triumphant from any predicament. Someone cried, *"Goombye,* Mr. Keplen!" A voice said, "Oi! I'll die!"—and Mrs. Moskowitz retorted, "Yas! By henging!"

Mr. Kaplan smiled bravely; it was heartrending. Mr. Parkhill rapped on the desk with a pointer.

"No, Mr. Kaplan," he said kindly. "Reception hall is not a proper noun, so it doesn't require capital letters. Reception, by the way, is spelled r-e-*c*-e. No, it's the meaning of your sentence that's at fault. Hang *yourself* in the reception hall, Mr. Kaplan? You don't say *that* to your guests, do you?"

Apparently Mr. Kaplan did. "I'm tryink to make mine gasts fillink at home."

Mr. Bloom's mocking laugh boomed across the room. "Kaplan means Hang your *things* in reception hall!" The startled look that leaped into Mr. Kaplan's eyes showed that Norman Bloom had hit upon the very word which he had meant to use. "But hang yoursalf? Kaplan is som host!"

The gaiety was unconfined.

Mr. Kaplan suddenly smiled and rested his gaze first on Mrs. Moskowitz, then on Miss Mitnick, and then—his eyes dancing with meaning—

Mrs. Moskowitz

on Norman Bloom. The noises vanished into an expectant silence.

"Maybe mine santence isn't *altogadder* a mistake. If *som* pipple came to mine house dat vould maybe be *exactel* vat I should say."

With ten minutes left after the exercise on idioms was completed, Mr. Parkhill put the class through a vigorous written spelling drill. (Spelling drills served admirably as fillers.) He noticed that Mr. Kaplan did not seem to be participating in the exercise with his customary enthusiasm. He was scratching little patterns, aimlessly, on a page torn out of his notebook.

"Restaurant," Mr. Parkhill called.

Mr. Kaplan seemed to have retired to some reverie of thought. The shame of those three sentences burned in Mr. Kaplan's soul.

"Carpenter."

Mr. Kaplan smiled, of a sudden, and began writing. His smile was lofty, with the quality of a private pleasure in some precious joke. Mr. Parkhill announced the next spelling word as if it were a reprimand. "Confess!"

The final bell rang. The students handed in their papers and the room became a jumble of "Good-nights." Mr. Kaplan's farewell was almost lighthearted.

Mr. Parkhill took his attendance report to the principal's office and started home. On the subway train he started to correct the spelling exercises. Miss Mitnick had done very well, as usual. Mr. Bloom had managed to get an 80, his average mark. Mr. Scymzak had misspelled only six out of fifteen words—a splendid performance for Mr. Scymzak. Mrs. Moskowitz was still confusing English with some other, unrevealed language.

Mr. Parkhill frowned when he saw that the next paper in the pile was blank. Some student had made a mistake, handing in an empty page instead of his spelling drill. Mr. Parkhill turned the page over, to see if there was some mark of identification. He beheld a bizarre conglomeration of words, designs, figures, and strange drawings, and all were executed in crayons of a gaudy variety.

Mr. Parkhill wrote a sentence on the page. "Mr. Kaplan: Please submit your spelling drill next time!" He was about to pass on to the next paper when something caught his eye. The scribbled words that were almost lost in the hieroglyphics seemed to *say* something. The writing appeared to be—it was!—*poetry*. Mr. Parkhill adjusted his glasses and read:

> *Critsising Mitnick*
> *Is a picnick.*
>
> *Bloom, Bloom,*
> *Go out the room!*
>
> *Mrs. Moskowitz.*
> *By her it doesnt fits*
> *A dress—Size 44.*

It was a terrible vengeance which Mr. Kaplan, mighty even in defeat, had wreaked upon those who had tried to cast dishonor on his name.

Mr. K★A★P★L★A★N's
Dark Logic

FOR A LONG TIME Mr. Parkhill had believed that the incredible things Mr. Hyman Kaplan did to the English language were the products of a sublime and transcendental ignorance. That was the only way, for example, that he could account for Mr. Kaplan's version of the name of the fourth President of the United States: "James Medicine." Then Mr. Parkhill began to feel that it wasn't ignorance that governed Mr. Kaplan so much as *impulsiveness*. That would explain the sentence Mr. Kaplan had given in vocabulary drill, using the word orchard: "Each day he is giving her a dozen orchards." But then came Mr. Kaplan's impetuous answer to the question, "And what is the opposite of rich?"

"Skinny!" Mr. Kaplan had cried.

Now a less conscientious teacher might have dismissed that as a fantastic guess. But Mr. Parkhill, who stopped at nothing in his pedagogical labors, thought it over with great care and he realized that to Mr. Kaplan wealth and avoirdupois were inseparable aspects of one natural whole: rich people were fat. Grant this major premise and the opposite of rich *must* be skinny.

The more Mr. Parkhill thought this over the more he was convinced that it was neither ignorance nor caprice which guided Mr. Kaplan's life and language. It was logic. A secret kind of logic, perhaps. A private logic. A dark and baffling logic. But logic.

Any final doubts Mr. Parkhill might have felt on the whole matter were resolved once and for all when Mr. Kaplan conjugated the verb to die as "die, dead, funeral."

IT WAS ON A Monday night, several weeks after Mr. Kaplan's incomparable analysis of to die, that Mr. Parkhill was given a fresh glimpse of the dialectical genius of his most remarkable student. The class was making three-minute addresses. Miss Rochelle Goldberg was reciting. She was describing her experience with a ferocious dog named, according to Miss Goldberg, "Spots." He was a "Scotch Terror."

"Was he a beeg, wild dug!" Miss Goldberg said, her eyes moving in recollective fear. "Honist, you would all be afraid somthing tarrible! I had good rizzon for being all scared. I was trying to pat Spots, nize, on the had, and saying, 'Here, Spots, Spots, Spots!'—and Spots bite me so hod on the—"

"Bite is the *present* tense, Miss Goldberg."

A look of dismay wandered into Miss Goldberg's eyes.

"You want the—er—*past* tense," Mr. Parkhill spoke as gently as he could; Miss Goldberg had a collapsible nervous system. "What *is* the past tense of to bite?"

Miss Goldberg hung her head.

"The past tense of to bite—anyone?"

Mr. Kaplan's Samaritan impulses surged to the fore. "Isn't bited, ufcawss," he ventured archly.

"No, it isn't—er—bited!" Mr. Parkhill couldn't tell whether Mr. Kaplan had uttered a confident negation or an oblique question.

Miss Mitnick raised her hand, just high enough to be recognized. "Bit," she volunteered quietly.

"Good, Miss Mitnick! Bite, *bit*, bitten."

At once Mr. Kaplan closed his eyes, cocked his head and began whispering to himself. "Mitnick gives bit. . . . *Bit* Mitnick gives. . . . My!"

This dramaturgic process indicated that Mr. Kaplan was subjecting Miss Mitnick's contribution to his most rigorous analysis. Considering the ancient feud between these two, to allow one of Miss Mitnick's offerings to go unchallenged would constitute a psychological defeat of no mean proportions to Mr. Kaplan.

"Bite, *bit*, bitten? . . . Hmmmm . . . Dat sonds awful fonny. . . ."

It was no use for Mr. Parkhill to pretend that he had not heard; the whole class had heard.

"Er—isn't that clear, Mr. Kaplan?"

Mr. Kaplan did not open his eyes. *"Clear,* Mr. Pockheel? Foist-cless clear! Clear like gold! Only I don' see *vy* should be like dat. . . . It don' makink *sanse!"*

"Oh, it doesn't make *sense,*" Mr. Parkhill repeated lamely. Suddenly he glimpsed a golden opportunity. "You mean it isn't—er—*logical?"*

"Exactel!" cried Mr. Kaplan happily. "Dat bit isn't logical."

"Well, Mr. Kaplan. Surely you remember our verb drills. The verb to bite is much like, say, the verb to hide. To hide is conjugated hide, hid, hidden. Why, then, isn't it—er—logical that the principal parts of to bite be bite, bit, bitten?"

Mr. Kaplan considered this in silence. Then he spoke. "*I* tought de pest time bite should be—bote."

Miss Mitnick gave a little gasp.

"Bote?" Mr. Parkhill asked in amazement.

"Bote," said Mr. Kaplan.

Mr. Parkhill shook his head. "I don't see your point."

"Vell," sighed Mr. Kaplan with a modest shrug, "if is write, wrote, written so vy isn't bite, bote, bitten?"

Psychic cymbals crashed in Mr. Parkhill's ears.

"There is not such a word bote," protested Miss Mitnick, who took this all as a personal affront. Her voice was small but desperate.

"Not-soch-a-void!" Mr. Kaplan repeated ironically. "Mine dear Mitnick, don' *I* know is not soch a void? Did I said *is* soch a void? All I'm eskink is, isn't logical *should* be soch a void!"

The silence was staggering.

"Mr. Kaplan, there is no such word, as Miss Mitnick just said." (Miss Mitnick was in agony, biting her lips, twisting her handkerchief, gazing with bewilderment at her shoes. Her plight was that of common humanity, faced by genius.) "Nor is it—er—logical that there *should* be such a word." Mr. Parkhill recapitulated the exercise on regular and irregular verbs, giving the principal parts of a dozen samples. He spoke with earnestness and rare feeling. He spoke as if a good deal depended on it.

By the time he had finished his little lecture, Mr. Kaplan had seen the light and submitted, with many a sigh, to the tyranny of the irregular verb; Mrs. Moskowitz was fast asleep, and Miss Goldberg, completely forgotten in the clash between two systems of thought, had taken her seat with the air of one washing her hands of the whole business.

Recitation and Speech went on.

Mr. Sam Pinsky delivered a short address on the mysteries of his craft, baking. (It came out that Mr. Pinsky had produced literally thousands of "loafers of brat" in his career.) Mrs. Moskowitz, refreshed by her slumbers, indulged in a moving idyll about a trip she was hoping to make to a metropolis called "Spittsburgh." Then the recess bell rang.

The second student to recite after the recess was Hyman Kaplan. He hurried to the front of the room, glowing with joy at the opportunity to recite.

"Ladies an' gantleman, Mr. Pockheel," Mr. Kaplan began, with customary éclat. "Tonight, I'll gonna talkink abot noose-peppers, does movvellous—"

"Pardon me." Mr. Parkhill knew it would be nothing short of fatal to give Mr. Kaplan free rein. "It's *newspapers*, not noose-peppers." Mr. Parkhill went to the board and printed NOOSE, PEPPER, and NEWSPAPER. He explained the meaning of each word. When he pointed out that pepper was a strong condiment, everyone smiled, including Mr. Kaplan, who was amazed by the ingenious combination (noose-pepper) which he had brought into being.

"Vell," Mr. Kaplan took up his tale after Mr. Parkhill was done, "de *newspapers* is to me de finest kind ting ve have in tsivilization. Vat *is* a newspaper? Ha! It's a show! It's a comedy! It's aducation! It's movvellous!" Rhapsodically, Mr. Kaplan painted the glory and the miracle of journalism.

"Even de edvoitismants in de paper is a kind lasson. An' ufcawss de odder pots a newspaper: de hatlininks, de auditorials, de cottoons, and de fine pages pitchiss on Sonday, dat ve callink rotogravy sactions."

"Rotogra*vure!*"

"An' in newspapers ve find ot all dat's heppenink all hover de voild! Abot politic, crimes, all kinds difference *scendels* pipple making, abot if is goink to be snow or rainink, an' ufcawss—'spacially in U.S.—all abot sax!"

Mr. Parkhill closed his eyes.

"Mitout newspapers vat vould ve humans be?" Mr. Kaplan paused dramatically. "Ha! Sawages ve vould be, dat's vat! Ignorant ve vould be, dat's all. No fects! No knolledge! No aducation!" A shudder passed through the body scholastic at the mere thought of such a barbaric state.

"Vell, dis mornink I vas readink a noos—a *news*paper. English newspaper!" Mr. Kaplan paused, awaiting the acclaim of his colleagues. They were inert. "I vas readink abot how vill maybe be annodder Voild Var. So vat de paper said? Vell, he said dat—"

"Mr. Kaplan," Mr. Parkhill interrupted. "It's *it* said, not *he* said!"

Mr. Kaplan was stunned. "Not he?"

"No, not he. It! Er—you know the rules for pronouns, Mr. Kaplan. He is masculine, she is feminine. Sometimes, of course, we say she for certain objects which have no sex—a country, for example, or a ship. But for newspapers we use the neuter pronoun." Mr. Parkhill had an inspiration. "Surely *that's* logical!"

Mr. Kaplan sank into mighty thought, shaking his head at regular intervals. Then, "Plizz, Mr. Pockheel. I unnistand *fine* abot mascoolin, faminine, an' neutral; but—"

"Neu*ter*, Mr. Kaplan!"

"Neu*ter*. But is maybe all right ve should say he abot *som* papers? Ven dey havink mascoolin *names?*"

Mr. Parkhill frowned. "I don't see what the name of the paper has to do with it. We say of *The New York Times*, for instance, It said. Or of the New York *Post*—"

"*Dose* papers, yassir!" Mr. Kaplan cried. "But ven a paper got a real *mascoolin* name?"

Mr. Parkhill spoke with calculated deliberation. "I don't understand, Mr. Kaplan. Which newspaper would you say has a—er—*masculine* name?"

Mr. Kaplan's face was drenched with modesty. "*Harold Tribune*," he said, just as the recess bell rang.

"Now we shall devote the rest of the period to our—er—examination," Mr. Parkhill announced as the students returned to the room.

It was not really necessary for Mr. Parkhill to go through the formality of an examination. He knew, many weeks before the end of the year, which of the students in the beginners' grade deserved to be promoted to Miss Higby's Composition, Grammar, and Civics class and which students would have to be held back. Miss Mitnick, for example, was unquestionably the best student in the class. There was no doubt about her right to promotion. At the other extreme there were students like Mrs. Moskowitz. By no stretch of the pedagogical imagination could poor Mrs. Moskowitz be considered ready for Miss Higby. Nor could Mr. Hyman Kaplan.

Mr. Parkhill frowned as he thought of Mr. Kaplan. Mr. Kaplan was certainly his most energetic and ebullient pupil. He never missed a class; he never grew discouraged; the smile of undaunted hope and goodwill never left his cherubic face. But unfortunately, Mr. Kaplan never seemed to *learn* anything. His spelling remained erratic, his grammar deplorable, his sentence structure fantastic. As for Mr. Kaplan's speech, if anything it grew more astounding from day to day. Only last week Mr. Kaplan had announced that his wife suffered "from high blood pleasure." And in a drill on adjectives he had given the positive, comparative, and superlative forms of cold as "cold, colder, below zero." Mr. Parkhill often wondered whether there wasn't something sacrilegious in trying to impose the iron mold of English on so unfettered an intelligence.

Mr. Parkhill could go right through the class that way, picking the promotion-worthy from the promotion-unworthy. He needed no examination to aid him, but Mr. Parkhill realized that examinations lent a certain dignity and prestige to the American Night Preparatory School for Adults. They had a valuable *psychological* effect. And this was the time for which the examination had been announced.

"Please clear the arms of your chairs of everything except paper. Keep plenty of paper, please, and pens or pencils."

Smiles, frowns, and grins appeared on the faces of the students, according to their individual expectations. Eyes alert, hearts pounding nervously, pens and pencils poised like falcons, the beginners' grade awaited the fateful event. In the eyes of some students there were already visions of Composition, Grammar, and Civics, and Miss Higby.

"The first part of the examination will be a combined spelling-vocabulary test," said Mr. Parkhill. "Write a short sentence with each word I call off. Underline the word used. Is that clear to everyone?"

From the agonized expression on Mrs. Moskowitz's face it was *too* clear.

"Very well, *knees.*" Mr. Parkhill waited a moment and repeated, *"knees!"* being careful to pronounce it as distinctly as possible: "Neez."

The class attacked knees. Mr. Kaplan promptly leaned his head back, closed his eyes, and held solemn communion with himself, whispering in a semipublic tone, "Neez . . . neez. . . . A fonny void. . . . So be careful. . . . Neez. . . . Aha! Has *two* minninks. . . . Vun, a pot mine lag. . . . Also mine brodder's daughter is mine nee—"

"Mr. Kaplan!" Mr. Parkhill said. *"Please* do not disturb the class."

"I back you podden," murmured Mr. Kaplan with an injured air.

Since Mr. Kaplan could think clearly *only* by whispering to himself, as if consulting a more rational self, Mr. Parkhill's edict was tantamount to an intellectual death sentence for him.

"Heat," said Mr. Parkhill, not daring to meet Mr. Kaplan's melancholy gaze. "Heat!"

"Heat," whispered Mr. Kaplan automatically. Then he caught himself, pressed his lips together resolutely, and wrote in silence. He looked pale and he seemed to grow even paler as he maintained the silence.

"Pack . . . excite . . . throat."

Spelling-vocabulary continued on its even course. Mr. Parkhill announced the words slowly and with laudable precision, allowing as much as three minutes for a word.

When the first part of the examination was over, a wave of relief swept through the class as the students handed in their papers.

Mr. Parkhill began to sort the papers. He noticed that Miss Mitnick had, as usual, done excellently. When Mr. Parkhill came to the paper headed "H★Y★M★A★N K★A★P★L★A★N," he sighed automatically. He scanned the sentences that Mr. Kaplan had contributed.

1. My brother Maxs' little girl (I am Uncle) is my <u>neece</u>.
2. I <u>heat</u> him on the head, the big fool.
3. I am buyink a fine <u>peck</u> potatoes.
4. In a theatre is the Insite, the Outsite and the <u>Exite</u>. (for Fire).

Then Mr. Parkhill read no more. He turned to the class. The students looked serious, a trifle worried, and tense. Mr. Parkhill, the cadences of Mr. Kaplan's bizarre sentences still ringing in his ears, *felt* serious, a trifle worried, and tense. But Mr. Kaplan beamed with some inner joy. He seemed to have forgiven and forgotten the heartless edict against his whispering. Mrs. Moskowitz was moaning, as if in pain.

"I'm shaking insite, Mr. Kaplan," she said.

Mr. Kaplan raised his head with a gallant flourish. "*Stop* shakink insite!" he cried. "Lissen, Moskovitz. Kipp high de had! Kipp couratch! Dis pot haxemination vill be a tsinch, a *snep*. Dat's all, a *snep*."

Mrs. Moskowitz took a deep sigh, admiring Mr. Kaplan's morale. "I vish I had your noives, honist."

Mr. Kaplan accepted this tribute with a gracious nod. "I'll *halp* you

mit de haxemination," he confided in a megaphonic whisper. "An'
ven you fillink blue, remamber de song dey sinking in U.S.: 'Heppy
Dace Is Here Vunce More!' " Mr. Kaplan hummed a few bars of that
classic ballad to lend weight to his counsel. "Vill give you strangt!
'Heppy Dace *Is* Here Vunce More!' "

Mr. Parkhill rapped his pencil on the desk at this point, interrupting an immortal conversation. Mr. Kaplan nodded encouragement
to Mrs. Moskowitz again and cried a last buoyant word across the
room. "Don' give op de sheep, Moskovitz!" It was like a call to the
colors.

Mr. Parkhill explained the second part of the examination. "A one-
page composition," he said firmly. "On any subject."

Several fallen faces testified to the magnitude of this assignment.

"Please do *not* talk during this part of the examination. I shall not
be able to answer any questions, so please do not ask them. And do
not—er—try to get help from your neighbors." Mr. Parkhill sent a
searching look in the general direction of Mr. Kaplan. Mr. Kaplan
nodded loyally, and then shrugged his shoulders toward Mrs.
Moskowitz, who looked as if the last psychic leg had been cut from
under her. "I suggest you begin at once. You will have the rest of the
period for the composition."

Silence fell like a pall upon the beginners' grade. The wheels of
creative imagination began to turn—rather slowly. Mr. Parkhill waited
a little while for the students to adjust themselves to their new
problem, then sauntered down the aisle to see how the compositions
were progressing. All the students were hard at work, grimacing
through the opening paragraphs of their prose—all except Mrs.
Moskowitz. She sat with a look of dumb, bewildered anguish in her
eyes. Little beads of sweat on her upper lip proclaimed the effort of
thought.

"Is anything wrong, Mrs. Moskowitz?" whispered Mr. Parkhill
anxiously.

Mrs. Moskowitz raised a haggard face. "I ken't think of a sobject!"

"Oh," murmured Mr. Parkhill. "Er—why not try 'My Ambition'?"
"My Ambition" was a *very* popular topic.

Mrs. Moskowitz shook her head. Apparently Mrs. Moskowitz had
no particular ambition.

"Er—how about 'My First Day in America'?"

"I'm sick of telling about dat," sighed Mrs. Moskowitz.

"I see," said Mr. Parkhill miserably. It was a desperate situation.

Suddenly a gentle whistle soared through the air. It was soft, but it had a haunting vibrance. Everyone looked up. The whistle caressed the lilting refrain of "Heppy Dace Is Here Vunce More."

"Mr. Kap—"

A disembodied whisper rose from the front row. "Sobjecks for composition . . . 'Should Ladies Smoke?' . . . 'Is Dere a God, Ectual?' . . . Tink abot a *qvastion*."

"Mr. Kaplan!" said Mr. Parkhill severely.

But the mysterious process of communication had been consummated. A light shone in Mrs. Moskowitz's eyes. "I'll write about a *quastion*," she said.

Mr. Parkhill moved on. He felt quite helpless.

It was with relief that Mr. Parkhill began to arrange the composition papers in a pile after the final bell had rung and the students were gone. The titles at the tops of the pages paraded before him. "My Friend's New House." "A Sad Night in Hospitel." "Should Be Dad Panelty for Murdering?" (That looked like an unmistakable Kaplan title; no, it was Mrs. Moskowitz's paper, but it showed Mr. Kaplan's advisory influence all too clearly.) "My 4 Children Make Me a Happy Life." "Liberty Stateu." "Thinking About."

Mr. Parkhill started. He read the title again. There it was, in bold letters: "Thinking About." Mr. Parkhill raised the sheet a little above the rest of the pile.

"Thinking About"
(Humans & Enimals)
by
H★Y★M★A★N K★A★P★L★A★N
1.

Somtime I feel sad about how som people are living. Only sleeping eating working in shop. Not <u>thinking</u>. They are just like Enimals the same, which dont thinking also. Humans should not be like Enimals! They should Thinking! This is with me a deep idea.

Now we are having in school the axemination—a Comp. Mostly, will the students write a story for Comp. But I am asking, Why must allways be a story? Mr. P. must be sick and tierd from storys. Kaplan, be a man! No story! Tell better about <u>Thinking</u> somthing! Fine. Now I am thinking.

2.

In the class was som students asking if is right to say Its Me or Its I— (because maybe we will have that question in axemination). Its Me or Its I—a plenty hard question, no? Yes.

But it isnt so hard if we are <u>thinking about</u>! I figgure in this way:

If sombody is in hall besides my door, and makes knok, knok, knok; so I holler netcheral "Whose there?" Comes the anser "Its Me." A fine anser!! But who is that Me? Can I tell? No! So is Its Me no good.

Again is knok, knok, knok. And again I holler "Whose there?" Now comes the anser "Its I." So who is now that I?? Still can I (Kaplan) tell?? Ha! Umpossible! So is Its I rotten also.

So it looks like is no anser.

But must be some kind anser. So how we can find him out??? BY THINKING ABOUT. (Now I show how Humans isnt Enimals)

3.

If I am in hall and make knok, knok, knok; and I hear insite (insite the room) somebody hollers "Whose there?"—I anser strong "<u>Its Kaplan!</u>"

Now is fine! Plain, clear like gold, no chance mixing up Me, I, Ect.

By <u>Thinking</u> is Humans making big edvences on Enimals. This we call Progriss.

THE END

Only after he had read the composition twice did Mr. Parkhill notice that there was a postscript to this expedition into the realm of pure logic. It was like the signature to a masterpiece.

ps. I dont care if I dont pass, I <u>love</u> the class.

THE SECRET
OF SANTA VITTORIA

The
Secret
of Santa
Vittoria

A Condensation of the Novel by
Robert Crichton

Illustrated by Don Daily

Life in Santa Vittoria hadn't changed
in a thousand years. Despite the war, the
simple hill people worked each day as
they always had, to grow the grapes and make
the bold black wine of the region. Then,
suddenly, World War II is on their
doorstep, and the Germans try to claim their
wine. *One million bottles of it!*
Stunned, the people try to hide it—under
beds, in cupboards, on rooftops. In the
uproarious confusion that follows, it is—of
all people—Bombolini the clown who
comes forth with a better plan.
And the result is a rich, robust comedy that
throbs with energy and wit.

Robert Crichton's first published book
was the nonfiction best-seller *The
Great Imposter*. His first novel, four years
in the writing, was *The Secret of Santa Vittoria*, and
it too became a top best-seller.

THE BEGINNING OF THE BEGINNING

THE ORIGINAL MANUSCRIPT of this book was left outside the door of my hotel room in Montefalcone, in Italy, in May 1962. It arrived in the manner of the classic foundling. Wrapped in coarse brown paper and held together by cheap twine, the bundle literally fell into my life when I opened the door one morning. A note pinned to it read, "In the name of God, do something with this."

As with most foundlings, this one was a bastard. The note was not signed, the manuscript had no professed father. It was not a manuscript at all, but a collection of disorganized notes. I let it lie in a corner of the room for several days, since I resented it as an intruder in my life, but as it also is with most foundlings this one cried out to live, and one night I untied the twine and began to read the notes. They were written in a bad hand in English and in the Italian dialect of this region, and sometime in the night I realized that it might prove to be my burden to raise another man's child.

What to label this book has been the subject of argument. The collector of the notes, whom I now know to be Roberto Abruzzi, calls it a history. The title page reads: *THE SECRET OF SANTA VITTORIA, THE DIARY OF A TRUE EVENT*

Some important things have been found to be true. There is a town of Santa Vittoria. The great central incident around which this story revolves—the secret—is history, and some of the people named in the book are alive and still tend grapevines on the side of the mountain Santa Vittoria clings to. But others have never existed. Much is made about a green light that burns in the Piazza of the People in memory of the martyr Babbaluche, but there is no such flame. And just when one is tempted to doubt there ever was a cobbler named Babbaluche, his name is found carved on a wall in the rock quarry where he is said to have given his life.

The difficulty in finding the truth lies with Santa Vittoria itself. The city, as the residents like to call it, is an isolated Italian hill town—parts of it unreachable except by mule or on foot, a huddle of gray and white houses pressed up against the side of a mountain as if they were sheep fearful of falling off it, which they sometimes do. The people have no tradition of outsiders and no procedures for handling them. History has proved that to talk to strangers sooner or later leads to trouble or ends up costing money, and so history has rendered them incapable of telling truths to outsiders. They don't lie, but they never of their own will provide the truth. And some are capable of denying knowledge of the town fountain when it can be heard bubbling behind their backs.

If one hopes to reach the people, Italian is the wrong language. Italian is the language of Rome and, as such, the tongue for taxes and trouble and misunderstanding. For the native of a hill town, Italy is somewhere beyond him. The walls of his town and the fields around them are his Italy, the main piazza is his Rome, and the local dialect is his language. His loyalty is to himself and to his family, and if there is any left over it might extend to his street and even to his section of town. In times of crisis such as Santa Vittoria knew, loyalty might extend to the entire town. But beyond that there is nothing more. Loyalty ends with the last grapevines at the foot of the mountain.

And Santa Vittoria is grapevines; it is wine. That is all there is. Without the wine, as they say here, even God Himself could not invent a reason for Santa Vittoria.

As for Roberto Abruzzi, I have never seen him, but I have talked with him on the telephone. Abruzzi is an American who cannot go back to the United States, or thinks that he can't go back, because of something that he had done during the war. In return for food and the use of a house he was later asked by the people of Santa Vittoria to tell their story and record for them the great thing the people of that city did there in that summer and fall of the war. They asked Abruzzi because, as an American, he was supposed to know how to do such things.

It wasn't easy for Roberto Abruzzi to begin. No one in Santa Vittoria had ever written a book and not too many had read one, but everyone knew how this book *should* be written. Vittorini, the old soldier and the most cultured man in Santa Vittoria, told him, "Long books are better than short ones. Say anything, just so you say it beautifully." And the priest, Padre Polenta, said to him, "Remember this, Roberto. One's words must glide across the page like a swan moving across the waters."

It was enough to stop him for a month. But in the end Roberto wrote what he did because he had a stronger reason for doing it than to satisfy the vanity of Santa Vittoria. He wished to tell his own story, which he feels is a shameful one but which he knew had to come out of him before it consumed him. It was his hope that if he told his story, some people might be able to understand him and what he did. This is the price that he asks the reader to pay in return for the story of Santa Vittoria. It is not a high price to pay.

Here, then, is the foundling that I agreed to adopt. From the ragged bundle of notes of Roberto Abruzzi has grown this book.

Montefalcone, 1962
New York, 1965

I

THE BEGINNING

THE HOUR THIS STORY begins is known. The minute, the exact moment, is recorded. To some this might not appear to be remarkable, but when it is considered that there are entire generations in the history of Santa Vittoria about which nothing at all is known, the statement becomes remarkable.

It was Padre Polenta who recorded the moment. He had been working in his wood-paneled room at the top of the bell tower when he first saw the light coming down the River Road from Montefalcone. At times the beam of light would be sharp and clear, and then it would enter a patch of fog and become a round wet globe, like a lantern dropped in a lake, or the moon before a snow. The light was a bicycle lamp, and it annoyed the priest. Like many people who don't sleep at night he felt the night belonged to him. He left the window of the tower and made an entry in his daily record.

1:21 a.m. Cavalcanti the Goat on the prowl again. Tell his mother to keep him home before her boy is found dead.

Beneath this he added, in purple ink and underlined three times:

The winter fogs have come again. Ha! A new record.

The priest hated the fogs. He lived in the top of the bell tower because of them. He felt that his lungs were lined with a kind of fungus that absorbed water, and he had given up a rich parish in the north of Italy and taken this poor place to escape the wetness of the northern winter.

"What about fogs?" he had asked the people of Santa Vittoria. "Do you have fogs?"

The members of the parish committee had all looked at one another as if the word *fog* was one they had never heard before. "Oh, there are the winter fogs," one of them finally said. "They last a few days or a week. I suppose you could go away for a week."

The first year was good, but in the second year the winter fogs came up from the valleys and slid down from the mountains in October and lasted until April. With the fogs a bitterness had come to the priest, and it grew deeper with the years. With the last of his money he repaired the ancient campanile in the Piazza of the People and paneled the room at the top where the lookouts had once stayed. The top of the tower floats above the fog line, and one day years ago the shepherd moved into the tower, away from his flock, and came down only when necessary—to say mass, give the last rites and bury the dead.

After the priest had made the entry, he went back to his work. He was occupied with restoring the Great Ledger of the Parish of Santa Vittoria, in an effort to re-create some kind of history for the people and the city. For one night Polenta had made a discovery that amused and even excited him. He found that if he took a page from the Ledger—one filled with births and deaths and marriages—from one century, and then took a page from a hundred years before and a hundred years later, it was impossible to tell which page belonged to which century. The same names were on them all. The same first names, middle names and last names. The same people were getting born and getting married and getting buried. The rest of the world might have been changing over those centuries, but it would be impossible to prove it by Santa Vittoria.

This night he had three pages on his worktable, one from 1634, one from 1834 and one from 1934, and he was counting the family of Pietrosanto. In 1634 there were recorded the names of forty-six members of that family. Three hundred years later there were thirty-eight Pietrosantos, but this did not include the three who had gone off to war someplace and were listed as missing. After all the plagues and the wars, and the fires and the landslides and the fights and feuds of three centuries, there were five fewer Pietrosantos in the city (Thank God for that much at least, Babbaluche the cobbler would have said), and almost all of them were living in the same houses on the same lanes, as solid and as sturdy, as stubborn and as bullheaded, as ever before.

Facts are facts and they are usually lifeless things, but one fact was beginning to depress the priest. The more he worked on the Ledger, the more it became clear to him that with the exception of the Sicilian Boob, Italo Bombolini, he himself was the only person who had come here by choice. For in Santa Vittoria one arrived through the natural passage of the womb and one left in a box of wood through the Fat Gate out to the cemetery beyond the walls of the town just above the vineyards on the terraces. In between those times you tended the vines and grew the grapes and made the wine and lived the best way you could.

PADRE POLENTA WOULD insist he wasn't asleep. But the truth is that he never heard the rattle of the bicycle being pushed across the cobblestones of the piazza below, nor that the young man pushing it had to shout four or five times before the priest heard him and went to the window. "If it's someone dying," Polenta shouted down, "he can die just as well in the morning."

"No one is dying, Padre. It's me, Fabio. Fabio della Romagna."

"What do you want?"

"I want to ring the bell, Padre. I want to wake up the town."

"It will be morning in two hours."

"It's Mussolini, Padre. The Duce."

"What about the Duce? Do you want me to come down into that fog for the Duce?"

"He's dead, Padre," Fabio called up. "They say the Duce is dead."

The priest went away from the window. He lit a tallow candle and wrote in the daily log.

2:25 a.m. Cavalcanti the Goat turns out to be F. della Romagna. I learn that they are saying the Duce is dead.

He took the candle and started down the steep, winding stone steps of the tower. Fabio met him at the door. The young man was sweating and tired, but he was happy. "You should see them in Montefalcone," he said, and described how the people were dancing in the streets and setting fire to portraits of Mussolini and to Fascist symbols, and how the soldiers had deserted their barracks and how even the *carabinieri* had gone to the hills.

"I suppose they'll go after the churches next," Polenta said. "They usually do."

Fabio was shocked. "They're going into the churches to pray, Padre, to give thanks for their deliverance."

"I'm sure. Go on, go ring your bells." He allowed Fabio to come into the bell tower, but he wasn't sure how he felt about Mussolini. The Duce had signed the Lateran Treaty and by that act had done more for the Church than any one other leader of Italy. But the Duce had been a fool and a clown, two traits the priest despised above all others.

Despite the fog the priest started across the Piazza of the People toward his church, Santa Maria of the Burning Oven, to be there in the event of any trouble. He was near the fountain when he heard the bell begin to peal. It thundered out over Santa Vittoria, swinging free and out of control, the entire tower trembling. The windows of the houses around the piazza trembled too. But no one came into the piazza. Fabio left the tower and ran to Santa Maria. "The people," he called to the priest. "What's the matter with the people?"

"You've been away at the school too long," Polenta said. "They don't believe the bell any longer."

The summer before, when the bell had begun to ring, the people had run to the Piazza of the People thinking to help fight a fire. When most of the town had collected, torches were lit and they found themselves surrounded by a company of Blackshirts from the barracks at Monte-falcone. "We shall now proceed to pay our back taxes," the officer announced. And they went through every pocket and every house in Santa Vittoria until every unburied lira in the city was taken.

"This is no city to catch fire in," the priest told Fabio. "Now when the bell rings, everyone gets up and bolts the door."

But there is something about the truth that makes itself understood. When the bell ceased ringing, Fabio ran up and down the piazza, calling to everyone to come out, that he had good news for them. Gradually lights were lit, and finally some of the Pietrosantos, those who live along the lanes leading into the piazza, seeing it was Fabio, opened their doors.

It must be understood that whatever happens in Santa Vittoria is known by everyone as soon as it happens. Some say it is because the walls of the houses are so thin that what is said in the first house is heard in the second and passed through the walls to the third, down through Old Town and up through High Town. Others say it happens because everyone is related to everyone else, and so what is experienced by one is felt by the next. Whatever it is, once the Pietrosantos went into the piazza, the others followed. They put Fabio up on the steps of Santa Maria of the Burning Oven, and Pietro the Bull, the oldest and still the strongest of the Pietrosantos, hung Fabio's bicycle from the statue of the turtle on the fountain so that the beam of the bicycle lamp would shine on the young man. It threw Fabio's shadow back onto the church façade, and when he held up his hand before speaking, the hand was twenty feet high on the stones.

"A great thing has happened today," Fabio called out. "A great thing for us. A great thing for Italy."

The people leaned forward to hear him, because good news is not a common commodity in this place. "Benito Mussolini, the tyrant, is dead!" Fabio cried.

There was no sound at all from the people. The face of Fabio showed that he was puzzled.

"The Duce has been put to death this day," he called.

Still the silence, the only sound the water pouring from the fountain. Then, "What is that to us?" a man shouted at last. "Why did you get us out of bed? Why did you ring the bell?"

Fabio's face was anguished. It is a fine face, long and clean and narrow like the blade of a new axe, the eyes deep and dark like ripe olives, and his hair so dark that it seems blue at times. Fabio's skin is white and fine, not the color of copper pots like most of the faces here.

"What does it mean to *us?*" the man shouted again.

"It means freedom," Fabio said, and he looked down.

The people respect Fabio, who is the only person in Santa Vittoria to have gone to the university, but they were annoyed by what he had done. He went down the steps of the church and they cleared a path for him so that he could get his bicycle down from the Fountain of the Pissing Turtle.

"You've been away too long, Fabio," a man said. "We don't go to school here, Fabio. We work. We grow grapes. You shouldn't have waked up the people."

"Excuse me," he said. "I'm sorry. I'm sorry."

"It's the books," a woman told him. Everyone nodded, because it is a known fact here that a few books are all right, like wine, but too much can be bad. Books break down the brains.

It was the cobbler Babbaluche who saved things, although it is usually his role to ruin them. "Leave the light there," he ordered Fabio. He has a voice that sounds as if his throat was plated with brass; it is always irritating and it is always heard. He limped— because he is a cripple—to the steps of the church. "I'll tell you what it means to you, you socks filled with dung."

Under the laws of Italy it is not allowed to put down on paper, even on paper that is not to be published, all the things Babbaluche calls the people of Santa Vittoria. He can say these things because of something that happened to him years ago in front of all the people and which they allowed to happen.

"How many of you would like to sink your boot in Copa's backside?" Babbaluche shouted. There was a cheer then, for that was the ambition of everyone in the piazza.

"As of this morning you have that right," he said. "Who wants Mazzola?" There was another cheer, for the ruination of Mazzola. He went through the rest of the city leaders, the members of the local Fascist party who were known as The Band.

There was nothing political any longer about The Band. They had long ago ceased contributing to the national party or to Rome. They kept Santa Vittoria for themselves and stole from it—not too much at a time, but all of the time.

The loudest cheer of all was reserved for Francucci. When Copa had taken over as mayor twenty years before, he had made his one speech. "Bread is the staff of life," he told the people. "Bread is too sacred to be left in the hands of greedy individuals. No penny of profit shall ever be made by any individual from the exploitation of the people's bread so long as I am mayor, so help me God."

He closed all of the bakeries in Santa Vittoria and opened the Citizen's Nonprofit Good Bread Association and put his brother-in-law, the mule drover Francucci, in charge. Francucci's first act was to reduce the amount of wheat that went into a loaf, and his second was to raise the price. Within a year the families of Copa, Mazzola and Francucci had moved out of the wet dark caves of Old Town, where they had lived for one thousand years, and up into the sunlight of High Town, where the gentry, what there is of gentry in Santa Vittoria, live.

"I offer you the backside of Francucci," Babbaluche went on. There was a terrible roar from the crowd.

They would turn the irrigation water for the terraces back on. The Band had turned it off years before, when the people refused to pay for their own water. They would fix the Funny Scale on which all of the grape growers had to weigh their grapes before selling them to the Citizen's Wine Cooperative.

The people began to get angry. It is impossible to guess what the crowd might have gone on to do had not Francucci chosen that moment to come down from High Town into the piazza.

"Why was the bell ringing?" he asked. ". . . Why are you looking at me like that? Take your hands off me!"

Like a soccer ball the baker went from one end of the piazza to the other, and every player along the way had a penalty shot at him. Then they called his family to come and take him away. Fabio helped them get him back up the steep lane to High Town, more dead than alive. That is the way Fabio is.

When he returned to the piazza the people were already starting back to their houses. "They shouldn't have done that," Fabio said to Babbaluche.

"The people are entitled to their blood," Babbaluche said. "Now give them big blood, important blood. Tell them how the Duce died."

"They don't want to hear that. They want to go home."

"The people always want to hear when the mighty stag is brought to the ground by a pack of common dogs."

The cobbler was right. Fabio told them how the Fascist Grand Council had gathered in a palace in Rome the night before and how one man, the Count Dino Grandi, rose to his feet and in the face of Mussolini began to read a resolution.

"Resolved: The members of the Grand Council and the people of the glorious nation of Italy, having lost all confidence in the ability of the leader to lead any longer, convinced that he has destroyed the will of the army to fight any longer and the people to resist . . ."

The people sat on the wet stones of the piazza and listened to Fabio. "Die," one of them shouted. "How does he die?"

Fabio told them what he had heard, how they took the Duce in a long black ambulance through the ancient burning city, past all the monuments to the Caesars, until they came to the walls of Rome and the Appian Way, the route that all the conquerors have taken to Rome. At a crossroads the ambulance stopped and the people from the village there looked inside. "An old man is dying," one of them said.

Mussolini said one sentence. "The people of Rome have always destroyed their greatest sons."

And Fabio told how after that they drove into mountains where the snow never ends, and two men took his arms and two took his legs, and they lowered him into a hole they had cut into the hard ice and began shoveling snow into the upright grave until only the great head was not buried.

"You dishonor Italy," the Duce said to them.

"No, we honor the dead of twenty years by doing what we do." So, Fabio tells them, the Duce had died, frozen to death in the snow.

When he was through with the story some of the women were crying, not for the Duce, but for the men of Santa Vittoria who had been sent to the mountains. They had left one morning in May 1941, twenty-three young men, marching down the mountain, singing all the way to the Montefalcone road, the feathers on those silly hats bending with the breeze. Not one of them was ever seen or heard from again.

We know now that this isn't how the Duce died, nor when, but the people always tell it thus because his death this way seems more fitting to them.

THERE WAS NO WAY to keep the people in the piazza after that, because the sun had come up. They could see it touching the tile roofs of the houses, and when the sun comes up here it drives the people out of the houses and down to the terraces to tend the vines.

"No one works today," Babbaluche shouted. "A day of holiday."

"A day of celebration," the wine seller Bombolini called. But the people didn't listen to either of them. They poured out of the piazza and down the streets to get their tools, deaf to anything but the needs of the grapes, and in a few minutes there were only five or six of them left. These men went to sit around the edge of the fountain while Fabio climbed up and took down his bicycle.

"For twenty years I dreamed of this day," Babbaluche said, "and now look at it." He swept his hand around the empty piazza. "This is the kind of people you have in this place, Fabio. Don't ever allow yourself to forget it."

They sat and listened to the sound of the water for a while.

"To think that I, Ugo Babbaluche, outlived Mussolini," the cobbler finally said. "I'm alive and that bastard's dead."

"It calls for a drink," Bombolini announced, and all of them at once stood up and began to follow the wine seller across the piazza to his wineshop. He was unlocking the folding iron gate over the front door when his wife looked out of the window above.

"See that you make them pay," she said. He was embarrassed.

"She lacks a sense of history," he said.

It was damp and chilly in the shop, but the warm air from the piazza and the warmth from the wine soon warmed them.

"What do you think is going to happen?" one of them asked.

"The Germans will come," Fabio said. But he felt suddenly shy. He had never spoken much with the men before, and now he was one of them.

"No they won't," a man said. "Why would they want to come here?"

"If Italy gets out of the war," Fabio said, "the Germans aren't going to leave Italy for the Americans and the English."

"No," Pietrosanto said. "There's nothing here for the Germans."

"There's nothing here for *us*," Bombolini said.

Fabio could only shrug his shoulders. But he told them about the tanks and armored cars he had seen coming into Montefalcone.

"Montefalcone is Montefalcone and Santa Vittoria is Santa Vittoria," the cobbler said. "One is a jewel and one is a dung heap."

They drank to this.

"Only a man born in Santa Vittoria can ever learn how to make a living out of it," someone said. "What would the Germans do here?"

They drank to this as well.

The wife of Bombolini came down the back stairs and into the wineshop. She looked at their glasses. "Did they pay?"

"They paid," Bombolini said.

"Let's see the money." She went to the drawer in the table by the big wine barrel. There was nothing in it.

"This is a historic day," Bombolini said. "You don't ask for money on a day like this and you don't accept it."

They nodded their heads at Rosa Bombolini. But they were afraid of her. She has the toughest tongue in the city and no shyness about putting it to use. She began taking the glasses from them and moving them toward the door. "What a bunch of patriots! Take your patriotism out into the piazza where it belongs. That's the trouble with this country. The whole place is filled with penniless patriots."

When they were out in the sunlight, they could hear the sound of a drum coming from one of the lanes in High Town that leads down into the piazza. Capoferro the town crier was announcing the Duce's death. There was a roll on his goatskin drum and then a blast from the automobile horn that he carried.

Capoferro has some kind of trouble with his speech and sometimes it takes two and three people to understand him, but at least what he says is remembered. Now he was coming into the piazza, beating the goatskin drum. "Nido Muzzlini dead."

Barrrombarrrummmbarrrum. A squeeze on the horn.

"Tyrant dead. All Idly weeps."

Barrrombarrrummmbarrrum. Horn.

"No, no," Fabio said. "Italy is happy."

"Oh," Capoferro said. He struck himself on the head with his drumsticks. He looked at the men. "You want to celebrate? For some wine I drum you a dance."

"Wait," Bombolini said. He went around to the back entrance of the wineshop, on the Street of D'Annunzio the Poet, and returned with two bottles of wine. "Keep your backs to the shop," he warned them.

It was good vermouth. They passed the bottles around and Capoferro took a very long drink and he began to drum.

At first none of them did anything, but then Babbaluche the cobbler began to dance. Because he is crippled, he dragged himself across the stones of the piazza in a slow rhythm.

"I never thought I'd dance at his funeral," he shouted.

The sun was hot now and they had had nothing to eat since the night before, and the wine began to go to their heads. After a while Bombolini started to dance with the cobbler, going around and around the Fountain of the Pissing Turtle while Capoferro beat the goatskin drum and the rest of the men clapped their hands.

Babbaluche's daughter had come up from Old Town into the piazza, and when she saw her father she seized his arm and marched him across the piazza toward the Corso Mussolini, which leads down into Old Town. He had passed his bottle to one of the other men and that was a mistake, because Rosa Bombolini saw it and came out of the wineshop. "You sons of thieves!" she cried, and she took the bottle and stalked off.

"You had better leave," Bombolini said to them. The men began to move away, and soon only Fabio and the wine merchant were left in the Piazza of the People—besides the children and the oxen and the old women getting water from the fountain. They had little to say to each other.

"The best thing I can do right now," Bombolini said, "is to go back to bed. Good-bye, Fabio."

It was the end of the celebration. Fabio was alone. He decided to go down into Old Town and sleep on a mat in his cousin Ernesto's house. It was very hot as he started down the steep corso.

An old woman was sitting in the darkness of the doorway next to Ernesto's door. "What was all the noise about?" she shouted at him. She was hard of hearing.

"A death," Fabio shouted back at her. "Someone died."

"Who?"

"Mussolini. Benito Mussolini."

She shook her head. "No," she mumbled, "no, I don't know him."

"It's nobody from here," Fabio told her.

"Oh." Her face became as dark and blank as the doorway.

The house smelled. Ernesto was no housekeeper. There was a pot of hard cold beans over the fireplace and Fabio ate them. Then he found a mat and stretched out on it and fell asleep. It was nine o'clock in the morning.

Thus did the twentieth year of the glorious reign of the Everlasting Imperial Fascist Empire come to a close in the city of Santa Vittoria.

FABIO WOKE IN THE early afternoon. He was still tired, but he woke because he was hungry. He looked around the small house, but there was nothing in it to eat, not even a piece of stale bread, and he went out into the Corso Mussolini and started up toward the Piazza of the People to try to buy some bread and cheese and wine. The midday sun blinded him and he was forced to hold on to the walls of the houses until his eyes could adjust to the glare. When he reached his destination, he was conscious of groups of people looking back down toward Old Town, but he was too blinded to see what it was they were looking at.

The Piazza of the People is the center of Santa Vittoria. It is a flat plateau of cobblestones that divides the city in two parts. Above the piazza is High Town where the houses sit on a saddle of land in the sun. The people who live in High Town are called Goats. The people who live around this piazza are called Turtles because of the fountain. Below the Piazza of the People is Low Town, or Old Town—the medieval section of the city—and that's where the Frogs live, because in the spring, after a rain, little green frogs hop in the dank, moss-green streets until the rats and the cats and the children get to them. Frogs almost never marry Turtles and Turtles don't speak to Goats. That's the way they are here.

The city is steep. The Corso Mussolini, which runs through Old Town up to the Piazza of the People, is so steep in places that the street becomes flights of stone stairs. The corso also runs down to the Fat Gate, the main passage through the Fat Wall, which the Romans built and which encircles Santa Vittoria. There is another way out, the Thin Gate, used mainly by small boys since the track that leads down the mountain from it is so steep.

If you stand in the center of the Piazza of the People, where Fabio was standing, you are almost at eye level with the second pride of Santa Vittoria, the one achievement of the Fascist movement here, the tall soaring cement-skinned water tower that rests on three great long thin steel legs over a lower piazza, the Piazza Mussolini, like the head on the top of an enormous spider. Written on one side of the cement tank in black block letters were these words: MUSSOLINI IS ALWAYS RIGHT. On the other side was: DUCE DUCE DUCE DUCE DUCE DUCE DUCE DU.

Below the tower in Old Town, near the Thin Gate, was the first pride of the city, the Citizen's Cooperative Wine Cellar, and on the roof of the cellar was a large blue and red sign which read CINZANO, since most of the wine made here is sold in the end to the Cinzano family.

Fabio went into the wineshop. It was dark and he was blinded again. He had passed Rosa Bombolini, standing in the doorway with her arms crossed and staring toward Old Town, but she had not followed him inside. He waited for his sight to return, and as he sat he heard someone crying in the darkness.

"Can I help you?" Fabio said. The girl didn't answer him. "Do I bother you?" He waited. "Is it you, Angela?"

"Yes, it's me."

He tried to say something that would sound helpful or sensible, but he could think of nothing. Not a single word would come to him.

There was this about Fabio, then. Although he had never actually spoken to this girl alone or said her name aloud before, he was in love with Angela Bombolini. This kind of thing happens here more often than in other places. For there is a kind of love here that is called "thunderbolt love."

A girl looks out the window and she sees a boy she has seen ten thousand times before, and all at once a thunderbolt hits her and she realizes that she is madly in love with him. From that moment she dedicates her life to him, even though he might not know her name or that she exists.

The great torture of the thunderbolt lover is that the one he loves will not return the love. Life would be unbearable then. So great is the fear of being rejected that many thunderbolt lovers never admit to their love at all. Most people, girls and boys, when struck by the thunderbolt, show the effects as clearly as if they had been struck with a true bolt. But Fabio is more clever than most people. All that he did was blush. When Angela's name was mentioned he turned scarlet, or if he passed her in the piazza he turned a deep red, but no one so far was conscious of what was taking place.

He was still trying to think of the proper thing to say when he realized that Angela's mother was standing over him.

"Did she get what you want?"

"Oh. Oh, no. I want some bread and cheese and wine."

"Why didn't you get him what he wants?" Rosa Bombolini shouted at Angela. "He sits here dry while you wet the floor."

She returned to her doorway and Angela went into the back room. His heart flew out to her. He had now managed to say a few words and get her in trouble. When she came back she put a plate of cheese in front of him and a glass of wine.

"No bread," she said.

"Why not?" It wasn't what he had wanted to say.

"Francucci," she said.

"Oh, yes. The baker. Of course." He felt his face turning red. He sat at the table and ate the cheese, listening to her cry. "Why are you crying?" he said at last.

"You know why," Angela said. "Why are you torturing me?"

He found himself turning red once more and wondering what it was he did that caused him to harm the person he least in the world wished to harm.

"I don't know why," Fabio said.

"Him," she said. "You saw him."

She nodded her head in the direction of the door and the piazza beyond. He went across to the window and cleaned a section of it with his hand and peered out. Groups of people were in the piazza, all looking toward Old Town. He could see nothing at first, but finally his eyes were able to pick out the movement and he felt his heart jump.

He made the sign of the cross. Two-thirds of the way up the water tower, still at least one hundred feet below the concrete tank and the safety of a little iron railing that runs around it, not moving at all now, silhouetted against the sky and the mountains beyond Santa Vittoria, gripping the narrow rusty ladder that climbs up to the tank itself, clung Italo Bombolini.

"What is your father doing up there?"

She began to cry again, and Fabio knew two things: that someone was going to have to help Italo Bombolini, and that it was going to be himself.

The figure was moving once more, moving with a terrible slowness upward. Fabio went outside and tapped Rosa Bombolini on the shoulder. "Do you have a length of rope? A good strong one?"

"Oh, no," Signora Bombolini said. "You don't risk your life to save his fat pride. He's going to fall. Let him fall."

"He's still going up."

"Because the idiot can't come down," she said.

Fabio turned red again. He had never heard a woman talk about her husband in this fashion before. "I'm going whether you get me the rope or not," he said.

In the end she got him the rope—two good lengths of rope and also a basket containing cheese and some olives and two bottles of wine and a *fiasco* of grappa—a flask of that strong raw brandy the peasants distill here.

"I can't carry all of this," Fabio said.

"Angela will meet you in the corso with a knapsack," Signora Bombolini said. Angela passed them then, still crying, and because she was running she was forced to lift up her skirts, and despite the fact that it was a matter of life and death, all that Fabio could seem to keep his mind on was the quality of her legs.

"Why are you so red?" Signora Bombolini asked him. "Are you sure you are all right?"

I am very much all right, Fabio thought. I am about to save the father of the woman I love, and she will be grateful to me for the rest of my life.

He met Angela Bombolini at the curve in the Corso Mussolini, and she handed him a black knapsack made of imitation leather that had once been the property of the Young Fascist Scouts. "I'll pray for you, Fabio," she said. It was the first time he had ever heard her use his name.

Fabio reached the base of the water tower. The ladder shocked him. It was narrow and inadequate, not a ladder at all, but lengths of pipe joined together into which small round iron spikes had been fixed at intervals to serve as foot and handholds.

"Don't go up. You can't help him," someone said to him.

He tightened his belt so his shirt would stay in and slung the ropes around his shoulders and tied the bottoms of his pants around his ankles with rough twine so they wouldn't flap.

"You're a fool to go, Fabio. Why should you get killed for him?"

Fabio pulled himself onto the pipe. He looked up and was astonished to see how far the fat wine seller had managed to pull himself. He took a deep breath and began to climb. It was not hard for him at first, but he was surprised how narrow the little spikes were; they felt even smaller than they looked. Something wet touched his hair and he realized it was paint from the bucket Bombolini had yoked around his neck.

All at once there was a tremendous shout from the people in the Piazza Mussolini below. Fabio pulled himself in against the pipe and waited for the body of Bombolini to rush by him.

When nothing happened he looked up, and he could see Angela's father hanging out away from the pipe like a door that the wind has blown open. Bombolini had missed his footing; but somehow, instead of falling, he had managed to hang on with one foot and one hand and now he swayed there, back and forth, trying to pull himself back to the pipe. Fabio could feel the pipe trembling from the effort and it frightened him, and then he heard a second cheer and he looked up and Bombolini was climbing upward again.

ACROSS THE PIAZZA FROM the wineshop, in the cellar of the Leaders' Mansion where The Band had barricaded themselves, they heard the shouting.

"It won't be much longer now," Copa the mayor said. "The mob is feeling its muscle. It's only a matter of time."

All of them were there: Copa and Mazzola, their families, their children and even Francucci, his eyes swollen shut, his lip split. With them, too, was Emilio Vittorini the mail clerk. He was not a Fascist, but he was a paid employee of the state, a "functionary" as he preferred to call himself, and since Vittorini is above all things a man of form, he felt it his duty to be counted with the recognized legal machinery of government.

"Maybe they won't come," Mazzola said. "Maybe they're cheering something else."

"They won't hurt *us*," the wife of Francucci said. "We've already paid the price."

"What, for twenty years of rotten bread?" Vittorini said. "You have only paid the first installment."

"If we knew who was leading them, we might be able to figure out something," Mazzola said. "Every man has his price."

"Where the hell is Pelo?" Copa asked. "I'll break his neck."

They had sent Romano Pelo, the least offensive of men, a shadow of a human being, to find out what all the noise was about. He had not come back. Now they sat and waited in the darkness, behind barricaded doors.

"If we can only last into the night," Mazzola said. "They'll forget us. The people's memory is short."

There was another shout from the piazza and it made the baker weep. "All I ever did was to bake their bread and now they want to harm me," Francucci said. He was becoming obsessed with the idea that the people wanted to put him in his own ovens and bake him alive.

"We must find a way to surrender to them before they can come to us," Vittorini said. "We must seize the initiative."

Little by little, as the day wore on, the mail clerk was assuming command in the cellar. The most impressive fact about Vittorini, more impressive even than his character, is the uniform he is entitled to wear, and which he wears on all state and religious holidays, and which he had the wisdom to put on this morning. It is from one of the fine regiments, although no one remembers the name of it now. It was made from a white whipcord twill that had been cleaned and bleached so many times that it was impossible to look directly at Vittorini in the sunlight. Across his chest was a silken sash, and on the sash a gold medal that swam in the silk like a sun rising from the sea. There were black patent-leather boots, a sword in a golden scabbard that clinked against the cobblestones when he crossed the piazza, epaulets trimmed with gold braid, and a hat of shiny black patent leather with a stubby little visor, from the top of which cascaded a fall of cock's plumes—a shiny black and green shower of them—so that when Vittorini walked, Vittorini rippled.

"We must discover the nature of the enemy," Vittorini told them, "and capitulate to it. They must not come and take; we must *give*. It is the only way." He shook his head to emphasize his point, and the dark river of feathers began to run.

THE SUN HAD BEEN BURNING down for half the day, and the iron grillwork of the catwalk that circles the top of the water tower was hot to the touch. But Bombolini never felt the burning when he crawled up onto the walk. He sank onto the hot iron and almost at once he slept. He had no intention of ever getting off the tower. He had prepared himself to die. He knew the people in the piazza were waiting for his last peformance and he wouldn't disappoint them, but at the moment he was too tired even to contemplate dying.

When he woke he could see from the shadows of things below him that a good deal of time had passed. I am thirsty, he thought. I am dying of thirst.

He could see the people working on the terraces in the vineyards, deep among the vines. And he could hear the sound of water bubbling by his ear, just on the other side of the thin concrete skin of the water tank. I am being driven crazy, he thought.

And finally he became conscious that someone else was on the tower with him. From the other side of the tank came a rhythmic sound, a soft and steady slapping like waves on the side of an anchored boat. Before I roll off I will find out who is on the tower, he told himself.

Then his eyes saw a wine bottle, the cork out of the neck, standing at attention like a little soldier a few inches from his hand. I will drink a little of this wine and then roll off, he told himself.

The wine was hot from the sun, but it didn't bother Bombolini. He could feel the wine run down his throat and begin to course through the bulk of his body as if it were the sun, the source of life itself running inside him. The second swallow was easier, and each one after that became easier, every mouthful exploding inside him like a small hot sun. The wine was working for Italo Bombolini the way a transfusion works for a man who has lost too much blood. When he was through with the bottle he found he could sit up, and he leaned against the concrete and all at once allowed his legs to drop over the side of the catwalk, which caused a great shout from the piazza.

"Who's on the tower?" he said.

"Fabio."

The sound, the *slap, slap* of a paintbrush against the concrete, continued.

"I knew if anyone came for me it would be Fabio. Fabio?"

"Yes?"

"How far are you?"

Fabio had already painted out MUSSOLINI IS ALWAYS RIGHT and was halfway through the eight DUCE's.

"Four more to go," Fabio said. "Whoever did it, overdid it."

"I did it," Bombolini said.

Fabio was silent. It embarrassed him to think of a man risking his life to climb a tower and write DUCE DUCE DUCE all over the side of it.

"I was young once, you know," Bombolini was saying. "I was tall and lean. When I was through I wasn't even tired."

Fabio went on with the painting. He could not imagine this man as ever having been young.

"I know what you're thinking, Fabio, but you have to try and understand how it was then. He was beautiful at first. He made promises to us."

They felt the tower tremble and they gripped the iron railing, but then it passed. The mountain rises and falls here, a little bit each day, like a giant shifting in his sleep.

"And what promises, Fabio. They were going to help us build a school and pay for teachers, help us build a road, and plant the hillsides with grass and trees so the land would stay on the hills and the water would stay on the land and there would be no more landslides. We *believed* that, Fabio."

"How could you believe?" Fabio said.

"Because he believed too. I really think Mussolini believed."

"And then none of it happened."

"Some of it happened. This thing, this tower, happened. Oh, we were going to be like America here. Fabio, can you see Scarafaggio from where you are?" Fabio said that he could. "When the tower was built they fell down in the streets with envy. 'Our turn next,' they said. 'It's happening. The miracle is happening.'"

He told Fabio of the famous morning when the tower was to be dedicated. The dignitaries had come from Montefalcone in cars and been taken up the mountain in oxcarts decorated with flags and flowers. A great flag had covered the top of the tower, and when the string was pulled and the tank was revealed, there, shining fresh and black in the morning sun, was *MUSSOLINI IS ALWAYS RIGHT* and all the *DUCE*'s, and on the catwalk was Italo Bombolini.

"I was a hero once, for a few days, and then they turned the water off," Bombolini said. "After that I was a fool."

When the leaders from Montefalcone were gone, The Band had assumed control of the water tower and began to charge for the water. When the grape growers refused to pay, the water was turned off, and the people went back to the old way, praying to God to send rain. The people forgot about the tower.

While he talked Bombolini threw the bottle off the tower, and there was a shout from the people as it arched out over the town and finally crashed in a tinkle of glass on the roof of the Cooperative Wine Cellar. A minute later an old man with white hair and a face as red as wine came out onto the roof and shook his fist at them. It was Old Vines the cellar master—the keeper of the wine.

"I've upset the sleep of the wine," Bombolini said. "If he had a rifle he would shoot us off this tower. Are you almost done?"

"Yes," Fabio said. "Two more *DUCE*'s and one *DU*."

"I ran out of paint. . . . No, we didn't blame Mussolini at first. It was the water. The country might have been falling apart, but we couldn't see it. You know what The Master says. 'Men are apt to deceive themselves in big things, but they rarely do so in particulars.'"

"I don't know who The Master is."

"Niccolò Machiavelli," Bombolini said. "He's my master. I have read his work *The Prince* forty-three times."

The young man was astonished. His father had once told him that beneath Bombolini's clownish exterior there was a better mind than anyone could expect, but Fabio had never seen any sign of it.

"I don't suppose there is any more wine?" Bombolini said.

Fabio thought about it. If Bombolini got drunk, it might be the end of them both, and yet the wine had made the journey down seem possible. He uncorked the second bottle and slid it along the catwalk.

"God shower blessings on you, Fabio. Rain them down on you. Flood you with them, Fabio. God drown you in blessings." And he began to drink the hot red wine. "When I'm through with this bottle I'm going off this tower, Fabio."

"Oh, no," Fabio said. "I didn't come up here for nothing."

"I can't disappoint my audience. Look at them down there.

They've been waiting for me all day. Can you imagine what they would say? The poor idiot can't even *fall* off the tower."

The young man began to paint more swiftly. If he was ever to get Angela's father down, it would have to be done soon, before he got too tired, before darkness fell.

The men and the women were on their way up from the terraces by then, so when Bombolini let fly the second bottle, the noise from the lower piazza, and from the Piazza of the People as well, was the loudest of the day. Fabio by then was on the last letter. It was strange, but there was exactly enough paint left in the bucket to paint out the last letter, the *u*, and not a brushful more.

"Now throw the bucket," Bombolini said. Fabio threw the bucket far out over the town, out over the Fat Wall, so that no one could get hurt.

"Now the brush." He threw the brush. There was a shout from the crowd. He threw the cheese and then the olives, and each time, the crowd roared and the noise grew louder and by the time he threw the knapsack the people were in an uproar.

Fabio had counted on the excitement to stir the wine seller. "All right, let's go now," he shouted. He came around the tank to where Bombolini sat, and as he did, the rusted iron bolts that held the catwalk to the concrete suddenly cried out, *screamed*, in protest. He quickly climbed onto the spiked pipe so that his weight was no longer on the catwalk. Now the people were silent. There was no sound from the city at all.

"They don't want you to fall, do you see?" Fabio said. "If they wanted you to fall they would be shouting for you."

While he talked he reached up and began to work the lengths of rope under the arms and across the back and around the waist of Bombolini. His plan was to tie the wine seller to the pipe, literally lash him to it, and then bring him down one foot at a time, spike by spike. He made Bombolini slide down until his feet could find the spikes to stand on. Even from where they were, so high above the city, they could hear the people suck in their breaths.

"Why are you doing this for me, Fabio?" Bombolini asked. Fabio didn't answer. How could he? He wondered if he would have been on this pipe now for anyone else's father, but then he realized that only Angela's father would be doing such a thing.

"Why, Fabio?"

"Because you are a man in trouble. It is people's responsibility to help others in trouble."

"Oh, Fabio," Bombolini said. "I don't know where you get ideas like that. It is people's responsibility to look after themselves and nothing more. Let us try a step."

Fabio lifted Bombolini's right foot and brought it down to the spike below, and then he climbed up so that his head was level with Bombolini's waist and he worked the ropes down the pole a foot or more. They did it several times and rested.

"Fabio? I want you to know one thing. If I ever get off this tower alive, if there is one thing in the world that you want and I can give it to you, I will give it to you."

Why couldn't he say it right then? Why couldn't he be honest with himself and say, "Yes, I want your daughter, Angela, in marriage." Instead, he could feel himself turning red.

IN THE LEADERS' MANSION they could hear the shouts of the people, and the cheering, but none of them was ready to believe what Pelo had come back and told them, that it was for Italo Bombolini the wine seller, the Sicilian Boob. And ever since then the noise had grown louder and with it had grown the need for The Band to know who was the leader so they could plan some kind of counteraction.

"I want the priest," Francucci the baker said, and he began to weep again. "I want to make my last confession."

"Shut up and start acting like a man," Copa shouted at him.

"I don't know how," Francucci sobbed.

"He's right, though. We need the priest," Vittorini said. "Every member of the *fiancheggiatori* must be united for the common defense." The *fiancheggiatori* is the alliance of the Crown and the Vatican with the bureaucracy and big business, which forms the traditional combination of power in this country. As Babbaluche had pointed out one day, the only thing missing from the combination was the people.

The leaders sent a young boy off to summon the priest. "Tell him someone is dying," Mazzola said.

They put Francucci in a far corner of the cellar, in the deepest part of the darkness, but even from there he could be heard saying over and over, "They are going to roll me in flour and sprinkle me with water and put me in an oven and bake me like my bread."

When the boy came back with the priest, Padre Polenta told them, "It's true. The people are cheering Bombolini."

"But why? Why Bombolini?"

"It is in the nature of mobs to cheer fools," the priest said. "Now where is the dying man?"

Mazzola waved his hand around the room. "Everywhere," he said. "All of us. It is only a matter of time."

There was a great shout from the piazza, followed by another one and yet another, until Francucci himself could no longer hear his own litany.

The shouts were the counting. Fabio had gotten Bombolini three-quarters of the way down the pipe when someone counted the number of rungs still to go. There were fifty of them, and the people began to shout the number left. "Forty-nine. Forty-eight." Great explosions of sound. "Forty-seven, forty-six . . ." Like a steam engine waiting in the station.

The crowd had come to see Bombolini fall off the tower, but now the mood had changed. Now they were cheering him down. When there were only thirty-four or thirty-five spikes still to go, however, Bombolini found his strength was gone. His leg muscles had become like strands of wet pasta. He hung from the ropes on the pipe like a quarter of beef in the marketplace.

What happened then must be seen at least as having the hand of God behind it. The grappa flask that Fabio was carrying clinked against the pipe. He had forgotten about it, but at the moment he needed it, at a time truly of desperation, something caused the bottle to strike the metal.

The grappa they distill here is strong. It can be used in a cigarette lighter or in a blowtorch. Fabio took the flask from his shirt and reached up, and because Bombolini was now too tired even to drink, began pouring little surprises of grappa down his throat.

The effect of the brandy was immediate. Bombolini's color, which had passed through purple into the whiteness of the dead, began to return to him. He got his feet back onto the spikes and was able to keep them there. "Give me the bottle," Bombolini said, and he began to pour the grappa down his own throat. In minutes the flask was emptied and he hurled it down into the piazza. There was another great cheer from the people below.

Then Bombolini began to work the ropes off himself, and when they were loose he threw them to the people and started down on his own. He was slow, but he also was steady and careful.

"Thirty-four!" Another step. "Thirty-three!" They could hear the sound all the way up the Corso Mussolini, they could hear it in every corner of the Piazza of the People, they could hear it through the barred doors of the Leaders' Mansion.

"It's starting again," Copa the mayor said. "They're getting ready to come. It's stronger now."

"I have a plan." Vittorini spoke so vigorously that the feathers in his hat rustled and it was reassuring. "I will make Bombolini take our surrender. It is now a matter of timing."

"And don't forget one thing," Copa added. "The Italian soldier is a *master* at the art of surrender."

It made them feel better, and the feeling lasted until they heard a noise, the loudest noise almost certainly ever heard in Santa Vittoria.

Bombolini had gotten down by himself, and then his feet touched the stones of the Piazza Mussolini. At that moment there was a great cheer and he had fallen forward and the crowd caught him before he hit the stones and began to carry him through the piazza toward his cart. It was a great solid oak two-wheeled Sicilian cart painted pink and blue, its oak wheels rimmed with iron, and it was at this time that he said the eight words that were the occasion for the greatest single sound in the history of the city.

Before telling you the words, it is necessary to understand one thing about this place and its people. Life here is hard. No one gets anything without working for it. Because of this, the greatest joy of these peasants is to get something they didn't work for: to get something for nothing. So this noise—now it can be understood. The crowd had put Fabio in the back of the cart and they propped Bombolini up in the high front seat and began to push the cart up the Corso Mussolini, when Bombolini cleared his throat and called out, "Free wine for the people of Santa Vittoria."

Then he slumped down in the seat, face forward, and it is doubtful if either he or Fabio ever heard the sound itself that greeted the words, the sound that soared up the corso and cascaded into the

Piazza of the People and thundered against the door of the Leader's Mansion.

The corso is steep and narrow. At the stone steps the men were forced to stop and rock the big iron-rimmed wheels back and forth to gain momentum to get up over the stones, and as they did they began shouting in time—*"Bom bo li-i-i-i ni."* The people behind them took up the shout, and soon the corso and then the whole of Santa Vittoria was vibrating with it. *"Bom bo li-i-i-i ni! Bom bo li-i-i-i ni!"* Someone said it sounded like a trombone announcing the angel of death.

In the Leaders' Mansion they were ready for Bombolini. They stood behind the heavy oak door and listened to the shouts of the people and waited for the proper moment. The barricades had been pulled aside and the door was opened a crack to allow Vittorini to see into the Piazza of the People. Copa stood just behind the old soldier with the medallion of the office of mayor held in his hand. Mazzola, behind Copa, held the great brass key to the city, which unlocks nothing here. Polenta, because he thought he had been coming to offer the last rites, had his tall silver crucifix with him, and the women had stripped the Mansion of every religious statue and holy picture the house possessed. Those who had no picture or soapstone saint to hold were given a baby or young child to carry in their arms. Vittorini himself had taken the Italian flag from a hallway and had worked the flag down the edge of his sword so that it hung like a banner when the blade was extended.

Before anything else, they saw through the crack in the door Bombolini's head rise from the Corso Mussolini, and then they saw his neck and his shoulders and finally, as the cart came up into the Piazza of the People, they saw the bodies of the people pushing him.

"My God," Copa said. "He comes like a king from the East."

Someone in the Leaders' Mansion moved toward the door, but Vittorini held him back. "Not yet, not yet," he shouted.

The cart, once out of the corso, rolled out of control into the center of the piazza, propelled by the pressure of the people behind it, and continued toward the Fountain of the Pissing Turtle.

"Now!" Vittorini commanded.

The door of the Leaders' Mansion was thrown wide open. The old soldier was the first to go through it, his sword held out in front of him with the flag fluttering in the evening wind. Copa came behind him, the imitation gold of the mayor's medallion glinting in what still remained of the sun. Mazzola was next, holding up the key to the city of Santa Vittoria. After him came Padre Polenta with the silver crucifix held aloft, and then came the women with statues and holy pictures and babies held at their breast.

The flag fluttered. Mazzola waved the key, and Copa flung the medallion up and down, and all the pictures and all the statues and all the babies waved up and down.

Nothing happened. The cart continued toward the fountain.

But Copa is a man of action, and action was required. "They ignore our surrender," he shouted to Vittorini. And he ran back into the Mansion. When he came outside again he held a double-barreled shotgun. The cart was no more than ten feet away from the fountain now, and he unloaded his first shot over the crowd. The second was lower, so low that several people were cut and stung by the bird shot. The movement in the piazza stopped, the pushing stopped, the cart stopped.

Copa put two more shells in the gun. He fired into the bell tower and the pellets caused the bell to go *ping* and *cling* and then the bell itself to rock lightly back and forth, with the clapper just touching the brass and sounding a mournful *blung, blung*.

"Once more," Vittorini said, and all of the pictures and the medallions and the sacred cross and the babies started to rise and fall again.

And allow this much for Bombolini. Although he was drunk and exhausted, it was he—of all the people in the piazza—who knew at once what was taking place.

Give this much for Bombolini, then. He saw his chance and he took it on the spot. "To the Leaders' Mansion," he called.

There was a moment when it seemed that the crowd would resist. The will of the crowd was for wine. But the people had a decency about them; they were willing to wait for their wine, and with a great effort Bombolini and the Sicilian cart were turned and began to bounce along the cobblestones of the piazza in the direction of the Leaders' Mansion.

"By the powers vested in me by the legitimate government of the city of Santa Vittoria . . ." Vittorini began. His voice, like that of all good soldiers, was loud and carried command.

Vittorini was impressive in defeat. The old soldier talked for al-

most a half hour without seeming to take a breath. The people didn't understand the purpose of the talk, but they liked to hear the words because they were beautiful and Vittorini was full of eloquence. The details were this: that in exchange for a sacred and a solemn vow by Bombolini that the persons and the property of those who had gone before—which meant The Band—would be respected, he, Italo Bombolini, would be handed the key to the city and the medallion of the office of the mayor.

"Have I your sacred and solemn vow?" Vittorini finally asked.

Someone prodded Bombolini. "You so have my solemn pledge."

Vittorini turned directly toward the people in the piazza then, and while Polenta sanctified the pledge by making the sign of the cross, Vittorini lifted his sword and the flag. "Citizens of Santa Vittoria," he cried out to them. "I give you your new leader."

There was almost no response from the people. They had not understood. What response there was—a few cheers and a few groans, a shout of laughter from Babbaluche, the sound of snoring from Fabio in the back of the cart—soon died away in the rush of the evening wind.

It was beginning to grow dark in the piazza, although the sun was still bright on the rooftops of the surrounding houses. Vittorini made a small sign with his hand; he turned it upward as if to say to Bombolini, "I have done my job, the rest is up to you." Then Copa pushed up behind the old soldier.

"Get the medallion," he said. "They don't want him. Get the medallion back. We have made a terrible mistake."

But at that moment Copa was proven wrong. Bombolini had turned around on the cart and back to his people and had said something to them, and this was followed by an enormous cheer and a great surge of movement as men seized the great cart to turn it around and drive it back across the piazza.

"And what would you call that if he isn't the leader?" Vittorini said.

The women lowered the holy pictures and the statues, and Padre Polenta began to walk across the clearing piazza to the bell tower. The others turned around and went back inside the Leaders' Mansion, because one of the promises Vittorini had made was that they would be out of the Mansion by sundown that evening.

The wine seller had said four words: "And now your wine."

When Rosa Bombolini heard the sounds coming up the corso, she had locked the iron gate that guards the front of the wineshop and then had gone upstairs and stood behind the shuttered windows, from where she could see into the Piazza of the People without being seen. Now her husband's cart stopped twenty feet from the wineshop.

"Open the gates," Bombolini demanded. When there was no answer, someone handed Bombolini a cobblestone that had been pried out of the piazza. Bombolini gave the stone to one of the Pietrosantos and made a sign, and the young man sent the stone crashing against an upstairs shutter. "Open the gates," Bombolini shouted again.

The shutter opened a little and his wife looked down from the window. "I open no gates to no mob!"

"This is no mob. These are the citizens of Santa Vittoria. I *order* you to open these gates."

"Order?" She made that laugh that all Santa Vittoria is familiar with, the one they are afraid of. "Whose order?"

"The order of the mayor of the city of Santa Vittoria." Bombolini held up the key to the city and the medallion of the office of mayor and the people cheered.

She opened the shutters wide then. "To hell with the indescribable mayor of this indescribable city!"

The new mayor looked very tired then and sad. He pointed to the gates. "Down," he said. "Pull them down."

"You s.o.b., I own this house!" she shouted. "I own this wineshop! You touch those gates and you'll never walk in here again."

This would be his first decision as mayor. He didn't look up at her when he made it. "Down," he ordered. "Take them down."

It was the Sicilian cart that did the job. They lifted Bombolini and Fabio out of the cart and then they ran it back and forth to build up the proper rage, like a bull preparing to make his charge, and all at once they released it. The old iron gate of the wineshop was no match for the cart. It gave almost at once, and after that the front door gave too. The reign of Italo Bombolini had begun.

It would be gratifying to be able to write that the people of Santa Vittoria acted in some other way than they did that night. But because the wine was free, everyone drank too much. Someone nearly set fire to a stall, and someone threw a bottle from a roof and cut someone. But it was not all bad. Some of the young people had accordions, and although they don't often dance here, the men danced and then the women and finally even the men with the women.

There was an omen for Santa Vittoria that evening. While the first barrel of wine was being drunk, just after the sun had gone down, a strange early evening star was seen glittering to the north and east of the city. It hung up above the mountains there, shining in the last gold of the setting sun before dipping down into the shadows of the mountains. Everyone agreed it was a good sign.

Long before midnight the dancing stopped and the piazza began to empty. No matter how much wine was drunk, the people would be down on the terraces in the morning when the sun rose. One of the young men found Fabio sleeping on the wet stones by the Fountain of the Pissing Turtle. "You'd better get up," he told him. "You'll die in the night air."

"I have no place to go," Fabio said. He was more tired than drunk.

The young man pointed him in the direction of the Leaders' Mansion. "There's room for you in there. Bombolini is living there now. His wife has thrown him out."

Fabio crossed the piazza to the door. He knocked, very lightly, and when no one answered he tried the door and it opened and he went inside. He was surprised to see Bombolini sitting on a box, with a tallow candle by his side, reading a book. He wanted to say something but could not think of the right thing, and he continued across the room until he was behind the mayor.

The book was old and grimy. It had been abused by use and time. Lines of the text were underlined in different colors, with all kinds of notes written in the margin. One read, *No, not true in Santa Vittoria.* Another said, *How very true* and *Try and tell that to the Fascists.*

"Oh," Bombolini said. He closed the book.

"I didn't mean to scare you."

"Well, you succeeded."

Fabio came around in front of the new mayor. "You were reading your Machiavelli."

"I need him now. He's going to have to tell me what to do."

Fabio sat down on a large wooden bench. "I want to stay here for the night if I may."

"Fabio, you may stay here for the rest of your life." Bombolini picked up the candle and took Fabio upstairs to a room where several blankets and an old coat were stretched out on the floor. "I want you to take my bed," he said, and when Fabio refused he forced him to lie down on it and went away with the light. Fabio had no idea how long he was there before the mayor returned.

"Fabio? Are you awake? Listen to this." He thumbed through the book and held up a hand with one finger extended, a gesture Fabio was to recognize later as the sign that Bombolini was about to quote from Machiavelli. " 'The wise ruler ought never to keep faith when by doing so it would be against his interests!' "

Fabio sat up. "What are you telling me?"

"Do I have to keep those promises I made to Vittorini?"

"You gave your word," Fabio said. "Your *sacred* word."

Bombolini closed the book with a loud noise. "I knew I should have asked Babbaluche," he said.

There was darkness, and Fabio slept. But when he woke again there was a light in the room once more.

"Just one other sentence, Fabio. An interpretation." The mayor held up his hand, his finger extended again. " 'Men must be either caressed or annihilated. They will revenge themselves for small injuries, but they can't do so for great ones. The harm the leader does must be such that he need not fear revenge.' What do you make of that?"

Fabio did not want to be part of any bloodletting, but he was tired and the words seemed to have only one meaning. "I think it means you're supposed to kill The Band."

"I think you are right." Bombolini said it sadly, because he had little stomach for blood and at the same time a respect for the words of The Master.

When next Fabio awoke, the room was light again, but this time the light came from the window. He had been able to sleep for several hours and he felt better because of it.

"Fabio della Romagna, I want you to join my cabinet," Bombolini said to him. "I want you to be a minister in the Grand Council of the Free City of Santa Vittoria."

"I am flattered," Fabio said, and it was the truth, "but my place is in Montefalcone. I have to finish my studies at the university."

"Just for the emergency," Bombolini said. "For the duration. I need you. I need educated men. That's what you will be, Minister of Education. No. Minister for Advanced Education. You can live right here. We'll get a bed for you and a desk, and Angela will bring us something in the morning and make us supper at night."

It was the thunderbolt again. It was all at once the most amazing idea that Fabio had ever heard—Angela carrying his breakfast; Angela preparing food for him with her own hands; Angela meeting him by error and design and chance in all those ways that can only occur when two people are alone in a house.

"I don't know," Fabio said. He could barely talk.

"Everything will be upset in Montefalcone. You said the Germans were taking over the town."

"Yes."

"Then I can put you down," Bombolini said. He took out a soiled card from his pocket and at the bottom added Fabio's name to the list of names. The card was old and the names on it were old and only Fabio's looked freshly placed, and he realized with a start that this man, whom they called the Sicilian Boob, the least likely man in all of Santa Vittoria to ever become a leader, had for months and perhaps years been walking about with a fully formed government in his pocket.

"You should sleep," Bombolini said. "But think about this while you sleep. The Master says it is necessary to rule by fear or rule by love. One way or the other. I want you to think about which course I should follow."

When Fabio awoke, the sun was fully up and the old blankets were hot against his skin. He thought about the night: the wine; the dancing—he had watched others dance with her; the strange star in the sky, and he thought about the new thing, Angela and himself in this house. As he lay on the floor he became conscious of a sound coming from the piazza, a tinkling of glass. When he looked out the window, he could see a group of old men and women with long-handled brooms sweeping up the broken glass of the previous night. Such a thing had never happened before in Santa Vittoria; God's winds swept and God's rare rains washed. He was still watching the work with admiration when Bombolini came into the room, clean now and refreshed, although he could not have slept.

"The Public Works Corps," Bombolini said. "I stole the idea from the Fascists."

"But how do you pay them?"

Bombolini smiled broadly and he handed Fabio a square piece of paper.

3   THREE   3
SANTA VITTORIA LIRE

This paper redeemable for
legal currency at the
end of the emergency

ITALO BOMBOLINI
MAYOR
THE FREE CITY OF SANTA VITTORIA

"Do you really intend to honor it?" Fabio asked.

Bombolini was shocked by the suggestion. "You can fool the people about many things, but only a fool would be foolish enough to fool the people about money."

"The Master," Fabio said. "I'm getting to recognize him."

The mayor was clearly flattered. He said, "In truth, Fabio, it was myself."

Fabio was impressed. "You should write those down."

"Fabio, I don't write that well. If someone else could write them down for me . . ."

It was in this manner that *The Discourses of Italo Bombolini* came into being. There are still several copies in Fabio's hand somewhere in the city.

"The people are saying we were born under a lucky star. A good omen, a good sign."

"I hope they are right," Fabio said. But all he could think about now was when Angela would come with some broth or pasta.

Bombolini leaned toward him. "Do you remember I asked you to think about whether I should rule by fear or rule by love?"

Fabio told him that he did, but that he had had no thoughts.

"Well, rest your brain then, Fabio," Bombolini went on, "because I have made my decision. I have decided to be lovably fearful."

II

BOMBOLINI

THE STAR THEY SAW was me, Roberto Abruzzi. I was the omen sent to Santa Vittoria. This is the place where I enter the story. It is the price I ask you to pay in return for hearing the story of Santa Vittoria, which is admittedly a better story than my own. It is something that I have wanted to say to my own countrymen, *my* people, for twenty years; an apology written in the hope that some will understand and that I might someday be able to go back home to America and rebuild what is left of my life.

On the morning that Fabio told the story of the death of Mussolini, I was flying in the *Odessa Darling*, a B-24 Liberator bomber, somewhere over Italy. It was our fourth mission. We had bombed Pantelleria and another island in the Mediterranean, and this was to be the first flight over mainland Italy. We had crossed the sea from Africa early that morning, flying with the sun, coming in low over the blue-green water. I never saw Italy until it came upon us, a surprise from the water, all green, so different from Africa, darkly green like the underside of grape leaves. We followed the coast, rushing along over the cliffs and the little towns strung along their steep sides, and somewhere we suddenly turned inland. After that I didn't look at the land much, because my aim was to see and to shoot an Italian plane. The reason for this was that the other members of the *Odessa Darling* didn't trust me.

It was one night after he had been drinking in the Officer's Club that Captain Buster Rampey came to my barracks and said, "Tell me one thing true, Abruzzi. If you was to see an Eyetalian plane in the air you wouldn't fire on it, would you?"

I told him that I would, and I can recall every word the captain said to me and the way he said them. I remember that he pronounced the word "fire" as *far*.

"You don't have to lie about it, Abruzzi. I won't hold that against you. You think if my people left Texas and some war came up that I would go back and shoot at Texas people?"

I said that I thought he would if he were ordered to do it. He gripped me by the front of my shirt. "Shoot *my* brothers? Shoot at *my* flesh and blood?" He let go of my shirt in disgust. "I just wish you would be honest about it."

After that I was accepted by the crew as a built-in handicap. They even had a plan for me called Plan Paisan, in case of an attack by Italian planes. Lieutenant Marvell was to leave his post as navigator and man my machine gun. There was nothing personal about it.

But I was looking then to prove them wrong. If Italian planes were sighted, I wanted to fire at them and hit them before Lieutenant Marvell could relieve me of my weapon. Then sometime that morning, while passing over a patch of dark pinewoods, the *Odessa Darling* flew into a grove of budding flak—puffs of black smoke and little flowerings of metal. The sky bloomed with them. I had thought we were through this dangerous garden and all of the bursts were behind us, when the plane leaped in the air, shuddered and started down in one great sudden dip, as if someone had pulled a plug in the sky.

"Please, God, don't let there be fire," someone said.

There was a thudding sensation, a series of bumps, and then we held; the plane had gotten hold of the sky again.

Captain Rampey was a good pilot. It is strange now to think that I owe my life to him.

For a long time we flew in silence, trying only to hold the plane in the sky, fearful of trying to turn or even to lift it, and the mountain towns came floating up at us and then faded away like islands in a high green sea. After a while—how long it was I couldn't even guess—Captain Rampey began to make the turn back again, to wheel the *Odessa Darling* around in a huge slow arc in the sky.

There was no talking. We listened to the strange sounds the plane was making. They frightened us, and then Rampey called to Marvell. "I want you to pick me out a nice little town on the way back. One directly on the line to home."

From my post I could see Lieutenant Marvell carefully checking his maps. "I got you one," he said. "We won't even have to bank for it. Name of . . . name of . . ."

"I don't *want* to know the name," the captain said. "Just tell me before we get there."

"Yes, sir."

"We didn't come this far for nothing."

"No, sir."

"Got to ditch these bombs *some*place."

"Yes, sir."

When we were five minutes from the target area, Lieutenant Marvell announced that it was time to begin to ease the *Odessa Darling* down. "It's just on the other side of that mountain," he said. The plane started down.

It was a good-sized town, a city really, about three or four times the size of Santa Vittoria. It was on the other side of the mountain, but it sat on a smaller mountain of its own, and it covered the crest of it, all white and orange tiles, ringed by a wall, so that in the sunlight it seemed to be a crown on the crest of the mountain.

"Marvell?"

"Sir?"

"You picked us a *jewel*, hear?"

There was trouble with the doors of the bomb bay; the flak had damaged the mechanism that controlled them. The bombardier was trying to work them open, but before he succeeded we were already over the city.

"I can get you a target further down the line," Marvell said.

"No," Rampey said. "I want this one."

We were low then, and I could see the city clearly. The piazza was crowded with people and carts and animals and children. At one end of the piazza was a large building that I took to be the town hall. At the other end stood the tower of the cathedral.

The shadow of the *Odessa Darling* slid across the wall of the city and over the piazza and the church façade, over the orange roofs and then over the other wall, like a dark messenger. When the shadow crossed over them the people looked up; some went back to their work and some waved to us.

When the bomb bay doors were open, the *Odessa Darling* swung around and came back for the town. As the plane passed over the city wall Captain Rampey said, "Kick 'em on out."

All of us became bombardiers. We rolled the bombs through the door and kicked them out with our feet, and they began to follow each other down upon the city, wigwagging back and forth the way bombs do.

When the explosions began we were low enough to see the confusion of the people in the piazza. Not knowing what to do, they would run first in one direction, and then they would turn and run back toward the place they had just left. Eventually they must have found their heads, because the second time we turned back over the city the people were gone. This was the run on which the five-hundred-pound delayed-action demolition bomb would be used. This bomb is the heart and even the very soul of the *Odessa Darling*.

"You have it ready and I'll tell you when," Captain Rampey told the bombardier. "Now!" he said; and on that word the bomb was pushed out. For a moment it seemed to fly along with the *Odessa Darling* before arching over the town and suddenly dipping down, and as it did, every one of us could see that it was going to be a success.

It appeared to just touch the gray slate roof of the cathedral and then to go through it so swiftly that the hole it made in the roof seemed to close behind it the way water does over a rock. Then the bomb exploded somewhere down among the dark cellars where a great many people from the piazza must have been hiding. First the great circular stained-glass window that was the front of the cathedral came apart all at once, flowering out onto the stones of the piazza. After that the fire began, a spurt of flame from the bowels of the church that took a great part of the slate roof with it. When we began to pull up, only the far walls of the cathedral still stood and the center of the city was engulfed in flames.

A soldier does his duty, and this was mine. We had banked away from the city to avoid the pillar of fire and smoke that was rising from it, and then we turned back toward Africa.

"That concludes the afternoon program," Captain Rampey said.

"I will tell you one thing," Marvell said. "We did us a job."

Those were the last words that I remember hearing on the *Odessa Darling*. I have no recollection beyond that, no recollection at all of stepping out through the bomb bay doors or of pulling the rip cord on my parachute. My first recollection is of dropping down onto Italy, the last rays of the sun glowing in the white nylon of my canopy as if I were hung to a silken lantern, and it must have been this that caused me to glitter in Santa Vittoria, far to the south of me then, like a star or an omen in the evening.

I was happy at that time; sometimes it seems like the happiest moment of my life. At other times I see it as the saddest, because it cut me loose from myself, perhaps forever.

I dropped out of the sun into the shadow of a mountain and I struck the terraced side of the mountain that was no longer farmed. The earth was hard there, and when I hit it I heard a bone snap in my leg. The cool evening wind caught in my canopy and I was dragged down and across the terraces until I finally became tangled in some old vines and was held by them. I pulled the parachute around me and made a nest for myself as a wounded animal would do.

Later, during the night, I was wakened by some small dark men who smelled of manure and wine. They said nothing, but lifted me up and put me in a large grape basket on the back of a mule and took me up the mountain. I thought they were going to kill me, and I didn't care then. I was a deserter now, I had declared my personal end to the war and I was ashamed of myself. Who was I to have attempted such a thing? I would close my eyes and as soon as I did I would see the people and the church and the flames. As I look back on it now, there was little reason to wonder why I wanted to die.

They kept me in a little twig and straw hut in a field for I have no idea how long. They fed me some kind of runny white goat cheese and hard bread and bitter olives and wine. One night they came and got me and put me in the basket on a mule again, and by morning I was in some sort of town. They dumped me here then, in the shredded old grape basket, in the Piazza of the People at the door of the Leaders' Mansion. Italo Bombolini was mayor of the city, as I was to learn, and had been mayor for several weeks by then.

IN *THE DISCOURSES OF ITALO BOMBOLINI* is the following:

The duty of the people is to tend to their own affairs.
The duty of government is to help them do it.
This is the pasta of politics.

The inspired leader, the true prince, no matter how great, can only be sauce upon the pasta.

Two weeks after Italo Bombolini had taken over as mayor of Santa Vittoria, everyone—with the exception of the priest, Padre Polenta, who despised him, and the cobbler Babbaluche, who wasn't prepared to see him as he was—recognized one thing about him. Bombolini was a leader; he was a born leader, a natural leader. He was, in his own words, "sauce upon the pasta." From his first day he seemed to have a feeling for the correct thing to do. He had the streets swept. He had the fountain repaired and the water-catch cleaned of all its mold and moss and all the old glass and potato peelings that washed around in it. One morning the people woke up and found that all the old slogans in Santa Vittoria had been changed in the night. The one in the Piazza of the People that read BELIEVE, OBEY, FIGHT had been changed to

TRANQUILLITY

CALMNESS

PATIENCE

THE THREE GREAT VIRTUES OF THE ITALIAN PEOPLE
—A public service
Italo Bombolini

In High Town, where for years the sign had read LIVE DANGEROUSLY, *D'Annunzio*, Bombolini had added BUT DRIVE CAREFULLY, *Bombolini*, even though there were no cars in Santa Vittoria then.

And in the Corso Mussolini, BETTER TO LIVE ONE DAY AS A LION THAN 100 YEARS AS A LAMB had been changed to BETTER TO LIVE 100 YEARS—*Bombolini, Mayor*.

It is impossible now to know whether the things the wine seller did came to him from study and thought or whether they were the reactions of instinct. It doesn't really matter. The important point is that he did them.

The trouble with government in this country is that it is composed of the Ins and the Outs. When the Outs get in, they kick all the Ins out, and the new Outs do everything in their power to destroy the programs of the Ins, even when they might help them. It is almost always exciting and usually no good for the town, but that is the way it always has been.

Bombolini's genius—for that is what it was—was that instead of throwing people out he invited everyone in. He formed the Grand Council of the Free City of Santa Vittoria and in two days every faction and force that could be counted upon to fight one another had a member in the government. Everyone was an In.

Giovanni Pietrosanto was made Minister of Public Waters, which meant that he was in charge of the fountain and the water tower. Under his direction the spillways were cleared and the pump was repaired, and for the first time in years there was water on the terraces for the vines—not a great deal, but enough to keep a dry spell from becoming a drought.

Under his brother Pietro, who has a voice that can break windows, the organization called Minute Men of Santa Vittoria was formed. At the start people laughed at the army, but as the twenty men drilled in the piazza, the people began to turn out to watch them. The drill was impressive. Every soldier was allowed to wear a red arm band and to sport a hawk's feather in his hat, and soon every young man in Santa Vittoria was hungry for a feather.

There was also a Commissioner of Sanitation, a Minister for Bread and Pasta, a Minister for Advanced Education and others.

Bombolini closed the second meeting of the Grand Council with these words. "A wise man once said, 'The first impression one gets of a new ruler and his brains is from seeing the men he has chosen to have around him.' Men of Santa Vittoria, by these standards I submit that I must be judged a genius."

They were, of course, flattered.

The morning I came to Santa Vittoria I would have died if it hadn't been for Fabio della Romagna, because the first people to find me assumed that I *was* dead and that the body should be taken someplace and buried. But Fabio took one look at me in the grape basket and knew that I was alive. So, instead of burying me, they took me into the Mansion of the Leaders and put me in a bed.

I have no idea how long I stayed there. Three or four times a day the girl, Angela, came and held my head in her lap and spooned broth and pasta and soft sopping bread into my mouth, and sometimes she poured me a small glass of wine. I had no hope that I ever would get well. I leaned toward death. The bone in my leg had joined together, but it had come together all wrong, and I would lie on the bed for hours at a time in darkness and in pain and never make a move.

After a week or two I began to realize that, with no effort on my part or any consciousness of it, I was beginning to understand the language that I heard around me. It was the language of my parents that I had learned as a small boy, and it was returning to me. I knew it was a dialect and that my parents must have come from some village in this region, but I didn't even know the name of it. That's the kind of son I had been to them.

I still dreamed at night about the bombs, and the fat mayor or his daughter would have to come and restrain me while I would cry out and pound against the wall and hide beneath my blanket. But I knew that somewhere I had decided to try and live, when one morning the girl was late coming with the broth and I was first hungry and then anxious and finally angry with her. And when she came, surrounded by all her smells, hot broth and good bread and strong soap and the freshness of herself, I found I was smiling. And I wanted to say good morning and talk with her, but I was afraid to begin. During all of this time I had allowed no one to know that I knew the language. I was too tired and too uninterested to want to speak.

Only once did I come close to revealing myself. Bombolini and Fabio were in my room with some young men who wanted to look at me. There is very little to do in Santa Vittoria, and I was an object of curiosity. The young men were about to leave when one of them looked down into the piazza from the low window beside my bed and said, "Oh, my God, the Malatestas are back!"

They all ran to the low window and knelt down by it.

"It's the tall one," one of them said. "The snotty one. What's her name?"

None of them could remember at first. They all had a nickname for her—Long Legs, the Icicle. Bombolini called her "the Hawk."

"Caterina," one of them finally said.

"Caterina," everyone agreed. "Yes. Caterina."

She was crossing the Piazza of the People toward the street that leads down from High Town, carrying two heavy suitcases. No one made an effort to help her with them, and she didn't ask for any. The women waiting in line at the fountain all saw her, but they gave no sign that they had. I know little about clothes, but even a very ignorant person would know that hers cost money and are what is called high style.

"The Germans must be giving them hell in Rome," Bombolini said.

"They only come back when they're in trouble. They must have put her husband in jail. What was his name?" No one knew.

"They must have killed him," someone else said, and they all nodded and were silent for a moment.

"She's a beast. She's no good for anything," they were saying now. "If you married her you'd have fun in bed and starve to death."

There is a saying here in Santa Vittoria—"What you can't have, abuse." And this is what they were doing.

"But she's very beautiful," I said in Italian, and not one of them noticed. She was the most beautiful woman I had ever seen.

One morning I awoke and found that it was cool in the room, and when I leaned out of bed and looked out the window and across the piazza and over the houses to the mountains beyond, I could see that they were covered with snow. Sometime in the night, unseen and unheard by us, a great storm had raged up there. When Angela came in with the broth I said, "If you go to my window, you'll see something beautiful."

She put down the broth and went to the window, and at that moment I noticed that she also was beautiful in the way of simple things. "I don't see anything," she said.

"On the mountains. There's snow this morning."

"Ah, the new wind. It has blown summer away." She turned back to me. "It's good for the grapes." She spoke to me in dialect and was not at all surprised that I could answer her back or understand her.

"Aren't you surprised at my talking?" I asked.

"We were wondering when you would begin to talk. After all, you've been here for weeks."

"But I talk rather well, don't you think?"

She shrugged. "Little babies speak at two years. You're a man."

However, she went down and told them that I was now talking and there was interest and even excitement, because now they could do business with me. Bombolini, followed by some other members of the Grand Council, came running up the stairs to my room.

"They say you talk very well," he said to me. "Good." He seized my hand and pumped it so violently that it caused my leg to ache. He turned to the others. "What did I tell you? This is someone very special. We are in the presence of a superior human being." He left without ever hearing me say a word.

Of all the people that I could hear downstairs only Fabio did not seem to be impressed by my language. "It's a kind of trick really," he explained. He told anyone who would listen about an idiot they had hired at the university to clean chamber pots who had learned German in one month. "The ability to learn languages in this way is in some cases actually a sign of idiocy."

"Fabio, you sound as if you have something against the man," Bombolini said.

"I have nothing against him," Fabio said. "I only want to correct the record."

No one understood what Fabio was trying to tell them, and neither did I, then. What despair I caused Fabio in those days, and I should have known it.

Although the mayor had not stayed to listen to me speak on the first day, nothing could seem to stop him from coming back on the days that followed. He came in the afternoons, when I was asleep, and at night, asking me questions about how they did things in America. I came to dread the sound of his step on the stairs. More than the intrusion and the effort involved was my shame at my ignorance.

"I don't know about that," I would say. Or, "I can't answer that. I never studied it."

"It's a wise man who can say 'I don't know,' " Bombolini would say to me. "Good man." But I would turn my head toward the wall in embarrassment.

It was Fabio who was finally able to figure out why Bombolini acted that way toward me. The reason for Bombolini's amazing success at government, which had changed him from a clown to a prince in one night, was that Bombolini was no longer Bombolini at all but someone else who had lived five hundred years before. When faced with any problem or any decision, he would go back to Machiavelli to provide the answer. Bombolini was only a body and a mouth for The Master.

But somewhere along the line there were problems for which The Master couldn't provide answers, and it was these gaps in The Master's knowledge that frightened Bombolini. To close them he needed a representative of the New Ways. And who better than me, Abruzzi the American, a dropper-in from the New World? As soon as I was able to stand with the aid of a crutch Babbaluche the cobbler had made for me, I was invited downstairs to sit in on sessions of the government, and after a week I was invited to join the Grand Council as a full member, as a Minister Without Portfolio, to advise on current affairs. I used to wonder what they would think in Benjamin Franklin High School, which I left when I was a junior, if they could see me then.

This was the state of things when one night Babbaluche came into the middle of a meeting and began pointing his finger at me. "Look at him," he said. "Feast your eyes on him." They looked at me. "Because of this man each one of you stands to go to jail and to lose your vines."

The loss of the vines struck fear in their hearts.

"Do you know what this man represents? This man is an enemy of the state."

"He seems like a good man to me," Giovanni Pietrosanto said.

"An enemy of the state."

The argument was that America was still at war with Italy, and by making me a member of the Grand Council each member was guilty of collaborating with the enemy.

"You are collaborators," Babbaluche told them. "Do you know what they do to collaborators?"

Everyone knew. They took away your home, impounded your land and tore up your vines. And it would have been understandable for Bombolini to have deserted me then. He could have had me taken to Montefalcone and turned over to the authorities. It would have ended his troubles and even earned him some small favors, but he fought for me. They sent me from the room, so I never heard the debate. I understand that it was bitter. Sometime early in the morning it finally became a question of confidence in the government and in the ability of its leader any longer to lead, and Babbaluche rose and proposed that Bombolini resign.

They voted after this, and the count must have been close. Whatever it was, Italo Bombolini managed to do what Benito Mussolini had failed to do; he had endured. For show they took away my membership in the Grand Council and I became an ex-minister without anything.

Why did Babbaluche bring the charge, he who hated the Germans and the Fascists above all the rest of us? It was, as Vittorini later told

242

me, in Babbaluche's nature to embarrass and destroy governments. The nation is filled with people like him. It is in this way that they find their dignity. It is their only business and their only true passion.

There was never a serious challenge to Bombolini after that. The next day, in a show of strength, he had himself named Captain of the People instead of Mayor, an old and honored title in this region, and after a time even Babbaluche came to call him Captain.

SOMEWHERE IN *THE DISCOURSES OF ITALO BOMBOLINI* the following appears:

> Anyone can be great with money.
> With money greatness is not a talent but an obligation.
> The trick is to be great without money.
>
> Anyone can make an omelet with eggs.
> It takes a great man to make one with none.

Those months—the summer in Santa Vittoria—were good. There was hunger in Italy but there was no hunger here. There was still good wine to trade and sell. Most of the wine here is vermouth, which is a blend of wines and aromatic herbs, and the vermouth made in Santa Vittoria is one of the best in the world. It is aged for a year or even two years, depending on the amount of sugar in the grapes and the amount of acid, on the time of month the grapes were picked, the position of the moon during the harvest, and the whisperings of the gods of the grape into the ears of Old Vines, the cellar master, who alone can hear them. Usually this wine is sold to the Cinzano family, who sell it all over the world, but because of the war the wine was still in Santa Vittoria. When the people needed food three or four carts were loaded with bottles and sent to Montefalcone where there was always a market for their wine. The carts would come back up the mountain the next day filled with flour for bread and pasta, with bags of onions and salt, green peppers and red peppers, tins of sardines, wheels of cheese, sometimes baskets of fruit from the north, sausage, salami, olives and cheap black wine, since their own wine is too good to drink every day. When the carts came back up the mountain you would not know there was a war on.

But something was happening in Italy. "There are more tanks in

Montefalcone than people," the men who went to get the food would tell the others. "There are more Germans than our own people."

The people felt it, but it didn't concern them. There was food and the grapes were fattening on the vines, and if the Italian nation was in danger of coming apart, the city of Santa Vittoria had never seemed closer together. And for this, Italo Bombolini must take all the credit. He had embarked the city on a program for greatness. Beside his bed in the Leaders' Mansion he had hung this sign:

NOTHING CAUSES A PRINCE TO BE SO MUCH ESTEEMED AS A GREAT ENTERPRISE. IT KEEPS THE PEOPLE'S MINDS UNCERTAIN AND ASTONISHED AND IT KEEPS THEM OCCUPIED IN WATCHING THE RESULT.

The mayor's problem, as he put it, was how to uncover greatness in a city so poor that one man will provoke another into an argument just so that his donkey can eat the other man's grass as they argue.

Bombolini began by changing the names of all the streets. There were public hearings, there were contests, there were votes and more votes, speeches and arguments, until the city was in a state of civic uproar and excitement. In the end, streets were named for Garibaldi, for Mazzini, for the Redshirts. The Piazza Mussolini became the Piazza Matteotti, named for the first famous victim of the Fascist regime. It was a very popular decision. The Corso Mussolini became the Corso Cavour, because every town must have something named after the famous statesman, Cavour, and the Leaders' Mansion was renamed the Palace of the People.

The effort was a great success. It had cost nothing, but had brought the people closer together. When the last of the streets and piazzas and lanes had been renamed and there were no more left, perhaps the only saddened person was Bombolini himself. "The people have entertained the vice of ingratitude," he told Fabio one day. "They didn't even name an *arch* after me."

It is said somewhere that the art of art is to make the work seem artless, and this is what Captain Bombolini did with Santa Vittoria. With the exception of Fabio and occasionally myself, no one had any idea at all of the work and thought that went into the things he did.

"Fabio," he said, "get your notebook. You are going to see a man make an omelet without eggs and I want you to see how it is done."

IT WAS FABIO WHO WAS responsible for getting Caterina Malatesta to repair the bone in my leg. I didn't understand it at the time, but he wanted my leg made well so that I could go away from Santa Vittoria.

Fabio was not the person he had been before. Even I, a stranger, could notice it. He was moody and sullen, and finally openly angry almost all the time, and he had begun to drink too much wine. We didn't know then that it was the sight of Angela Bombolini feeding me broth and the sound of Angela Bombolini talking to me while I stretched out on my bed that was destroying Fabio.

Bombolini himself had gone up to High Town to see the Malatesta, as they called her, and she had laughed in his face. Even after that, as shy as he was, Fabio went to see her, and for reasons we don't know, the Malatesta agreed to come and see me. It was a measure of how desperate Fabio must have been.

She was not a doctor in the sense that she had a license to practice, but she had gone to medical school in Rome until the final year, when her father, to save the family, forced her to leave school and marry a rich young Roman noble, who was also a rising Fascist. Her family had once been a great family in this region, with large holdings of land. But they had begun to lose the land, plot after plot, and by the time of the marriage they were reduced to a few parcels of land and several houses in the region, one of which was in High Town, to which various Malatestas retreated from time to time to lick their wounds.

No one knew how the marriage came out. There is a picture of the rich husband in the Malatesta house, but it is assumed by all that he died when Mussolini was ousted.

When the Malatesta came into my room she never really saw me. She took off the smelly bandages that had been put on the wound and threw them on the floor. I was ashamed of my wound because it stank and I began to apologize for it. She didn't hear me. "This wound will have to be opened," she told me. "The infection will have to be cleared up and the bone be rebroken and set again."

"If you say so, it has to be done."

"It doesn't have to be done. If you want a leg it has to be done."

"I want a leg."

"It will hurt a great deal." I shrugged. "You don't know the pain I am talking about," she said. "Americans aren't prepared for pain.

They think they have a right to avoid pain. The people here know different. They know that pain is the natural condition of life."

She came back several days later, with no warning. She came with some local anesthetic and a bottle of grappa, with Fabio as a helper, and a half hour after she arrived she cracked the bone in my leg. (It pleases me to this day to think that she was impressed when I didn't cry out.) Then she began to reset the bone. During all that time she never said a word to me. Afterward she said, "You lie in bed for one week and then you get up and try and walk. The sooner you walk on this the better it will be." She went to the door of the room and turned. "But I doubt that you will do it," she said.

It was this, of course, that sent me stumbling into the Piazza of the People, my face stiff with pain, exactly one week later. I began to go down through the streets and finally down to the wall and through the Fat Gate and down onto the terraces, where I would stop and talk with the people.

The more I walked the stronger the leg became. In the end I would go all the way down the terraces to the foot of the mountain and then rest in the enormous ancient wine cellar at the base before climbing up again. I had never seen anything like the wine cellar before, and I came to love it for its coolness and quiet. It had been built by the Romans, and rebuilt entirely sometime in the Middle Ages, and then finally abandoned in the eighteenth century.

There were three rooms actually. A small opening in the mountainside led into an enormous room hollowed out of the mountain itself, and it was called the Great Room. It was as large as the inside of a cathedral. From the back wall of the Great Room two long deep wine cellars were cut into the bowels of the mountain. The cellars themselves were filled with water, but the Great Room was cool by the entrance and I would often lie there on the dry sand and nap before going back up.

I was the only one in Santa Vittoria who ever went into the Great Room of the old wine cellar. The people were afraid of the spirits who lived in there and they feared for my life. When nothing happened to me it didn't lessen their belief in evil spirits. It only convinced them that Italian spirits and ghosts were not in the least interested in non-Italian people.

During the week that I had spent in bed before walking, I had worked on the radio of Vittorini the mail clerk. They had brought it to me to fix because I was an American and Americans are supposed to be able to fix new inventions such as radios. I knew nothing about radios, but there is a certain logic about anything that is broken. Sooner or later you find that if something isn't connected, and if it can be connected, then perhaps the thing may be made to work again. I finally got the radio to work.

In those days we received an hour of electricity a day from a power station at San Rocco del Lago. Some days it never came at all. But one day when it did come I heard a broadcast from Egypt that was sent to Italy by the British. The Americans, they said, were almost all the way across Sicily, and the invasion of the mainland was to be expected any day. I grew very excited, and I shouted out the news before I realized that the last thing I wished was to be liberated. But it didn't matter in any case. Fabio had no interest, and Bombolini was far too interested in cooking his eggless omelet.

THE OMELET BOMBOLINI was preparing was intended to feed the entire city, and he succeeded in doing it. He kept the people's minds astonished and occupied at a cost of nothing.

The patron saint of this place is not Santa Vittoria, as you would have a right to expect, but Santa Maria of the Burning Oven, a local peasant girl who did the kinds of things that saints do to get themselves canonized, and who was then thrust upon this city. One story about her concerned a baker who, while pulling out his loaves, fell headlong into his ovens. His screams could be heard all over the city, but there was nothing anyone could do for him except to hope that he didn't ruin the day's bread. But then the little girl Maria walked right into the blazing oven and picked up the baker and carried him into the street. Neither suffered a burn, and the bread that night was said to be the best ever baked in the city.

Bombolini's plan, as simple as possible, was to turn Santa Vittoria into a shrine for all the bakers of the world. What novice baker would wish to begin a career without first coming to Santa Vittoria for a few days and praying to God through Santa Maria to favor him? Old bakers would want to come too, and give thanks for their success. And bakers who were in trouble would want to come and get Santa Maria on their side.

The idea of Santa Vittoria as a national shrine became a craze here. It was all that anyone talked about. If a shrine was proclaimed, the pilgrims who came would need places to stay and places to eat. Every home was a potential inn, every woman a potential cook, every vine pruner a potential waiter going around in a white jacket and soft shoes collecting tips for doing next to nothing. There would also be a need for curio shops selling such things as clay ovens and satin pillows with pictures of the Little Saint, as Bombolini began to call her. It was even felt by some that within ten years' time only a fool would ever have to go down to work on the terraces again.

Most leaders would have stopped there, but Bombolini knew things most leaders never learn. "The wise prince," he told Fabio, with his finger in the air, "must foment some enmity so that by suppressing it he will augment his greatness." It was this that led him to declare war on Scarafaggio. It also led to Fabio's leaving Santa Vittoria.

Scarafaggio! You have only to say the word and you can picture the town. There is no beauty to it. It sits across the valley on the other mountain, a feeble imitation of Santa Vittoria. It cowers there, filled with fleas and ticks and roaches. There are bedbugs here, but they only survive; in Scarafaggio they flourish.

In the first week of September that year, Captain Bombolini called a meeting and everyone assembled in the Piazza of the People on a Sunday, and he asked them to look out over the valley at Scarafaggio. The people of Scarafaggio are thought to be fools by those in Santa Vittoria, but he said, "They're laughing at us over there. For two hundred years they have been going around, every day, laughing at us."

It was hard to believe this astonishing news. He allowed them a few minutes to study the miserableness heaped up across the valley, and then the bell in our tower rang out. "Do you hear that?" Bombolini asked them. Everyone nodded. "Well, so do they." He pointed across the valley. "They get up by our bell. They go to Mass by our bell. *We* pay for the bell and *they* use the sound and laugh. It is as simple as this. Scarafaggio is stealing our sound."

If the best thing in the world is to get something for nothing, it follows that the worst is to give away something and get nothing back. The people were violent about it. Pietrosanto was all for calling out the Santa Vittoria army and marching on Scarafaggio. "Take down the bell," someone else shouted. "Better no bell than to give away our sound." There was a roar of approval.

"Keep the bell, but cut the rope so no one can ring it," another cried. That made even more sense.

To his credit, Bombolini was able to restrain the angry people. He pointed to the new sign at the end of the piazza. "Remember the three true virtues of the Italian people: 'Tranquillity. Calmness. Patience.' Restrain yourselves. Your captain has a solution. The old wrong will be righted." But he did not tell them the solution.

So the city was excited after that. The people, as The Master said they should be, were curious. But Fabio, to whom Bombolini had already told the solution, said, "If you go through with this I leave Santa Vittoria. I resign from the Grand Council. I'll return to Montefalcone, where I belong."

Bombolini was hurt by this because Fabio, in a way, is the conscience of Santa Vittoria.

"It's an evil thing. It appeals to the people's worst instincts."

"That's not such a bad instinct, Fabio, to want what is yours."

"It's a rotten instinct and you know it." Fabio put on his hat to show that he was leaving.

It was not known at the time—no one understood Fabio then—but he wanted an excuse to leave the city and he had found it. He came to see me in my room before he left. "All right," he told me. "I'm leaving. You can have her now."

I told him I didn't know what he was talking about. In a way I didn't, and yet in a way I did.

"You know what I mean," he said. I had never seen him this angry before. "Angela. She eats you up with her eyes. She devours you."

"I never asked her to."

"Oh, no. You lie there and lead her on, because you Americans don't have manners as we do."

I was thankful that it was dark in my room. I had meant nothing by the little games I played with Angela, although something seemed to take place between us when we played them. "Why do you think an American wouldn't marry you?" I would say to Angela.

"Oh, Americans don't go for girls like me. They want rich girls."

"It helps. But they like pretty girls too."

"Then I'm not pretty enough."

"Maybe not," I would say. "Then again, stand up there by the window and let me see you."

She was so simple and so sweet that of course she would go and stand by the window. "Americans want women like the Malatesta," she would say.

"Oh, all men want women like the Malatesta. But if you can't get the Malatesta you have to get someone else. Someone like . . . someone like . . ." And she would turn scarlet. I didn't know then that men and women didn't talk to each other this way in Santa Vittoria unless they were going to be married.

"She never sees me," Fabio said. "She has forgotten my name. I'll tell you what she has done." He was close to shouting. "For two weeks she has failed to bring me my plate of beans!" And the next morning Fabio della Romagna left the city for Montefalcone.

He did not take his bicycle, because it was dangerous to be on the roads with a bike without a pass from the Germans or without a good reason. The few things he did take were in a small, crude knapsack on his back.

When he had reached the base of the mountain and was heading for the River Road that leads to Montefalcone, some men he knew from Santa Vittoria came running toward him. "Fabio," one of them shouted. "Fabio, it's marvelous. Look." Fabio turned around so that he was looking back up the mountain at the city. Someone on the Fat Wall was waving what appeared to be Vittorini's flag. "You see? You understand, Fabio?" the man said to him. "That means it's ringing and we can't hear a thing. You should have seen them in Scarafaggio. 'What happened to the bell?' they were asking. 'What's the matter with the bell?' "

"And not a *sound*, Fabio," another man said. "The greatest moment in the history of the city of Santa Vittoria."

None of them understood when Fabio broke loose and began to trot and then run to the River Road.

In Santa Vittoria the people were celebrating. One of the Pietro-santos was in the campanile pulling the rope. Each time the clapper met the bronze bell there was a low muffled sound, not the good clear *bong* of before.

Cork! A cork clapper. The people looked at one another and

began to smile, and as the muffled sound went on they began to laugh out loud and finally to hit each other on the back while tears began to run down from their eyes.

It was recognized for what it was, an act of inspiration, even an act of genius. The members of the Grand Council lined up in the piazza to shake Captain Bombolini's hand, and soon a good part of the city was in the line. After shaking his hand they went up the steep winding stairs to the top of the bell tower itself to feel the clapper.

The Grand Council authorized some young men to go down to the Cooperative Wine Cellar and withdraw two hundred bottles of wine, and the celebration for the cork clapper began. In all of the history of Santa Vittoria, in a thousand years at least, the people had never been more united or the government in more capable hands.

III

VON PRUM

ON THAT SAME NIGHT, the night of the cork clapper, Captain Sepp von Prum, of the Financial Affairs Division of the Headquarters Staff of the Fifth Panzer Brigade, with headquarters in Montefalcone, was finishing the last of his letters. Since it was not late, he decided to take them down to the Piazza Frossimbone to have them stamped and censored by Colonel Scheer, his commanding officer. He wrote a good letter, and unlike a lot of other junior officers he did not mind having the letters censored.

He went down the narrow stone stairs of the house in which he was billeted more swiftly than he usually did and it caused him pain. He was still recovering from wounds he had received the year before. All the men stationed with his unit in Montefalcone had been damaged in some serious fashion in North Africa or in Russia. Despite the pain, he continued quickly into the piazza. There had been a rumor that the Americans and the British had made a landing somewhere south of Rome that morning and that the Italians were about to declare themselves in a state of war with Germany. At eight o'clock the news would be broadcast by the British in Cairo, and he wanted to be with the others when Colonel Scheer turned it on.

It is a fortunate thing that Captain von Prum made copies of everything he wrote—military records, his diary and log, letters to his brother on the eastern front in Russia, and even letters to his fiancée, Christina Mollendorf, which were filed under the heading "Love Interest." He preserved the copies in an old gray file cabinet that he was forced to leave behind when he left Santa Vittoria, and from them it was possible to obtain a picture of the captain.

From the notes to his brother Klaus it was learned that during the fighting along the Dneiper, several of Klaus's soldiers broke and ran in the face of Russian tanks. Although they later returned to the field of battle, the young men were shot as an example to the others. Klaus von Prum, being the officer who reported them, was badly shaken by the action.

Dear Father:

Mother writes to ask if I am happy. It can only be German mothers who write to ask if their sons are happy at war.

Actually I am happy to be alive, happy to still have my leg. I won't be climbing any mountains, but each day the leg grows stronger.

You ask how it is here in Montefalcone. Pleasant but dirty. The money here comes from wine and I can tell you this much. Under sound German management the gross product of the region could be doubled. But these people go on in their old ways. They have a positive affinity for duplication and waste.

If nothing else, the work improves my Italian. I even speak the dialect now, to the amazement of one and all.

> Respectfully,
> Sepp von Prum
> Captain, Infantry

Darling Christina, ma petite chou:

You ask about the Italian women. Well, let me put it in this fashion. Some of these women are beautiful. But one soon loses interest in them because there is always this feeling (I am sorry to be crude) that their underwear, if indeed they have any on at all, is not clean.

You may cease blushing now. And then do this for me. Put down this letter at once and go to your mirror and then look into it and know this, that the little face in that glass, those clear blue eyes and those full lips and that soft white complexion, belong to the kind of woman that appeals to me.

> Lovingly,
> Sepp von Prum

Klaus:

What kind of nonsense is this you have written home? You have upset your family. Let us try to isolate one thing. You are not a young poet in love, you are an officer in the Army of the Third Reich.

You ask what you should have done and I tell you. You do your duty. If your commanding officer says the deserters should be shot, they are shot. It is as simple as that. Duty is one's responsibility to an idea larger than the self. This cancer of the self! The putting of one's conscience beyond one's duty is the true sickness of our time.

You say you feel "chained" by the Germanic sense of duty. Duty does not bind one, it frees one from personal responsibility. All kinds of acts become possible. There is only one question: Does my act help the Fatherland or not? There is nothing complex about it. Duty *becomes clear.*

Once you have done your duty you will feel better, because self-doubt will have vanished. So get on with your soldiering and do your duty and take care of yourself.

Your brother,
Sepp

The captain was disappointed when Colonel Scheer stamped his letter to Klaus "Approved" without so much as glancing at it. It was the kind of letter a junior officer might wish his senior officer to see.

"And now, shall we tune in Radio Cairo? Just to see what lies they are telling, of course," the colonel said.

It was a standing joke, since it was accepted by all of them that the British provided the most reliable news. When the radio began to operate, officers from other rooms gathered in the doorway.

The rumors had been correct. Landings had been made by the British and the Americans in a place called Salerno, south of Naples. The Italians had declared themselves out of the war and would soon come in again on the side of the Allies.

When the broadcast was finished, the colonel turned off the radio and faced his officers. "There have been no official orders as yet, but as of this moment, Plan A is in effect. Unless I am seriously wrong, Operation Clutch will commence in a day or two."

Plan A was a full combat alert, in which the Italians would be treated like the people in any occupied territory, as the enemy and a source of potential danger. Operation Clutch was the formal plan designed to occupy Montefalcone and the rest of the outlying area.

Captain von Prum left headquarters and went back to the building in which his men were billeted. He looked into a large cluttered room.

The soldiers were startled by the presence of an officer in their quarters, and they got to their feet in confusion. "Come to attention," Sergeant Traub shouted at them.

The captain took this chance to examine his detachment. It was not a reassuring sight. There were only eight of them, and all had been seriously wounded and were now on limited duty. The senior of them, Sergeant Gottfried Traub, had been hit in the face by shell fragments, and the muscles had been severed, so it was impossible to know what the sergeant was thinking from his expression.

"We're all going to become soldiers again," the captain said. "We are at war with Italy."

He took out a map of the region. It was so typical, von Prum thought, that the only reliable map of the area had been sent to him by his father from Mannheim. His slender finger touched the city of Montefalcone. "We are here." The soldiers, who were timid about doing it at first, began to gather around the map. "We eventually will be *here*." He began to move his finger down the line from Montefalcone and out to the Mad River and along the red line on the map which marked the River Road.

Corporal Heinsick was leaning over the map. His thick stubby finger touched the city and then crossed the map to the road. "There's no line to it. There's no road."

"There's a road. It is a track, really. For oxen and carts. But our equipment will be equal to it. Are there other questions?"

The soldiers were silent because they were not accustomed to asking their officers questions. It bothered them and made them nervous. But one thing had been troubling them from the beginning and they looked at Sergeant Traub, and so he finally said, "Sir? There are only eight of us, not counting yourself."

"That is correct."

Again there was an embarrassed silence.

"Captain Pfalz has fifty in his command. They feel they need fifty to take and hold their town, sir."

"We need only eight."

They knew that it was the end to the questions, and they made a show of gathering around the map again to exhibit interest. Traub touched the name on the map. "Sanda Viddoria," he said.

"Yes. Santa Vittoria," echoed the captain.

LONG BEFORE FABIO reached Montefalcone it was dark. A few soldiers riding in trucks shouted at him, but Fabio did not respond. The gate into the city was, as before, guarded by an Italian and a German. Fabio thought they might arrest him, but he didn't really care.

"You're not going to learn much at the academy," the Italian guard told him. "It's closed."

He only shrugged and they passed him through.

The city was filled with trucks and armored vehicles pressed up alongside the walls of the houses for protection. Some of them had men in them, sleeping under camouflage nets.

Fabio didn't know where he was going. He decided to try to reach the house of Galbiati, an instructor he had been fond of and who had been fond of him. He went down the corso directly into the Piazza Frossimbone. Soldiers sitting in the darkness of doorways said things to him, but he walked on at his own pace. It is hard to frighten anyone who has no more use for life.

At one side of the piazza a large sign had been put up. A group of German officers and noncoms were gathered around discussing what it said and taking notes, and Fabio joined them.

The sign was a big, carefully drawn map of the Montefalcone region, and on it were the names of all the towns that would be occupied within the next several days. Included were the names of the occupying units, the day they would take over the town and the hour in which they would arrive. Fabio, even in his condition, could appreciate the thoroughness of the work. He saw that the Germans would arrive in Santa Vittoria on Wednesday, at 1700 hours.

Three days. Not quite three days. At five o'clock in the afternoon. "They can ring their cork bell when they come," Fabio told himself.

He went through the dark little park in the center of the piazza, and as he did he heard a girl struggling with a man. "Don't do that to me," she said. "You promised. You gave your word to my mother." Then he heard her crash through the underbrush, and from the other sounds he knew the German had also run off.

Fabio didn't know where she was, and when he went to find her she had already gone. Girls who went with German soldiers deserved what they got, he thought, although he knew the soldiers sometimes went to the girls' houses and made it impossible for the families to refuse.

"Oh, God," he said aloud. Angela. They would do it to Angela. He knew at once—the same way he had known when he had seen Bombolini on top of the water tower—that he would have to be the one to go to Santa Vittoria and warn them.

Now that he cared, he found that his heart was beating hard, but he knew exactly what he wanted to do. He got the rest of the way across the piazza without being seen and moved deeper into the city where the workingmen lived. He found the house he was looking for, and when his knock was not answered he tapped on the window. The shutter was opened by a young woman who did not seem to be wearing any clothes. Fabio looked down.

"Oh," he said. "I wanted Gambo. I was expecting Gambo."

"He's in the hospital. A rock fell on him in the quarry."

"Oh. I'm sorry." Fabio cleared his throat. "Is his bike here? He said I could use it whenever I needed it."

"Come here and let me see you." She made him stand near the window and hold up his head. "Wait here," she said, and in a moment Fabio could hear the chain coming down from the door. "Now come in."

When he went in he could see the bicycle chained to an iron ring in the stone staircase, and when he looked further into the room he could see the girl and was surprised to find that she was wearing only a shirt, one of Gambo's shirts. The shirt was not buttoned all the way to the top. He turned back to the bike. "A nice bicycle," he said. "Gambo always took good care of his bicycles."

The woman laughed and asked him who he was.

"Fabio. Just call me Fabio."

"Just Fabio? I can't loan a bike to someone called 'just Fabio.'"

"Bombolini. Fabio Bombolini," he said. "From the Resistance."

She motioned him to come away from the door and into the room, and he looked at her quickly, because he had never seen anything like her, but when she sat down on the bed he looked away again. The shirt was almost completely open.

"How long have you known Gambo?"

"Oh, for years and years and years," Fabio said. "How long has he been in the hospital?" Fabio could feel his heart pumping.

"Oh, for weeks and weeks and weeks," she said, and he blushed.

They talked about Gambo for a while, and Fabio found that the woman barely knew him.

"Why don't you ever look at me?" she said.

"I'm looking at you. It's just that I was interested in the bike."

"The bike is more interesting than me?"

"It's a beautiful bike," Fabio said. The nature of the silence, the coldness behind it, informed Fabio that he would have to say more. "You seem beautiful too," he said.

"Then look at me."

He turned his eyes away from the bike and looked at her as calmly as he could, determined to examine her in all objectivity. But he felt that the pounding of his heart must be loud enough to make a sound in the room.

"The key to the bike. See?" She held up a small key chain that hung around her neck. "If you want it you can come and get it."

He had heard about things such as this. There would be a game to get the key. Sex games, his father had called them. He realized he would have to play, but he didn't know how to begin and he didn't know the rules.

Nevertheless, the game went swiftly enough after that, for she was expert at it. I will think only of Angela while I do this, Fabio promised himself. No, no, no. I will think only of the bicycle. I will remember that I am doing this only in order to get the bicycle.

He was conscious of the woman but he tried not to allow himself to enjoy the consciousness. In a way, it was a patriotic act performed in the line of duty, Fabio told himself. But somehow he was investing himself beyond the point of duty.

"I suppose I should know your name," Fabio said at last.

"Gabriele."

"Gabriele. What a beautiful name! It is very fitting."

"Someday you'll make some woman a good lover," she said. He turned red, of course, and yet he found that he wasn't displeased. Despite himself, he was smiling as she reached up and worked the chain over her head.

When he got the bicycle out into the steep narrow street he was filled with elation. The bicycle rattled on the cobbles, and so he picked it up and put it on his back, and he barely noticed its weight. Fabio, he told himself, you are becoming a goat.

WHEN FABIO REACHED Santa Vittoria, some of the older men were still in the Piazza of the People, seated around the fountain, waiting to hear the cork clapper strike twelve. They could not feed enough on the sound. "Fabio," Bombolini said when he saw him, "I knew you would come back to me." The mayor embraced him.

"I pedaled all the way up the mountain. I have bad news. The Germans are coming." The faces around him were blank. "I have seen the orders. Elements of the German army will arrive in Santa Vittoria at five o'clock in the afternoon on this coming Wednesday."

It meant nothing to them, not even to Bombolini. Fabio threw the bicycle down onto the stones of the piazza. "All right. I've told you. I have done my duty. I risked my life. I have stolen a man's bike. I have done all that I can." For a moment he had the wild idea of riding back to the arms of Gabriele, *his* lover; but he was too tired.

He turned and walked away. Bombolini came after him.

"We know it's important, Fabio. We appreciate your coming and telling us. It's just that we have expected it all along and there's nothing much to be done about it."

"You could put your women away someplace."

"If they touch the women they'll pay for it and they know it."

"You could get that Abruzzi out of town before he gets us all shot."

"No, he's going to stay. He'll be dressed like one of us. No one will be able to tell."

"Do you think all these people can keep a secret like that?"

"When it is to our advantage to keep a secret we can keep one."

They were all the way across the piazza and at the edge of the Corso Cavour, where it drops down into Old Town, when Bombolini took hold of Fabio's arm. "Don't go away again, Fabio. We all need you here."

"Oh, I don't know. I'm thinking of going into the mountains." He hadn't thought of it before. "The Resistance, you know."

"When the Germans come, the policy here is going to be one of accommodation, do you understand?" Bombolini said. "When they push, we will give. We'll be like quicksand."

And I intend to be a rock, Fabio said, but to himself. He was tired. He had come back to save Angela, and they wanted to accommodate themselves to the Germans. So be it. The day hadn't been all wasted. There was Gabriele. If he hadn't been concentrating so hard on the bicycle, he probably could have shown her a thing or two. At least now he knew where his destiny rested. Up in the mountains.

And just then, since it was twelve o'clock, the cork clapper began to ping against the metal of the bell, weak and thin and colorless.

"Oh, God, what a people we are," Fabio said aloud.

SERGEANT TRAUB LOOKED down onto the Via San Sebastiano and shook his head. "It's not very much equipment, sir."

"It's enough for our needs," Captain von Prum said. In the street below them was one small truck and a motorcycle with a sidecar that appeared to have been used in the First World War. "We aren't going up there to wage war."

"That suits me," Traub said. The others nodded.

The captain looked at Traub closely. "What do you think of the Italians?" he asked in an offhand manner. It was, however, a crucial question to von Prum. He had chosen these eight men partly because they understood Italian, reasoning that a man doesn't learn another man's language in order to despise him.

"They're all right," Traub said. "I can live with them. I just got no respect for them." The others nodded again.

Von Prum was pleased. It was what he had wanted to hear. "I am not one given to generalizations," he said, "but there are certain truths about certain peoples that simple observation will bear out every time." And he went on to tell the men what these were—that the average Italian had no stomach for battle, that it was not so much a matter of courage as much as having nothing worth dying for. The Italian, when given the choice, would bargain and make deals to protect what he has rather than fight for it.

"They fought up at Castelgrande last night, sir." Traub's voice was as respectful as he could make it. "They had five dead up there."

"And you missed four words I said, Sergeant. *When given the choice.* Do you understand? Captain Moltke's detail marched into Castelgrande and began to take what they wanted without even asking. There was nothing for the people to do but to fight. That will be the difference with us. We aren't going to take, they're going to *give*. At Castelgrande they had fifty men. We have eight, and eight is all we will need. Ours will be a bloodless victory," and at once von Prum knew that this was the title of the report he would write.

BLOODLESS VICTORY: A TECHNIQUE FOR THE CONSERVATION OF MAN-POWER AND EQUIPMENT DURING THE CONFISCATION OF ENEMY ASSETS

> A report on the occupation of the city
> of Santa Vittoria under command of
> Sepp von Prum, Capt., Inf.

He even took time to write it down and then he said, "The only red I expect to see is the red of their wine."

WHEN FABIO HAD GONE and the bell had rung for the last time that night, Bombolini found he couldn't sleep. He thought of the city then as his city and of the people as his people, and he knew he carried their burdens on his back. It was the price the leader paid and one he was happy to pay.

After a time he went to Roberto Abruzzi's doorway. "Do you think the Germans will come here?" he asked.

Roberto was annoyed. It was three o'clock in the morning. "I don't know. I don't know about those things."

"There's nothing for them here."

Roberto nodded. "Only your wine," he said, and he was sorry to be disrespectful, but he closed his eyes and fell back to sleep.

"There's no road up here," Bombolini said. But the sound of Roberto's breathing told him his argument was being wasted. He went to his room and to bed.

When he woke again the sun still had not risen and so he knew he had not slept for more than an hour. Something had been troubling him, and he lit a candle and began going through *the* book.

"Men are apt to deceive themselves in great things while being scrupulous about the small ones," he read. He felt a cold hand rest on his heart and begin to squeeze it. He knew what the words meant. It was only that morning that Babbaluche had said to him, "We lie about the truth, that's what ruins us here. And do you know why we lie about the truth? Not because we like to, but because we are scared to death of it."

He got up then and went downstairs and out into the Piazza of the People. Old Vines was there and he began shouting at Bombolini. "Tell us the truth! Don't lie to us. The Germans are coming and they're going to take our wine."

Bombolini trotted across to Old Vines. "I know," he said. "But there's no sense in terrifying the people before we have a plan."

Others had heard though—the ones who get up in darkness, before the sun even—and when they heard the words they recognized them as the truth.

"What are you going to do?" someone else cried. "What can we do?"

Bombolini turned away as if he hadn't heard. He went back to the Palace of the People and woke Roberto. "You have to help me now," he said. "Don't let anyone in. I must go to sleep. It's all that I can do."

WHEN VON PRUM PRESENTED his idea to Colonel Scheer, the colonel had had misgivings about the wisdom of a bloodless victory. "No, it all stinks of an experiment," the colonel had said. "It's all right to experiment with Poles. It's all right to try things with Jews. It's not all right with someone like you, the grandson of Schmidt von Knoblesdorf. If anything happens to Captain von Prum, Willy Scheer will be the one to hang for it."

Scheer was a rare case, the peasant who had risen through the ranks to a position of power without discarding his peasant ways. His manner was rough and direct, his speech was coarse, and he looked as if he had been carved from a potato. It amused and flattered him to have aristocrats around him and beneath him.

"No, I can't let you do it," Scheer said. "You are the cream of our culture, the flower of our people." He was being sarcastic but good-natured. "What will you go armed with?"

"The culture of the German people. Our national sense of purpose. Our genius at working with disciplined order."

"Oh, you are such a fine, noble boy." Scheer was shaking his head by then. "Do you really believe this?"

"I really believe it," von Prum said. "It's the only sensible, practical way to do it. You'll see."

The words had angered Scheer, and he said to the captain, "You listen to me. We don't learn much in the turnip fields but we do learn some things, and one of them is that the one thing, the only thing, that gets respect is strength." The colonel thumped his hard brown stubby hand down onto the hard wooden table. "You think about it. There is no other way."

But in the end von Prum had won, as he knew he would win, because in the end he was what the race aspired to, and he knew this and knew that Scheer knew it and approved of it. His Nordic bleaching, as the colonel called it, the blondness and whiteness and the cold blueness of him, was not just the symbol of racial purity but the fact of it. Most Germans, like most of the people of the world, are dark and short, but unlike other people the Germans despise their darkness and their shortness. It is von Prum they put on all their posters, and when they have a baby it is von Prum they hope to produce.

"At least take a tank," Scheer had said. Von Prum shook his head. "My God you're stubborn." Scheer's voice became hard. "This experiment *must* work."

"I understand."

"If it doesn't, I come up there and do things my way. I'm committed for that wine and I want all of it."

"You will get your wine," von Prum said. "When the time comes I intend to have the people bring it out themselves."

"You expect the people to collaborate in their own robbery?"

"Yes," von Prum said, so quietly and with such little doubt that his arrogance caused the colonel to laugh aloud.

"I will tell you what I will do," Colonel Scheer said. "If you can get the people of Santa Vittoria to bring their own wine to the railroad here I will recommend you for the Iron Cross." Von Prum smiled at this. "Third class, of course," Scheer added, "but an Iron Cross nevertheless."

The captain was excused then, but at the foot of the stairs he turned back to the colonel. "As for you," he called, "I'll put your name on the cover of the *Bloodless Victory*."

"No, to hell with that," Scheer said. "After the war you invite me to your home for dinner. Let me come in the front door." He smiled his hard, tough smile. "Have me with that fellow you're always quoting." Von Prum was puzzled. "Nitcha," Scheer said. "Your friend Nitcha."

"Nietzsche," the captain said. "He's dead."

"I'm sorry to hear it. Have me with all the descendants then."

"I'll do that," Captain von Prum said. "And I will toast you with the wine of Santa Vittoria."

CONSIDERING THE STATE of things in Santa Vittoria they were good to Bombolini; they allowed him to sleep until eleven o'clock, and then they told Roberto to go and wake him.

"They're waiting for you down there," Roberto told him. "The whole piazza is filled with people."

"I had a good sleep, Roberto," Bombolini said, and attempted to brush down his mane of hair, which was wild, so wild that Babba-luche once claimed that a bird could nest in it and Bombolini would never know it until he got egg on his face. "God came to me, I think. He put something in here." He tapped his head. "Let's go down."

They went down the steps into the large room where all the members of the Grand Council were gathered.

"God put a story in my head. I want to tell it to you and you can tell me what it means. I think the answer is in the story."

A THOUSAND YEARS ago, Bombolini told them, some invaders from the north called barbarians came to conquer Italy under the leader-ship of a man named Barbarossa. Everything fell before the barbar-ians until they came to one walled city that refused to surrender. They surrounded the city to starve it out, and when winter came the people began to go hungry and everyone knew it was only a matter of time. It was then that a peasant named Gagliaudi went to the prince of the city with a plan. "Give me all the wheat and grain that is left and I will save the city. If I don't, then kill me."

Because there was nothing else to do, the prince gave the wheat and the grain to the peasant. The people were outraged when the peasant began to feed the precious food to his cow.

"Now bring me the last of the water," Gagliaudi ordered, and the cow drank and drank.

"Now bring me the last of the wine."

The people watched in rage as the peasant sat before them and got drunk. Then, early in the morning just before dawn, a little side gate in the wall was opened and the drunken peasant and his bloated cow slipped outside the city's walls. Along the road where the enemy camped, Gagliaudi began to sing and laugh and roar, and he kicked the cow so that it mooed and bellowed in protest. The enemy could not believe their eyes.

When the guards of Barbarossa seized the peasant he fell to his knees and cried, "Oh, God help me, what have I done?" He began to weep. "I was taking my cow to the grainery and I opened the wrong door. Oh, don't harm me. Please."

They dragged the weeping peasant to Barbarossa, and he looked with astonishment at the drunken man and the fat sleek cow.

"Please don't kill me, sir," Gagliaudi said. "I have a proposition for you. If you will let me go I promise to go back inside the walls with any soldiers you select and bring you back my twelve cows."

"Twelve like this?"

Barbarossa was sick at the thought of all that beef on the hoof. "Do you mean to tell me you have twelve more like that inside the walls?"

"Only my own, sir. Just my own. All of the others belong to someone else and I can't give them to you."

Barbarossa was above all things a good soldier, and a good soldier recognizes when he is beaten. The city clearly had enough food to last them for two more years at least. That afternoon he packed up his army and left. The city was saved.

THE MEN IN THE room all looked at one another. The answer was in the story, everyone felt that. But they were silent. "It's like those parables in the Bible," someone finally said. "Just when I seem to have it in my hands it hops away from me."

A long time passed. They heard the thin sound of the bell at midday, and still no one was any closer to the secret of Gagliaudi.

"To hell with this bum and his cow," Pietro Pietrosanto suddenly shouted. "I say fight."

There was a cheer from the others. Their minds were tired from the pressure of thinking, and the idea of fighting seemed good then. At least it was doing something.

"I say this to you," a young man shouted. "The German who touches my wine or my wife pays for his touch in blood."

A very big cheer then.

Bombolini was confused. The Master had said, *Cunning and deceit will every time serve a man better than force.* How could that be explained to the people? How to tell men bent on becoming heroes that it would be more heroic of them to practice being cowards?

Just as Fabio had been saved by Babbaluche the night he told the story of Mussolini's death, now Tommaso Casamassima, Rosa Bombolini's uncle, stood up in the room and struck the floor with his mulberry stick until there was silence.

"You forget who you are," he shouted. "You think you're warriors and you shout like heroes and you are a bunch of grape growers."

There was silence, because everyone knew that what Tommaso said was so.

"We have no heroes here. We can't afford them. Tend to your grapes. The one lesson that every Santa Vittorian has known for a thousand years is that brave men and good wine don't last long."

Everyone went outside after that. All idea of the fight was ended.

Bombolini stopped to talk with Roberto. "Have you figured out the story yet?" he asked. Roberto looked puzzled. "My dream. What does it mean? You're the American. You know everything—" He stopped then and looked at Roberto. "What are you doing?"

"Arithmetic. I'm figuring out the hours until they come."

"How many?"

"They'll be here in fifty-three hours."

"Quick, now," Bombolini said. "As fast as you can say the words. If you were me what would you do with the wine?"

"Hide it."

"You would hide it?"

"Yes, hide it," Roberto said.

"Oh, Roberto. So simple and clean and beautiful that it's almost stupid," the mayor said, and struck Roberto such a blow on the arm that it was weeks before he could raise it without pain.

THE EFFORT TO HIDE the wine was a failure. Within the first half hour of the experiment, before twenty thousand bottles had been brought from the Cooperative Wine Cellar up the Corso Cavour and into the Piazza of the People, it was clear the experiment was not worth going on with. The people had taken the bottles from the piazza and begun to hide them in their houses, in closets and under beds and in the drains and under loose tiles and then in the manure piles and on grapevines hung down the chimneys.

"Keep the wine in the shadows, the sun is bruising it," Old Vines shouted at the people. "Would you put a newborn baby in the sun? Don't shake the wine. Would you shake a newborn baby? This wine isn't even born yet."

Sometime in the early afternoon Bombolini summoned the courage to ask the keeper of the wine how many bottles remained to be hidden, and when Old Vines told him, it was a matter of several minutes before he could make himself hear the figures, and when he did he wrote them on a card—*1,320,000*.

Each time he looked at the number he found it hard to comprehend. He held the card up first on one side and then on the other, as if somehow, if he twisted it in enough ways, the value of the numbers might change. Even if they hid 100,000 bottles, which was impossible, it was only one-thirteenth of the wine. At four o'clock there was to be an inspection of the hiding, and the teams went out even though all the people knew what they would report. A few minutes later the first of them came back.

"It's no good, Captain," Longo's son said. "It isn't working right. You can see bottles everywhere. Every time you turn around in a house you sit on a bottle, you step on a bottle, you break a bottle. The beds are lumpy with bottles."

It was the same everywhere.

"Bring the bottles back out," Bombolini ordered, and he felt at that moment the dread of failure. He went across the piazza and bottles were piled everywhere. To the credit of the people he passed, none of them said anything to him. He had the weight of the city and of one thousand people and now of one million bottles of wine to carry. It was too much for any one man, he thought. He felt someone pulling on him and turned to look. It was Fungo the idiot.

"I have something to tell you," Fungo said.

"Tell. Tell me."

"Tufa's back. He's dying."

"How would you know that?"

"Someone told me."

"Who?"

"Tufa. And he should know." The boy told him then how he had gone to Tufa's house to see if he could find any bottles and how he had found Tufa there, in the dark, lying on the floor.

I will attend to Tufa, Bombolini thought. It was at least something positive to do, and he started down the Corso Cavour to Old Town and Tufa's mother's house.

Old Vines caught up with him. "Stop them!" he shouted. "We can't leave the wine out here."

"To hell with the wine," Bombolini said. "Do we have to have the wine at room temperature for the Germans when they come? To hell with it."

"Oh, you sin," Old Vines said. "You sin against the wine."

Bombolini fully expected the next bolt of lightning to strike him in the heart. But he pushed the cellar master aside. He had made up his mind to keep all his thoughts on Tufa.

There were strange things about Tufa. He was, for one, an officer in the army and a Fascist, but this had never stopped him from being a hero to the young people here and a person to whom the old were not afraid to turn for help when he was home.

The thing about Tufa was that he was a true Fascist, one who believed all the glorious words and tried to follow them, and that had made him a very strange person here and in all of Italy. As a young boy he had been chosen to be trained as a Young Fascist Scout. He had believed every word he heard at the camp. Later he became a soldier and after that was made an officer in one of the aristocratic regiments, a very rare thing to happen. He was a believer in a nation of nonbelievers.

When Bombolini arrived, the room was dark and it felt wet and it was dirty. It smelled bad. Tufa's mother had never been able to run a house.

"Where is he?" Bombolini asked. The soldier's mother pointed to one end of the room, where the mayor could eventually make out Tufa's shape lying on the floor facing the stone wall.

"He's going to die," the mother said.

Bombolini crossed the room and stood over Tufa's body, not knowing what to say to him. Tufa had never liked him because he had been a clown and Tufa didn't understand clowns. With a terrible slowness Tufa turned away from the wall and looked at Bombolini.

"Get out of here," he said. "I have always despised you."

"Tufa? Can you hear me?"

"Get out of here."

"I'm not a clown anymore, Tufa. I'm the mayor here now. Can you hear me? Can you understand that?"

"Get out of here."

The hatred in Tufa's eyes was so strong that it defeated Bombolini. He backed out of the house and started up the corso. Before he reached the piazza, Pietro Pietrosanto came down the steps toward him. "We can't put if off any longer," Pietrosanto said. "We've got to do something with The Band."

Bombolini took in a large breath. Pietro was correct, the time had come. It was the one problem he had been unable to face since the day he had taken office. Now, with the Germans coming, there was no room left for the luxury of indecision.

"Do away with them," Bombolini said.

Pietrosanto found this hard to believe.

"I don't understand you," he said.

Bombolini took Pietrosanto by the arm. "Do you have a rifle? You own a rifle, don't you?"

"Shoot them? Is that what you mean?"

"I don't mean to caress them," the mayor said. "Come." They both went back up toward the piazza. "Try and look as if we have a plan," Bombolini said. "It gives the people heart."

"I don't know about shooting," Pietrosanto was saying, but Bombolini didn't hear him. Now that he had ordered the final solution to The Band it didn't concern him anymore. He looked instead at the wine bottles stacked high in the piazza.

THAT EVENING BOMBOLINI asked Roberto to go and ask the Malatesta to take a look at Tufa. "She'll listen to you," Bombolini said. "You're not from here, and she thinks you're brave."

"She doesn't think I'm brave. She thinks I'm afraid of pain."

"Ah, but that's just it. *Because* you're afraid of pain, the way you reacted to it makes you a brave man," Bombolini said. "Besides, I think she has an eye for you. She thinks you're handsome."

"How do you know?"

"I heard her say so once."

It was a lie, a complete and shameless lie, which Roberto recognized as a lie and treated as one, and yet it made his heart beat faster despite himself. He dressed and went across the Piazza of the People.

It was dark. It was the first time he had seen all the bottles there and he wondered what they were doing in the piazza. At the street that runs up into High Town he heard someone whisper his name. It was Fabio.

"I thought you were up in the mountains," Roberto said.

"I am in the mountains. Five of us. The Petrarch Brigade, formally. The Red Flames, informally." He named four young boys who were with him. None was over fifteen years of age. "They're young, but they can fight," Fabio said. "They also are hungry."

With his own money and some of Fabio's, Roberto went to the wineshop and bought two loaves of bread for the Red Flames.

"Now you do a favor for me," Roberto said. He made Fabio go with him to face Caterina Malatesta. They walked up the hill in silence.

"How is she?" Fabio said at last.

"Who?"

"Angela," Fabio said.

"I don't know. I haven't seen her."

"You must have a lot of fun together, if you know what I mean."

"Oh, no, nothing like that. Angela isn't like that."

Fabio made a sound like a mule. "They're *all* like that," he said. "Don't tell me. I know them from top to bottom."

Caterina lived in the next to the last house on the mountain. When she came to the door and opened it, they were surprised at what they saw. She was wearing long slender pants and little slippers and a sweater that revealed the outline of her breasts. None of these things are worn by the women here, even today. She didn't wish to come and she resisted, but Fabio was persuasive and there is something about Tufa, even to those who had barely known him, that was special. She got her medical bag and went with them.

She didn't knock at the door of Tufa's house, but opened it and went in and put down the medical bag Roberto had carried for her. She took a lamp from the bag and when it was lit she could see Tufa, not lying down any longer but propped up against the wall, looking at her the way a wolf looks at someone coming for him from the back of a cave. In the light his teeth were as bright as his eyes, and he looked very sane and very mad at the same moment. When Caterina saw him she made a sound, a stifled sound of astonishment. She was not able to take her eyes away from him.

"You are hurt," she said.

"You aren't going to touch me." Tufa has the finest voice in the city, sweet and yet strong. Sometimes it sounds as if Tufa is whispering through the pipe of an organ.

"You're badly hurt. I can help you. You'd like to die, but your body won't allow you to."

Caterina moved toward him. There was an awareness of each other that was so acute and powerful and immediate that it went beyond anything we know as love. It is an understanding so total that there is nothing they don't know about one another, and they are able to share things with each other at once that they have never been able to share with anyone before. The attraction supplants all else, and yet there is no love, not even any tenderness, only the attraction and the understanding of one another.

When she touched him he stiffened. She didn't move her hand for a moment, but then she began to take off the officer's jacket he wore to examine the wounds in his chest and upper arms that he had received the week before from an exploding grenade. "They told me you were a good man," she said. She opened her medical bag. "How can you be a Fascist and a good man at the same time?"

For a long time Tufa said nothing, but it didn't seem to bother her. She was willing to wait. She started dressing his wounds.

"You can be," he said at last, "if you are a fool."

Caterina finished tending to the last of the wounds. Most of them were not deep, but several were infected.

"You're not going to get better here," the Malatesta said. 'You're going to have to get out of this room."

"Where are you going to take him?" Tufa's mother asked.

"Someplace where he can get better."

The mother got up from the box she sat on and began collecting her son's things. "I don't want him dying in here," she said. "Besides, you know what I have to feed him?" She tapped the side of an earthen pot. "I have ten or twelve olives. I can't count. I have one piece of bread and no oil to drip on it."

Caterina looked at Tufa. "Do you want to go with me?"

"Oh, yes. You know that," he said, and he began to get to his feet. When she helped him she was surprised to find that he was silently crying. "The first time," he said. "The first time ever."

He didn't know why he cried, but he wasn't ashamed of the tears. Later he was able to figure that he cried because he was giving up the death he had planned for himself and he knew that he was going to have to enter again into the life that had fooled him so terribly and that he had wanted to give up. He went past his mother and out into the Corso Cavour, where Fabio and Roberto quietly left them.

Tufa, although he was weak and sick, led the way up the corso, which is the way it is in this town. He was forced to lean against the walls and gasp for breath, but he led the way up. Finally he had to lean on Caterina. "I apologize for that," he said.

"You don't have to apologize to me," she said, and it caused both of them to laugh because it was a truth, and when you hear the truth it makes you laugh.

In the piazza, although it had begun to rain, Tufa was forced to stop and sit on the edge of the fountain. He looked up and let the rain run down his face. "I can feel the dust of Africa wash off me," he said.

She saw how beautiful his eyes were, the thick lashes, the dark brows, the large soft brownness of the eyes themselves.

"Do you think we can go?" Caterina was becoming chilled and wet.

"In a moment."

"Then tell me the story of the fountain while we wait."

Tufa looked up at the fountain and smiled for the first time. "It's an old story and not a nice one."

"I think I can bear it."

"It's very dirty."

"You're apologizing."

"No, I'm warning you." He took her hand. "Here, help me up." They started to walk across the piazza once again. "I don't think I'm going to tell you. Don't you know that that story is told to women who are thirty years old and who no longer are virgins?"

"I qualify then," Caterina said. He gripped her arm very hard, so hard that it took her by surprise and hurt her.

"No you don't," he said. "I know when you were born." She was amazed by this. "Your father gave my father a cup of wine, a tin cup of wine and some coins, on the day you were born. Do you think I would forget that?"

"Yes."

"My father didn't want them. He was insulted. And when my mother heard my father had turned down the money, she made me go up and tell your father that my father was wrong, that there was something wrong with his head and that we wanted the money."

"And you were ashamed."

"Of course I was ashamed. Everyone laughed. They never heard of such a thing before. So they gave me the cup of wine and the coins and they put a chicken around my neck for my father."

He was silent then, and she said nothing. There was no reason to apologize for her father, and both of them knew that.

"He never forgave my mother and he never forgave me," Tufa said. "We ate the chicken and he sat there and looked at us and went hungry. Then he went away and never came back. I was eight then and I am thirty-four now, and that makes you twenty-six."

"Why did you do that to my arm, grip me like that?"

"I don't want any lies. Even little lies."

"I'll try not to tell any lies," Caterina said. "I don't know if it will be easy or not. I don't think I ever tried before."

At the end of the piazza they came upon the rows of wine. "What the hell is all this?" Tufa said.

"The Germans are coming. They were trying to hide the wine."

"How do you know?"

"The mayor here, what's his name? The fat man. Italo Bombolini."

"I refuse to believe that that fat idiot is the mayor here."

"He is the mayor. The Captain of the People they call him."

"Oh, God!" Tufa said, and both of them laughed. He looked at the bottles glistening in the rain. "This is the work of some kind of idiot."

They went up the long hill and it was midnight when they finally reached the door of the Malatesta house. "I never thought I would go inside here again," Tufa said. He hesitated. "I never ate chicken again, not once from that day," he said, but then he went through the door.

It was cold inside and dark, and when Caterina managed to light the little lamp that was fed by ox fat, she found that Tufa was trembling from cold and wet and from exhaustion. "Take off your clothes and get into that bed," Caterina said. "My bed."

"I'm not used to taking orders." He made no move of any kind.

"Do you want me to turn away?"

"Of course." He sounded annoyed. "Of course."

She waited until she heard him get into the bed before turning back to him. Next to the bed was a small porcelain stove. There was no fuel for the fire, but she burned the stump of a broom and it gave good light, and for a while it heated the room. She found a bottle of anisette and the liquor warmed them both.

Tufa wanted to talk to her. The story he had to tell is not an uncommon one in Italy, although it is possible that Tufa would tell it with greater hurt than most others, since Tufa has more pride than most. He had wanted to be a good soldier and a good Italian. He had wanted to act with courage, he had wanted to keep his integrity and live with honor. It wasn't a great deal to ask of a state, but they wouldn't allow that, although Tufa couldn't admit it. He lied to himself about the failures in Albania and the disasters in Greece. He continued to encourage his men to die for a cause they couldn't believe in. Through his example young men, for him alone as a man, stood and fought and were maimed or killed. And then one night in North Africa, some of the men, his own men, shot him in the back.

"I'm sorry," the one who did the shooting said. "We have to do this to save ourselves."

Even then he wasn't willing to admit everything to himself. When he rejoined his regiment in Sicily the soldiers were frightened by the officer who was so brave that he would kill them to prove it. During the first attack his men deserted. He lifted his rifle, as he had been forced to do before, and they kept running, and for the first time he knew that they were right and he was wrong and that to shoot them would be to murder them. That night he himself ran, using the rifle to force a fisherman to take him to the mainland, and he had run in the night like some wounded animal trying to make his way back to his den to lick his wounds in secrecy and darkness or to die.

When he was through, the fire had gone out and the house was cold again, and it was Caterina who was shivering.

"I'm going to have to come to bed. I hope you will allow this," Caterina said. It was a matter of courtesy only.

"There is no choice, is there?"

She took off her clothes and came to the bed, and neither of them said anything after that. Tufa had begun trembling once more, from the cold and his tiredness and from the story he had told. The heat of her body warmed him and calmed him and the trembling lessened, and after a time he slept. Later he awoke and they made love. There was no surprise about it and no surprise about each other. When they had finished they lay back on the bed and looked at the darkness of the ceiling.

"I know everything about you," Caterina said, "except one thing. I don't know your first name."

"Perhaps we should keep it that way. You know what they say here: 'Love, but make sure to keep a wall between you.' "

"No, I want to know it. I feel I am entitled to that."

"Carlo," he said. "It's German, from *Karl*. I've come to despise it."

They could hear the rain running down from the roof tiles and the filled gutters, splashing down onto the cobblestones of the street.

"We have no wall between us," Caterina said.

"Maybe that is bad. Maybe that will destroy us."

"Why do you bring that up?"

He said that he didn't know. He said that he had lost faith and was no longer sure. "They say, 'Love as if one day you will hate.' Maybe they're right."

The rain began to come hard against the windowpane. The wind was changing, Tufa said, and that meant the rain would pass.

"I think I'm also entitled to hear the story of the fountain now," Caterina said, but Tufa had surrendered himself to sleep at last. "Tufa? Carlo?" She knew he wouldn't answer, but she wanted to talk to him. She had been watching his face, and she found that looking at it moved her. She wanted to touch it, but she was afraid to.

"You're going to make me be in love again," she said.

ROBERTO HAD SLEPT for perhaps an hour or more when Bombolini woke him. He was reluctant to move.

"Would you like some onions?" Bombolini said. *"Please."*

Roberto got up then because it frightened him to hear Bombolini beg him. Downstairs there was a pot of onions simmering in olive oil over the small fire the mayor had built. Bombolini ladled out the hot browned onions and poured the bubbling olive oil over bread while Roberto told him about Tufa and the Malatesta.

"You know there's only one bed in the house, don't you?" Bombolini said. Roberto shook his head. "*One* bed. Can you imagine it? A Malatesta copulating with a Tufa? You don't know what it means. A revolution, a new world entirely."

"How do you know they are doing it?" Roberto said.

"They're in the same bed, aren't they?" It is an Italian belief that if two people are in the same bed they must be making love to one another, not from desire necessarily, but because man is weak and unable to resist the natural urge. There is no court in Italy that is prepared to believe otherwise.

Roberto watched the mayor wiping the olive oil from his cheeks and chin and realized only then that he was crying, quietly but steadily, exactly as he had been eating. When the last of the bread and onions had been eaten Bombolini turned to Roberto.

"Don't let it alarm you," Bombolini said. "But, Roberto, tell me this one thing. What am I going to do?"

"Something will turn up. You watch."

"Americans always say that. That's the difference between us, Roberto. You think there has to be an answer. A thousand years has taught us differently. There isn't always an answer. Like with your idea about hiding the wine. It seemed like an answer but it didn't work." He said it as if it were an accusation and it angered Roberto, as if somehow America was responsible for the wine in the piazza.

"Of course, if you had put it in the right place, " Roberto said. "It might not work but at least you might have tried."

Bombolini did not want to ask him. He was becoming used to the idea that there was nothing that could be done to save the wine. It was comforting to him to admit surrender, and he wasn't willing to have the idea challenged.

"Where?" he finally asked, in a voice as thin as the sound of the bell.

"In the old Roman wine cellar."

Bombolini said nothing. He had an enormous urge to yawn.

"Down below the terraces," Roberto said. "At the foot of the mountain. The place with the two wine cellars."

"The two wine cellars," the mayor said.

"Put the wine in one of them and brick it over."

"Put bricks over the opening."

"Yes. So it looks just like the wall. Seal it off," Roberto said. "Instead of an opening you'll have a false wall."

Bombolini said nothing for a long time—so long that Roberto grew impatient with him. "It's all brick back there. You must remember it."

"Yes." He looked numb now, although his heart was racing and he was conscious of blood rushing through him. "But they'll find it out," the mayor said.

"I suppose so."

"They'll see through it at once. They aren't stupid people."

"I suppose there are stupid Germans and smart Germans, just like here," Roberto said.

"They want the wine. They'll do anything to get it."

"You want it too," Roberto said. "I thought it was worth the try."

"Worth the try, Roberto? Worth it?" He moved so swiftly toward Roberto that he struck a chair and knocked it over and didn't seem to notice it. Then he did something that is hard to make sense of. He struck Roberto such a blow in the face that the American fell to his knees and stayed there for a moment before going the rest of the way down to the stones on the floor.

"We'll build such a wall that God Himself won't be able to see it," Bombolini said. He came back to himself then from wherever he had been. There was blood on the stones and for a moment he made a gesture of stopping and helping Roberto, but he turned and started instead for the door.

"I'm sorry, Roberto, but there's no time for you."

He ran. When he reached the piazza he kept running until he got to the campanile, and when the bell tower door wouldn't open he pulled on it with such fury that the old iron handle came off in his hands and he was able to work the latch. He felt for the bell cord in the darkness, and when he felt the greasy hemp he began to pull on it as hard and as swiftly as he was able. There was the thin and muffled tone.

"Damn this miserable bell," he shouted. "Damn me for this miserable bell."

But it was strong enough to carry around the edges of the piazza and at least the people there heard it and they began to get out of bed, although it was an hour or two before it was time to get up. It was black in the piazza then.

Bombolini had no watch. "The time?" he shouted at the first people to come into the piazza. "What is the time? Tell me the time."

At last someone came who owned a watch. It was two o'clock in the morning. The people watched Bombolini while he counted. He used his fingers for the hours and his fist stood for an entire day. He did it over several times because he wanted to be certain.

"Thirty-nine hours," he told them. "The Germans will be here in thirty-nine hours."

IV

THE WINE

BEFORE THE SUN GOT into Santa Vittoria that morning, while all the cocks in the city were crowing as if they were inventing the morning, it was no longer possible to cross the Piazza of the People in a straight line. Every person in Santa Vittoria who was able to walk, every man and every woman and every child was in the piazza. Every cart in Santa Vittoria was in the piazza. Everything that could be pulled or pushed or had wheels was in the piazza. Every animal that could carry a bottle of wine was in the piazza. Every donkey and every mule and every ox in Santa Vittoria was in the piazza.

Up on the fountain itself, Pietro Pietrosanto, as head of the army, was shouting orders. "Get all of the people with the shoulder yokes and bring them to the fountain." In every corner a push and a shove began as the people with the yokes began their fight to get to the fountain.

"Will you ever get it organized?" Bombolini shouted to Pietro.

"I got it organized," Pietro said. "I know what I'm doing."

It was hard to see it, but in all the pushing and shouting and shoving there was a shape and a form. Already, for example, all the young men and the strong men had been lined in a file, so that when the time came to pick up the bottles and begin carrying them down the mountain to the Roman cellars they would be the first to go because they could do the most.

"When you're ready for me down there," Pietrosanto shouted, "I'll be ready up here."

By the time Bombolini and Padre Polenta and the members of the Grand Council started down the corso the young men were clapping their hands in time and shouting *"Let's go, let's go, let's go, let's go . . ."* and the sound followed them down the street as if a mob were bellowing through a pipe at them. They went out the Fat Gate and started down the track that goes through the terraces to the foot of the mountain. They were walking fast, and then they were running down.

"Pietrosanto will be starting now," one of them said. The sun came up then, all at once, and it glittered off the sign on top of the Cooperative Wine Cellar so that the sign was like a sun itself.

"You're certain you know how to do it, Padre?" Bombolini asked.

"It's in here, right here," the priest said. He tapped a book he held in his hand along with his silver cross. "All the rules of God."

After such a rain it should have been cool, but the wind had shifted and was coming from the south. "A very fine day for the grapes," someone said. Heat after rain is said to cause sugar to form and turn fat in the grapes. No one mentioned the other thing, that it would be a bad day for people. They went in silence until they reached the opening in the mountain that leads into the Great Room and the two cellars built into the back wall of the room. None of them would enter it then until the priest had gone in first.

"Hurry up, Padre, please," Bombolini said. "Run in there and sanctify the place."

"God's work will not be hurried," Polenta said. He opened the black book, licked a forefinger and started leafing through from page one.

"The index, Padre," Babbaluche said. "Can't you study the index? Look under D for Devils."

The priest went on the way he was going. The first men were already starting down the mountain with their loads of wine.

"Can't you make up a prayer, Padre?" Vittorini said in a gentle voice. "Something from the heart, not from a book."

"Yes," Bombolini said. "God would like that. If I were God I know that *I* would."

"There is a right way to cast out spirits and there is a wrong way," Padre Polenta said. "It's all in the book, and God goes by the book."

The first of the men had put down their wine on the sandy flat outside the entrance to the cellars and started back up the mountain when Polenta found what he was looking for.

"Exorcise," the priest said. He looked up at them. "Not under Devil. Not under Ghosts, not under Spirits. Under *Exorcise*."

It wasn't easy even after that. The priest read to himself for a long time and then announced that he needed water. There was no water and they offered him wine, but since the book said water it must be water. Fortunately the drainage ditch alongside the cart track to the road was filled with muddy water. They got some in Vittorini's feathered hat. Bombolini handed the hat to the priest.

"Now go in there and start blessing, Padre," he said.

Polenta went inside the entrance and several of the braver men went with him, but when he started farther in, back toward the two wine cellars, even Bombolini lagged behind, and so the priest was all alone when he stepped down into the first of the cellars and fell headfirst into four feet of water. When he came up again and shouted for help no one went to his aid at once, because it was felt that the battle between evil and good must have been joined there and that good was losing to evil, as sometimes happens. Finally Bombolini and Vittorini crossed the room and found the priest standing waist-deep in the water, and they led him out onto the dry sandy floor of the Great Room.

"It's all over now," Bombolini said. "There's nothing left to be done. The cellars are flooded."

Five people at least now claim to be the one who first suggested what to do. "Get Longo," someone said. "If anyone can do anything now it is Longo."

They seized his name and began to shout it in the Great Room, booming it off the rough stone walls. "Longo, Longo"—a miracle in their midst, one more twig to grasp for people who were drowning. There was now a steady line of people coming down the mountain with their burdens of wine, and each man turned and called the message back to the man behind him, and in this way the message flew up the mountain from mouth to mouth, leaping up at fifty feet a step. By the time Bombolini and the priest came out of the cave and looked up at the city, Luigi Longo was already on the way down.

Longo was a genius with electrical things, a first-rate electrician with tenth-rate equipment. There was no piece of wiring that Longo had not at some time restored or re-created. He looked at the first of the two wine cellars, and he went into the water and walked along the walls, and in total silence he came outside and drew some pictures in the sand and then he stood up and brushed the hair out of his long, tired, ravaged face and said, "I can do this thing."

There is no need to put down in detail all of the things that Longo did. There was an old generator here, which had been left behind by a traveling circus when a juggler had attempted to kill a tightrope walker over the love of a twelve-year-old acrobat, and everyone had cut everyone else and gone to the hospital or to jail. Longo told them to get the pump from the water tower and cut down all the electric wires that ran from the foot of the mountain to the Fat Gate and to bring the wire to the Great Room. After that he ordered that the two best bicycles in the city be brought down the mountain with four or five of the best young riders.

Bombolini went back outside the cave, because he didn't understand what Longo was doing and it made him nervous not to understand what was happening. The wine was now spread out all over the flat sandy place and was piling up back across the flat part of the valley. "How's it going?" the men who were carrying the wine would shout to the mayor.

"Fine. It's going well. It's going well."

They would smile then. They were happy and excited because they were doing something. Bombolini also made marks in the sand. There were 18 hours left in this day and there were 17 hours left in the day ahead. The total was 35. The anguish was there, in the numbers: 35 and 0. The Germans would arrive in 35 hours. Not one bottle of wine had as yet been hidden.

THE THINGS LUIGI LONGO did that morning will always be remembered here. By seven o'clock the pump and the generator and the old fire hose had been carried down the mountain, and the bicycles had been adjusted so that when they were pumped, they caused the drive wheels on the generator to turn and a dim light to appear in the bulbs. Fabio was among the bike riders.

"*Now* you have come back," Bombolini said.

"Only for today and tomorrow," Fabio said. "I won't be here to humiliate myself when the Germans come."

"We're going to do it, Fabio. We're going to save the wine."

"Even if you lose your honor."

Bombolini was hurt by the boy's bitterness. "You get on fire, Fabio," he said. "It's no good. Fire in the heart only ends up causing smoke in the head."

Fabio was disgusted. "Where are the real Italians?" he said, but no one answered.

When the generator had built up a store of energy, Longo connected it to the pump. At first nothing happened. The moving parts were heavy with old oil and stubborn like an old ox, but Longo began to move the parts by hand and then they began to move on their own after that, grudgingly, only as far as they had to go, but then a little more swiftly to gurgle and cough, and finally to thump now and then and all at once to go *thump, thump, thump, thump,* and water began to gush from the hose. They heard the cheer from the mouth of the Great Room all the way up the mountain.

Longo sat down after that with Bombolini in the warm sun. "We're going to do it," Longo said. "The first cellar will be empty in an hour."

Bombolini took Longo's hand and kissed him on both cheeks. "He says we're going to do it," he told the others.

"Yes. I heard him say it. We're going to do it."

Old Vines came out of the cave. "We're going to do it," Bombolini told him.

"Yes, we're going to do it," the cellar master said.

Bombolini started back up the mountain then for Santa Vittoria, and he was conscious that never in his life had he felt happier than he felt right then.

TUFA WAS LIKE THE others here. He had come awake with the sun, and although he wanted to stay in the bed, next to this woman, he heard the sounds in the piazza and he felt that he must get out of the bed. Now she was awake also, lying next to him, looking at him.

"You should go back to sleep," she said. "It's very important for you. You should lie here for days and get your strength back."

It caused him to laugh. "Do you really think I'd get my strength back lying here next to you all day?"

She smiled at him then. It was she who got up.

"What are you doing?" Tufa said.

"I'm going to get us something to eat," Caterina said.

"I'm not hungry for food right now."

He watched her come back across the room toward him. She had no clothes on and there was no consciousness of herself, and he knew that no other woman in Santa Vittoria would ever be able to walk that

way or do such a thing. He reached up and brought her to the bed.

When they were through he did sleep again, and it was her turn to listen to the sounds of the city and the morning. The sight of his stained, torn uniform saddened her, because it told by itself the ordeal Tufa must have endured. It would have to be done away with before the Germans came. Very quietly then she got out of the bed and went into a back room and came out with a suitcase full of clothes that had once belonged to her husband. She looked down on Tufa and at that moment knew real fear. Through Tufa she had invested in life again, and to the degree you invest, to that degree are you in danger of losing your investment.

When Tufa woke again he said he was hungry, truly hungry, not for her but for bread dripping with olive oil, for some good black olives and for an egg. Caterina went to the door.

"I am going to get you an egg if I have to sell myself to do it." She was conscious that he didn't approve of her joke.

"I'm going with you," Tufa said. He began to get out of bed.

"I've left you some clothes. They belonged to my husband."

He began to pick up the clothes. "He had good taste," Tufa said.

"He had money."

He put on brown corduroy pants with leather patches on the inside of the knees and a white linen shirt that opened at the neck and a large brown leather belt. He was very handsome and he knew it. "They'll think I'm a landowner," he said.

"It's better than knowing you're a Fascist officer. Come. You must be starving."

When they were halfway down the hill that goes into the Piazza of the People, Tufa stopped in amazement. "What in the name of God are they doing down there?"

"Something to do with the wine we saw last night," Caterina told him. When they came down into the piazza itself, he stopped and watched them.

"Look at the way they're loading those carts," he said to her. "They should take down the sides and then put the wine in and put the sides up again. They could go twice as fast."

"Come," Caterina said. "It's not our concern." She looked at him. "We have so little time, you know."

"Oh, you're right," Tufa said. "It's a habit. You see them doing it wrong and you want them to do it right." He took her by the hand in the daylight, something that isn't done here, and they started toward one of the lanes that leads out of the piazza. Before going down it, Tufa stopped to study the scene once more.

"Whoever is running this is an idiot," Tufa said, and he turned away from it and so failed to see Bombolini with several of the other leaders come up into the piazza, although they saw Tufa.

"Look at them," the priest said. "Everyone in Santa Vittoria knows there's only one bed in that house."

"Who would have believed it?" Bombolini said. "A Tufa with a Malatesta in one bed. That's democracy for you."

The traffic in the Corso Cavour had by then backed up so far and so deeply that the river of wine had become a trickle. It was because of a sharp turn in the road and because the men were becoming exhausted. The ox carts locked wheels in the turn and the traffic going down had to stop entirely to allow the traffic coming back up to pass.

"It's all going wrong," Pietro Pietrosanto said. "I don't know what's happening, but it's all going wrong. I'm going to ask Tufa."

"We don't need people to come in from the outside and tell us how to run our affairs," Bombolini said. He was openly hurt.

"Outside?" Pietrosanto shouted. "Outside? Tufa's one of *us*. Tufa's a Frog." He began running for the back lane, pushing and shoving people as he went. He seized Tufa by the shoulder.

"I saw you looking in the piazza. Do you know something to do?"

Tufa took a long time in answering. "Yes, I have a plan."

Pietrosanto perked up then. "I knew he would have a plan," he shouted at Caterina. "He has a head. A head. A head."

"It's very complicated," Tufa said.

"Will it save the wine?"

"If it works, it will save the wine."

Pietrosanto took off his hat, the one with the tall hawk's feather that marked him as the leader of the army of the Free City of Santa Vittoria, and put it on Tufa's head, and he took off his red arm band, which read Commander in Chief, and pinned it around Tufa's arm. Tufa looked at Caterina.

"What can I say?" Caterina said. "You look good in the hat."

"If it was anything else but the wine, do you understand?" Tufa said. "It's blood here, you know, and it's my blood as well as theirs."

"I'll go and get you the egg." She started down the lane.

Pietrosanto and Tufa went back toward the Piazza of the People. Tufa's name ran ahead of him the way they say it happens in Rome when the Pope passes. "Tufa . . . Tufa . . . Tufa's here. . . . Tufa's in charge. . . . It's going to be all right."

When they reached the piazza, although no one had been able to move before, a path was somehow opened in front of them. Give this credit to Bombolini. He came forward to meet Tufa. And give credit to Tufa. He could have seized command then with the approval of the people, but he deferred to the mayor, whom he knew only as a clown.

"Will you ask the people to clear the piazza?" Tufa said. "Tell them to get something to eat and to rest and to wait." Slowly the piazza cleared and the jam lessened. Tufa's second order was to take down the wall of the Cooperative Wine Cellar that faced the Fat Wall and the little opening through it that we call the Thin Gate.

"Take down the wall," the mayor ordered.

The men were not strong about it at first. They chipped delicately at the bricks and stones because they didn't like to break down something which had been built with so much effort and cost. But when the first bricks came out they began to throw themselves into the work, because there is always something exciting about destroying something and about tearing something apart.

"The corso is a pipe, you see?" Tufa said. "As with any pipe, it can take so much water and no more, no matter what the pressure behind it. You thought you could push it through by desire, because you wanted it. But there are laws—laws of nature."

"I see," said Bombolini.

"Now we have to find a stream that can handle a larger flow."

The wall was down then, and the wine in the cellar was exposed.

"Ring the bell," Tufa said. "Call out the people."

They rang the bell, what there was of it to ring, and the people came out of their houses and gathered first in the Piazza of the People and then in a long file down the Corso Cavour right to the broken wall of the Cooperative Wine Cellar. Some of them had managed to sleep for a few minutes and to eat, and they rubbed the sleep out of their eyes and the bread from their beards and lips.

As they came down, Tufa and Pietrosanto and the soldiers and

Bombolini began to make a line of them, beginning at the open wall and running down across the open area where the grapes are pressed at harvest and through the Thin Gate and then down the steep path that the goats take down the mountain.

"It's going to take courage," Tufa told the women. "It's going to take all your guts."

"We have guts," a woman answered him.

"When it comes to the wine we have guts," another said.

"I'm going to ask more of you than I ask of soldiers," Tufa said.

"I would hope so," someone replied. There is no respect for soldiers up here.

Down they came then, filing down the corso from the Piazza of the People, the true army of Santa Vittoria in the service of the wine. They mixed the old with the young, and the strong with the weak, so they could spell each other and make up for each other's weaknesses. If people were too old or sickly Tufa would take them out of the line. When Caterina came down Tufa stopped her. "Let me see your hands." She held out her hands. They were so long and beautiful. He sent her back up the mountain to get gloves.

At a few minutes after one o'clock on Tuesday afternoon Carlo Tufa was able to stand on the floor of the valley, one hundred feet from the entrance to the ancient wine cellar, and look back up the mountain, over the terraces, all the way to the Thin Gate, and see one continuous line of people that led into the heart of the cellar. He ran across the flat stretch in front of the opening.

"Are you ready in there?"

The men inside shouted back that they were hot to go. He ran outside then and back away from the base of the terraces so that Bombolini could see him and he gave the sign by a motion of his arm.

"Start them going," he shouted.

The bottles began to flow then, hand to hand, out of the cellar, down to the gate, through the wall and then down the mountain, a stream at first until they found the rhythm of the flow and then a river, a river of wine running down the mountain.

IN THE FIRST HOURS the enemy was the sun, which sat on the people's backs as if it were a hot iron pressing down on them, but later it became the mountain itself. To keep from falling off it, the people were forced to brace themselves with one leg and step up the steep flank with the other, and more than any other part of the body it was the legs that began to tire and then to sting with fatigue and finally to cramp and knot.

After the second hour the bottles began to break. There were tired hands and sweaty hands, and the bottles would slip or swing against a rock and there would be the sound of breaking glass and then the smell of wine. Then there was blood. Many of the people had no shoes, and although their feet are as tough as ox leather, glass will finally cut through leather, and blood began to run with the wine and the whole length of the line glittered with glass.

In the late afternoon, when the sun was not so direct and when a cooler breeze began to blow, the people passing the wine settled into a true rhythm. From time to time Tufa came down the line to encourage the people, and when he did he would take Caterina's place for a few minutes. One time when he had to go on, he found her asleep under a vine. He kissed her then, in front of others.

"You have to get up," he said. "But I am proud of you." Later, Tufa realized that it was the first compliment he had ever given to a woman, because the men don't learn to do that here.

At night the fog came and it moistened the ground and cooled the rocks, but as the fog got thicker there was new trouble on the line. When someone fell out it was hard for the replacement to find where the chain had been broken. People stepped on the glass and fell on the stones, and the bottles began to break again.

Sometime after ten o'clock, when the wine was moving badly, Tufa decided that the time had come to risk the use of light. Pine boughs were cut and bound with wire and dipped into barrels of ox fat and they were lit and passed down the mountain, one every fifty feet or so. It was dangerous; the line glowed like some flaming arrow pointing down from the city to the ancient cellar below, but it gave the people heart again.

And it was these lights which drew Roberto down to the wine-passing line. He had recovered from the blow and gone to bed, and when he awoke he went out to the piazza to clear his head. He had thought the city was asleep until he saw the lights. He went down the corso to witness what his words had begun.

"What happened to you?" Bombolini said.

"You know what happened to me," Roberto said.

"Oh, yes." It seemed to have taken place weeks before. "It was excitement. A blow of love. I am Sicilian, you understand."

"Being Sicilian must be a very strange thing," Roberto said. "It provides an excuse for everything."

He watched the wine going down the mountain and he could see that almost half or perhaps even more than half of the wine was gone by then and he could also see that the people on the line were working by instinct, like blind mules grinding grain at harvest.

"It's good that you are almost done," Roberto said. "The people can't go on much longer."

"What do you mean, done? There's still half of the wine to go."

"But you have to leave some for them."

"We don't leave a drop," a man shouted to Roberto from the line. "Don't give away *our* wine, friend."

He felt guilty not helping, and although his leg pained him he took a place in line from a woman and was pleased to find that he could do the work. While he passed the bottles he remembered something from his youth and he knew that he was right and that he also could tell it to the people in a way that they could understand.

When Roberto was a boy his father put in a large vegetable garden in the back of the house, because no Italian could stand the sight of soil going unused. At night the rabbits came and stole from the garden. The first year the garden was a failure, until some people told his father what the Americans did. They made their garden and they fenced it in, and then they made a second garden, smaller, with a low fence around it, for the rabbits. The rabbits came and ate the rabbit garden and never touched the main garden.

"Signora," Roberto said. "You have to take your place again." She was disgusted with him.

"You Americans," she said, "you have forgotten how to work."

He went to Bombolini and he told his story, and Bombolini knew at once that it was true. Santa Vittoria, if the Germans weren't to tear it apart brick by brick, needed a Rabbit Garden. The only question was how large the garden should be. They stopped the flow of wine and allowed the people to rest, and by the light of the pine torches they held a meeting of the Grand Council.

The council members looked into the wine cellar, and some of them walked around the bottles and tried to count them in their heads, and they came back outside with long faces.

"Ten thousand bottles," one of the older men shouted.

Everyone knew the number was wrong, but none of them wanted to be the one to give the wine away; it goes against everything in the blood. Pietro Pietrosanto is tougher than the rest and a realist, and it was he who began the bidding again.

"One hundred thousand bottles," Pietro called out.

One older man clapped his hand over his heart as if a knife had been put in it, and for a time after that no one dared to talk. Tufa and Roberto knew that a hundred thousand bottles were not enough, but it was Babbaluche who let them know it in the manner they could understand. He began by calling them penny-pinching peasant pigs and in the end he named a proper figure: 500,000 bottles.

He was correct and at the same time he was wrong.

No bearer of the blood of the men who cut the terraces an inch at a time out of the mountain, no sons of those whose sweat watered the vines that had first been planted here a thousand years before, was capable of giving away 500,000 bottles of wine, even if it was the correct thing to do. After more minutes of bidding and debate, during which men wept and threatened to put themselves to death, it was agreed to plant the Rabbit Garden with 300,000 bottles. At any other moment in the city's history such a figure would have led to rebellion, but the people were then too tired to rebel, and the truth, which was not admitted for a long time afterward, was that to many it meant 300,000 fewer bottles to carry down the mountain.

At a little after four o'clock in the morning, Tufa stepped in front of the man who had just bent once more and picked a bottle off the floor of the cooperative cellar and he took it out of his hands.

"This is enough," he said. "You can rest. This is the last bottle."

The last bottle. They started it down the line with tenderness, they handled it with enormous delicacy. "Don't drop it," they said, "this is the last." People expected it to look different from all the rest, but it was the same, and it was hard to believe that one more would not be coming after it. There was no sense of joy, but only one of emptiness.

"What do we do now?" a woman asked Tufa.

"We go home to our beds," he said to her.

They began to leave the line, the young helping the old, many so bent over they could not then straighten up. It was agreed that the city should sleep until four o'clock in the afternoon, and then some of them should go down onto the terraces so that the Germans would not be suspicious and some should be in the piazzas and the streets.

Tufa waited for Caterina to come up the line because he was too tired to go down after her. "This is the man who saved Santa Vittoria," Bombolini said to the Malatesta.

"We aren't saved yet," Tufa said, "and if we are, the people saved the people."

Caterina slept when she reached the bed. She had taken off her gloves, and Tufa could see the soreness and the blisters of her hands. On the table was the egg she had found, a small one, a jewel of an egg. He broke the shell and drank the egg and put his head back on the bed. He had no idea whether he had slept or not when there was a shout at the door and then someone was shaking him.

"Tufa? Tufa, you got to get up. You hear me?" Tufa nodded. "Something terrible has happened on the mountain."

THE EXPEDITIONARY FORCE to Santa Vittoria was ready to go by ten o'clock that morning. There was the motorcycle and behind it the small truck, and behind the truck as an afterthought trailed a small, battered 20-millimeter dual-purpose gun. They were dressed not for war, but as if they were going on parade.

"If I had flowers I would put flowers in your buttonholes, is that understood?" Captain von Prum had told them that morning. They had all nodded.

They were restless. They wandered from the convoy out into the piazza and back into the shadows and out into the sun again. From the piazza it was possible to see from Montefalcone across the river to where several villages and towns much like Santa Vittoria were hanging far up on the sides of their mountain.

"I have to admire those terraces, sir," Sergeant Traub said. "It must have taken work."

"Yes, hundreds of years of work," von Prum said.

"Sometimes it seems like a shame to take their wine," Traub said. The captain looked at him. "They work so hard for it, I mean."

"And then we come and take it."

"Yes, sir."

"You had better think of it this way. We are engaged in a war, and wars aren't pretty things to be engaged in. What we do we do to aid the state, the Fatherland. Whatever aids the state is good."

"Yes, sir."

"And now let me tell you something a very wise German once wrote, Sergeant. To put your mind at rest. 'The essence of life is a taking over.' Do you understand that?" Traub nodded. "We don't invent this fact. This is life itself." He paused to allow Traub to think about the words. "The people who are rising in the world take over. The ones who are sinking are taken over. The strong take; the weak surrender. It is the way of life."

THEY MET TUFA IN the Piazza of the People—Bombolini, Pietrosanto, Vittorini, Fabio and Roberto—and started at once down the Corso Cavour.

"It can't be described to you. You have to see it," Bombolini said.

On the sandy flat before the entrance to the Great Room the bricks had already been brought down and were stacked on the sand. Some men were beginning to mix the cement and lime and sand and water.

"They might as well stop that now," Bombolini said. "It's not going to do any good."

Tufa was unable at first to see what was causing the concern, and when he did he felt that it might only be some trick that the early morning sun was playing. From the Thin Gate down through the terraces and directly into the mouth of the cellar ran, unbroken, and growing darker and wider as it went, a brilliant purple stain.

"The wine," he said.

"Yes, the wine," someone answered him.

And making the purple even more brilliant to the eye, dazzling in truth, was the glitter of the sun on the pieces of glass from a thousand broken bottles. "If God Himself had made a sign to where the wine was hidden He could not have done a finer piece of work," Bombolini said. "There is no sense going on."

Suddenly Vittorini spoke up. He was already wearing his white uniform so that he might stand at Bombolini's side in the piazza when the Germans came, a representative of tradition, the kind of man another soldier might respect.

"We shall wash the mountain," the old soldier said.

"There isn't enough water," Guido Pietrosanto said.

"We'll pump some more," Vittorini said. "Longo? Can you get the pump back up the mountain?"

Longo was asleep against the wall. When they woke him he said he could get the pump and the generator up the mountain and that the bricklayers would have to go on by torchlight.

"I don't want to be the one to wake the people," Fabio said. "I couldn't bear to look at them."

"They've had two hours' sleep. It's all they need," Pietrosanto said. They began the long trek back up the mountain.

It would be fine to say that the people responded to the crisis with good humor, but it wasn't true. Most of them were angry at being awakened. "You lied to us," they said.

"Come on, get up," they were told. "Get your water jug, your chamber pot, your buckets. We're going to wash the mountain."

They got up, but they were angry. Once again there was a line on the mountain. And when the water came they filled the jugs and bottles and walked to the goat path.

At first it was no good. The water spread the wine and made it even brighter. There was nothing to do, however, but to go on, and finally at ten o'clock in the morning, after perhaps a hundred thousand gallons of water had been poured on the side of the mountain, the wine began to thin and the earth began to swallow the wine and the water. Young boys had been coming down the path with grape baskets strapped to their backs and these were filled with glass. The people's spirits kept rising, and by noon no one was able to tell what had taken place there.

After the washing it was time to re-lay the wine in the Cooperative Wine Cellar. It was Fungo the idiot who thought of a solution for this. In general there are two ways to put down wine, the tight way which is used here and the loose way which is used in wineries that have a great deal of room to spare. The loose way takes a good deal of room, more room than there is here, but it reduces the chances of bottles breaking when accidents happen. Where Fungo learned of it no one knows, because he wouldn't say. Some people think that Fungo hears holy voices that direct him; and who is prepared to prove they don't? Instead of going home to bed the wine layers were put to work in the cooperative cellar, and all that morning and afternoon they spread the last of the bottles, so by midafternoon the 300,000 bottles almost filled the large room and were made to look as if they were at least 600,000. Meanwhile there was time to put away things and hide signs that might be revealing, to sweep the sand around the entrance to the cellars, put back up the brick wall of the cooperative cellar, get the people out of the piazzas and down onto the terraces.

Most of the worry now was with the wall in the Roman cellar.

"How does it grow?" the people asked.

"It grows, it grows," Bombolini would say to them. But the work went slowly. The men were on the edge of exhaustion. It was two feet by eleven o'clock, and six feet by noon, and eight feet by the time the people had had their bread and soup. At one o'clock a boy rode up the mountain on a mule and he had good news to tell the town. The wall would be finished no later than two o'clock that afternoon, three full hours before the Germans came.

At fifteen minutes before two o'clock, Italo Bombolini and Tufa and Pietrosanto and Vittorini and Fabio and Roberto and twenty other members of the Grand Council of Santa Vittoria went through the Fat Gate and started down the mountain.

The men had done a good job. From the floor of the cellar entrance in the back wall of the Great Room to the arched ceiling, the bricks had been fitted with enormous care to the old bricks of the wall. What had been that morning a gaping entrance to a great ancient wine-filled cellar was now one solid blank wall. The cellar and the wine were gone.

Many of the men were already asleep on the floor, so almost none of them, the first time at least, heard what Tufa said.

"The wall will have to come down."

The ones who heard him turned around.

"Why did you say that, Tufa?" one asked.

"It's no good," he said. "It will have to come down."

No one noticed Luigi Casamassima, who had been the leader of the bricklayers, get up from along the wall and come behind Tufa and put his hands around his neck.

"You're crazy, Tufa," Luigi shouted. "You're a Fascist. You're in the pay of the Germans."

"You're doing that, Luigi, because you know it's true."

Casamassima took his hands away then, but Tufa turned to him and his voice was low and not cold. "You should have stopped, Luigi. You should have had the courage to stop."

"We couldn't stop," Luigi said. "We were too tired to stop. All we could do was go on."

When they turned back to the false wall, all of them could see the problem.

"It stands out like a new grave," Babbaluche said.

CAPTAIN VON PRUM ENJOYED the ride from Montefalcone. He was glad to be moving and was anxious to begin putting his ideas to the test. "And so begins the first phase of the bloodless victory," the captain said, and Sergeant Traub nodded.

When the convoy was on a cart track a mile from the River Road, von Prum raised his arm and signaled, and they came to a stop in the shade of a beech tree.

"We're early, we must wait," the captain said.

To the left of the road were low hills, and the captain and the sergeant got out of the motorcycle and walked across to a hill and went up it and when they were near the top they were able to see the mountain with Santa Vittoria on the top of it.

"That's it," Captain von Prum said. "That's your city."

"It's like all the rest," the sergeant said.

"Except it's *our* city." Von Prum had binoculars and he could see things all along the road and among the terraces and he could even make out the faces of people who were gathered about the Fat Gate.

"There are people going up the road, a whole group of them," Sergeant Traub said. He had been handed the glasses.

"Our welcoming committee." They started back down the hill toward the River Road and the convoy.

THE MEN THEY HAD seen on the mountain were Bombolini and Tufa and the others coming from the Roman cellar. They were halfway up the mountain then, and none of them had said a word. They were too tired and too disappointed.

"Let's not tell the people," Bombolini said. "It won't do them any good to know."

"Tell them," Tufa said. "They have a right to know."

Fabio was forced to smile at hearing the ex-Fascist putting his trust in the people. When they reached The Rest, the place where everyone always stops, they looked back down behind them into the valley.

"I won't let you quit," Tufa said. "If the Germans don't look in the entrance on their way up, if they don't look in the cellar tomorrow, the wall will be built."

"Ah, yes," Bombolini said. "The Germans won't look in the tunnel. They'll go right by and not look in."

It was too much to believe and too exhausting to hope. But the false wall was coming down. Even from where they were on the mountain they could hear the first of the bricks being dropped into the great copper kettles that are used to blend all the wines and ingredients that go into the vermouth.

The problem with the wall had been the bricks. They were not new, they were very old bricks, but they were bricks that had been bleached by several hundred years of sun and leached by thousands of winter rains and scoured by winds too numerous to be considered. So they stood out in the darkness of the rest of the back wall of the cellar. Now they were being dyed. The bricks were being dumped into the huge copper kettles which had been filled with several hundred bottles of our best red vermouth. "The wine will save the wine," Old Vines said.

Bricks drink. They absorbed the wine, and they turned a deep, rich, dark red, as dark and rich as the wine itself.

Bombolini and the others left The Rest and started back up again. When they neared the Fat Gate some of the people came down the path to meet them.

"How's the wall? How does it look? Is it all grown up?" they asked.

Bombolini looked at Tufa and Tufa stared back at him.

"It still grows. They're still working on the wall."

The people were astonished and frightened by what they heard. "But they said . . ."

Bombolini shook his head. "No. They were wrong. The wall still grows." It made him sad to tell them that. "I wish we had Mazzola back," he said to Pietrosanto.

"I wish we had Copa," Pietrosanto said. Although they had not done much work in recent years both Copa and Mazzola had once been the very best men in Santa Vittoria with stone and brick.

"You did what you had to do?" Bombolini said to Pietrosanto.

"Yes. The problem is solved. The Band is all taken care of."

Bombolini looked at Pietrosanto with a new respect. "Was it terrible? Did you find it hard to do?"

"No, it wasn't hard to do," Pietrosanto said, and then he stopped very suddenly, almost locked in motion, as if he had come face to face with an invisible barrier. "Did you hear it?" he asked. "Do you hear it now? Quiet!" he shouted.

The people by the Fat Gate and the people around them and they themselves were quiet, and then they heard.

The Germans were coming.

CAPTAIN VON PRUM's motorcycle started up through the terraces, the first motor vehicle ever to attempt to come up the mountain. When the captain looked back toward the base of the mountain, he saw Fungo sweeping the sand in front of the entrance to the Roman cellars.

"A place to examine," he said to Sergeant Traub. "It might make a good air-raid shelter."

Halfway up the mountain they stopped to allow the engines of their vehicles to cool. It was ten minutes before five o'clock. Just before they started up again Captain von Prum sampled some of the grapes that grew alongside the cart track and they were bitter. Paolo Lapolla had the bad fortune to be near them.

"What's the matter with your grapes?" von Prum asked Paolo.

At first Paolo found it impossible to find his tongue. "They aren't ripe yet," he finally said. "You came too soon."

It caused the Germans to laugh. "When would you have wished us to come, next year?"

"Later, later," Paolo said. "Much later."

ALL UP THE CORSO Cavour and up into the Piazza of the People the people were in the doorways and along the edges of the street and around the fringes of the piazza. They were silent and they were composed. Only Fabio seemed to be upset, and when the sound of the engines could be heard coming up the Corso Cavour, he left the piazza and went up into the mountains. There were, in the center of the piazza then, only two people: Italo Bombolini, the mayor, and

Emilio Vittorini in the dress uniform of his old regiment. And behind them was the Fountain of the Pissing Turtle.

The motorcycle was the first to come into the piazza. It came up onto the lip of the street where for a moment it seemed to hang suspended, half in the piazza and half in the corso. Then it seemed to catch hold of the cobbles of the piazza and explode out into it.

They circled the piazza, roaring along the rim of people, who were pressed back against the walls of the houses. Bombolini and Vittorini kept turning with them so that they would always be facing them, much as the matador does when a bull is on the loose in the arena. Once was not enough for the Germans, and they went around the piazza a second time, until the truck and the little gun had ground up into the piazza and could follow them. At a sign from the officer, the

truck pulled to one side of the square and the soldiers leaped from it. And when this was done, the motorcycle very sharply turned and headed directly toward the two men.

Vittorini's wife shouted for him to jump, but everyone knew Vittorini would never move. It seemed to us then that Bombolini would be forced to break and run if the machine was not to hit him, but he too stood in the piazza as if this was the ordained thing to do. The motorcycle, with a terrible screeching of brakes, came to a stop less than a foot away from them, at the edge of Bombolini's shoe.

"Welcome to the Free City of Santa Vittoria," Bombolini shouted above the sound of the engine. "We of this city know that in times of war . . ." It was the last they heard, as Traub raced the engine and the mayor's voice was lost beneath it.

"We know that in times of war—" Bombolini continued.

"Quiet!" Sergeant Traub shouted. He shut off the engine.

"I want you to know, sir," Bombolini said, "that we are willing and anxious to cooperate with you as guests of the city, exactly as we would do if we were running an inn."

Bombolini continued to talk, but they didn't hear him. The sergeant had gotten down from the seat of the motorcycle and had gone around and opened the door of the sidecar for the captain. The captain stepped out. The two men walked around the fountain and examined it carefully and came back. Von Prum stopped in front of the mayor.

"Why did you stop talking?" he asked.

"I had nothing further to say," Bombolini replied.

"Do you expect us to believe that?" von Prum said. "Would you like to hear what the sergeant said about you?" Bombolini nodded his head. "He said you were like the piazza; very large and very empty."

Someone in the piazza laughed. It was Babbaluche.

"It is my hope that we can find a way of living here that will be profitable for both of us," Bombolini said.

"I will *insist* on it," the German said.

He was back in the sidecar then, and Traub started up the motorcycle. It made a great noise, and then it broke loose. As it did the foot pedal on the left side of the cycle struck Bombolini's leg and it sent him moving backward. Had he fallen at once there would have been nothing funny in it, and it might have even alarmed the people. But he didn't go down at once. He began to fall and to run backward at the same time, going a little faster at each step, trying to keep his balance but losing it as he moved, going backward and down, clutching the air to hold him up. There must have been twenty desperate steps in this way before he was moving at such a speed and was bent over backward so far that in the end nothing could support him and he went down, flatly down, fully down, on his back, so that his legs flew up in the air and hovered there as if he were about to do a backward somersault.

He was stunned by the fall but not hurt by it, and then he could hear them beginning. Please God, he thought, don't let them do it.

But they did do it. It began as a titter but it soon became a laugh, and because of the way sounds carry in the Piazza of the People, it became a gigantic laugh, a thunderous, booming laugh that fed on its own noise, laughter creating new laughter until it went beyond anything that had to do with Bombolini lying on his back in the center of the piazza, but must have been a cry at everything they had done and knew they were going to have to do.

The Germans heard it, although they were already down in the Corso Cavour making their first reconnaissance of the city.

"I don't understand these people at times, sir," Traub said.

"It's because in many ways they are like children," Captain von Prum said, "and so they react like children."

Bombolini got to his feet and marked one cobblestone with the sole of his shoe. He looked at the people and nodded his head at them, over and over.

All right, he was saying to himself, you can laugh. Laugh now. One day, right here, on this stone, you will erect a monument to me.

V

THE SHAME OF SANTA VITTORIA

THOSE FIRST DAYS OF the occupation were good ones for the people of the city. They had set themselves for something bad to happen, and nothing bad had taken place. The weather for the grapes was good, and when this happens things are always good in Santa Vittoria, no matter what else may be happening. But beyond that was the fact that everyone was after the same thing. The Germans wanted the people to cooperate with them, and the people couldn't find enough ways to do it.

At the start it had been Captain von Prum's policy to show a strong, hard hand and then, when the people were properly conditioned, to show them that the rock in his breast was actually a heart. On that first day, for example, a curfew was set for eight o'clock that night. It was too late to warn the bricklayers, and when they came up the mountain at ten o'clock, after working on the wine-dark wall, they were jailed for breaking the curfew and they were whipped.

"I am sorry to have to do this, but these men have broken the rules and must be punished for it," the captain said.

"It's only correct," Bombolini said. "They deserve it."

The bricklayers didn't mind. They were so tired they were numb.

Some of them slept all through the three days of their confinement and never missed the food they were supposed to be deprived of.

Captain von Prum and Sergeant Traub moved into the home of Constanzia Pietrosanto, across the piazza from the Palace of the People. It was small but well built and clean and airy and light. Constanzia wept and cried, but then one morning, at the end of the week, she was delivered an envelope by Corporal Heinsick and in it was fifty lire, and they came every week after that. Under the rules of war the German had no need to pay, but he chose to pay.

The rest of the soldiers were quartered in the office of the Cooperative Wine Cellar. Von Prum might have put them in private homes, but he didn't. He paid the city of Santa Vittoria for the use of the wine cellar office. Each week he gave Italo Bombolini fifty lire, the only source of income in the entire city.

"You see?" Sergeant Traub would say to Bombolini. "He's firm but he's fair. You watch. You have a friend here, whether you know it or not. Just so you cooperate."

Cooperate. It was always that word. The captain didn't know then, and he never did know, that Bombolini's policy, which he had actually written down, was named Creative Cooperation. He didn't just go along; he tried to do it eagerly and willingly.

There was a great deal of smiling going on in Santa Vittoria those first weeks. The people smiled at the soldiers, and although they were supposed to be firm, the soldiers began to smile back. There was a great deal of saying "Good morning" and "Good evening." "Good morning, Captain von Prum." "How are you today, Captain von Prum?" When he walked down the Corso Cavour they said his name so often, von Prum, von Prum, von Prum, that it sounded as if someone was filling a barrel with apples.

And then there were the Good Time Boys. These were groups of younger men whose job it was to drink with the German soldiers and to play cards with them and smile at them. They met in the soldiers' quarters, in the wine cellar office. As Babbaluche said, what better place for rabbits than at the edge of the Rabbit Garden.

The Good Time Boys went in shifts. Some dropped around in the morning to share an eye-opener of grappa and some in the middle of the morning for a little pick-me-up of vermouth and some to bring wine for lunch and then an after-nap refresher, and in the evening the serious drinking began with the card playing. The result was that the Germans were drunk a good deal of the time and some of them were drunk all of the time.

Captain von Prum saw none of this. His mind was on other matters. The bloodless victory was proceeding so successfully that he finally felt he must speak to the Italian mayor, and he summoned Bombolini to his office on the evening of his eighth day in Santa Vittoria.

"You are so cooperative with us. Why?" von Prum said. "There must be a reason." He had intended to shock the mayor.

"The obvious one," Bombolini told him. "It is selfish, I suppose. If we help you, we hope that maybe you won't hurt us."

There was nothing for the captain to say except that it was a very realistic way of looking at things.

"We don't see this as our war," the mayor said. "It doesn't matter to us who wins or loses; all we stand to do is get hurt by it."

"So you would be willing to cooperate with the Germans if it meant preserving yourself?"

"The first duty of every Italian is to preserve himself," Bombolini said. "What good does it do me or my country if I get killed?"

"Very mature way of thinking," von Prum said. *Self-interest is their motivation,* he later wrote to his father. *Appeal to their sense of self-preservation. They love themselves more than their country. I have prepared a little test of the mayor's sincerity.*

The test was to make an inventory of Santa Vittoria; to count all the houses and all the people, all tools and machinery, and to report the number of bottles of wine in the Cooperative Wine Cellar.

"The wine?" Bombolini said. "Why the wine?"

"Yes, the wine. It's a property," the German said. "What makes you surprised about that? It's what you make your living on."

"Yes, but the wine . . . you see, the wine here . . ."

"You said you wanted to cooperate," von Prum said.

Bombolini shrugged his shoulders. "There's a lot of wine," he said. "We don't count so well."

"Then *we* can count the wine. You count the other things."

"No. Oh, no," Bombolini said swiftly. "We'll count the wine."

That night the German put in his log: "He has the bait and he is running with it. The counting begins tonight."

"How many are you going to tell him?" Old Vines asked Bombolini.

"How many bottles are there?"

"Three hundred and seventeen thousand."

"Tell him two hundred thousand," Pietrosanto suggested.

Everyone agreed that Pietrosanto was right.

It was very strange. At first everyone had been concerned with saving the wine in the Roman cellar and had already given the wine in the Rabbit Garden away. But as the days went by they began to hope that they could get away with saving half of the Rabbit Garden too. Bombolini was a little wiser than the rest of them. He went to the captain's headquarters the next night.

"Three hundred and two thousand bottles," Bombolini told him.

The German smiled at him. "The right number is three hundred and seventeen thousand bottles. We counted them last night."

Bombolini pretended to be greatly embarrassed. "I warned you that we don't count so well."

"Isn't it odd that the number would be too few and not too many?" Captain von Prum said. But they smiled at one another and Bombolini knew he had done the correct thing. It was only natural that he would lie. It was expected of him.

When Bombolini had gone, the captain called his sergeant in.

"He's a liar like all of them, but he's just a little one. Fifteen thousand out of three hundred thousand bottles is about right, Sergeant. I'd do the same myself, I think. He passed the test."

After that the attitude of the people changed. At first they were fearful that they wouldn't be able to keep the secret, but as the days and then the weeks passed and the secret held, it became a habit. The fact that all of the city shared it made it somehow simple.

They worked on the wall every day. Men were stationed all the way down the path in the terraces to sound an alarm if the Germans were to come down, but they never did. The bricklayers continued to paint the bricks until there no longer was any way to tell which part of the wall was old and which was new.

Then one morning, after a meeting of the Grand Council, the men went out into the Piazza of the People, where they saw a soldier putting up a strange-looking machine at one end of the piazza.

"What is it?" Bombolini asked.

"You turn the handle, see," the soldier said, "and sausage comes out the other end. Try it."

The mayor turned the handle and a terrible sound, a scream of loneliness, filled the piazza. Von Prum had joined them. "An air-raid alarm," he said. "Now all we need is the proper shelter."

Bombolini said afterward that at that moment there was the feeling of a shadow passing over his mind.

"The church would be good," Bombolini said. "It's strong and there's a deep cellar and, besides, they never bomb a church. God won't let them bomb a church."

It caused the German to laugh, and then he looked at them with disdain. "There is a better place than that," he said.

When he left they looked at each other, and none of them said anything, but the words formed on their lips. *He knows. He knows.*

Bombolini tried to work that afternoon. He was putting down the rules that would guide his policy with the Germans. There had been many rules and ideas, but he had reduced them to three.

All men can be reached by flattery, even God can. (What, after all, is prayer?)

All men can be led to believe the lie they want to believe.

All men can be corrupted, each in his own way.

He wrote them down on the back of a photograph, the last clean piece of cardboard he could find in the city. It was a picture taken on the day of his marriage to Rosa Casamassima. In the picture they appeared to be in love. At the bottom is printed: "May this marriage become a vine and produce a bountiful harvest." The words always caused Bombolini to wince. It had produced one grape, sweet and beautiful, and a wine barrelful of bitterness.

When he finished the three rules he lay down and tried to sleep, and the thought wouldn't go away from him. *He knows.* He was not surprised when Corporal Heinsick came to the Palace of the People and told him the captain wanted to see him. Bombolini went immediately.

Von Prum came to the point at once. "You have one of the finest air-raid shelters I have ever seen and you mention the church to me," the captain said. "I'm surprised at you."

Bombolini said nothing to this. He looked at the stones of the floor as if they were the most important objects in the world.

"Sometimes it takes an outsider to see things an insider cannot see," von Prum said.

"We don't go in there. It's filled with evil spirits."

"Oh. So you know where I mean?"

Why must he play this game? the mayor thought. "Yes, I know."

"It used to be an ancient wine cellar, I believe," von Prum said.

"I wouldn't know. No one goes in there."

"Someone goes in there." Von Prum's voice was harsh now. "There are electric light bulbs in there. What are you hiding? Who uses it?"

Bombolini could bring himself to say nothing.

"The Resistance," von Prum said. "You allow them in there."

"No, it isn't true," Bombolini said, but it was a shout. I must not laugh. Oh, God, I must not laugh aloud.

"It's true," the German said, and Bombolini lowered his head. Von Prum laughed at him. "They say the Italians are good liars, that you are all good actors. It isn't so. You're a rotten liar."

Instead of laughing, Bombolini found that he wanted to weep.

"You will get them out of there and keep them out of there."

"Yes."

"You lied to me about the wine."

"Yes. Not much of a lie."

"And you lied about this."

"Yes." Then he looked up at the captain and was serious. "You are right, I am not a good liar," he said. "I won't lie to you again."

It was the happiest Bombolini had ever felt in his life.

BUT THE GERMANS DIDN'T get into the cellar, not then at least, because the next morning a messenger arrived in Santa Vittoria with two papers for Captain von Prum. The people found out later what they were. One was a note that said:

Von Prum:
    Here is your chance to earn your medal!
    The time of the wine is upon us.
    May Schmidt von Knoblesdorf have reason to be proud of you.
                            Scheer

The second paper was the official order authorizing the taking of the wine. Von Prum summoned Bombolini that afternoon.

"Sit down," he said. The captain picked up the order. "Can you read this?" Bombolini said that he couldn't. "It is a pity, since it would make my work easier." The captain stood and turned away from Bombolini. "It is your fate to be a civil authority and it is mine to be a soldier. What do soldiers do?" Bombolini didn't answer. The German turned around then.

"Soldiers take orders. I want you to remember one thing now. I do not want to do this personally. This is not my business. I can only follow my orders because I am a soldier."

Bombolini dropped his head.

"It is also true," von Prum went on, "that we are at war with one another and in a war someone gets hurt. Someone pays a price."

"I know who pays," Bombolini said. "What is it they want?"

"They want your wine."

It is not necessary here to put down all the things Bombolini did after that. He did what was expected of him, he did what he had been rehearsing every night since they had hidden the wine. He slapped his hand over his heart as if he were suffering a stroke and shouted, "The wine! They want our wine?" and he fell to the floor.

It was only the start. It is embarrassing today to put down all the rest that he did—the running into the piazza and the bathing of his head in the fountain, the cries and the tears, the hitting of his head against a stone wall, always with cries of "No . . . no. . . . Never. It is too much, too much." In the end he collapsed, as he had planned, on the floor of Constanzia's house, where von Prum could talk to him.

It was the signal, of course. Everyone knew then. The Rabbit had gone over the fence. The Rabbit was in the garden.

"In the name of God," Bombolini shouted. "The wine is *us*. The body and blood of my people." He tried to sit up. "Captain von Prum. I want you to shoot me, to destroy me now."

The captain wouldn't listen to him. Instead, he would try the last trump, short of violence, that he held in his hand.

"I have a proposition to make to you," he said.

Bombolini succeeded in sitting up, and the captain told him. In payment for the cost of occupying and thus protecting their town, the town would be required to surrender its stock of wine.

"It's like paying an intruder to sleep in your bed with your wife," Bombolini said.

Part of the wine would be considered a payment, but part would be considered a loan to the German government, which would be returned with interest when the war was won.

"What if you lose?" Bombolini said.

Von Prum went on then to the proposition. Because transportation was becoming increasingly hard to obtain, any city that would volunteer to bring its own wine to the railhead at Montefalcone could retain for itself some part of the wine.

"How much?" Bombolini said.

They began at twenty percent.

"I can't ask my people to rape themselves for that amount."

"I could force them."

"No, this can't be done by force," Bombolini said, and the German knew he was correct. "I ask you one thing. Has this been done by any other town?"

The German was honest about it. He told him that it hadn't.

"Then the price will be fifty percent for us."

"It's high," the German said. "I don't know if they will accept it." He went to the window and looked out into the piazza. Bombolini hoped the people weren't gathered in the piazza looking at the house. At last he came back and when he did he was smiling.

"We will help each other," the German said.

There was a good feeling in every part of Santa Vittoria after that, and it remained until the morning they were due to carry the wine to Montefalcone. The feeling remained even when it was found that the order von Prum had shown to Bombolini had required him to requisition only fifty percent of the wine in the first place.

Maybe the people are realists. They were content with their victory; it was more wine than they had counted on, and they were content to let the German have his.

No ONE HERE LIKES to look back on the journey to Montefalcone. It began as though they were going on a picnic, and it ended in misery. Tufa tried to tell them. "This will be a terrible day for Santa Vittoria," he had said, but no one listened, because no one wanted to hear him.

Tufa alone seemed to know what was involved in carrying 150,000 bottles of wine so many miles by so many mules and donkeys and oxen and carts and people and backs all the way to Montefalcone.

The people were actually gay at the beginning.

"They should be crying," Sergeant Traub said. "I tell you, I don't understand these people."

"They have accepted what can't be changed," Captain von Prum said. "As this Bombolini says, the people are realists."

"I don't know," Traub said. "I don't know." By his standards it was carrying realism too far.

The trip down the mountain, even in the dimness before dawn, was easy. When the people reached the River Road the sun was up and the column opened up and began to spread out. The wine baskets on the people's backs began to get hot and heavy even then. When the column began to fall apart and the older people to drift back through it, Tufa, from habit as much as anything, attempted to keep the long march organized. It was the first time the Germans noticed him. There was a manner about him that made itself apparent. "That man is a soldier," Traub said. "We're supposed to turn them in."

Von Prum had been watching. There was a kind of wildness hiding just beneath a mask of discipline that the German found interesting in a man, and almost always fatal. He's one of the men destined in advance to commit the destructive act that ruins, the captain thought.

"Meanwhile, he's doing our work," he said. "We'll watch him."

"There's something wrong about the other one as well, sir," Sergeant Traub said, referring to Roberto. "He has hands like a girl."

The argument had no meaning for Captain von Prum. He also had hands like Roberto. They had never pruned vines or worked the harvest or washed dirty clothes in cold water with strong lye soap. The women were envious of the hands of Roberto and the captain.

It is something the men of Santa Vittoria don't like to admit about their women, but it is true. Whenever the German went through the streets the women didn't look at him directly, but when he passed they followed him and undressed him with their eyes. He was so clean, so white and blond and cool, which the men here are not. He was in truth all that the women talked about for some time.

There is one other thing that must be told: In Italy all the men are unfaithful, because, as is known by all Italians, all Italian men are by nature and birth great lovers.

And, of course, just because they *are* such, all the women are faithful. The faithless woman can be killed and no one will lift a hand to defend her, because she has committed the unpardonable sin, the worst of all crimes—she has dishonored the man. It is naturally because the woman must not so much as look at another man that they do look at him, that they fall in love with him at a distance.

There is only one question that has never been answered: If all Italian men are faithless and sleep with all the women in the town, how is it that all the women are faithful? It is a very great mystery.

At the first of the hills the first of the people began to fall out of the line of march. The Germans had made some effort to keep order on the way. "I don't care where it is or what it is," Sergeant Traub said, "a line of march is a line of march." But at the hills it was no good. The soldiers stopped prodding the people with their rifles. "I take it back," the sergeant said. "A line of march is a line of march everywhere but in Italy."

By midday those who could march had settled into themselves and had developed a rhythm, an almost silent, shuffling cadence that pulled people along with it, the same way it had been on the day of the passing of the wine. People came down along the road to watch, but they said nothing.

Sometime in the evening, fourteen hours after the march had started, the first of the people began to climb up the steep side road into Montefalcone itself.

This was the cruelest part. The word had gone down the river that the people of Santa Vittoria were surrendering their own wine and bringing it in on their backs. The streets of Montefalcone were lined with people and they were making a great noise, and for a moment it was thought they were cheering for the marchers. But the first one was a butcher. He came out in front of the line, his apron spattered with blood, and he was holding the skull of a goat in his hands and he was screaming. "Tell me these are lying." He put his bloody hands to his eyes. "Tell me I'm not seeing what I see."

"Don't look at him," Tufa said.

"Just tell me. I will believe you." He shoved the goat's head into Tufa's face and tried to pull the wine off his back. "No son of Italy could be doing what you are doing. Tell me you are Greeks."

And this was the beginning. It is too painful to tell the rest. They spat on the people of Santa Vittoria, grabbed their hair and lifted up their heads so that their faces, looking down at the stones, could be seen. The priests in the streets turned away from them and an Italian soldier in the pay of the Germans aimed his rifle at their heads.

When they came into the Piazza Frossimbone on the way to the railroad yards in back of the city, Colonel Scheer was on the steps of his headquarters with other officers of his command. The line passed in front of them with the wine, now *their* wine, in the same manner that Fabio says the slaves were marched in front of Caesar when the armies came back from their wars.

"I salute you," Colonel Scheer called to Captain von Prum. "We all salute you." The people of Santa Vittoria, bent with their loads and with their shame, filed by the German officers.

The Captain stopped. "I don't know how you have done this," the colonel said to him. "Unless I am mistaken you are soon to be Major Sepp von Prum. How does that sound?"

Captain von Prum told him that it sounded very pleasant.

"And about the other thing"—Colonel Scheer tapped the region of his chest where a medal would go—"I haven't forgotten. I don't go back on my word."

It was one of the few times that anyone ever saw the captain smile.

The long march back is remembered now as the time when Captain von Prum first met Caterina Malatesta. The captain had promised that he would use his truck and his scarce gasoline to help carry the women and the children back to the foot of the mountain. The Malatesta, against Tufa's wishes, had helped carry wine and her feet had become a mass of blisters so that she was no longer able to walk. "I'm going to have to go with the German," she said to Tufa. "Don't be angry with me. I don't want to leave you."

"It's all right," Tufa said. But when the truck came he didn't feel that way. The back of the truck was filled with women, and when it stopped, the officer motioned for Caterina to get in front with himself and Sergeant Traub.

"Go the next time," Tufa said. Caterina pulled away from him and climbed in next to the officer. Tufa looked into the cab at them. "I *asked* you—" he said to the Malatesta, and the truck pulled away.

"Did you see the eyes on that one?" Sergeant Traub said. "He's one to watch."

"Find out his name," the captain said.

They rode in silence for miles until finally von Prum put on the little running light inside the cab of the truck. Caterina had worn the clothes of a peasant woman, but the effort to pass as a peasant had been in vain. There are women who are so beautiful by nature that they do not know what to do to make themselves less beautiful.

"I haven't seen you before," the captain said.

"Oh, yes. Many times."

"No," he said.

Just no, she thought. The perfect Germanness of it, blunt and uncharming. The fact that he was correct did not concern her.

"I assure you of one thing," von Prum said. "Had I seen you I would not have forgotten you. Thus, I haven't seen you."

She shrugged her shoulders. How German of him and how Italian of me, Caterina thought. To her annoyance she realized that she had spoken to him in Italian and not in the dialect. But also to her annoyance she found that she liked to talk in good Italian, and that she was enjoying sitting next to someone who smelled so clean.

"You aren't like the others here," he said.

She shrugged her shoulders once again.

"No, you aren't like them. Any more than I am like them. We are strangers here, you and I."

When they neared the foot of the mountain, von Prum touched Caterina on the arm. "Now I'm going to tell you something," he said. "One is that you are an extraordinarily beautiful woman; but you know that, and it is merely a formality to get out of the way. The other is that sometime this winter, when you have had nothing to eat for weeks on end and your body is chilled so that you become afraid to touch anything, on that day you will look down on my house in the piazza and see the smoke coming from the fireplace and you'll think of the brightness of the rooms and the beds with sheets and the hot water in tubs and warm, clean clothes, and at that moment you'll want to be there."

They had stopped then and she pulled away from him.

"Not because of me, not at first at least. But because that will be where you belong," von Prum said. "Life owes that to people like yourself. The oxen can survive, but not the racehorses of the world."

When she got out of the truck he opened the map compartment

and handed her a pair of gray woolen socks. "You'll need these to get up the mountain," he said. "It's all right. You can bring them when you come."

AFTER THE WINE HAD been taken, the days continued good. Each day the grapes grew fatter. Old Vines said that he could hear them growing in the warm nights, fattening in their skins, pushing out against their sides. The wine had been taken and even if the false wall was noticed, which no longer seemed likely, there would be no reason to be concerned about it. Why should anyone be looking for something, the people asked each other, when nothing was missing?

One of the strange things was the growing friendship between von Prum and Italo Bombolini. It is said that every German has a desire to sweep his neighbor's dirty steps, and in this sense von Prum was no exception. He began by remaking the mayor. He saw to it that the mayor shaved each day and that his hair was cut and kept trimmed. In September, on Bombolini's forty-eighth birthday, the German sent his measurements to Montefalcone and a few weeks later a suit came back purchased with von Prum's money.

"If you are going to share the leadership of the city," von Prum said, "then I want you to be worthy of me."

The captain was then at work on the first draft of *Bloodless Victory*, and he began to discuss with Bombolini the ways of the people here and the reasons for things. The subject that seemed of interest to him above all others was why the star of Germany was rising so high and why that of Italy had sunk so low. Why were the people of Germany so vigorous and virile and young, and those of Italy so decadent and corrupt and tired? "Look at your soldiers. Why do all Italian soldiers run away in battle?"

At times like these Bombolini would study the floor. There was a certain truth in these things. Even Tufa now had left the battlefield and was in bed in a woman's arms. "Perhaps it's because our soldiers love life more than your soldiers do," Bombolini said.

It caused von Prum to laugh. "But what good is life without honor?"

"I don't know. I don't think I ever tried one with honor yet. It's a very great luxury for people like us."

There is no question that these conversations bothered Bombolini.

But soon they all became unimportant. One morning Captain von Prum received a message, a message that was to change things in Santa Vittoria swiftly and terribly.

SERGEANT TRAUB STOOD in the doorway with an envelope in his hand and von Prum did not look up. He was working on *Bloodless Victory*, and his notes were spread over the packing case he used as a desk. Although Traub was aware that he was not to interrupt when the captain was at work on his report, he decided this time to risk it.

"I think I have good news, sir," the sergeant said. "I think by this time tomorrow I might be calling you Major von Prum, sir."

Inside the envelope were two messages. One, from his brother Klaus, had been forwarded from Montefalcone.

Dear Brother:
I think that I am going mad. What do you have to tell a young German boy who is going mad?

Your brother

Because von Prum knew that the other message contained good news, he was sorry that he had opened Klaus's letter because it took some of the joy away. The question of Klaus's madness, in which he believed, he decided to think about later. He opened the second letter and was surprised to find that his hand was trembling. It was not an official letter and it was written by hand.

Von Prum:
This is not what you expected to receive; it is not what I expected to send. I submitted your name for promotion and decoration as promised. Both requests were rejected. They have ridiculed your performance and through it my endorsement.
A study of sales figures for the past twenty years obtained from wholesalers in this city and from the Cinzano family reveals that your quota of wine should have approached 600,000 bottles and not the 150,000 bottles that you so "miraculously" brought to Montefalcone.
The question is very simple: Where is the rest of the wine? An accounting will be expected from you by ten o'clock tomorrow morning.

Scheer

He closed his door and was not seen again until evening. There were obvious conclusions. They would claim that he had managed to get the people to carry the wine by letting them keep most of it. Or that it was a simple case of thievery, that he had taken the wine not for the Fatherland but for personal gain. It could be seen as a case of cowardice, fear of the people—that if the wine went, no matter what, he would die.

Or there could be wine hidden somewhere in the city and he had been fooled. He was not ready to believe any of this. The answer, he was convinced, lay somewhere else.

He made a mistake that afternoon. He left his office and began to walk through the city, looking up the lanes, sizing up the town, moving swiftly and restlessly, like a fox seeking a hiding place, and so informing the people. Now everyone knew. The element of surprise, which every good soldier covets, was lost to him. In the evening he came back up into the Piazza of the People, and Bombolini and the others knew and were waiting around the fountain. He went directly toward them. His voice was cold and level and impersonal.

"I know now," he said. "Where is the rest of the wine?"

"The rest of what wine?" Bombolini said. His face showed shock and anger.

"The rest of *all* the wine."

"You can't have the rest of the wine. That wine is our wine," Bombolini said. He was beginning to shout. "You promised us."

"Not that wine," the German was forced to say. "We don't take that wine. My word is my bond on that. The other wine."

All of them played their parts well. They came around him then with their mouths open and their eyes dazed, as if trying to see something and not being able to make it out.

And so the German had to tell them about the records and the one million or more bottles of wine, and as he talked they looked at one another and they said, in low bewildered voices, "No, oh, no, it couldn't be . . . there is something wrong." When he was through, one of them said that no people in the world could be that rich; and they all nodded and were silent.

And so they convinced him. He already believed them, when Pietrosanto asked the question, "But if we had a million bottles—*if*, mind you—where would we put them? How do you hide one million bottles of wine?"

The captain went to his room and wrote to Colonel Scheer.

I say this much with no fear of contradiction.

For reasons that I am now unable to understand I am forced to conclude that you have been falsely informed and that any further investigation by you can only bear this out.

On the following I stake my professional reputation, my personal reputation, my good name and that of my family which, as you know, is considerable.

Upon my word of honor: There is no wine in the city of Santa Vittoria except that which the people have been authorized to keep.

The letter was sent to Montefalcone that evening and an answer from Colonel Scheer was returned that night.

Dear von Prum:

Upon receipt of your letter I myself am forced to conclude that I have been misinformed and that a further investigation by our office can only bear this out. Sleep well this night at least.

Before going to bed he answered Klaus's letter as well as he could. There was, he said, nothing to tell a young German going mad except not to do it.

VI

THE NOOSE GROWS TIGHTER

IT MIGHT BE THOUGHT that the question of the missing wine would have separated the Germans from the Italians and made them suspicious of each other, but that wasn't the way it happened. It became as important to the Germans as it was to the Italians that there be no other wine. They discussed it with each other, even talked about where it could have been hidden. "The logical place," Bombolini actually said, "would be the old Roman wine cellar. It's the only place big enough. But the wine isn't there."

After that the talk advanced to the question of why someone would want to say that the wine was hidden. It was decided that some of the wholesalers had altered their figures so that after the war they could file some kind of claim with the German government for confiscated wine which, of course, had never existed. It sounded so sensible that many of the people here began to believe it.

Something was happening with the war. From time to time the

booming, rolling sounds of heavy guns were heard from far away. Then one evening planes came over the city and dropped bombs. Most of them landed down in the terraces and damaged some vines, although not many. No one knew whether it was the Germans, the British, the Italians or the Americans. Two or three old people were killed and seven or eight others were badly hurt. Tufa turned the Palace of the People into an emergency hospital and put it under Caterina Malatesta's direction. It was not very nice there. She worked with the help of Bombolini, who could not bear to look at the wounded, and Roberto Abruzzi and Angela Bombolini. There were no drugs to help relieve the pain and no medicines to stop infection.

"You will have to go to the German and make him get us supplies in Montefalcone," Caterina told the mayor.

"I don't think he wants to do that," Bombolini said.

"You tell him that as commander of the city he is responsible for the health and welfare of the people in it under the articles of the Geneva convention of war. Tell him that if he doesn't do it he will be held accountable as a war criminal when this is over."

"You should tell him this. You're the one he will listen to."

"I will never beg anything from any German," Caterina said.

Bombolini reluctantly talked to von Prum, and the captain went that same day to Montefalcone. He returned with most of the things that were needed. After that he came every day to help in the hospital. He was capable and quick, and he had no fear of blood, unlike Roberto and Bombolini. During that time von Prum and the Malatesta almost never exchanged a word that didn't have to do with the people they were treating. There was no outward sign at all that the captain was slipping into love.

It was the night after the bombing that the Roman cellar was turned into the air-raid shelter for the city of Santa Vittoria. It was decided that the people would take bedding and a few things to heat food in and that the city of Santa Vittoria would be moved into the Roman cellar at night, within breathing distance of their wine.

The afternoon before the move Bombolini went down with Sergeant Traub and Corporal Heinsick and Captain von Prum.

"It's a remarkable place," the captain said. "It could take direct blows from any airplane in the world and everyone would be safe. Why is it so large?"

"It is said that it was the collection point for all of the wine in the region," Bombolini said. "It all belonged to one man. I think it was Julius Caesar. Yes, that's who it was."

"It's a very peculiar shape," the captain said. "I wonder what was the need of that wall along there?"

Bombolini said that he didn't know.

The people started down that evening. They carried mattresses and straw mats and blankets and anything that anyone could lie on. It was a mass migration of lice and bedbugs probably not equaled in this part of the world before. They took down jugs of water, bread and bottles of wine and pots of cooked beans and baskets of onions. Longo started up the lights again, and by the pale dimming lights the false wall looked more natural than ever before.

At first the people were afraid to talk loudly, as if the vibration of their voices might cause a brick to pop loose. They were even afraid to look at the wall. But that passed. As the old Roman wine cellar became crowded with pots and pans and bedclothes and people, it ceased to be a wine cellar at all and became an air-raid shelter, run like some monstrous underground inn from the Dark Ages.

Other things helped. The captain did not come to the cellar but stayed in his room and worked on *Bloodless Victory*. Von Prum was given to questions and curiosity. His soldiers were given to drink. The Good Time Boys set them up in a running card game well away from the wall and in such a way that their backs were almost always toward it. Such precautions were not a waste of time. It was just this arrangement that saved the people from ruin the first time.

It began early in the evening. The bombs were heard by the river, giant strides of bombs, coming in the direction of Santa Vittoria. Several of the German soldiers stopped playing and went outside and came back again when the bombs came closer.

"These are the big ones," they called. "The Americans."

"Yes," Roberto said. "B-24s." It was his only slip in all his time in Santa Vittoria. They didn't hear him.

After that the bombs came louder and louder, and their force was stronger. They could feel the explosions then, through their feet, and dust began to fall from the arches above. The cellar was rumbling from the pressure of the explosions.

And then everyone seemed to see it at once—everyone except the

card players—and they were unable to take their eyes away from it. The bombs were dropping on the side of the mountain, and as they exploded the false wall began to swell and to puff out, and then all at once to sink back into place again until the next bomb landed.

Then there was one great explosion, the heaviest of them all, and this time the bricks swelled out so far from the rest of the wall that it seemed impossible not to hear the sound that was dreaded more than any in the world, the *snap*, the sound of the first brick springing out from its framework in the wall.

The next explosion was a little less and the one after that far less, and everyone waited and waited until finally there were no more sounds at all and it was over.

The next morning the people found that the mortar holding the bricks in place had shivered itself apart. If one man unknowingly had leaned against the wall, the entire structure would have come down on top of him and exposed the treasure. In the morning some of the men took a cartload of bricks down to the wine cellar and they rebuilt part of the wall twice as thick as before.

They learned something that day. When the bricklayers came back up from the field with the empty cart, Corporal Heinsick asked, "What did you do with the bricks?"

"Fixed something," one of the men said.

"That's good. It's always good to fix something."

The Germans weren't really interested in what the people did. They only cared about themselves. They didn't see the people of Santa Vittoria as people at all.

ON THE FIFTH DAY of October the wine began to explode. Not all at once—a bottle now, several a few minutes later, a long pause perhaps, and then a succession of explosions.

Something had gone wrong with the weather. In October it is dry, hot in the day and cool in the night. But the wind began to come from the southwest, hot and steaming and moist, and it settled on the city like a wet hot shawl. By afternoon the moist heat had worked its way down to the valley floor, and then the first of the bottles began to explode. The people could only guess that it was the result of some imbalance in the fermentation process caused by the hot moist air. The sound of the explosions, which carried across the terraces and up into the streets of the city, was a sickness and a terror in their hearts.

When they first heard it in the Piazza of the People, Bombolini felt that he knew what it was. Fabio and the Petrarch Brigade must have decided to fight.

Sergeant Traub came over. "What the hell is that?"

"From the rock quarry," Babbaluche said. "Kids shooting off blasting caps." Sergeant Traub seemed satisfied.

With the setting of the sun and the cooling of the day the explosions stopped and they felt safe, at least until the next day. But when the people came in from the terraces to settle in the cellar for the night the heat of their bodies was enough to cause the bottles to begin exploding again.

To most of the people, the only explanation for what took place is that a miracle occurred. On this night, as if stationed there by God, spread out along the floor of the wine cellar just in front of the false wall, were the families of Constanzia Muricatti and Alfredo del Purgatorio, who were preparing for the couple's marriage. The people were very gay and very loud because everyone was happy about this marriage.

When the first bottle exploded behind the false wall, the German soldiers turned from their card game. "What's going on back there?" Corporal Heinsick asked.

One of the Good Time Boys winked at him. "The celebration has begun," he said. "They're popping the corks. There will be some action in here tonight."

They sent wine to the soldiers, and a little later, when the music and dancing began, they knew they were safe. Bombolini ordered every musician in the city to play. There were tambourines, mandolins and an accordion; there were Capoferro's drums and the singing and the dancing and the clapping of hands. If you listened with your ear to the wall you might be able to hear a bottle explode now and then, but this was the only way it could be heard.

At nine o'clock that night the dancers, who had worked all day in the vineyards, grew tired and the wine was having its effect and the musicians wanted a rest. "Play," Bombolini ordered. "Dance. Sing," he told them.

"We can't go on," they said.

"You have to go on," the mayor told them. "The whole city is depending on you now."

At eleven o'clock, when they would normally have been asleep for hours, the dancing still continued. It went in shifts now, with fresh dancers every fifteen minutes or so. At midnight, while taking a walk in the Piazza of the People, Captain von Prum heard the noise and went down the mountain to see what it was. No one knows how long he might have watched from the entrance to the Great Room.

"They don't seem to be having much fun," the captain said.

"They're tired now, but they'll get a second wind, you'll see," Bombolini said. Pietrosanto and some of the others went quietly around to the back of the cellar and gave new orders.

"Get a smile on your faces," the people were told. "Get some spring into your steps. Start having fun and don't you dare forget it."

"Now, you see," Bombolini said to von Prum. "Now they're perking up. They can go all night."

And they did.

The dance, Bombolini explained to von Prum in the morning, was a tradition in Santa Vittoria. It might go on for days, he said.

"What happens to your work? You can't dance all night and all day and do your work."

"What does it matter about the work if it helps to create a beautiful marriage?" Bombolini said.

"The Italian mind," von Prum said. "You jump from realism to romanticism in the middle of one sentence."

"Oh, it's realistic," Bombolini said. "It keeps up our population. It grows future grape growers." And the German was forced to admit that there was a hard peasant wisdom behind it all.

And then began some of the hardest days and nights ever spent by the people of Santa Vittoria. As long as the city sat stewing in the heat wave, the party would have to continue, all the time, dancing at eight o'clock in the morning, singing and dancing in the heat of the day, wine flowing until people were sick of wine.

"One more night of joy and I shall go mad," Angela Bombolini said, and she was no different from all the rest.

"The gaiety has died down, the laughter has cooled," von Prum remarked on the fourth day of the wedding celebration.

"It's coming to the end now," Bombolini told him.

But it wasn't to be for another two days. The mandolin players wore pruning gloves and hit the strings with their knuckles. Several del Purgatorios had already had fights with Muricattis. If there had been a vote then, it is possible that the people might have surrendered the wine, anything to stop the wedding party.

Then one night the wind shifted, now coming into the mouth of the Great Room, and after that came the rain and the thunderclaps and the flashes of lightning. And then came a hard, cool wind with a hard, cold rain. In the morning they held the wedding of Constanzia Muricatti to Alfredo del Purgatorio. It was the most popular wedding ever held in our city.

"They are very sweet," von Prum said, "and very tired."

"Very tired," Bombolini said.

"Now you have no music? A week of music and just when they're married the music ends. It's just the opposite with us."

"Now is the time to sleep and to sleep and to sleep. There's no more need for music. The party is over, you see."

THE CITY STILL SLEPT when the Germans came, two cars of them, four Germans and four Italians in each car. The cars parked at The Rest and the men proceeded on foot. The Germans were all officers and looked as if they ate a great deal of meat. The Italians were all civilians, dressed in little thin dark suits stained with wine and pasta. Word had gone up the Corso Cavour to Captain von Prum, and by the time they arrived at the Fat Gate the captain was there to meet them. Colonel Scheer made no response to his greeting. He pointed to the Italians. "They say the wine is here."

"With all respect, sir, they can say what they wish, but I am forced to stand on my statement," Captain von Prum answered.

"It cost them a lot of teeth to say that and to stand by it," Colonel Scheer said, and he went across to one of the Italians and he forced open the man's mouth. His gums were torn and his teeth were gone. "We took them out one by one and he stayed with his story. I'm inclined to believe a man like that."

There was nothing for the captain to say.

"So I decided I had better come and see for myself." Scheer turned to the youngest of the Italians. "Show the captain the papers."

At first the young man was shy with Captain von Prum, but as the papers began to tell the story of the wine, he found courage in them and he grew excited by what they revealed. There were warehouse receipts showing bottle deliveries; there were bills of lading and transportation orders. In every case they told the same story. In some years the amount of wine ran as low as 800,000 bottles, but in good years it ran to a million bottles and even more. Because of the war, since deliveries had not been made the season before, it was safe to assume, the Italian said, that well over a million bottles, perhaps a million and a half bottles, could be found in Santa Vittoria.

Von Prum studied the papers carefully, and finally he faced Colonel Scheer. "There can be only one explanation," he said. "The papers are a fraud."

The Italian, who had grown arrogant now, answered for the colonel. "In order for these papers to be a fraud it would take hundreds of people to be involved in the deception. It would take people in the wineries, the warehouses, the railroads, the wholesale companies." It was apparent that he might have gone on for a long time. He was very convincing.

"Now they want to see the wine you have," Scheer said, and they started up the corso to the lane that turns off into the Cooperative Wine Cellar. Bombolini had been warned, and when von Prum saw him he told him to come along in case questions would need to be answered. When they could see the bottles in the cellar the Italians began to smile at one another. Bombolini tried to catch their eyes and shake his head, but he knew it was hopeless.

"It is what you would expect," one of them said. "There are two ways to put down wine. We will show you." They began to put down the bottles in the tight way, and when they had finished several rows it was clear that the cellar had been made to handle ten times the amount of wine that it now held.

"There is no need to go on," Colonel Scheer said, and he turned to von Prum. "The question being then, Captain, what happened to the rest of the wine?" He turned back to the young officers who were with him. "Get me a wop," he said. "From the town."

"There's one right here," von Prum said. "The mayor."

"Who could be better than the mayor?" the colonel said. "Come over here."

Bombolini was afraid and he tried not to show it. To his surprise, however, he found that he was not afraid for himself or what was about to happen to him, but only afraid that he might reveal something even against his wishes.

"We are not a cruel people," the colonel was saying to him. "If you are honest and generous with us you will find that we are honest and generous with you. Now then. Where is the wine?"

Bombolini held out both of his hands, palms upward. His eyes were as wide open as his mouth. "This is our wine."

Scheer raised his dark hard fist and struck the mayor in the mouth. "Where is the wine?"

When Bombolini held out his hands again the colonel hit his face once more, as hard as the first time, breaking his nose and breaking one tooth from the bridge of his mouth and causing him to fall on the stone floor of the wine cellar. The first blow had caused a lump the size of a pigeon's egg to form below Bombolini's eye, and the colonel touched it with the sandy tip of his boot.

"Now if you want to lose your eyesight to protect something that will be found out in the next few hours, I will oblige you with my boot," the colonel said. He turned on von Prum. "Don't turn away. Is this too crude for someone with such fine blood as yours?"

"It isn't that," the captain said. "It's the failure of what I wanted to do here. I wanted to rule without violence."

"This will not fail." Scheer slammed his hard fist into the palm of his other hand. "You'd be surprised how well it works."

"It wasn't the way I wanted to do it."

Scheer was angered by the statement. "You may think you're different, but you're one of us," he said. "You are a German. Those who can use the fist have a right to use the fist, they have a responsibility to use the fist if the fist can help the Fatherland. Who do you think you are?"

The colonel's anger and scorn were hard to take. The captain lowered his eyes and looked at the floor, not conscious of the mayor's body lying on it.

"Get him up and hit him," Colonel Scheer said. Several of the soldiers lifted Bombolini to his feet. He was in great pain, and yet he was pleased with himself. He had discovered that he would say nothing despite the pain.

"It isn't the hitting, Colonel. I can hit." Von Prum surprised them by pulling back his arm and smashing his fist into Bombolini's face. "I believe you now," Captain von Prum said. "The wine is here. I am humiliated. I ask one thing."

"Will you hit him again? Would you knock an eye out?"

"Yes," von Prum said.

"Then ask."

"I want a chance to restore my honor in my own way. I want to find the wine and bring it to you by myself."

"And if you don't?"

"I'll find it."

"I give you five days."

VON PRUM WAS CONFIDENT. Now that he had no doubt that the wine was in Santa Vittoria, he had no doubt that it could be found.

"It is a matter of reason and logic and science," the captain told his men. "I want no force and no violence."

The matter of violence had become important to him, because of the *Bloodless Victory*, and—something he was not prepared to consider then—because of Caterina Malatesta and the respect he wanted from her, and the love. He wanted to find the wine easily and gently, to touch the right place almost sadly and say, "The wine is here. I'm very sorry, it was a good effort but it wasn't quite enough."

Instead of beginning the search at once, in a haphazard fashion, the Germans sat down and made a detailed map of Santa Vittoria, which is still the best map available of the city, and it showed the sections where the wine might be hidden.

"It is a simple process of logical anticipation followed by logical elimination, which in the end will leave no other possibility except the place where the wine *must* be, and so, *will* be."

"Oh, we'll find it all right," Corporal Heinsick said. "If *they* hid it, sir, then *we'll* find it."

The first "logical anticipation" was the Roman wine cellar, as the most obvious and convenient place to put the wine, and it was the first to be eliminated. Sergeant Traub told the other soldiers, "Even these people are too smart to put their wine down there." And they went on to the second anticipation, which was that some stretch of the Fat Wall had been hollowed out and was being used as a massive container for the wine. In the morning they began going over the wall brick by brick, striking the sides with bayonets, listening for that hollow sound that would tell them the brick front was false and the wine was behind it. By the middle of the morning they were still not halfway around the city. When Heinsick suggested ways to speed up the process, they were rejected by von Prum.

"Carefulness is the keystone of our method here, Corporal. Thoroughness. Time is on our side, not on theirs. Each time we finish one area the remaining areas grow smaller. The noose draws tighter."

They were good words, and the soldiers liked them. *"The noose draws tighter."* It offered a satisfaction, even when the search revealed nothing. At each failure they inked out a section of the map, and it meant they were that much closer to the end.

When they were through with the Fat Wall, they began to investigate the possibility that the wine was in some fashion buried in the very bowels of the city, in some old storage place built in ancient days that could be reached by stairways and trapdoors in the floors and cellars of the old houses or through the church or the Palace of the People. So they began a systematic, door-by-door examination of every house in Santa Vittoria, starting in High Town.

The search of the houses took longer than they had thought, and von Prum began to urge them to go a little faster and a little faster, and the stop for lunch was only ten minutes long and they ate their supper while they worked. At night the people still went down the mountain and, since the evenings were becoming cool, it was comfortable in the Roman cellar. If they were quiet they could hear the sound of hammers on stone all the way down the mountain.

DURING THESE DAYS Bombolini slept. They had carried him up to his old bed in his old home above the wineshop, so that Angela Bombolini could take care of him. On the third day he was able to sit up and take some soup, and they made him a chicken soup in which an entire chicken had been used, a very great thing here. When he finally awoke for good, although he could not see because of the swelling of his face, everything seemed clear to him; all the answers were simple and clear. It was he, for example, who knew at once what must be done with The Band.

As the Germans neared the houses in Old Town, Pietrosanto came to him in terror. Pietro hung his head in shame. "I tried to kill them.

I had my rifle ready, and then I looked into those big stupid ox eyes of Francucci's, and I couldn't make my finger pull the trigger." Instead of killing them, he had hidden them in the cellar of one of the oldest houses by the wall at the bottom of Old Town. The Band had no idea of all the things that had taken place in Santa Vittoria under Bombolini.

"As soon as it is evening," Bombolini said, "put them in the cellar of Copa's old house. They'll be safe there. The Germans will never come back to High Town." Because of the systematic manner of the German search everyone always knew where they were going and where they had been. A criminal might have stayed one house ahead of them or one house behind and been perfectly safe all the while.

And when Fabio came down from the mountains, Bombolini knew what to do with him.

"This deed must be avenged," Fabio said. "The time for crawling has passed, the time to act is at hand."

Fabio had grown a beard in the mountains, and since it was the same deep black color as his hair, the beard against the long whiteness of his face made him look like a martyr.

Bombolini allowed his fingers to touch the swelling of his face and his tongue tipped his broken tooth.

"I agree with you, Fabio," he said. "The time to act has come."

A plan was made at once. The Petrarch Brigade—known as the Red Flames—would come down out of the mountains that night and gather in back of Copa's house. At two o'clock, at the sound of a goat, Pietrosanto and the other soldiers would join forces with them and prepare the assault on the enemy. Fabio was moved to tears. "You don't know how long I have waited for this," he said. "The hour has come when we will repay acts of dishonor with deeds of honor." Fabio then kissed Bombolini on both swollen cheeks.

It was Bombolini who began the silent evacuation of the city. They wrote down the names of all the people they felt could not keep their silence if the Germans turned to violence. These people would be allowed to work in the terraces but never to come up into the city. In the next two days they sent down almost all of the women and the old men and people like Fungo the idiot, and Capoferro because he was crazy, and Roberto Abruzzi because they were afraid he might cry out something in English if they tore out a fingernail. And because the Germans were the way they were, because they didn't really know what the people were doing, they never noticed the women gone, the children vanished, the old out of sight.

Because of what had happened to Bombolini there was a good feeling in the city about the prospects of physical violence.

"If *Bombolini* can take it, then *I* can take it," the men said.

Only Tufa, who said nothing aloud to all this, had no faith. "They don't know," he told Caterina Malatesta. "They don't know what's going to happen to them." He told her that they would send for the professionals, for the Gestapo or the SS secret police. "Then they all break," Tufa said. "No man can stand it."

"But Bombolini stood it," Caterina said.

"No, no, no, no. He stood *nothing*. After five minutes with the SS he will beg them to break his jaw or put out his eye if only they will stop what they are doing to him."

Caterina persuaded him to go to Bombolini and tell him. And what the mayor heard saddened him, because he had been feeling confident about himself and about his people.

"So there is no hope."

"There is no hope. They *all* break sooner or later."

And then Tufa was astonished and even angered to see that Bombolini, to the best of his ability, was trying to smile at him.

"I have some men who won't break," Bombolini said.

IT WAS ALMOST DAWN when Pietrosanto reported to Bombolini what they had done with Fabio and the rest of the Red Flames. They had led them to the cellar, the same one in which The Band was hidden, and they had bound and gagged the young men and put them in the darkness beneath the house.

"How did they take it?" Bombolini asked.

"They vowed to kill first you and then the Germans," Pietro said.

"Did you explain that it was for the wine?"

"I told them."

"And how did they react?"

"The same as a pig I once told that he'd be more help to everyone as bacon," Pietro said. "He didn't want to understand me."

Bombolini smiled his painful smile. "Well, I feel safer now," he said. "This was no time for valor."

"What gets into people like Fabio?" the head of the army said. "He knows this is no place for honor."

"In some ways Fabio wasn't raised right," Bombolini said.

THEY FINISHED THE SEARCH of the houses on the evening of the third day. "So much for *that*," Captain von Prum said. "Now the noose grows truly tight."

They had a good meal that night for the first time in several days, but the captain found that even though he was hungry he could not eat and although he was tired he could not sleep. He allowed himself a nap, and it was while lying on his bed, in between the worlds of sleep and waking, that he received the first of his inspirations. He got up very swiftly.

"Traub." He woke the sergeant. "Where else but the bell tower? The entire middle part of the tower could be filled with wine."

They crossed the piazza, moving swiftly and silently. Sergeant Traub pounded on the door and when the priest was slow in answering the knocks, Captain von Prum told the sergeant to shoot the lock off the door. He fired three shots in all, and then Padre Polenta opened the door.

"We should have looked here first," the captain told the priest.

Traub was already running up the steep stone stairs, but when he could see well enough all the way up the tower to where the bells hung and all the way down to where the captain stood, he came slowly back down and then the two men went out into the Piazza of the People and back across it to Constanzia's house.

"It was worth the effort," the captain said. They got out the map of the city and with a good deal of satisfaction they eliminated the campanile from the list of possible hiding places.

It was educational to the people of Santa Vittoria to watch what was happening to the captain. He became a lesson to them; and to this day, when a person runs about trying vainly to do the impossible they say that he is "doing a von Prum." They didn't understand it then, but his trouble was that he didn't know how to fail.

Von Prum changed in those five days. He didn't eat and he didn't sleep, he lost weight, and all at once the fine lines of his face appeared not fine but bony and old. Because his clothes had been tailored for him, when he lost weight the uniforms so tightly fitted before sagged on him. "If he lasts one more week," Constanzia Pietrosanto, who did his cooking, said, "he'll die of old age."

The people began to worry about him then. If under the pressure his mind were to break, they would be the ones to suffer for it. So they tried their best to calm him down and help him sleep and eat. If someone was fortunate enough to stumble on something good to eat he gave it to Constanzia to cook for him. She made him little dishes, the way one gets a child to eat, a fresh salad from the field, a trout from the Mad River, and then, since it was late October and the songbirds were flying south, the people netted tiny finches and nightingales and cooked them to a crisp in olive oil so the little bones would crunch in the mouth. He looked at the plate of finches and he cried for them.

"He's like a toy now that's been wound too tight," Babbaluche warned. "One more turn of the key and the spring will snap."

On the afternoon of the fifth day a messenger came from Montefalcone. There were two messages in all, and they are in the archives of the city. One was from his brother Klaus. It is not a letter at all, but a card, on the top of which, in black crayon in the hand of a child, is drawn a dark wing. The card said:

The angel of death calls me and I fly to her.
Good-bye, Sepp, my brother.

It is signed only "K."
The other was from the office of Colonel Scheer.

The hunting season is over. Bring in your pelts or bring in yourself by sundown tomorrow evening.

He read the messages several times, and then he put them in his files. After that he took the pages of the *Bloodless Victory* and ripped each one in pieces, one after another, and then he burned them, and after that he began to cry. He cried for his brother, but most of all he cried for himself, and everyone was frightened then because a man who cries is capable of any evil.

THAT SAME NIGHT, VON Prum left Constanzia's house and crossed the piazza to the wineshop and ran up the stairs to Bombolini's room, where he found him in bed, with his wife seated by his side.

"The game is over," von Prum said. "I did my best. I have played fairly. My hands are clean." He appeared to be relieved. "I want you to remember that I gave you your chance until the end, Captain Bombolini." It was the first time he had ever honored the mayor with his title. "Tomorrow the new team comes."

He turned then and went out of the room, and when he crossed the piazza his stride was strong and rapid. He seemed to be a new person. Perhaps an hour after that the sound of the motorcycle engine was heard and Captain von Prum left Santa Vittoria.

"It's time for me to get up," Bombolini said. "You had better leave, Rosa, before the captain comes back."

"No," Rosa Bombolini said. She began to help him with his clothes. His entire body was sore although only his face had taken the beating. She pointed at his face. "If you could take that I can take it."

"Do you care at all for me?" he said.

"No," she said. She was aware that she had hurt him.

"You couldn't bring yourself to say something good, something nice at a time like this?"

"Because your face looks like an ox stepped on it, does that mean I should care now?"

He sighed both at the effort of dressing and at her words, and he put his arm on her strong shoulder and told her that she would have to help him down the stairs.

"Well, did you ever—care?" It embarrassed him to continue. It was difficult to say the word. "Did you ever love me?"

"I don't know," Rosa said. "There was a time, I guess. Then you became a clown, and a woman can't love a clown."

"Not one like you," Bombolini said. They were in the room with the wine barrel now and he leaned on it and asked for a glass of wine. "So you don't think then, when this is done, providing of course that I am here, that you and I might, oh, come back to each other."

"No."

He was hurt once more. On a night such as this, he thought. He drank a second glass of wine.

"And what about her?" He pointed in the direction of Angela's room. As always, the wine made him feel better.

"She's going to marry the American."

"Roberto? Abruzzi?"

"Is there another one?"

Bombolini laughed, because it was so perfect a response. All of their life together she had done it, and he laughed because he knew the words she would say before she said them.

"He doesn't know it yet but he's beginning to fall for her," Rosa Bombolini told him. "I see to it that they're together."

Bombolini was angered by that. "You don't even know what kind of man he is," he said.

"He'll take her to America. What does it matter what kind of man he is, just so he takes her to America?"

"And Fabio. Have you ever considered that Fabio della Romagna is sick with love for your daughter and that he is a fine boy and that I have promised him anything he wants for saving my life?" He drank another entire glass of wine after that.

"Fabio is an Italian. As such he is no good for my daughter," Rosa said. "There is no Italian man who is good for a woman."

It made him laugh. "I don't feel so all alone then," he said.

"To feel like a king it is necessary for them to make the woman into an ox."

"I didn't do that to you."

"You tried," she said, "but you couldn't. I escaped."

Bombolini put down his glass. He had drunk enough. When he was at the door to the shop he turned back to her. "Tell me one thing," he said. "These past months. I did surprise you, didn't I?"

It made her smile, because it was true. "Yes, you surprised me."

"You know," he said, "that was the best thing you ever said to me."

VII

THE RAT IN THE THROAT

WHEN THEY CAME, THE four of them, von Prum and Traub and two young soldiers from the SS, Bombolini was alone in the Piazza of the People. They came on the motorcycle and in a small compact truck that held the SS men's equipment. Sergeant Traub stopped the motorcycle and Captain von Prum stepped out of the sidecar. As von Prum came across the piazza toward Bombolini, even the most unobservant among the people could see that some change had taken place in him. The age that had altered his face seemed to have passed, and his motions were slow and controlled; the stiffness that had caused him to move like an overwound toy was gone and with it the wildness about the eyes.

"So. You put everyone away this morning," Captain von Prum said. "Or did they run away?"

"No, sir. I hid them."

"The same as your wine."

"No, Captain."

"We'll soon find out." The captain started toward the Palace of the People, and Bombolini went along with him. "I'm going to use your place because it's bigger."

They stood in the doorway of the palace and examined the large dark room, and Bombolini could see von Prum's disapproving face.

"And because it's very filthy," the captain said. "They bleed and vomit, and all of the rest of it."

Bombolini understood that this would be his one opportunity to do what he had to do, and he seized the chance. "Which is why I have this one thing to ask of you," he said. "I don't want to have to be responsible for picking any man, so I told the people not to come into the piazza until after you had arrived."

"And? What about it?"

"The first one who comes into the piazza is the one who will have to taste it first. That way I don't have to have his blood on my head. And you don't have to choose, Captain. God will decide. Or fate."

"I would have said the devil, not God." But von Prum was smiling. The idea appealed to him. Sergeant Traub had come into the room followed by the two SS men. Bombolini was surprised to see how youthful they were. Von Prum then explained the situation to the one who appeared to be the leader.

"It makes no difference," the soldier said. "They all talk."

The two SS men were very young and very clean and strong. They weren't dressed the same as the other soldiers. Their uniforms were black with white piping. The darkness of their dress made their skins seem fairer, their eyes bluer, their blondness more striking.

They unloaded their equipment from the back of the truck, and in a very short time had set it up. The last piece was a wooden table—a narrow, thin plank of wood not much wider than an ironing board. At one side of this table was a portable generator to which they began attaching coils of wire with little metal clips that had rows of teeth like ferrets. On the other side was a smaller table on which rested pincers and pliers and various other tools of their trade.

"You're young but you know your business, you interrogators," Captain von Prum said.

"We like to think of ourselves as a truth squad," the younger one, Otto, said. "Going about the land uncovering truth."

They laughed. There was nothing solemn about them.

"Now hand me the rubber gloves, Hans," Otto said. He seemed to be the one in charge.

"I have a special treat for you, Captain Bombolini," von Prum said. "I am going to allow you to watch it all. *All* of it."

Bombolini went to the window and looked out into the piazza. It was still empty. By then there should have been some sign of Pietrosanto coming down the hill from High Town.

Captain von Prum was looking at the table of instruments. "Do you actually use these?" It seemed to be a stupid question.

"Not often," Hans said. "This does the job, you see." He pointed to the generator to which a magneto had been attached. As a test a wire was run from the magneto to the handle of a metal hammer to which the wire was clipped. He nudged the brass arm of the magneto, and there was a sputtering sound, and sparks began to shoot from the head of the hammer, and the hammer itself actually began to leap on the wooden table. "People do the same thing. And so they always tell the truth," Hans went on. "But we aren't allowed to take just one man's word. We have to do a second and a third. Sometimes we do five. Just to look good."

"Although one would be enough," Otto said.

"We'll do five." Captain von Prum turned to Bombolini. "Did you hear that?"

"If one will do . . ." the mayor began.

"I want five," von Prum said, wetting his lips. His voice was hard and cold.

"Where are they, sir?" Otto said. "We're ready for them."

There was no one in the piazza but Germans. Bombolini found that he was trembling and that he felt sick.

"All right," von Prum said. "We'll give fate a minute or two, and then we'll have to go and get someone."

"Just don't send us any heroes," Otto said to Bombolini. "It's boring, you know, these heroes. They come in with their jaws sealed together. Then we put the clamps on them and give them a little juice and all at once they want to talk. It's very sad actually."

"I will send you such cowards," Bombolini suddenly said, surprising even himself, "men who will tell you such lies you won't know what is true and what is false."

Traub had come from the piazza and he called in through the door. "Here comes one."

They went to the door and looked out at what fate had delivered to them. He had come down the steep hill from High Town and paused for a moment at the edge of the piazza. When he saw the German soldiers he made no effort to avoid them, but instead went directly toward them.

"A martyr. It's one of the martyr types," Hans said.

They watched the man say something to Corporal Heinsick and then the German brought the man to the terrace of the palace and pushed him inside. "He says he's glad to see us," Heinsick said. "I told him *we* were glad to see *him.*"

It was Giuliano Copa, the former mayor of Santa Vittoria. When he saw Captain von Prum he made a Fascist salute.

"Oh, God. *This* kind," Hans said. "The loyal, true Fascist." He turned to the others. "He was really for us all along, you see."

They laughed at Copa, and his eyes grew large with suspicion and with fear.

Then he saw the interrogation tools and he began to shout. "I am a loyal Fascist. A member of the party. There has been a mistake—"

"Quiet!" Hans suddenly yelled at him.

"I don't understand!" Copa said. He was brave. He was still in command of his voice, and his body gave no outward sign of fear.

Otto seized the top of Copa's shirt and in one sudden motion ripped it from his body. Then they placed Copa on the narrow wooden table and strapped him to it with leather straps. Otto leaned over him now. "We don't want to do this to you. It will be more terrible than you know. At the moment it begins you will want to die. But we won't let you die, and you don't want to die."

To Bombolini's horror he saw that Copa was nodding yes, yes to the German.

"Sometimes they tell us the truth before we ever touch them," Hans said to von Prum.

"Now," Otto was saying. He began attaching the wires to Copa's body. "We only want you to tell us the truth."

"Yes, I want to tell you the truth. Now," Copa said. "I'll tell you what you need to know."

Otto looked up at the captain with an embarrassed smile. "What was it we wanted to know?"

"About the wine. Where is the rest of the wine?"

He asked and Copa said that he didn't understand the question and that he didn't know what they were asking him, and it was the truth.

"Now?" Hans said. "Now," Otto said.

Otto made a movement with his finger on the magneto, a very slight movement with the brass handle, and at the same moment Copa came flying up from the table against the leather straps and after what seemed a long time, he released a terrible scream.

They were through with Giuliano Copa when there was no way to revive him, and it was the turn of Mazzola, another of The Band. A few minutes before, Pietro Pietrosanto and Vittorini had released Mazzola from the cellar in High Town, and he had gone down, as he thought, to meet with Copa in the piazza. So terrible was his suffering that Bombolini found that he was crying for the people who had been his enemies.

Bombolini had tried to tell himself that what was happening to these men was only what they deserved, that in one sense true justice was being carried out and that they had brought it upon themselves. But even as he convinced himself of it, he knew that what he was thinking was a lie, because he knew that what was happening to Copa and to Mazzola should never happen to any man.

The baker Francucci appeared next and they turned to him.

"If there was wine this one would have told us," Otto said to Captain von Prum.

Finally Hans said to von Prum, "Do you still insist the wine is here?"

"The wine is here," von Prum said. "But he's too brave. My God, some people are too brave for their own good." He went to the table and began to shout at the man. "What are you doing to yourself? You have no right to be this brave." He turned to Bombolini. "In the name of God, Bombolini, tell him to tell us."

Bombolini could only hold his hands palms upward and turn away.

"Do you *still* insist there is wine?" Hans asked von Prum.

"There is wine," he said.

The young SS men were damp with sweat and they were tired. One of them looked at von Prum. "Either there is no wine or we have failed."

"And we have never failed," the other said.

"What is there for lunch?"

"And we have never missed our lunch."

"I want my five," Captain von Prum said. "I *know* the wine is here."

"All right," Otto said. "You're going to *get* your five."

The two young soldiers glanced at one another, and it was meant to be seen by the captain. It was a form of contempt fitting for anyone who was not a member of the SS.

It was while they ate lunch that Bombolini learned that the Red Flames, who had been held in the cellar with The Band, had gotten out and were on their way down into the Piazza of the People. Fabio and Cavalcanti the Goat were the next ones taken in. Bombolini was unable to look at them.

"There is no dessert, eh?" said Hans.

"All right," Otto said. He got up and washed his hands in a bowl of water. "I suppose you two are also members of the Fascist Party. Would you like to show me your cards and medals first?"

"I am a citizen of the Italian nation," Fabio said.

Bombolini felt his heart try to break, and almost without his realizing it he came between Fabio and the Germans. "I want to volunteer myself in place of the boy," he said. "I want to save his life. He once saved mine."

"All that you have to do to save his life, Bombolini," von Prum said, "is to tell us where the wine is."

Bombolini looked at Fabio, who had by then been put on the table. He had lost weight in the mountains, and because of the darkness of his hair he seemed whiter than ever before and thin and weak and breakable. There was no sign of fear on Fabio's face, and yet it is not wrong to write that Fabio was trembling.

Bombolini's problem was a very simple one. He believed now that under the pain of the torture all men would break. If he told and spared Fabio the pain and the brutality that were waiting for him, Fabio would not forgive him nor would the people of the town. If he allowed Fabio to endure the pain and then to tell, Fabio could never live with himself again.

"Before you begin," Fabio said, "I have something to say to you." They stared at him in complete amazement. "You have no right to do this. This is a crime against people and you will someday pay for it."

They smiled then. They asked him his name.

"Fabio," he told them.

"Fabio," Otto said. "Meet Hans. Hans, Fabio. I am Otto. I will help you tell the truth for once in your life."

Bombolini found that he was weeping for Fabio's courage and that he was trembling and his body was bathed in sweat. They started Fabio much higher up on the magneto scale than they had the others. Bombolini wanted to die. He could see that von Prum was looking at Fabio as he had not looked at the others.

Fabio, of all of them, had been able to keep from shouting at first, but then he began to scream. "I'll tell you, I'll tell. Just stop it."

Perhaps it is true that Fabio wanted to tell them. He had tried to speak but could not. Finally they were forced to undo the straps and help him sit up. And perhaps, now that he had had a moment to discover himself again, he found that he would rather be dead than open his mouth to them.

Fabio said, "You have no right. What are you doing to me? And you," Fabio said to von Prum. "You are the worst of them because you know better."

"Put him down!" Hans shouted. "Put him back down."

There is no more sense and no more use in going on about Fabio. The SS men no longer believed in what they were doing. They advanced then on Cavalcanti the Goat, the one who cared only about stealing a night with some woman who could not resist him. Yet it was the Goat who, more than all of them, remained defiant and who suffered the worst for it. There is no need to say what happened to Cavalcanti, but there is need to mention the meaning of it. And the truth is this: If only one man among the rest will not break, as Fabio and then Cavalcanti did not break, then those who so despise men that they believe all men can be broken and all men can be bought, *those* are the ones who have failed and are defeated. So, no matter what else happens here, they have this reason at least to be proud.

Cavalcanti was taken and thrown along the wall with the others. "That ends it. Five of them." Hans and Otto moved with their usual swiftness. They were extremely tidy and neat in what they did.

"You understand what it means, sir," Hans said. "You have to accept it. There is no wine."

"No, there is no wine here," Otto said.

They had finished their packing and were putting a camouflaged tarpaulin over the equipment in the back of the truck when Caterina Malatesta came down from High Town to attend to the men in the room. The soldiers stopped when they saw her.

"Sometimes we make it six," Otto said.

"Not this one," the captain told them, and they looked at him with some surprise.

"Oh. Oh, I see," Otto said. He studied the Malatesta. "I don't blame you," he said. "You have nice taste."

They got into the truck and started the engine.

"So, you are vindicated then," Hans said. "You were right all along. The SS will vouch that there is no wine."

"Yes, I am vindicated," von Prum said. He watched them drive away, then went back to the Palace of the People and there was no sense of triumph or even of belief in him. The room smelled very bad. Caterina Malatesta was already at work, treating Fabio. Von Prum stood behind her for several minutes.

"I'm sorry about what happened here," he said. "We are at war and war has never been pretty."

She said nothing.

"I saved you from something," he said to her. "I expect you to remember that. It wasn't an easy thing to do."

When she still didn't answer he turned to leave; the smells were now too strong for him and he felt tired. Before he left, however, Cavalcanti motioned to him. It was a wild and thoughtless thing to do, but who can condemn Cavalcanti for it? His voice was low and the words came with difficulty, so Captain von Prum was forced to bend near Cavalcanti to hear him.

"I know where the wine is," Cavalcanti said. He smiled at the German through his distorted lips.

"You lie," von Prum said.

Cavalcanti shook his head and continued to smile. "You know I know where the wine is," he said.

"There is no wine!" von Prum shouted, and because he couldn't stand the sight of that smile, he kicked Cavalcanti's face with his boot. Then he turned and ran.

"For that he dies," Copa said. "For that one thing, of all the rest, he dies."

"No, no, no," Fabio said. "You don't undertand how we do things. For that he must live."

DESPITE WHAT HAD taken place the mood of the people was forgiving, for the hand of death had rested on the city and then it had been taken away. But more than that, it was because the harvest was closing upon them and it was a good harvest. There isn't the luxury of time to hate during harvest. The grapes demand attention, and they demand to be picked; the wine demands to be made, and the people are helpless before it because their blood has been bred over the centuries to heed it. So it wasn't that the people forgave the Germans, because they have never done that, but that, because of the harvest, no one cared any longer.

It was for this reason that, when Captain von Prum went down the mountain with Sergeant Traub to Montefalcone, some of the people actually waved to them as they went.

"I don't understand them," Sergeant Traub said. "They shouldn't act this way after what happened to them."

"It is a matter of values," von Prum said. "They are deficient in values. I've come to despise them."

Things had been changing in Montefalcone. Many of the units stationed in the city had pulled back to the higher mountains in the north, where it was said the Germans would attempt to establish a winter line that would be easy to defend. Captain von Prum reported to Colonel Scheer, and the colonel was pleased to see him. He pointed to a report on his desk.

"They clear you," Colonel Scheer said. "They vindicate you."

"But that's what I came to see you about," von Prum said. "I am still convinced the wine is in the city."

"Don't be a fool," Colonel Scheer said. "The SS says there is no wine, there is no wine. The file is closed, von Prum is exonerated."

"But if it's there, I want to find it."

"Why?" The colonel was sarcastic then. "Your honor? Duty? A matter of principle, perhaps. What do we care about the wine, just so we aren't held responsible for it."

"Because," Captain von Prum said, "if the wine is there they're laughing at me. Bombolini is laughing at me."

Colonel Scheer looked at his junior officer. "And so, as we say where I come from, you have a rat in your throat."

"If you wish to put it that way."

"And what would you do with the wine if you found it? It's too late for us to do anything with it. We couldn't steal it if we wanted to."

Von Prum's voice was loud and for the moment he lost the poise that the colonel had admired in him. "I'd smash it," he said. "If we couldn't take it from there, I'd break every bottle it was in my power to break."

Scheer smiled at him. "Then what you have to do—and never say that I suggested it—is to take a hostage. Put the hostage on view in the public piazza so that he is never out of their minds. You put his life on the conscience of the people. There's a very simple choice for them. If they tell you what you want to know, the hostage lives. If they don't, he dies and by their silence they have killed him."

The captain was conscious that his heart was beating swiftly at the prospect of what was ahead. He asked the colonel for written permission to choose a hostage in Santa Vittoria.

"My very dear von Prum," Scheer said. "It's your honor you're trying to salvage, not mine."

"Does it work?"

"Almost every time," Colonel Scheer said. "Of course in case we lose the war, just in case, understand"—he began to smile again—"you might have to justify what you've done."

"I understand that, sir. It's a risk I'm prepared to run."

Von Prum wished to go right then, but the colonel held him and they talked of the progress of the war, although von Prum could barely hear him. That was another war, which no longer belonged to him; his own was being waged within himself and with some people on a mountain.

At the door the colonel held him again. "Try and get someone with a good family life," he said. "You will find that it is especially difficult for children to stand and watch their fathers die before them, all for the sake of a few words. And von Prum?"

"Yes."

"You didn't say it, Captain."

Von Prum came to attention. "Heil Hitler," he said.

"Heil Hitler," Scheer said.

The captain could hear the colonel laughing when he was at the motorcycle, and it ceased only when Sergeant Traub started up the engine.

There was never any doubt who the hostage would be. When they reached Santa Vittoria Captain von Prum turned to Sergeant Traub.

"Go now," he said, "and get me the one called Tufa."

THEY TIED HIM TO the tail of the dolphin that swims down one side of the Fountain of the Pissing Turtle soon after the sun was up, to allow the people to see him on their way to work. There was no need to announce the reason for his being tied up. At first the people didn't want to leave the piazza, but it was Tufa who ordered them to go down to the grapes, and in a way the people were gratified, because the harvest was upon them and the pull of the grapes was strong.

Bombolini did what could be done. He hid Tufa's mother so that no one could find her and so that she couldn't go to von Prum to save her son, and then he went to see Caterina Malatesta.

"I don't believe that I have to worry about you," Bombolini said.

"I have only one question. Why was it Carlo? Why not someone else? Why not a Pietrosanto with fifty members in his family?"

"I don't believe I have to worry about you," Bombolini said again. She nodded.

"That's why Carlo Tufa," he said.

The soldiers were decent about Tufa. They didn't believe there was wine, and they recognized Tufa as one of their own kind. They gave him cigarettes from Spain and oranges from Portugal. They set up a canvas roof in the daytime to shield him from the sun. There is something strange about looking at a young man in good health who you know will be dead the next day. You watch him because you watch yourself. But there was nothing to be seen in Tufa. He gave no sign of being worried. One thing alone bothered him, and it was

Caterina. "Where is she?" he asked Bombolini. "Why doesn't she come to see me?"

The mayor had no answer for him.

"I never told her the story," Tufa said. He motioned with his head to the fountain above them. "Sometime when I'm gone I want you to tell her the story and tell her that I asked you to tell it to her."

"I'll tell her, Carlo," Bombolini said, and he kissed Tufa on one cheek and then the other.

During the whole of that day it was possible at almost any time to see the figure of Captain von Prum through the windows of Constanzia's house. He would work over his letters and his logs for several minutes at a time, and then he would be drawn once more to the window.

At times he found comfort in a line Nietzsche wrote and which he quoted in his notes and log that day, that in the long haul of history one life was worth nothing.

It was this line Bombolini had once chosen to answer. "Then that is the difference between us," he had said. "To us nothing is worth one life."

It is not easy even now for people to believe that the city slept that night. But Bombolini slept, and they put a straw pallet down on the cobblestones and Tufa slept, and the people looking from the windows around the piazza began to go to sleep. Across the piazza the captain was awake and, although he had gotten ready to go to bed, he got up again and, for a reason he could not explain, dressed himself. His intuition was good, because at the time he was dressing, Caterina Malatesta was coming down from High Town.

She carried her shoes in her hand so she would make no noise, and she stayed in the shadows of the houses. The old women and old men who stay at the windows at night because for them sleep doesn't come must have seen her moving along in the darkness, but they said nothing. When she was across the piazza from the fountain she attempted to see Tufa, but it was too dark for that. At the door to Constanzia's house she put on her shoes—they were shoes from the city, with heels, and not made for here—and when she was ready she scratched on the wood of the door with her fingernails.

In the manner of such things, the captain knew at once what the sound meant. He was pleased that Traub was not in the outer room where he often slept, but was in the piazza guarding the hostage. Before he went to let her in, the captain lit a second tallow candle which he put before a mirror so that it gave off a warm good light, and then he went to the door.

He realized that ever since he had first heard the word "hostage" in Montefalcone, without ever admitting it he had been preparing for this moment. But even so, he was unprepared for her beauty. In the books and stories it says that men are made breathless by the great beauty of a woman, and in this case it was as the books say. He was overpowered by it. She had spent the day in the classic way of great beauties, in warm baths, in oils. She had washed her hair and brushed it so often that the light reflected from it, and she had dressed in the kind of dress no other woman has ever worn here because no other woman would know how to buy one or how to wear one, or would ever have the money to own one.

When he had dreamed of this moment he had dreamed that he would surrender, but that in surrendering, as it should be with any good soldier, the price would come high. He knew that what he was doing would in some way, perhaps a serious way, damage him; and yet he also knew that in the end he couldn't care about that.

"So you've come as I said you would come," von Prum said.

"Not in the way you said," Caterina replied.

"No. Not from the snow or the rain or the cold. But you came. That's what is important. None of *them* came."

"None of them had anything to offer you."

"They could have brought me the answer to the secret."

"There is no answer."

He smiled at her. "You too, eh? No, it's because they know that after he dies, in a month or two they will have forgotten, because they know that in a month or two they themselves would be forgotten. They have souls of leather. I don't say that in disrespect."

"And we? We have souls of what?"

"I don't know if we have souls. Maybe that's why we put such an importance on living and dying."

The conversation was not going the way he had heard it in his mind before this night, and he didn't like it. It was Caterina who was wise enough to redirect it. "Have you any wine?" she asked.

345

He looked at her with genuine pleasure and went into the other room. "What do you have to offer?" he said when he came back with glasses and some brandy.

"Myself," Caterina said.

He allowed the brandy to work in him before he spoke again.

"Do you really think that is enough for what I will have to do?"

"Yes, I will be enough for you."

He looked away from her, because when he watched her the things he wanted to say were weakened by her. She had taken off her scarf and a dark outer coat she had chosen to wear, and she came across the room toward him.

"Where do you stay?" Caterina asked. He motioned with his head in the direction of his room and she went past him and into the room, where she began to undress. He came to the door and stood in the entrance. She moved with the assurance of those who are beautiful in their bodies and as if he were not there. When she was halfway through undressing she asked for more brandy and she drank it.

"As long as we're doing this," she said, "there is no reason why it should be unpleasant."

When he was beside her he began to tremble.

"That won't do," Caterina said. "Why are you trembling?"

"Because you're what I have wanted all my life," von Prum said, which was the moment of his surrender.

"Then we understand," the Malatesta said. "It is me for him."

"Yes."

"You won't regret it."

"No, I won't regret it. But I will have to take another hostage," he said. "You understand that."

"That isn't what I came for," she said.

Caterina woke him before dawn because he had asked her to wake him then, before the people were up, and he got dressed and went out into the darkness to the fountain and woke Sergeant Traub. Tufa was awake, lying on his back, looking up into the night.

"Take the ropes off him," von Prum said. "He's going free."

It pleased Traub. He turned to Tufa. "You heard him?"

"Yes," Tufa said. "I don't know whether to thank someone or despise someone."

It was still dark when Tufa crossed the piazza and started up to

High Town. There was no Caterina Malatesta waiting for him, of course. When he reached the house some of the people were already up, and he asked them about her, but none of them would answer. It was a long time, a day or two at least, before anyone in Santa Vittoria found enough heart to tell him.

WHEN DAWN CAME AND it was found that Tufa had been freed, there was fear in Santa Vittoria. But when it was found that the wine was safe, the fear became joy. The town learned about the Malatesta and the contract she had made and the people approved of it. It was a very good bargain.

"She can always bring her body back when it's all over," Babbaluche said. "It's more than Tufa would have been able to do."

But as the morning wore on, a new consideration occurred to some of the people and the joy died. "Now someone else has to die in Tufa's place," Pietrosanto said. And everyone knew it was true.

By afternoon, work on the terraces had almost come to a stop. Everyone was preparing for someone else's death and praying to God that it wouldn't end up being his own. By evening the city was in such a state that Bombolini was forced to speak to Captain von Prum. He was surprised to be invited inside Constanzia's house.

"I'm sorry to have to bother you on this day," Bombolini began, and he was embarrassed. He had almost said on your wedding day. He told the captain about the state of the city. "If you must have a hostage, and it is a very bad idea, the people want you to pick one. Until you do the entire city is condemned. We have been tortured enough."

The German smiled. "There never really was any other choice from the start," he said. "I had always thought of you, Bombolini."

During all of this time it had never once entered Bombolini's mind that he would be the hostage.

"No," he said. "That wouldn't be a good idea. The city would lose a good leader." It was a simple fact.

"And who would you suggest then?" von Prum asked.

Bombolini could hear Caterina moving in the other room and wondered if she was listening. He wondered if it had occurred to her that the next death would belong to her.

"I think the only way to do it is the way we did it before," Bombolini said. "Take it out of our hands and put it in God's hands. Let Him make the choice."

"The first one in the piazza?"

"No, I have in mind something different. A lottery." He could see that the idea appealed to the captain. "Put the names of all the people in a wine barrel and then let the priest draw out the name."

"You might call it a lottery of death," von Prum said.

They said the words over in their minds—a lottery of death. There was an excitement to the words.

"Would the priest involve himself in something like this?"

"Oh, yes," the mayor said. "This is God's work now. No matter who puts his hand into the barrel it will be God who chooses the winner."

The German called to Caterina in the next room. "And what if Tufa is picked by God this time? What would you do then?"

"Then I'd threaten to leave you."

Von Prum smiled, and to his own surprise Bombolini found that he was smiling also.

Before Bombolini left they drew up the rules for the lottery. The honor of dying would belong to all men between the ages of sixteen and sixty, the same ages that the Italian government in the north of Italy had set for the conscription of soldiers.

"When?"

"The drawing must be held tomorrow morning so the people will be able to go to work," Bombolini said.

And so it was agreed.

When the mayor was at the door Caterina called to him and he went back inside and stood at the door of her room.

"Does he know yet?" she said to him. "How does he seem?"

Bombolini told her that he was tired and confused, but that he didn't know.

"Do you think he will understand?" Caterina asked, and Bombolini was surprised by her question.

"You know Tufa. You know how he is made," Bombolini said.

"I couldn't let him die when I had a way to save him."

"It doesn't matter," the mayor said. "You put the horns on his head. To buy his life, you sold his honor."

"He knows I love him."

"It doesn't matter," Bombolini said. "You broke the rules."

BEFORE AN HOUR HAD PASSED, Bombolini had called a meeting of the Grand Council, and they met in Santa Maria of the Burning Oven, going in through the side doors one at a time so as not to attract any attention. They gathered to pick the winner of the lottery.

"I don't like to say this, because I admire you, Bombolini," one of the older men said, "but at a time like this, doesn't honor require that the leader make himself available to his people?"

Bombolini was gratified when the members of the council voted the idea down before he had to answer. It is not easy to turn down the role of martyr when it is offered to you.

It was surprising, the number of people the Grand Council felt were qualified to die for the city and the wine.

"Take Enrico R——," one of them said. "He has no friends, he has no land, he doesn't owe anyone money. He's got no real reason to live. I'm sure he would be glad to do this for us."

"You forget," another member of the council said, "Enrico happens to be married to my sister. She wouldn't let him do it."

They started down the list of names in Padre Polenta's record book, one by one. For a time they thought they had found the right man, the perfect winner of the lottery, in N.

No one liked N., and N., as far as anyone knew, liked no one in return. His own family despised him. If N. were selected, his own family would hold a celebration. "The beauty of N.," Bombolini said, "is that, bad as he is, he is a man of courage."

"And a miser," Pietro Pietrosanto said. "He will die with a smile on his lips before he gives those bastards one bottle of his wine."

But it was pointed out that N. was also related by blood to fifty-six people in Santa Vittoria, and some of them were a little crazy. It was impossible to tell when one of them might have some kind of religious vision or other symptom of madness and go to the Germans to save N.'s life if not his soul.

At the end of it all, one name came up again and again.

"But who has the courage to face him?" someone asked. "And what if he refuses, as I know he will?"

The delegation, when it was finally formed, consisted of Bombolini, Vittorini as a representative of tradition, Roberto Abruzzi as a representative of the outside world, Angelo Pietrosanto as a representative of the youth of Santa Vittoria, and Pietro Pietrosanto as a member of the military. They met before Vittorini's house in the Corso Cavour and started down to Babbaluche's house to ask the cobbler if he would be good enough to agree to win the lottery of death and die the next day for the people of Santa Vittoria.

They stood outside his door for a long time. No one wanted to knock or be the first to go inside. In the end it was the Captain of the People who had to do it. Such is the price of leadership.

Babbaluche was smart—as smart as some of the cocks here who always know when you are coming to get them and manage to die of old age on the rooftops before they see the inside of a pot. The moment the door opened he knew why they had come.

"You've come to tell me something," the cobbler said. "I only hope it's good news."

Bombolini made the error of looking down at his shoes at that moment, and as if the movement were a magnet drawing the others with it, every other head went down. "There is going to be a lottery tomorrow," the mayor managed to mumble.

"And you want me to serve on the committee," Babbaluche said. There was a long deep silence. They could hear Babbaluche's wife breathing in the next room, and the stomach of his ass, whom he kept with him in the house, rumbling.

"It's a strange lottery, eh?" Babbaluche said. His voice was hard and cold. "All the losers are winners and the winner is a loser."

The silence again.

"I know what you want," Babbaluche said after that. "You want me to pick the name, because I'm the one who has no reason to protect anyone. I hate them all."

"Something like that," Roberto said.

"Or is it the other way around?" Babbaluche said. "There's no reason to protect the cobbler, because they all hate him?"

No one could take his eyes away from the pieces of leather scattered all over the floor. If for no other reason than for the words he said next, forgetting all the other things he did for them, the people of the city would have to honor Bombolini.

"Babba," the mayor said, "we have chosen you because we think that you can do it best."

You must someday hear a peacock scream at the dawn to know the sounds that came from the cobbler's throat. The screams of defiance and wild joy and bitterness came, not once, but over and over again. It was the finest joke of all his life.

"It would be an act for all of Italy," Vittorini said, and the peacock screamed again. His wife and children came to the door of the room and he motioned them away.

"Where was all of Italy when they were doing this to me?" he shouted at them. He tapped his crippled legs. He had been the first in the city to be mutilated by the Fascists. A few Blackshirts from Montefalcone had come into the Piazza of the People and had seized him and in view of the people they had broken his legs one after the other. Since then Babbaluche had been a shame for Santa Vittoria to carry on its bent back.

"Let's go," Angelo Pietrosanto said. "We've made a mistake."

But the cobbler wouldn't let them go that easily. "Tell me," he said, "give me five good reasons why I should die for all of you?"

They tried to say things about love of country and of neighbor and brother, and the words were so much sawdust in their mouths. How is it possible to tell a man who has purged himself of love that in the end he should die for it? They began to back away and make the motions of leaving then.

"Sometimes the only decent thing a man can do is to die," Roberto said. He wanted to tell the cobbler that he knew, that he had tried it once. He knew that if he closed his eyes he would see the bombs and the running people and the burning town. Perhaps there was something in his voice that made itself heard to the cobbler.

"Now you are saying something," Babbaluche said. "Aren't you ashamed of yourselves, leaving it to an outsider to say something?"

"We know that you are going to die soon, Signor Babbaluche," Roberto said. "You know it as well. That is why we came to you."

"And that's just it," Babbaluche answered. "I am old and sick. I want to die my own way. I don't want to give them the satisfaction of killing me." We could hear his wife and her two daughters moaning and crying in the next room.

Roberto didn't know what to say because his mind doesn't work in the right ways for this place, but Bombolini knew what to say after that. "But that *is* just it, Babba." His voice was triumphant now. "When they kill you, you cheat them. They demand a life and we give them a corpse."

351

And the cobbler began to laugh, from the stomach and not from the throat the way he had done before.

"You make fools of them," Bombolini said.

Now everyone was excited. It was the ancient thing here, something for nothing all over again, this time turned inside out.

"You make them do what God would do next week, and they must *pay* for it," Vittorini said.

Babbaluche told them to keep God out of it.

"Will you tell them? Will you make sure that they know?"

"No," Bombolini said. "Absolutely not. They must carry the shame and guilt of Babbaluche the cobbler around in their minds and in their hearts until the day comes for them to die."

The cobbler actually tried a little leap in the air. "Italo, you are marvelous!" he shouted. "You are so clever."

Then he was sad. As bright as he had been, the light had gone from him, and they could all read at once that death was indeed already sitting inside his body, waiting. "But they'll know," he said. "They'll take one look at me and know."

Bombolini had thought of that. "We're going to paint your face so you look fresh and healthy. We'll put walnuts in your cheeks to make them bulge. We'll stuff things under your shirt to make you look fat."

The cobbler was brightening again. "Italo," he said, "we should have been friends. We could have done terrible things together."

Bombolini shrugged. "I was a clown and you didn't like clowns."

"But I should have seen through your mask."

"Yes, but I was a clever clown and so I wore a clever mask."

They made the plans for the morning, which was by then not too far away. As few as possible should know, so that when the name was picked from the wine barrel it would come as a shock to the people. They thought at first that every name in the barrel should read "Babbaluche," but realized that would be a dangerous thing to do in case any German put his hand into the barrel. It was decided to put all the names into the barrel and to have Padre Polenta hold Babbaluche's name in the sleeve of his cassock.

"But would the priest do such a thing?" Roberto asked. They looked at him as if he were crazy.

"Have you ever known a priest to lose at cards?" Babbaluche said.

The others left then, all except Bombolini, to start making a list of all the names and to set up the wine barrel in the Piazza of the People and to send Angela Bombolini down to paint the cobbler's face.

"Oh, I look forward to this," Babbaluche said. "My last trick on life, my death." The two men smiled at each other.

"Do you know what is even better?" Bombolini said. "Do you know what will happen over this? You will become a martyr. You will become a hero—the story will go all over Italy—the little cobbler who died for the secret of the wine."

Babbaluche laughed. "Oh, if only I could be here to see it."

"You can't have it both ways, Babba," Bombolini said.

"It's the one problem of being a martyr. You never know for certain if they put you in the book."

"We'll put up a plaque to you, Babba: 'Santa Vittoria. The city where Babbaluche the cobbler surrendered his life for his people.' " The mayor was quite excited then. "Perhaps we won't have to make this a shrine for bakers after all. People might come here to see the home of the heroic cobbler."

"You might make it a shrine for cobblers. That would be better yet. Put a statue up with a halo on my head."

They sat for a time enjoying the wonderful joke. The cobbler got a bottle of grappa and they shared it, drinking for a time in silence. Because they had both had nothing to eat for a long time they got a little drunk very easily.

"You know," Babbaluche said, "I *am* going to die tomorrow. In the joke I forget that sometimes." He looked around the room. "Think. All of those years of work and pain and sickness, all the hopes I had as a young man, and this—this—this is the end. Isn't that strange?"

After that, Babbaluche said something that was truly strange for him, and many people wonder if he really ever said it.

He said that he was afraid, not of death, but of not being remembered. And then he told about the thing that had impressed him most in his life. He had once been able to go to Venice, and when he was there he saw a bridge on which there hung a blue light. An innocent man had been hanged from the bridge and ever after that time the people had kept the light lit in his memory and his honor and in payment for their mistake.

"I want you to put a light, a green light, in the Piazza of the People for the mistake of my life," Babbaluche said. "I want this under it:

So That All Should Learn
In memory of the cobbler Babbaluche
He lived his life wrong but had the
good fortune to die his death right.
What a waste of a life!

"Now get out of here," Babbaluche said. "I'm tired and sick and a little drunk, and I have a great deal of acting to do tomorrow. When will Angela come to make up my face?"

"Just before dawn. The lottery is at dawn."

"Two or three hours of sleep. It's a funny thing to need sleep in order to die. But, of course, I have to be fresh for my death."

Bombolini couldn't bring himself to smile at a joke like that. At the doorway he held the handle for a moment and then turned back to Babbaluche. He was very serious. "Babbaluche?"

"What is it?"

"Make me one promise," the mayor said. "Promise me not to die on us tonight."

The cobbler was shocked and his face showed it. "What? And spoil a good joke?"

Bombolini could hear him laughing even when he reached the top of the corso. Although it was still dark, he could see that the wine barrel was already standing there.

An hour before the sun came up Rosa Bombolini went down to Babbaluche's house and woke him from his drunken sleep.

"I thought Angela was coming," the cobbler complained. "At least I could have that on my last day."

"You get me," Rosa said.

She rouged his sunken yellow cheeks and darkened his eyebrows and brushed his hair. She used wax from the top of wine kegs to pad out his cheeks and old sweaters under his shirt to hide the bones of his chest and back. When he peered in the mirror he was pleased. He must have looked something like this years before.

"You know, I wasn't bad looking," Babbaluche said. "It's fortunate for you you didn't know me then."

"I knew you," Rosa Bombolini said. "You weren't so much."

He looked at her with admiration. "If it weren't for you, Rosa Bombolini, I would lose all faith in life."

"You still have one day to do it in," she said.

"Anyone else would have said, 'That's right, Babba, you were a pretty gay dog, God's gift to women.' But not you. That would be asking too much with still a whole day to go." He shook his head.

"You're like the rest. I don't care if you're going to die tomorrow or ten years from now. Why should I have to lie for you?"

"All right," Babbaluche said. "I'm not so much. I begin to have an idea of what hell must be like, and it frightens me."

He had to lean on her in order to get up to the piazza, and when they arrived almost all of Santa Vittoria was already there, even though it still was dark. All eyes were on the wine barrel. Sergeant Traub was going through the names and he was satisfied that most of the eligible men were represented.

Padre Polenta came across the piazza and he made the sign of the cross over the people as he came. A young man began to stir the names in the barrel with a long stick.

Captain von Prum had decided it would be wiser if he wasn't present, so Sergeant Traub took charge. "Let's get this over with," he said to the priest.

"This is a terrible thing to ask a priest to do," Polenta said.

"I didn't ask you to do it. I'm only a soldier. I carry out orders. My hands are clean. Pick the name."

Capoferro began to beat a slow march on his drum, and then Polenta's arm went up in the air and suddenly dipped down into the barrel. Capoferro rolled the drum louder as the priest swirled his hand around inside the wood. The people strained forward. And then the arm came back out of the barrel and the drumming stopped and the priest held up the paper. The silence was broken by a blast on wild old Capoferro's horn.

The priest looked at the paper as if he could not believe what he read on it, and he passed it to Bombolini, who in turn passed it along to the sergeant. Sergeant Traub looked at it one way and then the other and he checked the pronunciation of the name with Bombolini and after that came to full attention.

Babbaluche.

It is strange how in a crowd, a mob even, the people always know where to look. The ones around the cobbler turned toward him first, and then all the others turned and then they began to back away from him, as if by being close they might be included in his fate or as if death might be catching.

"No," Babbaluche cried. "It can't be me. They don't want me. You have read it wrong."

The sergeant gave the paper to someone in the crowd, and it was passed along, from person to person, until the cobbler held it in his hand and read his own name. There was a scream—it was his wife— and then there were the cries of his two daughters, and they fell to the stones; they grabbed the sergeant and pleaded with him, they attacked Padre Polenta and demanded that he intercede with Captain von Prum and with God Himself. After that, they were taken out of the piazza and put away so no one could find them and they could find no one. They led Babbaluche then to the Fountain of the Pissing Turtle and they tied him to the dolphin in the place where Tufa had been tied.

From Constanzia's house the captain could see what was taking place in the piazza.

"Did you have to do it?" Caterina asked him.

"I had to do it."

"Thank God it's an older man," she said.

"He isn't dead yet. If he chooses to talk, he has life." The captain suddenly turned on her. "If you choose to talk he will live. He's there only because of you."

It was not a good night for the people of Santa Vittoria. Now that Babbaluche was going to die, the people began to know that they would miss him. He lived that night on grappa, since he could keep nothing else down.

"I wouldn't do that; you're going to have a terrible hangover," Traub said to him.

"Yes, but what a cure I have," Babbaluche told him. "A little drastic, but complete."

Padre Polenta came and asked him if he could bless him, that it might be a form of fire insurance, but the cobbler wouldn't allow it.

"If God personally shows me a miracle between tonight and tomorrow morning I'll let you sprinkle holy water on my head."

"But there are hundreds of millions of people. God can't show each one a miracle. He'd run out of ideas."

"Oh you of little faith," Babbaluche said.

They came and got him even before the sun was up the next morning. They took the rope off and asked him if he would like to go down in a cart or on a donkey's back, but he told them he would rather limp along.

The Germans were in their parade uniforms. They wore their tunics and steel helmets. At a few minutes after five the procession marched out of the Piazza of the People, the soldiers going ahead, Babbaluche limping along behind them, followed by Bombolini, Vittorini in his dazzling white uniform, and Capoferro behind them tapping on his goatskin drum.

No one planned what happened, but if there is ever another execution here we will do it this way. The people had lined themselves up all the way down the Corso Cavour, and as Babbaluche started down they reached out to touch him and say good-bye, to catch his eye for a last time, and he smiled at them and waved back.

They came through the Fat Gate and started toward the rock quarry, which was their destination. If one must be shot, the rock quarry is a good place for it. The pit is in the shape of a horseshoe, and there was room for all the people. They tied the cobbler to the stake they had put up for Tufa and stepped back from it. Capoferro ceased his drumming, and the only sound then was of the crunching of the Germans' hobnailed boots on the loose shale. Sergeant Traub asked if he wanted a blindfold.

"I'm entitled to all the sun I can get," the cobbler told him. "It warms me and I'm going to need it."

The sergeant stepped forward then and took out a card and read from that in Italian.

"You are here provided one last chance to preserve your life. Answer one question only in return for it. Where is the wine?"

Babbaluche made no sound. He began to smile at Traub, and some of the people began to smile also, until the whole city was smiling.

"You have the right to say something," Traub said.

The soldiers had leveled their rifles at the cobbler and he began to smile once more.

"Why do you laugh?" Traub asked. "This is a serious business."

"The rifles," Babbaluche said. "Those six little black eyes looking for my heart." He gazed at us. "They know," he said, "I don't have one."

Traub looked at his watch.

"Take the cork clapper off the bell," Babbaluche said. "Give Scara-faggio back their sound."

Then it was done. The shots were fired and the noise was enormous, and then the cobbler was leaning forward against the ropes of the stake. The smoke rose from the ends of the rifles and the people were very silent. The silence was in its manner as enormous as the firing had been, and so the sergeant ordered his men to reload at once, and they formed a close rank and turned and started out of the rock pit as fast as they could march without seeming to run from us.

"Long live Babbaluche," Bombolini shouted.

"Long live Babbaluche," the people of the city shouted.

We carried the body out of the rock pit and back up the goat path to the burying ground. Babbaluche's wife and children were there, but they had done their crying and now they were silent.

"How did he go?" the wife asked.

"Fine," Bombolini said. "He went just like Babbaluche."

The people turned away then and went back out of the burying ground. Captain von Prum was there. His face was flushed and it was clear that he had been running, since his breathing was hard and his words came in gasps.

"I tried to stop it," the captain said. "I ran all the way."

They only looked at him, and some of them looked away.

"I wanted to stop it. I made up my mind it was wrong."

They started to walk past him then.

"I ran all the way. I ran as hard as I could go. I have a bad leg, too, you understand."

Bombolini alone of them stayed behind with von Prum. In the background he could hear the priest praying.

"Do you know Machiavelli?" Bombolini asked.

"Yes. We've talked about that."

"Do you know what he said? He said—and pay attention—'It is well that when the act accuses you, the result excuses you.' "

He started toward the city again, and the German came along behind him. Bombolini wanted to tell him another one, that to an unjust government a martyr is more dangerous than a rebel, but then he decided the German would have to find that out for himself.

When they came into the Corso Cavour the bell began to ring. They had not changed the clapper, but someone was beating the side of the bell with a metal hammer and it occurred to Bombolini how clear and pure the tone was, and he knew that Babbaluche was right, as Babbaluche had been all morning.

VIII

THE TRIUMPH OF SANTA VITTORIA

AFTER THAT THE WHOLE spirit changed. The people were the way Babbaluche had been with Sergeant Traub the morning of his death; there was nothing left the Germans could do to them. Even if they found the wine, the people knew and the Germans understood that they would be killed. It was possible that if they found the wine they would say nothing about it at all.

The people no longer saw them or heard them. The soldiers spent all of their time in the wine cellar, playing cards among themselves and drinking and trying to apologize with their eyes.

It didn't matter. The people wouldn't allow them to apologize and that is a terrible thing to do to men.

Besides, there were the grapes, and the harvest was upon them.

There is *one* moment only—known by men like Old Vines—when it is right to begin to pick the grapes, and when that moment is reached nothing else exists for Santa Vittoria. Everyone who can move goes down to the terraces and cuts the fat grapes free from the vines and puts them in the baskets, which are carried to the carts and taken up the mountain to the wine presses. The liquid runs clear and with no taste to it, into the great oak barrels. On the third day the liquid begins to "storm," and the process of fermentation has begun. And when the storm is over, in a week or ten days, depending on the quality of the grapes, Old Vines will dip his glass into the barrel and hold it to the sun, and at that moment everyone will know what the entire year has meant, whether they will go hungry in the winter ahead or eat when the snows come.

In the early days everyone works. Bombolini goes down to the terraces and sweats. Vittorini goes down. This year, for example, Roberto, although his leg pained him, worked with Rosa and Angela and the Casamassima family from dawn until dark. He liked working by Angela's side, sweating together in the October sun, walking up the mountain together in the coolness of the evening. Once, next to her in the darkness of the leaves, he put his hands on her hips and then around her waist and kissed her on the back of the neck.

"You shouldn't do that," she said. "The boy who does that to the girl here means he wants to marry her." He told her that maybe he would marry her but she said no and pointed to her bare feet. "Americans don't marry girls with bare feet. Besides, what would I do there? I only know how to pick grapes."

"Do you know how to go to the movies?"

"Yes."

"You could go to the movies all day."

"No, I wouldn't like that. I like to pick the grapes."

"I was joking with you. They do more than that in America. You think about it."

There was excitement on the terraces. No one could remember heavier grapes or fatter clusters. The wine was plentiful, and if it was good too, it could be the finest year in the memory of any person in Santa Vittoria. There was excitement, but there was a humor too, since as the new wine began to run, a hundred thousand gallons down the wooden spillways, the answer to the first part of the secret, whether there was wine or not, was being spilled out in front of the Germans, and they were unable to see it, because they had no eyes for the wine.

When the harvest was almost over, Bombolini decided on a daring thing. He went across the Piazza of the People and invited Captain von Prum and the soldiers to share in the harvest festival.

"It's a very great honor," Caterina said.

"The greatest we have," the mayor added.

So Captain von Prum, in his soldiers' name, accepted the offer.

"Some of the traditions are a little strange and I hope you understand that," the mayor said. "It would dishonor the people if you didn't go along. We're very strong on our traditions."

Captain von Prum promised to obey.

THE WINE IN THE first of the barrels stopped storming on the fifth day. All of the grapes except the ones that would be used for the traditional wine pressing had already been picked.

On the ninth day Old Vines dipped his wine taster into one of the barrels, and the wine he drew out was almost clear.

"Get ready," he ordered. "I taste the wine in the morning."

It is hard to put down what goes on here then. Three men were sent off to get Lorenzo the Magnificent, Lorenzo the Wine Presser, and bring him back with them. Three more were sent to a neighboring town, San Marco della Rocca, to the prison to get the band that always plays for us in return for a small barrel of new wine. Others went to get Marotta the Blaster, who would set off the fireworks with his son.

"Get to bed, go to sleep," all the mothers shouted; but it is almost a law here that no child sleeps the night before the festival. The old ladies, whose job it is, began to get out the straw hats for the oxen and the mules and to go pick flowers that they make into chains to hang around the beasts' necks. The young girls work on their hair and dresses, and the older ones try to make the traditional costumes respectable for one more time. The men do almost nothing. They scrape the mud and the manure from their boots and feet, and get out their black suits, those who own them, and they stand about and talk about the wine, over and over, endlessly, never tiring of it. They talk about whether it will be thin or fat, sharp or round, heavy or light, and whether it will have the true bouquet of the fruit, and most important, whether the wine this year will have the true *frizzantino*—the thing that makes the needles jump on the tongue.

It began, the day of the festival, in the darkness of the morning at a few minutes past four o'clock. It didn't begin in the sense that a day usually begins, by degrees, a little at a time; it began all at once. It erupted; the day exploded.

A child ran into the Piazza of the People. "Here they come," he shouted. "I saw them. They're at the Fat Gate now."

And right after that they were heard coming up the Corso Cavour as if they were trumpeting through a megaphone. The San Marco Penitentiary Thieves and Guards Brass Band, good men, reliable men, who must have walked the whole dark night through until there they were, at the Fat Gate, blowing their lungs and hearts out. By the time they got to the piazza there were a thousand people gathered there to shout a welcome to them.

Eight men in all, eight in green and gold uniforms, eight good musicians, some of the finest thieves and bravest guards in all of Italy. Five thieves and three guards: one piccolo, one trombone, one clarinet, two trumpets, cymbals, one bass drum, who would be supported by our own Capoferro, and the leader, the maestro Stompinetti, the Rock of San Marco.

Bombolini welcomed them to the city of Santa Vittoria.

"I heard you were mayor. I couldn't believe it," Stompinetti said.

"The best we ever had," Pietro Pietrosanto added.

"Ah, well, I've heard crazier than that," the Rock said. "God bless the mayor, God bless the people, God bless the wine."

The people were preparing to file into the church, when there was a command in German from Constanzia's house, and then a second, and finally the German soldiers began to file out into the piazza, lined up in rows of two. On a command from Captain von Prum they began to march in the direction of the church.

They were dressed in their parade uniforms. The leather on their wide black belts was polished as was the leather of their boots, and the silver buckles shone. They carried their rifles slung over the shoulder and wore their metal helmets. The Germans were impressive. At the church door Bombolini welcomed them as guests of honor at the festival.

"Wait until the Resistance gets their hands on this Bombolini," Stompinetti said. "What kind of an Italian is this?"

"Just wait," the people near him said. "He knows what he's doing."

Polenta began the Mass of the Grapes and he made it brief. It was his belief that if God wanted to come down and bless the grapes and wine He would come down whether the people spent an hour on their knees or ten minutes. The Mass was over in fifteen minutes.

On the way out of the church they could see the statue of Santa Maria resting in the back of a large open cart, hung with clusters of red and white grapes, entwined with vines and dressed with thousands of grape leaves which fluttered in the early morning wind. And which soon, Padre Polenta hoped, would be further dressed with lire.

"The spirit of the harvest," Bombolini explained to von Prum.

"We honor it," the German said.

At the foot of the church steps a large black wooden coffin was placed on two wine barrels.

"The first of our traditions," the mayor said. "It holds the corpse of the old year gone by. We destroy the old year and in that way give birth to the new that lies ahead. Would you and your men care to act as honor guard?"

"We should be glad to."

From the church door there is a wire which runs down the steps and through an opening into the coffin. For reasons no longer remembered, a white dove is attached to the wire and then sent skidding down into the black box. When the bird goes through the opening it trips another wire, which sets off a bag of explosive powder, which in turn explodes the coffin. The Germans had stationed themselves alongside the box, three soldiers on each side, von Prum and his noncommissioned officers a little in front of it.

"The old is dead," Padre Polenta said from the top of the church steps. "The new"—and the dove began to skid down the wire, tied to it upside down by its pink feet—"is born."

The noise is raspy and sometimes the dove cries out, but it made no sound this year. The explosion, however, was as loud and complete as ever. Pieces of the coffin went straight up into the air and others flew out in all directions into the piazza. The smoke was so dense that from the center of the piazza it became impossible to see the front of Santa Maria. When it did clear the people could see the Germans, all nine of them, face down on the piazza stones. There was a great cheer then, an enormous cheer, because this officially opens the festival. Some of the people ran to help the soldiers to their feet and tried to brush the manure off their uniforms, but without much success. Bombolini said something to the captain and he smiled and patted him on the back, but nobody was able to hear what he said because of the roaring in their ears.

In the center of the piazza, near the fountain, a platform had been built in the night and on it stood the first of the wine barrels, and by the barrel stood Old Vines. Padre Polenta said a prayer and then a young girl, all white in her Communion dress, took a copper pitcher and turned the barrel tap and filled the pitcher with wine, and when it was full she handed it to Old Vines. There was no sound at all in Santa Vittoria. Even the animals, who exist by the wine as much as the people do, seem to know enough to be silent. He held the pitcher in the air and then he began to pour the new wine into a large crystal wineglass which he then raised over his head.

"It is *vino nero,*" Old Vines called out. "Good and black." There was a roar from the crowd, but not a great one. It was a good sign, but not enough.

Now he lifts the glass to his lips and the people push forward, because they demand not only to see it but to hear the wine washing around in his mouth and being kissed by his tongue and lips, and then he spits it out and no one moves.

They knew it was good. He could not hide the look that began to spread out on his red face. The question now was, how good?

"*Frizzantino!*" the old man shouted. And then there was the roar, the true roar, almost as great as the one that had greeted Bombolini so many months before. "The wine is alive," he shouted. "It dances. The needles on the tongue."

"Give us, give us!" the people shouted, reaching for the glass.

"It is a good wine," he said. The first of the desirable categories.

"It is a great wine." The cheering grew louder. They waited for the third category, which is almost never awarded.

"It is a wine too good for men to drink," Old Vines told them. He was holding the glass up to the gods that only he recognized.

"We have grown a wine fit for the saints."

No one cheered then; it was a moment for reverence, it had gone beyond cheering.

Now the oldest of each family comes forward with a pitcher and the wine is taken back to the family and sipped and tasted and then drunk by all, from the oldest down to the youngest. The San Marco brass band broke into a gay mountain song and the time for reverence was past, and the uproar began in the piazza.

"Now comes a real treat," Bombolini shouted into von Prum's ear. "No outsiders have ever done this before. You are going to be allowed to help carry the statue of Santa Maria."

Three teams of eight men each carry the statue, and it is considered an honor to be chosen. It is not a heavy statue, but the distance is long, around the Piazza of the People, down the Corso Cavour through the Fat Gate and across the terraces. Polenta, in the lead, blesses the doorways and the windows and on the terraces he blesses the vines. And when the day is hot it can prove to be work fit only for the strong. To many, carrying the statue is a kind of penance. It was as if they were saying to God, "I sweat for You, You sweat for me." It is also one of the ugliest statues in all of Italy and possibly the world. It was made of wax and cheap paint and plaster a hundred years ago in Montefalcone, and when a team of men left here to get it, on the way back they stopped in a roadside inn for some wine and left the statue out in the sun and the rain and it melted and turned black. When the people saw it they were horrified.

"No, no," the men who had carried it said. "It was a miracle. This must be the way Santa Maria really looked, all black and roasted. It was God's wish."

To this very day the city is divided between those who think Santa Maria's melting was a miracle and those who think the melting was a simple case of drunkenness, stupidity, lying and criminal neglect. It was also hollow, whether by design or by deceit is not known.

The first team carried the statue around the piazza and down the corso, and the people pinned lire to the statue and left food in her arms and in the cart that came along behind.

At the Fat Gate a second team took over the statue and it went down to the terraces. Most of the men were older men, some as old as sixty, but they held the statue high and went at a good pace. Young girls were picking the last of the grapes, and the German soldiers, getting into the spirit of things, helped them fill the baskets.

"You had better take it easy," Pietrosanto warned them. "You're going to be next with the statue."

"If those old men can carry it, we can carry it," Heinsick told him.

"They know how to do it. It's harder than it looks," Bombolini said.

"With one hand," one of the soldiers said. "One hand."

In the center of the terraces the statue was set down on the cart and the men and women and the soldiers walked through the vine-yards for the blessing of the vines. When the prayers were done and they came back, Bombolini asked Captain von Prum if his men were ready to accept the honor of carrying the statue.

"We have been looking forward to it," von Prum said, and the people applauded. They lifted it up easily and put it on their shoulders and they started back toward the Fat Gate at a good pace. Sergeant Traub counted the cadence even though he was one of the men under the statue.

"One two three four, one two three four"—in German, loud and clear and strong. It went very well then for at least a hundred steps, but after that Traub ceased to count, and then the steps slowed a little and the band, following behind the statue, had to play a little slower. Soon some of the people, even older men, began to go past the men carrying the statue.

"What's the matter with you?" von Prum called to them. "Keep it moving. Pick up the step."

For a short time after that they were able to pick up the step and Traub began to count again. But then it seemed to be too much for them once more and the step slowed and finally, still a long way from the Fat Gate, it became a kind of clump.

"Pick it up," von Prum said. "You're disgracing yourselves."

It didn't work this time, however. The pace remained the same.

"I think we should relieve you now," Pietrosanto said.

The captain wouldn't consider it.

"It's these uniforms, sir," Corporal Heinsick said. "They're strangling us." His face was the color of the *vino nero*, a deep rich red.

"The first man to drop out receives a summary court-martial," von Prum said, in a low voice that only his men were meant to hear.

It is true that if the desire to live were enough, no man, for example, would ever drown. But there comes a time when the body can no longer do even what it deeply desires. The Germans' legs were quivering, and it was only a matter of a few more steps before at least one of the sixteen legs would quiver too much and go under, which is what happened. For one moment they stopped and teetered, they started to go backward and held themselves and they ran forward a step or two, and there was a second at least when they came within a foot of plunging down into the terraces with Santa Maria on their backs.

"The sacred statue," Bombolini shouted. "In the name of God, hold it."

The old women began to cry out. They shouted to the Mother of God to reach down and save Santa Maria, and in the end the Germans held, although their eyes were bulging.

"Who did it?" von Prum shouted.

"Me, sir," one of the soldiers said. "I can't go on."

"Get out then," the captain said, and he pulled the soldier away and took his place beneath the statue. "It's not so heavy. What's wrong with you men? I know what it is, too much drinking."

He was a tonic to them, for five steps. A man with a bad leg such as Captain von Prum possessed should never allow himself to get under a statue. Since his legs were not even, at every second step the statue would shift slightly and rest on his shoulder and it was as if an iron bar were pressing down on him. "You are doing fine," Bombolini shouted in his ear. "Only four hundred more steps to go."

At those words Captain von Prum, for at least the second time in Santa Vittoria, looked into the face of failure. But the Germans did not go down without a great fight.

"All right," von Prum shouted at them. "We are going to go *up*. At the count of three, we step off again. One, two, three, *step*," he called out. "*Step. . . . Step. . . . Step.*"

One of the soldiers, each time the captain called out *step*, answered, "I die, I die, I die."

"Only three hundred and fifty more, Captain," Bombolini called.

No one could say why they stopped. "*Step*," the captain called out, and no one took a step. They stood where they were, and the statue shook with the effort simply to keep it from falling.

Six young men then—it was important to Bombolini that there were six and not eight—eased the poles off the Germans' shoulders and not one of them made a protest, not even Captain von Prum, and they slung the statue on their shoulders and started up toward the Fat Gate at a fast pace.

The Germans fell where they had stood, sprawled out in the white dust of the path. They were still that way when Lorenzo the Magnificent, the one who was to press the grapes in the old way, came up the mountain with the men who had gone to get him.

Lorenzo is mad. By his own admission he is mad, but he is also, as his name says, magnificent. There is no man in the world who does not recognize that Lorenzo is something very special and is not afraid of him or impressed by him. He is like a steel coil, his body and his mind drawn so fine and hard that if he ever breaks, pieces of himself will fly all over Italy.

"What's the matter with those bastards lying in the dust?" he said.

"Quiet. They're Germans," one of the men said.

"I can see that. All I asked was why they're lying there like pigs."

When Lorenzo got up to the Piazza of the People, the statue of Santa Maria, which had been carried by nine or ten different groups by then, was being placed up on the platform on which Old Vines had first tasted the wine that morning. And when they were sure that none of the Germans had managed to recover and come back inside the Fat Gate, they took out the great boulder that had been put in the saint's belly and dropped it in a cart and took it away so that it would never be seen again. After that, they carried Santa Maria back into the dimness of the church, where Polenta began to strip her of the lire that had honored her. She had served her people well.

FOR THE GERMANS THE day seemed to have ended, but the festival was only beginning. There was the noon meal of cold cooked beans and raw onions spread on fresh bread and the new wine washing it down. After lunch the people slept, except for those who still had business to do. Longo and a crew of men were converting the Fountain of the Pissing Turtle so that it would run with wine that evening. Marotta and his son were preparing the fireworks display, and Lorenzo, with some of the young men, was putting up the enormous barrel in which the last of the grapes would be pressed.

At four o'clock the fountain began to run with wine and when the men cheered, the people began to wake up and come back into the piazza. When the first of the Germans, Captain von Prum and Sergeant Traub, came back up into the Piazza of the People, Lorenzo the Magnificent Wine Presser was standing knee-deep in the grapes. Marotta fired a Roman candle out over the people's heads, and as the little colored balls of flame began to hit the walls and drop among them, Stompinetti broke into the "Wine Presser's Song" and the festival was underway once more.

It is a strange song, a slow dance, since wine pressing is hard and heavy work. The trampling of the grapes must be done in a slow rhythm, in a swaying movement that goes back and forth and side to side. There is a genius to everything in the world and Lorenzo was this way with the grapes. He knows how to make people use themselves to take from the grapes all that God put in them.

He began the dance as he always did, with his own woman, a Gypsy who looks as if she had spent one life already as a wolf, and when she was tired, he began to point at people in the crowd and they would come up and get into the barrel and begin to dance with Lorenzo. There is no turning away when you are summoned to the press. It would insult the wine and it would insult Lorenzo, neither of whom must be insulted. Anything is allowed to Lorenzo. The women hold up their skirts and show their legs and even their thighs, and Lorenzo holds them by the hands and by the arms and around their waists.

He doesn't dress the way other men do. He wears very tight pants, like a bullfighter's, that stop at the knee. His chest is covered only by a vest that is decorated with silver and gold threads, and his arms and his chest are as hard as bone. But it is his face and his eyes that people watch. As the dance continues, Lorenzo becomes possessed by the motion of it, and finally he is mad and at the same moment under control. He doesn't seem like one of the people then; he is superior to them. There is no end to his energy, he can dance on and on, because, as they say, he isn't human then, he is an animal and a god.

"You," he points, and the woman comes and he seizes her by the wrist and they begin to move to the music. He dances with a woman until she surrenders herself completely, and he can move her to the left or right or in any way he wishes her to go by a flicker of the eye, a breath, the touch of a finger. She belongs to Lorenzo then, and when she does he discards her.

The same goes for the men. It is a challenge with the men, and he never loses. He dances not until the man surrenders, but until the man can go on no longer. Then, when the moment is right, Lorenzo flings the man aside and the people shout and jeer at the victim, and he goes on to the next. He had been dancing for almost an hour when he motioned for Angela Bombolini to come into the press. When she raised her skirts, the men applauded her legs, and it surprised Bombolini. Why should they cheer the legs of a little girl? he thought.

It was a good battle. At first Angela danced with Lorenzo but not for him, and her face was innocence, but there was the moment— and everyone knew exactly when it took place—when the face of innocence was replaced by something else and Angela began to dance for Lorenzo and the barrier that had been between them was broken.

"She's no virgin now," a woman shouted. Bombolini turned to look at her.

"It's no use, Italo. He's making love to her with his eyes," a man said, and when Bombolini turned away because it was too much for a father to see, he saw Roberto at the side of the wine press, gripping the wooden staves and staring at Angela in amazement and anger. He knew what Roberto was going to do, and he held him back.

"Don't get in there, Roberto," he whispered in his ear. "You can't get in until you are invited."

"But he's . . . he's . . ."

"I know that," Bombolini said. "It's what happens here. Do you think it's any easier for the father to watch?"

There was a shout from the crowd. He had released her; he had taken his fill of Angela, the surrender was total, the victory complete. She stood among the grapes as another woman came up into the press, and when the world began to come back to her, she shook her head as if she had come back from a long sleep, and still unsteady she began to wade through the grapes to the side of the press.

"Angela," Roberto said. He held up his arms to help her out of the barrel, but she didn't see him. Instead, she climbed over the side of the barrel and down onto the cobblestones, her bare feet dripping with the juice of the grapes, and went past his arms and into those of Fabio della Romagna. No one except Roberto and Bombolini saw them, because there was something greater to watch. Captain von Prum had come out of the doorway of Constanzia's house. He had washed himself and changed into a fresh uniform, and he looked like the captain once more. Behind him in the doorway was Caterina Malatesta, and Lorenzo saw her and made a motion with his head.

"Stay where you are," von Prum said. "I don't want you to go."

"I have to go. He's seen me. It would insult the wine."

"I don't want you to go," the German said; but there was no way to stop her and he knew it. She started across the piazza and it grew quiet. Everyone could see at once that it would be a battle.

There is no way to describe the dancing of Lorenzo and the Malatesta. Her legs are long and very strong and her feet narrow, and this is good for the grapes. He had clapped his hand around her wrist with force, and it was understood that he would not let go until he had won. And he did win because in the end he wanted her more than the Malatesta wished to deny him.

"You are good," the Malatesta said. "You win."

"I am truly great," Lorenzo said.

He helped her to the side of the press and lifted her over it. It was the greatest honor he ever gave to anyone in Santa Vittoria. He was tired after that, because it had not been easy for him. He wanted to rest, but the German was in the wine press.

"Try me," von Prum said. "Dance with me."

"I'm tired now."

"Try me," he ordered.

Lorenzo shrugged his shoulders. "Take off your boots," he said. "You bruise the grapes."

Von Prum took off his boots and his socks and shirt, and the women near the press said "Aaah" at the smooth whiteness of his arms and chest. He was not a weak man, but against Lorenzo's hard darkness he seemed like a child pitted against a man.

"You needn't hold my wrist," von Prum said.

"I need to," Lorenzo told him. "You won't know how to move in the grapes." His fingers locked on the German's wrist.

They began to dance.

Caterina didn't wish to see it, to watch him being humiliated in front of the people. But it was something else, also, as if she knew that Tufa would be waiting for her in Constanzia's house. She went back to it and he was there, in the darkness of the room, when she entered. Even in the darkness she could see the wildness of his eyes.

"If you're going to do something to me I want you to do it at once, without talking," Caterina said to him. He held a knife in his hand.

"And so you gave yourself to him too," Tufa said. "In front of the entire city."

"All women give themselves to Lorenzo. I'm no different."

He crossed the room and stood at the entrance to the small bedroom. "And this is where you sleep with him," Tufa said. His voice held anger and disgust.

"What do you want to do with me?" Caterina asked.

There was laughter coming from the piazza, and she knew they were laughing at the captain. Tufa had gone into the room and he was prodding the bed with the toe of his shoe. What do you say to him?" He came back toward her. "Maybe sometimes you forget and call him Carlo, eh? Do you ever do that?"

She had turned away. "Do what you have to do, Carlo. If you have to use the knife, use the knife, but in the name of God, do it."

It angered him. "You're so damn brave, Caterina, so above us," Tufa said. "Do you know what they do here when a woman dishonors her man? Do you know what they do with their knives?"

She turned back toward Tufa. "They cut them," she said. "So they can't dishonor again."

"Yes," Tufa said. "It's very ugly and very effective."

She decided to try. "I didn't dishonor you," Caterina said. "I came here because I honor your life."

"You stole my honor from me," he shouted at her. "Who do you think you are, to take what is *mine?*"

The knife entered her stomach. The pain was not as bad as she had thought it would be, and the feeling she had above all others was relief that it was over. She knew also that she would live.

All of Tufa's anger was gone. He pointed to the wound.

"Every man you give yourself to will know why that was done," Tufa said. "They'll hate you for it."

"No, some man will love me for it," the Malatesta said.

"I'm sorry I had to do that, Caterina, but it was something that had to be done."

"I understand," she said. "Don't apologize to me." There was a great deal of blood from the wound, but she was unwilling to tend to it until he was gone.

"I have my honor back," Tufa said. He went to the doorway. The people were making a great deal of noise, and it would be a good time for him to go. "You were brave, but I have my honor back."

"Go," she said. "For God's sake go."

"I'm sorry," Tufa said. "But it had to be done."

It was necessary to stop the bleeding then, and she went into the bedroom and took the bed sheet, and when she came back he was still there. "What do you want of me?" she shouted.

He said her name. It was an effort for him, and he couldn't say what he wanted, but at that moment she understood.

"I see," she said. "You want me to forgive you. People who do such things shouldn't ask for forgiveness, but I forgive you, Tufa."

When he was gone she stopped the flow of blood and then she found her medicine bag. The cut was clean, and she was able to sew it with the good gut provided by the German army and to bandage it with the good bandages provided by them as well. When she had changed her clothes, she went to the doorway to look into the piazza and was pleased to find that her legs trembled no more than when she had climbed out of the wine press.

It was growing dark but she could see Lorenzo and von Prum still dancing. If Lorenzo had allowed the German to drop, he would have dropped down into the grapes, but Lorenzo held the German in his arms and danced him. It was ugly to watch the way he did it, making a puppet of a human being.

"All right, I want to sit now," the German said. "I want to rest." But Lorenzo didn't want him to sit or to rest; he wanted him when he let him go to drop in the grapes and to lie in them and not be able to get up. A short time after the Malatesta came to the door of Constanzia's house, Lorenzo let him go and von Prum fell face forward onto the grapes. The German tried to get up, but each time he did so, the grapes gave way and shifted beneath him and he fell again and again, until he could no longer make even the effort to rise.

"Turn him over," Bombolini called to Lorenzo. "He'll drown."

"Let him drown," people shouted. "Let him drown."

Lorenzo reached down and turned the German over, because even Lorenzo, who doesn't come from here, knew the town couldn't afford to have people drown in their wine. The fireworks began to go off then, and had von Prum been able to open his eyes from his bed of grapes he could have seen the first of the rockets soar up out of Santa Vittoria. Then the dancing started, but even over the sound of the band and the voices, Bombolini could hear guns sounding in the south. Something very big was underway.

THE DANCING ENDED AT two o'clock in the morning and the Germans came at five. These were, as Pietrosanto said, the real Germans, hard, bearded men from the Hermann Goering Parachute Division and they were running for their lives. They never looked at the people. In little half-tracks they moved through them with the assurance of men who knew that if so much as one shot was fired at them by some Resistance fighter, they would burn the town to the ground. They ran along the top of the Fat Wall and they studied the countryside from the bell tower and from the houses that faced the valley, and finally three or four of the highest officers gathered in the Piazza of the People and compared what they had found.

"It's no good," one of the officers said, and the others agreed.

"What's the name of that place?" a German asked Vittorini. He pointed across the valley toward Scarafaggio.

"Scarafaggio," Vittorini replied "It has a good command of the Montefalcone highway."

"Yes, Scarafaggio is the place you want to fight in," Bombolini said to them.

The German looked at them as if they were a circus animal act. "Shut your *mouths*," he said. "Who is in command here?"

"Do you mean the Italian in command or the German?" Bombolini asked.

"Italian?" the officer said. "Italian?" His rage was so swift and so genuine that Pietro Pietrosanto for a moment was certain he would kill Bombolini on the spot.

They led the officer across the piazza and they pointed toward Constanzia's house. What happened after that was unfair to Captain von Prum. They found him in bed with Caterina Malatesta. They pulled him out of the bed, his hair mottled with wine, his body dyed purple with it. He was too stunned and too sick to protect himself.

"This is the garbage we leave behind to run things while we fight," the parachute officer said. He slapped Captain von Prum in the face and there was nothing the captain could do but stand in the room and look at the floor. "Where are the rest of your men?"

"I don't know," von Prum said.

The officer seized von Prum by the nose and pulled his head to the left and the right. "He doesn't know," he said. "He doesn't know." He stepped away and kicked von Prum in the groin, and the captain went down to the floor.

"You make me sick," the officer said. "Consider yourself under arrest." He told the captain that when they stabilized the line at San Pierno von Prum was to report to him there for disposition of his case after he had withdrawn his men and equipment from Santa Vittoria. The captain tried to get up from the floor.

"Stay down," the officer shouted at him. "Don't rise. You aren't permitted to stand with men. What is your name?"

"Mollendorf," von Prum said. "Captain Hans Mollendorf." One of the younger officers wrote down the name.

"This is the kind of scum who is destroying us," the parachute officer said. They left then, and within ten minutes all of them were in the Corso Cavour and going back down the mountain.

The people helped the soldiers who were left collect their helmets and tunics and personal things and carry them up the corso to the Piazza of the People. Von Prum was already there, putting his things into the back of the truck and into the sidecar of the motorcycle. He moved very slowly; he was in pain and he was confused. He ordered them to load his cabinet of files, but when they had difficulty getting it into the truck, they put it down in the piazza and forgot about it.

"What about this?" Bombolini asked. It was the air-raid siren.

"You can keep that," Sergeant Traub said.

"Once each year we'll sound it and think back on these days."

Some of the soldiers were already in the back of the small truck, crowded among their packs, hunched on the hard wooden seats. Vittorini came up into the piazza then and stood next to Bombolini, dressed in the uniform with the sword drawn and the Italian flag suspended from its blade.

It was very quiet in the piazza. The people had always dreamed that the day they left would be a day of great celebration, but it was not. Captain von Prum came back from the motorcycle. For a moment it looked as if he was getting into the sidecar and that it was time to go, but he had stopped and come back toward Bombolini.

"You did this to me," Captain von Prum said to Bombolini.

"Whatever was done was done inside of you. We did nothing here," the mayor replied.

"I came here to treat you with decency and respect and honor, and it's come to this. I made a mistake."

It was more than Bombolini was willing to hear. "We have a saying here," the mayor said. " 'If the dove chooses to fly with the hawk, his feathers stay white but his heart turns black.' It was in you all along."

"I treated you with honor, and you returned it with humiliation."

"You ordered the electricity for Fabio."

Von Prum was silent. He looked as if he wasn't hearing what was being said, but he must have heard.

"And you put our cobbler to death."

The Malatesta was in the doorway and the captain saw her. There was a moment when it seemed that he was going to go to her, but he stayed where he was.

"What you people have to remember, your kind, is that there is no cure for birth," Bombolini said.

Von Prum turned and started toward the motorcycle.

"And there is no cure for death," Bombolini said, "if you think about it."

The German stopped; perhaps the mayor had touched something in him. He was angry and confused at the same time.

"If you think about that," Bombolini said, "you might think about becoming human beings for a change. Now get out of our city."

The engines of the truck and the motorcycle had already been started up, and the captain got into the sidecar. As on the day that it had come, the motorcycle didn't go directly to the corso but began a tour of the piazza. But von Prum didn't see the people this time. His eyes were so set and so cold and so distant that it was hard at the time to believe that they would ever close again, even on his death. Vittorini was saluting, but von Prum didn't see it. As before, the motorcycle came toward Bombolini and Vittorini and halted.

It startled them when von Prum spoke. His lips barely moved. There was no expression of any kind in his voice or in his face. "Is there more wine or not?"

Bombolini smiled at him.

"Is there more wine or not?"

They all were smiling at the captain then, but they didn't know whether he saw the smiles.

"Is there?"

Traub started to move again and very slowly this time he drove past Italo Bombolini and Vittorini, who still stood with his salute unanswered. The captain's lips were moving. He must have been asking the question again, but it was not possible to hear the words over the sound of the engine.

At the Fat Gate one of the things that are fated to take place here happened. It was done by the younger men, whose warm blood leads them into errors of taste. They lack the proper sense of things that a man like Bombolini, whose blood has cooled, has learned. They stopped the motorcycle, and before Traub could start it up again they handed the captain a wicker basket in which was packed twelve bottles of Santa Vittoria's best wine. On top of the fresh straw around the bottles was a card written in Fabio's finest hand:

Take this wine as well.
Don't thank us for it.
We won't miss it.
There are one million—
1,000,000—
one million more bottles where these came from.

The people of Santa Vittoria

"Where?" Traub said.

"That we can't tell you," Fabio said.

"We don't want it. We just want to know *where*."

Fabio shook his head at them. He was very gentle about it. "No, no. That will be your torture. Don't you see?"

Traub nodded.

Fabio turned directly to von Prum then. "Ten years from now, if you are alive, you will wake up in the night and you will start going over the city again, house by house and street by street, and it will begin to drive you mad. Where did you fail? you will ask yourself. And you will know only one thing for certain."

Fabio paused to be sure that von Prum was hearing him.

"What?" Traub said. "Certain of what?"

"That we are laughing at you. That we were laughing at you when you came and that we will always laugh at you."

The people had gathered on the wall, and when the motorcycle went through the Fat Gate there was a little cheer from them. There was the beginning of a feeling of joy, but as long as the Germans were still on the mountain no one would allow himself to go beyond that. Of all the people on the wall only Bombolini wasn't happy. People saw it and it puzzled them.

"What's the matter, Italo? Why are you sad?" they asked him, but he couldn't tell them, and they turned away to watch the progress of the motorcycle winding its way down the path and through the terraces. He left the wall and went back up into the Piazza of the People where he was alone, until Fabio came up from the Fat Gate.

"So you told them of the wine," Bombolini said.

"But not where it was," Fabio said. "That's the true torture."

Bombolini shook his head. "It lacks perfection, Fabio. But it doesn't matter. Nothing matters now." He began to walk across the piazza to the Palace of the People.

"Where are you going?" Fabio said.

They could hear another cheer, and Fabio guessed that the motorcycle was halfway down the mountain.

"I'm going away, Fabio. I'm leaving."

Fabio was astonished.

"This was my great moment. It's all over for me now." The mayor held up his hand. " 'In time of trouble men of talent are called for, but in times of ease the rich and those with powerful relations are desired.' You see? There's no place for me here."

Fabio didn't know what to say to him.

"You'll miss my wedding," he finally said.

Bombolini shrugged. "I don't want an ending that lacks perfection," he said. "The curtain is down, and it's time for the actors to get off the stage."

They had passed the fountain when Roberto came into the piazza.

"This is a great day for you, Roberto," Bombolini said.

"Yes," Roberto said, but his face was as long as Bombolini's.

"You'll be leaving us, Roberto."

"I guess so."

"Never stay in a place where you don't belong."

They heard a very loud cheer from the top of the wall. The motorcycle must be near the bottom of the mountain. The mayor turned to Fabio. "One rule, Fabio. One law that must be respected. Never grow old where you once have been great."

There was still another cheer, and this one was very loud. Bombolini turned around. "I had better take a look," he told Fabio. He began to walk toward the lane that leads down to the wall. "Just a peek," he said. "A last look and then I'll be gone." He was moving very fast and almost broke into a run. "Remember what I said, Roberto." He was running by then. "I'll be leaving myself."

Fabio and Roberto watched him go.

"He'll never leave," Fabio said. "You'll be gone, but Bombolini will be here. You're the lucky one, Roberto. You'll be gone, and he'll grow old."

The next time they saw him he was on top of the wall, and the people were silent. The motorcycle had reached the foot of the mountain and had stopped forty or fifty yards from the entrance to the Roman cellar. There had always been a belief here that the

Germans knew, that the last great joke would be the Germans' joke, and that their last act would be to destroy the cellar with the wine.

It is the belief now that Captain von Prum stopped to choose whether to go south toward the advancing armies or to go north toward his Fatherland and the punishment that awaited him there. He turned north, toward the dark open mouth of the cave and then past it and over the goat trail that crosses that part of the valley.

Fabio and Roberto could still see them, not the men or the motorcycle itself, but the high white plume of chalk that rose up behind them, a towering flag above the vineyards that marked the movement of the enemy through the grapes on the other mountain as surely as the wake of a ship in the sea. And then even that was gone.

THE PEOPLE HEARD THE soldiers before they saw them. The soldiers crossed the valley and started up the mountain, a long column of men in battle dress led by two bagpipers wearing kilts. When they came into the piazza, they were hot and tired and thirsty.

"Royal Sutherland Highlanders," their leader said. Even Roberto found it hard to understand what he said. The soldiers had crowded around the Fountain of the Pissing Turtle, and they looked at it but it was dry. There was no wine and there was no water.

"Have you anything to drink?" the officer asked.

"He wants to know if we have anything to drink," Roberto told Bombolini. The mayor turned to the people in the piazza.

"Do we have anything to drink?" he shouted to them. The people began to smile at each other and then to laugh. "He wants to know if we have anything to drink. Do we have anything to drink?"

There was such an outburst then, of shouts and laughter, that the soldiers became worried. They had never seen anything like this before. Bombolini turned to Roberto and although they were only a few feet apart he shouted. "Tell them this, Roberto," the mayor shouted. "Tell them God, yes, we have something to drink."

SELECTED
SHORT SUBJECTS

★ JAMES THURBER
★ ERMA BOMBECK
★ S.J. PERELMAN
★ ROBERT BENCHLEY

SELECTED
SHORT SUBJECTS

Illustrated by Bob Bugg

In the following pages America's
best-loved humorists take us, by way of
comic essays, through the familiar
and the wildly funny in everyday life.
JAMES THURBER, internationally acclaimed for his
very literate brand of fun, creates household havoc
with a ghost and a grandfather
in "The Night the Ghost Got In." For homestyle
hilarity of another sort, the ever-popular
ERMA BOMBECK gives us her wise and witty
views on family life in "The Family
That Plays Together Gets On Each
Other's Nerves" and "Out of the Nest." Then a
punster who is also known for his zany sketches,
S. J. PERELMAN has us chuckling at the
frustration of assembling on Christmas
morning an impossible-to-assemble toy in
"Insert Flap 'A' and Throw Away." Finally,
ROBERT BENCHLEY, actor, critic, playwright—
but above all a wryly amusing author—
romps through a mercifully forgettable
Spanish town to celebrate "Carnival
Week in Sunny Las Los."
    Taken all together, these essays represent
humor at its outrageous best.

THE NIGHT THE GHOST GOT IN

by James Thurber

THE GHOST THAT GOT into our house on the night of November 17, 1915, raised such a hullabaloo of misunderstandings that I am sorry I didn't just let it keep on walking, and go to bed. Its advent caused my mother to throw a shoe through a window of the house next door and ended up with my grandfather shooting a patrolman. I am sorry, therefore, as I have said, that I ever paid any attention to the footsteps.

They began about a quarter past one o'clock in the morning, a rhythmic, quick-cadenced walking around the dining-room table. My mother was asleep in one room upstairs, my brother Herman in another; Grandfather was in the attic, in an old walnut bed, and I had just stepped out of the bathtub and was busily rubbing myself with a towel when I heard the steps. They were the steps of a man walking rapidly around the dining-room table downstairs. The light from the bathroom shone down the back steps, which dropped directly into the dining room; I could see the faint shine of plates on the plate rail; I couldn't see the table. The steps kept going round and round the table; at regular intervals a board creaked, when it was trod upon. I supposed at first that it was my father or my brother Roy, who had gone to Indianapolis but were expected home at any time. I suspected next that it was a burglar. It did not enter my mind until later that it was a ghost.

After the walking had gone on for perhaps three minutes, I tip-toed to Herman's room. "Psst!" I hissed, in the dark, shaking him. "Awp," he said, in the low, hopeless tone of a despondent beagle—he always half suspected that something would "get him" in the night. I told him who I was. "There's something downstairs!" I said. He got up and followed me to the head of the back staircase. We listened together. There was no sound. The steps had ceased. Herman looked at me in some alarm: I had only the bath towel around my waist. He wanted to go back to bed, but I gripped his arm. "There's something down there!" I said. Instantly the steps began again, circled the dining-room table like a man running, and started up the stairs toward us, heavily, two at a time. The light still shone palely down the stairs; we saw nothing coming; we only heard the steps. Herman rushed to his room and slammed the door. I slammed shut the door at the stairs' top and held my knee against it. After a long minute, I slowly opened it again. There was nothing there. There was no sound. None of us ever heard the ghost again.

The slamming of the doors had aroused Mother: she peered out of her room. "What on earth are you boys doing?" she demanded. Herman ventured out of his room. "Nothing," he said gruffly, but he was, in color, a light green. "What was all that running around downstairs?" said Mother. So she had heard the steps, too! We just looked at her. "Burglars!" she shouted, intuitively. I tried to quiet her by starting lightly downstairs.

"Come on, Herman," I said.

"I'll stay with Mother," he said. "She's all excited."

I stepped back onto the landing.

"Don't either of you go a step," said Mother. "We'll call the po-lice." Since the phone was downstairs, I didn't see how we were going to call the police—nor did I want the police—but Mother made one of her quick, incomparable decisions. She flung up a window of her bedroom which faced the bedroom windows of the house of a neigh-bor, picked up a shoe, and whammed it through a pane of glass across the narrow space that separated the two houses. Glass tinkled into the bedroom occupied by a retired engraver named Bodwell and his wife. Bodwell had been for some years in rather a bad way and was subject to mild "attacks." Most everybody we knew or lived near had *some* kind of attacks.

It was now about two o'clock of a moonless night; clouds hung black and low. Bodwell was at the window in a minute, shouting, frothing a little, shaking his fist. "We'll sell the house and go back to Peoria," we could hear Mrs. Bodwell saying. It was some time before Mother "got through" to Bodwell. "Burglars!" she shouted. "Burglars in the house!" Herman and I hadn't dared to tell her that it was not burglars but ghosts, for she was even more afraid of ghosts than of burglars. Bodwell at first thought that she meant there were burglars in his house, but finally he quieted down and called the police for us over an extension phone by his bed. After he had disappeared from the window, Mother suddenly made as if to throw another shoe, not because there was further need of it but, as she later explained, because the thrill of heaving a shoe through a window glass had enormously taken her fancy. I prevented her.

The police were on hand in a commendably short time: a Ford sedan full of them, two on motorcycles, and a patrol wagon with about eight in it and a few reporters. They began banging at our front door. Flashlights shot streaks of gleam up and down the walls, across the yard, down the walk between our house and Bodwells'.

"Open up!" cried a hoarse voice. "We're men from headquarters!" I wanted to go down and let them in, since there they were, but Mother wouldn't hear of it. "You haven't a stitch on," she pointed out. "You'd catch your death." I wound the towel around me again. Finally the cops put their shoulders to our big heavy front door with its thick beveled glass and broke it in: I could hear a rending of wood and a splash of glass on the floor of the hall. Their lights played all over the living room and crisscrossed nervously in the dining room, stabbed into hallways, shot up the front stairs and finally up the back. They caught me standing in my towel at the top. A heavy policeman bounded up the steps. "Who are you?" he demanded. "I live here," I said. "Well, whattsa matta, ya hot?" he asked. It was, as a matter of fact, cold; I went to my room and pulled on some trousers. On my way out, a cop stuck a gun into my ribs. "Whatta you doin' here?" he demanded. "I live here," I said.

The officer in charge reported to Mother. "No sign of nobody, lady," he said. "Musta got away—what'd he look like?" "There were two or three of them," Mother said, "whooping and carrying on and slamming doors." "Funny," said the cop. "All ya windows and doors was locked on the inside tight as a tick."

Downstairs, we could hear the tramping of the other police. Police were all over the place; doors were yanked open, drawers were yanked open, windows were shot up and pulled down, furniture fell with dull thumps. A half-dozen policemen emerged out of the darkness of the front hallway upstairs. They began to ransack the floor: pulled beds away from walls, tore clothes off hooks in the closets, pulled suitcases and boxes off shelves. One of them found an old zither that Roy had won in a pool tournament. "Looky here, Joe," he said, strumming it with a big paw. The cop named Joe took it and turned it over. "What is it?" he asked me. "It's an old zither our guinea pig used to sleep on," I said. It was true that a pet guinea pig we once had would never sleep anywhere except on the zither, but I should never have said so. Joe and the other cop looked at me a long time. They put the zither back on a shelf.

"No sign o' nuthin'," said the cop who had first spoken to Mother. "This guy," he explained to the others, jerking a thumb at me, "was nekked. The lady seems historical." They all nodded, but said nothing; just looked at me. In the small silence we all heard a creaking in the attic. Grandfather was turning over in bed. "What's 'at?" snapped Joe. Five or six cops sprang for the attic door before I could intervene or explain. I realized that it would be bad if they burst in on Grandfather unannounced, or even announced. He was going through a phase in which he believed that General Meade's men, under steady hammering by Stonewall Jackson, were beginning to retreat and even desert.

When I got to the attic, things were pretty confused. Grandfather had evidently jumped to the conclusion that the police were deserters from Meade's army, trying to hide away in his attic. He bounded out of bed wearing a long flannel nightgown over long woolen underwear, a nightcap, and a leather jacket around his chest. The cops must have realized at once that the indignant white-haired old man belonged in the house, but they had no chance to say so. "Back, ye cowardly dogs!" roared Grandfather. "Back t' the lines, ye damn lily-livered cattle!" With that, he fetched the officer who found the zither a flat-handed smack alongside his head that sent him sprawling. The others beat a retreat, but not fast enough; Grandfather grabbed Zither's gun from its holster and let fly. The report seemed to crack the rafters; smoke filled the attic. A cop cursed and shot his hand to his shoulder. Somehow, we all finally got downstairs again and locked the door against the old gentleman. He fired once or twice more in the darkness and then went back to bed. "That was Grandfather," I explained to Joe, out of breath. "He thinks you're deserters." "I'll say he does," said Joe.

The cops were reluctant to leave without getting their hands on somebody besides Grandfather; the night had been distinctly a defeat for them. Furthermore, they obviously didn't like the "layout"; something looked—and I can see their viewpoint—phony. They began to poke into things again. A reporter, a thin-faced, wispy man, came up to me. I had put on one of Mother's blouses, not being able to find anything else. The reporter looked at me with mingled suspicion and interest. "Just what the hell is the real lowdown here, Bud?" he asked. I decided to be frank with him. "We had ghosts," I said. He gazed at me a long time as if I were a slot machine into which he had, without results, dropped a nickel. Then he walked away. The cops followed him, the one Grandfather shot holding his now-bandaged arm, cursing and blaspheming. "I'm gonna get my gun back from that old bird," said the zither-cop. "Yeh," said Joe. "You—and who else?" I told them I would bring it to the station house the next day.

"What was the matter with that one policeman?" Mother asked, after they had gone. "Grandfather shot him," I said. "What for?" she demanded. I told her he was a deserter. "Of all things!" said Mother. "He was such a nice-looking young man."

Grandfather was fresh as a daisy and full of jokes at breakfast next morning. We thought at first he had forgotten all about what had happened, but he hadn't. Over his third cup of coffee, he glared at Herman and me. "What was the idee of all them cops tarryhootin' round the house last night?" he demanded. He had us there.

THE FAMILY THAT PLAYS TOGETHER GETS ON EACH OTHER'S NERVES

by Erma Bombeck

FOR YEARS, MY HUSBAND and I have advocated separate vacations. But the kids keep finding us.

We have always said if we could just mail ourselves to where we are going, we might arrive in a gayer holiday mood. But it's all the miles in between that makes traveling as giddy as the Nuremberg trials. (We once picked up a hitchhiker who wrote us a check to let him out.)

Although each vacation spot is a new, exciting experience, the trip by car is rather predictable.

First, there is the blessing of the car, followed by Captain Daddy's "Give 'Em Hell" speech.

"All right, gang," he says, resting his foot on the front of the bumper, "you're probably wondering why we're gathered here to-day. We're about to embark on what can be a wonderful vacation together. That depends on you.

"First, I want to make a few remarks about the car. You'll notice it

has a floor in it. That is for your feet. At no time, repeat, no time do I want your feet resting on my shoulders. A good driver is an alert driver and I cannot be at my best with a pair of yesterday's socks in my face.

"Second, we will not play car roulette at any time during the trip. There is nothing more frustrating than for me to look through my rearview mirror and see bodies hurling through the air like the Flying Wallendas. As your captain, I will make window assignments each morning. If there is any quarrel with these assignments, feel free to file a grievance.

"May I also remind you this car is not a trough. Any candy wrappers, banana peelings, stale bread, apple cores, broken straws, paper cups or breakfast rolls must be wrapped and thrown away or buried. I will not tolerate another fruit-fly assault like last summer.

"Third, transistors must be turned off while you sleep. Also, the occupants of the car will not be subjected to more than ninety-nine choruses of 'Ninety-nine Bottles of Beer' in a twenty-four-hour period.

"And last, there will be no reading of *Mad* magazine, *Sports Illustrated* or *Mag Wheels Digest* while we are touring breathtaking mountain ranges, historic monuments or indescribable cathedrals. Remember, you are going to have a wonderful time if I have to break every bone in your bodies. We are ready to start our motor. Good show."

Once Captain Daddy's speech is out of the way, we are in for five hundred miles of the Disaster Lady.

The Disaster Lady is our teenage daughter who didn't want to make the trip in the first place and who threatens to join a convent the minute the car slows down. Her fatalistic approach to a vacation makes it as much fun as diarrhea.

The car is barely out of the driveway before she lifts her head in a dramatic jerk and whispers, "Did you hear that? I thought I heard a knock under the hood. Cecily Ainsworth's dad had that same knock under his hood and the car blew up at the end of the driveway."

If she isn't predicting hurricanes as far inland as Indiana, she's telling you an amusing story of a shark that showed up in some freak way at the lake where we plan to stay.

When you are half a day out from home, she will stir restlessly in the back seat and yell, "Mom, did you remember to unplug your coffeepot and your iron? The last time I saw them they were on." Or, "Daddy, did you get a confirmation on the hotel room? I wonder if it's one of those places where you have to bring your own linens? I sure hope someone remembered to take the cat next door."

Occasionally, she will unplug the transistor from her ear and sigh, "Gee, that's too bad."

"What's too bad?" we ask.

"About the weather."

"What about the weather?"

"The extended forecast predicts two solid weeks of rain where we are going. But I don't mind really," she adds.

I'm almost afraid to ask, "Why not?"

"Because I was exposed to German measles thirteen days ago."

In between Captain Daddy and the Disaster Lady, we have Happy Mouth.

Happy Mouth is the eleven-year-old who is one of the best testimonials to Planned Parenthood I can think of. There is something disgusting about a kid who wakes up happy and goes steadily uphill the rest of the day.

"Hey, do you want to hear the poem I read on the last rest-room wall?" he chirps.

"No," says the car in unison.

"It said, 'Violets are blue, roses are red, If you can read this, you're standing on your head.' "

"That's enough."

"There was also a phone number underneath it. Can I call it when we stop?"

"No."

"Can I plug in the electric back scratcher I bought at the last souvenir shop?"

"No, you'll run the car battery down."

"Can I take a picture of your teeth?"

"No."

"Anyone want to play Monopoly?"

"No."

"I'll roll up all the windows so the money won't blow around."

"Mom, will you hush him up?"

Happy Mouth may be put down on the average of once every three minutes, but he is undaunted. "Hey, this looks like a neat restaurant," he exclaims.

I grimace. "Are you kidding? This place will have to be cleaned before they can condemn it. Let's move on to something else."

"I want to eat here," shouts Happy Mouth. "There's a real neat dog inside, see him?"

"I should," I say dryly. "He's sitting in a booth."

"Aw c'mon, Mom."

"Okay," I relent, "but let me give you one word of advice. This place is a filthy dump. I bet they haven't had a customer since the septic tank backed up. We'll be fine if we order something safe like cheese or peanut butter. Remember now. Something safe."

Happy Mouth is the first to order. "I'll have the roast turkey and dressing." He grins. Then, "May I use your rest room?"

The waitress blows an enormous bubble and pops it. "You walk past the jukebox and turn and go through those two big double doors. You walk through the kitchen and out of the back into a gravel parking lot, then walk through that field about an eighth of a mile down the road."

"Isn't that the service station?" I ask.

"Right," she says.

Happy Mouth is absolutely jubilant when he gets back. "You should see the kitchen."

"I don't want to talk about it," I say, picking at my cheese sandwich.

"It's got a stove with big pots on it and a neat fire extinguisher on the wall."

"It's probably a stomach pump," snarls my husband.

"And the dog out there is real neat."

All eyes focus hard on Happy Mouth. He senses our animosity. "Guess what?" he says cheerfully, "I didn't sit on the toilet seat."

Another fun occupant in the car is the Teenage Grumbler. Nothing, it seems, is as much fun as he anticipated. He came on the trip with a change of underwear and a single word in his vocabulary, "Gross."

The tours are gross, the statues are gross, the motels and the food are gross, the girls are gross and the weather and the towns are gross. You get the feeling if he had been present while the Red Sea was being parted, he'd have whipped a pocket comb out of his shirt, yawned and said, "That's gross."

Efforts to introduce him to scenic phenomena of the world are in vain. "Would you look at that?" gasps his father. "Those faces carved in the side of a mountain are fantastic."

The Grumbler speaks. "They're gross."

"No, they're Roosevelt, Washington, Lincoln and Jefferson," says his father. "Look here, boy, I don't think you have the proper attitude for this trip. Here we have driven seventeen hundred and fifty miles to show you a breathtaking view and you slouch in your seat and clean your fingernails with a matchbook cover."

"I saw a breathtaking view already yesterday," he grumbles. "When do we eat?"

"We ate yesterday," snaps his father and drives on.

If you did not know the background of the Grumbler, you would vow he was sired by a Bank Americard, born in a jet and weaned on Wall Street. Throughout the entire trip, he spews out his displeasure. "That swimming pool isn't heated." "Can't we get a motel with a phone in the bathroom?" "You can't get a decent TV picture in this cabin." "That stupid drugstore hadn't even heard of the *Mag Wheels*

Digest." "They only have three kinds of soft drinks at this gas station." "Make him keep his feet on his side of the car." "I've been keeping tab, Dad. This is your 87th wrong turn, your 18th detour and your 467th profane word."

His father turns his head angrily and opens his mouth.

"That's 468th," he says. "That's gross."

Naturally, I have saved the Family Mother of the trip until last. Upon her frail shoulders rests the responsibility of dispensing discipline, maintaining order, keeping track of the gas and oil mileage, reading road maps and of course getting Captain Daddy to make pit stops with some regularity.

"Don't you think we should stop and get a bite to eat?" I ask.

"Why?" answers the captain. "We just got rolling."

"We got rolling at five this morning," I say. "It is now two thirty in the afternoon and my vision is beginning to blur."

"You exaggerate," he said. "I wanted to make Goose Fork by four. If we stop you'll all want to go to the bathroom, stretch your legs and get out of the car to eat and that will blow another twenty minutes."

"I feel like I am in a getaway car. We are only human. We have a body that requires food and rest. Our muscles must be exercised or they become useless. We have plumbing that must function. We are mortal. We bleed like anyone else."

"NOT ON THOSE NEW SEAT COVERS!" he yells over his shoulder.

"That was just an expression," I say. "Frankly, I don't understand you at all. Why don't you get hungry once in a while? Are you sure you aren't pilfering food from somewhere like the fat guy in *The Diary of Anne Frank?*"

"Really," he snorts, "if you are going to make such a big deal about it, look for a place to eat. When you see one, just yell."

"There's a plaaaaaaaaaaaaaaace. . . ."

"Where?"

"Back there."

"I can't stop on a dime, you know."

"Not going seventy miles an hour you can't."

"Look," he growled, "you pick out a beanery the size of a flea's navel and expect me to see it and drive at the same time. Besides, it looked like a hole in the wall."

"I thought you didn't see it."

"I could smell the grease when I went by. Believe me, I know when they fry the shrimp and the french fries in the same vat."

"Oh, really."

Two hours later, we are still looking for a place to eat. Family Mother has her head wedged in the no-draft peering into the darkness for a lighted sign. The children are sprawled out on the seats to conserve energy as their stomachs bloat.

Finally, Mother rummages in her handbag. "I'm in luck," I shout. "Here are three breath mints, one for each child. Here is a sticky coughdrop for me and here's a piece of chocolate for Daddy."

Daddy smiles as he devours the square of chocolate. "This should hold us until we get to Goose Fork."

"Don't count on it," I say, taking a deep breath. "I just fed you a laxative."

From the back seat came three voices.

"When laxatives are old, they lose their effectiveness," said the Disaster Lady.

"That's neat. I'm going to buy some when we stop and use them as tricks," laughs Happy Mouth.

"You're all gross," snarls the Grumbler.

OUT OF THE NEST

by Erma Bombeck

WE CALL HIM THE BABY.

He weighs forty pounds, stands stove-high, and can kick a football higher than the house. Somehow, I have the feeling we will call him the baby when he is forty, has children of his own, and a hairline like the coast of Florida.

This day, in particular, is special. It's the day when the baby goes to school for the first time. I don't know why I feel so irritable. One minute I'm yelling at him, "You slam that door once more, fella, and I'll mail you to a school in Nebraska with no return address."

The next, I'm scooping him to my bosom and saying, "Let's run away to never-never land, you and I, where little boys never grow up and I could get the job of Peter Pan that Mary Martin gave up."

This should be a happy morning. I remember all those promises I made to myself just six short years ago while sloshing over diaper pails and shaking boiling hot milk over my wrists at two a.m. Just wait, I told myself. When this whole mess is behind me, I'll go back to bed in the mornings, have lunch with someone who doesn't eat his meat with a spoon, shed fifteen pounds, do my nails, learn how to play bridge, and blow this firetrap called home that has held me a virtual prisoner.

I nurtured this dream right through measles, fractures, tensions, traumas, Dr. Spock, and nursery school. And now that I am so close to its realization, I feel guilty. What am I doing? Sending this *baby* off to learn calculus before the cord is healed. How does the state of Ohio know my son is ready for the first grade? They look at him and what do they see? A birth certificate and a record of immunizations.

I look at him and I see a smile . . . like Halloween. I see two short legs that won't get him a drink of water without a stool under them. I see two pudgy hands that can't work together to hold a slippery bar of soap. I see a shock of red hair that doesn't come up to his father's belt buckle. I see a little boy who never went to the rest room all during nursery school because he didn't want to admit he couldn't spell the difference between B-O-Y-S and G-I-R-L-S on the doors.

From this day forward his world can only widen. An existence that began in a crib, grew to a house, and extends over a two-block bicycle ride will now go even beyond that. I will share him with another woman, other adults, other children, other opinions, other points of view. I am no longer leading. I am standing behind him ready to guide from a new position.

Who is this woman who will spend more daylight hours with him than I? Please, Miss Chalkdust or whatever, give him the patience and gentleness he needs. Please have a soft lap and a warm smile.

And please don't be too pretty or too smart, lest I suffer from the comparison.

A note. Maybe I should pin a note on his sweater to make sure she understands him. I could say, "Dear Miss Chalkdust or whatever: I submit to your tender, loving care my son who is a little shy and a lot stubborn. Who can't cope with zippers that stick or buttons on sweaters that don't come out even. One who makes his 5's sideways but works seriously and in earnest. I may sue you for alienation of affection, but for the moment, God bless you!"

There is no time for a note. The bus is here. It's such a big bus. Why would they send their largest bus for someone so small? He is gone. He didn't even look back to wave.

The house is so quiet. It's what I've always wanted, isn't it? A quiet house. I wonder who my tears are really for. I hate to admit it, but I think they're for myself.

I think I'm afraid. What kind of a woman am I? Am I going to be the woman who wanders through the house, unfulfilled and bored, occasionally sobbing, "My baby, my baby!" Will I dust and vacuum the house every day by ten thirty, only to sit and drink coffee and watch for the big yellow bus to deposit my brood at the curb, that I may once again run and fetch like a robot that has been programmed for service?

Will my children go on being my excuse for not stirring from this house? Will I dedicate my entire life to their comforts?

Or could I be like that robin last spring? I watched that little feathered mother-to-be as she and her mate built the nest and she perched on her eggs to wait. Then, day of days, the babies were born and both she and the father scratched and carried to fill the demands of those ever-open mouths.

Finally the day came when the parents lined up the babies, and one by one they flew. At first they hesitated and hung back until they were nudged out of the nest. Then they swooped up and down like an early prop plane gone out of control. They exhausted themselves flapping their wings. Some set down in makeshift landings that were unbelievable. Others perched precariously near the danger of cats and barking dogs, but the mother never budged. She just watched and observed, her snappy black eyes never missing a move. Day by day the birds flew more, flew better, and flew farther, until they were ready to take their place in the sky with the parents.

I thought of my friends and I remembered the ones who were as wise as the robin. They too nudged their youngsters out of the nest, and then the youngsters sprouted their own wings and led the way. My friends emerged from a cocoon existence of peanut butter and naps into great beautiful butterflies. The sound of the school bell was like V-E Day to them. They assumed leadership, developed, and grew into active citizens in the community, unearthed talents that surprised everyone (including themselves), and set about restoring order to their lives.

The bus! It's here so soon. I've scarcely had time to get my bearings. There he comes, hopping off the step and yelling excitedly, "I passed!" It's such a small bus. Why would they send such a small bus for such a group of big, boisterous boys? Or could it be . . . the same bus they sent this morning and my son just grew a lot?

INSERT FLAP "A" AND THROW AWAY

by S. J. Perelman

ONE STIFLING SUMMER afternoon last August, in the attic of a tiny stone house in Pennsylvania, I made a most interesting discovery: the shortest, cheapest method of inducing a nervous breakdown ever perfected. In this technique (eventually adopted by the psychology department of Duke University, which will adopt anything), the subject is placed in a sharply sloping attic heated to 340° F and given a mothproof closet known as the Jiffy-Cloz to assemble. The Jiffy-Cloz, procurable at any department store or neighborhood insane asylum, consists of half a dozen gigantic sheets of red cardboard, two plywood doors, a clothes rack, and a packet of staples. With these is included a set of instructions mimeographed in pale-violet ink, fruity with phrases like "Pass Section F through Slot AA, taking care not to fold tabs behind washers (see Fig. 9)." The cardboard is so processed that as the subject struggles convulsively to force the staple through, it suddenly buckles, plunging the staple deep into his thumb. He thereupon springs up with a dolorous cry and smites his knob (Section K) on the rafters (RR). As a final demonic touch, the Jiffy-Cloz people cunningly omit four of the staples necessary to finish the job, so that after indescribable purgatory, the best the subject can possibly achieve is a sleazy, capricious structure which would reduce any self-respecting moth to helpless laughter. The cumulative frustration, the tropical heat, and the soft, ghostly chuckling of the moths are calculated to unseat the strongest mentality.

In a period of rapid technological change, however, it was inevitable that a method as cumbersome as the Jiffy-Cloz would be superseded. It was superseded at exactly nine thirty Christmas morning by a device called the Self-Running 10-Inch Scale-Model Delivery-Truck Construction Kit Powered by Magic Motor. About nine on that particular morning, I was spread-eagled on my bed, indulging in my favorite sport of mouth breathing, when a cork fired from a child's air gun mysteriously lodged in my throat. The pellet proved awkward for a while, but I finally ejected it by flailing the little marksman (and his sister, for good measure) until their welkins rang, and sauntered in to breakfast. Before I could choke down a healing fruit juice, my consort, a tall, regal creature with her foot entangled in a roller skate, swept in. She extended a large, unmistakable box covered with diagrams.

"Now don't start making excuses," she whined. "It's just a simple cardboard toy. The directions are on the back—"

"Look, dear," I interrupted, rising hurriedly and pulling on my overcoat, "it clean slipped my mind. I'm supposed to take a lesson in cross-hatching at Zim's School of Cartooning today."

"On Christmas?" she asked suspiciously.

"Yes, it's the only time they could fit me in," I countered glibly. "This is the big week for cross-hatching, you know, between Christmas and New Year's."

"Do you think you ought to go in your pajamas?" she asked.

"Oh, that's okay." I smiled. "We often work in our pajamas up at Zim's. Well, good-bye now. If I'm not home by Thursday, you'll find a cold snack in the safe-deposit box." My subterfuge, unluckily, went for naught, and in a trice I was sprawled on the nursery floor, surrounded by two lambkins and ninety-eight segments of the Self-Running 10-Inch Scale-Model Delivery-Truck Construction Kit.

The theory of the kit was simplicity itself, easily intelligible to Kettering of General Motors, Professor Millikan, or any first-rate physicist. Taking as my starting point the only sentence I could comprehend, "Fold down on all lines marked 'fold down;' fold up on all lines marked 'fold up,' " I set the children to work and myself folded up with an album of views of Chili Williams. Then I was ready for the second phase, lightly referred to in the directions as "Preparing the Spring Motor Unit." As nearly as I could determine after twenty minutes of mumbling, the Magic Motor ("No Electricity—No Batteries—Nothing to Wind—Motor Never Wears Out") was an accordion-pleated affair operating by torsion, attached to the axles. "It is necessary," said the text, "to cut a slight notch in each of the axles with a knife (see Fig. C). To find the exact place to cut this notch, lay one of the axles over diagram at bottom of page."

"Well, *now* we're getting someplace!" I boomed, with a false gusto that deceived nobody. "Here, Buster, run in and get Daddy a knife."

"I dowanna," quavered the boy, backing away. "You always cut yourself at this stage." I gave the wee fellow an indulgent pat on the head that flattened it slightly, to teach him civility, and commandeered a long, serrated bread knife from the kitchen. "Now watch me closely, children," I ordered. "We place the axle on the diagram as in Fig. C, applying a strong downward pressure on the knife handle at all times." The axle must have been a factory second, because an instant later I was in the bathroom grinding my teeth in agony and attempting to stanch the flow of blood. Ultimately, I succeeded in contriving a rough bandage and slipped back into the nursery without awaking the children's suspicions. An agreeable surprise awaited me. Displaying a mechanical aptitude clearly inherited from their sire, the rascals had put together the chassis of the delivery truck.

"Very good indeed," I complimented (naturally, one has to exaggerate praise to develop a child's self-confidence). "Let's see—what's the next step? Ah, yes. 'Lock into box shape by inserting tabs C, D, E, F, G, H, J, K, and L into slots C, D, E, F, G, H, J, K, and L. Ends of front axle should be pushed through holes A and B.'" While marshaling the indicated parts in their proper order, I emphasized to my rapt listeners the necessity of patience and perseverance. "Haste makes waste," I reminded them. "Rome wasn't built in a day. Remember, your daddy isn't always going to be here to show you."

"Where *are* you going to be?" they demanded.

"In the movies, if I can arrange it," I snarled. Poising tabs C, D, E, F, G, H, K, and L in one hand and the corresponding slots in the other, I essayed a union of the two, but in vain. The moment I made one set fast and tackled another, tab and slot would part company, thumbing their noses at me. Although the children were too immature to understand, I saw in a flash where the trouble lay. Some idiotic employee at the factory had punched out the wrong design, probably out of sheer spite. So that was his game, eh? I set my lips in a grim line and, throwing one hundred and fifty-seven pounds of fighting fat into the effort, pounded the component parts into a homogeneous mass.

"There," I said with a gasp, "that's close enough. Now then, who wants candy? One, two, three—everybody off to the candy store!"

"We wanna finish the delivery truck!" they wailed. "Mummy, he won't let us finish the delivery truck!" Threats, cajolery, bribes were of no avail. In their jungle code, an inexpensive gewgaw bulked larger than a parent's love. Realizing that I was dealing with a pair of monomaniacs, I determined to show them who was master and wildly began locking the cardboard units helter-skelter, without any regard for the directions. When sections refused to fit, I gouged them with my nails and forced them together, cackling shrilly. The side panels collapsed; with a bestial oath, I drove a safety pin through them and lashed them to the roof. I used paper clips, bobby pins, anything I could lay my hands on. My fingers fairly flew and my breath whistled in my throat. "You want a delivery truck, do you?" I panted. "All right, I'll show you!" As merciful blackness closed in, I was on my hands and knees, bunting the infernal thing along with my nose and whinnying, "Roll, confound you, roll!"

"Absolute quiet," a carefully modulated voice was saying, "and fifteen of the white tablets every four hours." I opened my eyes carefully in the darkened room. Dimly I picked out a knifelike character actor in a Vandyke beard and pencil-striped pants folding a stethoscope into his bag. "Yes," he added thoughtfully, "if we play our cards right, this ought to be a long, expensive recovery." From far away, I could hear my wife's voice bravely trying to control her anxiety.

"What if he becomes restless, Doctor?"

"Get him a detective story," returned the leech. "Or better still, a nice, soothing picture puzzle—something he can do with his hands."

CARNIVAL WEEK IN SUNNY LAS LOS

by Robert Benchley

YOU HAVE ALL DOUBTLESS wanted to know, at one time or another, a few of the quaint customs which residents of the continent of Europe seem to feel called upon to perpetuate from one century to another. You may know about a few of them already, such as child-bearing (which has been taken up on this continent to such an alarming extent) and others of the more common variety of folk mannerisms, but I am very proud and happy to be able to tell you today of some of the less generally known customs of the inhabitants of that medieval Spanish province Las Los (or Los Las, as it was formerly called, either way meaning "The The" *pl.*) where I have had the extremely bad fortune to be spending the summer.

Las Los, nestling, as it does, in the intercostal nooks of the Pyrenees, makes up into one of the nicest little plague-spots on the continent of Europe. Europe has often claimed that Las Los was *not* a part of it, and in 1356 Spain began a long and costly war with France, the loser to take Los Las and two outfielders. France won and Spain built an extension onto the Pyrenees in which to hide Los Las and they succeeded in hiding it from view.

It was in this little out-of-the-way corner of the world, then, that I set up my easel and began painting my fingers and wrists. I soon made friends with the natives (all of whom were named Pedro) and it was not long before they were bringing me their best Sunday knives and sticking them in my back for me to try to tell which was which. And such laughter would go up when I guessed the wrong one! All Latins, after all, are just children at heart.

But I am not here to tell you of the many merry days I myself spent in Las Los, but of some of the native customs which I was privileged to see, and, once in a while, take part in. They rather resent an outsider taking part in most of them, however, for there is an old saying in Las Los that "when an outsider takes part, rain will surely dart," (meaning "dart" from the clouds, you see) and above all things rain is abhorred in that section of the country, as rain has a tendency to cleanse whatever it touches, and, as another old proverb has it, "clean things, dead things"—which isn't exactly accurate, but appeals to these simple, childish people, to whom cleanliness is next to a broken hip.

First of all, then, let us tiptoe up on the natives of Las Los during their carnival time. The carnival week comes during the last week in July, just when it is hottest. This makes it really ideal for the Los Lasians, for extreme heat, added to everything else, renders their charming little town practically unbearable. This week was chosen many hundreds of years ago and is supposed to mark the anniversary of the marriage of old Don Pedro's daughter to a thunderbolt, a union which was so unsatisfactory to the young lady that she left her husband in two days and married a boy named Carlos, who sold tortillas. This so enraged the thunderbolt that he swore never to come to Los Las again, and, from that day to this (so the saying goes, I know not whether it be true or not) that region has never had any locusts. (This would almost make it seem that the repulsed bridegroom had been a locust, but the natives, on being questioned, explain that the *patois* for "thunderbolt" *[enjuejoz]* is very much like the *patois* for "locust" *[enjuejoz]* and that the thunder god, in giving his order for the future of Los Las, put the accent on the wrong syllable and cut them off from locusts instead of thunder storms).

This may, or may not, be the truth, but, as I said to the old man who told me, "Who the hell cares?"

The first day of the Carnival of the Absence of Locusts (just why they should be so cocky about having no locusts is not clear. Locusts would be a godsend compared to some of the things they *have* got) is spent in bed, storing up strength for the festival. On this day all the shops, except those selling wine, are closed. This means that a little shop down by the river which sells sieves is closed. People lie in bed and send out to the wineshops for the native drink, which is known as *wheero*. All that is necessary to do with this drink is to place it in an open saucer on the windowsill and inhale deeply from across the room. In about eight seconds the top of the inhaler's head rises slowly and in a dignified manner until it reaches the ceiling where it floats, bumping gently up and down. The teeth then drop out and arrange themselves on the floor to spell "Portage High School, 1930," the eyes roll upward and backward, and a strange odor of burning rubber fills the room. This is followed by an unaccountable feeling of intense lassitude.

Thus we may expect nothing from the natives for the first two days of the carnival, for the second day is spent in looking for bits of head and teeth, and in general moaning. (A sorry carnival, you will say— and *I* will say, too.) But later on, things will brighten up.

On the third day the inhabitants emerge, walking very carefully in order not to jar off their ears, and get into a lot of decorated oxcarts. They were not very crazy about getting into these oxcarts, but it is more or less expected of them at carnival time. Pictures are taken of them riding about and are sent to the London illustrated papers, and if they were to pass up one year without riding in decorated oxcarts, it wouldn't seem like carnival week to the readers of the London illustrated papers. You can hardly blame a man with a *wheero* hangover, however, for not wanting to bump around over cobblestones in an old two-wheeled cart, even if it has got paper flowers strung all over it. One of the saddest sights in the world is to see a native, all dressed up in red and yellow, with a garland of orange roses around his neck, jolting and jouncing along over hard stone bumps with a girl on his knee, and trying to simulate that famous Spanish smile and gay abandon, all the time feeling that one more bump and away goes that meal he ate several days ago, along with his legs and arms

/

and portions of his lower jaw. No wonder Spaniards look worried.

However, there is a great deal of shouting and cawing among those who can open their mouths, and occasionally someone hits a tambourine. This is usually frowned upon by the person standing next to the tambourine-hitter and a remark, in Spanish, is made which could roughly be translated as: "For the love of God, shut up that incessant banging!"

The carnival, which is known as *Romeria,* is supposed to be a festival of the picnic type combined with a religious pilgrimage to some sort of shrine. This shrine, however, is never reached, as along about noon of the third day some desperate guy, with a hangover no longer to be borne, evolves a cure on the "hair of the dog that bit you" theory, and the *wheero* is brought out again. The village watering trough is filled with it and a sort of native dance is held around the trough, everyone inhaling deeply. Those who are still unable to inhale are carried to the edge of the trough and a little *wheero* is rubbed on their upper lips, just under the nose. Then it is "good night all, and a merry, merry trip to Blanket Bay," for the festive villagers, and the carnival is shot to hell. A week later business is quietly resumed.

On the fifth day of the carnival there is supposed to be a bull chase

through the streets. The principle of the thing is that a bull is let loose and everyone chases it, or vice versa. As, however, there was nobody fit to chase a butterfly, much less a bull, on the fifth day of this carnival, I had to take care of the bull myself. The two of us sat all alone in the public square among the cadavers drinking a sort of lemon squash together.

"A dash of *wheero?*" I asked the bull.

Well, you should have heard him laugh!

After that, I got up on his back and rode all around the town, visiting the points of interest and climbing several of the better-looking mountains. Pretty soon we were in Turkey, where we saw many interesting sights and then, swinging around through the Balkans, I got back just in time for me to scramble into bed. I must have hit my head on the footboard while pulling up the sheet, for the next morning (or whenever it was) when I awoke, I had quite a bad headache.

Thank heaven I knew enough to lay off that *wheero,* however. I'm no fool.

MR. BLANDINGS
BUILDS HIS DREAM HOUSE

MR. BLANDINGS BUILDS HIS DREAM HOUSE

A CONDENSATION OF THE NOVEL BY

ERIC HODGINS

DRAWINGS BY WILLIAM STEIG
TITLE PAGE ILLUSTRATION BY BRUCE STARK

Mr. and Mrs. Blandings are city dwellers
who yearn for a home of their own
in the country—a cozy rural nest in which
to raise their fledgling daughters.
And the Hackett place, a sweet old
farmhouse on a hill, is a dream come
true. But first they must deal with a
realtor who proves wilier than a coyote,
a brace of country bankers who don't
like city folk, and even a sparkling
stream that won't cooperate!

With faith, hope and hilarity, the
Blandings muddle on, even as soaring costs
and cosmic confusion threaten to turn
their dream into a comic nightmare.

Eric Hodgins, a prominent magazine
editor, published *Mr. Blandings* in 1946,
and it became an immediate best-seller.
Although its prices may seem quaintly
low today, anyone who has ever
built a house or tried to fix one up
will smile in sympathy and howl
in recognition at the Blandings' mirthful
misadventures.

CHAPTER ONE

THE SWEET OLD farmhouse burrowed into the upward slope of the land so deeply that you could enter either its bottom or middle floor at ground level. Its window trim was delicate and the lights in its sash—those twelve little square panes of glass—were a bubbly amethyst. Its ridgepole seemed to sway a little against the sky, and the massive chimney that rose out of it tilted a fraction to the south. Where the white paint was flecking off on the siding, there showed beneath it the faint blush of what must once have been a rich, dense red.

In front, rising and spreading along the length of the house, was the largest lilac tree Mr. and Mrs. Blandings had ever seen. Its gnarled, rusty trunks rose intertwined and burst into billowing clouds of blossoms, a haze of blues and purples. When the house was new, a hundred and seventy years ago, the lilac must have been a shrub in the dooryard—and house and shrub had gone on together, side by side since the 1770's.

"If the lilac can live and be so old, so can the house," Mrs. Blandings said to herself. "It needs someone to love it, that's all." She flashed a glance at her husband, who flashed one back at her.

Using a penknife as a key, the real-estate man unlocked the door. As it swung back, the top hinge gave way and the door lurched against Mr. Blandings and gave him a sharp crack on the forehead. The damage was repaired in an instant, and Mr. Blandings, a handkerchief at his temple and his wife by his side, stood looking out through the amethyst window lights at an arc of beauty that made them both cry out. The land rushed downward to the river a mile away; then it rose again, plane after plane of hills and higher hills beyond them. The air was luminous, and there were twenty shades of browns and greens in the plowed and wooded and folded earth.

"On a clear day you can see the Catskills," said the real-estate man.

Mr. and Mrs. Blandings were not such fools as to exclaim at this revelation. Mrs. Blandings flicked a glove in which a cobweb and free-running spider had become entangled; Mr. Blandings, his lips pursed, was a picture of controlled reserve; strong, realistic, poised. But by the way the two of them said "Uh-huh?" the real-estate man knew that his sale was made. The offer would not come today, of course; it might, indeed, not come for a fortnight. But it would come; it would come with all the certainty of the equinox. He computed five percent of $10,275 in his head and turned to the chimney footing.

"You'd have to do a little pointing up here," he said, indicating a compact but disorderly pile of stone in which a blackened hollow suggested a fireplace that may have once been in good working order. Mrs. Blandings, looking at the rubble, saw instead the kitchen of a wayside inn: a spindle plump with flax lying idly on the polished hearth; copper pots and skillets pegged to hang heads downward near the oven wall; a pig glistening on the spit.

What Mr. Blandings saw broke through into speech. "With a flagstone floor in here it'd be a nice place for a beer party. You could put the keg right over in that corner." He laughed a mild laugh, which meant to say that if his thought was frivolous, so, indeed, was the whole occasion. The notion that he might buy this old farmhouse, or any other, anywhere, ever, was nonsense.

The real-estate man refused to take Mr. Blandings' suggestion so lightly. "You could at that," he said, awe and rumination in his voice, as though he had just heard a brilliant restatement of nuclear theory. He quickly did five percent of $11,550 in his head, and aloud he said, "You haven't seen what's on the other side, either."

Mr. and Mrs. Blandings stepped across a mound of rubbish on the cold earthen floor and saw the second fireplace, an even more impressive example of masonry in disarray. But it was the work of a moment for Mr. Blandings to set everything to rights and swing a polished black kettle on its crane over the glowing ashes of an oak that he himself had sawed and quartered. In a minute he would have a mug of hot rum to banish the cold from his ten-mile plunge through the snowdrifts to rescue the heifer his hired man had abandoned for lost. . . .

"They must have done their own slaughtering down here years ago," said the real-estate man. "You don't see an old kettle like that every day in the week, not even in this part of the country."

The Blandings followed his forefinger and saw, to the right of the hearth, a huge hemisphere of somber metal. Mr. Blandings thumped it lightly with his fist and it gave forth a hushed, whispering boom.

"I think they filled that full of boiling water and scalded the hide off the pig before they roasted it. Anyway, they must have hung their hams and sides of bacon on those hooks up there."

Mrs. Blandings, whose broiling chickens came to her kitchen frozen and packed into neat rectangles from the store near her city apartment, contemplated the slaughtering of a 300-pound hog with ease, and observed the slender beauty of the hooks sunk deep in the old beams; hooks that had been shaped and pointed on some anvil lost in the tall grasses of a century ago.

"Mind your head as we make the turn," said the real-estate man, leading his prospects now into a gloom in which a stairway could be faintly discerned. "I want you to see the living room just the way it's been left ever since old Mr. Hackett died." Despite the injunction, Mr. Blandings failed to stoop sufficiently, and a beam dealt his head a vibrant blow; but his dizziness soon left him, and he was able to join his wife in the admiration she thought she was concealing by her silence.

The living room was not quite like anything the Blandings had ever seen before. Another huge fireplace jutted from the massive central chimney; it had been carefully boarded up, and the boards plastered over with the same wallpaper that ran around the room from ceiling to floor, covering all moldings and ornaments of the past. The wide oak planks of the floor, rounded and buckled here and there, and the magnificent hand-hewn beams, were obviously unchanged since Revolutionary times. But the furnishings were in general of the era of William McKinley, with here and there a final, crowning touch of Calvin Coolidge. The old house had been lived in through successive eras of changing custom and decoration; here was the residue, left when at last one final patriarch had died, and somehow that had been the end of a long story.

Mrs. Blandings was moving in and out of a confusion of tufted-horsehair furniture to gaze at an assortment of photographs on the walls: one was a large bright-tinted portrait, in an oval frame, of an elderly curmudgeon slicked up to the nines. Old Man Hackett, the last patriarch, Mrs. Blandings surmised. There was a family group in a surrey that must have been the height of country style in the 1890's, and in the background could be seen, neat and perfect in a morning sun, the barns that now, on the other side of the road, presented only an aspect of ghostly ruin.

"They just moved out and left things this way when the old man died," said the real-estate man. "After they buried him, his wife and son moved back down into the valley, and the place has stayed this way ever since. That was nearly twenty years ago, around 1926."

"What sort of price is the owner asking for the property?" Mr. Blandings inquired. The sham of his casualness was apparent even to his wife, whose preoccupation with another of the photographs was itself no masterpiece.

The real-estate man's response was casual, too, but it had the benefit of twenty years of practice. "I think he's asking $15,000," he said, "but if you want my opinion, I think you could get it for less."

He turned a gaze of steady, manly frankness on Mrs. Blandings. "Maybe for a whole lot less," he said very quietly, and with a smile that Mrs. Blandings knew he was not in the habit of using on everyone, "if he really took a shine to his prospective buyers."

Mrs. Blandings combined innocence and worldliness in her return gaze, and the real-estate man went on. "These country people, you know, when they have to let their family homes go, they want to see people get them that'll, you know, sort of want to carry on with them in the same spirit."

The smile the Blandings exchanged with the real-estate man was partly in gentle condescension of country people, partly in dissociation of themselves from all other city people who had ever before come up from New York to Lansdale County hunting for a quick bargain in real estate. It was a smile of perfect understanding.

The real-estate man let a little minute of silence go by, to mark the

"Let's go and take a look at your orchard," said the real-estate man.

intimacy into which they had all so happily fallen. When he spoke again, it was as if he had put a precious instant away in his book of memories and was returning now, because he must, to more mundane things.

"Let's go up the hill and take a look at your orchard," he said, clearing his throat. "There's an interesting story connected with . . ."

The effect of the possessive pronoun "your" was as a fiery liquor in Mr. and Mrs. Blandings' veins.

MR. AND MRS. BLANDINGS traveled back to New York City in a heavy flush; in a flush, still, they sat in the New York apartment which had been home to them until that afternoon. It was home no longer; the old Hackett place on Bald Mountain was home now. They wanted it as once, fifteen years ago, they had wanted each other: ravishing desire at one instant; at the next, a sick hopelessness that the desire would ever be fulfilled.

The Blandings had always been city folk. When Mr. Blandings, fresh out of Yale, landed his first job with an advertising agency, he had taken a little one-room-and-bath apartment for himself in the East Thirties. When after a few years of menial writing he was promoted, he had permitted himself to expand to two rooms. He had married not long after that; as newlyweds, Mr. and Mrs. Blandings took up quarters in the East Fifties. When their first baby arrived, they skipped fifteen blocks and moved to the East Seventies. There they stayed. Neither the arrival of their second child two years later nor a series of modest but gratifying promotions by the now celebrated agency of Banton & Dascomb had budged them a foot farther north.

Suddenly, this whole mode of living had become unsatisfactory; Mr. Blandings was beginning to have what seemed like a very nice income. His name had earned a considerable respect in the inner circle of the hardworking, highly competent, and deeply miserable men who wrote advertising copy. While still a relatively young man in his profession, Mr. Blandings had been lucky enough to hit upon a three-word slogan for a laxative account. So compulsive did these three simple monosyllables become, iterated and reiterated to the metabolizing public from print and electronic media, that within three years' time a fading cathartic had come to stand with Ivory Soap, Wrigley's Chewing Gum, and Campbell's Soup as one of the dozen most widely recognized brand names in America.

The happy agency had rewarded Mr. Blandings most generously since the three portentous words had first occurred to him. The client himself made it clear that if ever Mr. Blandings wanted to leave Banton & Dascomb for greener fields, the account would go with him. Mr. Blandings loathed his calling with a deep, passionate intensity, but he was not the man to forgo all of the advantages. If a business of his own did not tempt him, something that he and his friends called "the good life" did.

About the time that a piece of Blandings' laxative copy won a Harvard Advertising Award for the exceptional power and beauty of its language, Mr. and Mrs. Blandings realized that not only could they now afford to expand their modest horizons, but that, in the eyes of their professional colleagues, they could not afford *not* to. And so they began a halfhearted search for land and an old house in the country. Then, suddenly, the land fever had seized them. They knew in a flash what had been wrong with them all those years, and it was just then that they had come upon the Old Hackett Property at the top of Bald Mountain.

"Farm dwelling, oak grove, apple orchard, trout stream, hayfields, four barns, seclusion, superb view, original beams, paved highway, acreage, will sacrifice," *The New York Times* advertisement had said. As the Blandings saw it, it was all utterly true—all, that is, except the very last, which remained an open and terrible question. When the Blandings tried to sleep that first night after their return from Bald Mountain, they could only thrash miserably on their pillows, tortured by visions of Old Man Hackett's son, Ephemus, surrounded by scores of jostling buyers screaming to be heard. Actually, if Mr. Blandings could have known, Ephemus W. Hackett was having a very quiet time of it: his friends had told Eph that he would probably have to wait a long time to sell his property at the price he wanted. But now the real-estate man from nearby Lansdale had called that afternoon to say that by all the signs a buyer was at hand. Pretty quick work, thought Mr. Hackett, who slumbered contentedly in the country airs while Mr. Blandings lay in torture on Manhattan Island, a hundred miles away, counting the minutes until he could stand once again on the height of Bald Mountain and clutch it to him as a child clutches the teddy bear without which life is not to be endured.

THE NEXT SATURDAY Mr. and Mrs. Blandings were on Bald Mountain early. With the real-estate man they once again wandered among the scattered snake fences and the slowly melting stone walls of the Old Hackett Property. "The owner said he'd be up this way sometime this morning," the real-estate man said, looking at his watch. From the vagueness of his utterance it was not to be gathered that he had delivered the most explicit instructions to Mr. Hackett the night before. "For God's sake don't get there a minute before half-past eleven, Eph," he had emphasized. "I want them to be restless."

While they trod the springy, water-bearing earth of the warm mountainside, the Blandings found new fascinations in the old Hackett place. They counted the barns across the road like auditors checking a voucher list; indeed, there were four barns, just as the advertisement had said. Not mentioned in the advertisement was a chicken house, the remains of what must once have been a pigpen, and a generous collection of privies.

"I must say," said Mrs. Blandings, thinking of the warm, sunlit pictures full of the order and prosperity of the 1890's she had seen on the living-room walls the week before, "I must say it all seems rather terribly ramshackle."

The real-estate man smiled at them. "You've got to be able to visualize," he said.

There was no more talk about order or repair. The real-estate man's remark had been genial and straightforward, but it was a rebuke, the Blandings felt, and a deserved one.

In the week that had gone by since the Blandings' first visit, the apple trees, neatly ranged in the orchard, had bedecked themselves like brides in their enchanting bloom. Robins filled the air with their sweet, vernal song. It was still too early for the burst of wildflowers now obviously poised for the early days of summer, but violets were wild in the fields and lilies of the valley dipped and nodded in the shady places. By the time Mr. Hackett put in an appearance, driving a surprisingly large, glossy Buick for the country bumpkin the Blandings had expected, the prospective purchasers were drunk on the sights and sounds of spring on Bald Mountain.

Mr. Blandings, hearing Mr. Hackett constantly referred to as the Hackett "son," was not prepared for a man of between fifty-five and sixty. He had expected him, also, to be taciturn, as befitted a Nutmeg Yankee, and Mr. Blandings was thrown off his stride to find him endlessly garrulous. The Hackett conversation, however, did not cohere; it was vacuous and shrewd, vague and incisive, by turns. Mr. Blandings discovered that he did not know on what level the conversation should be pitched, nor even with what assumptions it should begin. Mr. Hackett, after his father's death, had left Bald Mountain to establish a small feed store and lumberyard in the little town in the valley beneath them. Although the matter of house and land purchase was yet to be raised, Mr. Hackett would periodically mention the extremely favorable prices he not only *could* give Mr. Blandings but *would* give him, that very afternoon, if he could state without delay what quantities of building lumber he would be requiring.

The real-estate man, from long experience, said nothing. He was in effect the farmhand supervising a barnyard mating; if the parties were momentarily coy, coercion was worse than useless. Forces stronger than anything within his control would soon take over and carry matters to their inevitable conclusion. He had seen the process too often to be impatient of the seemingly aimless preliminaries.

The Blandings ended an hour's tour with Mr. Hackett breathless but frustrated. It had successively appeared that Mr. Hackett would not sell any of his property at any price; that he would sell part but not all, under incomprehensible circumstances; that he was open to any reasonable offer; and that he was unaware that any sale was under discussion. His desire to sell building materials to the Blandings, however, was not only clear but urgent. When he finally got into his shiny Buick to drive away, everything was much higher up in the air than before his arrival.

As his car vanished down the hill, the Blandings looked about for the real-estate man. They discovered him some distance away, throwing rocks at a dead cherry tree. "Well," he said cheerfully, "did you get down to business?"

"Well," said Mr. Blandings, "in one way we—"

"No, they didn't," said Mrs. Blandings crisply. "Men complain about women talking and then they—"

"Tell you what," said the real-estate man. "Eph Hackett is going to want a definite offer. If you wait for him to commit himself, you'll wait a century. But there's going to be a lot of real-estate activity up this way this year, by all the signs, and sooner or later somebody is going to come along and give him just about what he wants for this property. If you good people are seriously interested in it, my advice is to speak for it."

He looked at his watch. "I'm going to have to excuse myself in another couple of minutes," he said. "Some other people are coming up on the afternoon train, and I promised I'd meet them. They said they just sort of wanted to come up and look around."

Deep, black panic filled the souls of Mr. and Mrs. Blandings. These hateful Other People, nonexistent until that second, were instantly bodied forth as shrewd, sharp, and predatory; they would assay the Hackett acres in a flash, make a curt offer, and be instantly accepted. Then they would tear down the old house and erect a suburban villa with a varicolored asbestos-shingle roof on the ravished foundations of the immemorial Hackett manor. Mrs. Blandings wanted to cry but was too frightened. Mr. Blandings smiled a smile at the real-estate man that had all the insouciance of a sex fiend in the police lineup; a misshapen, terrible thing.

"Thanks for all your time and trouble," he twisted his mouth to say. "We'll think things over and write you from New York."

NEVER IN HIS LIFE had Mr. Blandings worked so hard on a piece of advertising copy as he now worked on the letter to the real-estate man; something that would convey the precise blend of active arousal, cool disinterest, and refusal to be carried away by daydreams that Mr. Blandings felt was called for.

But consideration of the letter as a work of art had to be postponed three separate times while a vast struggle went on to reexamine a question that had already been solemnly decided: Was a place in the country something the Blandings really *had* to have, after a married life of fifteen years in which, until six weeks ago, no lack of real estate had ever been felt? The process always brought forth the same answer, but never by the same route. What proved to be the final decision was arrived at via the Blandings' two children, concerning whom, Mrs. Blandings now admitted, both parents had been somewhat thoughtless.

Ever since the Blandings' daughters had outgrown their days of pail-and-shovel happiness at the seashore, the Blandings had packed them off to summer camp. They would be due, indeed, to take off again in a very few weeks, to stay until it was almost time for school to reopen in the fall. The girls had always come home after Labor Day lithe and brown, but it was not the most considerate way to treat your own flesh and blood, Mr. and Mrs. Blandings agreed, particularly now that adolescence had begun for one and was an imminent prospect for the other. Girls needed their parents now as they had seldom needed them before; if the ties of intimacy had been frayed by the headlong life of parents-on-the-make in the city, what else could so sweetly knit them up as a home in the country? Young men would be entering their daughters' lives in a year or two; it could almost be said that there was not a minute to lose.

The Blandings' daughters, Betsy and Joan, took the news of a possible country home with an appalling calm and some disdain. At thirteen, Betsy was finding her teeth braces a tragic hobble to approaching womanhood. Joan, at eleven, was a soberly intellectual child who appeared to be anxious to pick up where Madame Curie had left off. Mr. Blandings loved his daughters, but he sorely missed the affectionate childhood during which they both regarded him as God. There was certainly not much fun in them these days, he reflected. At present, it was obvious that both of them regarded him as a husk.

"Miss Stellwagon says that anybody who remodels an old colonial house in these modern times is no better than a dupe," said Betsy. "Is this a colonial house?"

"It is," said Mr. Blandings.

"Miss Stellwagon says that sort of thing is a form of totem worship," said Betsy.

"I am not asking for Miss Stellwagon's opinions," he said.

"There isn't any use sending the children to an expensive school and then undermining a teacher's authority in the parents' living room," said Mrs. Blandings.

"I'm not undermining anybody. I just get tired of hearing this woman's pronouncements. Stellwagon on Housing. Stellwagon on Isotopes. Stellwagon on—"

"I want to live in a Dymaxion house," said Joan. "It's built on a mast like a tent and it revolves with the sun. When it wears out you throw it away and get another one. Or if it isn't a Dymaxion it could be a Stout mobile home," she continued. "It comes all folded up, and when you find a place you like you unfold it and plug in for water and electricity, and when you get tired there you fold it up and find someplace else."

"Don't you kids want to live in something permanent and substantial?" asked Mr. Blandings. "Do you just want to live in upper berths and merry-go-rounds? This house we're talking about was built before this country became a nation. It has dignity."

"How gruesome!" said Betsy.

"Maybe we could hitch a Zamboni power unit onto it," said Joan. "It's the kitchen and bathrooms and heating unit and power generator all rolled up into the size of a refrigerator. You fasten it onto any old house, just the way you fasten a locomotive onto any old freight train, and *zip*—it makes the house *work*. They're going to start building them year after next. I read it."

"You'd have rooms of your own," said Mrs. Blandings, a touch of wheedling in her voice. "Nice big rooms that you could furnish and decorate yourselves, the way you liked best."

"Partitions in a house are obsolete," said Betsy. "An enlightened house has no interior walls—only screens you can move about at will, Miss Stellwagon says. Mother, won't you please ask Dr. Shields to take these torture things off my teeth before the commencement dance next week?"

"It's past bedtime for both of you," said Mrs. Blandings. "If we lived in the country, someday we could have a tennis court and a swimming pool, maybe."

The children brightened perceptibly. "That would be more like it," the two said in unison. They retired without protest and without further allusions to any subject except dentistry.

"The children will love it when they *see* it," said Mrs. Blandings, as soon as she and her husband were alone.

"The way they talked made me realize how much they need a place like Bald Mountain," said Mr. Blandings soberly.

"Joan could have a laboratory in the cellar if she's really set on being a physical chemist," said Mrs. Blandings. "Do you suppose she really will be?"

Mr. Blandings did not answer. A dreamy look had come into his eyes. "This is something we should do for the children, even if we disregarded ourselves," he said.

THE BASIC QUESTION being at last resolved on a high plane, there remained the problem, almost as weighty, of what to offer in the way of money for the Old Hackett Property. It had appeared that Mr. Hackett was "asking" $15,000. So the real-estate man had said, anyway. But had he not also said that Mr. Hackett might be persuaded to take less, or even "a whole lot less"? How much *was* "a whole lot less"? Where did an offer cease to be shrewd and become merely insulting? Mr. Blandings had few landmarks in these woods, save that on the occasions when he had felt it decorous to talk money with the real-estate man, a round, vague figure of $10,000 had now and again cropped up. Among his friends and acquaintances, Mr. Blandings could not discover a soul who had up to that time ever paid that sum for anything. The letter he finally mailed, with the grudging approval of his wife, was a seventeenth draft, in which every word had been weighed and tested.

"My wife and I," he wrote, "have been considering an offer we might feel disposed to make for the property described as the 'old Hackett place,' which we have several times had the pleasure of visiting with you. After due consideration I arrive at a value to me, for the property as it stands, of $9000. I am accordingly glad to propose a cash payment of $4500 and the assumption of a first mortgage which Mr. Hackett would hold to a like amount. If you will convey this proposal to the owner and let me have word at your convenience, I shall be much obliged."

Mr. Blandings considered this letter a masterpiece. He read it over one final time; it was curt but friendly, businesslike but open. It had a genial take-it-or-leave-it quality that could scarcely fail to impress itself on the real-estate man and old Ephemus Hackett. In picking the $9000 figure Mr. Blandings had, of course, placed himself heavily on the defensive with his wife, who was sure it was too low and would merely deliver the property to the Other People, who were still haunting her day and night. Mr. Blandings was equally haunted, but his position as a male did not permit so unshackled a display of his fears.

The Blandings waited, twitching, for a response from the real-estate man. When, after an aeon of seventy-two hours, it came, Mr. Blandings ripped open the envelope and read, sweatily, the blunt first paragraph:

Dear Mr. Blandings:
   I have conveyed your offer to Mr. Hackett and I am sorry to say that he is not interested. . . .

The Blandings swam in a mist of despair, but somehow read on:

   I hope you will not think me forward if I suggest that in my opinion you have somewhat undervalued the Hackett property. The old house has a definite antique value that is bound to increase. I know of no view more superb in all the state than that which the property commands, and although you have an unusual seclusion at the top of the mountain, you happen to be close to not one but two arterial highways. I do not want my own enthusiasms to influence you, but if you see your way clear to making a revised offer, I think I can present it in such a way as to recapture Mr. Hackett's consideration.
   I should point out that your letter did not mention any definite acreage to which your offer applied. The Hackett family has always owned a considerable amount of land on or near Bald Mountain, but I assumed that your interest applied to "the fifty acres, more or less," to which we alluded in our discussions on your several pleasant visits.

Disappointment, relief, and chagrin pursued one another through Mr. Blandings' vitals. The disappointment in the real-estate man's first two lines was mitigated by the suggestion that the way was still open to Mr. Hackett; the Other People, apparently, had not yet preempted everything. But if Mr. Blandings was relieved that the property still existed for him, he was mortified at the real-estate man's sharp remark about the acreage. Yet if he felt chagrined, he also felt instructed. Fifty acres. Certainly. That was really what he had had in mind all along.

Mr. Blandings spent the next two days writing another eight-line letter to the real-estate man. With various rhetorical throat clearings, he raised his offer to $10,500, of which $5500 would be cash, and said that yes of course he had been talking about the fifty acres they had discussed. He mailed it after another day's delay to indicate the casual quality of his interest, and lay sleepless each night until the answer came. Mr Hackett, the real-estate man then reported, had given this offer a more favorable consideration than the first but, after deliberation, had declined it.

That was all. No selling, no come-on stuff, no nothing. Obviously the real-estate man had lost interest in the whole proceeding. The hideous specter of the Other People rose up to torture the Blandings now more frightfully than ever. The man was a coarse, loud creature; the woman was a shrill bitch with ebony-tinted lips and fingernails. The property was theirs for certain, spirited out from under the Blandings' noses during a haggle over a few miserable pennies. Goaded by these nightmares, Mr. Blandings raised his ante to $11,000 in a letter that said, with a finality that made his hand shake as he signed it, that this was the last.

Utter silence ensued.

It was Tuesday morning of the following week when Mr. Blandings' office phone rang and the real-estate man's voice came over the receiver. Mr. Blandings gripped the desk and prepared for the blow that would crush him.

"I think I have good news for you," the real-estate man said. Mr. Blandings' vasomotor system relaxed and blood flowed again in his smaller capillaries. "Mr. Hackett says he'll accept that $11,000 proposition, provided it's net."

Mr. Blandings was instantly wafted from the fiftieth floor of a New York skyscraper to a position a little lower than the angels, but not much. But he did not forget to say, with the first frankness that had characterized him since he saw the Hackett acres, "What do you mean by 'provided it's net'?"

"That you pay the commission," said the real-estate man patiently.

Mr. Blandings was wafted from an office in a New York skyscraper to a position a little lower than the angels, but not much.

"It's five percent, you know."

With no more pause than J. P. Morgan sweeping aside a quibble involved in the creation of United States Steel, Mr. Blandings gave a noise of assent. He even made a remark about "not letting a little thing like that stand between us." What was five percent?

"Good," said the real-estate man. His computation, made five weeks before as the Blandings stood beside the fireplaces in the cellar of the old Hackett house, had turned out well within the limit of error he was in the habit of setting for himself.

CHAPTER TWO

MRS. BLANDINGS SAT under the hair dryer at Vincent & Henri's and dreamed a dream. The children had again been successfully packed off to camp, and she had some time, now, for fancies. The Old Hackett Property was securely hers and her husband's at last. No papers had yet been exchanged, but verbal assurances were enough to make it certain that the Other People had been vanquished. With them happily out of her way she could direct her thoughts to the creation, on the top of Bald Mountain, of enchantment simple and enchantment pure. The stone walls would be rebuilt, firm and square. The rail snake fences would be put to rights and gleam with whitewash. The drooping barns would become again what they had been in the photographs that attested to their handsome, square-shouldered past. The apple orchards would be pruned and sprayed and tidied; the brook cleaned to glint and ripple among its stones. Around the old house would be a velvet lawn, and in beds and pockets and artful places she would plant bulbs and tubers and seedlings that would make the place atop Bald Mountain a glowing altarpiece of flowers. The family would all bloom with country health, fed on country milk, country eggs, country butter. Inside the old house there would be a deep and beautiful peace. . . .

Impatience suddenly curdled in Mrs. Blandings. It would be *weeks* before she could begin this new life to which she had dedicated herself. Her husband and Mr. Hackett had first to sign a purchase agreement; then, after an infinite hocus-pocus that would involve her husband's young friend and attorney, Bill Cole, the deed would be signed in the Lansdale County Courthouse and the property "conveyed." It was tedious beyond belief.

Meanwhile, Bald Mountain was deteriorating day by day, it was only too obvious. She had seen, for example, half a dozen disgusting bowers of tent caterpillars in the lovely apple trees in the orchard. These were *her* trees the caterpillars were slowly munching. God knew what other insect depredations were going on here, there, and elsewhere, totally unknown to her, she reflected with rising dismay. It was hard not to worry, really very hard indeed. But soon Mrs. Blandings fell to work in imagining cretonne curtains, and presently she felt a little better.

When Mr. Blandings came home that evening he was grumpy, and had no conversation in him until the end of the second cocktail. Then it came out that the real-estate man had called him during the afternoon to say that "apparently Mr. Hackett has been a little overoptimistic about the acreage"; it was probably going to survey closer to thirty-five acres than fifty.

"It" had at first been a portion of the earth's surface indicated by Mr. Hackett's sweeping gestures, later somewhat more closely defined by a walk with him following the course of a puzzling alternation of walls, fences, scrub trees, and brush. It had seemed like a good, generous tract of land to Mr. Blandings, and since he and the real-estate man had always talked about "fifty acres" in the same take-it-for-granted way they would have discussed a pound of tea, Mr. Blandings had assumed that the two were one and the same. Now he had been made sharply aware that they were not, and that nobody had ever said they were; he was the victim of self-hypnosis, and he was consequently vexed with his wife.

Mr. Blandings' third cocktail mellowed his judgments a little; he was surprised and relieved when Mrs. Blandings pooh-poohed the whole thing and admitted she would actually be happier with thirty-five acres than with fifty. She had been thinking hard about tent caterpillars and was swiftly coming to regard acreage as a measure more of responsibility than of possession. "I don't know what we'd do with any more acres anyway," she said.

Mr. Blandings drained a final goblet, and the cosmos suddenly rearranged itself in more agreeable proportions. "Thirty-five acres still lots acres," he agreed buoyantly, as he rounded a chair that had interposed itself between him and the dining room.

"YOU'RE BEING FLIMFLAMMED," said Bill Cole. He leaned across Mr. Blandings' office desk and gestured earnestly with his silver pencil. "I don't like a client of mine to enter a verbal agreement to buy fifty acres and then have it turn out that he's going to buy thirty-five acres for the same price. I'm in favor of going to this Hackett-whoever-he-is and telling him the whole deal's off."

Mr. Blandings' blood turned icy cold. "No," he said. Just when he thought things were settled and the Hackett property was his to have and hold forever, here was the whole miserable business drifting loose again. "I couldn't possibly do that. I'm committed and I'm perfectly glad to be committed. I've told them to draw up a purchase agreement for thirty-five acres."

"What are you asking my advice for, then?" Bill Cole asked. "And why do you always wait to call me in until you've gone and committed yourself to something and there's nothing for me to do except try to clean up behind you? Remember the time you bought that carload of butter two years ago?"

Mr. Blandings had no wish to be reminded of the time he and a friend had taken a flier on the Chicago Mercantile Exchange, when Mr. Blandings did not even know how to buy a government bond. "That has nothing to do with our present topic," he said.

"It is identical to our present topic," said Bill. "I will write to this Hackett and tell him he can either kick in with those fifteen acres he's mislaid, reduce the price, or find another sucker."

"No," said Mr. Blandings, rigid in his chair. "Can't I make it clear to you that I *want* this property? It isn't just another chunk of real estate. It's something Muriel and I feel very deeply about. It's going to be our"—he swallowed suddenly—"home."

How, he thought to himself in a silent frenzy, can this young friend of mine be so colossally stupid? A graduate of Harvard Law School in the top tenth of his class, a Rhodes scholar after that, and now on his way to being head of the whole legal department of General Bag— and yet he can sit here and talk this way about what I have just been breaking my heart to acquire. Can't he *understand?*

Bill Cole laid down the pencil with which he had been doing some scratch arithmetic. "Have you any idea how much those brigands have traded you up already without your knowing that anything has happened to you?" he asked. "You offered $9000 for fifty acres the first time around, didn't you?"

Mr. Blandings nodded.

"That's $180 an acre," said Bill Cole. "I know that part of the country as well as you do, and $100 is the standard top-gouge price per acre to city slickers. However, we'll assume your $180 an acre is a fair price for the acreage plus various unimproved structures. You finally raised your offer to $11,000, which is $220 an acre. Then first they stick you for the commission, which brings you up to $231 an acre, and now they tell you that your money is only going to buy you thirty-five acres, which brings the price up to $330 an acre."

"When are you going to come to the point?" asked Mr. Blandings.

"*That* is my point," said Bill Cole. "This is a fifty percent increase over what you said was your final offer, and you don't even seem to know that this has been going on."

"Look," said Mr. Blandings. "If you're criticizing me for not having bought the whole of Manhattan Island for $24 and a bottle of Holland gin, you're not affecting me."

Bill took off his glasses, put them in the case, and snapped the case closed briskly. "Look," he said. "Every time you get a little tight, you weep on my shoulder about what a terrible thing it is to make your living out of bamboozling the American public. I would say that a small part of this victimized group has now redressed the balance. Humanly, I am willing to leave it at that. As your attorney, however, I insist that a letter of record go to Hackett *et al.*, in the matter of fifty acres versus thirty-five acres, and if it does not, you can get some other lawyer to put the deeds through."

After another half an hour of discussion, Mr. Blandings signed a cooled-off version of the scorching letter Bill Cole had composed. It emphasized that Mr. Blandings, having discussed the purchase of fifty acres, wished to purchase fifty acres. He mailed it that evening and waited anxiously for a reply.

"Mr. Hackett is nonplussed," the real-estate man wrote him with chilly decorum several days later, "to have a new proposition put before him at the instance of your lawyer just when the original one was about to be ratified. Subsequent to your offer he has had several other tempting proposals and has asked that I tell you he would be agreeable to the cancellation of any verbal agreements between you and him, should you be dissatisfied with the representations made."

Mr. Blandings spent a day cursing Bill Cole to the depths of nether hell, and then dispatched a letter of cordial disacknowledgment for what he had written at Bill's urging. But Bill had also planted in Mr. Blandings' mind the cancerous seed of suspicion, now growing to a certainty, that he *was* being flimflammed. He was being flimflammed and there was nothing he could do about it because he would rather be flimflammed and get the Hackett property than not be flim-flammed and not get it. Mr. Blandings would never admit to Bill that he had been so deftly frisked by an old windbag who seemed unable to keep his mind on any one subject for more than thirty seconds, but in his heart, Mr. Blandings knew it to be so. Hackett had looked him coolly up and down and taken his measure, for once, for all.

"THIRTY-FIVE ACRES, more or less—" that was what the purchase agreement, somewhat sulkily checked by Bill Cole, now told Mr. Blandings he was contracting to buy. That "more-or-less" phrase bothered him as he saw it embedded in the formal agreement, but he no longer felt in a moral position to share his uncertainty with Bill.

It had comforted Mr. Blandings to know that the property had to be surveyed with rod and transit and an official map made a part of the final papers, even though it had come to him as a surprise that the buyer, not the seller, was the one who bore the cost. However, he had cheerfully ponied up the $65 that met the bill of the local surveyor, and now he had before him the crisp blueprint of his boundaries. He studied the blueprint and three pages of closely typed description of how the boundaries ran. He felt a sense of calm and security as he saw his own name on the map; the surveyor's jargon made a soothing singsong in his ear: ". . . thence along said stonewall fence forming the East boundary of said Lansdale Road 21.84 feet to the end of said stonewall fence, thence along a wire fence N 16° 31′ W, 78.66 feet to a twenty-inch chestnut tree, thence in a straight line . . . stonewall fence . . . said boundary . . . to a total of thirty-one and one-half acres as certified by me this twelfth day . . . year of our Lord One Thousand Nine Hundred and—"

"To a total of *what?*" Mr. Blandings cried aloud.

He stared at the survey sheet without affecting in the slightest the figure of thirty-one and one-half acres as attested by the surveyor. Fortunately for Mr. Blandings' bursting indignation, Bill Cole answered his phone immediately.

"Fascinating," said Bill after Mr. Blandings had vented his first preliminary gasps.

"He can't *do* this," said Mr. Blandings.

"The time to fight about the acreage," said the attorney in an infuriating, flat voice, "was when I wrote that letter you first emasculated and then totally disacknowledged. If the survey shows thirty-one and a half acres, then the fact that this same area is loosely described elsewhere as thirty-five acres 'more or less' has very little to do with anything."

"There must be *something* to do," said Mr. Blandings.

"Your friend Mr. Hackett has an eye like Joe DiMaggio, that's all," said Bill. "He has a remarkable grasp of common fractions, too. Taking ten percent from thirty-five acres leaves thirty-one and a half acres. Here and there, there's a rough convention that ten percent on either side is the tolerance a court might regard as the limit of fair play. He seems to have hit that right on the button—couldn't have done better on a lathe."

"You don't seem disposed to be very helpful," said Mr. Blandings.

"There may be some sort of stink that could still be raised," Bill replied, "but the legal facts are pretty obscure by now, in view of your letter—and I don't want to get a reputation for ambulance chasing when my client doesn't even know he's been run over."

"Well," said Mr. Blandings, "maybe—"

"I'm looking forward to meeting Mr. Hackett," said Bill Cole in a tone that indicated the conversation could now close. "As of this minute he is getting a bonus of 104 percent, and this is the first faint yip of pain he's drawn so far. I'll see you at the train gate in the morning."

But the next morning Mr. Blandings found little to say to Bill as the train bore them northward to the Lansdale County Seat, and Bill seemed content to read two newspapers and a long legal document without pressing Mr. Blandings for conversation. When the two of them entered the bare, echoing room that served old Probate Judge Lester Quarles as his chambers, Mr. Blandings suddenly found himself feeling awed and embarrassed. The judge was brisk. The real-estate man carried himself with a strange sort of reverence. Mr. Blandings had been prepared to treat Mr. Hackett with a freezing hauteur and was therefore taken aback at the blaze of hostility in Mr. Hackett's eyes directed at *him*. Mr. Hackett's aged mother, there to affix a palsied signature to some necessary papers, contributed an occasional shower of tears that made Mr. Blandings feel like a criminal; this was, she made evident without comprehensible words, the occasion that bore out of her life and into the hands of a callous and pomaded barbarian (Mr. Blandings had had a haircut, which made him look unfortunately sleek) the home to which she had come on a bridal night some sixty years gone by; where she had borne three sons and a daughter and reared them all; where she had watched the maples leaf and the lilac flower, spring after spring after spring, since the days when

Mr. Hackett's aged mother contributed a shower of tears that made Mr. Blandings feel like a criminal.

the United States was a country newly made whole after a civil war.

Mr. Blandings was angry and guilty and apologetic and harassed all at the same time. There was nothing for him to do except sign his name occasionally where Bill told him to, and to stare uncomfortably about the room. Finally, the moment came when Mr. Blandings handed over to Judge Quarles his certified check for $5500. He sighed deeply. The judge immediately demanded four other checks—for tax adjustment, interest on something or other, the real-estate man's brokerage fee and the judge's own legal fee. They made a tidy sum in themselves. Bill Cole assented, and when the old judge had scrutinized them all he solemnly handed to Bill documents that Mr. Blandings was later to identify as an Administrator's Deed, a Quitclaim Deed, a Certificate of Title, and a handful of miscellaneous receipts. It was done.

"Well," said Bill to his shrinking client, "it's all yours now—subject, of course, to that mortgage." Judge Quarles cleared his throat in a terminal manner. Mr. Hackett shook hands with the judge and the real-estate man, nodded curtly to Bill Cole and Mr. Blandings, and guided his weeping mother out of the room. A moment later, Mr. Blandings and his young attorney were blinking on the steps of the courthouse in the bright noon sun of a flawless June day.

"That's that," said Bill Cole.

The real-estate man joined them for a moment on the steps, shook hands solemnly, and disappeared.

Standing there, Mr. Blandings could not escape the conviction that he had done something sneaky and illicit.

As TO A FEAST DAY, a Mardi Gras, Mr. and Mrs. Blandings had looked forward to the day when they alone, without benefit of the real-estate man, Mr. Hackett, or any other hangers-on, would be able to visit the old Hackett place and establish their ownership of it. "To have and to hold to him, the said Grantee, his heirs and assigns, to his and their own proper use and benefit forever"—those were the words of their deed, almost Biblically beautiful, the Blandings thought.

And now the day was here. Mr. Blandings felt gay to the point of song as he and his wife drove through the network of back-country roads that crisscrossed the happy hills and valleys of Lansdale County. He had never driven this tangle of roads himself, but he had watched closely the practiced turns and counterturns of the real-estate man's snappy convertible roadster. Right turn at the green mailbox; bear left when you come to the milk stand across from the bright red barn; straight ahead past the old cemetery; a sharp, hairpin left when you come to the great bole of the fallen chestnut that lay at the top of the rise where you could see a distant steeple.

It seemed to Mr. Blandings that he was a long time in coming to the fallen chestnut, and a few minutes later it struck him that perhaps he had never before in his life seen the deserted farm on his left. When he suddenly came to a sign saying SHRUNKS MILLS 2 MI. he realized he was lost. *He had bought a place in the country for $11,550 and now he could not find it!*

"I think we're lost," said Mrs. Blandings.

Her husband turned on her savagely, but discovered that he had no materials ready for a retort.

"Why do you always speed up when you've lost your way?" Mrs. Blandings pursued in her see-how-reasonable-I-am voice. "You don't give me any time to look for signposts."

Twenty minutes later, Mr. Blandings gave up and spread his humiliation on the record; he stopped and asked a lurching oaf on the roadway for directions. The roadside traveler had never heard of any such name as Hackett and knew nothing of the Old Hackett Property, but wondered if he could have a lift to Shrunks Mills.

While hunting for Shrunks Mills, Mr. Blandings had suddenly come on the Lansdale railroad station, whence he had started two hours ago. He set out for Shrunks Mills again to drop the wayfarer with whom he had become entangled, then returned to the Lansdale railroad station to start life anew for the third time. Not only could he not find his future home; he could not now find anything similar to what he had accidentally traversed before. Much later, Mr. Blandings got out of his car and knocked on a farmhouse door. "Excuse me," he said to a large woman with suds up to her elbows, "I wonder if you can tell me how close I am to the Old Hackett Property."

If he had displayed to his wife one tenth of the deference he now showed to this big, untidy, ferocious farm woman, she would have kissed and forgiven him in an instant. But a man could go just so far in self-abnegation, and no further.

"Somebody's bought it," said the woman.

"I know," said Mr. Blandings. "That is, I—" He stopped, entrapped on the brink of a new disaster.

"Did *you* buy it?" asked the woman, coming to the heart of the matter in an instant.

A lie would do no good. A lie would make everything worse, if possible. The woman knew. Mr. Blandings could feel himself turning the color of a new drainpipe. "Yes," he said.

The woman's contralto laugh brought six children instantly to the sagging door frame; six children and a hollow, saturnine man with a wad of tobacco in his cheek.

"So you're the fella Eph Hackett's unloaded his place on," the woman boomed. "And now you can't find it." She checked another echoing laugh. "Maybe you're lucky at that," she said.

Mr. Blandings detested her. "Which way is it?" he asked, attempting to reject all other conversational gambits.

"Lord, mister," said the woman, "I don't know whether I can help you or not. I never heard of anybody mislayin' where he lived before. Or where he's goin' to live, anyway. You goin' to *farm* it?" she asked, her eyes like arrow tips.

"Just a little, I guess," said Mr. Blandings. He was wishing he had become a monk that time back in 1919 when an adolescent fit of religious fervor had hit him. With a vow of poverty, he would never have been able to write a check to anybody for anything; a vow of chastity would have precluded Mrs. Blandings and the Blandings children; a vow of obedience . . .

"Go ahead and try farming something 'just a little' around this country," said the woman. Her tone was not hostile; she was merely blustering him as she would have blustered one of her children. "It'd do me good to get up at four o'clock in the morning 'just a little.' "

Suddenly she took pity on him. "Look," she said. "You want to get to Eph Hackett's place, I tell you what you better do. Go back to the Lansdale railroad station and ask somebody where Squantatuck Road is. Then . . ."

Mr. Blandings, in his agony, heard no word of the new directions. He returned to the car.

"What did she say?" asked Mrs. Blandings with the correctness of a Prussian in a conquered city. Mr. Blandings mumbled feebly and soon found himself again in Shrunks Mills, where his previous voyager, now leaning against a hardware-store window, regarded him with obvious relish.

It was near dusk when the Blandings reached their home on Bald Mountain. The new owners watched as a murmuration of starlings swooped and chattered in the fading sky; a woodchuck the size of a collie waddled across the road. He cast a sneering look at the estranged couple and faded into a tangle of brush. As if prodded by an invisible finger, a shingle high up on the old house roof broke loose from where it had lain since 1775 and slid with a scrambling noise down its fellows to the eaves, and there fell off. As the Blandings looked at the little scar of raw wood it had left behind, the top edge of the sun's red disk vanished behind the distant Catskills.

CHAPTER THREE

"LET'S SAY YOUR land'll cost you $10,000, round numbers," the real-estate man had occasionally said in the days before it had actually cost more. "And let's say it'll cost you $10,000 to restore the old farmhouse. So you've made a $20,000 investment that'll stand you all the rest of your life, to say nothing of having a home to live in. It's pretty hard to see how you're going to lose."

This lyric passage had served the Blandings in lieu of thought for several months until, one evening, Mrs. Blandings looked up from her mending. "Do you suppose it's worth our while to remodel that old house?" she asked in a faraway voice.

If she had risen in church to confess the illegitimacy of their daughters, she could scarcely have had a more thunderous effect upon her husband.

"I only mean," she went on in an effort to silence him, "that maybe somebody should look at it besides Mr. Funkhauser."

Mr. Savington Funkhauser was a young architect who had done some farmhouse restoration for friends of the Blandings, and Mr. Blandings discovered that he had retained him during the course of a cocktail party at which the two had met for the first time. Mr. Funkhauser had been enchanted with the old Hackett house and pronounced it one of the truest gems of Revolutionary architecture he had ever seen. By the time he had finished explaining to the

Blandings where the original front door had been, the probable date of the addition of the ell, and where the original twelve-light windows had been replaced with modern, double-hung windows, Mr. Blandings felt that his possibly impulsive choice of an architect was well ratified. After spending one rainy day on Bald Mountain, Mr. Funkhauser had since been covering reams of sketch tissue with the graceful swashes of a 6-B drawing pencil. The Blandings had found the results enchanting. "He's retained all the feeling of the old house," they would tell people, "in spite of all the changes. Look at the way he's blended that turret into the original lines. He really has an extraordinary instinct for what's right and what's wrong in that part of the countryside, and it's so remarkable he should have, coming from Brooklyn the way he does."

Mrs. Blandings' question seemed to alter this congenial footing. Sensing trouble, Mr. Blandings thrust out an immediate patrol. "What's the matter with Funkhauser?" he demanded. "Last time I heard, you were so crazy about his sketches you were practically getting into bed with him."

"I wish you could find some other expression to indicate sympathy and understanding between two people," said Mrs. Blandings. "I only mean that Mr. Funkhauser is so enthusiastic about everything that sometimes I think he gets carried away. I'd like to have some other sort of person take a look at the house, just to make certain that it's going to keep on standing up, and things like that."

In no time Mr. Blandings came to believe that he himself had had this prudent idea. By now he once again felt sufficiently at ease with Bill Cole to consult with him, and it turned out that Bill knew just the man—a good practical fellow who Bill guaranteed would not be carried away by anything. It was arranged that Mr. Fred Apollonio, construction engineer, would visit the Hackett property and give the Blandings the benefit of his advice.

Once, at three o'clock in the morning, it sleepily occurred to Mr. Blandings that if he was doing the right thing in calling upon Mr. Apollonio's experience, there must be some doubt as to whether he was doing it at the right time. He had bought his house and land for $11,550 and there were 31.5 acres of land; that was water over the dam. Since a city dweller could, as Bill had emphasized, buy all the *unimproved* land he wanted for $100 an acre, then the house had

"Sometimes I think Mr. Funkhauser gets carried away," said Mrs. Blandings.

cost him the difference between $11,550 and $3150, or $8400, and he was now about to call a witness to testify that it might be worth— *nothing?* Mr. Blandings sat up sharply in bed, a thin band of sweat across his brow. But no, it would not be that. It would not. That noble old farmhouse that the stout young Hackett men of Revolutionary days had hewn out of oak and ash, the adz marks still sharp on the stout, inflexible beams . . .

Besides, Mr. Blandings' thoughts continued, there were the barns; the barns and the shed and—and the privies, too, when you came to think of it. They were worth quite a tidy sum, probably. *"No, they weren't, either,"* said Mr. Blandings' demon in his ear. "You damn well know they're not, Blandings. When it came to the question of fire insurance (which took you somewhat by surprise, by the way; you hadn't dreamed the rates would be that high when the real-estate man suddenly turned insurance agent and asked to write your policies), you agreed that it wasn't worth insuring the barns at all, that $5000 was enough to carry on the old house. Why did you agree that the old house should be insured for so little?"

Mr. Blandings rose and groped for the bathroom. From the medicine cabinet he extracted a bottle of pills; he looked glumly for a minute at the red lettering on the label that said, CAUTION: MAY BE HABIT-FORMING, and swallowed two pellets.

MR. APOLLONIO VISITED THE OLD Hackett place with Mr. and Mrs. Blandings a week later. In his black shoes and dark business suit and derby, he made an odd picture among the roaming hills, particularly compared to Mr. Blandings in his slightly aggressive rural tweeds. But he was a mine of wisdom. He worked for the Port of New York Authority and had apparently been assistant chief of rivet design during the days of the building of the great bridge that now flung its exquisite steel shawl across the Hudson River. Mr. Blandings felt a little silly at the idea of asking this master to look at an old farmhouse, but Mr. Apollonio set all at ease by a wave of his thick, stubby, competent hand. "Glad to pick up the extra money," he said with simple candor.

On the site, Mr. Apollonio became wordless. He stood looking at the house from about a hundred feet away, his hands on his hips, his derby pushed upward on his forehead. After five minutes of silent contemplation, he went up to the house and kicked one corner of it. The Blandings winced in unison as something unidentified fell off.

Mr. Apollonio picked up the fragment, fumbled with it for a moment, and tossed it away. Then he opened the door through which Mr. and Mrs. Blandings had made their first ingress ever into their future home; when the door fell toward him as it had toward Mr. Blandings, Mr. Apollonio leaped aside as if he had encountered an African hartebeest. Mr. Blandings felt something give in the pit of his stomach when he reflected that this man who now recoiled from the door of their house was the same man who had regaled them that morning with the tale of how he had stood on a steel plate atop the final girder for the western tower of the George Washington Bridge in a thirty-five-mile wind.

When Mr. Apollonio emerged from the house and returned to his clients he was dusting his hands. He spoke to them in a soft voice.

"You oughtta tear it down," he said.

Mr. Apollonio, whose competency was hard to question, went on to state his reasoning. "If your chimney was shot and your sills were okay, I'd say go ahead, fix her up," he said. "If your sills were shot and your chimney was okay, again I'd say go ahead, fix her up. But your sills are shot *and* your chimney is shot, so I say okay, you better tear her down. You want a roof on your house? You won't have that one long, and if you did, you'd have to raise it a foot, foot 'n' a half, two foot, and it would cost you $2000 just for that—unless you want to keep midgets upstairs, maybe?"

His mellow laugh was a blasphemy in the everlasting hills.

"THAT STINKING ROUGHNECK has simply no feeling for antiquity," said Mr. Blandings, taking a spastic gulp out of his glass.

"I wish you wouldn't drink when you're upset," said Mrs. Blandings. She and her husband were back in their city apartment again. It was not only to exorcise the memory of Mr. Apollonio that Mr. Blandings now wished oblivion for the rest of the evening. The instant he entered his apartment he had written out a check for $50 to Mr. Apollonio's order, and dispatched it to him with a curt, correct note. Now Mr. Blandings was alone with God and Mrs. Blandings, and there seemed no concealing from either of them that he had paid a not inconsiderable sum for a structure that he had just been advised (for $50 more) to destroy.

In Mr. Blandings' view his wife was an accessory before the fact and God stood convicted of the grossest sort of negligence. But condemn them as he might, he could see no recourse from either of them, or from the real-estate man or from Ephemus Hackett. Yet the real-estate man, Mr. Blandings' conscience perversely told him, had uttered not the slightest word of misrepresentation; had, in fact, scarcely done anything at all except keep the channel clear for Mr. Blandings' own racing fantasies. As for Mr. Hackett, Mr. Blandings would like to fry him in hell—yet the record would show that Mr. Hackett had been a most reluctant seller, having rejected two offers and dictated the revision of a third before the purchase agreement was finally signed.

There remained, however, the luckless Mr. Funkhauser, still doodling happily on his sketch tissue, dreaming towers and battlements onto an old wreck of a farmhouse. Him, Mr. Blandings fired with a thunderclap suddenness that left, as one residue, a folder on file at the American Institute of Architects labeled "Funkhauser-Blandings Grievance Case." After a consultation with Bill Cole on the law of contracts, Mr. Blandings gave up any attempt to wave aside Mr. Funkhauser's claim to a fee, paid him $435 for the "Preliminary Plans for Restored Blandings Residence," and received the tracings and blueprints thereof.

*Mr. Perlasky said he would take
the house down, all neat and clean, and
not charge a penny more than $950.*

They were cold comfort. So was the report of Mr. Joe Perlasky, a local housewrecker and junkyard proprietor whom Mr. Blandings had consulted on the sly, in the hope of presenting to Mrs. Blandings the happy news that they could realize perhaps $2000 out of the salvaged materials. Mr. Perlasky, a stout little man with hands like frankfurters, had figured for fifteen minutes on the back of an old shirt cardboard and then announced that he would take the house down, remove all materials, and leave everything neat and clean around the foundations and not charge Mr. Blandings a penny more than $950.

"Charge?" cried Mr. Blandings. " 'At's right," said Mr. Perlasky, who explained his modest figure by saying that he would take a chance on being able to use the beams on another job.

It was at this point that Mr. Blandings' stout heart failed him. He put Mr. Perlasky off with paltering evasions, but when he faced Mrs. Blandings with the news he had no alternative but to be brave. The entire Blandings restoration project must be put off to another, happier time. They had their land; they could now afford the luxury of delay while they made up their minds about the next step. In any case, Mr. Blandings had no wish to begin until prices were "right," and currently, every trend curve in Wall Street counseled caution and postponement.

The forces that were to make prices "right" in the residential construction industry were not known to Mr. Blandings, but he did not know that he did not know them. He was sure, however, that the following spring would be the time to resume constructive thoughts. The summer had vanished anyway. The children were home from camp and back in school; by the strange alchemy of childhood, they were now full of gleeful excitement about a house in the country—the more utterly colonial the better. The Blandings were happy, but their children's new eagerness would not hurry them. Probably the worst and most frequent mistake of home builders, they agreed, was trying to rush things. What was the delay of one season compared to the everlasting satisfactions of having planned deeply and planned well? Mr. and Mrs. Blandings let the gray winter close in on them with an almost Oriental calm.

The calm was broken one February evening when Mr. Blandings engaged in figuring up his expenses to date. The first figures left him dissatisfied; he did the whole thing again, and the results were the same. Mr. Blandings then came face to face with the inexorable fact that in land cost, brokerage, and a round dozen other items, he had so far spent nearly $14,000—a great deal more than he'd ever expected to spend—and the sound of a saw or hammer was yet to be heard on Bald Mountain.

"WE CAN FIX UP that old house," said Mr. Simms, looking at it with affection. "Of course we can. You can fix up *any* structure that's still standing. The sills and the chimney certainly couldn't be worse, I grant you, but I'm amazed at how solid the beams are."

The Blandings inwardly exulted. They would "restore" their house after all, just as God had meant them to when first He brought them to it. Mr. Simms was saying they could.

Mr. Simms was the new architect, and the Blandings loved him. They had discovered him living not five miles away from Bald Mountain—a distinguished member of his profession, deferred to by men with names more publicized than his own, author of two books on local architecture, alert, vital, and humorous: the obvious answer to home builders in trouble.

"On the other hand," Mr. Simms continued, "fixing up any house as neglected as this one is going to cost a lot of money. Just about as much money as building a new house of the same size, I'd say, and I question whether you'd have what you want when you get through. My advice is to start afresh."

Very well, said the Blandings inwardly, we'll start afresh. Nothing so healthy as acknowledging an error and wiping the slate clean.

Later that morning Mr. Simms showed the Blandings a portfolio of houses he had designed, and the last lingering uncertainties in Mr. Blandings' mind about home building disappeared completely. The houses were superb. They clung low to the ground; their long horizontal lines were infinitely restful; they breathed peace and security, ease, charm, taste, quiet, and serenity. Even a stair rail or a porch rail, as Mr. Simms designed it, was lovely to look at. Mr. Simms was a cause for rejoicing.

Of course, Mr. and Mrs. Blandings had set out with the assumption that they had $20,000 to spend, half for the land and half for the house, and the arithmetic had seemed simple. It was somewhat more clouded now. Manifestly, they had overspent on the land, and they couldn't skimp by putting up a mere bungalow. No, that would be stupid. Prices were somewhat higher now, too, so that the cost of the house would have to be adjusted. It might come out a little on the high side, but you couldn't spend all your life worrying about $1000 here or $1000 there. When the Blandings' children got older they certainly wouldn't thank their parents for having built a house in which they couldn't entertain their young friends.

What the Blandings wanted, they explained to Mr. Simms, was simple enough: a two-story house in quiet, modern, good taste; something to blend with the older architecture of the countryside around them, but no slavish imitation. It would be, in effect, an updating of the old house, with obvious modifications dictated by the difference between the professions of farming and advertising.

"Excellent," said Mr. Simms. "You people really understand your problem."

On the first floor the Blandings wanted a good-sized living room with a fireplace; a dining room, pantry, and kitchen; a small lavatory. On the second, there would be four bedrooms and four accompanying baths. There must be a roomy cellar for various goings-on, vague but essential; a good attic for storage; plenty of closets and a couple of porches. "We're certainly asking for the minimum," said Mr. Blandings.

Mr. Simms said that if they really meant it, they could have this for very close to their revised figure, provided they cut out two of the four bathrooms, which ran into money in a dozen different ways. Mrs. Blandings said she was sorry, but two bathrooms would not do. That might as well be clear at the outset. Mr. Simms agreed that Mrs. Blandings had not left it ambiguous.

A series of lovely days began. For the approaching summertime, the Blandings rented a pleasant little cottage not far from the foot of their mountain. Mrs. Blandings would stay there until autumn; the children would stay until camp time, and Mr. Blandings would come up for weekends and his August vacation.

So in the sweet, warm afternoons, Mr. Simms and the Blandings would confer and plan together, and Mr. Simms would draw the scrupulously neat, light lines of his first tentative plans. Things went swimmingly. The Blandings were being lucky at last, and they reveled in their good fortune.

The Blandings girls saw in Mr. Simms a marked resemblance to Charles Boyer, except for an accent, and mooned after him endlessly. In the midst of the new happiness, Mr. Blandings had only one complaint. "Simms makes everything too small," he said. "I think his ideas are wonderful, but, my God, if there's one thing I don't want in the country, it's to feel *cramped*."

To this criticism Mr. Simms replied that he was watching the

In the sweet, warm afternoons, they would confer and plan together.

cubage. The Blandings had never heard of cubage before, but Mr. Simms explained. It was the overall cubic content that roof and walls enclosed. A rough rule of thumb was that, for the sort of house the Blandings obviously wanted, with quality materials and tasteful finish, the cost would be about forty-five to fifty cents a cubic foot. This sounded dirt cheap to Mr. and Mrs. Blandings. Mr. Simms, they felt (and told him), was holding a little too tight a rein on the cubage, good fault that it was.

Mr. Simms sighed a little. "Look," he said. "You ought to be fully aware that this $18,000 'more or less' "—Mr. Blandings winced inwardly—"that you're now calling the cost of your house doesn't get you moved in with light bulbs in all the sockets and a pack of cigarettes on every table. It's for the bare house, and it doesn't figure a stove or a refrigerator or a washing machine, and other things like that. And you've got a water supply to think of."

Good God, the water supply, thought Mr. Blandings. He had mentally turned on all the glittering chrome faucets in the bath a hundred times and they had gushed forth like Moses' rock, but he had somehow not traced their bounteous supply back to its source.

"I just don't want you to wake up some morning in a state of shock, that's all," he heard Mr. Simms conclude.

"Maybe we'd better cut out *one* bathroom," said Mr. Blandings, pleased with himself now that he had the water-supply problem well in hand.

"I will not hazard the children's health in a house with three bathrooms," said Mrs. Blandings. She looked so flushed with annoyance that Mr. Simms clamped his jaw shut on a decorously jocose remark that had just occurred to him about privies. There was a time for everything, but this was not it.

"WHERE," ASKED MR. BLANDINGS one weekend later, "are we going to *put* the house?"

It was a simple question, fraught with peril. It made suddenly apparent a flaw in understanding between client and architect. Mr. Simms had assumed that the three criteria for the site were level ground, a good view, and nearness to the road. He was too experienced an architect to make such an assumption without putting it into words, but somehow he had, and now there was hell to pay. For several days before this crisis arose, Mr. and Mrs. Blandings had been notably aloof from one another; they had obviously been having bad fourth-bathroom trouble and had spoken to one another in Mr. Simms' presence with cold infrequence. Suddenly, they had common cause: man and his mate against the hated stranger at the cave's mouth. What they had assumed all along, they said fiercely to Mr. Simms, was that the new house would burrow into the side of a hill just as the old house did. They saw no reason why this should alarm, discommode, or depress the architect in any way. It came to them only slowly, and with much feverish impromptu sketching by Mr. Simms, that if their house was to jut into a hillside, all the windows on its north side would be considerably below grade. Eventually the Blandings altered their concept of the site and the crisis abated. But Mr. Simms needed occasional heavy drafts of self-control over the next month when Mrs. Blandings would now and again refer to "Mr. Simms' mistake" in placing a handsome set of casement windows beneath the grass.

So, without too much unhappiness, the house was again planned to lie on the spot for which Mr. Simms had begun to design it. Thereupon another problem swiftly arose in the Blandings' minds. The new house was too close to the old house—the two buildings would clash impossibly.

"I certainly hate to see you tear that old house down," said Mr. Simms. "But I suppose you've got to face it; you've either got to tear it down or fix it up."

"I guess," said Mr. Blandings, "we'll tear it down. We'll tear it down right here and now before what I once heard described as its 'genuine antique value' costs me any more money to get rid of." His underlip suddenly quivered, like a mistreated servant girl's. Shortly, he put on a stolid mask and sought a new interview with Mr. Perlasky, and learned that the price of removing the house would now be $1075. Labor had gone up, and Mr. Perlasky no longer knew for certain of a job on which he could use the old beams.

Mr. Perlasky came to work a week later with two assistants, and within an hour the ground around the old house was strewn with ravished shingles. Mr. Blandings could not bear to look at the lovely old building as it became more and more ragged. There came a time when nothing but the frame remained, enclosing the stump of the chimney and the massive fireplaces around which Mr. and Mrs. Blandings had once planned to sit and rock and mull the wine and patch the quilts and roast the apples as, with graceful serenity, they entered the twilight of their lives.

"Watch it!" cried Mr. Perlasky, as a final load of filth flung itself out of the sky and landed at Mr. Blandings' country brogues. He glared at the blue vault of the heavens and then at the pile at his feet. "My equity," he said softly to himself. "My $8400; there it lies. Why didn't I light cigars with it? Spend it on liquor and women? I could have had quite a time on $8400."

As Mr. Blandings watched Mr. Perlasky and his men struggling to unship the doweled and mortised beams, he wondered whether he had done *anything* since the day he first saw the Old Hackett Property except follow one demented decision with another. The error of buying the house was not corrected by the error of tearing it down. He had obliterated a relic of history at a very large cost to himself, including $50 for the advice to take it down and $1075 for following the advice. The total was $9525 plus what he was sure were the beginnings of an obscure ailment in his stomach.

The evening came when the last truckload of rubbish rattled away down the mountain, and only an empty, stone-girded rectangle of earth remained to show where a living house had been. The great lilac tree stood alone now, its companion of the years gone from its side. Mr. Blandings remembered another evening, a year ago, when the first tiny, tentative question about the worth and fitness of the old house had been raised. He remembered who had raised it. He very much wanted to ask Mrs. Blandings if *she* remembered, and if she was pleased, now, with the finale. As he was about to clear his throat, he heard his wife sigh.

"I *hope* you were wise in taking down the old house," said Mrs. Blandings.

THE VIGOROUS YOUNG brook that went dodging down the rocks behind the building site had always been referred to, during real-estate negotiations, as "the trout stream." It came to Mr. Blandings now that the brook would be his source of water. Mr. Simms had looked dubious at this proposal, but had said only, "I think it dries up in August." When Mr. Blandings imprisoned some of the crystal waters in a five-gallon jug, he was disappointed at the brown swirling fragments of something or other that settled to the bottom.

For $6.50 the nearby Stoop Biological Laboratories rendered an analysis of the contents, warning him that the waters were unpotable; it suggested the presence of cows in an upper field as the reason behind the intense activity visible even under the lowest power of the microscope. Mr. Blandings had often seen the cows, he now realized; they belonged to a neighborhood farmer from whom he had expected to buy milk. He had thought of them happily, but as a source of nourishment, not of bacteria. As things were turning out, the laboratory said, he had better drill an artesian well.

Mr. Blandings sighed, but bowed to what must be. An artesian well sounded expensive, but it also sounded exciting. Even in his boyhood, he remembered, a shallow well had sufficed all but the wealthiest; ladies of the most fragile quality drank with impunity from wells and streams whose waters would fell a stevedore today. The race was certainly getting brittle, Mr. Blandings reflected.

Mr. Simms offered the name of a local well driller who would drill Mr. Blandings a well at $4.50 a foot for the first three hundred feet, and $6 a foot thereafter, if necessary. When a fortnight later one Mr. John Tesander, well driller, appeared on the Blandings' acres with a bright red drill rig, a new richness came into Mr. Blandings' life.

Mr. Tesander, who spoke English heavily tinctured by the mountains of Bosnia, was one of those skilled workmen who restored a man's faith in his kind. He wore gold-rimmed glasses and had a scholar's face, but his arms and chest were sculptured by a quarter of a century of heavy, cheerful toil. Mr. Blandings was momentarily dismayed by the method of selecting a well site. "I sinks she might as good go here as anywheres," Mr. Tesander had said, indicating a wide area seeming no different from any other on Bald Mountain. But once Mr. Tesander settled down to work, all doubts disappeared.

That Mr. Tesander had the skill of a surgeon and the equanimity of a llama was quickly apparent. As Mr. Blandings watched him maneuver his rig to the selected spot and begin to unload his gear, he felt new hope and cheer surge through him, not merely for the success of the well but for the whole great Blandings Project. The job would probably keep him on the site between five and seven weeks, Mr. Tesander said; Mr. Blandings' vacation was coming up, and he resolved that he himself would spend every available day between now and the completion of the well sitting on a grassy bank, in a pair of overalls, watching this quiet aristocrat of heavy labor at his craft. Mr. Blandings' soul needed it.

When Mr. Blandings hurried back to Bald Mountain after a perfunctory summer work week in the city, he found Mr. Tesander and his helper literally poised to begin the major job. They had dug a hole six feet by six, as far as they could go with shovels; they had jacked the drill rig up on its axles to level and secure it. As Mr. Blandings watched, Mr. Tesander and his helper unshipped the long, glistening 500-pound drill bit, and into its head they looped and rove the end of a 500-foot cable of twisted steel strands.

Mr. Tesander checked everything over one last time and steadied the huge free-swinging pendulum of drill and cable over the exact spot where water was someday expected to flow. His helper cranked the rig's heavy motor, and the moment had arrived. The motor roared; the rig shook with an ague; and Mr. Tesander cautiously let in a clutch. The drill bit rose, hung poised for an instant, then plunged and dealt the earth a staggering blow. Mr. Blandings' well was being drilled! At last there would be something to show for the passage of fifteen months, and for the tears and struggles that had so far been the lot of the Blandings on Bald Mountain.

MR. BLANDINGS SPENT hours watching his well in process. The drill bit had now sunk out of sight so that Mr. Blandings could create the illusion that it was already a hundred feet down; how wonderful it would be, he thought, if his well should suddenly blow in with a gusher of water that spouted to the top of the nearby oak. And hadn't people drilled for water and struck oil? He confided his fantasies to Mr. Tesander, who treated them kindly but warned against overoptimism. Both these things had happened in the history of well drilling, but infrequently, and never at twelve feet down.

Mr. Blandings discovered that any one of a dozen emergencies could flash into being any instant the rig was working. The worst, which was also the most likely, was that the drill would catch and jam on the rocky circumference of its close-fitting hole. Mr. Tesander recounted for Mr. Blandings the various jobs during the last twenty years on which this or some allied misfortune had befallen him. Once he had gone down a total of 850 feet and never encountered a drop of water. Mr. Blandings' mouth went dry at the thought. The client, Mr. Tesander explained, had been a wealthy, eccentric old tyrant who wanted his well there and nowhere else. At the 851st foot the cable had snapped. "Dann I loss' my schtring," said Mr. Tesander. ("String," Mr. Blandings discovered, was short for string of tools, which described the bit, stem, and mandrel of the drill.) "I go fishing for it, but I never catch my schtring again. Old man died same week. Cost me t'ousand dollar. Some yobs I make money, some I lose my shirt." He smiled happily at the memory of past ill fortunes and the hazards of his occupation, and carefully loosed a clutch to pay out another two inches of cable to the drill bit.

Father of us all, thought Mr. Blandings, from what deep wells of Your devising does this man draw his beautiful calm, his total equanimity? I pay him $4.50 for every foot he sinks this shaft for me, and he doesn't know whether he's going to make a hundred dollars or so with all his labor, or whether he's going to lose his string and his shirt with it. And it doesn't seem to bother him. He was put into the world to drill wells, so he drills 'em, and that's all that counts with him. Why can't everyone be like him? Why can't *I* be like him?

Mr. Tesander pulled an old envelope out of a pocket, from it stuffed a corncob pipe, and sat down on the bank beside Mr. Blandings, puffing in perfect comfort. "Warm day," said Mr. Tesander.

It was, Mr. Blandings agreed; he looked at Mr. Tesander's well-browned skin as it showed through his ripped and tattered undershirt, and saw, with a vast feeling of inferiority, that it was as dry as a granite statue. Well, he thought, someday, after he was a seasoned country dweller and could fell an oak in an afternoon, then he, too, would be able to work like that in a warm sun and not sweat.

CHAPTER FOUR

"THERE IS THE MOST hideous thing going on not half a mile from where our property ends," said Mrs. Blandings when her husband came back to the cottage from a satisfying vacation afternoon watching Mr. Tesander at the well site. "Right on the *road!* I'm just *sick* about it."

The way she spoke suggested in Mr. Blandings' mind the spectacle of a boa constrictor publicly squeezing the life out of a goat in the middle of the road that led to Lansdale. He said nothing but began to mix a martini. His wife faced him with obvious emotion.

"Somebody is building a *house!*" she burst forth.

Mr. Blandings set down the martini shaker with a crash. "What!" he cried. "Where? Who?"

"I've been telling you," said Mrs. Blandings, quivering. "Right before you turn off for the Grovers'. A horrid, nasty little house with two rooms and a porch *right on the road!*"

This was just about as bad as anything could be. Scarcely over a year after they had bought the top of a virgin mountain, blight had appeared. Their idyll of peace and solitude was being shattered.

"It's a horrid, beastly little *bungalow*," said Mrs. Blandings, "and it's going to have a tar-paper roof and they're going to paint it a bright *green*. That Hackett creature sold him two acres for it."

"Who is he? Where did you pick all this up?" asked Mr. Blandings.

"In the drugstore," said Mrs. Blandings. "It couldn't be worse. The man is a *stonemason*, and they have *ten* children, and *she* keeps goats. I could simply *weep*. If we're going to have a *shanty* right in our *backyard*, I guess we might as well give up the whole *thing*."

Even when buoyed up by the martini, Mr. Blandings could not help taking a drastic view of the invasion of Bald Mountain. There was no question that Mr. Hackett had done one more traitorous, treacherous thing to Mr. and Mrs. Blandings.

"What a nasty, mean-spirited thing to do," said Mrs. Blandings. "And stupid, too. He sold those two acres for a total of $65. It's just impossible to figure these country people out."

Next day, as they drove toward the town of Lansdale, Mr. and Mrs. Blandings stopped off to study the situation. An industrious young man in the gray costume of a stonemason was at work, nailing narrow tongue-and-groove siding to the frame of a structure that could not have been much more than fifteen feet square. "Howdy," he said as the Blandings stopped. "Thought I'd put me up a little shack where we could bring our two kids summers. Gets pretty hot right in the middle of the village, and this Bald Mountain is just about the finest country in the whole state, you ask me. You folks live up this way?"

Shack, thought Mrs. Blandings; that's certainly the word for it. She was relieved a trifle that the ten children of her overheard conversation were reduced to a more manageable quantity. But only a trifle. "Yes," she said. "We live farther up the road."

"I don't recognize you," said the young man. "I was born right down in town and I know every face within fifteen miles. I guess you must be city people."

This is ridiculous, Mr. Blandings thought. He's treating us like intruders. "That's right," he said with a sudden, synthetic country heartiness. "Our name is Blandings and we've bought the old Hackett place at the top of the mountain."

"Well, for God's sake," said the young man. "Speak of the devil! I was reading a piece about you folks in the newspaper just last night."

The Blandings exchanged lightning glances. They were subscribers to the Lansdale *Blade* and their weekly copy had arrived yesterday afternoon, to lie unopened on the living-room table.

"Too bad it had to happen, but you got one consolation, anyway," the young man went on. "A lot of people think old Mrs. Prutty is pretty hipped on that sort of business. Got too much time on her hands ever since her husband got run over by the milk truck down to Gatti's Tavern, where he didn't have no business anyway."

There wasn't the faintest clue in any of this for the uneasy Blandings, and they were becoming very uncomfortable in the young man's presence; they had come to observe and assess him, and perhaps to grant him, grudgingly if at all, the privilege of being their neighbor. But now it was he who had them on the defensive—about what they did not know and felt disinclined to inquire. Mr. Blandings sought to signify the end of the visit by putting his car in gear.

"I wouldn't take it too hard if I was you," said the young man. "It's just one of them tempests in a teapot. Don't let it get you down. Give 'em time and they'll forget it."

The Blandings exchanged worried speculations as they drove on down to Lansdale for the Saturday shopping. In the village, Mr. Blandings was certain that people were looking at him in a funny way, although the occasional how-de-do's of the shopping tour seemed friendly enough. While Mrs. Blandings pursued an endless conversation with the butcher, her husband tried to while away a moment at the soda fountain next door, but his request for a Coke was as tremulous as if he were asking for absinthe before breakfast.

Back in the seclusion of the summer cottage, he could, at first, find nothing in the Lansdale *Blade*. All the headlines seemed dull; a few were incomprehensible. Mr. Blandings scrutinized page one for the third time. He came again on:

HISTORICAL SOCIETY BLASTS "VANDALISM"

But that this could in any way apply to him never crossed his mind until beneath it, he suddenly saw:

Censure Vote Passed Re
Destruction of Famed
Bald Mountain Edifice

"Oh, my God," he groaned, and in fascinated horror read on:

The usually sedate semimonthly meeting of the ladies of the Lansdale Historical Society was turned into an uproar last Tuesday when Mrs. Bildad Prutty reported the total demolition by its recent New York buyer of the historic old home of the Hackett family situated atop Bald Mountain since some years before the town itself was founded. The old Hackett house was swiftly demolished and sold by the new owner for a junk value reported to be $1075, according to Mrs. Prutty. The aroused ladies quickly resolved that Mrs. Prutty head a committee and be authorized to visit the New Yorker responsible and express the official disapproval of the society.

Mrs. Prutty reminded her audience that several years ago the society raised the sum of $1900 for the purchase of the old Hackett house and property, to restore it to its original condition when General Horatio Gates stopped there to water his horses on the way to the Battle of Saratoga in 1777. The deal fell through by being $750 short of the sum of $2650 that Ephemus Hackett testified was the smallest reasonable sum he could accept as the executor of his father's estate, the local probate court upholding this contention. Mrs. Prutty also . . .

The stab of the telephone bell came to Mr. Blandings as a merciful severance. That Mr. Hackett had been willing to sell his whole property a couple of years ago to Mrs. Prutty's Amazons for $2650 had given him enough to absorb for that afternoon, all by itself. That these Amazons were on the brink of censuring him for paying over four times that amount—

*Mrs. Prutty was authorized
to express the official disapproval
of the Historical Society.*

"New York is calling," said the operator. "Go ahead New York."

"Hey, Jim," said Bill Cole's voice, "did you tear down that old what-do-you-call-it house without telling me?"

"Has the Historical Society retained you? I'd just like to know."

"I don't get you," said Bill. "Are you all right? Listen, what I'm calling for is to tell you I've just had a letter from your Mr. Hackett's lawyer."

"Oh," said Mr. Blandings.

"Listen," said Bill, "don't you know you can't tear down a house on which another man holds a mortgage without getting his express written consent? The old boy is serving notice that under the terms of the mortgage the whole balance of the purchase price is now payable on demand, and this is his demand."

"Deposit another thirty-five cents for another three minutes, please," said the operator. There was a sound in the receiver as of the fracture of a large stick of kindling.

Mr. Blandings held the suddenly blank instrument in his hand for a moment as if it had been a kitten run over by a tractor. Then he put it down and strode to the sideboard.

"I make it a point not to criticize your drinking habits," said Mrs. Blandings, "but when you tip the bottle up and I can hear it gurgle at least three times, I think I am bound to say that it strikes me as not only unwise, but vulgar."

During the next few days Mr. Blandings kept wondering if Banton & Dascomb might be persuaded to send him to New Guinea to establish an agency branch. Then he could liquidate all his personal affairs in the United States. But this phase soon passed; things became surprisingly better surprisingly soon, and he wondered whether everybody else's life was such a succession of roller-coaster plunges from elation to despair and back, or whether he was suffering from emotional instability. Anyway, he had not become the community pariah he had prepared himself to be. The next issue of the *Blade*, still not mentioning his name, had unexpectedly changed its tack and come to his defense. "Some of our good local ladies," the lead editorial said, "might perhaps reflect if they are not getting a little too high up on their horses. It seems they are all wrought up over the tearing down of the old Hackett house, but this particular landmark was going to racking ruin for a long time before it was sold to a purchaser from the city. The ladies should remember that quite a little retail trade is developing out of the money these big-shot newcomers are spending with us."

Very sound, Mr. Blandings thought. A little crass, but very sound. It gave him a wry sense of discomfiture to be called "big shot," even by inference, when his record of managing his own affairs was so totally incompetent, but perhaps he should take himself at the *Blade*'s assessment, not his own. As for the mortgage, Bill Cole had gone through a legal waving of hands as the result of which Mr. Hackett agreed to discontinue his demand for the principal sum of the mortgage provided Mr. Blandings immediately pay him $1000 for its reduction. Mr. Blandings had to do some scraping around to come quickly by this sum, but once he did he consoled himself that reducing a mortgage was, after all, a form of saving. He wrote a modest letter to the *Blade*, thanking the editor for his utterance and pointing out that in any event he had paid, not *been* paid, $1075 for the removal of the Hackett landmark.

Peace descended again on the exquisite landscape that was Bald Mountain; the bees droned in the warm air and sucked their nectar from a rippling sea of wildflowers. Mrs. Blandings flitted about their summer cottage in a sunbonnet, and Mr. Blandings went back to his study of Mr. Tesander, drilling at the well. His vacation was in midcareer, and he was resolved that nothing else should blemish it.

But much though he loved Mr. Tesander, he was beginning to feel some slight concern. Mr. Tesander was down 107 feet now, and

Mr. Tesander was encountering everything in an
omnipotent God's creation except water.

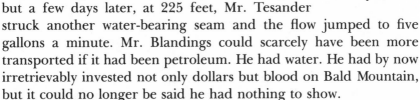

apparently drilling in iron; a concussion would
shake the earth every time the drill took its pulver-
izing bite. On a poor day Mr. Tesander might
make four feet; on a good day he might make
eighteen; but in his methodical progress through
the earth's crust, he was encountering everything
in an omnipotent God's creation except water.
"There ought to be a better way," Mr. Blandings
moaned one night after Mr. Tesander had announced that he was down 201 feet in a dry hole.
But Mr. Blandings' spirits rebounded next day on
the news that the well driller had encountered liquids; somewhere in the bowels of geology the drill
had struck a fissure through which one-half gallon
of water per minute was now flowing into the bore.
This was far from the twenty gallons per minute
Mr. Blandings had come to think of as desirable,
but a few days later, at 225 feet, Mr. Tesander
struck another water-bearing seam and the flow jumped to five
gallons a minute. Mr. Blandings could scarcely have been more
transported if it had been petroleum. He had water. He had by now
irretrievably invested not only dollars but blood on Bald Mountain,
but it could no longer be said he had nothing to show.

When the bluebells and the columbine faded, the meadow lilies
and the wild geranium took up the torch. These in turn gave way to
the black-eyed Susans and the evening primrose. It would soon be
time for the tall, waving asters and the goldenrod. August was well
along. "I wish I knew where the time has gone," sighed Mrs. Blandings. Her husband felt he knew, but forbore to say.

Throughout the weeks, Mr. and Mrs. Blandings and Mr. Simms
had toiled onward and upward with the plans for the house. "Mr.
Simms is a tower of strength," Mrs. Blandings repeated over and
over. Whatever misfortune overtook the Blandings, Mr. Simms was
somehow able to remember something much worse that had hap-

pened to somebody else, who had, however, lived to tell the tale. Mountains might diminish and rivers change their course, but Mr. Simms remained the Blandings' one foundation.

The preliminary designs were still going slowly. The Blandings would change their minds a dozen times a week; Mr. Simms' cheerfulness could not be dented. "It only costs us the price of an eraser to make our changes now," he would say as he obliterated one set of lines to make way for another. "Get them all out of your system early—they'll cost you real money as soon as the building starts." They took his advice to heart; change after change was made as the days wore on.

Mrs. Blandings came to realize, for example, that she had miscalculated the servant problem. Somehow the house was getting too big to be servantless, as she had planned; and thirty-one and a half acres was—well, in a way it was too much land, rather than too little, when you thought of the spraying and the pruning that every inch of it now appeared to need. So because the house was getting bigger than first planned, it had to get bigger still; the Blandings would be in obvious need of a hired couple: the man for outdoor work, his wife as cook and housekeeper. You couldn't just stick them in the attic, Mr. Simms warned; couples were getting pretty fussy. He got space for a small living room, bedroom, and bath at the kitchen end of the house by adding twelve feet to the house's long dimension.

It was in closets, perhaps, that Mrs. Blandings showed up most clearly as a woman of character. "All my life," she said with an air of speaking for all womankind, "I've wanted to have enough closets." Now she had her chance, and she was resolved. Her proposal, on which she would retreat not one inch, started with two closets per bedroom and two in every hallway, and went on to a total of thirty-one. Mr. Blandings specified a liquor closet, with spring lock. It all added up to thirty-two closets, and Mrs. Blandings would brook no counterproposals except the elimination, if people were *really* sincere about saving space, of the liquor closet.

To Mr. Blandings this closet was the one really indispensable storage compartment in the house, and its proposed elimination struck him as unfriendly. Mr. Simms bent over his drafting board with elaborate attention until the disturbance passed.

One evening he did a little multiplication and discovered that Mrs.

Blandings' closets accounted for almost as many cubic feet on his conscientious plans as the rest of the house, and for the first time the word "mansion" was used in conversation—facetiously, of course.

The Blandings watched their house grow more perfect every day. It was the embodiment of everything they had ever longed for. It looked like the old house in a way; it had the same clear, unadorned lines; a similarly massive chimney stack rose out of the broad, handsome roof. Yet it was not the old house, and owed little to it; it was a new house on reinforced concrete sills that neither moth nor rust could corrupt, with a solid copper termite pan to keep every stick of wood clear of the contagious earth. The Blandings loved it, but a phrase developed on their lips that Mr. Simms could hear in his sleep: "While we're at it, we might as well—"

It was on this philosophy that a study for Mr. Blandings on the first floor passed from dream stuff to stark necessity within a short period of forty-eight hours. It was no easy matter to add one entire room to a ground plan already agreed upon, but a solution occurred to Mr. Simms so deft and ingenious that he himself fell in love with it and became emotionally incapable of further objections. This in turn made it both necessary and possible to add a small cubicle off the master bedroom that Mrs. Blandings, in a moment of cuteness, referred to as a "sulking room"—something that would serve her as either dressing room or study.

"I sometimes wonder if you people know what you're heading for," Mr. Simms said one night as he was packing up his portable drafting board to go home. "Got your plans all laid for what bank you're going to rob?" But he and the Blandings were in a relaxed mood, with highballs in their hands. It was a bad evening for warnings, anyway; a little earlier Mr. Tesander, God bless his lovely, beautiful soul, had run crash into nine gallons of water per minute at 297 feet and had telephoned the joyful news. There would be no need now to pursue this quest below 300 feet, at which the cost per foot changed ominously from $4.50 to $6.

It had been a lovely day; a thunderstorm had threatened from the west in the afternoon, but the clouds had vanished, and as Mr. Simms drove away, the Blandings looked up into a night sky of late August that was powdery with stars. It was apparent at last that the plans would soon be finished. Now that John Tesander was dismantling his

*Mr. Tesander had run crash
into 9 gallons of water and had
phoned the joyful news.*

rig and preparing to leave forever, Mr. Blandings no longer felt quite such an urge for the country. It occurred to him that if he clipped ten days from his vacation now he could more profitably return for another "week or two" later on. He began to lay plans for a fury of continuous fourteen-hour stints in New York whereby he could, with luck, turn out enough laxative copy to last him until the really heavy season of intestinal stasis resumed around the first week in November, and then take a little extra vacation time.

The account's sales curves were going through the roof, Mr. Blandings discovered when he returned to the hot, disordered city. He brewed himself pot after pot of coffee and sat before his typewriter in his empty, echoing apartment. After six days he had drafted twenty pieces of new laxative copy and made crude little pencil drawings for the Banton & Dascomb art department. There were only some forty-five words to a piece of copy, but Mr. Blandings was a critical workman; he wrote and rewrote, and then re-rewrote over again, like the poet A. E. Housman agonizing over the quatrains of "A Shropshire Lad." When he had finished he was bound to admit that he had done his work extremely well, and he took a Tuesday afternoon train back to Lansdale.

THINGS HAD GONE well in his absence. "I always somehow seem to get more done when you're away," his wife said, not unkindly, but with a point. "Mr. Simms and I went all the way to Seagate in his car to look at hardware and then we went together to see that International Wallboard Exposition near Blyfield. I got a lot of pointers."

Mrs. Blandings, it turned out, had gotten so many pointers that Mr. Blandings could not seem to catch up with her. In the ten days he had been away his house had slipped out of his control. So if the details had irretrievably escaped him, he would take refuge in the Higher Generalities, the Broader Picture, as he had seen more than one founding businessman do as the day-to-day technicalities of the enterprise he had established slipped slowly from his grasp.

"When we build, let us think that we build for ever," someone once had written. Mr. Blandings heartily endorsed this view, and the Blandings' home, as it now lay on the drafting table, bore out the philosophies of quality and permanence. The floors were to be broad oak, the water lines red brass; the plumbing fixtures did not bear the trade name of Sphinx for nothing; the incombustible shingles were the same as those developed for Mr. Rockefeller for the restoration of Williamsburg, in Virginia; the hardware was to be supplied by the nearest thing to Benvenuto Cellini in the area.

One day it occurred to Mr. Blandings that his house on a mountain-top was beautifully situated to let him develop the hobby of amateur weather observation, which had always appealed to him; he plunged deep into half a dozen instrument catalogues, and immediately involved Mr. Simms in the redesign of walls to include pipes to carry the wires from the instruments on the roof to the gauges in the study.

It was getting late for this sort of thing, and Mr. Simms occasionally gave way to impatience. "Why don't you just get the Reconstruction Finance Corporation to build the whole house?" he asked. "I think it's a project on a scale that would appeal to them."

"But didn't you say it was less expensive to make our changes now?" Mr. Simms had had to grant the point, but his petulance had its effect. Mr. and Mrs. Blandings suddenly announced that they would present no further new ideas; prudence dictated it. "There'll be bugs in it, all right," the Blandings assured their new Lansdale friends, the Grovers, one evening at dinner. "We know that; but you can't foresee everything. Remember how the Longwells built that $75,000 palace of theirs and their architect forgot the chimney?"

Mr. Blandings and his auditors dissolved into laughter, but Mrs. Blandings looked suddenly serious.

"Heavens!" she said, a hand to her cheek. "Chimney! Lightning rods! *Mr. Simms has forgotten lightning rods on the chimney!*"

When Mr. Simms was faced with his oversight he remarked, with a trace of the satiric tendency that had recently come to mark him, that he had also forgotten to buy the Blandings' china for them; his implication seemed to be that there were matters that did not lie in the province of the architect and that here was one of them; if the Blandings wished a lightning protective system, they were welcome to it, and he would even put them in touch with a lightning-rod salesman. If they insisted that he draw some lines on his plans indicating rods and cables and ground connections, he would be glad to, but it would cost them ten percent of the cost of the installation and he, Mr. Simms, didn't think it would be worth it to them.

This was the first remark about money or compensation that had ever passed between architect and client, Mr. Blandings realized, and somehow he felt sober about it.

Then, one evening, Mr. Simms arose from his portable drafting board with a happy sigh of conclusion. One phase of home building was finished at last, he announced; another was about to begin. The sketches and specifications his clients and he had been tossing lightly about must now be reduced to the coldest and hardest literal fact. He shook hands, told the Blandings it had all been great fun so far, and made ready to vanish out of their lives.

How nicely this is turning out, thought the Blandings. Labor Day was almost at hand, and their children were momentarily due home from summer camp. Mrs. Blandings had before her an orgy of reoutfitting for their new school term, and other responsibilities connected with September. She would go back to New York for a week or two, collect and process the children, and then, before school opened, bring the whole family back again to the cottage at Bald Mountain's foot, to spend the balance of Mr. Blandings' hoarded vacation in the flamingly gorgeous days of early autumn.

It all worked out with an unaccustomed neatness, which Mr. Blandings took as the best possible augury for their future. Both children had put Dymaxion houses and mobile homes behind them, and seeing BETSY'S ROOM and JOAN'S ROOM in Mr. Simms' best architectural script on the plans, they became wholly proprietary and abandoned themselves in the evenings to interior decoration. Everything seemed to be on a very clear track indeed.

When Mr. Simms emerged from his seclusion into the Blandings' lives again, he had with him a set of tracings and blueprints that floored his clients flat. The papers were bound by a wooden rod into something the size and thickness of a book of wallpaper samples, and they were like nothing the Blandings had ever seen before. The simple drawings they had watched grow on the drafting board were superseded now by framing plans, and wiring diagrams, and detail sheets; by incomprehensible blueprints labeled "Section at A-A'." Along with the innumerable blueprints there was a set of specifications the thickness of a Chicago telephone directory.

It was now time, Mr. Simms informed his clients in a sepulchral voice, to ask for bids.

CHAPTER FIVE

JUST AFTER LABOR DAY John Tesander's bill arrived, inscribed in a lovely copperplate. The bill was for $1336.50. Mr. Blandings jumped when he saw the figure, but 297 feet at $4.50 a foot came to that, to the precise penny. There were no ingenious extras, and Mr. Blandings paid it with the first pleasure at disbursal he had so far experienced. But the neatly capped casing pipe, which was the only evidence that Mr. Tesander had left behind him, now gave Mr. Blandings a sudden thought as he looked at it. He went scurrying to Mr. Simms' neat plans and there confirmed a suspicion that might well, he reflected, have dawned upon him before. On the drawings of the cellar, a careful arrow and the words FROM PUMP HOUSE in architectural lettering made him realize that there was a gap between where Mr. Tesander left off and a plumber could begin. The gap would have to be filled, and only Mr. Blandings could fill it. It consisted of a deep-well pump, a snugly buried water tank beside it, and pipes running to the cellar.

Mr. Blandings simply did not know whether to be angry or dejected. For the second time, a vital matter in the domain of water supply had all but slipped his mind. But—*damn it!*—there was the exit of the main soil line on Mr. Simms' plans, and *it* was marked, TO SEPTIC TANK, SEE SPECIFICATIONS. Lo and behold, the specifications drooled on for two pages about the septic tank and its connections. . . . It must be lined with pitch, it must have a vitrified tile header, capped

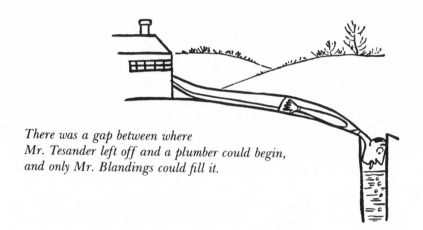

There was a gap between where
Mr. Tesander left off and a plumber could begin,
and only Mr. Blandings could fill it.

vent tiles, shear gates, and be bedded in straw, cinders, and gravel.

It sounds good enough to eat, Mr. Blandings thought disgustedly. If architects put septic tanks into their contract specifications, why didn't they put in pumps, and water-storage tanks, and the big copper tubes that would lead from pump house to cellar, and the trenches that would have to be dug for them? He looked to the heavens for answer and received none. Instead, the heavens suggested that he had better not postpone any longer the business of borrowing the money on which he was to build his house. He had better consult Mr. Anson Dolliver, President of the Lansdale National Bank.

Mr. Blandings had had the foresight, a year earlier, to open a checking account in Mr. Dolliver's bank: he had kept his balance there at a level he was sure a country bank would consider opulent. Mr. Dolliver had been cordiality itself the day Mr. Blandings first made himself a depositor; he had come out from behind the glassed enclosure that served as his office and introduced himself. He had complimented Mr. Blandings on his astuteness in buying that particular thirty-one and a half acres, and not a square foot more. "Took the very heart out of old Eph Hackett's land up there, 's what you did, like all you city people coming up here and clipping off mountaintops for yourselves."

He had put just the right blend of admiration and ruefulness into his voice, and Mr. Blandings felt himself swelling slightly. Then Mr. Dolliver had remarked that although some townsfolk resented the intrusion of city dwellers into the community, he, Mr. Dolliver, did not share this parochial view, particularly with the fine type of outlander represented by Mr. Blandings.

This happy initial conversation was repeated at regular intervals; the pattern grew more cordial, and Mr. Dolliver invariably ended such a chat with the warm suggestion, "If we can ever help you out, up there on the hill, just let us know."

"Well," said Mr. Blandings to himself as he drove into town on a Saturday morning, "now you can help me, up there on the hill, Mr. Dolliver, so here I come to let you know." Mr. Blandings envisioned from Mr. Dolliver cordiality in the extreme, the proffer of a fine cigar, and an open line of credit at a nominal rate.

What he encountered was nothing like that at all.

"So now you want some money for that enterprise of yours up there," said Mr. Dolliver, with an unpleasant stress on the word "enterprise." He bit off the end of a cigar for himself and spat daintily in Mr. Blandings' direction, but proffered nothing. He seemed puzzled and displeased that Mr. Blandings had brought up such a topic as money. Mr. Blandings began to murmur something about a need for cash and instantly loathed himself for its tentative, apologetic, and defensive quality.

"Why, great grief," said Mr. Dolliver, breaking in, "we're loaned full up to our legal limit right now; have been for longer'n I could tell you. Love to help you out, but . . ." He left the sentence unfinished, while Mr. Blandings dangled in midair. Then he added, as if a bright solution to an unusual problem had just occurred to him, "My brother's the president of the savings bank across the hall. *He* might be able to do something for you. . . ."

Mr. Blandings, thoroughly shaken, had three separate conversations with the savings-bank brother, at the end of which the second-string Dolliver admitted that there might be circumstances under which his bank would make a $10,000 mortgage loan to Mr. Blandings at six and a half percent. Mr. Blandings said that he had hoped for more money at a lower rate, and the road-company Dolliver had responded with a concise lecture on the risks involved in rural real estate that Mr. Blandings wished he had been able to think up for himself a year and a half ago. He swallowed, and contented himself with wondering aloud how soon he might have the money, since his bids were almost due and he hoped to begin breaking ground soon.

Mr. Dolliver snapped forward in his chair, his bland manner gone like a breath of ether in a gale. "You want this money for *construc-*

tion?" he asked in a tone that made Mr. Blandings feel that he had somehow offended him deeply. Mr. Blandings said he did.

"You've had me at a misapprehension," said Mr. Dolliver. "This bank *never* makes construction loans. If that's your situation and you have some government bonds, I think my brother in the commercial bank across the hall could work out something satisfactory for you."

It was at this moment that the original Dolliver strolled across the hall, intent on a word with his brother. He checked himself when he saw Mr. Blandings rising to take his leave.

"Well," he said, "get it all fixed up?"

Suddenly Mr. Blandings began to tremble with rage. Mr. Dolliver was not the first member of the community to attempt rape on him, but somehow he was the least lovable.

"We didn't get a damn thing fixed up," said Mr. Blandings. "I don't know what the hell you and your brother do in this bank that a pig couldn't do better."

A savings bank is designed for hush, and Mr. Blandings' voice would have carried well at Yankee Stadium.

"You can take your tin-pot bank and shove the assets down your throats two bits at a time," said Mr. Blandings in what was partly a yell and partly a sob. "All I want from you is a check for the balance in my checking account, and after I get it I wouldn't come back here if you had a pay toilet."

When it was all over and he stood outside, his cashier's check crumpled to a soggy ball in his hand, Mr. Blandings' rage began to turn to guilt, and the guilt to fear. He would go down in local history as the barbaric despoiler who had first torn down a sacred shrine on a cloud-wreathed mountaintop and then vomited on the altar of the high priest. He could picture his tombstone in the local burying ground. "James H. Blandings," it would say, "known as The Wretched; un-wept, unhonored, unsung."

He could scarcely tell a coherent story to Mrs. Blandings that evening, and it was several days before his turbulent memories al-lowed him to sit still in his easy chair. After a while he was able to begin hunting for a silver lining, and presently he found it. It had not been pleasant to deal with the Dollivers, but he could at least congrat-ulate himself that here was one episode that had not cost him any money. He merely did not have his loan.

Mr. Blandings was in a state of what seemed to be permanent depression, mixed with alternations of lethargy and irritation. He had been a man of substance in a mild way. He had accumulated some money, saved out of his own earnings. But the greater part of it had now been swallowed up or preempted by the demands of real-estate ownership, and he still had no house. He had not even the beginnings of a house, unless Mr. John Tesander's well could be counted.

What was more, the clash with the Dollivers had illuminated something for him with a lightning stroke: in the midst of the bucolic loveliness where he had wanted to live in peace and harmony with nature and his fellows, he was disliked. He did not think it was anything about him personally. He even doubted that it had much to do with the tearing down of the old house. It was just that he was an outlander. He could wear overalls or part his hair down the middle until kingdom come, and it would make no difference. The natives of Lansdale County would still know him for an alien. He would still be a City Man on masquerade.

He thought of all the little booklets of the nation's savings banks and their hymns about the joys of ownership—with halftone pictures of a placid man reading while a placid woman sewed and a placid child played beside a placid hearth—all order, convention, calm; the unanticipated and accidental events fleeing elsewhere to happen. *Damn it all*, why were his honest, earnest, yearning efforts to create such an El Dorado for the Blandings family so hampered and addled by every conceivable mischance and marplot within 500 miles?

"I think you ought to go away someplace and get a good rest," said Mrs. Blandings from her corner. "You're looking all drawn and tired. What you need is a little vacation."

"I'm *on* vacation," said Mr. Blandings. "Don't you remember that I went back to the city and did eight weeks' work in ten days so that I could be up here when the bids were due?"

"I forgot," said Mrs. Blandings.

Mr. Simms arrived on a Saturday morning, looking a little constricted about the mouth, but brisk. "We've got all our bids," he said. "I've summarized them on the top sheet."

Mr. Blandings opened the manila folder and leaped upward as

from a bayonet thrust through the bottom of the chair. "Great God in heaven!" he cried and let the folder slip from his grasp. Mrs. Blandings, who had borne the younger Blandings daughter without anesthetics on the grounds that she did not wish to miss the experience, calmly picked up the sheets as they slithered to the floor and bent a level gaze on them.

Estimates — Blandings Job — Bald Mountain

Antonio Doloroso, Builders	$32,117.00
Caries & Plumline	34,265.00
Julius Akimbo & Co.	37,500.00
Zack, Tophet & Payne	28,920.50
John Retch & Sons	30,852.00

"There are a couple of things to be noticed from this," said Mr. Simms, speaking in an even voice. "In the first place, Julius Akimbo obviously doesn't want the job or he wouldn't have put in any round-figure bid that size. As for that bid from Zack, Tophet & Payne, I wouldn't touch it with a ten-foot pole. They have a reputation for bidding low and then loading on the extras. That would leave John Retch low man, and I'd be happy to see him get the job; he's my idea of a sound, honest builder. Even so, I think we'll have to cut some of our costs."

This, Mr. Blandings thought in a blurred sort of way, was putting it mildly, and the cost-cutting job began that afternoon, early. What Mr. Blandings now discovered was that you could cut the cost of a $31,000 house *somewhat*—at the sacrifice of everything you wanted most—but there was no way on earth to cut a $31,000 house down to a $21,000 house. And yet there seemed nothing to do but try.

It was slow, dispiriting work. Moreover, some things were irreversible: you could no more reverse the growth process of the house than you could force an adolescent back into last year's clothes by denying him food.

What was worse, Mrs. Blandings was lending only the most faint-hearted efforts to cost reduction, and even the rectitudinous Mr. Simms was not killing himself with exertions. He had warned his clients at every step that they were insisting upon a house not specified in their budget, and they had gone their headlong way. Now Mr.

Simms had achieved a creation of which he was justly proud, and he would have been more than human had he been willing to throw it into the fire and start again.

Yet something had to be done. The house could not be abandoned. For one thing, although Mr. Simms had made only one brief, elliptical remark about his charges, and had seemed willing to go on designing the house forever, Mr. Blandings was aware that the standard architect's fee was ten percent of the cost of the house—and God knew that if anybody had ever earned $3100, it was Mr. Simms. Manifestly he could not now be asked to design a new, less expensive house and receive a lower fee. Mr. Blandings would owe Mr. Simms for the design of two houses, not one. It would be delightful, Mr. Blandings thought, to abandon Bald Mountain utterly and forever; to return to the city and move a final, cautious ten blocks farther north, and die of old age in a rented apartment in the East Eighties. But he could not do that now; he had passed the crucial mark known as the point of no return.

Yet despite all obstacles, some deflation of the house did set in: bronze casements changed to steel; red brass piping first became yellow brass, then galvanized iron. The roofing specifications came down in the world. The Sphinx plumbing fixtures became notably less elegant. A whole flagged terrace disappeared.

No one had heart for any of it. It depressed Mr. Blandings still further to observe that the elimination of the terrace, on which he had already, in anticipation, sat in the cool of the evening, saved him, on Mr. Retch's figures, only $172.50. "If I was *adding* the terrace it wouldn't cost me a cent less than $700," said Mr. Blandings savagely. But he said it to himself, for he no longer had anyone to talk to. He was being cheated, he was being made a fool of, but he could not find the villain, because everyone was a villain—his wife, Mr. Simms, the local bank, everyone—all had made him the butt and victim of a huge conspiracy, clever and cruel.

"There!" he heard Mrs. Blandings say to Mr. Simms a fortnight later. "We've got Mr. Retch's figures down some; that's more like it."

"What's more like *what?*" Mr. Blandings snarled, the milk of human kindness curdling within him.

"I think," said Mr. Simms tactfully, "we've pared it down as far as it will go. It's more money than you started out to spend, but you're

He could not find the villain, because everyone was a villain.

getting a fine house, if I do say so myself, and one that would be pretty easy to resell someday, if you ever had a mind to. Retch is an honest builder and that's about what your house will cost you—*if* you don't start getting into a lot of extras with him."

With one voice, Mr. and Mrs. Blandings assured Mr. Simms that there would be *no* extras. Far, far off in outer space, the Gods of Residential Construction offered a chirruping laugh.

Mr. Blandings' ego was powerfully restored a fortnight later on his visit to the big, impressive savings bank in the industrial city of Seagate, nearest metropolis to Lansdale. Thither Mr. Blandings and Bill Cole had gone to seek the needed capital. The chief mortgage officer congratulated him on Mr. Simms' excellent plans, and looked with satisfaction on Mr. Blandings' statement of salary and financial position. In no more than an hour's conversation the bank had agreed to advance Mr. Blandings $18,000 at five percent, the loan to be amortized over twenty years. That fell far short of Mr. Blandings' commitments, but Bill had advised against asking for more. To make up the balance, Mr. Blandings would have to hock a large chunk of the Banton & Dascomb stock he had been permitted to acquire. But *of course*, said the bank in conclusion, Mr. Blandings could have access to cash as soon as the bank's title attorneys had completed their search on the Old Hackett Property.

This last puzzled Mr. Blandings. "What did I pay old Judge Quarles $125 for when I bought the property from Hackett in the first place?" he said to Bill Cole as they left the bank together.

Bill explained that that had been a title search, all right. "But Seagate-Proletarian is a pretty big institution," he said. "They have to have their own guarantees, naturally. Their title attorneys are Barratry, Lynch & Virgo; they'll soak you $250, but it'll be worth it to have their stamp of approval, if you ever resell, for example."

This idea of resale that seemed to crop up so perpetually no longer had the jangling effect upon Mr. Blandings' nerves that once it had had when all the world was new. Now, in fact, he found it rather soothing; there was still a way out, after all.

Then on a crisp autumnal day the steam shovel arrived. Bill Cole was still fussing with the innumerable details of the building contract, but Mr. John Retch had allowed that he was not a man to stand on ceremony and wanted to get his shovel working while he could. He and Mr. Simms were both present for the ground breaking, and Mrs. Blandings was delighted with the rugged honesty and loud good humor of their contractor. "A rough diamond with a heart of gold," she averred.

Mrs. Blandings was also happy that Mr. Blandings seemed himself again, as indeed he did. Any man who could raise $18,000 in an hour's conversation with one of the biggest savings banks in the East had certainly no call to be as jumpy about his position in life as he had permitted himself to become. Again he could see himself sitting before his own fireplace, home after a Yale–Harvard game (Yale 28, Harvard 0), impressing his daughters' young admirers with the breadth and sanity of his views on a variety of topics. They would have formed the habit of calling him "sir," and the hair at his temples would be gray, but in his heart there would be serenity. . . .

"I wonder why the steam shovel isn't working," said Mrs. Blandings. It had been half an hour now since she had heard its snortings come drifting down the hill to the cottage.

"He's been at it for five hours," said Mr. Blandings, rousing himself and speaking of the villainous-looking man who had turned out to be Mr. Retch's excavating subcontractor. "Let's see what our hole in the ground looks like."

Hand in hand, like happy children, the Blandings climbed the hill—*their* hill, as Mrs. Blandings put it now. Thank God, *work* had at last begun. Nothing was so cozy, Mrs. Blandings thought, as the sight of workmen plying their trade on behalf of a home, where one day soon a woman and her breadwinner and the children of their love would dwell in peace and harmony together.

At one corner of the Blandings' building site, Mr. Giuseppe Zucca's steam shovel rested unevenly on its elephantlike treads. In the south portion of the staked-out ground it had dug a hole that went down six feet at the edges. Toward the north side, the excavation was ragged and uneven, and while the shovel operator sat in his cab and smoked, three men with spades were at work with the earth. As they dug, Mr. and Mrs. Blandings could see growing the outlines of what appeared to be a colossal ossified whale.

"Looka that," said Mr. Zucca.

"Boulder?" inquired Mr. Blandings genially.

"Boulder!" said Mr. Zucca in derision. "Atsa no boulder, atsa *ledge*. We go home now, come back next week, start blasting, keep on blasting plenty, yes, *sir*. One thing you never got to worry your house settle any, sitting on granite, no, *sir*." He bellowed an incomprehensible command and all work stopped.

When he got back to his fireside, Mr. Blandings looked up Mr. Retch's estimates on excavation. The job was to be done for $500 flat, except for the proviso, "If rock encountered, removal by blasting at $.24 per cubic foot; dynamite and caps extra." It had not seemed much, but now he took pencil and paper, to discover that an excavation sixty feet long, twenty-eight feet wide, and six feet deep contained 10,080 cubic feet.

Mr. Blandings was just beginning to wonder what sizable fraction of this figure should be multiplied by $.24, and how much a stick of dynamite cost, when the telephone rang. With a leaden hand he placed the receiver at an ear that did not wish to hear. Bill Cole's voice greeted him with what he instantly knew to be false cheer.

"I don't want you to fly off the handle, Jim," Bill said, "but there's a little hitch."

"What kind of hitch?" Mr. Blandings heard himself ask.

"I've just been talking to Barratry, Lynch's man, Hank Pugh, who's doing your legal job for the bank."

"And so what?" said Mr. Blandings.

"There's a flaw in the title," said Mr. Blandings' attorney.

THE MORNINGS HAD AN edge of chill now, for autumn was upon the land. Bald Mountain's swamp maples were scarlet, its ash trees and its elms golden. Among the wildflowers, only the asters and the Queen Anne's lace survived.

But very little of this, if any, did Mr. Blandings see. He was in bed. He had a cold that he was treating with a succession of strong hot toddies. He came to care less and less, in the three days of his invalidism, whether the hot toddy had any lemon or sugar in it, and eventually whether it was hot. After a number of curious symptoms, including occasional bursts of wild, sardonic glee, he arose and resumed most of the outward appearances of his former life. But whether he could ever again feel the calm and euphoria he had known before he had thought to build a country sanctuary against age and want, Mr. Blandings was far from sure.

From his bed, he had heard Mr. Zucca's crew setting off its blasts, one approximately every half hour. Now that his health again permitted it, he wished to have a look at things.

He toiled up the hill and arrived just as a blast was to be set off; he stopped abruptly, 200 yards away, warned by the blasting foreman's shouts and arm motions. Mr. Zucca's men took up discreet positions behind trees, and the foreman himself stood at the detonating machine. He looked about him, shouted *"Fire,"* and rammed the machine's handle downward with all his strength. Mr. Blandings, looking earnestly at his excavation, saw a portion of it momentarily blur, as if it had gone out of focus. Then the earth shuddered, and there was a boom.

A moment later, the echoes struck back from the hills. Mr. Blandings resumed his course, but paused as a light patter struck the leaves of a maple above him. Four thumps and a *thwack* halted him stock-still. The blast was dropping fragments half the size of cobblestones in a circle about his feet. Not until all had been silent for at least a minute did Mr. Blandings venture on again.

"When I say 'fire,' get the hell out of here," said the foreman.

Mr. Blandings bridled weakly. "I'm the new owner," he said, wondering why he said it with shame instead of with pride.

"Well, when I say 'fire,' get the hell out of here or you'll be the *old* owner." The foreman laughed harshly. "Got any liability insurance?"

"I don't know," said Mr. Blandings. Bill Cole was handling all the necessary policies, and he truthfully did not have any idea.

"You better have," said the foreman. "Old man from down the road was looking for you half an hour ago with fire in his eye."

"What's the matter?" asked Mr. Blandings.

"Claims a piece of rock come down on top of his prize laying hen quarter mile down the road and knocked her flatter'n a son of a bitch," said the foreman. "Ask me, I think he wanted chicken for supper and figured you might as well pay for her. Quarter mile is a long way for this stuff to travel. Look at that lousy ledge."

Mr. Blandings looked, and could see for himself that when the blasting crew set off a charge, the rock would crack and fragments would fly, but the mass would not shatter. Only a crew of men with long, ten-pound crowbars could pry the cracked ledge rock apart and spread it loose for the steam shovel to pick up.

Mr. Blandings set off slowly down the hill. Near his cottage he saw a gaunt, fierce old man carrying the plump body of a chicken whose white feathers were bespattered with blood. Apparently the old man did not recognize him as the owner whose rock blasting had cost the life of his precious hen, for he merely returned a blank, baleful glare to Mr. Blandings' tentative proffer of a good morning.

It surged over Mr. Blandings that he very much wished he were back in the city. He wanted the city's blessed anonymity, whereby if he saw an old man with a bloody chicken under his arm, he would merely pass by, unthinking and free of responsibility. And he wanted the noise of the city in his ears; the quiet of the countryside, he had learned, was merely the quiet of a capricious wrath, capriciously withheld until the supremely inopportune moment. True detachment was to be achieved not among rocks and rills but on the pavements of the harsh, uncaring city, across a mile of which a man with a dagger might pursue a screaming woman with a child in her arms and evoke, in the true city dweller, no feelings other than mild wonder and philosophic speculation.

That was where he wanted to be, thought Mr. Blandings, and that, by God, was where he was going when this week drew to its close. He heaved a small, tremulous sigh. The children were back in school and he would resume his city life; his wife would stay on in the cottage and keep an eye on the construction, while he came back for weekends. It was a good arrangement; things always went better when he was not around, as his wife had already made clear to him, and it was less harrowing to be told what *had* happened than to see it in its horrid process.

EXTRACTS FROM MRS. BLANDINGS' DIARY:

October 2

Every day they say the blasting will be finished, but every day it still goes on. It's a good thing Jim is back in the city. Mr. Simms and Mr. Retch and Mr. Zucca had a big fight today about how much rock had been removed so far. I couldn't make out whose side Mr. Retch was on. Six trucks arrived late yesterday afternoon and dumped huge piles of lumber all over the place. Mr. Simms took one look at it and said it all had to go back—checked or crazed or split or something. So am I, I guess.

October 7

I don't understand this trouble over the title to our property, which is still dragging along. A long letter from the lawyers came for Jim this morning and I opened it. They still seem to be saying they have nothing to show that Mr. Hackett was entitled to act as the administrator of *his father's estate*, from which it seems we bought. The law firm wants Mr. Hackett to post a $10,000 bond to guarantee his clearing up the final accounting and settlement of his father's estate before we get our loan, and he won't do it. Mr. Hackett doesn't speak to us anymore when we meet him, I don't know why. Nervous headache.

October 18

Mr. Retch came down with his first "requisition" this afternoon, all signed and attested by Mr. Simms, and it was for $3765! Mr. Retch said he could use it right away, please, because he had a terrible fight with Mr. Zucca over the blasting and Mr. Zucca offered to compromise his excavation bill for a flat $1900 instead of $2341 if it was paid within a week. Jim has already borrowed up to the hilt on his B & D stock to tide us over until we can get the title mess straightened out. There is something wrong with *this whole system*—I wish I knew what. It hasn't rained in weeks, but in the deepest corner of the excavation there's quite a pool of water, which I think is very odd.

October 29

It rained a little last night, just a shower, and the excavation has water in it out of all proportion. Today the cement contractor, I guess you call him, arrived, complete with concrete mixer and all sorts of pots and pans, to start the foundation. He looked at the excavation and said, "I should build a swimming pool?" and then he and his men just went away. Later, Mr. Simms explained the cement contractor had gone off to get a gasoline pump, although why it took four men on a two-ton truck to get a pump, I'm sure I don't know. Mr. Simms didn't like there being water in the excavation, and I must say there was a lot.

November 4

Jim came up from the city just in time to hear that we have a spring in our cellar! A bubbling, bubbling spring! The cement man finally had to hitch up three pumps, and when they had finally sucked all the water out, there in one corner was a place where water came *spurting* up through the rock. What I want to know is, why do men think they are so smart? They have to go down 297 feet to get water when it's right up *here*. Wonderful little creatures! They don't know what they're doing three quarters of the time, but they always manage to keep on acting like the lords of creation just the same.

November 14

So now we have a system of trenches around the foundation that looks like something on Mars, and Mr. Simms says our spring is diverted, "he hopes." Now it turns out that we have to get every one of the subcontractors to sign a "waiver of lien," a paper promising that they won't sue us if they don't get paid for their work, or we don't stand a chance of getting any money out of the savings bank. Why shouldn't they sue us? I bet every one of them will, anyway.

November 20

It *would* freeze in mid-November, so hard that the concrete man can't pour any of his stuff for the cellar walls! Jim fell into the excavation last night and hurt his knee. Glum weekend.

November 25

So it unfroze, and the men started pouring the cellar walls, but Mr. Simms came along and when he saw what they were doing, he stopped the whole show and tried to get Mr. Retch on the phone. They weren't putting more than a teaspoonful of cement into the sand and gravel, he said—a fine situation! Suppose Mr. Simms hadn't just happened to come around! Mr. Retch couldn't be reached—he was in Maryland on another job. Right after lunch a whole crew of painters arrived, and when they found there wasn't any house to paint, the foreman became *abusive!* He said they had come all the way from New Jersey in answer to what he claimed was an emergency telegram Mr. Retch sent him, God knows why, saying painting must start instantly.

December 1

Glory be! Bill Cole says the bank and its lawyers are almost ready for "the closing." This means we're going to get our money at last. We're pretty far behind with all of Mr. Retch's requisitions, and I certainly hope it's going to improve his disposition when this money business gets cleared up. All Jim has to do now, apparently, is give the title lawyers $500 "in escrow" in case anything goes wrong with those beastly "waivers of lien" from those subcontractors. Six toilets arrived today and they're lying all around the field. They look *unspeakably* vulgar.

December 10

The framing is going up and it's almost finished on the wing part, and I'm just sick about *everything!* It's all *miles* too high: it looks like a *grain elevator!* It just goes up and *up*. Mr. Simms was very short when I telephoned him about it, and suggested that I "take a pill or something." He is not himself these days. I know that somebody is making another terrible mistake. Three crates of lighting fixtures arrived today. I could scream.

*There wasn't
any house to paint.*

December 14

Soon I will be going back to the city for the winter, thank God. I was supposed to stay here to see that things didn't go wrong, but I don't see how they could have gone wronger if I had been in Kalamazoo. But I must admit *I* was wrong about the framing being too high. Now that it's all up, it looks very nice, and *just* right. Mr. Retch was a changed man today; he got a big check to bring things almost up to date, now that we have the mortgage money after all this endless waiting. Mr. Retch says he is going to hurry the men along now to get everything "closed in" before the snow flies, and that the whole job is going to go "like clockwork" from here on.

December 15

Just after Jim came up for the weekend, the men nailed a little tree to the top of the roof. Then they all knocked off work and came down to our cottage and stood around on one foot or another until one of them said right out that when the rooftree went up it was time for the owner to stand a round of drinks for all the workmen. Jim didn't seem to think much of this idea at first, but it's remarkable how he fell in with it after the first twenty minutes. He reached the friendly stage quite fast, and then he reached the bottoms-up stage with the boss carpenter whom he had hitherto described as "a stinking so-and-so." Fortunately, everybody left just before he reached the quarrelsome stage. To bed very late. Farewell, Bald Mountain. Only weekends now.

CHAPTER SIX

ANOTHER WINTER CAME to Bald Mountain, and Mr. and Mrs. Blandings saw their growing house only at irregular intervals. As he viewed it now, on a warm mid-January weekend, it made Mr. Blandings think of what a flayed elephant must look like—a nakedness of muscle, minus skin and fat.

It had been a mild January—"so far," Mr. Retch added with truculence—and more workmen swarmed inside the house and out than Mr. Blandings would have thought necessary to fit out a destroyer. As he and his wife stood uncertainly in what appeared to be a hallway, his ear could detect half a dozen different hammers going at once, each with a pitch and frequency determined by the wood and the workman concerned with it. Unattended and malevolent, a blowtorch roared and hissed at the Blandings like a cougar's cub, its wicked flame invisible in the winter sunlight. The house smelled of hot lead, pine shavings, turpentine, sweat, linseed oil, wet plaster, orange peels, garlic, mice, a lunch somewhere forgotten, and plumbing facilities prematurely used. It all blended into something not at all unpleasant.

A shower of broken glass rang musically on the planking—from where, the Blandings could not determine. No one paid the slightest attention.

"I wish you'd speak to someone about the men smoking all over the place with all this sawdust and shavings around," said Mrs. Blandings, in a nervous reaction from the broken glass. "I expect everything to go up in a puff of smoke any minute."

Mr. Blandings stepped half an inch too close to the gagging mouth of the blowtorch, and in a hypertonic reaction from this, engulfed his right hand in a can of putty. He was of no mind to answer his wife aloud, for he had just heard a voice in his inner ear whisper to him that he wished his house in hell, that he did not want it, *and never had.*

They went outside. Mrs. Blandings observed a pile of fragments of new, fresh-looking wood, went to examine the wreckage gingerly, and narrowly escaped a hurtling ejection from the upper story. "Stop it," she cried to the blank opening whence it had come.

An angry man appeared in the hole, his hands on his hips. "What's biting *you?*" he inquired.

From inside the house came a long, shrill whistle. Instantly, every sound of activity ceased, and the man in the siding hole disappeared with the suddenness of a catastrophe in a Punch-and-Judy show. "Okay, fellas, let's quit," yelled a voice. The front door opened and a horde of men poured out.

What have I done? thought Mrs. Blandings in an agony. I spoke too sharply. I have precipitated a strike. She could see a bored headline on an inner page of a future Lansdale *Blade:* BLANDINGS WORK STOPPAGE ENTERS SECOND YEAR. The workmen were struggling into their overcoats now, and striding for the dozen cars parked in disorder around the Blandings manse.

"*Why* are you stopping?" asked Mrs. Blandings of a saturnine man carrying a Thermos bottle and a Stillson wrench.

"Twelve noon Saturday, lady," said the man. "Whaddaya think this is, a chain gang?"

Mrs. Blandings put her hand to her heart and breathed a little "Oh!" in sheer relief.

The next day, Sunday, the Blandings had their house to themselves. Mr. Blandings was dismayed by the ragged lopsidedness of the holes where someday windows were to be. But worst of all to them both, the thing so bad that it produced only numb, wordless sympathy between them, was the apparently microscopic size of the rooms; of the spaces, that is, as defined by the studding. Even the largest such space they could discover seemed no better than a cubicle. "Is this the *living* room?" Mrs. Blandings wailed from amid a rectangular grove of two-by-fours. Mr. Blandings merely stared out through one of the random holes in the wall.

"I *guess* so," he said. "Simms warned us a room always looks this way before the partitions go up and the furniture goes in."

"Where would we have space for any furniture?" she sobbed.

"Where would we have money for any furniture?" he asked.

He wandered off in an aimless way, and a moment later Mrs. Blandings heard his step on the steep ladder that gave the only access to the second floor. "Don't you go up there," she said. "You'll never be able to get down."

Mr. Blandings concerned himself with evidences of plumbing. The second-floor bedrooms were outlined in only the vaguest way by vertical members here and there, and he was not walking on a floor at all but on a treacherous aggregation of loose planks; yet one bathroom seemed all but finished and the others far advanced. He looked into a bathtub. It held a jumble of crate slats, shingles, bent nails, and pipe ends. It also contained a dried sandwich.

Below, Mrs. Blandings picked her way in her high-heeled shoes over the ruts and cracks and blocks of wood, and from a convergence of piping and electrical cables, she judged that she must now be in her kitchen. It seemed long and narrow and dark, and two nail kegs appeared to fill it beyond its capacity. She tried to imagine moving about it with silent efficiency, and whisking a perfect dinner for eight into the candlelit loveliness of an adjoining dining room, but the picture would not come clear before she heard a distant pounding.

The pounding stopped a moment and then broke out again, redoubled. "Hey!" said her husband's voice. "*Hey!*"

She retraced her steps to the foot of the ladder and called, "Where are you?"

"I'm *here*, in our bathroom," said Mr. Blandings. "Come outdoors where you can see me."

Mrs. Blandings did as she was bidden, and stepped through the

"Is this the living room?"
Mrs. Blandings wailed from amid
a grove of two-by-fours.

doorway. Her husband was at a second-floor opening in the back wall of the house, and was not at his ease.

"I'm stuck in this bloody bathroom," he said. "A gust came up and slammed the door and it's stuck shut and there isn't any hardware on it and I've busted all my fingernails trying to claw it open. Somebody's got to come up here and give it a push."

"I can't come up there," said Mrs. Blandings. "I have on high heels and I can't climb that rickety ladder and even if I could, I could never get down again. I told you not to go up there in the first place."

Mr. Blandings wanted very much to get out of the bathroom, but he had no plan for bringing his wife down the ladder if, indeed, she could be persuaded to come up it. There was a long pause. Then a car came bounding and scrabbling up the Blandings' driveway-to-be and stopped. Out stepped two ladies. One was older than Mrs. Blandings, the other a few years younger. Both looked large and purposeful; discerning them, Mr. Blandings, a prisoner in his lavatory, shrank from the window space.

"Hello," said the younger lady. "They told us down in the village we'd probably find you up here mooning over your castle. You got a wonderful place up here, and you got to take care of it and protect it from a lot of crackpots and meddlers down there in Washington that want to fix it so's people can't build their own house without getting some college professor's say-so. That's why Mrs. Ortig and me are here right now to get a contribution for the Republican State Committee from anybody's got the brains and money to build a beautiful home right here on top of this mountain that they got to protect if they want to save their God-given right to enjoy it."

"My husband is stuck in the bathroom," said Mrs. Blandings, whose mind changed subjects slowly under certain conditions.

The ladies turned a hearty gaze on the shrinking object in the second-story hole in the siding. "Why, blessums little heart," said the younger one. "Why don't you get him out? He looks real nice."

Mr. Blandings' position as a hostage to the Republican State Committee swept over him with a clarity akin to nausea. "Jump," said the younger one. "Mama'll catch you."

Mr. Blandings' attempts to live up to the occasion were so piteous that in a moment the younger woman strode into the house and scurried up the ladder with the agility of a squirrel. A thump of her palm swung the bathroom door ajar, and Mr. Blandings walked out into freedom—freedom save for a moral commitment to the Republican State Committee that needed no emphasis in any of the four minds that contemplated it.

"Thanks," said the younger apostle of right thinking as she snapped her purse shut on the pledge card on which Mr. Blandings had written the word "fifty." "If you ever get stuck in the john again, just yell for Isabella Rorty and I'll come a-running."

The women departed in a breeze of good humor, leaving the newly enrolled member of the Republican Party to wonder what he should have done instead of what he had done.

"WE ENCLOSE," SAID THE LETTER, "our check for the final payment on the amount of $18,000, which we have been happy to advance to you on your property on Bald Mountain. . . ." It was the mortgage officer for the Seagate-Proletarian Savings Bank addressing Mr. Blandings on his institution's crackliest engraved stationery. "You are building a fine house in an impressive location, and I hope you will live to enjoy the fruits of your industry and imagination for many years."

It just couldn't have been a nicer letter, the Blandings agreed. "By God, we're going to come out of this all right," said Mr. Blandings, and he took from a shelf Mr. Simms' original drawings.

There was nothing so, well, so *aphrodisiac*, as a set of building plans, Mr. Blandings said to himself. His head buried in Mr. Simms' exquisite draftsmanship, Mr. Blandings was dreaming again; dreaming happily. The vexations and frustrations were all in the far and insignificant background; something for a hearty laugh in the days when the Blandings' house would be a mellowed, weathered shrine; ivy-shrouded, garlanded with lilac, the shade trees casting their waving silhouettes upon the pure green suede of an English lawn.

The next weekend visit to Bald Mountain sustained the owners' recaptured calm. It had snowed hard earlier in the week, and now it was clear and cold. The dry snow blew like smoke across the fields, and around every tree trunk was a circle of flashing bits of ice.

The house was quiet. The house was far too quiet. Where a dozen workmen had been scurrying like ferrets the week before, today there was not a soul to be seen, and the house appeared to have made the least possible progress consistent with not vanishing.

A faint jangle from the cellar had Mr. Blandings clumping down the rough steps to search it out. Sitting cross-legged on a plank was a young man with his back to Mr. Blandings. He was surrounded by a welter of tubes and sheets of thin metal, and as he flourished a pair of heavy tin snips in his right hand, he whistled a toneless tune. Apparently he had heard no visitor approach.

"Morning," said Mr. Blandings. The young man turned around, and Mr. Blandings was confronted with the stonemason from down the road whose shack was so deep a source of distress to him.

"Howdy," said the young man. "Wondered when I'd be bumping into you again. How's things with you and the hysterical society? All blowed over like I told you, I guess."

"Yes," said Mr. Blandings, feeling embarrassed and not knowing precisely why. "All blowed over, so far as I can see, just like you said."

"Some people seem to like to spend all their time sticking their nose into other people's business," said the young man. "Now you take me, I wouldn't care what you're up to, so long as you leave me go *my* way, like I leave you go yours."

"That's right," said Mr. Blandings.

"You take some of the workmen around here," said the young man. "They got themselves all lathered up about you. They—"

"About *me?*" said Mr. Blandings.

"Sure," said the young man. "They go 'round muttering what's this Blandings guy think he's up to, building an ark up here top this mountain that's been Hackett's mountain ever since God was a small boy. I tell 'em this is a free country, ain't it? I don't know who this Blandings is, I tell 'em, but if he's got money to pay me a day's wages, I'll give him a day's work and not ask any questions."

"I thought you were a stonemason," said Mr. Blandings.

"I work at that summers," said the young man. "Winters I cut these paper dolls out of sheet metal for Woskowski."

Mr. Blandings recognized the name of the plumbing-and-heating subcontractor. "Where's everybody else today?" he asked.

"Too cold for 'em, I guess," said the young man. "But it ain't going to get any warmer in here until I get these ducts so that we can set the furnace. You could do with some windows in your house, too."

"I sure could. I guess everybody doesn't like to work as much as you do. Maybe that's because they're not as good workmen."

The young man rode roughshod and unheeding over the compliment. "Listen," he said. "You got some very good mechanics on this job, but you got some fairly lousy ones, too. It ain't up to me to tell you which is which, but I kid 'em when I see 'em cutting corners on you. I tell 'em, listen, the owner's human, too, you know, even if he is a millionaire, so don't cheat the poor bastard *every* time he turns around, I tell 'em; just every other time."

"I appreciate that," said Mr. Blandings. He meant it. He had a slight taste of wormwood in him from the venom he had held for this young man as a neighbor. "Maybe," he said in a compensating burst of friendliness, "maybe when we've got the house finished you and your wife will come up to see us. You only live half a mile away."

"Sure we'll be up," said the young man. "My wife'll bring your wife some seedlings to get her garden started with, or something."

"Well," said Mr. Blandings, warm with friendship, "so long, then." He started up the stairs and paused on the third step. "I guess I don't know your name," he said.

"Hackett," said the young man. "Old Eph is one of my uncles. Don't never trust him further than you can throw a grand piano. Him and that Mrs. Prutty is cousins, and old Anson Dolliver you tangled with down to the bank, he's her son-in-law. Just o-n-e b-i-g family you got mixed up with. Someday I'll give you the password."

I am making progress, Mr. Blandings thought. Someday I will really know the ins and outs of this community, after all. A few more happy encounters like this one, and I will be able to get around without a sheepdog. But first I must get my house finished, and to do that I must have some windows, as the young Hackett chap so succinctly pointed out.

So first thing Monday morning he phoned Mr. Retch. By some miracle Mr. Retch was in his office and not supervising a job in Vermont. He turned out to be in a state of sympathetic irritation about the windows, and assured Mr. Blandings he wanted them worse than anybody else. How could he build a house and collect the money he sorely needed without a little cooperation from suppliers?

The next thing Mr. Blandings knew he was so mixed up with his windows that there seemed little room in his life for anything else, and care once again perched on his shoulder.

The window truck had left the factory and would be on the site

485

tomorrow. No, the truck had not left; there was no truck. The windows had been shipped by freight as all windows are the world over. No, the windows would be shipped *when* they were ready; this would not be for another five weeks. No, the windows could be nowhere but on the site, and must have been mislaid by the contractor.

When, just a few days later, a great load of windows arrived by truck, Mr. Blandings experienced a supreme but impermanent pleasure. They were apparently for a house being built by a man named Landers in Fishkill, New York. A long-distance telephone call to Mr. Landers revealed that Mr. Landers had just received a huge consignment of windows addressed to "Blankenthorn Job, Pueblo, Colorado," and was himself suffering from vexation; he deeply resented any suspicion that he had Mr. Blandings' windows, he wanted his own windows, he wanted them quick, and as God was his witness, he was going to get them if he had to pry them out of Mr. Blandings with a pinch bar.

Mr. Blandings felt a strong sense of triumph when suddenly enough windows arrived to build a biscuit factory. Some days later two window installers arrived, quite drunk, bearing with them the tools of their skilled profession, which turned out to be hatchets. They hacked away with cheerful abandon at the two-by-fours in the vicinity of the roughed window openings, and into these enlarged and irregular holes they began jamming the delicate steel frames.

After about a week the installers announced that the condition of their health would make their further attendance impossible. They departed in the early afternoon, staggering slightly and suggesting to Mr. Blandings that they were going to sue him for permitting penal working conditions on his job. They left behind them eight window frames still uninstalled in random locations.

It was at about this time that Mrs. Blandings discovered all the bathtubs in the house to be deeply and disfiguringly scratched.

Not even Mr. Retch and the plumbing subcontractor, when Mrs. Blandings faced them, could deny the facts. Most of the rubbish in the tubs had been thrown out the windows, but the heavy protective paper glued to the tubs' interiors had not been enough to keep a profusion of glacial grooves from the porcelain surfaces. Nor did it take any heavy inductive process to determine how the scratches had got there: the windows in all four bathrooms were directly over the

*The plumbing subcontractor fell
into a passionate torrent of abuse.*

bathtubs; anyone working at the windows would have had to stand in the tubs, but need not have stood in them with hobnail boots.

The plumbing subcontractor, until now a quiet and orderly Pole, fell into a passionate torrent of abuse directed at Mr. Retch, and vowed that any attempt to fix the responsibility for the tub damage on *him* would only result in deep misfortune for all. Mr. Retch allowed that *somebody* was going to have to replace the tubs. He would, that is to say, happily replace the tubs at a per diem rate when new ones were obtained, but who was going to pay for the new ones? The plumbing subcontractor declaimed that this was just what he had suspected: the beginnings of a conspiracy against him.

Since the plumbing subcontractor was also the heating subcontractor, he immediately ordered a cessation of all his work on the premises, and the faint current of warmed air that had begun at last to circulate through the partially closed-in Blandings job immediately ceased. Conditions then reverted to approximately what they had been a month or more before, except that the Blandings now had some of their windows more or less installed, but had traded this advantage for the necessity of having four 500-pound bathtubs ripped out of the tiled walls and floors into which they had for some weeks been securely affixed, and new ones installed, subject to some future delivery.

It remained to be seen who would pay for what. Mr. Retch faced the window company with the responsibility for its vagrant workmen. Just what Mr. Retch said to the window company over the telephone Mr. Blandings did not know. But with lightning speed the window company called Mr. Blandings direct to say that his contractor had been grossly abusive on the general subject of bathtubs, which was obviously no concern of theirs since they were manufacturers and installers of window frames; that even if bathtubs *were* their concern, they would still resent having been treated insolently by this chiseling contractor; that finally and furthermore they would within the next three days send a special crew from their headquarters to remove from the house *and* from the site every window that bore their trademark, since the check for $1407.56 with which Mr. Retch had paid for the windows had been returned to them marked "insufficient funds." When Mr. Blandings relayed this intelligence to Mr. Retch, Mr. Retch went rooting in a vast pile of papers and produced a check for the precise figure under discussion, stamped and canceled by the bank as paid. He added that in his thirty years in the construction industry this was the first time an owner had ever accused him of fraud, and that if Mr. Blandings would like to, they could settle the affair outside; if Mr. Retch lost, he would build the rest of Mr. Blandings' house at his own expense.

It was about this time, too, that Mrs. Blandings discontinued her diary with the notation that she was taking the children to Sarasota for the balance of the winter and installing them in an outdoor school for the benefit of their sinuses. She did not mention the house at all.

WHILE SHE AND THE children were away, Mr. Blandings had occasion to write the following letter to Mr. John Retch:

It is some time since my wife or I have visited the house and my hope is that the work is progressing as fast as the receipt of money requisitions from you would seem to indicate. We hope to get up again as soon as the weather moderates.

Meanwhile, I am considerably disturbed by the number of "extras" accumulating on your bills. So far as my wife and I are aware, we have authorized only two changes from the original plans. I am at a loss to understand the multitude of other matters being billed me, or even what the items specified refer to at all. I herewith quote and comment on the following from your latest requisitions:

Redesign of doorways No. 102, 107, 108, 112 .... *$220.00*
(Mr. Simms asssures me that there was no redesign on any doorways on the job whatsoever.)

New installation of well casing *$96.50*
(If, according to your own explanation, the well casing installed by Mr. John Tesander was cracked by the blasting done by your excavation subcontractor, I fail to see why I should bear the cost of the replacement.)

Substitution of 220-volt switch panel in cellar *$139.89*
(What is the meaning of this? It is another of the innumerable extras on the electrical work. You told me that the electrical subcontractor was a good man "but liked to bid low and add extras." *You suggested that I add $500 to his contract figure before he started work* because "that'll please him and you'll save in the long run." I would like to know what I have saved by this charitable contribution, since I cannot imagine getting more extras than I have had, anyway. As to this switch panel, why has something been substituted for something else without my knowledge until it comes time to pay for it?)

Furring down ceiling for kitchen cabinets *$102.00*
(Insofar as I understand this charge, I consider it outrageous. You have known the dimensions of the kitchen cabinets from the beginning; if you did not, then you were guilty of negligence. And yet you have the effrontery to put this on my bill as an extra!)

Installing one Zuz-Zuz Water Soft-N-R *$265.50*
(I will not have any such piece of equipment in my house. Who authorized it? So far as I am concerned it can be taken out immediately. Nor will I pay any subsequent extra labeled "Removal of Zuz-Zuz Water Soft-N-R.")

Extra Screws *$3.00*
(A very modest sum, but are your accounting methods so accurate that you know this should cost me $3.00 instead of $2.99 or even $3.01?)

All this totals $826.89—a not inconsiderable sum. I will expect to hear from you directly and to have these evident misunderstandings cleared up without cost to me. Also, I wish you would ask your bookkeeper to stop writing "Please!" in red ink across the bottom of these bills. I am cleaning up your legitimate charges as quickly as I find it possible.

The letter to Mr. J. H. Blandings from John Retch said in part:

. . . only time in our experience that an owner has taken any such position. We have passed up many extra items without bill, because we wanted you to be satisfied all along the line. Pardon our suggestion that you and Mrs. Blandings ought to get together, but furring down of kitchen ceiling was discussed with her, and she told us kitchen cabinets had to fit exactly "at all costs." We could have installed a lighter electrical switch panel against advice of electrical contractor, who is a specialist in such things, and leave the resulting fire hazard up to you, but preferred to take the honest course of making the equipment adequate to the heavy electrical load your lines will be carrying and bill you in the open, after calling architect's attention to same. The Zuz-Zuz people make a fine water softener and we put it in because we were looking out for your interests in not letting your boilers and water lines be ruined by your water, which the plumbing man assured us was the most corrosive water he's seen in his entire experience in the trade. We discussed this with Mr. Simms and he said he would explain these circumstances to you, which it appears he did not. As to the well casing . . .

Mr. Blandings replied: "I enclose a check for $826.89, but will positively not be responsible for any further . . ."

"WE'LL RAISE A BIG fund," Mr. Simms was saying to Mr. & Mrs. Blandings in a tired voice. "I'll contribute to it myself, as generously as I can. So will every other architect in the country. We'll use it so that every man, woman, or child who wants to build a house can build a practice one, free of charge. As soon as it's built, it gets torn down, and *then* if the state gives you a certificate of competency, you can build a house for keeps at your own expense."

490

"That is very amusing," said Mr. Blandings, who had developed a noticeable twitch in his right eyelid. "But what I'm trying to talk about is this latest, final, outrageous piece of larceny from your colleague, Mr. Retch."

He waved the bill he was holding in his tremulous hand, feeling the same tendency to scream and smash as when he had first unfolded it. On the bill was typed only one line:

Changes in closet *$1247.00*

"I would venture to say," said Mr. Blandings, "there is no closet in the Taj Mahal that ever cost $1247 to construct *new*, to say nothing of merely *changing* it." He glared at the architect.

"On my copy there's a notation that says it refers to changes on Detail Sheet No. 135," said Mr. Simms. "Let me find that sheet."

Mr. Simms made for the table on which his great volume of blueprints lay curly and dog-eared. Mrs. Blandings, who had returned with the children from her sojourn in Florida, had been sitting quietly sewing in a corner. Now she arose as he did. Making for the sideboard, she poured herself a generous slug of whiskey, downed it at a gulp, and resumed her seat. Her husband watched her with amazement. Mrs. Blandings drank only when her duties as a hostess made her think it the part of graciousness.

"Well, it really isn't a closet at all," said Mr. Simms. "It's that recess with the flower sink off the back entryway. We designed it while we were working on the closets, and I guess it's always stayed that way on Retch's charts. But God knows why there'd be any changes there."

Mr. Blandings continued to glare at him. Mrs. Blandings, returned to her sewing, was mouselike in the corner, but a flush had crept into her cheeks.

"Wait a minute," said Mr. Simms, looking up from his blueprints. "There was a bluestone floor with a drain in there when I looked at it the other day, and I said to myself I must be slipping; I could have sworn we just had a wood floor in there. But right here on my detail it shows a wood floor, just as I thought."

Mr. Blandings, who could be extremely slow to add two and two when on the defensive, could also be as swift as a striking cobra when his own conscience was clear. His wife's silence, her flush, the incredible

"What—have—you—done?"
demanded Mr. Blandings.

gulp of whiskey, and the flower sink, a pet and favorite project from the day she had first thought of it, arranged themselves suddenly in his mind. He knew he had something. He pivoted slowly and faced his wife. He had been the prisoner in the dock for a year; suddenly he was the guardian of Justice—black-robed, bewigged, and awesome.

"What–have–you–done?" demanded Mr. Blandings.

"I never heard of anything so ridiculous," said Mrs. Blandings. "I haven't done a thing, and what I did has nothing to do with what we're talking about and I don't see why I should be bullied about my flower sink."

It was said too fast, and it did not hang together. Even Mr. Simms began to look stern.

"All I did," said Mrs. Blandings, "all I did was one day I saw four big pieces of flagstone left over from the porch that were just going to be thrown away and I asked Mr. Retch if he wouldn't just put them down on the floor of the flower sink and poke a little cement between the cracks and give me a nice stone floor so that I could splash around with my flowers if I wanted to. And Mr. Retch was as nice as could be, and said, 'You're the doctor,' and that's all anybody ever said to anybody about anything."

Mr. Simms closed his eyes and put his head in his hands. Mrs. Blandings, who expected to be told that she had done something only mildly wrong, stared at the silent suffering of her architect with a wild feeling of alarm. Mr. Blandings looked from his wife to Mr. Simms and back again, and a thick, towering silence grew and grew.

After a while Mr. Simms took his hands down from his face and shook his head as if to clear his ears. "All right," he said. He seemed better, now the uncertainty was over. "I think I can tell you everything that happened, just as if I'd seen it all myself. First, the carpenters had to rip up the floorboards. Those planks run under the whole width of the pantry, so Retch had to knock the bottom out of the pantry wall to get them out. Then he had to saw them off. Then he had to relay floorboards in the pantry. Then he would have had to chop out the tops of the joists under the flower-sink space to make room for a cradle. I guess he bought some iron straps and fastened them to a big pan to give him something to hold the cement he was going to lay those flagstones up in. What with that added load on the weakened joists, I'll bet he had to put a lally column down below it for support, too. Do you mind if I have a drink?"

In the absence of any response from his hosts, Mr. Simms went to the sideboard, mixed himself a highball and resumed his chair.

"Well," he said, "the main soil pipe runs right under there in the cellar, so Retch had to get his plumbing man back to take out a section of the pipe so he could get that cradle set. I guess that meant he had to change the pitch of the soil pipe from one end of the house to the other; you can't just put a sag in it, you understand, unless you want the sewage to run backward. And then, of course, he had to put in another pipe section with a Y in it, so he could hitch up that drain he was putting in the floor for you. There are hot- and cold-water pipes hooked to the joists right under there, too, so I'll bet my bottom dollar he had to relocate *them*. And I guess the electrician had to rip out about sixty feet of armored cable between the main panel and the junction box by the oil burner. Oh, yes, and there was a heating duct in the way, too. I'll bet that duct took somebody three days to fiddle with, all by itself."

Mr. Simms took a long pull on his glass. "So then he put his cradle in, and then he called back his mason contractor and got him to lay that stone, including the work around the drain, which was a nice dainty-looking job, as I saw it."

He paused. There was no sound from Mr. or Mrs. Blandings.

"I guess that was about the size of it," said Mr. Simms. "Except then Retch had to repair the pantry wall and that meant getting a plasterer back, and the wire-lath man, too. And—I forgot all about it—the doors wouldn't clear the new floor, and I guess he sent them back to the mill for adjustment. Quite an undertaking. Let's see—carpenters, plumber, electrician, plasterer, lather, mason, tinsmith for the ducts, a couple of floor layers—it took all those people on the site, plus a blacksmith and a millworker in their own shops, to get those four flagstones laid down in that little recess. . . . If I can't get Retch to knock $75 off his extra, I'll certainly sweat $50 out of him."

"Does—" said Mrs. Blandings.

"Be quiet," said Mr. Blandings.

"Now look," said Mr. Simms. "The trouble with virgin builders like you people is that you don't even know when you're saying good morning to the contractor and when you're authorizing him to spend over a thousand dollars of your money. If you weren't to pay Retch's bill for this, and if he were to sue you for it, and you were to tell in court what you've just told me, the judge would instruct the jury to find for Retch."

"Does—" said Mrs. Blandings.

"Be quiet," said Mr. Blandings. "I wouldn't mind about women so much if it wasn't that they wanted to *chatter* all the time."

"Well," said Mr. Simms, "I've got to be going. It's a lot later than I thought. I guess Retch saw a fairly good thing in this, and a chance to make up some money he might have lost someplace else on the job and kept his mouth shut about. At that, there's nothing that's not legitimate. You gave him a chance, and he took it."

He paused at the door. "Don't worry. If I can't get $50 out of him, I'll get $25 or know the reason why. Good night."

IT WAS ALL, Mr. Blandings decided several days later, a blessing in disguise. It had cost a lot of money, but in exchange he had newly acquired a pliant wife—quiet, cooperative, deferential. And perhaps it would not cost so much money after all. Mr. Simms had telephoned to say that he had read the riot act to Mr. Retch for responding so literally to the whims of an owner's spouse; that furthermore Mr. Retch was yearning to get the contract for a mansion that a wealthy manufacturer was soon to build fifteen miles from Bald Mountain— and that if Mr. Blandings were to write this gentleman a letter expressing admiration for Mr. Retch's unwavering rectitude as a contractor, it might well be discovered that Mr. Retch would be as putty in Mr. Blandings' hands when it came to a discussion of the cost of flower-sink flagstones.

Mr. Blandings did not convey this to his wife; not in full, at least.

The opportunity for marital discipline was too bright to tarnish with subjunctives.

"Sweetheart," said Mrs. Blandings softly. "I'm—"

It was impossible for her voice to achieve, ever again, the shy tentativeness, the captivating hesitancy, it had had seventeen years ago; but this was not bad, Mr. Blandings thought, not bad at all.

"I'm in the most desperate trouble," he heard his wife conclude.

"What's up?" asked Mr. Blandings, as to his elder daughter.

The color scheme for the house was up. Mr. Simms had called Mrs. Blandings to say that the boss painter was getting finished with sizing and priming the plaster, the woodwork, and the window frames and now wanted to talk turkey about the actual, the final colors. Mrs. Blandings was aghast at the range of choice before her.

"Why don't you just paint all the rooms a nice buff and not fuss about it?" said Mr. Blandings.

The first veil of the New Acquiescence fell. "I'm afraid that wouldn't be practicable," said Mrs. Blandings.

What did seem to her practicable, Mr. Blandings could not discern. His wife had spent a frantic week collecting, rejecting, and recombining color samples from every paint company east of Denver, and studying the colors with which the houses in the Williamsburg, Virginia, restoration had been painted. She seemed to want something like them but "better," she explained.

There had been a time when the Blandings had assumed that newly purchased furnishings would garnish their home in the country. Imperceptibly, this hope had faded; the Blandings had nothing left but a deficit to cover the budget for any furnishings at all. They had never said a word to one another about this; each merely assumed, and knew that the other shared the assumption, that they would just move up to the country the "city furniture" with which they had been invested at the time of their marriage.

It made Mrs. Blandings a little sad that she could not make a clean sweep of some of their more unfortunate earlier acquisitions, but she bore it bravely; she was now resolved that with brand-new colors she would accomplish what she had in her mind's eye after all. It was only the interior of the house that bothered her; the exterior was to be an "off-white" with the tiniest imaginable addition of raw umber to give it an almost imperceptible putty tinge. The front door was to be "off-eggplant." The venetian blinds, which had to be painted before they left their own factory, would be further "off" the "off-white" of the house on their outsides; on their insides they would be—gracious, there was so much to think about.

Deeming consultation with Mr. Blandings as no more useful than seeking the True and Beautiful in a penny arcade, Mrs. Blandings sat down to compose to the boss painter a letter of instructions on which he could not possibly go wrong.

"Dear Mr. PeDelford," she began. She bit the pen top and a dreamy look came into her eyes as she gathered her powers:

> I am enclosing the samples for the paint colors. To make things so clear that there can be no misunderstanding I will list them below, room by room.
>
> *Living room.* The color is to be a soft green, not as bluish as a robin's egg, but not as yellow as daffodil buds. The sample enclosed, which is the best I could get, is a little too yellow. It should just be a sort of grayish apple green.
>
> *Dining room.* To be yellow, and a very *gay* yellow. Just make it a bright sunshiny color and you cannot go wrong. Simply get a pound of butter and match it *exactly.*
>
> *Mr. Blandings' study.* Color must be masculine. The enclosed beige sample is quite a bit too pink, so do not follow it literally.

Mrs. Blandings took a new sheet of paper. Whereas her pen had moved haltingly in the beginning it now flew fast, for inspiration was upon her.

> The bedroom colors are the only ones that may give you any trouble. For our bedroom I am enclosing a small sample of chintz, which I have tagged MBR (Master Bed Room), but I do not want you to match any of the flower colors. There are some dots in the background, and it is *these dots* I want the paint to match exactly. The other samples of chintz are for the other bedrooms. The front one, that I call the "pink room," is to match the little rosebud next to the delphinium—*not* the bud near the hollyhock leaf. The other bedroom, the "blue room," should be like the delphinium blossom second from the top on the stem.
>
> For the guest room please match the piece of thread that I

have wrapped in the bit of tissue paper enclosed. Be sure to get an exact match, because the whole effect depends on the walls matching the little touches of the same color.

Then in the master bath, the color should suggest apple blossoms *just* before they fall. For the guest bath I am enclosing a pressed forget-me-not flower, which should be a good guide for you except that it should be quite a little lighter. The paint must be easy to wash but it must *not* gleam. I wish you would please . . .

CHAPTER SEVEN

THE ROOMS GOT PAINTED. It was surprising how well the rooms got painted, considering an unpromising start. Mr. PeDelford, the boss painter, did not know how to take Mrs. Blandings in the beginning, nor did his ambivalence ever completely disappear. "We couldn't take time off to go pickin' wildflowers all over the county to get a match for some of these here," said Mr. PeDelford. "How's this for that back room?" He gestured with a cigar toward a bucket of delicate puce. Half an inch of the cigar's dense ash fell into it, but when Mr. PeDelford stirred the mixture vigorously with a split shingle

Half an inch of dense cigar ash fell into a bucket of delicate puce, but little or no change resulted.

coated with dead leaves, little or no change resulted. Generous supplies of oats, dandruff, iron filings, sawdust, and earth kept falling
into Mr. PeDelford's paint buckets as the job proceeded, but Mrs.
Blandings got used to the procession of these mishaps and discovered that they somehow made very little difference.

"Oh, dear," said Mrs. Blandings. "I can't tell until I see some of it
on the wall."

It turned out that she couldn't tell then, either. "I'll have to wait
until it dries," she said. When it dried there was something wrong
with it, but it was hard to say what. To Mrs. Blandings it was too dark;
to Mr. Blandings it was too light. To Mr. PeDelford it was the finest
color that had been mixed since the life and times of the artist
Botticelli. Under the pressure of his salesmanship, and his increasingly extravagant remarks about Mrs. Blandings' "color sense," it
went on the walls. It was followed, one by one, by its companions,
most of which turned out to be indistinguishable from the paint
company's standard samples, as designated by number and made up
in thousand-gallon batches at the factory.

The Blandings were happy to discover that it was restful to visit the
house now. The weather was growing milder. The swarming workmen were mostly gone, except for the painters, who produced only a
gentle swish and slap, swish and slap. The marks of haste and
carelessness all faded slowly away as the colors spread and glowed.

"It's beginning to look simply *lovely*," said Mrs. Blandings, whose
memory of the flagstone episode had by now totally vanished. "When
will you be getting to work on the floors, Mr. PeDelford?"

The oaken floors, which someday must gleam under their scatter
rugs, were dull with spilled liquids, ground-in plaster dust. The
house had not yet been swept out, but at least it had been shoveled
out, and the footing was less hazardous.

"They ain't in *my* contract," he said with simple innocence.

Indeed they were not, Mr. and Mrs. Blandings discovered. They
were not in anybody's contract. They had just been forgotten. Mr.
PeDelford allowed as how, since he had his crew right on the site, he
could do the floors with stain, wax, and polish for $225.

Mr. Blandings was discovering that getting a house finished was a
horror of the same intensity, but of different order, as getting it
started. The problems of starting a house were vast, few, and insolu-

ble; the problems of finishing it were small, multitudinous, and insoluble. Deciding which was worse was like deciding whether you preferred death through being crushed by a bulldozer or torn apart in a threshing machine. By the time the interior painting was finished, the house was indubitably ninety-five percent done, and ninety-five percent of Mr. Retch's requisition payments were indubitably due him. But a house that was ninety-five percent finished could not be lived in. Lighting fixtures, medicine cabinets, the kitchen stove, were not yet in place.

If there was anything in the world that Mr. and Mrs. Blandings now wanted to see, it was their house with its outside painted. Until it was, they would not know whether they liked it or not, whether the whole vast project was a success or a failure. With bare brick and wood showing in their native states and colors, the Blandings could not see their house steady or see it whole.

But Mr. PeDelford could not paint the outside. Four rows of redwood siding near the eaves were missing; enough had been damaged in handling to make Mr. Retch's supply short by just that much. The mill would supply him when next he had a big enough job to make delivery worthwhile; in the meantime the painters betook themselves to other quarters, to return God only knew when.

ONE LATE AFTERNOON as the sun was fading, the house was seized with a convulsive and sustained shudder. Mrs. Blandings cried out; Mr. Blandings made an elaborate pretense of calm. The seizure lasted a long half minute and passed away. Before the Blandings left, the same racking spasm again shook their home from ridge to footing, and the plaster dust, still unswept, danced in the cracks of the floor. Mr. Blandings made an alarmed telephone call to Mr. Simms, who said he would come over and investigate as soon as he could: other homes for other people were beginning to be on his mind and his drawing board, he gently implied.

When Mr. Simms got around to visiting the house, it stood serene and still; no such visitation as the Blandings had described could even remotely be imagined. After a week of periodic visits, it at last obliged with its seizure late one afternoon, as owners and architect were about to give up their vigil. Mr. Simms then swiftly traced the trouble to the oil burner, starting up in answer to the call of its thermostat as the afternoon warmth faded. The bolts that held its motor base to the concrete had never been screwed home; this, plus a flutter in the smoke-pipe damper, had set every inch of hot-air duct work to quivering as the motor first revolved. Mr. Simms, with a wrench and a piece of twisted wire, banished the ague in five minutes.

"If I were you, I'd start doing things like that for myself," he said. "That's one way; the other is to spend hours tracing John Retch on the phone, then waiting three to ten days before he gets a man back here to find out what it's all about. Then you have another little extra for work that Retch can say was outside the contract."

Mr. Simms cleared his throat; he had intended to say nothing more, but perhaps this was the best occasion he would ever have for a formal leave-taking.

"If you don't mind my saying so, one of the hardest jobs an architect has is weaning the owner when the time comes. I hope I'll always be seeing a lot of you, for after all I don't live far away; but these other people whose plans I have on my drawing board right now—they stand about where you and your plans stood a year ago. They want to see a good deal of me—do you remember how it was?"

Yes, Mr. Blandings thought with a sigh. He had a house; now he must grow up to it. His cares were not ending, it appeared, but, in a realer sense, just beginning. He mopped his brow and told Mr. Simms that indeed he understood, and immediately began a careful round of all equipment designed to flow, spin, or reciprocate. There was a lot of it.

The turning on of a tap produced spasmodic gushes of a liquid that was the color of weak coffee but fizzed like champagne. He assumed that this condition would someday right itself, and turned his attention to one of his brand-new, unbelievably filthy toilet bowls—the newest and most inaudible type known to science.

Mr. Blandings pushed the flush lever on the stylishly low porcelain tank. There was an almost imperceptible click, and then the waters in the uncleansed bowl began a silent, lovely swirl; implacable but beyond the limits of human audibility. This is marvelous, Mr. Blandings thought. The swirling waters gathered themselves up, silent still, and sluiced themselves out of his sight forever. Without warning there then emerged from the toilet's deepest inwardness so harsh and terrifying a *yawp* as to make Mr. Blandings leap backward into the hall. He tried all the other toilets and was similarly rewarded, first by the enigma of the silent whirlpool, then by the horror of the final, climactic withdrawal. From his pocket he pulled a little notebook and in it he wrote a pungent criticism, for Mr. Simms' benefit, of what he had just observed. The notebook had a dozen close-packed pages already, but he knew that after a while he would tear them all up, that in a year or two he would get used to the toilets and to the progress they exemplified, and that he would grow old with them as gracefully as was possible.

Then the day came at last when the Blandings' house was to become the Blandings' house, and none other's. The ceremony of the architect's final certification and the owner's acceptance was at hand. Bill Cole had insisted on such an endless legal hocus-pocus before giving Mr. Retch his final check that even Mr. Blandings thought his friend was carrying things too far. Then he thought of what the Messrs. Barratry, Lynch & Virgo had done to him over the title while he was waiting, wasted and pale, for his money, and he relaxed again. It was Mr. Retch's turn to fume. Somehow, Mr. Bland-ings felt, Mr. Retch fumed to better effect than he. Then after a few days Bill suddenly said that everything was now all right, the check could be passed.

The check was passed. And now Mr. Blandings and his wife were on their way to possess their house, and it was once again the flowering spring. Mr. Blandings drove through lanes of dogwood and banks of violets and dripping bushes of forsythia, and smiled at the recollection of how he once had lost himself in a tangle of back-country roads.

The last familiar turn was made. The Blandings saw their house and a cry escaped them. It was a cry of joy. Mr. PeDelford's work was completed; there stood their creation in all its gleaming whiteness, lovelier than the fairest drawings that ever Mr. Simms had drawn. It seemed to wait for them as a girl would wait, with downcast eyes, for her lover's first shy kiss. The Blandings entered the citadel and stood with reverence upon their shining oaken floors.

OF COURSE, THERE were little misfortunes here and there. The suave, silent mercury switches in the lighting system had all been ripped out and replaced with switches whose onward *click* and offward *clack* had the attention-commanding value of a circus clown's slapstick: a three-wire master-switch arrangement on which Mr. Blandings had insisted, whereby he could turn on all the hall and outside lights at once if he smelled a smell or heard a sound, had made use of the silent switches impossible, but nobody had told him.

The "very advanced" fluorescent lighting in the dining room hummed so loudly from its hidden ballasts that conversation would obviously not be possible. "We have never recommended this type of lighting equipment for rooms of low noise level," the Nadir Electric Supply Company wrote tartly in answer to Mr. Blandings' protest. "Had your contractor informed us of the use contemplated for this equipment we would have warned against it." It was later discovered that the lighting turned a healthy roast of beef into a purple mass of putrescence on the dining table, and the whole installation was eventually removed and replaced by the more conventional type of lamp invented by Thomas Alva Edison in 1879.

There was, too, window hardware that would not work. All the doors stuck except those that would not latch at all, and one (in the cellar) would open only a meager distance before its swing was blocked by the air duct which had been altered in the cause of Mrs. Blandings' flower-sink flagstones.

Mrs. Blandings had achieved a pretty fair approximation of the colors of rosebuds, of apple blossoms about to fall, of forget-me-nots in desiccation, with which she had faced the skeptical Mr. PeDelford, but in her eagerness for soft and delicate colors she had either misunderstood or never heard the mumbled and ambiguous warning from her boss painter. She had a horror of gloss in her colors, so there was none; it had not occurred to her that the coats of flat paint as they dried on the wall would become culture surfaces for thumbprints. She could not touch one of her own delicate and ultra-clean fingertips to a wall without it looking as though a bootblack had splayed his palm against it.

Then there was the insect world to cope with. The spring was still early and the screens were on the windows, but it was nevertheless apparent that Mrs. Blandings' paints held a deep fascination for an assortment of small flying and crawling creatures. They had hurled themselves upon the paint in one assault wave after another, and it was theirs.

But the Blandings had built a good house—a very fine house indeed by any standards. Considering its process of development, Mr. Blandings vaguely remembered that it had all sprung from the old Hackett farmhouse on which $10,000 was to be spent for "restoration." Only Mr. Blandings—and he not altogether—would someday know how much money he had really spent on the eventually emerged dwelling. In the far, far back of his head, there rang a figure of $56,000 that he preferred, for the moment, not to examine further.

THE CHRISTMAS HOUSE issue of *Home Lovely* lay open before Mr. Savington Funkhauser, professional architect, who was wondering why, after a hard day at the drafting board, he had opened it at all. "Our problem was to create a home of modern implications in a community dominated by fine old colonial farmhouses from Revolutionary days and before," he read, "and to accent a youthful spirit without offending the traditions of those stout forebears whose indomitable strivings . . ."

"Spittle," said Mr. Funkhauser in a toneless voice. He looked for a title and saw *Home Lovely*'s *December House-of-the-Month Is Tribute to Taste and Ingenuity with Materials Old and New*. There seemed here no conveyance of information whatsoever, and Mr. Funkhauser read on in a sort of mild hypnosis.

"It was a challenge to our ingenuity, but my husband and I tackled the difficulties with a will, and out of a combination of carefully budgeted planning and the most friendly three-way cooperation among architect, owner, and builder, we were able to achieve our aims with a minimum of those unforeseen expenses that occasionally mar the joys of building that sine qua non of all couples' ambitions, the Home of One's Own."

"Whose bilge *is* this?" Mr. Funkhauser asked of the fireplace. On the instant, a picture caption answered him. "Mrs. J. Holocoup Blandings, whose delightful mountain dwelling is this month's *Home Lovely* choice as . . ."

Mr. Funkhauser's right arm moved suddenly, and the Christmas House issue described a graceful arc, disappearing into his wastebasket. A moment later the young architect fished it out again and turned back to the interview with "the chic and attractive Mrs. Blandings, mistress of 'Surrogate Acres.' " For some five wordless minutes he studied the dim halftones and spidery linecuts on the chalky paper. Suddenly he came on something familiar, and a flush darkened his face. He muttered for a moment, and then, taking pen and paper, he commenced the draft of a letter.

> Dear Mr. Blandings,
>   In the Christmas issue of Home Lovely I note the display of your new residence and an interview with your wife. In it, on page 166, I notice a reference that says ". . . once the impracticalities of an earlier designer had been discarded as wholly unsuitable . . ." I would scarcely have credited this to be a reference to myself were it not that on the following page an illustration at the top labeled "Discarded Study" is an obvious and offensive caricature of a rendering I submitted to you on—

Mr. Funkhauser left the date blank for filling in and went to his filing cabinet to examine the documents bearing on the Funkhauser-Blandings grievance case of long ago. Then he resumed:

> Taken in conjunction, the sentence and drawing offer to my professional standing an affront and damage that I cannot afford to pass unnoticed. I am in consequence instructing my attorneys, the Messrs. Barratry, Lynch & Virgo, to communicate with you regarding possible steps toward redress which . . .

Miles away, on Bald Mountain, in the midst of Surrogate Acres, beneath an uninsulated roof which creaked slightly now and then under the growing snow load of a winter storm, Mr. Blandings smiled uneasily in his sleep. He was dreaming that his house was on fire.

THE HOT ROCK

THE
HOT ROCK

A Condensation of the Novel by
Donald E. Westlake

Illustrated by Don Daily

The Balabomo Emerald was worth
a lot of money to someone. It was also the
closely guarded treasure of a new
African nation. So it seems unlikely that even
criminal mastermind John Archibald
Dortmunder could steal it. But with the full
resources of a rival nation behind him,
and with the right team of expert crooks to
help—why then, he just might pull it off.
The caper he organizes to snatch
the stone (and then to storm a police station,
invade an insane asylum, kidnap a slippery lawyer,
and avoid a double cross) will have
you alternately sitting on the edge of your
chair in suspense, and falling off
it in laughter.

   Donald E. Westlake is the author of many
popular books, among them the award-winning
God Save the Mark. With a mind that surpasses
even Dortmunder's at hatching madcap
schemes, he is considered the undisputed
master of comic suspense.

PHASE ONE

DORTMUNDER BLEW HIS nose. "Warden," he said, "you don't know how much I appreciate the personal attention you been paying me." There wasn't anything for him to do with the Kleenex, so he just held it balled up in his fist.

Warden Outes gave him a brisk smile, walked around from behind his desk, patted Dortmunder on the arm, and said, "It's the ones I can save that give me the most pleasure." He was a latter-day civil service type—college-trained, energetic, idealistic, reformistic, and chummy. Dortmunder hated him.

The warden said, "I'll walk you to the gate."

"You don't have to do that, Warden," Dortmunder said. The tissue was damp against his palm.

"But it will give me pleasure," the warden said. "To see you walk out that gate, and know you'll never slip again, never be inside these walls again, and to know I had some small part in your rehabilitation, you can't imagine how much pleasure that will give me."

Dortmunder was feeling no pleasure at all. He'd sold his cell for three hundred bucks—having a hot-water faucet that worked and a tunnel to the dispensary made it a bargain at the price—and the money was supposed to be passed to him on his way out. He couldn't have taken it before then or it would have been found on him in the final shakedown. But how could it be delivered with the warden standing right next to him?

He said, playing a little desperation ball, "Warden, it's in this office that I've always seen you, in this office that I've listened to your—"

"Come along, Dortmunder," the warden said. "We can talk on our way to the gate."

So they went out together. On the last lap, crossing the big yard, Dortmunder saw Creasey, the trusty with the three hundred, start in his direction and then abruptly stop. Creasey made a small gesture that meant, There's nothing to be done.

Dortmunder made a small gesture that meant, Damn it to hell, I *know* there's nothing to be done.

At the gate, the warden stuck his hand out and said, "Good luck, Dortmunder. May I say I hope I never see you again." It was a joke, because he chuckled.

Dortmunder took the warden's hand and said, "I hope I never see you again either, Warden." It wasn't a joke, but he chuckled anyway.

Dortmunder turned away. The big gate opened, he stepped outside, the big gate closed. He was free, his debt to society was paid. He was also out three hundred fish. Damn it. He'd been counting on that dough. All he had was ten bucks and a train ticket.

Disgusted, he threw the tissue on the sidewalk.

Littering.

KELP SAW DORTMUNDER walk out into the sunlight and then just stand there on the sidewalk a minute, looking around. Kelp knew what that feeling was, the first minute of freedom, free air, free sun. He waited, not wanting to spoil Dortmunder's pleasure, but when Dortmunder finally started to walk off, Kelp started the engine and steered the long black car slowly down the street after him.

It was a pretty good car, a Cadillac with side curtains, air conditioning, a gizmo that would switch down your high beams at night when another car was coming—all sorts of labor-saving devices. Kelp had preferred to drive up here today rather than take the train, so he'd gone shopping for a car last night, and he'd found this one on East 67th Street. It had MD plates and he always automatically checked those, because doctors tended to leave the keys in the car. Once again the medical profession had not disappointed him.

It didn't have MD plates now, of course. The state hadn't spent four years teaching him how to make license plates for nothing.

He glided along after Dortmunder now, the long black Caddy purring, tires crunching the dirty pavement, and Kelp thought how surprised and pleased Dortmunder would be to see a friendly face the first thing on hitting the street. He was just about to sound the horn when Dortmunder suddenly spun around, looked at the silent black car with side curtains following him, got a panicky look on his face, and began to run like hell along the sidewalk, cowering against the gray prison wall.

There were four buttons on a control panel in the car door, and they operated the four side windows of the Cadillac. The only trouble was, Kelp could never remember which button operated which window. He pushed a button and the right rear window slid down. "Dortmunder!" he shouted, hitting the accelerator, the Caddy leaping forward along the street. There was no one else in sight, only the black car and the running man. The prison wall loomed tall and gray. Across the street the small grimy houses were closed and silent.

Kelp was veering all over the street, his attention distracted by his confusion over the window buttons. The left rear window rolled down, and he shouted Dortmunder's name again, but Dortmunder still couldn't hear him. Kelp's fingers found another button, pushed, and the right rear window rolled up again. The Caddy jounced up over the curb, and then was angling straight for Dortmunder, who turned, flattened himself against the wall, spread his arms out wide, and screamed like a banshee.

At the last second, Kelp hit the brakes. They were power brakes, and the Caddy stopped dead, bouncing Kelp off the steering wheel. Dortmunder reached one shaky hand out and leaned on the Caddy's quivering hood.

Kelp tried to get out of the car, but in his excitement he'd hit another button, the one that automatically locked all four doors. "Damn doctors!" he cried, pushed every button in sight, and finally lunged from the car like a skin diver escaping from an octopus.

Dortmunder was still leaning forward slightly, supporting himself with one hand on the car hood. He looked gray, and it wasn't all prison pallor. Kelp walked over to him. "What are you running for, Dortmunder?" he said. "It's me, your old pal, Kelp." He stuck his hand out. Dortmunder hit him in the eye.

"All you had to do was *honk*," Dortmunder said.

ON THE HIGHWAY TO New York, the Caddy's speed set at sixty-five miles an hour, Dortmunder was still feeling aggrieved. Three hundred bucks down the drain, scared out of his wits, almost run down by a damn fool in a Cadillac, and skinned his knuckle on Kelp's cheekbone, all on the same day.

"What do you want, anyway?" Dortmunder said. "They give me a train ticket, I didn't need no ride."

"You need work, I bet," Kelp said. "Unless you got something lined up."

"I don't have anything lined up," Dortmunder said. Now that he thought about it, that irritated him too.

"Well, I got a sweetheart for you," Kelp said. He was smiling all over his face.

Dortmunder decided to stop grousing. "All right," he said. "I can listen. What's the story?"

Kelp said, "Did you ever hear of a place called Talabwo? It's a country. In Africa."

"I never heard of it," Dortmunder said. "I heard of the Congo."

"This is near there," Kelp said. "But the job isn't over there, it's right here in the good old U.S.A."

"Oh." Dortmunder sucked his skinned knuckle, then said, "Then why talk about this other place?"

"Talabwo?"

"Yeah, Talabwo. Why talk about it?"

"I'll get to that," Kelp said. "You ever hear of Akinzi?"

"He's that doctor did that sex book," Dortmunder said. "I wanted to get it out of the library in stir, but they had a twelve-year waiting list. I put my name on, just in case I got turned down for parole."

"That's not what I'm talking about," Kelp said. "I'm talking about another country. It's called Akinzi." He spelled it.

Dortmunder shook his head. "Is that in Africa too?"

"Yeah, it's another country in Africa," Kelp said. "There was this British colony that went independent, but there was trouble because there were two big tribes and they both wanted to run the government, so they had a civil war and finally decided to split into two countries. So that's the two countries, Talabwo and Akinzi."

"You know an awful lot about this stuff," Dortmunder said. "But I don't see any caper in it yet."

"I'm coming to that," Kelp said. "It seems that one of these tribes had this jewel, this emerald, and they used to pray to it like a god, and these days it's their symbol. Like a mascot, something like that."

"An emerald?"

"It's supposed to be worth half a million bucks, maybe more."

"That's a lot," Dortmunder said. "But you couldn't fence a thing like that. It's too well known."

"True. But that's the caper," Kelp said. "To heist the emerald."

Dortmunder found himself getting irritable again. He took his pack of Camels out of his shirt pocket. "If we can't fence it," he said, "what the hell do we want to lift it for?"

"Because we've got a buyer," Kelp said. "He'll pay thirty thousand dollars a man to get the emerald."

Dortmunder stuck a cigarette in his mouth and pushed in the cigarette lighter on the dashboard. "Who is this guy? Some collector?"

"No. He's the United Nations ambassador from Talabwo."

The cigarette lighter popped out of the dashboard and fell on the floor. Dortmunder picked it up and lit his cigarette. "He's who?"

Kelp repeated himself.

"Explain," said Dortmunder.

"Sure," Kelp said. "When the British colony split into two countries, Akinzi got the city where the emerald was being kept. But Talabwo is the country where the tribe is that always had the emerald. The U.N. sent in some people to referee the situation, and Akinzi paid some money for the emerald, but money isn't the point. Talabwo wants the emerald."

Dortmunder shook the cigarette lighter and flipped it out the window. He said, "Why don't they go to war?"

"The two countries are even Steven. They're a pair of welterweights—they'd ruin each other and nobody'd win."

Dortmunder dragged on the cigarette, exhaled through his nose. "If we cop the emerald and give it to Talabwo," he said, "why won't Akinzi go to the U.N. and say, 'Make them give us back our emerald'?" He sneezed.

"Talabwo won't let on they got it," Kelp said. "They don't want to display it or anything. They just want to have it. It's symbolic with them. Like those Scotchmen that stole the Stone of Scone years ago."

"The who that did what?"

"It's a thing that happened in England," Kelp said. "Anyway, about this emerald heist. You interested?"

"Depends," Dortmunder said. "Where's it kept at?"

"Right now," Kelp said, "it's in the Coliseum in New York. There's this show, all sorts of stuff from Africa, and the emerald's part of the display from Akinzi."

"So we're supposed to swipe it from the Coliseum?"

"Not necessarily," Kelp said. "The display's going on tour in a couple weeks, traveling by train and truck. We'll get plenty of chances to get our hands on it."

Dortmunder nodded. "All right," he said. "We cop the emerald, we turn it over to this guy—"

"Iko," Kelp said, pronouncing it *eye-ko*, accent on the first syllable.

Dortmunder frowned. "Isn't that a Japanese camera?"

"No, it's the name of the U.N. ambassador from Talabwo. And if you're interested in the job, that's who we're going to go see."

Dortmunder said, "He knows I'm coming?"

"Sure," Kelp said. "I told him what we needed was an organizer, a planner, and I told him Dortmunder was the best organizer in the business and if we were lucky, we could get you to set things up for us. I didn't tell him you were just finishing a stretch."

"Good," Dortmunder said.

MAJOR PATRICK IKO, stocky, black, mustached, studied the dossier he'd been given on John Archibald Dortmunder and shook his head in amused contempt. He could understand why Kelp hadn't wanted to tell him that Dortmunder was just finishing a prison term, that one of the plans Dortmunder was famous for had failed to go precisely according to blueprint. But hadn't Kelp realized the Major would automatically look into the background of each of the men under consideration? He naturally had to be selective about the men to whom he would entrust the Balaboma Emerald. He couldn't take a chance on picking some dishonest types who, having rescued the emerald from the Akinzi, would then steal it for themselves.

The great mahogany door opened and the Major's secretary, a slender, discreet, ebony young man whose spectacles reflected the light, came in and said, "Sir, two gentlemen to see you. Mr. Kelp and another man."

"Show them in."

"Yes, sir." The secretary backed out.

The Major closed the dossier and put it away in a desk drawer. He then got to his feet and smiled with bland geniality at the two men walking toward him across the great expanse of Oriental rug. "Mr. Kelp," he said. "How good to see you again."

"Nice to see you too, Major Iko," Kelp said. "This here is John Dortmunder, the fellow I told you about."

"Mr. Dortmunder." The Major bowed slightly. "Won't you both be seated?"

They all sat down, and the Major studied Dortmunder. In terms of facts, Major Iko knew quite a bit about him. He knew that Dortmunder was thirty-seven, that he had grown up in an Illinois orphanage, had served in the army in Korea but had been on the other side of the cops-and-robbers game ever since, and that he had twice been in prison for robbery, the second term having ended with a parole just this morning. He knew that Dortmunder had been arrested at other times for robbery, but that none of those other arrests had stuck. And he knew that Dortmunder had never been arrested for any other crime, and that there didn't even appear to be any rumors concerning murders, arsons, or rapes that he might have performed. And he knew that Dortmunder had been married in San Diego some years ago to a night-club entertainer called Honeybun, from whom he had won an uncontested divorce two years later.

What did the man himself show? He was sitting now in the direct sunlight streaming in the park-view windows, and what he looked most like was a convalescent. A little gray, a little tired, face a little lined, thin body rather frail-looking. His suit was obviously new and obviously the cheapest quality made. His shoes were obviously old but had obviously cost quite a bit when new. The clothing indicated a man who had been used to living well but for whom times had recently turned bad. The eyes, as they met the Major's, were flat, watchful, unexpressive. A man who would keep his own counsel, the Major thought, and a man who would make his decisions slowly and then stand by them.

And stand by his word? The Major thought it worth taking the chance. He said, "Welcome back to the world, Mr. Dortmunder. I imagine freedom feels sweet right now."

Dortmunder and Kelp looked at each other.

The Major smiled and said, "Mr. Kelp didn't tell me."

"I know," Dortmunder said. "You been checking up on me."

"Naturally," the Major said. "Wouldn't you, in my position?"

"Maybe I ought to check up on you," Dortmunder said.

"Perhaps you should," the Major said. "They'd be happy to tell you about me at the U.N. Or call your own State Department. I'm sure they have a file on me over there."

Dortmunder shrugged. "It doesn't matter. What did you find out about me?"

"That I can probably take a chance on you. Mr. Kelp tells me you make good plans."

"I try to."

"What happened the last time?"

"Something went wrong," Dortmunder said.

Kelp, rushing to his friend's defense, said, "Major, it wasn't his fault. It was just rotten luck. He had it figured for—"

"I've read the report," the Major told him. "Thank you." To Dortmunder he said, "It was a good plan, and you did run into bad luck, but I'm pleased to see you don't waste time justifying yourself."

"Let's talk about this emerald of yours."

"Let's. Can you get it?"

"I don't know. How much help can you give us?"

The Major frowned. "Help? What kind of help?"

"We'll probably need guns. A car or two, maybe a truck, depending on how the job works up. We might need some other stuff."

"Oh, yes," the Major said. "I could supply any matériel you might need, certainly."

"Good." Dortmunder nodded and pulled the crumpled pack of Camels from his pocket. He lit a cigarette and leaned forward to drop the match into the ashtray on the Major's desk. "About money," he said. "Kelp tells me it's thirty G's a man."

"Thirty thousand dollars, yes."

"No matter how many men?"

"Well," the Major said, "there should be some sort of limit on it. I wouldn't want you enlisting an army."

"What's the limit?"

"Mr. Kelp spoke of five men."

"All right. That's a total of a hundred fifty G's. What if we do it with less men?"

"It would still be thirty thousand dollars a man."

Dortmunder said, "Why?"

"I wouldn't want to encourage you," the Major said, "to attempt the robbery with too few men. So it will be thirty thousand per man no matter how many or how few men are involved."

Dortmunder nodded again. He said, "Plus expenses."

"I beg your pardon?"

"This is going to be a full-time job for a month, maybe six weeks," Dortmunder said. "We need money to live on."

"You mean you want an advance on the thirty thousand."

"No. I mean I want expense money over and above the thirty thousand."

The Major shook his head. "No, no," he said. "I'm sorry, that wasn't the agreement. Thirty thousand dollars a man, and that's all."

Dortmunder got to his feet and stubbed out the Camel in the Major's ashtray. It smoldered. He said, "See you around," and, "Come on, Kelp," and started for the door.

The Major couldn't believe it. He called, "Are you going?"

Dortmunder turned at the door and looked at him. "Yeah."

"But why?"

"You're too cheap. It'd make me nervous working for you. I'd come to you for a gun, you wouldn't want to give me more than one bullet." Dortmunder reached for the doorknob.

The Major said, "Wait."

Dortmunder waited, hand on knob.

The Major thought fast, adding up budgets. "I'll give you one hundred dollars a week per man living expenses," he said.

"Two hundred," Dortmunder said. "Nobody can live in New York City on one hundred a week."

"One-fifty," the Major said.

Dortmunder hesitated, and Kelp, who'd just been sitting there all this time, said, "That's a fair price, Dortmunder. What the hell, it's only for a few weeks."

Dortmunder shrugged and took his hand off the knob. "All right," he said. He came back and sat down. "What can you tell me about how this emerald's guarded?" A wavering ribbon of smoke extended up from the smoldering Camel. The line was directly between the Major and Dortmunder, making him feel cross-eyed when he tried to focus on Dortmunder's face. But he was too proud to stub out the cigarette, so he squinted one eye and went on to answer.

"All I know is, the Akinzi have it very well guarded in the Coliseum," the Major answered.

"All right. We'll go take a look at it. Where do we get our money?"

The major looked blank. "Your money?"

"This week's hundred fifty."

"Oh." It was all happening a little too fast. "I'll call our finance office downstairs. You can stop in there on your way out."

"Good." Dortmunder got to his feet. "I'll get in touch with you if I need anything," he said.

The Major was sure of that.

"IT DOESN'T LOOK MUCH like half a million bucks to me," Dortmunder said.

"Just so it's thirty thousand," Kelp said. "Each."

The emerald, many-faceted, deeply green, a little smaller than a golf ball, nested in a cloth of red satin on a table completely enclosed in glass. The glass cube was about six feet square and seven feet high, and at a distance of about five feet out from it a red velvet rope looped from stanchions to make a larger square to keep the gawkers at a safe distance. In each corner of this larger square stood a guard in a dark blue uniform with a holstered gun on his hip. A small sign on a stand said BALABOMO EMERALD in capital letters and gave the stone's history.

Dortmunder studied the guards. They looked bored, but not sleepy. He studied the glass, and it had the slightly olive look of glass with a lot of metal in it. Bulletproof, shatterproof, burglarproof. Each of the edges of the glass cube were lined with strips of chromed steel and so was the line where the glass met the floor. In that steel rim between glass and floor were four locks, one in the middle of each side of the cube.

They were on the second floor of the Coliseum, the ceiling about thirty feet above their heads. The Pan-African Culture and Art Exhibit was spread throughout four display floors, with the main attractions here on the second floor. The high ceiling bounced back a general stirring of sound as people shuffled by the exhibits. The Balabomo Emerald stood in a fairly exposed position, miles from any exit.

"I've seen enough," Dortmunder said.

They left the Coliseum and went across Columbus Circle and into Central Park. They took a path that headed for the lake and Dortmunder said, "That would be tough, taking it out of there."

"Yeah, it would," said Kelp.

"I wonder maybe we should wait till it goes on the road," Dortmunder said.

"That won't be for a while yet," said Kelp. "Iko won't like us sitting around doing nothing at a hundred fifty bucks a week per man."

"Forget Iko," Dortmunder said. "If we do this thing, I'm the one in charge. I'll handle Iko, don't worry about it."

"Sure, Dortmunder," said Kelp. "Anything you say."

They walked to the lake and sat on a bench there. It was June and Kelp watched the girls walk by. Dortmunder sat looking at the lake. He didn't know whether he liked this caper or not. He liked the idea of the guaranteed return, and he liked the idea of the small easily transported object of the heist, but on the other hand he had to be careful. He'd fallen twice now; he didn't want to fall again, to spend the rest of his life eating prison food.

So what didn't he like? Well, for one thing, they were going after an item valued at half a million dollars, and it only stood to reason an item valued at half a million dollars was going to get some pretty heavy guarding. It wasn't going to be easy to get that rock away from the Akinzi. The four guards, the bulletproof glass—that was probably only the beginning of the defenses.

For another thing, if they did manage to get away with the stone, they could count on very heavy police activity. The cops would be likely to spend considerably more energy tracking down a half-million-dollar emerald than going after somebody who copped a portable television set. There would also be insurance dicks all over the place, and sometimes they were worse than the cops.

And finally, how did he know Iko could be trusted? There was something a little too smooth about that bird. He said, "What do you think of Iko?"

Kelp, surprised, looked away from a girl in green stockings and said, "He's okay, I guess. Why?"

"You think he'll pay up?"

Kelp laughed. "Sure he'll pay up," he said. "He wants the emerald, he *has* to pay up."

"What if he doesn't? We wouldn't find any buyer anywhere else."

"Insurance company," Kelp said promptly. "They'd pay a hundred fifty G's for a half-million-dollar rock any day."

Dortmunder nodded. "Maybe," he said, "that would be the better system anyway. We let Iko finance the job. But when we get the emerald we sell it to the insurance company instead."

"I don't like that," Kelp said.

"Why not?"

"Because he knows who we are," Kelp said, "and if this emerald is this big symbolic thing for the people in his country, they could get awful upset if we cop it for ourselves, and I don't want some whole African country out to get me, money or no money."

"Okay," Dortmunder said. "Okay. We'll see how it plays."

"A whole country out to get me," Kelp said and shivered. "I wouldn't like that."

"All right."

"Blowguns and poison arrows," Kelp said and shivered again.

"I think they're more modern now," Dortmunder said.

Kelp looked at him. "Is that supposed to make me feel better? Tommy guns and airplanes?"

"All right," Dortmunder said. "All right." To change the subject, he said, "Who do you think we should bring in with us?"

"As the rest of the team?" Kelp shrugged. "I dunno. What kind of guys do we need?"

"It's hard to say." Dortmunder frowned at the lake, ignoring a girl going by in a tiger-stripe leotard. "No specialists," he said, "except maybe a lockman. But nobody for safes, nothing like that."

"We want five or six?" Kelp asked.

"Five," Dortmunder said. He announced one of the rules he lived by: "If you can't do a job with five men, you can't do it at all."

"Okay," said Kelp. "So we'll want a driver, and a lockman, and a utility outfielder."

"Right," said Dortmunder. "For the lockman, there was that little guy in Des Moines. You know the one I mean?"

"Something like Wise? Wiseman? Welsh?"

"Whistler!" said Dortmunder.

"That's it!" said Kelp and shook his head. "He's in stir. They got him for letting a lion loose."

Dortmunder turned his head away from the lake and looked at Kelp. "For what?"

Kelp shrugged. "Don't blame me," he said. "That's just what I heard. He took his kids to the zoo. He got bored. He started to play around with the locks kind of absentminded, like you or me might doodle, and the first thing you know he let a lion loose."

"That's nice," Dortmunder said.

"Don't blame me," Kelp said. Then he asked, "What about Chefwick? You know him?"

"The railroad nut. He's crazy out of his head."

"But he's a great lockman," Kelp said. "And he's available."

"Okay," Dortmunder said. "Give him a call."

"I will." Kelp watched two girls in various shades of green and gold go by. "Now we need a driver," he said.

"How about Lartz? Remember him?"

"Forget him," Kelp said. "He's in the hospital."

"Since when?"

"A couple weeks ago. He ran into a plane."

Dortmunder gave him a long slow look. "He did what?"

"It ain't my fault," Kelp said. "The way I heard it, he was at the wedding of some cousin of his out on Long Island, and he was coming back into town, he took the Van Wyck Expressway the wrong way by mistake, the first thing he knew he was out to Kennedy airport. He was a little drunk, I guess, and—"

"Yeah," Dortmunder said.

"Yeah. And he got confused by the signs, and he wound up on taxiway seventeen and he ran into this Eastern Airlines plane that just come up from Miami."

"Taxiway seventeen," Dortmunder said.

"That's what I heard," Kelp said.

Dortmunder pulled out his Camels and stuck one thoughtfully in his mouth. He offered the pack to Kelp, but Kelp shook his head and said, "I gave them up. Those TV cancer commercials got to me."

Dortmunder paused with the cigarettes held out in midair. He said, "I haven't seen any television in four years."

"You missed something," Kelp said. "Scare the life out of you. Wait till you see one."

"Yeah," Dortmunder said. He put the pack away and lit the cigarette. "About a driver," he said. "Did you hear about anything odd happening to Stan Murch lately?"

"Stan? No. What happened?"

Dortmunder looked at him again. "I was asking you."

Kelp shrugged in bewilderment. "Last I heard he was fine," he said.

"Then why don't we use him?"

"If you're sure he's okay," Kelp said.

Dortmunder sighed. "I'll call him and ask."

"Now," Kelp said. "About our utility outfielder."

"I'm afraid to mention anybody," Dortmunder said.

Kelp looked at him in surprise. "Why? You got good judgment."

Dortmunder took a deep breath. "How about Ernie Danforth?" he asked.

Kelp shook his head. "He quit the racket," he said.

"He quit?"

"Yeah. He became a priest. See, the way I heard it, he was watching this Pat O'Brien movie on the Late—"

"All *right!*" Dortmunder got to his feet. He snapped his cigarette into the lake. "I want to know about Alan Greenwood," he said, his voice tight, "and all I want is a yes or a no."

Kelp was bewildered again. Blinking up at Dortmunder, he said, "A yes or a no what?"

"Can we use him!" Dortmunder shouted, and an old lady, who had been glowering at Dortmunder since he'd thrown his cigarette into the lake, suddenly blanched and hurried away.

"Sure we can use him. Why not? Greenwood's a good man."

"I'll call him!" Dortmunder shouted.

"I can hear you," Kelp said. "I can hear you."

Dortmunder looked around. "Let's go get a drink," he said.

"Sure," Kelp said, jumping to his feet. "Anything you say. Sure."

THEY WERE ON THE straightaway now. "All right, baby," Stan Murch muttered through clenched teeth. "This is it."

He was hunched over, his fingers in their kid gloves clutching the steering wheel, his foot tense on the accelerator, his eyes flicking down to the instrument panel, reading the dials there, checking it all out: speedometer, odometer, tachometer, fuel gauge, temperature, oil pressure, clock. He strained against the chest harness holding him against the seat, willing his car forward, seeing the long sleek nose come closer and closer to the guy in front of him. He was going to pass on the inside, by the rail, and once past this one it would be clear sailing.

But now the other guy was aware of him closing the gap, and Murch sensed the other car pulling away, keeping ahead of the danger.

No. It wasn't going to happen. Murch checked the rearview mirror, and everything was all right back there. He tromped down on the accelerator and the Mustang went into passing gear. He shot on past the green Pontiac, angled across two lanes and let his foot ease on the accelerator. The Pontiac roared by on his left, but Murch didn't mind. He'd established who was who, and this was his exit coming up. "Canarsie," the sign said. Murch steered his car off the Belt Parkway, around the circle, and out onto Rockaway Parkway, a long, broad, flat bumpy street lined with housing projects, supermarkets, and row houses.

Murch lived with his mother on East 99th Street, just a little ways off Rockaway Parkway, on Long Island. He slowed when he came to the middle of the block, saw his mother's cab was in the driveway, and rolled on by to a parking space down near the far corner. He got his new record album—*Sounds of Indianapolis in Stereo and Hi-Fi*—out of the backseat and walked to the house. It was a two-family row house, in which he and his mother lived on the first floor and various tenants lived on the second floor.

The current tenant, a fish handler named Friedkin, was sitting in the air at the head of the outside steps to the second floor. Friedkin's wife made him sit out in the air any time there wasn't actually a blizzard or an atomic explosion going on out there. Friedkin waved, an aroma of the sea wafting from him, and called, "How you doing, boychick?"

"Yuh," said Murch. He wasn't too good at talking to people. Most of his conversations were held with cars.

He went on into the house and called, "Mom?" He stood there in the kitchen.

She'd been downstairs, in the extra room in the semi-finished basement that Murch had turned into a bedroom for himself. She came upstairs now.

"Look what I got," Murch said and showed her the record.

"So play it," she said.

"Okay," he said.

They went into the living room together and while Murch put the record on the turntable he said, "How come you're home so early?"

"Aahhh," she said in obvious disgust. "Some wise-guy cop out at the airport."

"You were taking more than one passenger again," Murch said.

She flared up. "Well, why not? This city's got a shortage of cabs, don't it? You oughta see all those people out there at the airport, they got to wait half an hour, an hour, they could fly to Europe before they could get a cab to Manhattan. So I try to help the situation a little. The customers don't care. And it helps me. I get two, three times the price on the meter. And it helps the city, it helps their image. But try to tell a cop that. Play the record."

"How long you suspended for?"

"Two days," she said. "Play the record."

"Mom," he said, holding the tone arm above the record, "I wish you wouldn't take those chances. We don't have all that much dough."

"You got enough to throw it away on records," she said. "Play the record."

"If I'd known you were gonna get yourself suspended for two days—" he began.

"You could always get yourself a job," she said. "Play the record."

Stung, Murch put the tone arm back on its rest and his hands on his hips. "Is that what you want?" he said. "You want me to get a job at the post office?"

"No, never mind me," his mother said, suddenly contrite. She went over and patted his cheek. "I know something'll come through for you pretty soon. And when you do have it, Stan, nobody on God's green earth spends it as free or as open as you do."

"Damn right," Murch said, appeased but still a little grumpy.

"Put the record on," his mother said. "Let's hear it."

Murch put the record on and the room filled with the shrieking of tires, the revving of engines, the grinding of gears. They listened to side one in silence, and when it was done Murch said, "Now, that's a good record."

"I think that's one of the best, Stan," his mother said, "I really do. Let's hear the other side."

Murch went over to the phonograph and picked up the tone arm, and the phone rang. "Hell," he said.

"Forget it," his mother said. "Play the other side."

"Okay." Murch put the other side on, and the ringing of the phone was buried in the sudden roar of twenty automobile engines turning over at once. But whoever was calling wouldn't give up. In the lulls in the record the ringing could still be heard, a disturbing presence. A racing driver going into the far turn at one hundred twenty miles an hour shouldn't have to answer the telephone.

Murch finally shook his head in disgust, shrugged at his mother, and picked up the phone. "Who is it?" he said, yelling over the sounds of the record.

A distant voice said, "Stan Murch?"

"Speaking!"

The distant voice said something else.

"What?"

The distant voice shouted, "This is Dortmunder!"

"Oh, yeah! How you doing?"

"Fine! Where do you live, in the middle of an expressway?"

"Hold on a second!" Murch shouted and went to turn off the record. "I'll play it in a minute," he told his mother. "This is a guy I know, it might be a job."

"I knew something would turn up," his mother said. "Every cloud has a silver lining."

Murch went back to the phone. "Hello, Dortmunder?"

"That's a lot better," Dortmunder said. "What did you do, shut the window?"

"No, it was a record. I turned it off."

There was a long silence.

Murch said, "Dortmunder?"

"I'm here," Dortmunder said, but he sounded a little fainter than before. Then, stronger again, he said, "I wondered if you were available for a driving job."

"I sure am."

"Meet me tonight at the O. J. Bar and Grill on Amsterdam Avenue," Dortmunder said.

"Fine. What time?"

"Ten o'clock."

"I'll be there. See you, Dortmunder."

Murch hung up the phone and said to his mother, "Well, looks like we'll have some money pretty soon."

"That's good," said his mother. "Play the record."

"Right." Murch went over and started side two from the beginning.

"TOOT, TOOT," SAID Roger Chefwick. A short and skinny man of late middle age, Chefwick was seated on a high stool at his grand console, his practiced hands moving over an array of transformers and special switches. His three H-O gauge trains were all in motion at once, traveling hither and yon around the basement. Relays tripped, electrical signals were given. Flagmen slid out of their shacks and waved little flags. Bells rang at highway-railway crossings, bars went down, and when the train had gone by, the bars went back up again. Cars coupled and uncoupled. All sorts of things went on.

"Toot, toot," said Roger Chefwick. The waist-high plywood platform, four feet wide, flanked the wall on three sides of the basement, so that Chefwick, in the middle of it all, was like a man in the ultimate Cinerama. Model houses, model trees, even model mountains gave veracity to his layout. His trains traveled over bridges, through tunnels, and around intricately curved multilayers of track.

"Roger," said his wife.

Chefwick twisted around and saw Maude standing on the cellar stairs. A vague, fussy, pleasant woman, Maude was his perfect mate and he knew how lucky he was.

"Yes, dear," he said.

"Telephone, Roger," she said.

"Oh, dear." Chefwick sighed. "One moment," he said.

"I'll tell them," she said and turned to go back upstairs.

Chefwick faced his console again. Train number one was in the vicinity of the Chefwick freight yards, so he rerouted it from its original destination, Center City, and sent it instead through the Maude Mountain tunnel and on into the yards. Since train number two was just approaching the Rogerville station, he simply ran it onto a subsidiary track there to leave the main line open. That left train number three, currently heading through Smoke Pass. It took some intricate planning, but he finally brought it out of the Southern Mountains and shunted it onto the spur track leading to the old Seaside Mining Corporation. Then, pleased with his work, he shut off the master switches on the console and went upstairs.

The kitchen, tiny and white and warm, was full of the aroma of fudge. Chefwick said, "Mmm. Smells good."

"Be cool in just a little while," Maude said.

"Can't wait," he said, knowing it would please her, and went through the tiny house to the living room. He sat down on the doily-covered flower-pattern sofa, picked up the phone on the end table, and said mildly, "Hello?"

A rough voice said, "Chefwick?"

"Speaking."

"This is Kelp. Remember?"

"Kelp?" The name did ring a bell, but Chefwick couldn't exactly remember why. "I'm sorry, I—"

"At the bakery," the voice said.

Of course, the robbery at the bakery. "Kelp!" he said. "How good to hear from you again. How have you been keeping yourself?"

"Little a this, little a that, you know how it is. What I want to know is, are you available."

"One moment, please," Chefwick said. He put the phone down, got to his feet, and walked out to the kitchen, where he said to his wife, "Dear, do you know offhand the state of our finances?"

Maude dried her hands on her apron, looking thoughtful, and then said, "I believe we have just about seven thousand dollars left in the checking account."

"Nothing in the basement?"

"No. I took the last three thousand at the end of April."

"Thank you," Chefwick said. He went back to the living room, picked up the phone, and said, "I am quite interested."

"Good. We're meeting tonight at ten o'clock at the O. J. Bar and Grill on Amsterdam Avenue."

"Fine," Chefwick said. "See you then." He hung up and went back to the kitchen and said, "I'll be going out awhile this evening."

"Not late, I hope."

"Not tonight, I don't believe. We'll just be discussing things." Chefwick got a sly look on his face, a pixie grin on his lips. "Is that fudge ready yet?"

Maude smiled indulgently at him. "I believe you could try a piece."

"So THIS IS YOUR apartment!" the girl said.

"Mmm, yes," said Alan Greenwood, smiling. He shut the door and pocketed the keys. "Make yourself comfortable," he said.

The girl stood in the middle of the room and turned in a big admiring circle. "Well, I must say," she said. "It certainly is well kept for a bachelor's apartment."

Greenwood, walking toward the bar, said, "I do what I can. But I do feel the lack of a woman's touch." He switched on the fireplace. "What's yours?" he said.

"Oh," she said, shrugging, doing the coquette a little, "just anything light."

"Coming up," he said. He made her a Rob Roy just sweet enough to hide the deadliness of the Scotch. "Here's your drink," he said. He raised his own—light on the Scotch, heavy on the water—and said, "To you." Then, with hardly any pause, he added, "Miranda."

Miranda ducked her head in embarrassed pleasure. "To us," she whispered.

He smiled his agreement. "To us." They drank.

"Come sit down," he said, leading her to the white sheepskin sofa.

"Oh, is that sheepskin?"

"So much warmer than leather," he said softly and took her hand, and they sat down.

Seated side by side, they gazed a moment into the fireplace, and then she said, "My, that is realistic, isn't it?"

"And no ashes," he said. "I like things—clean."

"Oh, I know what you mean," she said and smiled brightly at him.

He put his arm around her shoulders. She lifted her chin. The phone rang.

Greenwood closed his eyes, then opened them again. "Ignore it," he said.

The phone rang again.

"But it might be something important," she said.

"I have an answering service," he said. "They'll get it."

The phone rang again.

"I've thought about getting an answering service," she said. She sat forward a bit, dislodging his arm, and turned half toward him, one leg tucked under her. "Are they expensive?"

The phone rang a fourth time.

"Around twenty-five a month," he said, his smile becoming a bit forced. "But it's worth it for the convenience."

Fifth time.

"Oh, of course," she said. "And not to miss any important calls."

Sixth.

Greenwood chuckled realistically. "Of course," he said, "they aren't always as reliable as you'd like."

Seven.

"Isn't that the way with people nowadays," she said. "Nobody wants to do an honest day's work for an honest day's pay."

Eight.

"That's right."

She leaned closer to him and said, "Is that a tic in your eyelid? The right eye."

Nine.

He jerked a hand to his face. "Is it? I get that sometimes . . . when I'm tired."

"Oh, are you tired?"

Ten.

"No," he said quickly. "Not in particular. Maybe the light in the restaurant was a bit too dim, I might have been straining my—"

Eleven.

Greenwood lunged at the phone, yanked the receiver to his head, shouted, *"What is it?"*

"Greenwood? Alan Greenwood?"

"Who's this?" Greenwood demanded.

"Is that Alan Greenwood?"

"Yes, damn it! What do you want?" He could see from the corner of his eye that the girl had risen from the sofa, was standing looking at him more than a little warily.

"This is John Dortmunder."

"Oh," he said, much calmer. "How are things?"

"Fine. You available for a piece of work?"

Greenwood looked at the girl's face while thinking of his bank accounts. Neither prospect was pleasing. "Yes, I am," he said. He tried a smile at the girl, but it wasn't returned.

"We're meeting tonight," Dortmunder said. "At ten. You free?"

"Yes, I think I am," Greenwood said. Not happily.

DORTMUNDER WALKED INTO the O. J. Bar and Grill on Amsterdam Avenue at five minutes to ten. Two of the regulars were having a game at the bowling machine, and there were three more at the bar. Behind the bar stood Rollo, tall, meaty, balding, blue-jawed, in a dirty white shirt and dirty white apron.

Dortmunder had already set things up with Rollo on the phone this afternoon, but he stopped at the bar a second as a courtesy, saying, "Anybody here yet?"

"One fellow," Rollo said. "A draft beer. I don't think I know him. He's in the back."

"Thanks."

Rollo said, "You're a double bourbon, aren't you? Straight up."

Dortmunder said, "I'm surprised you remember."

"I don't forget my customers," Rollo said. "It's good to see you back again. You want, I'll bring you the bottle."

"Thanks again," Dortmunder said, and walked on down past the rest rooms and past the phone booth and through the green door at the back into a small square room with a concrete floor. Practically the whole room, floor to ceiling, was taken up with beer and liquor cases, leaving only a small opening in the middle big enough for a battered old round table with a green felt top and half a dozen chairs. One bare bulb with a tin reflector hung low over the table on a long black wire.

Stan Murch was sitting at the table, half a glass of draft beer in front of him. Dortmunder shut the door and said, "You're early."

"I made good time," Murch said. "Instead of goin' all the way around on the Belt Parkway, I went up Rockaway Parkway and over Eastern Parkway and right up Flatbush Avenue to the Manhattan Bridge. Then up Third Avenue and through the park at Seventy-ninth. At night you can make good time that way."

Dortmunder looked at him. "Is that right?" he said and sat down.

The door opened and Rollo came in with a glass and a bottle. He put them in front of Dortmunder and said, "There's a fellow outside I think is maybe with you. A sherry. Asked for a fellow name of Kelp. That the Kelp I know?"

"The same," Dortmunder said. "He'll be one of ours, send him on in."

"Will do." Rollo looked at Murch's glass. "Ready for a refill?"

"I'll string along with this for a while," Murch said.

Rollo gave Dortmunder a look and went out, and a minute later Chefwick came in, carrying a glass of sherry. "Dortmunder!" he said in surprise. "It was Kelp I talked to on the phone, wasn't it?"

"Kelp should be here in a minute," Dortmunder said. "You know Stan Murch?"

"I don't believe I've had the pleasure."

"Stan's our driver. Stan, this is Roger Chefwick, he's our lockman. Best in the business."

Murch and Chefwick nodded to each other, and Chefwick sat down at the table. "Will there be many more of us?" he said.

"Just two," Dortmunder said, and Kelp came in, carrying an empty glass. "Sit down," Dortmunder invited. "You all know each other, don't you?"

They did. Everybody said hello, and Kelp poured bourbon from the bottle into his glass. Murch took a tiny sip of beer.

The door opened and Rollo stuck his head in. "There's a Dewar's and water out here that asked for you," he said to Dortmunder.

"Ask him if he calls himself Greenwood," Dortmunder said, "and if he does, send him on in here."

"Right." Rollo looked at Murch's beer. "You all set?"

"I'm fine," Murch told him, though the beer left in the glass didn't have a head anymore. "Unless I could have some salt," he said.

Rollo gave Dortmunder a look. "Sure," he said and went out.

A minute later Greenwood came in, a drink in one hand and a salt shaker in the other. "The barman said the draft beer wanted this."

"That's me," Murch said.

Murch and Greenwood had to be introduced, and then Greenwood sat down. Murch sprinkled a little salt into his beer, which gave it back some head. He sipped at it.

Dortmunder said, "Now we're all here." He looked at Kelp. "You want to tell the story?"

"No," said Kelp. "You do it."

"All right," Dortmunder said. He told them the story, and then he said, "Any questions?"

Murch said, "If we get a hundred fifty a week until we do the job, then why do it at all?"

"Three or four weeks is all we'd get out of Major Iko," Dortmunder said. "Maybe six hundred apiece. I'd rather have the thirty thousand."

Chefwick said, "Do you want to take the emerald from the Coliseum or wait till it's on the road?"

"We'll have to decide that," Dortmunder said. "Kelp and I went over there today and it looked well guarded, but they might be even more security-conscious on the road."

Greenwood said, "Once we get this emerald, why turn it over to the good Major at all?"

"He's the only buyer," Dortmunder said. "Kelp and I have already been through all the switches we might want to pull."

"Just so we're flexible in our thinking," Greenwood said.

Dortmunder looked around. "Any more questions? No? Anybody want out? No? Good. Tomorrow you all drift over to the Coliseum and take a look at our prize, and we'll meet back here tomorrow night at the same time. I'll have the first week's living expenses from the Major by then."

Greenwood said, "Couldn't we make it earlier tomorrow night? Ten o'clock breaks into my evening pretty badly."

"We don't want it too early," Murch said. "I don't want to get caught in that rush-hour traffic."

"How about eight?" Dortmunder said.

"Fine," said Greenwood.

"Fine," said Murch.

"Perfectly all right with me," said Chefwick.

"Then that's it," said Dortmunder. He pushed back his chair and got to his feet. "We'll meet back here tomorrow night."

Everybody stood. Murch finished his beer, smacked his lips, and said, "Aaaahhh!" Then he said. "Anybody want a lift anywhere?"

IT WAS TEN MINUTES to one of a weeknight, and Fifth Avenue across from Central Park was deserted. An occasional cab showing its off-duty sign rolled south, but that was about it. A spring drizzle was leaking out of the black sky, and the park across the way looked like the middle of a jungle.

Kelp trotted up the steps of the Talabwo mission to the U.N. and rang the bell. Lights showed in the first-floor windows, but it took a long while for someone to come open the door, and then it was a silent black man who motioned Kelp in with long slim fingers and led him through several opulent rooms before finally leaving him alone in a bookcase-lined den with a pool table in its middle.

Kelp waited three minutes, standing around doing nothing, and then decided the hell with it. He racked up the balls, selected a cue, and began to play a little rotation with himself.

He was just about to sink the eight ball when the door opened and Major Iko came in. "You're later than I expected," he said.

"I couldn't find a cab," Kelp said. He put down the cue, patted various pockets, and came up with a crumpled sheet of lined paper. "This is the stuff we need." He handed the Major the paper. He went back to the table and picked up the cue and sank the eight ball.

The Major said, "About these uniforms—"

Kelp put the cue down and turned to Iko. "Anything wrong?"

"The uniforms," the Major said. "It says here four uniforms, but it doesn't say what kind."

"Oh, yeah, I forgot." Kelp pulled some Polaroid prints from another pocket. They showed guards at the Coliseum from various angles. "Here's some pictures," he said, handing them over. "So you'll know what they look like."

The Major took the prints. "Good. And what are these numbers on the paper?"

"Everybody's suit size," Kelp said.

"Naturally. I should have realized." The Major tucked the list and the prints into his pocket and smiled crookedly at Kelp. "So there really are three other men," he said. "Dortmunder forgot to tell me their names."

Kelp shook his head. "No, he didn't. He told me you'd probably try to pump me on that."

The Major, in sudden irritation, said, "Damn it, man, I ought to know who I'm hiring. This is absurd."

"No, it isn't," Kelp said. "You hired Dortmunder and me. Dortmunder and me hired the other three."

"But I need to check them out," the Major said.

"You already talked this over with Dortmunder," Kelp said. "You know what his attitude is."

"Yes, I know," said the Major.

Kelp told him anyway. "You'll start makin' up dossiers on everybody. You make up enough dossiers, you'll attract attention, maybe tip the whole thing."

The Major shook his head. "This goes against my training," he said, "against everything I know. How can you deal with a man if you don't have a dossier on him? It isn't done."

Kelp shrugged. "I don't know. Dortmunder says I should pick up this week's money."

"This is the second week," the Major said.

"That's right."

"When are you going to do the job?"

"Soon as you get us the stuff." Kelp spread his hands. "We weren't just sittin' around for a week, you know. We earned our money. Go to the Coliseum every day, sit around and work out plans every night. We've been doin' that for a week now."

"I don't begrudge the money," the Major said, though it was clear he did. "I just don't want it to drag on too long."

"Get us the stuff on the list and we'll get you your emerald."

The Major let Kelp out, and he stood ten minutes in the rain before he got a cab.

THE NEW YORK COLISEUM stands between West 58th Street and West 60th Street facing Columbus Circle at the southwest corner of Central Park in Manhattan. On the 60th Street side, there is an entrance for the Coliseum staff. A blue-uniformed private guard is always on duty inside the glass doors of this entrance, day and night.

One Wednesday night in late June, at about three-twenty in the morning, Kelp came walking along West 60th Street wearing a tan raincoat, and when he was opposite the Coliseum entrance he suddenly had a fit. He went rigid, and then fell over, and then began to thrash around on the sidewalk. He cried, "Oh! Oh!" several times, but in a husky voice that didn't carry far. There was no one else in sight, no pedestrians and no moving automobiles.

The guard inside had seen Kelp through the glass doors and knew that he had been walking very calmly until he had his fit. The guard hesitated a moment, frowning, but Kelp's thrashing seemed to be increasing, so at last the guard opened the door and hurried out. He squatted beside Kelp, put a hand on his twitching shoulder, and said, "Is there anything I can do, Mac?"

"Yes," Kelp said. He stopped thrashing and pointed a .38 Special Colt revolver at the guard's nose. "You can stand up very slow," he said, "and you can keep your hands where I can see them."

The guard stood up and kept his hands where Kelp could see them, and out of a car across the street came Dortmunder and Greenwood and Chefwick, all dressed in uniforms exactly like the one the guard was wearing.

Kelp got to his feet, and the four marched the guard into the building, where they tied and gagged him. Kelp then removed his raincoat, showing yet another uniform of the same type, and went back to take the guard's place at the door. Meanwhile Dortmunder and the other two stood around and looked at their watches. "He's late," Dortmunder said.

"He'll get there," Greenwood said.

Around at the main entrance there were two guards on duty, and at this moment they were both looking out at an automobile that had suddenly come out of nowhere and was hurtling directly toward the doors. "No!" cried one of the guards, waving his arms.

Murch was behind the wheel of the car, a two-year-old Rambler Ambassador sedan, dark green, which Kelp had stolen just that morning. The car had different plates now, and other changes had also been made.

At the last possible second before the impact Murch pulled the pin on the bomb, shoved the door open, and leaped clear. He landed rolling, and continued to roll for several seconds after the sounds of the crash and the explosion.

The timing had been beautiful. No eyewitness—there were none but the two guards—would have been able to say for sure that Murch had leaped before the crash rather than been thrown clear because of it. Nor would anyone suppose that the stains and smears on Murch's face and clothing had been carefully applied almost an hour ago.

The crash was magnificent. The car had leaped the curb, had crossed the wide sidewalk and lunged into and through the glass doors, had thudded to a grinding halt, half in and half out, and then burst at once into flame. Within seconds the fire reached the gas tank—this having been assured by some alterations Murch had made—and the explosion shattered what glass the car had missed. Dortmunder and the others heard it, and they smiled at one another and moved out, leaving Kelp behind to guard the door.

Their route was roundabout, involving several corridors and two flights of stairs, but when they at last got to the second floor exhibit area, they saw their timing had been perfect. There wasn't a guard in sight anywhere.

They were all out front, by the fire. Several of them were clustered around Murch, whose head was in a guard's lap and who was obviously in shock, lying there twitching, muttering, "It wouldn't steer . . . it wouldn't steer . . ." and moving his arms vaguely, like a man trying to turn a steering wheel. At least four guards went to four different telephones to call various hospitals and police stations and fire departments.

Inside, Dortmunder and Chefwick and Greenwood made their way quickly and silently through the exhibits toward the Akinzi display and the glass cube containing the Balabomo Emerald. Only a few lights were on, and in the semi-dark they went to work. They'd studied this for a week now, they knew what to do and how.

There were four locks to be undone, one in the middle of each side of the glass cube, down at the base, in the steel rim between glass and floor. Once these locks were opened the glass cube could be lifted out of the way.

Chefwick had with him a small black bag of the sort country doctors used to favor, and this he now opened, revealing many slender metal tools of the sort most country doctors never saw in their lives. While Greenwood and Dortmunder stood on either side of him watching the exit doors on the far wall, and the stairs and the escalator, Chefwick went to work on the locks.

The first one took three minutes, but after that he knew the system and he did the other three in less than four minutes more. But still, seven minutes was a long time. The noise from downstairs was ebbing; soon the guards would be coming back to their duties. Dortmunder refrained from telling Chefwick to hurry, but only with difficulty.

At last Chefwick whispered a shrill "Done!" Still kneeling, he hurriedly put his tools back into his bag.

Dortmunder and Greenwood got on opposite sides of the glass cube. It weighed close to two hundred pounds, and there was no way for them to get a really good grip on it. They could only press their palms against it at the edges and lift. Straining, sweating, they did so, each gazing at the other's tense face through the glass. When they got it up two feet, Chefwick slid under and grabbed the emerald.

"Hurry up!" Greenwood said, his voice hoarse. "It's slipping!"

"Don't leave me in here!" Chefwick rolled quickly out from underneath the cube.

"My palms are wet," Greenwood said, even his voice straining. "Lower it. Lower it."

"For God's sake, don't let it go," Dortmunder called.

"It won't—I can't—it's—"

The glass slid out of Greenwood's grip. With the pressure gone from the other side, Dortmunder couldn't hold it either. The glass cube dropped eighteen inches and hit the floor.

It didn't break. It went bbrrrooo*ooonnnn*NNNNNNNNNNGGG-GGGGGGGGINGINGING*inging*ing.

Shouting from downstairs.

"Come on!" Dortmunder yelled.

Chefwick, rattled, shoved the emerald into Greenwood's hand. "Here. Take it." He grabbed up his black bag.

Guards were appearing at the head of the stairs. "Hey, you!" one of them called. "You stop there, stay where you are!"

"Scatter!" Dortmunder cried and ran to the right.

Chefwick ran to the left. Greenwood ran straight ahead.

Meanwhile, an ambulance had arrived. The police had arrived. The fire department had arrived. A policeman was trying to ask Murch questions while a white-garbed ambulance attendant was telling him to leave the patient alone. Firemen were putting out the fire. Someone had taken from Murch's pocket the wallet full of false identification he had put in there half an hour ago. Murch, still apparently only semiconscious, was repeating, "It wouldn't steer. I turned the wheel and it wouldn't steer."

"It looks to me," the policeman said, "like you panicked. Something went wrong with the steering and instead of hitting the brake you tromped on the accelerator. That happens all the time."

"Leave the patient alone," the ambulance attendant said.

Finally Murch was put on a stretcher and loaded into the ambulance and driven away, the siren screaming.

Chefwick, racing pell-mell for the nearest exit, heard the siren screaming and doubled his speed. The last thing he wanted was to spend his declining years in jail. No trains. No Maude. No fudge.

He yanked open the door, found a staircase, raced down it, found a corridor, raced along that, and suddenly found himself face to face with an entrance and a guard. He tried to turn around while still running, dropped his bag, fell over it, and the guard came over to help him up. It was Kelp, saying, "What's wrong? Something go wrong?"

"Where's the others?"

"I don't know. Should we take off?"

Chefwick got to his feet. They both listened. There was no sound of pursuit. "We'll wait a minute or two," Chefwick decided.

"We better," Kelp said. "Dortmunder's got the keys to the car."

Dortmunder, meanwhile, had run around a thatched-roof hut and joined the chase. "Stop!" he shouted, running along in the middle of a pack of guards. Up ahead he saw Greenwood duck through a door and shut it behind himself. "Stop!" shouted Dortmunder, and the guards all around him shouted, "Stop!"

Dortmunder got to the door first. He yanked it open, held it for all the guards to run through, then shut it behind them and walked over to the nearest elevator. He rode this to the first floor, walked along a corridor, and came to the side entrance where Kelp and Chefwick were waiting. "Where's Greenwood?" he said.

"Not here," said Kelp.

Dortmunder looked around. "We better wait in the car," he said.

Meanwhile, Greenwood thought he was on the first floor but wasn't. He was on a mezzanine between the first and second floors. Greenwood didn't know about the mezzanine. He had been on the second floor and had taken a staircase down one flight and therefore thought he was now on the first floor.

The mezzanine consisted of offices and a corridor that went all the way around the building. It was along this corridor that Greenwood was now running, the Balabomo Emerald clutched in his hand as he searched in vain for an exit to the street.

In his ambulance, meantime, Murch was socking his attendant on the jaw. The attendant sagged into sleep, and Murch settled him on the other stretcher. Then as the ambulance slowed to make a turn, Murch opened the rear door and stepped out onto the pavement.

The ambulance tore away, siren shrieking, and Murch hailed a passing cab. "The O. J. Bar and Grill," he said. "On Amsterdam Avenue."

In the getaway car Dortmunder and Kelp and Chefwick kept worriedly studying the West 60th Street entrance. Dortmunder had the engine running and his foot was nervously tapping the gas pedal. Sirens were coming this way now, police sirens.

"We can't wait much longer," Dortmunder said.

"There he is!" cried Chefwick, as a man in a guard uniform came out. But then half a dozen other men in guard uniforms came out too.

"That's not him," said Dortmunder. "None of them is him." He put the getaway car in gear and got away.

Up on the mezzanine, Greenwood was still loping along like a greyhound after the mechanical rabbit. He could hear the thundering of pursuit behind him, and now he could also hear the thundering of pursuit from around the corner in the corridor up ahead.

He stopped. He was caught and he knew it.

He looked at the emerald in his hand. Roundish, many-faceted, deeply green, a trifle smaller than a golf ball.

"Drat," said Greenwood, and he ate the emerald.

AT THE O. J. BAR AND GRILL Rollo had loaned them a small portable radio, and on it they listened to reports of the caper on an all-news station. They heard about the daring robbery, they heard about Murch having made his escape from the ambulance, they heard about Alan Greenwood having been arrested and charged with complicity in the robbery, and they heard that the gang had managed to get away successfully with the stone. Then they heard the weather, and then they heard a woman tell them the price of lamb chops in the city's supermarkets, and they turned the radio off.

Nobody said anything for a while. The air in the back room was blue with smoke, and their faces in the glare of the light bulb looked pale and tired. Finally Murch said, "I wasn't brutal." He said it sullenly. The announcer on the radio had described the attack on the ambulance attendant as brutal. "I just popped him on the jaw," Murch said. He made a fist and swung it in a small tight arc. "Like that. That ain't brutal."

Dortmunder turned to Chefwick. "You definitely gave the stone to Greenwood."

"Definitely," said Chefwick.

"Why?"

Chefwick spread his hands. "I really don't know. In the excitement of the moment— I had the bag to carry and he didn't have anything and I got rattled, so I handed it to him."

"But the cops didn't find it on him," said Dortmunder.

"Maybe he lost it," said Kelp.

"Maybe." Dortmunder looked at Chefwick again. "You wouldn't be holding out on us, would you?"

Chefwick snapped to his feet, insulted. "Search me," he said. "I insist. Search me right now. In all the years I've been in this line, in I don't know how many jobs I've been on, no one has ever impugned my honesty. Never. I insist I be searched."

"All right," Dortmunder said. "Sit down, I know you didn't take it. I'm just a little bugged, that's all."

The door opened and Rollo came in with a fresh glass of sherry for Chefwick and more ice for Dortmunder and Kelp, who were sharing a bottle of bourbon. "Better luck next time, boys," Rollo said.

Chefwick, the argument forgotten, sat down and sipped his sherry.

"Thanks, Rollo," Dortmunder said.

Murch said, "I could stand another beer."

Rollo looked at him. "Will wonders never cease," he said and went out again.

Murch looked at the others. "What was that about?"

Nobody answered him. Then Kelp said to Dortmunder, "What am I going to tell Iko?"

"We didn't get it," Dortmunder said.

"He won't believe me."

"That's kind of tough," Dortmunder said. "You tell him whatever you want to tell him." He finished his drink and got to his feet. "I'm going home," he said.

Kelp said, "Come with me to see Iko."

"Not on your life," Dortmunder said.

PHASE TWO

DORTMUNDER CARRIED A LOAF of white bread and a half-gallon of homogenized milk over to the speed checkout. The cashier put the bread and milk into a large bag and Dortmunder carried it out of the supermarket with his elbows held close to his sides, which looked a little weird but not terribly so.

The date was the fifth of July, nine days since the fiasco at the Coliseum up in New York, and the place was Trenton, New Jersey. The sun was shining and the air was pleasantly hot without humidity, but Dortmunder wore a light basketball jacket over his white shirt, zipped almost all the way up. Perhaps that was why he looked so irritable and sour.

He walked a block from the supermarket, and then he stopped and put the bag on the hood of a handy parked car. He reached into the right-hand pocket of his jacket and pulled out a can of tuna fish. He reached into the left-hand jacket pocket and pulled out two packets of beef bouillon cubes; he dropped them into the bag. From his left trouser pocket he pulled a tube of toothpaste and dropped that into the bag. Then he zipped open his jacket and took out a package of sliced American cheese and a package of sliced baloney and dropped them into the bag. Then he picked the bag up and carried it the rest of the way home.

Home. Home was a fleabag residence hotel downtown. Dortmunder walked into his room and gave it a dirty look and put his groceries away. The place was neat, anyway. He had learned about neatness during his first stretch and had never gotten out of the habit. Having things orderly and clean made even a small gray room like this bearable.

For a time, for a time. The three hundred bucks he'd received from Major Iko was long since gone and he was really scrimping now. He was looking for a score.

Dortmunder put water on for instant coffee and then sat down to read the paper. Nothing in it, nothing interesting. Greenwood hadn't made the papers for almost a week now, and nothing else in the world caught Dortmunder's attention.

He'd reported in to the parole office here as soon as he'd hit town—no point making unnecessary trouble for himself—and they'd gotten him some sort of cockamamie job at a municipal golf course. He worked there one afternoon, trimming the edges of a green, the color reminding him of the stinking Balabomo Emerald, and wound up with a sweet sunburn on the back of his neck. That was enough of that. Since then he'd been making do on slim pickings.

Like last night. Out walking around, looking for whatever might come his way, he'd hit on one of those all-night Laundromats. The attendant, an old woman in a faded print dress, was sitting in a blue plastic chair sound asleep. In he'd gone and quietly tapped the machines one by one and walked out with twenty-three dollars in quarters in his pockets, damn near weight enough to pull his pants off. If he'd had to run away from a cop right then, it would have been no contest.

He was sipping his coffee and reading the funnies when the knock came at the door. He started, looking instinctively at the window, and then he remembered he wasn't wanted for anything right now and got up and opened the door, and it was Kelp.

"You're a tough man to find," Kelp said.

"Not tough enough," Dortmunder said. "Come in." Kelp walked in and Dortmunder shut the door after him and said, "What now? Another hot caper?"

"Not exactly," Kelp said. He looked around the room. "Livin' high," he commented.

"I always throw it around like this," Dortmunder said. "What do you mean, not exactly?"

"Not exactly *another* caper," Kelp explained.

Dortmunder looked at him. "The emerald again?"

"Greenwood stashed it," Kelp said.

"The hell," Dortmunder said.

"I'm only telling you what Iko told me," Kelp said. "Greenwood told his lawyer he stashed the stone, and sent the lawyer to tell Iko. Iko told me and I'm telling you."

"Why?" Dortmunder asked him.

"We still got a chance for our thirty G's," Kelp said. "And the hundred fifty a week again while we get set up."

"Set up for what?"

"To spring Greenwood," Kelp said.

Dortmunder made a face. "Somebody around here is hearing bells," he said. He went over and picked up his coffee and drank.

"Greenwood doesn't stand a chance to beat the rap and he knows it. And they'll give him the book because they're sore about the stone being gone. So either he turns it over to them to lighten the sentence or he turns it over to us for springing him. So all we have to do is bust him out and the stone is ours. Thirty G's, just like that."

Dortmunder frowned. "Where is he?"

"In jail," said Kelp.

"I know that. I mean, which jail?"

"Oh, there was trouble at the jail in Manhattan, so they moved him to some dinky can out on Long Island."

Dortmunder studied him suspiciously. Kelp had said that too off-hand, he'd thrown it away a little too casually. "Some dinky can on Long Island?" he said.

"It's a county jug or something," Kelp said. "They're holding him there till the trial."

"Too bad he couldn't get bail," Dortmunder said.

"Maybe the judge could read his mind," Kelp said.

"Or his record," Dortmunder said. He walked around the room, gnawing his thumb, thinking.

Kelp said, "We get a second shot at it. What's to worry about?"

"I don't know," Dortmunder said. "But when a job turns bad I like to leave it alone. Why throw good time after bad?"

"Do you have anything else on the fire?" Kelp asked him.

"No," Dortmunder said. The doubts still nagged him, but he shrugged and said, "What have I got to lose? You got a car with you?"

"Naturally."

"Can you operate this one?"

Kelp was insulted. "I could operate that Caddy," he said indignantly. "The damn thing wanted to operate itself, that was the trouble."

"Sure," said Dortmunder. "Help me pack."

MAJOR IKO SAT at his desk, shuffling dossiers. Besides the dossiers on Kelp and Dortmunder, there was also the one on Alan George Greenwood, which the Major had requested the instant he'd learned the man's name in the course of television reports of the robbery. And now there was a fourth to be added to what was becoming a bulging file, the dossier on Eugene Andrew Prosker, attorney at law.

Greenwood's attorney, in fact. The dossier described a fifty-three-year-old lawyer with an office in a building way downtown near the courts and with a large home on several wooded acres in an extremely expensive area of Connecticut. E. Andrew Prosker, as he called himself, had a reputation for shadiness in the Criminal Courts Building, and his clients tended to be disreputable, but no public complaint had ever been lodged against him and within certain specific boundaries he did appear to be trustworthy. As one former client reportedly had said of Prosker, "I'd trust Andy alone with my sister all night long, if she didn't have more than fifteen cents on her."

The photos in the dossier showed a paunchy, jowly sort of man with a loose cheery smile. The eyes were too shadowed to be seen clearly, but it was hard to make that happy-go-lucky smile jibe with the facts in the dossier.

The dossiers pleased the Major. He liked to touch them, to shuffle them around. The dossiers were not functional in the normal sense; they just soothed the Major's fear of the unknown by their presence.

The secretary, light reflecting from his glasses, opened the door. "Two gentlemen to see you, sir. Mr. Dortmunder and Mr. Kelp."

The Major tucked the dossiers away in a drawer. "Show them in."

Kelp seemed unchanged when he came somewhat jauntily in, but Dortmunder seemed thinner and more tired now, and he'd been both thin and tired before. Kelp said, "Well, I brought him."

"So I see." The Major got to his feet. "Good to see you again, Mr. Dortmunder," he said.

"I hope it's good," Dortmunder said. He gave no indication that he expected a handshake. He dropped into a chair, put his hands on his knees, and said, "Kelp tells me we get another chance."

"More than we anticipated," the Major said. Kelp had also taken a seat now, so the Major sat down again. He put his elbows on the desk and said, "Frankly, I had suspected you of perhaps taking the emerald yourself."

"I don't want an emerald," Dortmunder said.

The door opened again and the secretary came in, saying, "Sir, a Mr. Prosker is here."

"Send him in."

The secretary withdrew, and an instant later Prosker came striding in, smiling, carrying a black attaché case. "Gentlemen, I'm late. I hope this won't take long. You're Major Iko, I take it."

"Mr. Prosker." The Major stood. He recognized Prosker from the dossier photos, but now he saw what the photos hadn't been able to show. It was Prosker's eyes. The mouth laughed and said words and lulled everybody, but the eyes just hung back and watched and made no comment at all.

The Major made the introductions, and Prosker handed both Dortmunder and Kelp his business card, saying, "In case you're ever in need, though of course we hope it won't come to that." He chuckled, and winked. Then they all sat down again and Prosker said, "Gentlemen, I rarely give my clients advice that doesn't come out of the lawbooks, but with our friend Greenwood I made an exception. 'Alan,' I said, 'my advice to you is tie some bedsheets together and get the hell out of here.' They didn't find this emerald on him, but they didn't need to. He was caught in a guard uniform and he was identified by half a dozen guards as being near the emerald at the time of the robbery. Gentlemen, they have Greenwood cold, there isn't a thing I can do for him, and I told him so. His only hope is to depart the premises."

Dortmunder said, "What about the emerald?"

Prosker spread his hands. "He says he got away with it. He says Chefwick handed it to him, he says he hid it on his person before being captured, and he says it is now hidden away in a safe place that no one knows about but him."

Dortmunder said, "And the deal is, we break him out and he hands over the emerald for everybody to split again, same as before."

"Absolutely."

"And you'll be liaison."

Prosker smiled. "Within limits," he said. "I do have to protect myself."

Dortmunder said, "Why?"

"Why? Because I don't want to be arrested, I don't want to be disbarred, I don't want to be occupying the cell next to Greenwood."

Dortmunder shook his head. "No, I mean why be liaison at all. Why stick your neck out even a little bit?"

"Oh, well." Prosker's smile turned modest. "One does what one can for one's clients. And, of course, if you do rescue young Greenwood, he'll be able to afford a much stiffer legal fee, won't he?"

"Sort of an illegal fee, this time," Kelp said and cackled.

Dortmunder turned to the Major. "And we go back on the payroll, is that right?"

The Major nodded reluctantly. "It's becoming more expensive than I anticipated," he said.

"Don't strain yourself, Major," Dortmunder said.

The Major said, "Perhaps you don't realize, Dortmunder, but Talabwo is not a rich country. Our gross national product has only recently topped twelve million dollars. We cannot afford to support foreign criminals the way some countries can."

"Now, now," Prosker said, being jolly, "the important thing at the moment is Alan Greenwood and the Balabomo Emerald. I have some things . . ." He picked up his attaché case and unsnapped the lid. "Shall I give these to you, Dortmunder?"

"What have you got?"

"Some maps that Greenwood made up of the interior of the prison. Some photos of the outside that I took myself. A sheet of suggestions from Greenwood concerning guard movements and so on." Prosker took three bulky manila envelopes from his case and handed them over to Dortmunder. There was a little more talk, and then everybody stood up and shook hands and they all left.

Major Iko stayed in his office and chewed the inside of his cheek. He was angry at himself and worried. That had been a slip, to tell Dortmunder how poor Talabwo was. Would he remember it later and begin to wonder? Begin to put two and two together?

"Nice place," Kelp said.

"It's not bad," Dortmunder admitted. He shut the door.

It *wasn't* bad. It was a lot better than the place in Trenton. This one, a furnished one-and-a-half-room apartment on West 74th Street half a block from the park, was a long step up from that. To begin with, there was no visible bed at all, only a tasteful sofa that opened up at night into a comfortable double bed. Where in Trenton Dortmunder had had a hotplate, here he had an honest-to-God kitchenette, with a stove and a refrigerator and dishes and a drain rack. But the main thing was the air conditioning, and Dortmunder kept it going night and day. Outside, New York City was suffering July, but in here it was perpetual May.

Kelp commented on it right away, saying, "Nice and cool in here." He wiped sweat from his forehead.

"That's what I like about it," Dortmunder said. "Drink?"

"You bet." Kelp stood in the doorway of the kitchenette while Dortmunder got out ice cubes, glasses, bourbon. Kelp said, "What do you think of Prosker?"

Dortmunder opened a drawer, reached into it, held up a corkscrew, looked at Kelp, put the corkscrew away again.

Kelp nodded. "Me too. That's a geometric figure, that bird, he don't exist without an angle."

"Just so it's Greenwood he puts it to," Dortmunder said.

"You mean we get the rock, get paid, he turns Greenwood back in and takes the thirty grand for himself?"

"I don't know what he's up to," Dortmunder said. "Just so he isn't up to it with me." He handed Kelp his drink and they sat on the sofa.

Kelp said, "We'll need both Chefwick and Murch, I suppose. You want to call them, or you want me to?"

"This time," Dortmunder said, "I'll call Chefwick and you call Murch."

The phone was on the stand next to Kelp. He looked up Murch's number in his little book, dialed, and Dortmunder faintly heard two rings, then clearly what sounded like the Long Island Expressway.

Kelp said, "Murch?" He looked at Dortmunder, baffled, and louder he said, "Murch?" Then he shouted into the phone. "It's me! Kelp! *I said Kelp!*" Then he cupped the mouthpiece and said to Dortmunder, "Is it a phone in his car?"

"It's a record," Dortmunder said.

"It's a what?"

Dortmunder heard the sudden silence from the phone. "He turned it off," he said.

Kelp took the phone away from his head and studied it as though the thing had just bitten him on the ear. A tinny voice came from it, saying, "Kelp? Hello?"

Kelp said doubtfully, "That you, Stan?"

Dortmunder went out to the kitchenette and began to put cheese spread on Ritz crackers. When he went back to the living room, Kelp was just hanging up. Kelp said, "He'll meet us at the O. J. at ten."

"Good. Hand me the phone, I'll call Chefwick. At least he doesn't make car noises."

Dortmunder dialed Chefwick's number, and Maude answered. He said, "Is Roger there? This is Dortmunder."

"One moment, please."

After a while, faintly, Dortmunder could hear a voice saying, "Toot toot." He looked at Kelp, but didn't say anything. The toot-toot voice came closer, then Chefwick said, "Hello?"

Dortmunder said, "Roger, you know that idea we had that didn't work out?"

"Oh, yes," Chefwick said. "I remember it clearly."

"Well, there's a chance we can make it work after all," Dortmunder said. "If you're still interested."

"Well, I'm intrigued, naturally," Chefwick said. "I suppose it's too complicated to go into over the phone."

"It sure is," Dortmunder said. "Ten o'clock at the O. J.?"

"That will be fine," Chefwick said.

DORTMUNDER AND KELP walked into the O. J. Bar and Grill at one minute after ten. The regular customers were draped in their usual positions on the bar, watching the television set, and Rollo was wiping glasses with a towel that was once white.

Dortmunder said, "Hi, anybody else here yet?"

"The beer and salt is back there. You expecting the sherry?"

"Yeah."

"I'll send him along when he comes in. You boys want a bottle and glasses and some ice, right?"

"Right."

"I'll bring it on in."

"Thanks." They walked into the back room and found Murch there reading his Mustang owner's manual. Dortmunder said, "You're early again."

"I tried a different route," Murch said. "I went over to Pennsylvania Avenue and up Bushwick and Grand and over the Williamsburg Bridge and up Third Avenue. It seemed to work out pretty well." He picked up his beer and drank three drops.

"That's good," Dortmunder said. He and Kelp sat down, and Rollo came in with the bourbon and glasses. While he was putting them down, Chefwick came in. Rollo said to him, "You're a sherry, right?"

"Yes, thank you."

Rollo went out, not bothering to ask Murch if he was ready for another, and Chefwick sat down, saying, "I'm certainly intrigued. The emerald's lost, isn't it?"

"No," Dortmunder said. "Greenwood hid it. We don't know where, but that means we can get back on the track."

Murch said, "There's a gimmick somewhere, I can smell it."

"Not a gimmick exactly," Dortmunder said. "Just another heist. Two for the price of one."

"What do we heist?"

"Greenwood."

Murch said, "Hah?"

"Greenwood," Dortmunder repeated, and Rollo came in with Chefwick's sherry. He went out again and Dortmunder said, "Greenwood's price is we bust him out. His lawyer tells him there's no way to beat the rap, so he's got to beat a retreat instead."

Chefwick said, "Does that mean we're going to break *into* jail?"

"In and back out," Kelp said.

"We hope," Dortmunder said.

Chefwick smiled in a dazed sort of way and sipped at his sherry. "I never thought I'd be breaking *into* jail," he said. "It raises interesting questions."

Murch said, "You want me to drive, huh?"

"Right," said Dortmunder.

Murch frowned and drank a whole mouthful of beer.

Dortmunder said, "What's wrong?"

"Me sitting in a car, late at night, outside a jail, gunning the engine. I don't feature it. It don't raise any interesting questions for *me* at all."

"If we can't work it out," Dortmunder said, "we won't do it."

Murch said, "I got to be careful, that's all. I'm the sole support of my mother."

Dortmunder said, "Doesn't she drive a cab?"

"There's no living in that," Murch said. "She just does that to get out of the house, meet people."

Chefwick said, "What sort of jail is this?"

"We'll all go out there, one time or another, take a look at it," Dortmunder told him. "In the meantime, this is what I've got." He spread out on the table the contents of the three manila envelopes.

THE EBONY MAN WITH the long thin fingers led Kelp to the room with the pool table in it, shut the door after Kelp, and went away. Kelp had dropped twelve balls with only four misses and was taking aim again when the Major came in.

Kelp put the cue down on the table. "Hi, Major. Got another list for you."

"It's about time," said the Major. He frowned at the pool table and seemed irritated by something.

Kelp said, "What do you mean, 'about time'? It's been less than three weeks."

"All I know," said the Major, "is I have so far paid out three thousand three hundred dollars in salaries, not counting the costs of materials and supplies, and so far I have nothing to show for it."

"That much?" Kelp shook his head. "It sure mounts up, doesn't it? Well, here's the list."

"Thank you."

The Major sourly studied the list while Kelp went back to the table. He sank the thirteen ball with enough backspin on the cue ball to practically put it inside his shirt, and the Major said, "A truck? That's an expensive item."

"We're going to need one," Kelp said. He sighted on the nine ball. "And it can't be hot, or I'd go out and get one myself."

"This will take a while," the Major said. "The other things should be no problem. You're going to scale a wall, eh?"

"That's what they've got there," Kelp said.

The Major glanced at the pool table. "If you're finished . . ."

"Unless you'd like to try it with me."

"I'm sorry," the Major said with a dead smile. "I don't play."

FROM HIS CELL WINDOW Alan Greenwood could see the blacktopped exercise yard and the whitewashed outer wall of the prison. Beyond that wall hunkered the small Long Island community of Utopia Park, a flat Monopoly board of houses, schools, churches, shopping centers, Italian restaurants, Chinese restaurants, and orthopedic shoe stores, bisected by the rails of the Long Island Railroad. Inside the wall sat and stood and scratched those adjudged to be dangerous to the Monopoly board, including Alan Greenwood. Next to his cell window someone had written on the cement the question, "What did the White Rabbit know?" Greenwood was yet to figure that one out.

He was spending most of his time at the window because he liked neither his cell nor his cell mate. Both were gray, scabrous, dirty, and old. The cell mate spent hours picking at his toes. Greenwood had been here nearly a month now, and his patience was wearing thin.

The door clanged. Greenwood turned and saw a guard standing in the doorway. The guard looked like the cell mate's older brother, but at least he had his shoes on. He said "Greenwood. Visitor."

"Goody."

Greenwood went out, the door clanged again, and he and the guard walked down the metal corridor and down the metal spiral stairs and along another metal corridor and through two doors, both of which had to be unlocked by people on the outside and both of which were locked again in his wake. Eventually he came to a room painted light brown where on the other side of a wall of wire mesh sat Eugene Andrew Prosker.

Greenwood sat opposite him. "How goes the world?"

"It turns," Prosker assured him. "It turns."

"And how's my appeal coming?" Greenwood didn't mean an appeal to any court, but his request for deliverance.

"Coming well," Prosker said. "I wouldn't be surprised if you heard something by morning."

Greenwood smiled. "That's good news," he said.

"All that your friends ask of you," Prosker said, "is that you meet them halfway. I know you'll want to do that."

"I sure will," Greenwood said, "and I mean to try."

"You should try more than once," Prosker told him. "Anything that's worth trying is worth trying three times at the very least."

"I'll remember that," Greenwood said. "You haven't given my friends any of the other details, I guess."

"No," Prosker said. "As we decided, it would probably be best to wait till you're free before going into all that."

"I suppose so," Greenwood said. "Did you get my stuff out of the apartment?"

"All seen to," Prosker said. He got to his feet, gathering up his attaché case. "Well, I hope we'll have you out of here in no time."

"So do I," Greenwood said.

AT TWO TWENTY-FIVE A.M. the morning after Prosker's visit to Greenwood, the stretch of Northern State Parkway in the vicinity of the Utopia Park exit was very nearly empty. Only one vehicle was in the area, a large dirty truck with the words PARKER'S RENT-A-TRUCK lettered on both cab doors. Major Iko had done the renting, through untraceable middlemen, just this afternoon, and Kelp was doing the driving at the moment. As he slowed now for the exit, Dortmunder, in the seat beside him, leaned forward to look at his watch in the dashboard light and say, "We're five minutes early."

"I'll take it slow on the bumpy streets," Kelp said, "on account of everything in back."

"We don't want to be there too early," Dortmunder said.

Kelp steered the cumbersome truck off the parkway and around the curve of the exit ramp. "I know," he said. "I know."

In the prison at this same time Greenwood was also looking at his watch, the green hands in the darkness telling him he still had half an hour to wait. Prosker had told him Dortmunder and the others wouldn't be making their move until three o'clock. He shouldn't do anything too early that might tip their mitts.

Twenty-five minutes later the truck, headlights off, rolled to a stop in the parking lot of an A&P supermarket three blocks from the prison. Streetlights at corners were the only illumination, and the cloudy sky made the night even blacker. You could barely see your hand in front of your face.

Kelp and Dortmunder got out of the cab and moved cautiously around to open the doors at the rear. The interior of the truck was pitch-black. While Dortmunder helped Chefwick out, Murch handed a ten-foot ladder out to Kelp. Kelp and Dortmunder stood the ladder up against the side of the truck while Murch handed out to Chefwick a coil of gray rope and his little black bag. They were all dressed in dark clothing and they communicated in whispers.

Dortmunder took the coil of rope and went up the ladder first, Chefwick following him. When they were both on top of the truck, Kelp pushed the ladder up after them. Dortmunder laid the ladder lengthwise on the truck top and then he and Chefwick lay down on either side of it. Kelp went around and shut the doors, then got back into the cab, started the engine, and drove the truck slowly around the A&P and out to the street. He didn't turn the headlights on.

In the prison Greenwood, looking at his watch and seeing it was five minutes to three, decided the time had come. He sat up, throwing the covers off. He was already fully dressed. He got to his feet, looked at the sleeping man in the top bunk for a few seconds—the man was snoring slightly, mouth open—and then Greenwood hit him in the nose.

The old man's eyes popped wide open, and for two or three seconds he and Greenwood stared at each other, their faces no more than a foot apart. Then the old man blinked, and his hand sidled up from under the blanket to touch his nose, and he said, in surprise and pain, "Ow."

Greenwood, shouting at the top of his voice, bellowed, *"Stop picking your feet!"*

The old man sat up, his eyes getting rounder and rounder. His nose was starting to bleed. He said, "What? What?"

Still at top volume, Greenwood roared, *"And stop fingering your nose!"*

The old man took his fingers away from his nose and looked at them, and there was blood on the tips. "Help," he said tentatively, as though to be sure that was the word he was looking for. Then he let fly with a raucous string of helps, putting his head back, squeezing his eyes shut, yipping like a terrier, *"Helphelphelphelp—"*

"I can't take it anymore," Greenwood raged, taking the baritone part. *"I'll break your neck for you!"*

"Helphelphelphelphelphelphelp—"

Lights went on. Guards were shouting. Greenwood began to swear, to wave his fists in the air. He yanked the blanket off the old man, wadded it up, threw it back at him. He grabbed the old man's ankle and began to squeeze it as though he thought it was the old man's neck.

The big clang came that meant the long iron bar across all the cell doors on this side of the tier had been lifted. Greenwood yanked the old man out of bed by his ankle, being careful not to hurt him, clutched him around the neck with one hand, raised his other fist high, and stood posed like that, bellowing, until the cell door opened and three guards came rushing in.

Greenwood didn't make it easy for them. He didn't punch any of them because he didn't want them to lay him out with their truncheons, but he did keep poking the old man at them, making it difficult for them to come around through the narrow cell and get their hands on him.

Then, all at once, he subsided. He released the old man, who sat down on the floor and clutched his neck, and Greenwood stood there slump-shouldered, vague-eyed. "I don't know," he said fuzzily, shaking his head. "I don't know."

The guards put their hands on his arms. "We know," one of them said, and the second said quietly to the third, "Flipped out. I wouldn't of thought it from him."

Not too many walls away, the rented truck had rolled silently and blackly to a stop against the outer wall of the prison. There were towers at both corners of the wall and there was a great deal of light on other parts of the wall, but here there was silence and darkness only intermittently broken by a searchlight sweeping along the length of the wall from the inside. The reason was, there were no cells or entrances near this part of the wall at all, according to Greenwood's maps, only the prison heating plant, the laundry, the kitchens and dining halls, various storage sheds and the like. No part of the wall was left totally unguarded, but the security in this area was the most perfunctory.

As soon as the truck came to a stop, Dortmunder got to his feet and leaned the ladder against the wall. It reached almost to the top. He hurried up it while Chefwick held it steady, and at the top he peeked over, watching for the searchlight. It came, it showed him a layout of building roofs that matched Greenwood's map, and he ducked out of sight just before it swept past. He went back down the ladder and whispered, "It's all right."

"Good," Chefwick whispered.

Dortmunder joggled the ladder to be sure it would hold still with no one at the bottom, and then he went back up, Chefwick following close behind. Dortmunder carried the coil of rope over one shoulder, and Chefwick toted his black bag, moving with an agility surprising in a man of his appearance.

At the top, Dortmunder shook out the coil of rope, holding on to the end tied to a metal hook. The rope was knotted every few feet and dangled to about eight feet from the ground. Dortmunder attached the hook to the top of the wall and tugged the rope to be sure it was solid.

As soon as the searchlight glided by the next time, Dortmunder zipped up the rest of the ladder and straddled the top of the wall to the right. Chefwick hurried up after him, hampered slightly by the black bag, and straddled the wall to the left, facing Dortmunder. They reached down, grabbed the ladder, pulled it up until it would tilt over the wall, and then slid it down the other side. About nine feet down was a flat tar roof, over the prison laundry. The ladder touched the roof and Dortmunder immediately took the black bag from Chefwick and hurried down the ladder. Chefwick scrambled down after him. They put the ladder down next to the low wall that edged the roof and then lay down where they would be in that wall's shadow the next time the searchlight came by.

Outside, Kelp had been watching in the dark. He had seen them vaguely, huddled on the ladder, one time when the searchlight went by on the other side of the wall, but the next time it went by they were gone. He nodded in satisfaction, got into the cab, and drove away, headlights still off.

Dortmunder and Chefwick, meantime, used the ladder to get from the laundry roof to the ground, then hurried for the main prison building looming up in the darkness ahead of them. They had to duck behind a wall once, to let the searchlight go by, but then trotted on, got to the building, found the door where it was supposed to be, and Chefwick took from his pocket the two tools he'd known he would have to use on this door. He went to work while Dortmunder kept watch.

Dortmunder saw the searchlight coming again, running along the face of the building. "Hurry it up," he whispered, and heard a click, and turned to see the door opening. They ducked inside, shut the door, and the searchlight went by. "Close," Dortmunder whispered.

"I'll take my bag now," Chefwick whispered back. He was completely unruffled.

The room they were in was totally black, but Chefwick knew the contents of his bag well. He squatted on the floor, put the two tools away in the bag, took out two others, closed the bag, stood, and said, "All right."

Several locked doors away, Greenwood was saying, "Don't worry. I'll come quietly."

"We're not worried," one of the guards said.

It had taken them all quite a while to get everything sorted out. After Greenwood had suddenly gotten calm, the guards had tried to find out what it was all about, but all the old man could do was sputter and point, and all Greenwood would do was stand around looking vague and shaking his head and saying, "I just don't know any more." Then the old man said the magic word, "feet," and Greenwood erupted again.

He was very careful about how he erupted. He did nothing physical, all he did was scream and shout and thrash a bit. He kept it up until he saw that the guards were about ready to apply a local anesthetic to his head; then he calmed down again and explained about the old man's feet, being totally lucid and reasonable.

What they did was humor him, and that was what he wanted. And when one of them said, "Look, fellow, why don't we just find you someplace else to sleep tonight?" Greenwood smiled in honest pleasure. He knew where they would take him now, to one of the cells over in the hospital wing. He could cool off there until morning, and then be handy for the doctor to see.

That's what they thought.

Greenwood said a smiling good-bye to the old man, who was holding a sock to his bleeding nose now, and out he marched amid the guards.

The early part of the route was the same as when he'd gone to see Prosker. Down the metal corridor, down the metal spiral stairs, along the other metal corridor and through two doors, both of which had to be unlocked by people on the outside and both of which were locked again in his wake. After that the route changed. They went down a long brown corridor and around a corner to a nice lonely spot where two men dressed all in black, with black hoods over their heads and black pistols in their hands, came out of a doorway. One said, "Don't nobody make a sound."

The guards looked at Dortmunder and Chefwick, for indeed it was they, and blinked in astonishment. One of them said, "You're crazy."

"Not necessarily," Chefwick said. He stepped to one side of the doorway and said, "In here, gentlemen."

"You won't shoot," the second guard said. "The noise would attract a lot of attention."

"That's why we have silencers," Dortmunder told him. "That's this thing like a hand grenade on the front of the gun. Want to hear it?"

"No," said the guard.

Everybody went into the room and Greenwood shut the door. They used the guards' belts to tie their ankles, their ties to tie their hands, and their shirttails to gag them. When they left the room, Chefwick carefully locked the door behind him, and the three of them loped down a corridor and through a heavy metal door that had been locked for several years until Chefwick had gotten to it.

They retraced the route that Dortmunder and Chefwick had taken coming in. Four more doors stood in the way, each having been unlocked by Chefwick on the way in and each now being locked again on their way out. They came at last to the exit from this building and waited there, clustered around the doorway, looking at the black cube of the laundry across the way. Dortmunder checked his watch and it was three twenty. "Five minutes," he whispered.

Four blocks away, Kelp looked at his watch, saw it was three twenty, and got out of the truck cab again. He closed the door quietly, went around back, and opened the rear doors. "Set," he whispered to Murch.

"Right," Murch whispered back and began pushing a long two-by-twelve board out of the truck. Kelp grabbed the end of it and lowered it to the ground so the board leaned against the rear edge of the truck body in a long slant. Murch pushed out another board and Kelp lined it up parallel to the other one about five feet away.

They had chosen the most industrial area of the neighborhood for this part of the plot. The streets directly contiguous with the prison were all shabby residential, but starting two or three blocks to the south, for block after block, there was nothing but the low brick buildings in which sunglasses were made, soft drinks were bottled, newspapers were printed, signs were painted, and foam rubber was covered with fabric. There was no traffic at night, there were no pedestrians, a police car prowled through only once an hour. There was nothing here at night but the factories and, parked in front of them, hundreds of trucks. Up this street and down that, nothing but trucks, bumpy-fendered, big-nosed, hulking, empty, silent. Trucks.

Kelp had parked his truck in with all the other trucks, making it invisible. He had found a space just beyond a fire hydrant so there would be room behind the truck, and it pleased him.

Now Kelp stepped up on the curb and waited. Murch had disappeared into the blackness inside the truck again, and after a minute there was the sudden chatter of an engine starting up in there. It roared a brief second, then settled down to a quiet purr, and out from the truck nosed a nearly new dark green Mercedes-Benz 250SE convertible. Kelp had run across it earlier this evening on Park Avenue. Because it wasn't going to be used very much, it still bore its MD plates. Kelp had decided to forgive doctors.

The boards bowed beneath the weight of the car. Murch, behind the wheel, looked like Gary Cooper taxiing his Grumman into position on the aircraft carrier. Nodding at Kelp the way Coop used to nod at the ground crew, Murch tapped the accelerator and the Mercedes-Benz went away, lights out.

Murch had spent some of his idle time in the back of the truck with a flashlight, reading the owner's manual he'd found in the car's glove compartment, and he wondered if the top speed of one hundred eighteen miles an hour was on the up-and-up or not. He shouldn't test it now, but on the way back maybe he'd have enough of a straightaway to find out.

Back in the prison, Dortmunder had checked his watch again, found that five minutes had passed, and said, "Okay." Now the three of them were trotting across the open space toward the laundry, the searchlight having flashed by just before they started.

Dortmunder and Chefwick put up the ladder and Greenwood led the way. The three got to the roof, pulled the ladder up after them, lay down in the lee of the low wall, held their breaths while the searchlight went by, and then got to their feet and carried the ladder over to the outer wall. Chefwick went up first this time, toting his black bag, went over the top and down the rope hand over hand, the handle of the black bag clamped in his teeth. Greenwood went up next and Dortmunder followed. Dortmunder straddled the top of the wall and began pulling the ladder up. The searchlight was on its way back.

Chefwick dropped to the ground just as Murch arrived in the convertible. Chefwick took the bag from his teeth, which were aching from the strain, and climbed into the back of the convertible.

Greenwood was coming down the rope. Dortmunder was still pulling up the ladder. The searchlight reached him, washed over him like magic water, passed on, stopped dead, quivered, and shot back. Dortmunder was gone, but the ladder was in the process of falling onto the laundry roof. It went *chack* when it hit.

Meantime, Greenwood had reached the ground and jumped into the front seat of the convertible. Dortmunder was coming very fast down the rope. A siren said *Rrrrrr*—and began getting louder. Dortmunder kicked out from the wall, let go of the rope, dropped into the backseat of the convertible, and called, "Go!"

Murch hit the accelerator.

Sirens were starting up all over the place, and Kelp, standing by the truck with an unlit flashlight in his hands, began to chew his lower lip.

Murch had turned on the headlights, since he was going too fast now to depend on the occasional streetlights. Behind them, the prison was coming to life like a yellow volcano. Any minute it would start erupting police cars.

Murch made a left on two wheels. He now had a three-block straightaway. He put the accelerator on the floor.

There are still milkmen who get up very early in the morning and deliver milk. One of these, standing at his steering wheel, *put-putted* his stubby white traveling walk-in closet into the middle of an intersection, looked to his left, and saw headlights coming at him too fast to think about. He yipped and threw himself backward into his cases of milk, causing a lot of crashing.

Murch went around the stalled milk truck like a skier on a slalom and kept the accelerator on the floor. He was going to have to brake soon, and the speedometer hadn't broken a hundred yet.

No good. He'd have to brake now, or overshoot. He released the accelerator and tapped the brakes. The four-wheel disc brakes grabbed and held.

Kelp didn't hear the engine over the screaming sirens, but he did hear the tires shriek. He looked down at the corner and the convertible slid sideways into view, then leaped forward.

Kelp switched on his flashlight and began to wave it madly. Didn't Murch see him? The convertible kept getting larger.

Murch knew what he was doing. While his passengers clung to the upholstery and each other he shot down the block, tapped the brakes just enough at the right split second, nudged the wheel just enough, rolled up the boards and into the truck, tapped the brakes again, and came to a quivering standstill two inches from the far wall. He shut off the engine and switched off the lights.

Kelp, meanwhile, had put away his flashlight and was quickly shoving the boards back into the truck. He slammed one of the doors. Hands reached down to help him up into the truck, and then the other door was shut.

For half a minute there was no sound in the blackness inside the truck except five people panting. Then Greenwood said, "We've gotta go back. I forgot my toothbrush."

Everybody laughed at that, but it was just nervous laughter. Still, it helped to relax them all. Murch turned the car's headlights on again, since they knew no light from in here could be seen outside the truck, and then everybody shook hands with everybody, congratulating everybody on a job well done.

They got quiet and listened as a police car yowled by, and then Kelp said, "Hot on our trail."

They all grinned.

They'd done it. From here on it was simple. Everybody was feeling pleased and happy and relieved. They sat around in the convertible and told jokes and after a while Kelp brought out a deck of cards and they started to play poker for high paper stakes.

Along about four o'clock Kelp said, "Well, tomorrow we go get the emerald and collect our dough."

"We can start working on it tomorrow, I guess," Greenwood said. "Three cards," he said to Chefwick, who was dealing.

Everybody got very quiet. Dortmunder said to Greenwood, "What do you mean, we can start working on it?"

Greenwood gave a nervous shrug. "Well, it isn't going to be all that easy," he said.

Dortmunder said, "Why not?"

Greenwood cleared his throat. He looked around with an embarrassed smile. "Because," he said, "I hid it in the police station."

PHASE THREE

MAJOR IKO SAID, "In the police station?" He stared at them in blank disbelief.

They were all there, all five of them. Greenwood, the one they'd gotten out of prison last night, was sitting in front of his desk between Dortmunder and Kelp. And two new ones, introduced as Roger Chefwick and Stan Murch. A part of Major Iko's mind fondled those two new names, could hardly wait for this meeting to be over so he could give the orders for two new dossiers to be made up. But the rest of his mind was given over to incredulity. He stared at everyone, and most especially at Greenwood. "In the police station?" he said, and his voice cracked.

"It's where I was," Greenwood said reasonably.

"But surely—at the Coliseum you could have—"

"He swallowed it," Dortmunder said.

The Major looked at Dortmunder, trying to understand what the man had just said. "I beg your pardon?"

But it was Greenwood who explained why and how. He said, "In the Coliseum, I was in a hall. No place to hide anything. I didn't want them to find it on me, so I swallowed it. Next day, when I had the emerald again, I was in a cell in a precinct on the Upper West Side, in one of the detention cells on the top floor."

"And that's where you hid it?" the Major said faintly.

"There wasn't anything else I could do, Major. I didn't dare keep it on my person, not in jail."

"Couldn't you have just kept on swallowing it?"

Greenwood gave a greenish smile. "Not after the first time. It's rather large," he said.

"Mmmm," the Major admitted reluctantly. He looked at Dortmunder. "Well? What now?"

Dortmunder said, "We're divided on going after it again. Two for, two against, and one uncertain."

"But—" The Major spread his hands. "Why wouldn't you go after it? If you've successfully broken into a prison, surely an ordinary precinct house—"

"That's just it," Dortmunder said. "My feeling is we're pushing our luck. We've given you two capers for the price of one as it is. We can't just keep busting into places forever. Sooner or later the odds have to catch up with us."

The Major said, "Odds? Luck? But it isn't odds and luck that have helped you, Mr. Dortmunder. It's skill and planning and experience. You still have just as much skill and are capable of just as much planning as in last night's affair—"

"I just have a feeling," Dortmunder said. "This is turning into one of those dreams where you keep running down the same corridor and you never get anywhere."

"But surely if Mr. Greenwood hid the emerald, and knows where he hid it, and—" The Major looked at Greenwood. "It is hidden well, is it not?"

"It's hidden well," Greenwood assured him. "It'll still be there."

The Major spread his hands. "Then I don't see the problem. Mr. Dortmunder, I take it you are one of the two opposed."

"That's right. Chefwick is with me. Greenwood wants to go after it, and Kelp is on his side. Murch doesn't know."

"I'll go along with the majority," Murch said. "I got no opinion."

Greenwood said to Chefwick, "It's a cinch. I tell you, it's a precinct house. You know what that means, the joint is full of guys typing. It'll be easier than the jug you just got me out of."

"Besides," Kelp said, also talking to Chefwick, "We've worked at the damn thing this long, I hate to give it up."

"I understand that," Chefwick said, "and in some ways I sympathize with it. But at the same time I believe we should consider ourselves very lucky to have done as well as we have, and I believe we should retire and consider some other job somewhere else."

"Say," said Kelp, "that's just the point. We're still all of us on our uppers, we've still got to find a caper somewhere to get us squared away. We know about this emerald, why not go after it?"

Dortmunder said, "Three jobs for the price of one?"

The Major said, "You're right about that, Mr. Dortmunder. You are doing more work than you contracted for, and you should be paid more. We'll make it—" The Major paused, thinking, then said,

"Thirty-two thousand. An extra ten thousand to be split among you."

Dortmunder snorted. "Two thousand dollars to break into a police station? I wouldn't break into a tollbooth for money like that."

Kelp looked at the Major with the expression of a man disappointed in an old friend and protégé. "That's awful little, Major," he said. "If that's the kind of offer you're going to make, you shouldn't say anything at all."

The Major frowned, looking from face to face. "I don't know what to say," he admitted.

"Say ten thousand," Kelp told him.

"A man?"

"That's right. And the weekly amount up to two hundred."

The Major considered. But too quick an agreement might make them suspicious, so he said, "I couldn't make it that much. We're straining the national budget as it is."

"How much, then?" Kelp asked in a friendly, helpful sort of way.

The Major drummed his fingers on the desk top. He squinted, he closed one eye, he scratched his head above his left ear. Finally he said, "Five thousand."

"And the two hundred a week."

The Major nodded. "Yes."

Kelp looked at Dortmunder. "Sweet enough?" he asked.

Dortmunder chewed a knuckle, and then said, "I'll look it over. If it looks good to me, and if it looks good to Chefwick, all right."

MURCH, OBVIOUSLY VERY drunk and holding a nearly empty pint bottle of apricot brandy in his hand, stepped off the curb in front of the police car, waggled his other hand at it, and cried, "Takshi!"

The police car stopped. It was that or run over him. Murch leaned on the fender and announced loudly, "I wanna go home. Brooklyn. Take me to Brooklyn, cabby, and be fast about it." It was well after midnight and except for Murch this residential block on Manhattan's Upper West Side was quiet and peaceful.

The nondriving policeman got out of the police car. He said, "C'mere, you."

Murch staggered over. Winking hugely he said, "Never mind the meter, pal. We can work out a private arrangement. The cops'll never know."

"Izzat right?" said the cop. He opened the rear door. "Climb aboard, chum," he said.

"Right," said Murch. He lurched into the police car and fell asleep at once on the rear seat.

The cops didn't take Murch to Brooklyn. They took him to the precinct house, where they woke him without gentleness, trotted him up the slate steps between the green lights and turned him over to some other cops on the inside. "Let him sleep it off in the tank," one of them commented.

There was a brief ritual at the desk, and then Murch was trotted down a long green corridor and shoved into the tank, which was a big square metal room full of drunks. "This isn't right," Murch told himself, and he began to shout. "Yo! Hey! What the hey! Police!"

All the other drunks had been trying to sleep it off as they were supposed to, and all that shouting woke them up and irritated them. "Shut up, bo," one of them said.

"Oh, yeah?" Murch said and hit him in the mouth, and pretty soon there was a good fight going on in the drunk tank. Most people missed when they swung, but at least they were swinging.

The cell door opened and some cops came in, saying, "Break it up." They broke it up, and worked it out that Murch was the cause of the trouble. "I ain't staying here with these bums," Murch announced, and the cops said, "Indeed you aren't, brother."

They took Murch out of the drunk tank, being not at all gentle with him, and ran him rapidly up four flights of stairs to the fifth and top floor, where the detention cells were.

Murch was hoping for the second cell on the right, because if he got the second cell on the right that was the end of the problem. Unfortunately, there was somebody else already in the second cell on the right, and Murch wound up in the fourth cell on the left. They pushed him in at high speed and shut the door behind him. Then they went away.

There was a little light, not much, coming from the end of the corridor. Murch sat down on the blanket-covered metal bunk and opened his shirt. Inside, taped to his chest, were some sheets of typewriter paper and a ballpoint pen. He removed these from his chest, wincing, and then made a lot of diagrams and notes while the information was still fresh in his mind. Then he taped it all back to his chest again, lay down on the metal bunk, and went to sleep.

In the morning he was given a good talking to, but because he had no record and he apologized and was very chagrined and embarrassed and decent about it all, he was not held.

Outside, Murch looked across the street and saw a two-year-old Chrysler with MD plates. He went over and Kelp was behind the wheel, taking photographs of the front of the station house. Chefwick was in the back, keeping a head count on people going in and out, cars going in and out of the driveway beside the building, things like that.

Murch got in beside Kelp. He said, "Boy, don't ever be a drunk. Cops are death on drunks."

A little later, when they were done, Kelp and Chefwick drove Murch across town to where his Mustang was parked. "Somebody stole your hubcaps," Kelp said.

"I take them off when I come to Manhattan," Murch said. "Manhattan is full of thieves." He opened his shirt, removed the papers from his chest again, and gave them to Kelp. Then he went to his car, got in and drove home. It was a hot day, full of sun and humidity, so when he got home he took a shower and then went downstairs to his bedroom and lay on the bed in his underwear and read a magazine article about the new chevy models.

THE EBONY MAN WITH the long thin fingers and light-reflecting glasses took Kelp to the room with the pool table right away, bowed his head slightly, and left, closing the door behind him. Kelp walked over to the pool table and racked up the balls. He didn't feel like much of anything tonight, so he just practiced breaks.

When the Major came in he said, "You haven't progressed very far tonight."

"Just fooling around this time," Kelp told him. He put the cue down and took a damp and crumpled sheet of paper from his hip pocket and handed it to Iko, then turned back to the table. He'd put three balls away when Iko squeaked, "A helicopter?"

Kelp put the cue down again. "We weren't sure you could get your hands on one of those, but if you can't we don't have any caper. So Dortmunder said I should just bring you the list like always and let you decide for yourself."

Iko was looking a little strange. "A helicopter," he said. "How do you expect me to get you a helicopter?"

Kelp shrugged. "I dunno. But the way we figured, you've got a whole country behind you."

"That's true," Iko said, "but the country behind me is Talabwo, it is not the United States."

Kelp said, "Talabwo doesn't have any helicopters?"

"Of course Talabwo has helicopters," Iko said irritably, his national pride stung. "We have seven helicopters. But they are in Talabwo, naturally, and Talabwo is in Africa. The American authorities might ask questions if we tried to import an American helicopter from Talabwo. Are you sure you have to have one?"

"The detention cells," Kelp said, "are on the top floor. You go in the street entrance, you've got five floors of armed cops to go through before you ever reach the cells, and then you've got the same five floors of cops to go through all over again before you get back to the street."

"I see," said Iko.

Kelp picked up his cue. "So our only chance is to come down from the top. Get on the roof, and go from there down into the building. The detention cells are right there, handy, and we don't even see most of the cops."

Iko said, "But a helicopter is very loud. They'll hear you coming."

"No, they won't," Kelp said. He leaned over the table, dropped the four ball, straightened, and said, "There's airplanes going over that neighborhood all day long. Big jets, a lot lower than you'd think. We know who the regulars are, and we'll drift in while one of them is going by." He sank the twelve.

"All right," Iko said. "I can see where it could work."

"And nothing else can work for a minute," Kelp told him, and dropped the fifteen.

"Perhaps," Iko said. He frowned, troubled. "But the problem is, where am I going to get you a helicopter?"

"I don't know," Kelp said, sinking the two ball. "Where'd you get your helicopters before this?"

"Well, we bought them, naturally, from—" Iko stopped, and his eyes widened. A white cloud formed above his head, and in the cloud a light bulb appeared. "I *can* do it!" he cried.

"Good," Kelp said and put the cue down. "How you going to manage it?"

"We'll simply order a helicopter," Iko said, "through normal channels. I can arrange that, though it could take a while. When it arrives in Newark for transhipment by boat to Talabwo, it will spend a few days in our warehouse space. I can arrange for you to borrow it, but not during normal working hours."

"We wouldn't want it during normal working hours," Kelp assured him. "About seven-thirty in the evening is when we figure to get there."

"That will be fine, then." The Major was obviously delighted with himself. "I will have it gassed up and ready," he said.

"Fine."

"The only thing is," the Major said, his delight fading just a trifle, "it could take a while for the order to go through. Three weeks, possibly longer."

"That's okay," Kelp said. "The emerald will keep. Just so we get our salary every week."

"I'll get it as quickly as I can," Iko said.

Kelp motioned at the table. "Mind?"

"Go ahead," Iko said. He watched Kelp sink the last two balls and then said, "Perhaps I ought to take lessons in that. It does look relaxing."

"You don't need lessons," Kelp told him. "Just grab a cue and start shooting. Want me to show you how?"

The Major looked at his watch, obviously torn two ways. "Well," he said, "just for a few minutes."

DORTMUNDER WAS SORTING money on his coffee table, a little pile of crumpled singles, a smaller pile of less-crumpled fives, and a thin pair of tens. His shoes and socks were off and he kept wiggling his toes as though they'd just been released from prison. It was late evening, the long August day finally coming to an end outside the window, and Dortmunder's loosened tie, rumpled shirt, and matted hair demonstrated he hadn't spent much of that day here in this air-conditioned apartment.

The doorbell rang.

Dortmunder got heavily to his feet, went over to the door, and peered through the spy hole. Kelp's cheerful face was framed there, as in a cameo. Dortmunder opened the door and Kelp came in, saying, "Well, how's it going?"

Dortmunder shut the door. "You look pleased with life," he said.

"I am," Kelp said. "Why not?" He glanced at the money on the coffee table. "You don't seem to be doing too bad yourself."

Dortmunder limped back to the sofa and sat down. "You don't think so? Out all day, walking from door to door, chased by dogs, jeered at by children, insulted by housewives, and what do I get for it?" He made a contemptuous wave at the money on the coffee table. "Seventy bucks," he said.

"It's the heat slowing you down," Kelp said. "Want a drink?"

"It isn't the heat," Dortmunder said, "it's the humidity. Yeah, I want a drink."

Kelp went to the kitchenette and talked from there, saying, "What sort of dodge you working?"

"Encyclopedias," Dortmunder said. "And the problem is, you ask for more than a ten-buck deposit they either balk or they want to write a check. As it is, I got one ten-dollar check today, and what the hell am I going to do with that?"

Kelp came out of the kitchen with two glasses containing bourbon and ice. "Why you doing encyclopedias?" he asked.

Dortmunder nodded at the slender briefcase over by the door. "Because that's what I got the display case on," he said. "You can't sell a thing without a lot of bright pieces of paper."

Kelp handed him a glass and went over to sit down in the armchair. "Hell," Kelp said, "why not take it easy? You can make ends meet on Iko's two hundred."

"I want to build a stake," Dortmunder said, keeping his eyes closed. "I don't like living on the bone like this."

"That's a hell of a stake you'll build," Kelp told him, "at seventy bucks a day."

"Sixty yesterday," Dortmunder said. He opened his eyes. "We've been tapping Iko four weeks since Greenwood got out. How much longer you think he'll ante up?"

"Till he gets the helicopter," Kelp said.

"If he gets it. Maybe he won't get it at all. He didn't sound happy when he paid me last week." Dortmunder drank some bourbon.

"And I'll tell you something else," he said. "I don't have the belief in this job I have in some things. I've got my eyes open for something else, I've spread the word around I'm available. Anything else comes along, that rotten emerald can go to hell."

"That's the way I feel too," Kelp said. "That's why Greenwood and me are matching coins up and down Seventh Avenue. But I believe Iko's going to come through."

"I don't," Dortmunder said.

Kelp grinned. "You want to put a little side bet on it?"

Dortmunder looked at him. "Whyn't you call Greenwood over and I can bet you both?"

Kelp looked innocent. "Say, don't be in a bad mood," he said. "I'm just kidding with you."

Dortmunder emptied his glass. "I know it," he said. "Build me another?"

"Sure thing." Kelp came over and took Dortmunder's glass and the phone rang. "There's Iko now," Kelp said, grinning, and went out to the kitchenette.

Dortmunder answered the phone and Iko's voice said, "I have it."

"Well, I'll be damned," Dortmunder said.

THE LAVENDER LINCOLN with the MD plates nosed slowly amid the long warehouses on the Newark docks. The setting sun cast long shadows across the empty streets. Today was Tuesday, the fifteenth of August; the sun would set this evening at two minutes before seven. The time was now six thirty.

Murch, who was driving, found the sun reflected into his eyes from the rearview mirror. He said irritably, "Where the hell is this place anyway?"

"Not much farther," Kelp said. He was holding the typed sheet of instructions and was sitting beside Murch. The other three were in back. They were all in their guard uniforms again, the policelike costumes they'd worn at the Coliseum. Murch, who didn't have a uniform like that, was wearing the jacket and cap of a Greyhound bus driver.

"Turn there," Kelp said, pointing ahead.

Murch shook his head in disgust. "Which way?" he said with studied patience.

"Left," Kelp said. "Didn't I say that?"

"Thank you," Murch said. "No, you didn't."

Murch turned left, into a narrow blacktop alley between two brick warehouses. It was already twilight in here, but sun shone orange on stacked wooden crates at the far end. Murch steered the Lincoln around the crates and out to a large open area of weedy dirt surrounded on all sides by the backs of warehouses. In the middle of the empty space stood the helicopter.

"That's big," Kelp said. He sounded awed.

The helicopter looked huge, standing out there all alone like that. It was painted a dull army brown, had a round glass nose, small glass side windows, and blades that hung out like wash lines.

Murch jounced the Lincoln over the rough ground and stopped near the helicopter. Up close it didn't look as gigantic. They could see that it was just a little taller than a man and not much longer than the Lincoln. Squares and rectangles of black tape covered the body here and there, apparently to hide identifying numbers or symbols.

They all got out of the cool car into the hot world and Murch rubbed his hands together as he grinned at the machine in front of them. "Now, there's a baby that'll go," he said.

Dortmunder, suddenly suspicious, said, "You *did* drive one of these things before, right?"

"I told you," Murch said, "I can drive anything." He kept grinning at the helicopter.

"Yeah. You *can* drive anything," Dortmunder said. "That's what you told me. But the question is, *did* you ever drive one of *these* things before?"

"Don't answer," Kelp said to Murch. "I don't want to know the answer. Come on, let's load up."

"Right," said Murch, and they all started to carry things from the trunk of the Lincoln over to the helicopter. Chefwick carried his black bag. Greenwood and Dortmunder carried the machine guns and then between them, toted by its handles, a green metal box full of detonators and tear gas grenades and miscellaneous tools. Kelp carried a cardboard carton full of handcuffs and strips of white cloth. Murch locked the Lincoln up tight, then followed carrying the portable radio jammer—a heavy black box about the size of a beer case, bristling with knobs and dials and retracted antennas.

Inside the helicopter were two padded bucket seats up front and a long seat across the back, with stowage space behind the backseat into which they shoved everything. Then they arranged themselves with Murch at the wheel, Dortmunder beside him, and the other three in back. They shut the helicopter door and Dortmunder studied Murch studying the controls. After a minute Dortmunder said in disgust, "You never even *saw* one of these things before."

Murch turned on him. "Are you kidding? I read in *Popular Mechanics* how to *make* one, you don't think I can *drive* one?"

Dortmunder looked over his shoulder at Kelp. "I could be peddling encyclopedias right now," he said.

Murch, having been insulted, replied, "Come on, now, watch this. I hit this switch here, see? And this lever. And I do this."

A roaring started. Dortmunder looked up, and through the glass bubble he could see the blades starting to rotate. They went faster and faster until they became a blur. Abruptly, Murch smiled and sat back and nodded and pointed out. Dortmunder looked out and the ground wasn't there. "Oh, yeah," Dortmunder said softly, though no one could hear him. "That's right."

Murch fiddled around for a couple of minutes, getting used to things, but then he settled down and they began to move northeast at a good clip. They passed over Newark Bay and Jersey City and Upper Bay and then Murch figured out how to steer and he turned left a little and they followed the Hudson River north, Manhattan on their right, New Jersey on their left.

After the first few minutes, Dortmunder liked it. Murch didn't seem to be doing anything wrong, and aside from the noise it was kind of nice to be hanging up in the sky here like this. The guys in back were nudging each other and pointing at things like the Empire State Building, and Dortmunder turned at one point and grinned at Kelp, who shrugged and grinned back.

Murch pointed to the right. Over there was another helicopter, with a radio station's call letters on the side. The pilot waved, and Dortmunder waved back.

Far away on their left the sun was sinking slowly into Pennsylvania, the sky turning pink and mauve and purple. Manhattan was already in twilight, and Dortmunder checked his watch. Seven twenty. They were doing well.

The plan was to come at the police station from the rear, so the cops out front wouldn't get a glimpse of the helicopter landing on their roof. Murch kept following the Hudson north, therefore, until Harlem stood snaggle-toothed on their right, and then he made a wide sweeping U-turn. He had figured out the altitude adjustment now, and eased down over the Upper West Side, figuring out the street they wanted from landmarks like Central Park and the meeting of Broadway with West End Avenue. And then, dead ahead, there stood the black rectangle of the police station roof.

Kelp leaned forward and tapped Dortmunder's shoulder and pointed to the sky on their right. Dortmunder looked up and saw the jet they had planned to use as cover coming out of the west, sweep-winged, sparkling, noisy. Dortmunder grinned and nodded.

Murch put the helicopter down on the roof as gently as he'd put a beer glass on a bar. He cut the engine and in their own sudden silence they could hear the passage of the jet, sliding down the sky above them toward LaGuardia Airport. "Last stop," Murch said, and the jet noise faded away to the east.

Dortmunder opened the door and they all clambered out. Chefwick hurried over to the door in the small shacklike construction atop the roof while the others unloaded the machine guns and equipment from the helicopter. Kelp took a pair of cable shears, went over to the front left edge of the roof, lay down on his belly, reached down and out, and cut the phone wires. Murch set the portable jammer down on the roof, turned it on, put earphones on, and began twiddling the dials. All radio broadcasting from this building promptly became unintelligible.

By now Chefwick had the door open, and Dortmunder and Greenwood had picked up the machine guns and stuffed their pockets with detonators and tear gas grenades, and they followed Chefwick down the stairs to the windowless metal door at the bottom. Chefwick studied this door a second, then said, "I'll have to blast this one. Go on back up."

The two of them hurried up to the roof, where Murch had left the jammer and was sitting near the front edge, several detonator caps beside him. He looked over at them and waved. In return Dortmunder showed him two fingers, meaning he should wait two minutes, and Murch nodded.

Chefwick came upstairs. Kelp, carrying the handcuffs and strips of white cloth, said to him, "How we doing?"

"Three," Chefwick said in a distracted sort of way. "Two. One."

Phoom, said a noise.

Grayish smoke drifted lazily up the stairwell and out the door.

Dortmunder dashed downstairs through the smoke, found the metal door lying on its back at the bottom, and hurried through the doorway into a short square hall. Straight ahead, a heavy barred gate blocked the end of the hall where the stairway went down. An astonished-looking cop was sitting on a high stool there, just inside the gate, with a paper-filled lectern beside him. He was thin and elderly, and his reflexes were a little slow. Also, he wasn't armed. Dortmunder knew, from both Greenwood and Murch, that none of the cops on duty up here were armed.

"Take him," Dortmunder said over his shoulder to Greenwood, and then turned the other way, to where a stout cop with a ham and cheese sandwich on rye in his hand was trying to close another gate. Dortmunder pointed the machine gun conversationally and said, "Stop that."

The cop looked at Dortmunder. He stopped and put his hands up in the air. One slice of rye dangled over his knuckles like the floppy ear of a dog.

Greenwood meanwhile had the elderly cop standing beside his lectern with his hands up while Greenwood tossed three detonator caps and two tear gas grenades through the bars and down the stairs, where they made a mess. The idea was that no one was supposed to come upstairs.

There was one more officer on duty up here. He'd been sitting at a scarred wooden desk reading, in an area beyond the second gate. This one looked at Dortmunder and Greenwood in bewilderment, got to his feet, raised his hands over his head, and said, "You sure you got the right place?"

"Open up," Dortmunder said, gesturing with the machine gun at the second gate. Through there, in the detention block, arms could be seen waving through cell bars on both sides. Nobody in there knew what was going on exactly, but they all wanted to be part of it.

"Brother," cop number three told Dortmunder, "the hardest case we got in there is a Latvian sailor hit a bartender with a fifth of

Johnny Walker Red Label. Seven stitches. You sure you want one of our people?"

"Just open," Dortmunder told him.

The cop shrugged. "Anything you say."

Meanwhile, on the roof, Murch had started tossing detonator caps at the street. He wanted to make noise and confusion without killing anybody, which was easy the first couple of times but increasingly difficult as the street filled up with cops running around trying to figure out who was attacking who and from where.

In the precinct captain's office, on the second floor, the quiet evening had erupted into bedlam. The captain had gone home for the day, of course, and the prisoners upstairs had been given their evening meal. The lieutenant in charge had been relaxing down into that slow, quiet period of the day Dortmunder had been counting on. Suddenly people had started to run into his office.

The first one was the patrolman on the switchboard, who said, "Sir, the phone's gone dead."

"Oh? We'd better call the phone company to fix it pronto," the lieutenant said. He liked the word "pronto," it made him feel like Sean Connery. He reached for the phone, and there wasn't any sound. Then he became aware of the patrolman looking at him. "Oh," he said."Oh, yes." He put the phone back on its hook.

He was saved, momentarily, by the patrolman from the radio room, who came running in, looking bewildered, to say, "Sir, somebody's jamming our signal!"

"What?" the lieutenant had heard the words but hadn't comprehended their meaning.

"We can't broadcast and we can't receive."

"Something's broken," the lieutenant said. "That's all." He was worried, but he was damned if he was going to show it.

There was an explosion somewhere in the building.

The lieutenant leaped to his feet. "My God! What was that?"

"An explosion, sir," the switchboard patrolman said.

There was another explosion, and then there was a third.

A patrolman ran in, shouting, "Bombs! In the street!"

The lieutenant took a quick step to the right and then a quick step to the left. "Revolution," he babbled. "It's a revolution. They always go for the police stations first."

Another patrolman ran in, shouting, "There's tear gas in the stairwell, sir! And somebody's blown up the stairs between the fourth and fifth floors!"

"Mobilize!" screamed the lieutenant. "Call the governor! Call the mayor!" He snatched up the phone. "Hello, hello! Emergency!"

Another patrolman ran in. "Sir, there's a fire in the street."

"A what? A what?"

"A bomb hit a parked car. It's burning out there."

"Bombs? Bombs?" The lieutenant looked at the phone he was holding, then flung it away as though it had grown teeth. "Break out the riot guns!" he shouted. "Get all personnel in the building to the first floor, on the double. I want a volunteer to carry a message through the enemy lines!"

"A message, sir? To whom?"

"To the phone company, who else? I've got to call the captain!"

Upstairs in the detention block, Kelp was using the handcuffs to lock the cops' wrists behind their backs and the lengths of white cloth to gag them. Chefwick, having taken the keys to the cells from the desk, was unlocking the second cell on the right. Dortmunder and Greenwood were keeping alert, machine guns at the ready, while the clamor from the other cells increasd to near pandemonium.

Inside the cell Chefwick was opening, staring out at them all with the blank astonished delight of someone whose most outlandish wish-fulfillment fantasy has just come true, was a short, wiry, bearded, dirty old man in a black raincoat, brown trousers, and gray sneakers. His hair was long and shaggy, and so was his beard.

Chefwick opened the cell door. The old man said, "Me? Me, fellows?"

Greenwood went in, his machine gun carried casually in his left hand, and headed directly to the rear wall, brushing by the old man. The rear wall of the cell, being the outer wall of the building, was stone. Greenwood stood on tiptoe, reached up to just under the ceiling, and plucked out a small piece of stone that didn't look any different from any other part of the wall. He then reached in behind where this stone had been.

Kelp and Dortmunder, meantime, had hustled the three cops into the detention block and were waiting just outside the cell to put the cops in there.

Greenwood, his fingers in the hole in the wall, looked around at Dortmunder and gave a very glassy smile.

Dortmunder said, "What's the matter?"

"I don't under—" Greenwood's fingers were scrabbling around in the hole like spiders. Faintly from outside they could hear detonator caps going off.

Dortmunder said, "It isn't there?"

The old man, looking from face to face, said, "Me, fellows?"

Greenwood looked at him, sudden suspicion on his face. "You? Did you take it?"

The old man suddenly looked fearful. "Me? Me?"

"He didn't take it," Dortmunder said. "Look at him. He couldn't reach up there, for one thing."

Greenwood was beginning to get wild. "Who, then?" he said. "If not him, who?"

"The thing was there almost two months," Dortmunder said. He turned to Kelp. "Ungag one of them."

Kelp did so, and Dortmunder said to the cop, "When did this bird take occupancy?"

"Three a.m. this morning."

Greenwood said to Dortmunder, "I swear I put it—"

"I believe you," Dortmunder said. He sounded tired. "Somebody found it, that's all. Let's get out of here." He walked out of the cell, a troubled Greenwood coming behind him, frowning

The old man said, "What about me, fellows? You're takin' me along, ain'tcha, fellows?"

Dortmunder looked at him, then said, "Maybe you ought to stay here." He turned to the cops. "Go on in there with him."

The cops went in, Chefwick locked the door, and they left. There was no one at all at the head of the stairs, but they tossed two more tear gas grenades down there anyway. They hurried up the stairs to the roof, following the getaway plan just as though they had the Balabomo Emerald, and at the top Dortmunder dropped three detonators down the stairwell and shut the door.

Murch was already in the helicopter, and when he saw them coming he started the engine. The rotors began to spin and roar, and Dortmunder and the others ran through the wind to the side of the helicopter and climbed in.

Down on the first floor, the lieutenant paused in his supervising of the handing out of riot guns to listen to the unmistakable *chuff-chuff* of a nearby helicopter. "My God!" he whispered. "They must be supplied by Fidel Castro!"

As soon as everybody was aboard, Murch lifted the helicopter into the air, curving north and west over Harlem again, then dropping low over the Hudson River and heading south.

Murch was the only one who didn't know about the missing emerald, but when he saw that no one was happy he began to understand that something must have gone wrong. He kept trying to find out what, paying no attention to the controls or the dark water rushing by just below the flimsy craft they were in, so Dortmunder finally put his cupped hands against Murch's ear and bellowed out the facts.

They were on the ground again at the starting point at ten past eight. They all climbed out feeling stiff, and walked over to the Lincoln. There was very little talk on the drive back to Manhattan. They let Dortmunder off at his apartment and he went upstairs, made himself a bourbon on the rocks, sat down on the sofa, and looked at his briefcase full of encyclopedia brochures.

Dortmunder sighed.

PHASE FOUR

"NICE DOGGY," DORTMUNDER SAID.

The German shepherd wasn't buying any. He stood in front of the stoop, head down, eyes up, jaws slightly open to show his pointy teeth, and said, "Rrrrrr," softly in his throat every time Dortmunder made a move to come down off the porch. The message was clear. The damn dog was going to hold him here until somebody in authority came home.

"Look, doggy," Dortmunder said, trying to be reasonable, "all I did was ring the bell. I didn't break in, I didn't steal anything, I just rang the bell. But nobody's home, so now I want to go to some other house and ring the bell."

"Rrrrrr," said the dog.

Dortmunder pointed to his attaché case. "I'm a salesman, doggy," he said. "I sell encyclopedias. Books. Big books. Doggy? Do you know from books?"

The dog didn't say anything. He just kept watching.

"All right now, dog," Dortmunder said, being very stern. "Enough is enough. I don't have time to fool around with you. I have places to go. I've got to make my rent money. Now, I'm leaving here and that's all there is—" He took a firm step forward.

"Rrrrrrrr!" said the dog.

Dortmunder took a quick step back. *"Damn it,* dog!" he cried. "This is ridiculous!"

The dog didn't think so. He was one of those by-the-book dogs. Rules were rules, and Dortmunder didn't rate any special favors.

Dortmunder looked around, but the neighborhood was as empty as the dog's mind. It was not quite two in the afternoon, September the seventh—three weeks and two days since the raid on the police station—and the neighborhood children were all in school. The neighborhood fathers were all at work, of course, and God alone knew where all the neighborhood mothers were. Wherever they were, Dortmunder was alone, trapped by a stupid overzealous dog on the porch of a middle-aged but comfortable home in a middle-aged but comfortable residential section of Long Island, about forty miles from Manhattan. Time was money, he had none to spare of either, and the dumb dog was costing him both.

"There ought to be a law against dogs," Dortmunder said darkly. "Dogs like you in particular. You ought to be locked up somewhere."

The dog was unmoved.

"You're a menace to society," Dortmunder told him. "You're lucky I don't sue the hell out of you. Your owner, I mean."

Threats had no effect. This was clearly the kind of dog that would accept no responsibility. "I was just following orders," that would be his line.

Movement attracted Dortmunder's attention, and he looked down the block to see a brown Checker sedan with MD plates rolling slowly in his direction. The Checker's horn honked. An arm waved from its side window, and there was Kelp's head, also sticking out the side window. Kelp shouted, "Hey, Dortmunder!"

"Right here," Dortmunder shouted back. He felt like a sailor stranded on a desert island for twenty years when a ship finally heaves to just offshore. He waved his attaché case over his head. "Here I am! Right here!"

The Checker heaved to just offshore, and Kelp called, "Come on over here. I got news for you."

Dortmunder pointed. "Dog," he said. "The dog won't let me off the porch."

Kelp frowned. "How come?"

"How do I know?" Dortmunder said in irritation.

Kelp got out of the car, and on the other side Greenwood climbed out, and the two of them slowly approached. The dog watched the new arrivals warily.

Greenwood pointed at the animal and said, "Sit."

The dog cocked his head, puzzled.

More firmly, Greenwood said, *"Sit."*

Still puzzled, the dog stood looking at Greenwood. Who, he was clearly thinking, was this stranger who knew how to speak Dog?

"I told you to sit," Greenwood said, "and I mean *sit.*"

The dog could almost be seen to shrug. When in doubt, obey orders. It sat.

"Come on," Greenwood said to Dortmunder. "He won't bother you now." Dortmunder started down off the porch. "Just don't act afraid of him."

Dortmunder said, "It isn't an act."

The dog looked at Dortmunder, at Greenwood, at Dortmunder, at Greenwood. "Stay," said Greenwood.

Dortmunder stopped.

"Not you," Greenwood said. "The dog."

"Oh." Dortmunder came down off the stoop and walked on by the dog, who glowered at his left knee as though to be sure he'd remember it the next time they met.

"Stay," said Greenwood again, pointing at the dog, and then he turned around and all three got aboard the Checker, Dortmunder in back, and Kelp drove them away from there. The dog, still in the same place before the porch, watched them carefully until they were out of sight. Possibly memorizing the license plate.

"I appreciate that," Dortmunder said. He was leaning forward with his forearms on the top of the front seat.

"Any time," Kelp said airily.

"What are you two doing out here anyway?" Dortmunder asked.

"We're looking for you," Kelp said. "You said you'd probably hit this neighborhood today, and we've got news for you. Anyway, Greenwood has."

Dortmunder looked at Greenwood. "Good news?"

"The best," Greenwood said. "Remember that emerald job?"

Dortmunder sat back as though the front seat had suddenly filled with snakes. "Take me back to the dog," he said. "I know when I'm well off."

"I don't blame you," Greenwood said. "I almost feel the same way. But damn it, I've put so much effort into that stinking emerald, I hate to give up now. I had to change my name, pay out of my own pocket for a complete line of new identity papers, renounce an entire bookful of telephone numbers, give up a really good apartment at the kind of rent you can't get anymore in New York, and we still don't even have the emerald."

"That's the whole point," Dortmunder told him. "Look what's happened to you already. You really want to go back for more?"

"I want to finish the job."

"It'll finish you," Dortmunder said. "I'm not usually what you'd call the superstitious type, but if ever there was such a thing as a jinxed job, this one is it."

Kelp said, "Will you at least listen to what Greenwood has to say? It seems he held out on us a little."

"I didn't hold out," Greenwood said. "Not exactly. The thing was, I was embarrassed. I got played for a sucker, and I hated to tell anybody until I could make up for it. You know what I mean?"

Dortmunder looked at him. "You told Prosker," he said.

Greenwood hung his head. "It seemed like a good idea at the time," he mumbled. "He was my attorney and all. And the way he explained it, if something went wrong while you guys were springing me, he could get his hands on the emerald anyway and turn it over to Iko and use the money to try to spring the whole bunch of us."

Dortmunder made a sour face. "He didn't sell you any gold-mine stock, did he?"

"It seemed reasonable," Greenwood said plaintively. "Who knew he'd turn out to be a thief?"

"Everybody," Dortmunder said.

"The point is," Kelp said, "now we know who has the emerald."

"It's been over three weeks," Dortmunder said. "How come it took so long to deliver the news?"

Greenwood said, "I wanted to try to get the emerald back myself. I figured you guys did enough, you went through three operations, you sprang me out of prison, I owed it to you to get it back from Prosker myself."

Dortmunder gave him a cynical look.

"I swear," Greenwood said. "I wasn't going to keep it for myself, I was going to turn it over to the group."

"That's neither here nor there," Kelp said. "The point is, we know Prosker's got it, and he's holding on to it till the heat's off and then he'll peddle it to the highest bidder. So all we got to do is go take it away from Prosker, turn it over to Iko, and we're back in business."

"If it was that easy," Dortmunder said, "Greenwood wouldn't be here without the emerald."

"You're right," Greenwood said. "There's a little problem."

"A little problem," said Dortmunder.

"After we didn't find the emerald at the police station," Greenwood said, "I went looking for Prosker. That's what I've been doing the last three weeks. Two days ago, I found out where he was. The problem is, he's going to be a little bit difficult to get at. It's going to take more than one man."

Dortmunder lowered his head and put a hand over his eyes. "You might as well go ahead and tell me," he said.

Greenwood cleared his throat. "The day we knocked over the police station, Prosker committed himself to an insane asylum."

There was a long silence. Dortmunder didn't move. Then he sighed and lowered the hand from his eyes. He looked very tired. He tapped Kelp on the shoulder. "Kelp," he said.

Kelp looked in the rearview mirror. "Yeah?"

"Please take me back to the dog. Please."

Two DAYS LATER Dortmunder sat for one of his regular interviews with his New York probation officer, an overworked, balding man named Steen. Steen said, "Well, it looks as though you're really going straight this time, Dortmunder. That's very good."

"I've learned my lesson," Dortmunder said.

"It's never too late to learn," Steen agreed. "But let me give you one little piece of friendly advice. In my experience, the thing you've got to look out for most of all is bad companions."

Dortmunder nodded.

"Now," Steen said, "that may seem like a strange thing to say to a man your age, but the fact of the matter is, more recidivism is caused by bad companions than just about any other factor. You want to remember that, in case any of your old chums ever come to you with that just-one-more job that's supposed to put you on Easy Street."

"I've already turned 'em down," Dortmunder said heavily. "Don't you worry."

Steen looked blank. "You what?"

"I said no."

Steen shook his head. "No what?"

"No, I wouldn't do it," Dortmunder told him. He looked at Steen and saw that Steen remained unenlightened, so he told him, "The just-one-more-job guys. I told them no dice."

Steen gaped at him. "You were approached? For a robbery?"

"Sure."

"And you turned it down?"

"Damn right," Dortmunder said. "There comes a point when you got to give anything up as a bad job."

"And," said Steen, so stunned his voice was cracking, "you're reporting it to *me?*"

"Well, you brought it up," Dortmunder reminded him.

"That's right," Steen said in a vague sort of way. "I did, didn't I?" He gazed around the bleak battered office with its grimy furniture and the faded inspirational posters on the walls, and his eyes were shining with an unaccustomed glow. He could be seen to think, It *does* work! The probation system, the paperwork, the irritation, the crummy offices, the surly parolees, by God, it *works!* A parolee has actually been approached to take part in a crime, and has actually turned it down, and has even reported it to his probation officer! Life *does* have meaning after all!

Gradually Dortmunder began to grow impatient. He cleared his throat. He tapped his knuckles on the desk. He developed a coughing fit. Finally he said, "If you don't need me anymore—"

Steen's eyes slowly refocused on him. "Dortmunder," he said, "I want you to know something. I want you to know you have made me a very happy man."

Dortmunder had no idea what he was talking about. "Well, that's good," he said. "Anytime I can help out."

Steen cocked his head to one side, like that dog the other day. "I don't suppose," he said, "you'd want to tell me the names of the people who contacted you?"

Dortmunder shrugged. "It was just some people," he said. He was a little sorry now he'd brought it up. Usually he wouldn't have, but this emerald business had gotten him rattled over the last few months, and the habits of a lifetime were gradually going to hell. "Just some people I used to know," he amplified, to make it clear he wasn't saying any more than that.

Steen nodded. "I understand," he said. "You still have to draw the line somewhere. Still, this has been a red-letter day for crime prevention, I want you to know that. And for me."

"That's good," Dortmunder said. He wasn't following, but it didn't matter.

Steen looked down at the papers on his desk. "Well, let's see. Just the usual questions left, I guess. Are you still going to that machinists' school?"

"Oh, sure," Dortmunder said. There was no machinists' school.

"And you're still being supported by your cousin-in-law, is that right? Mr. Kelp."

"Sure," Dortmunder said.

"You're lucky to have such relatives," Steen said. "Well, that's about it for this time. Keep away from those bad companions."

"I'll do that," Dortmunder said and went home, and found them all sitting around his living room, drinking his booze. He shut the door and said, "Who let you birds in?"

"I did," said Chefwick. "I hope you don't mind." He was drinking ginger ale.

"Why should I mind?" Dortmunder said. "It isn't like it's a private apartment or anything."

"We wanted to talk to you," Kelp said. He was drinking Dortmunder's bourbon, and he held out a glass of the stuff, saying, "I brought out a glass for you."

Dortmunder took it and said, "I'm not breaking into any insane asylum. You people want to, you probably ought to be there anyway, so go right ahead."

Kelp said, "All the rest of us are in it, Dortmunder. Everybody's willing to give it one more try except you."

"What do you need me for?" Dortmunder said. "Do it without me. You've got four men."

Kelp said, "You're the planner, Dortmunder, you're the organizer. We need you to run things."

Dortmunder said, "You could do it yourself. Or Greenwood. Chefwick could do it. I don't know, maybe even Murch could do it."

Murch said, "Not as good as you."

Dortmunder thought about that for a few seconds, then nodded heavily and said to the room at large, "I hope you guys'll be very happy here. I'll let you know where to send my stuff." He turned and headed for the door.

Kelp said, "Hey! Wait a second!"

Chefwick ran around in front of Dortmunder. "I understand how you feel," he said, "but we need you. It's as simple as that. With you running things we can get this job done once and for all."

Dortmunder looked at him. "Job? Jobs, you mean. Do you realize we've already pulled three heists for that stinking emerald, and we still don't have it? And no matter how many heists we pull, our take is still the same."

Greenwood had come over to the door now, where Chefwick and Dortmunder were standing, and he said, "No, it isn't. At first it was thirty a man, then for the police station it went up to thirty-five."

Kelp came over too, saying, "And the Major will go up again, Dortmunder, I already talked to him. Another five thousand a man. That's forty G's for walking into an insane asylum and walking back out with crazy-like-a-fox Prosker."

Dortmunder turned to him. "No, it isn't," he said. "That would be the fourth heist, and that one's a kidnapping, which is a federal offense and they can give you the chair for it. But even just talking economics, that's the fourth heist, and four heists for forty grand is ten thousand dollars a caper, and I haven't worked a job for ten grand since I was fourteen years old."

Chefwick said, "I think we should put our cards on the table."

Greenwood shrugged. "I suppose so," he said.

Murch, the only one still seated and still sipping away at a beer, called, "I told you that in the first place."

Kelp said, "I just didn't want to put pressure on him, that's all."

Dortmunder, looking around at everybody with grim suspicion, said, "What now?"

Chefwick told him. "Iko won't finance us without you."

Greenwood said, "He's sold on you, Dortmunder, he knows you're the best man around."

"Damn," said Dortmunder.

Kelp said, "All we want you to do is look at it. We could take the train up there tomorrow, if you're willing. After that, if you say no go, we won't bother you anymore."

They all stood there and watched Dortmunder and waited for him to say something. He glowered at the floor, chewed his knuckle, then walked back to the table where he'd put down his bourbon. He took a healthy swallow, and turned to look at them all.

Greenwood said, "You'll go take a look at the place?"

"I suppose so," Dortmunder said. He didn't sound happy.

Everybody else was happy. "That's great!" Kelp said.

"It'll give me chance to get my head examined," Dortmunder said and finished his bourbon.

"TICKETS," SAID THE CONDUCTOR.

"Air," said Dortmunder.

The conductor stood in the aisle. He said, "What?"

"There's no air in this car," Dortmunder told him. "The windows won't open and there isn't any air."

"You're right," the conductor said. "Could I have your ticket?"

"I need air," Dortmunder said.

"You could get off the train at the next stop," the conductor said. "Lots of air on the platforms."

Kelp, sitting next to Dortmunder, tugged his sleeve and said, "Forget it. You're not gonna get anywhere."

Dortmunder looked at the conductor's face and saw that Kelp was right. He shrugged and handed over his ticket, and Kelp did the same, and the conductor made holes in them. He did the same for Murch, across the aisle, and for Greenwood and Chefwick in the next seat back. The five were the only occupants of this car. The conductor left by the door at the far end.

Dortmunder looked around and said, "Anybody carrying?"

Kelp looked startled, saying, "Dortmunder! You don't bump off a guy for no air!"

"Who said anything about bump off? Isn't anybody heavy?"

"Me," said Greenwood, and from inside his Norfolk jacket—he was the spiffiest dresser in the group—he produced a Smith & Wesson .32 caliber revolver with a two-inch barrel. He handed it over to Dortmunder, butt first, and Dortmunder said, "Thanks." He took the gun, reversed it to hold it by the barrel and chamber, and said to Kelp, "Excuse me." Then he leaned across Kelp and punched a hole in the window.

"Hey!" said Kelp.

"Air," said Dortmunder. He turned and handed the gun back to Greenwood, saying, "Thanks again."

Greenwood looked a little dazed. "Anytime," he said and looked at the butt, studying it for scratches. There weren't any, and he put the weapon away again.

It was Sunday, the tenth of September, and they were on just about the only passenger train running in this direction. The sun was shining outside, the fresh air blowing in through the hole Dortmunder had made was pleasantly scented with the odors of late summer. All in all it was the sort of leisurely excursion you just can't find too often in the twentieth century.

"How much longer?" Dortmunder said.

Kelp looked at his watch. "Another ten or fifteen minutes," he said. "You'll be able to see the place from the train. On this side. It used to be a factory."

Dortmunder nodded.

The train stopped just then and they looked out at some old men, who looked back. The train started up again, and Kelp said, "We're the next stop. New Mycenae. It's named after an old Greek city."

"I don't want to know why," Dortmunder said.

Kelp looked at him. "What's the matter with you?"

"Nothing," said Dortmunder.

A few minutes later the conductor popped in to call, "Next stop New McKinney," then disappeared again.

Dortmunder said, "I thought you said the next stop was us."

"It's supposed to be," said Kelp. He looked out the window and said, "Sure it is. There's the place."

Dortmunder looked and saw a large sprawling red brick building off to the right a ways. A tall chain-link fence enclosed the grounds, with metal signs attached to it at intervals. Dortmunder squinted, but he couldn't make out what they said. He asked Kelp, "What do the signs say?"

"Danger. High voltage."

Dortmunder looked at him, but Kelp was gazing out the window, refusing to meet his eye. Dortmunder shook his head and looked out at the asylum again, seeing a set of tracks that curved away from the tracks that their train was on and angled around to go under the electrified fence and across the asylum grounds. The tracks were orange with rust, and within the grounds they'd been incorporated into the design of a formal flower bed. A couple of dozen people in white pajamas and white bathrobes were strolling around the grass in there, and they were being watched by what looked like armed guards in blue uniforms.

"So far," Dortmunder said, "I wouldn't say it looks easy."

"Give it a chance," Kelp said.

The train had started to slow as the asylum moved into the background, and now the door at the far end of the car opened again and the conductor stuck his head in to call, "New McKinney! *Newwww* McKinney!"

Kelp and Dortmunder frowned at each other. They looked out the window, and the platform was just edging into sight. The sign on it said, NEW MYCENAE.

"New McKinney!" yelled the conductor.

"I think I hate him," Dortmunder said to Kelp. He got to his feet, and the other four got up after him. They went down the aisle as the train creaked to a stop, and the conductor glowered at them as they disembarked.

As the train started up and stumbled slowly away, Dortmunder and the others walked through the station and out the other side.

"We can walk it," Kelp told Dortmunder. "It isn't far."

It wasn't. They walked about seven blocks and came to the main entrance, with a sign that read, CLAIR DE LUNE SANITARIUM. The electrified fence was set back from the road here, with another chain-link fence five feet in front of it. Two armed guards sat on folding chairs inside the main gate, chatting together.

Dortmunder stopped and looked at it all. "Who've they got in there?" he said. "Rudolf Hess?"

"It's what they call a maximum security bughouse," Kelp told him. "For rich nuts only. Most of them in there are what they call criminally insane, but their family has enough money to keep them out of some state asylum."

"I've wasted a whole day," Dortmunder said. "I could of sold half a dozen encyclopedias today. Sunday's a good day for encyclopedias, you got the husband at home, you tell the husband you'll throw in a bookcase that comes unassembled and he can put it together himself, and he'll hand you his wallet."

Chefwick said, "You mean it can't be done?"

"Armed guards," Dortmunder said. "Electrified fences. Not to speak of the inmates. You want to mix with *them*?"

Greenwood said, "I was hoping you'd see some way. There oughta be a way to get in there."

"Sure there's a way to get in there," Dortmunder said. "You drop in with a parachute. Now let's see you get *out*."

Kelp said, "We got an hour to kill before our train back. We might as well walk around. Maybe we'll see something."

Dortmunder shrugged. "All right, we'll walk around."

They walked around, and they didn't see anything encouraging. When they got to the rear of the building, they had to leave the blacktopped road and walk across a scrubby field, stepping over the rusty orange tracks.

Murch said, "Look, one of the loonies is waving at us." It was true. One of the figures in white stood by the flower bed and waved at them, and he was smiling to beat the band. They started to wave back to him, and then Greenwood said, "Hey! That's Prosker!"

Everybody stood there with his hand up in the air. Chefwick said, "So it is." He pulled his hand down, and everybody else followed suit. In there by the flower bed Prosker waved and waved, and then he bent over and slapped his knee and went into a fit of laughter. He tried to wave and laugh at the same time and almost fell over.

Dortmunder said, "Greenwood, let me borrow it again."

"No, Dortmunder," said Kelp. "We need him to give us the emerald."

"Except we can't get at him," Murch said. "So it doesn't make any difference."

"We'll see about that," said Dortmunder, and he shook his fist at Prosker, who as a result laughed so hard he sat down on the ground. A guard came over and looked at him, but didn't do anything.

Kelp said, "I hate it that we're beaten by a louse like that."

"We aren't," Dortmunder said grimly.

They all looked at him. Kelp said, "You mean—?"

"I mean he can't laugh at me," Dortmunder said. "I've had enough, that's all."

"You mean we're going in after him?"

Dortmunder looked at Kelp. "You go tell Iko to put us back on the payroll." He looked back at Prosker, who was now rolling on the ground, clutching his ribs and beating his heels into the turf. "If he thinks he can stay in that place," Dortmunder said, "he's crazy."

WHEN THE EBONY MAN showed Kelp in, Major Iko was leaning over the pool table sighting down the cue like a sniper with a musket.

"Well?" he barked, straightening up. "It's been two weeks since Dortmunder agreed to do the job. Money keeps going out, but no emerald ever comes in."

"We're ready again," Kelp said, and pulled a tattered list from his pocket. "This is the stuff we need."

"No helicopters this time, I hope."

"No, it's too far from New York. But we thought about it."

"I'm sure you did," the Major said dryly and took the list.

Kelp said, "Mind if I sink a couple?"

"Go ahead," the Major said, looking at the paper.

Kelp picked up the cue, dropped the three, and the Major screamed, "A *locomotive?*"

Kelp nodded and put the cue down again. Turning to face the Major, he said, "Dortmunder thought there might be some question about that."

"Question!" The Major looked as though he'd been poleaxed.

"We don't actually need a big diesel locomotive," Kelp said. "What we need is something that runs on standard gauge tracks under its own power. But it's got to be bigger than a handcar."

"Bigger than a handcar," the Major said. He backed up till his legs hit a chair, on which he sat. The list hung forgotten in his hand.

"Just a small locomotive. Chefwick is our railroad expert," Kelp said. "So if you want to talk things over with him, he'll let you know exactly what we need."

"Of course," the Major said.

"He could come over tomorrow afternoon," Kelp suggested.

"Of course," the Major said.

Kelp frowned at him. "You okay, Major?"

"Of course," the Major said.

"Well." Kelp looked around a little helplessly. He felt the need to say something. "I'll call you later on about when Chefwick should come over," he said, and backed to the doorway.

"Of course," the Major said.

MAJOR IKO STOOD beside the truck, forehead furrowed with worry. "I've got to give this locomotive back," he said. "Don't lose it, don't hurt it. It's only borrowed."

Chefwick said, "You have my personal word of honor, Major, that no harm will come to this locomotive. I think you know my feeling about locomotives."

The Major nodded, somewhat reassured, but still worried. A muscle in his cheek was jumping.

"Time to go," Dortmunder said. "See you later, Major."

Murch drove, of course, and Dortmunder sat beside him, in the cab of the truck, while the other three got in back with the locomotive. The Major stood watching them and Murch waved to him and drove the truck down the dirt road from the deserted farmhouse and out to the highway, where he turned north, toward New Mycenae.

It was a very anonymous truck, with an ordinary red cab and a trailer completely swathed in olive drab tarpaulins, and no one they passed gave them a second look. But underneath the tarps lurked a very gaudy truck indeed, its sides combining brightly painted pictures of railroading scenes with foot-high red letters running the length of the trailer and reading, FUN ISLAND AMUSEMENT PARK—TOM THUMB. And underneath, in slightly smaller black lettering, THE FAMOUS LOCOMOTIVE.

What strings the Major had pulled, what bribes he'd paid to get this locomotive, Dortmunder neither knew nor cared. He'd gotten it within two weeks of the order, and now Dortmunder was going to go wipe that laugh from Attorney Prosker's face. Oh, yes, he would.

This was the second Sunday in October, sunny but cool, with little traffic on the secondary roads they were traveling, so they made good time to New Mycenae. Murch drove them through town and out on the road toward the Clair de Lune Sanitarium. They rode on by, and Dortmunder glanced at it as they went past. Peaceful. Same two guards chatting at the main gate. Everything the same.

They traveled another three miles down the same road, and then Murch turned right. Half a mile later he pulled off to the side of the road and stopped, leaving the engine running. This was a woodsy, hilly area, without houses or other buildings. A hundred yards ahead stood a set of white crossbars, warning of a railroad crossing.

Dortmunder looked at his watch. "Due in four minutes," he said.

During the last few weeks, he and the others had been all over this territory. They knew which roads were well traveled and which were generally empty. They knew where a lot of the dirt side roads went, they knew what the local police cars looked like and where they tended to spend their Sunday afternoons, they knew four or five good places in the neighborhood to hide out with a truck, and they knew the railroad schedule.

The train they were waiting for was almost five minutes late. But at last they did hear it hooting in the distance, and then slowly it appeared and began to trundle by, the same passenger train Dortmunder and the others had ridden up here some weeks ago.

"There's your window," Murch said and pointed at a holed window gliding by.

"I didn't think they'd fix it," Dortmunder said.

When the final car went by and the track was once again clear, Murch looked at Dortmunder and said, "How long?"

"Give it a couple minutes."

They knew the next scheduled occupant of that track would be a southbound freight at nine-thirty tonight. On Sundays most trains stayed home.

After a minute or two of silence, Dortmunder dropped his Camel butt on the truck floor and stepped on it. "We can go now," he said.

"Right." Murch put the truck in gear and eased forward to the tracks. He jockeyed back and forth till he was crosswise on the road, blocking it, and lined up on the tracks and then Dortmunder got out and went around back to open the rear doors. Greenwood and Kelp at once began to push forward a wide metal ramp with a set of railroad tracks on it. The far end clanged on the rails below, and Greenwood came down to help Dortmunder get the ramp's tracks lined up with the railroad company's tracks. Then Greenwood waved to Kelp on the tailgate, who turned around and waved into the interior, and a few seconds later a locomotive came out.

And what a locomotive! This was Tom Thumb, the *famous* locomotive, or at any rate an exact replica of the tiny Tom Thumb, built back in 1830 and the first regularly working American-built steam locomotive. Well, maybe not exactly exact, since the original Tom Thumb ran on steam from a coal-fired furnace while the replica ran on gasoline in an engine from a 1962 Ford. But it looked legit, something like a flatcar with a smokestack on it, and that was the important thing.

The locomotive came complete with its own coal tender, a wooden affair like a box on wheels, empty except for an arms case and a green-handled push broom in one corner.

Chefwick was at the controls as Tom Thumb came slowly down the ramp, and he was in seventh heaven, smiling and beaming around in sheer delight. In his mind he was running a model train *in person.* He grinned out at Dortmunder and said, "Toot, toot."

"Sure thing," Dortmunder said. "Up a little more."

Chefwick eased Tom Thumb forward a few more feet.

"That's good right there," Dortmunder said and went back to help slide the ramp back up into the truck. They shut the truck doors and hollered to Murch, who drove the truck off the tracks and stopped it beside the road. So far there'd been no other traffic at all.

Chefwick and Greenwood and Kelp were wearing divers' wet suits, the black rubber gleaming in the sun. They weren't wearing the face masks or gloves or headpieces yet, but otherwise they were completely encased in rubber. So much for electrified fences.

Dortmunder and Greenwood and Kelp all climbed aboard the tender, Chefwick said, "Toot, toot," and Tom Thumb began to perk along the track.

The other wet suit was waiting for Dortmunder on the arms case.

He put it on and said, "Remember. When we go through, keep your hands over your faces."

They reached the Clair de Lune Sanitarium in no time. Chefwick pulled to a stop just before the turnoff where the old spur track angled away toward the sanitarium. Greenwood jumped down, threw the switch beside the tracks, and then climbed back aboard.

It had taken two nights of oiling and straining and heaving to get the old switch to work again. Rust had been the only problem here, and the switch now turned like a dream.

They all put on their headpieces and gloves and face masks, and Chefwick accelerated over the bumpy orange track toward the sanitarium fencing. Tom Thumb, tender and all, was still lighter than the Ford from which his engine had come, and he accelerated like a go-cart, hitting sixty before he hit the fence.

Snap! Sparks, sputters, smoke. Live wires whipping back and forth. Tom Thumb's wheels shrieking and squealing along the twisty old rails, then shrieking even louder when Chefwick applied the brakes. They'd breached the fence like a sprinter breasting the tape, and now they screamed and scraped to a stop in the flower bed, surrounded by chrysanthemums.

In the office on the opposite side of the building, Chief Administrator Dr. Panchard L. Whiskum sat at his desk rereading the piece he'd just written for the *American Journal of Applied Pan-Psychotherapy* entitled, "Instances of Induced Hallucination among Staff Members of Mental Hospitals," when a white-jacketed male nurse ran in shouting, "Doctor! There's a strange-looking locomotive in the garden!"

Dr. Whiskum looked at the male nurse. He looked at his manuscript. He looked at the male nurse. He said, "Sit down, Foster. Let's talk about it."

In the garden, Dortmunder and Greenwood and Kelp had emerged from the tender in wet suits and masks, carrying tommy guns. All over the lawn, patients and guards and attendants were running around in circles, shouting at each other, grabbing each other, bumping into each other. Bedlam was in bedlam.

Dortmunder pointed his tommy gun in the air and let go with a burst, and the silence after that was like the silence in a cafeteria just after somebody has dropped a thousand metal trays on a tile floor. Silent. Very silent.

The lawn was full of eyes, all of them huge. Dortmunder looked among them and finally found Prosker's. He pointed the tommy gun at Prosker and called, "Prosker! Get over here!"

Prosker kept on standing there, pretending Dortmunder wasn't looking at him. Dortmunder called, "Do I shoot your ankles off and have somebody carry you? Get over here."

But Prosker continued to stand there, feigning innocence, until a guard near him took a quick step and shoved him, shouting, "Will you get over there? Who knows if his aim is any good? You want to kill innocent people?"

A chorus of yeahs followed that remark, and the tableau of people turned itself into a sort of bucket brigade, pushing Prosker on from hand to hand all across the lawn to the locomotive.

When he got there, Prosker suddenly became voluble. "I'm not a well man!" he cried. "I've had illnesses, my memory's gone. Why would I be here if I wasn't a sick man. I tell you, my memory's gone, I don't know anything about anything."

"Just get up here," Dortmunder said. "We'll remind you."

Very reluctantly, with much pushing and pulling, Prosker got up into the tender. The others held him while Dortmunder told the crowd to stay where it was until they made their escape. "Also," he said, "send somebody to put that switch back after we're gone. We don't want to derail any trains, do we?"

A hundred heads shook no.

Dortmunder told Chefwick, "Back her up."

The locomotive backed slowly out of the flower bed. Dortmunder and Kelp and Greenwood surrounded Prosker, grabbing him by the elbows and lifting him a few inches into the air. He hung there, pressed in by wet suits on all sides, his slippered feet waggling inches above the floor, and said, "Why are you doing this?"

"So you don't get electrocuted," Greenwood told him. "We're about to back through live wires. Cooperate, Mr. Prosker."

"Oh, I'll cooperate," Prosker said. "I'll cooperate."

"Yes, you will," Dortmunder said.

MURCH STOOD BESIDE the tracks, smoking a cigarette and thinking about railroad trains. In the last fifteen minutes one vehicle had gone by, an ancient green pickup truck with an ancient gray farmer at the wheel. A lot of metal things in the back had gone *klank* when the truck had crossed the track.

The other noise had come a minute or two later, being a brief stutter of tommy-gun fire, faint and faraway. Murch had listened carefully, but it hadn't been repeated. Probably just a warning, not an indication of trouble.

And now, here came something down the tracks. Murch leaned forward, peering, and it was good old Tom Thumb, backing down the rails.

Good. Murch flipped away the cigarette and ran over to the truck. He backed it around into position, and had it all ready when Tom Thumb arrived.

Chefwick eased the locomotive to a stop a few yards from the rear of the truck. While Greenwood stood guard over Prosker in the tender, the others, no longer in their wet suits, got the locomotive back up into the truck. Dortmunder shut the door and went around to get into the cab. Murch said, "Everything okay?"

"No problems."

"Nearest place?"

"Might as well," Dortmunder said, and Murch started off. Two miles later he made a sweeping left onto a narrow dirt road, one of the many they'd checked out in the past weeks. This one trailed off into the woods without ever getting much of anywhere, and finally petered out entirely, with no signs of man except a couple of meandering lines of stones that had once been boundary fences. Murch drove the truck in as far as he dared and stopped. "Listen to the silence," he said. It was late afternoon now, and the woods were without sound.

Dortmunder got out of the cab and walked back and opened the rear door. He and Murch climbed inside, then shut the door again. The interior of the trailer was lit by three frosted glass lights spaced along the top, and the place was very, very full of locomotive. Dortmunder and Murch went along to the front of the tender and stepped aboard. Prosker was sitting on the arms case, his innocent-amnesiac expression beginning to fray a bit at the edges. Kelp and Greenwood and Chefwick were standing around looking at him. There were no guns in sight.

Dortmunder went over to him and said, "Prosker, it's as simple as can be. If we're out the emerald, you're out of life. Cough it up."

Prosker looked up at Dortmunder, as innocent as a puppy who's missed the paper, and said, "I don't know what anybody's talking about. I'm a sick man."

Greenwood, in disgust, said, "Let's tie him to the tracks and run the train over him a few times. Maybe he'll talk then."

"I really doubt it," Chefwick said.

Dortmunder said, "Murch, Kelp, take him back and show him where we are."

"Right." Murch and Kelp took Prosker ungently by the elbows off the tender and to the rear of the truck. They pushed open a door and showed him the woods, with the sunlight making diagonal rays down through the foliage, and when he'd seen it they brought him back and sat him down once more on the arms case.

Dortmunder said, "We're in the woods. Am I right?"

"Yes," Prosker said and nodded. "We're in the woods."

"You remember about woods. That's good. Look up there in the driver's part of the locomotive. What's that leaning against the side?"

"A shovel," Prosker said.

"You remember shovels too," Dortmunder said. "I'm glad to hear that. Do you remember about graves?"

Prosker's innocent look crumpled a little more. "You wouldn't do that to a sick man," he said and put one hand feebly to his heart.

"No," Dortmunder said. "But I'd do it to a dead man." He let Prosker think about that for a few seconds and then said, "I'll tell you what's going to happen. We're going to stay here tonight, let the cops look for a locomotive someplace. Tomorrow morning we're going to leave. If you've handed over the emerald by then, we'll let you go and you can tell the law you escaped and you didn't know what it was all about. You won't mention any names, naturally. You know now we can get you wherever you hide, don't you?"

Prosker looked around at the locomotive and the tender and the hard faces. "Oh, yes," he said. "Yes, I know that."

"Good," Dortmunder said. "How are you with a shovel?"

Prosker looked startled. "A shovel?"

"In case you don't give us the emerald," Dortmunder explained. "We'll be leaving here without you in the morning, and we won't want anybody finding you, so you'll have to dig a hole."

Prosker licked his lips. "I," he said. He looked at the faces again. "I wish I could help you," he said, "but I'm a sick man. I had business reverses, an unfaithful mistress, trouble with the Bar Association. I had a breakdown. Why do you think I was in the sanitarium?"

"Hiding from us," Dortmunder said. "You committed yourself. If you could remember enough to commit yourself to a maximum security insane asylum, you can remember enough to turn over the emerald."

"I don't know what to say," Prosker said.

"That's all right," Dortmunder told him. "You've got all night to think it over."

"IS THIS DEEP ENOUGH?"

Dortmunder came over and looked at the hole, now knee-deep. Prosker was standing in it in his bathrobe, sweating. It was another sunny morning, with the crisp air of the woods in autumn, but Prosker looked like August and no air conditioner.

"That's shallow," Dortmunder told him. "You want a shallow grave? That's for mugs and college girls. Don't you have any self-respect?"

"You wouldn't really kill me," Prosker said, panting. "Not for mere money. A human life is more important than money, you have to have more humanity than—"

Greenwood came over and said, "Prosker, *I'd* kill you just out of general irritation. You conned me, Prosker, *you* conned *me*. You gave everybody a lot of trouble, and I'm to blame, and in a way I hope you keep pulling the lost memory bit right up till it's time to leave."

Prosker looked pained and glanced along the trail the truck had come on. Dortmunder saw that and said, "Forget it, Prosker. If you're stalling, waiting for a lot of motorcycle cops to come racing through the trees, just give it up. It isn't gonna happen. We picked this place because it's safe."

Prosker studied Dortmunder's face, and his own face had finally lost its pained-innocence expression, which was replaced by a look of calculation. He thought things over for a while and then flung the shovel down and briskly said, "All right. You people wouldn't kill me, you aren't murderers, but I can see you aren't going to give up. And it looks like I won't get rescued. Help me up out of here, and we'll talk." His whole manner had changed, his voice was deeper and more assured, his gestures quick and firm.

They gave him a hand out of the hole, and Greenwood said, "Don't be so sure about *me*, Prosker."

Dortmunder said, "The emerald."

Prosker turned to him. "Let me ask you a hypothetical question. Would you let me out of your sight before I handed over the emerald?"

"That isn't even funny," Dortmunder said.

"That's what I thought," Prosker said, and spread his hands, saying, "In that case, I'm sorry, but you'll never get it."

"I *am* gonna kill him!" Greenwood shouted, and Murch and Chefwick and Kelp strolled over to listen.

"Explain," Dortmunder said.

Prosker said, "The emerald is in my safe-deposit box in a bank in Manhattan on Fifth Avenue at Forty-sixth Street. It takes two keys to open the box, mine and the bank's. The bank regulations require that I go down into the vault accompanied only by an officer of the bank. The two of us have to be alone, and in the vault I have to sign their book, and they compare the signature with the specimen they keep on file. In other words, it has to be me and I have to be alone. If I gave you my word I wouldn't tell the bank officer to call the police while we were down there, you wouldn't trust me, and I wouldn't blame you. I wouldn't believe it myself. You can mount a perpetual watch on the bank if you wish, and kidnap and search me every time I go into it and come out, but that only means the emerald will stay where it is, useless to me and useless to you."

"Damn it," said Dortmunder.

Prosker shrugged. "The problem is insoluble," he said. "I put the stone where neither of us can get it."

Dortmunder said, "Where's your key?"

"To the box? In my office in town. Hidden. If you're thinking of sending someone in my place to forge my signature, let me be a good sport and warn you that two of the bank's officers know me fairly well. It's possible your forger wouldn't meet either of those two, but I don't think you should count on it."

"Damn it to *hell*," said Dortmunder.

Kelp said, "You know what this means, Dortmunder."

"I don't want to hear about it," Dortmunder said.

"We get to rob a bank," Kelp said.

"Just don't talk to me," Dortmunder said.

"I am sorry," Prosker said briskly, "but there's nothing to do." Greenwood hit him in the eye and he fell backward into the hole.

"Where's the shovel?" Greenwood said, but Dortmunder said, "Forget that. Get him up out of there and back in the truck."

Murch said, "Where we going?"

"Back to the city," Dortmunder said. "To make the Major's day."

PHASE FIVE

"I AM NOT HAPPY," the Major said.

"On the other hand," Dortmunder said, "I'm giggling all over."

They had arrived in time to interrupt the Major's lunch. Prosker, in dirt-stained pajamas and bathrobe, was sitting in the middle, where everyone could see him. Dortmunder and the others were grouped in a semicircle facing the Major.

Prosker said, "I continue to be sincerely sorry. It was shortsighted of me, but I moved in haste and now regret in leisure." He had a nicely developing black eye.

"Just shut up," Greenwood told him, "or I'll give you something else to regret."

"I hired you people in the first place," the Major said, "because you were supposed to be professionals, you were supposed to know how to do the job right."

Kelp, stung, said, "We are professionals, Major, and we did do the job right. We've done four jobs, and we did them *all* right. We got away with the emerald. We broke Greenwood out of jail. We got into the police station and back out again. And we kidnapped Prosker from the asylum. We've done everything right."

"Then why," the Major said angrily, "don't I have the Balabomo Emerald?" He held a hand out, empty palm up.

"Circumstances," Kelp said. "Circumstances have conspired against us."

The Major snorted.

Chefwick said, "Major, I won't speak for myself, but I will tell you that in my twenty-three years in this business I have gotten to know a large number of people engaged in it, and I assure you this team could not be improved upon anywhere."

"That's right," Kelp said. "Take Dortmunder. That man's a genius. He's sat down and worked out four capers in four months and brought every one of them off. There isn't another man in the business could have organized the Prosker kidnapping *alone*, much less the other three jobs."

Greenwood said, "And what Chefwick said about the rest of us goes double for Chefwick, because not only is he one of the best lockmen in the business, he is a first-class railroad engineer."

Chefwick blushed with pleasure and embarrassment.

The Major said, "Before you all start proposing toasts to one another, let me remind you that I *still do not have the Balabomo Emerald*."

"We know that, Major," said Dortmunder. "We still don't have our forty grand each either."

"You're getting it an inch at a time," the Major said angrily. "Do you realize I have so far paid out over twenty thousand dollars to you people in salaries and supplies? And what do I have to show for it? The operation was successful, but the patient died. It just won't do anymore, and that's final."

Dortmunder heaved himself to his feet. "That's all right by me, Major," he said. "I came down here willing to give it one more try, but tomorrow's an anniversary for me, I'll be out of the pen five months, and all I've done in all that time is run around after that emerald of yours. I'm sick of it, if you want the truth."

Kelp was on his feet, saying, "Dortmunder, don't get mad. You too, Major, there's no point everybody getting mad at everybody. This time we know for sure where the emerald is."

"If Prosker isn't lying," the Major said.

"Not me, Major," Prosker said.

"Shut up, you," Greenwood said.

"He isn't lying," Kelp said. "He knows if we get into that bank and there's no emerald, we'll come back to see him and this time we'll get rough."

"A smart lawyer knows when to tell the truth," Prosker said.

Greenwood leaned over and rapped Prosker on the knee. "You didn't shut up yet," he said.

Kelp was saying, "The point is, this time we know for sure where it is. We've got the only guy who could move it, and we're holding on to him. If we just do our jobs like we always do, the stone is ours. So we don't have to get mad at each other. One more caper and we're done, it's over, and everybody's still friends."

"A bank on Fifth Avenue in Manhattan," the Major said, "could very well be the most difficult job you've ever attempted."

"It definitely is," Dortmunder said. "The New York City banks got the most sophisticated alarm and camera systems in the world, plus grade-A guards, plus plenty of city cops just outside the door. Plus the traffic jam that midtown is always in the middle of, that you can't even make a getaway."

"You know all that," the Major said, "but you still want to go on with it?"

"We all do," Kelp said.

"It's a matter of honor," Murch said. "Like not gettin' passed on the right."

"I want to go on with it," Dortmunder said, "to the point that I want to look over the bank and see is there anything I can do about it. If I can't, then that's it."

The Major said, "You'll want to be on salary while making up your mind, is that it?"

Dortmunder looked at him. "You think I'm here for the two hundred a week?"

"I don't know anything for sure anymore," the Major said, "but there's no need to hurry. Take your time. I'm just upset, that's all, just as all of you are upset. And Kelp is right, we shouldn't fight among ourselves."

"Why not?" Prosker asked, smiling at them.

Greenwood leaned over and knuckled Prosker behind the ear. "You're starting up again," he said. "Better don't."

The Major pointed at Prosker. "What about him?"

Dortmunder said, "He told us where to find the key in his office, so we don't need him anymore. But we can't let him go yet. You got a basement here?"

The Major looked surprised. "You want *me* to hold him?"

"Temporarily," Dortmunder said.

"I don't like keeping him here, but I suppose you have no other place." The Major shrugged. "Very well then." He got on the intercom. Prosker sat in the middle of the room, smiling amiably at everybody, and a few minutes later two burly black men came in and saluted the Major.

"I'll be in touch, Major," Dortmunder said, and went on out, followed by the other four.

The Major, in his native language, told the two burly men to lock Prosker in the basement. They proceeded to obey, picking Prosker up by the elbows, when Prosker said conversationally to the Major, "A nice bunch of boys, but awfully naïve. Do you realize that it hasn't occurred to even one of them to ask himself if you really intend to pay off when you get the emerald?"

"Moka!" said the Major, and the burly men stopped. The Major said something else, and the burly men turned Prosker around and carried him back to his chair and sat him down in it. Then the burly men left the room.

Prosker sat there smiling.

The Major rose, "Did you give them any such idea?"

"Of course not," said Prosker.

"Why not?"

"Major," said Prosker, "you are black and I am white. You are a military man, I am an attorney. You are African, I am American. But somehow I sense a kinship between us that I just don't feel between myself and any of those five worthy gentlemen who just left."

The Major slowly sat down again behind his desk. "What's in it for you, Prosker?" he said.

Prosker smiled again. "I was hoping *you'd* tell *me*, Major," he said.

NINE O'CLOCK WEDNESDAY EVENING, two days after the meeting in Major Iko's office, Dortmunder walked into the O. J. Bar and Grill and nodded to Rollo, who said, "Good to see you again."

"Anybody else here?"

"Everybody except the beer. The other bourbon has your glass."

"Thanks." Dortmunder walked to the back room, where Kelp, Greenwood, and Chefwick were sitting at the round table under the green metal-shaded light. The table was covered with photographs and sketches and even blueprints of the branch of the Capitalists & Immigrants National Bank at 46th Street and Fifth Avenue.

Dortmunder sat down in front of the empty glass and poured some bourbon. He drank, put the glass down, and said, "Well? What do you think?"

"Bad," said Kelp.

"Rotten," said Greenwood.

"I agree," said Chefwick.

The door opened and Murch came in. Everybody said hello, and he said, "I made a mistake this time." He sat down in the vacant chair and said, "I took another route and it didn't work out. There was a lot of bad traffic there and I got caught by the lights a lot. Otherwise I'd of been here ahead of time."

Dortmunder said to him, "The question is, what do you think of this bank job?"

"Well, you're not going to make a getaway," Murch told him, "that's one thing for sure. Now, Forty-sixth Street is one way eastbound, and Fifth Avenue is one way southbound, which gives you only half the usual directions just to begin with. Then there's the problem of traffic lights. There's a traffic light at every intersection in Manhattan, and they're all red. On the avenues they've got staggered lights, but even so they're set for something like twenty-two miles an hour, and you just don't make a getaway at twenty-two miles an hour."

Dortmunder said, "What about at night?"

"Less traffic," Murch said, "but just as many lights. And there's always cops around midtown, so you don't want to run any lights, and even if you do, you'll get hit by a cab in the first ten blocks. Day or night, you don't make any getaway by car."

Greenwood said, "Helicopter again?"

Kelp answered him, saying, "I thought about that, but it's no good. It's a forty-seven-story building, with the bank on the ground floor."

Dortmunder nodded and said to Chefwick, "What about locks?"

Chefwick shook his head. "I haven't been down in the vault, but from what I could see on the main floor they don't have the kind of locks you pick. It would take blasting, probably some drilling. A lot of time, and a lot of noise."

Dortmunder nodded again and looked around at Kelp and Greenwood. "Any suggestions? Any ideas?"

Kelp said, "I thought about going through walls, but you take a look on that blueprint there, you'll see not only is the vault underground, surrounded by rocks and telephone cable and power lines and water pipes and God knows what all, but the walls are eight-foot-thick reinforced concrete with sensor alarms that ring at the local precinct house."

Greenwood said, "I spent some time working out what would happen if we just walked in and pulled guns and said this is a stick-up. But the downstairs entrance to the vault is always barred shut, and there's two barred doors with a room in between, and they never have both doors open at the same time. So even if we could work out some kind of getaway, there's no job there to make a getaway from."

"That's right," Dortmunder said. "I came to the same conclusion as you guys. I just wanted to hear did any of you think of something I missed."

"We didn't," Chefwick said.

"You mean that's it?" Kelp said. "We give it up? The job can't be done?"

"I didn't say that," Dortmunder said. "I didn't say the job couldn't be done. But what we've all said is that none of us could do it. It isn't a place for a frontal attack. We've hit up Iko for trucks, for a helicopter, for a locomotive, I'm sure we could hit him up for just about anything we'd need. But there's nothing he could give us that would do the trick. He could give us a tank and it wouldn't help."

"Because we'd never get away in it," Murch said.

"That's right."

"Though it might be fun to drive one," Murch said thoughtfully.

Kelp said, "Wait a minute. Dortmunder, if you say none of us could pull this job, you're saying the job can't be done. We're shot down whatever way you say it."

"No, we're not," Dortmunder said. "If none of the five of us could get that emerald out of that bank, that doesn't mean nobody in the world could do it."

Greenwood said, "You mean bring in somebody new?"

"I mean," Dortmunder said, "bring in a specialist. This time we need a specialist outside the string."

"What kind of a specialist?" Greenwood said, and Kelp said, "Who?"

"Miasmo the Great," Dortmunder said.

There was a little silence, and then everybody began to smile. "That's nice," Greenwood said.

THE MAJOR WAS LEANING over the pool table when Kelp was shown in by the ebony man with the light-reflecting glasses, and Prosker was sitting at his ease in a leather chair to one side. Prosker was wearing a neat business suit and nursing a tall drink that tinkled.

The Major said, "Ah, Kelp! Watch this, I saw it on television."

Kelp walked over to the pool table. "Do you think it's all right to have him walking around?"

The Major glanced at Prosker, then said, "There's nothing to worry about. Mr. Prosker and I have an understanding. He has given me his word not to try to escape."

"His word and half a dollar will get you a cup of coffee," Kelp said, "but it tastes better with just the half a dollar."

"Additionally," the Major said casually, "the doors are guarded. Now, really, you must watch this."

The Major set up a trick involving three balls against a cushion and a fourth at the far end. Clack. Clackety-clackety-clack. Balls rolled hither and yon. Ball number one dropped into a pocket, two and three followed, and number four hit the shoulder, teetered on the edge, spun slowly, reluctantly, and fell into the pocket.

The Major put down his cue with obvious pleasure. "Now," he said, rubbing his hands together, "Dortmunder called last night and said he thought there was a way to do it. That was fast work. You have a list for me?"

"No list this time," Kelp said. "All we need is cash. Five thousand dollars."

The Major stared. "Five thou—" He swallowed. "For what?"

"We have to hire a specialist," Kelp said. "We can't do this one like the other ones, we need a specialist. He gets a flat fee of five grand. Dortmunder says you can take it off our payments when we give you the emerald because he's an extra man you didn't count on."

The Major glanced at Prosker, then looked at Kelp again. "How soon do you need it?"

"The sooner we get the money," Kelp said, "the sooner the specialist goes to work."

"Who is this specialist?"

"He calls himself Miasmo the Great."

The Major was taken aback. "What on earth does he do?"

Kelp told him, and the Major and Prosker exchanged a quick startled glance. The Major said, "You mean on Prosker here?"

"No," Kelp said, not noticing how they both relaxed. "We don't trust Prosker, he might be able to fake it."

"That's good," Prosker said amiably. "Never be too trusting, that's what I say."

The Major gave him a dirty look. "I will have the money by two o'clock tomorrow afternoon," he said to Kelp.

"Good," Kelp said. "Well, I'll be seeing you, Major. I know my way to the door."

"My best to Greenwood and all the boys," Prosker said cheerfully as Kelp closed the door behind him.

The Major turned angrily to Prosker, saying, "You are not amusing."

"They don't suspect a thing," Prosker said easily. "None of them."

"They will if you keep being playful."

"No, they won't. I know where to draw the line."

"Do you?" The Major lit a cigarette with nervous angry movements. "I don't like toying with those people," he said. "They could all be very very dangerous."

"That's why you like having me around," Prosker said. "You know I know how to deal with them."

"We'll see," the Major said. "We'll see."

IN SUIT AND TIE, Dortmunder could look like a slightly seedy small businessman, as though he operated something like a Laundromat in a poor neighborhood. It was good enough to carry him through his errand to the bank.

Dortmunder walked into the bank a little after two, and walked over to one of the uniformed guards, a slender white-haired man sucking his false teeth. "I want to see about renting a safe-deposit box," Dortmunder said.

"You'll want to talk to an officer of the bank," the guard said and escorted Dortmunder over behind a rail.

The officer was a soft young man in a dandruff-flecked tan suit, who told Dortmunder the box rental was eight dollars and forty cents a month, and when that didn't seem to stun Dortmunder, he gave him a form to fill out, full of the usual questions—address, occupation, and so on—which Dortmunder answered with lies prepared for the occasion.

After the paperwork was done, the young man escorted Dortmunder downstairs to look at his box. At the foot of the stairs was a uniformed guard at a desk. The young man explained to Dortmunder the signing-in procedure he would have to follow every time he visited his box. The first gate was then unlocked and they stepped through into a small room where Dortmunder was introduced to a second guard, who would take over from here. The young man shook Dortmunder's hand and went back upstairs.

The new guard, who was named Albert, said, "Either George or I will always serve you, any time you want to get to your box."

"George?"

"He's the one on the sign-in desk today."

Dortmunder nodded. Albert then unlocked the inner gate and they went into a room that looked like a Lilliputian morgue, with rank upon rank of trays for the tiny dead bodies.

Dortmunder's drawer was low and to the left. Albert used his own master key first, then asked for the key Dortmunder had just received from the young man upstairs. Dortmunder gave it to him, he unlocked the drawer, and at once gave the key back to Dortmunder.

The safe-deposit box was actually a drawer, about an inch high, four inches wide and eighteen inches deep. Albert slid it most of the way out and said, "If you wish privacy, sir, I can carry it into one of the side rooms for you," motioning to the small chambers off the main morgue.

"No, thanks," Dortmunder said, "not this time. I just want to put this stuff in." He took from his inside jacket pocket a sealed white envelope containing seven unused Kleenex tissues. He carefully placed this in the middle of the drawer and stood back while Albert shut it up again.

Albert let him out the first gate and George let him out the second, and Dortmunder went upstairs and outside, where it seemed strange somehow that it was still daylight. He checked his watch and hailed a cab, because he now had to get uptown and then come all the way back with Miasmo the Great before the bank's employees started going home for the day.

"NEW YORK IS A lonely city, Linda," Greenwood said.

"Oh, it is," she said. "I know that, Alan." He had kept his first name, and his new last name also started with G, which was safe enough and very convenient.

Greenwood clasped his arm tighter around the girl beside him. "When one meets a sympathetic soul in a city like this," he said, "one doesn't want to let go."

"Oh, I know what you mean," she said and snuggled more comfortably against him, her cheek resting against his bare chest, the covers warm over their bodies.

"That's why I hate it that I have to go out tonight," he said.

"Oh, I hate it too," she said.

"But how did I know a treasure like you would come into my life today? And now it's too late to change this other thing. I just have to go, that's all there is to it."

She lifted her head and studied his face. The artificial fireplace in the corner of the room was the only source of light, and she peered at him in its uncertain red glow. "Are you sure it isn't another girl?" she asked. She was trying to make the question light, but wasn't entirely succeeding.

He cupped her chin in his hand. "There is no other girl," he said. "Not anywhere in the world." He kissed her lightly on the lips.

"I do want to believe you, Alan," she said. She looked sweet, and plaintive, and yearning.

"And I wish I was permitted to tell you where I am going," he said, "but I can't. I just ask you to trust me. And I should be back in no more than an hour." He kissed her again.

After the kiss she murmured, "How much time do we have before you go?"

He had been squinting at the bedside clock over her shoulder, and he said, "Twenty minutes."

"Then there's time," she whispered, nibbling his ear, "to make doubly sure you won't forget me."

"Mmmmmm," he said, and the result was that when the doorbell sounded, one long, two short, twenty minutes later, he hadn't finished dressing.

Chefwick was waiting on the sidewalk. "You were quite some time," he said, gently chiding.

"You don't know the half of it," Greenwood said. "Which way?"

"This way."

Murch was at the wheel of his Mustang parked around the corner. Chefwick and Greenwood got into the car and Murch drove downtown to Varick Street, where all the office buildings had been shut down for hours. He parked across the street from the one they wanted, and Greenwood stood watch while Chefwick opened its front door. Then they went in and up the stairs—the elevators were not working now—to the fifth floor. They went down the hall, Greenwood lighting their way with a small pencil flash, until they found the door marked DODSON & FOGG, ATTORNEYS AT LAW. On the lower left corner of the frosted glass were five names, the second of which was E. ANDREW PROSKER.

Chefwick went through this door so fast it might as well not have been locked at all. Now they followed the map Prosker had drawn for them, finding his office, finding the furniture arranged as Prosker had said. Greenwood sat down at the desk and opened the bottom right-hand drawer all the way. To the back was taped a small yellow envelope. Greenwood smiled and took the envelope and shook it over the desk pad. A small key dropped out, looking exactly like the one Dortmunder had been given at the bank earlier today.

"We've got it," Greenwood said. "Isn't that amazing?"

"Perhaps our luck has changed," Chefwick said.

"And it's Friday the thirteenth. Fantastic."

"Not any longer, it's after midnight."

"Is it? Let's go. Here, you'll give this to Dortmunder."

Chefwick put the key in his pocket and they left the office, Chefwick relocking doors. Back on the street, they got in Murch's car and Greenwood said, "Would you mind dropping me first? I've got a little something going on back at my place."

"It's perfectly all right with me," Chefwick said.

"Sure," said Murch. "Why not?"

They drove back uptown and let Greenwood off in front of his building. He hurried inside.

HOME FOR ALBERT CROMWELL, safe-deposit-box guard at the 46th Street branch of C & I National Bank, was a twenty-seventh-story apartment in a thirty-five-story building on the Upper West Side, and he traveled there by subway and elevator. Today, Thursday, the nineteenth of October, as he entered the elevator on the final leg of his homeward journey, a tall and imposing man with piercing black eyes, a broad forehead, and thick hair, jet-black except for the gray at the temples, boarded with him. Albert Cromwell hadn't noticed, but the same man had entered the elevator with him every evening this week. The only difference today was that this was the first time the two of them were alone.

They stood side by side, both facing front. The doors slid shut and the elevator began to rise. "Have you ever noticed those numbers?" the imposing man said. He had a deep and resonant voice.

Albert Cromwell looked at the other man in surprise. Strangers didn't talk to one another in the elevator. He said, "I beg your pardon?"

The imposing man nodded at the row of numbers over the door. "I mean those numbers there," he said. "Take a look at them."

Puzzled, Albert Cromwell took a look at them. They were small glass numbers running from left to right in a long chrome strip over the door, and they lit up one at a time to indicate which floor the elevator was at. Right now, for instance, the number 4 was on; when that number switched off number 5 switched on in its place.

"Notice how regular the movement is," the imposing man said in his resonant voice. "How pleasant it is to see something so smooth and regular, to know that each number will follow the one before it. So smooth. So regular. So restful. Watch the numbers. Count along with them, if you wish, it's very restful after a long hard day. It's good to be able to rest, to be able to look at the numbers and count them and feel one's body relaxing, to know that one is relaxing, to know that one is safe in one's own building, safe and relaxed and calm, watching the numbers, counting the numbers, feeling every muscle relax, every nerve relax, knowing that one can now let go, one can lean back against the wall and relax, relax, relax. There's nothing but the numbers now, nothing but the numbers and my voice. Nothing but the numbers and my voice. The numbers and my voice."

The imposing man stopped talking and looked at Albert Crom-

well, who was leaning back against the rear wall of the elevator, gazing in a bovine way at the numbers over the door. The number 12 switched off and the number 14 switched on. Albert Cromwell watched the numbers.

The imposing man said, "Can you hear my voice?"

"Yes," said Albert Cromwell.

"One day soon," the imposing man said, "a man will come to you at your place of employment. At the bank where you work. Do you understand me?"

"Yes," said Albert Cromwell.

"The man will say to you, 'Afghanistan banana stand.' Do you understand me?"

"Yes," said Albert Cromwell.

"What will the man say?"

"Afghanistan banana stand," said Albert Cromwell.

"Very good," said the imposing man. The number 17 lit briefly over the door. "You are still very relaxed," said the imposing man. "When the man says to you, 'Afghanistan banana stand,' you will do what he tells you to do. Do you understand me?"

"Yes," said Albert Cromwell.

"What will you do when the man says, 'Afghanistan banana stand'?"

"I will do what he tells me to do," said Albert Cromwell.

"Very good," said the imposing man. "That's very good, you're doing very well. When the man leaves you, you will forget that he was there. Do you understand?"

"Yes," said Albert Cromwell. "When the man leaves me, I will forget he was there."

"Excellent," said the imposing man. The number 22 lit over the door. "You are doing fine," said the imposing man. He reached out and pushed the button for the twenty-sixth floor. "When I leave you," he said, "you will forget our conversation. When you reach your floor, you will feel rested and very, very good. You will not remember our conversation until the man says to you, 'Afghanistan banana stand.' Then you will do what he tells you, and after he leaves, you will again forget our conversation and you will also forget that he was ever there. Will you do all that?"

"Yes," said Albert Cromwell.

The number 26 lit over the door, and the elevator came to a stop. The door slid open. "You did very well," the imposing man said, stepping out to the corridor. The door slid shut again, and the elevator went up to the twenty-seventh floor. The door opened, and Albert Cromwell shook himself and stepped out into the hall. He smiled. He felt very good, very relaxed and rested. He walked down the hall with a buoyant step, feeling great.

DORTMUNDER WALKED INTO the bank, remembering what Miasmo the Great had told him last night when reporting success at last with Albert Cromwell. "If at all possible," he had said, "do your work tomorrow, while the suggestion is fresh."

So here it was tomorrow. Tomorrow afternoon, in fact. Dortmunder had come here once already today, but when he'd walked by the stairway and looked down, it was Albert on duty outside, which meant George would be inside, and George hadn't been primed. Now Dortmunder got to the head of the stairs and looked down and there was George at the desk outside. They must have shifted posts after lunch. Dortmunder didn't hesitate. He trotted down the stairs, said hello to George, signed in, and was let through the first gate.

There was no one in the small in-between room, and for just a second Dortmunder felt the cold touch of apprehension. He could see himself locked in here by a gloating George, everything known, being held here until the police arrived. A fitting end to the Balabomo Emerald quest.

But then George said, "Albert will be with you in just one moment, sir," and Dortmunder's paranoia faded like mist. He nodded, and George shut the gate after him and went back over to his desk.

Dortmunder stood where he was, and after a couple of minutes the farther door opened and a stout elderly lady emerged, clutching a Pekingese to her fox fur, and followed by Albert, who shut the gate and said to Dortmunder, "Just one moment, sir."

"Take your time," Dortmunder said.

Albert opened the other gate and let the lady out, then turned to Dortmunder. "If you'll follow me, sir."

They went through the inner gate and directly to Dortmunder's box. Albert inserted his key, asked to borrow Dortmunder's, opened the box, and at once gave Dortmunder his key back.

"I just wanted this," Dortmunder said, and took out the envelope full of tissues. He tucked it away in his inside jacket pocket.

Albert used the two keys to lock the now-empty box, gave Dortmunder back his key, and said, "This way, sir."

"Afghanistan banana stand," Dortmunder said.

Albert stopped where he was. He turned to Dortmunder, and he looked calmly prepared to be of service. "Yes, sir," he said.

Dortmunder took out Prosker's key. "Now we'll open this box."

"Yes, sir." Albert took the key and turned away. Dortmunder followed him down the aisle. Albert opened Prosker's box, then stood there continuing to look calm and alert and ready to be of service.

There were a lot of papers in Prosker's box, deeds and birth certificates and one thing and another. In with all the rest was a black plush box of the kind cuff links and earrings come in. Dortmunder picked up the black plush box, and opened it.

The Balabomo Emerald. Filling the box and winking at Dortmunder under the bright fluorescent lights. Grinning to itself inside the box.

Dortmunder slipped the box into his left-side jacket pocket. He said to Albert, "All right, shut it up again."

Albert shut the drawer and gave Dortmunder Prosker's key, continuing to look alert, calm, ready to serve.

Dortmunder said, "That's all. I'm ready to leave now."

"Yes, sir," Albert said and led the way to the first gate. He opened it and stood aside for Dortmunder to go on through. Then Dortmunder had to wait while he closed it again before crossing the small anteroom and opening the outer gate. Dortmunder walked past him, and outside George said, "Have a good day, sir."

"Thank you," Dortmunder said. He went upstairs and out of the bank and caught a cab. "Amsterdam Avenue and Eighty-fourth Street," he said.

The cab went down 45th Street and got itself snarled in a traffic jam. Dortmunder sat in the back and slowly began to smile. It was incredible. They had the emerald. They actually had the emerald, at long last. Dortmunder saw the cabby puzzling at him in the rearview mirror, wondering what a passenger caught in a traffic jam had to smile about, but he couldn't stop. He just went right on smiling.

PHASE SIX

AROUND THE TABLE in the back room at the O. J. Bar and Grill sat Murch and Kelp and Chefwick. Murch was drinking beer with salt and Kelp was drinking straight bourbon, but since it was midafternoon Chefwick was having a diet cola, and he was nursing it. Greenwood was out in the bar, showing Rollo how to make a vodka sour.

The three in the back room had been silent five or six minutes when Murch suddenly said, "You know, I've been thinking about it."

"That's a mistake," Kelp said. "Don't think about it. It'll give you a rash."

"I've been sitting here," Murch persisted, "and I've been trying to think what could possibly go wrong this time. Like maybe they moved the bank since yesterday."

Chefwick said quietly, "I agree with Kelp. I think you should stop thinking about it at once. Or at least stop talking about it."

Greenwood came in with his vodka sour. Murch said, "But there's nothing I can think of that sounds like the kind of snafu that happens to us. I'm almost ready to believe Dortmunder is actually going to walk through that door over there with the emerald in his hand." Murch pointed at the door, and it opened, and Dortmunder walked in with an empty glass in his hand.

Everybody stared at him. Dortmunder stared at the finger pointing at him, then moved out of its line of fire and walked around the table to the vacant chair and the bourbon bottle. He sat down, poured bourbon into his glass, and took a swallow. Everybody watched, unblinking. The silence was so pure he could be heard swallowing.

He looked around at them. His face was expressionless, and so were theirs. Then Dortmunder smiled.

THE EMERALD LAY IN the middle of the table, looking like a beautiful egg laid by the green metal-shaded hanging light directly overhead. That light was reflected and refracted in the prisms of the stone, so that the emerald looked as though it was silently laughing and chuckling in the middle of the table there.

The silence in the back room at the O. J. Bar and Grill was both reverential and ecstatic. The five men sitting there had an air of awed solemnity about them, and yet they were all smiling. From ear to ear. Gazing at the winking, laughing stone and smiling back at it.

Kelp sighed. He said, "There it is."

The others shifted position, as though waking from a trance. Murch said, "I never thought it would happen."

"But there she is," Greenwood said. "And isn't she a beauty."

"I wish Maude could see that," Chefwick said. "I should have brought my Polaroid to take a picture of it."

"I almost hate to get rid of it," Kelp said.

Dortmunder nodded and said, "I know what you mean. Nevertheless, the time has come to turn that rock over to Major Iko and collect our money."

Murch said, "You want us all to go? I got my car."

"No," Dortmunder said. "The five of us together might attract attention. Besides, if something goes wrong there should at least be some of us still on the loose and ready to help. Kelp, this was your job first, you brought the rest of us into it, you were the first one the Major contacted. You want to bring him the stone?"

"Sure," Kelp said. He was pleased. "If you guys all think I can make it across town."

"Murch can drive you," Dortmunder said, "and we three'll stay here." He picked up the emerald and put it back into its black plush box. He handed it to Kelp, who took it and said, "If we're not back in an hour, God knows where we are."

"We'll wait till we hear from you," Dortmunder said. "After you go, I'll call the Major and tell him to open his safe."

"Good." Kelp put the box in his pocket, finished his bourbon, and got to his feet. "See you later," he said, and went out. As Murch followed him, the others heard him saying, "The question is, do we go through the park at Sixty-fifth Street, or—" And the door closed.

Dortmunder went out front to the phone booth and called the Talabwo mission. He had to talk to two other people before Major Iko at last got on the phone, and then he said, "We're making delivery this afternoon."

"Are you really?" The Major was obviously delighted. "That is good news. I'd about given up hope."

"So had we all, Major. You understand it's COD."

"Naturally. I have the money waiting in the safe."

"The usual guy is bringing it."

"Not all of you?" The Major sounded disappointed. "Well, it will all work out, I'm sure. Thank you for calling. I'll be expecting our friend."

"Good," Dortmunder said. He hung up and left the booth.

Rollo looked over at him as he started for the back room again and said, "You're lookin' cheerful today."

"It's a cheerful day," Dortmunder said. "Looks like we won't be using your back room anymore for a while."

"*Mazel tov*," Rollo said.

"Yeah," Dortmunder said, and went into the back room to wait.

THE USUAL EBONY MAN with the light-reflecting glasses let Kelp in, but he did not lead him to the usual room. "Office today," he said.

"Oh? Yeah, I guess today is special. Okay, lead on."

The ebony man opened the office door and Kelp went inside and the Major wasn't sitting behind the desk at all. Prosker was, sitting there as though he owned the joint, smiling amiably at Kelp like a spider smiling at a fly.

Kelp stopped just past the door, but a hand in the middle of his back pushed him on. "Hey!" he said and turned around, and the ebony man had come in after him, had shut the door, had drawn an automatic from his pocket, and was pointing it at Kelp's nose.

Kelp stepped backward farther into the room, putting more air between himself and that automatic. "What's going on here?" he said, and now he saw two more black men with guns in their hands, standing against the back wall.

Prosker chuckled, and Kelp whirled and glared at him. "What'd you do with the Major?"

Prosker broke up entirely. "With the *Major!* Oh, my word. You people are babes in the woods, babes in the woods! What did I do with the Major!

Kelp took a threatening step forward. "Yeah, what did you do with the Major? What are you up to?"

"I am working for the Major now," Prosker said, sobering, "and the Major thought it would be better if I took over the task of explaining the facts of life to you, which you could then take back to your friends. Besides, I made up a good deal of the plot myself."

"Plot? What plot?" Kelp demanded.

"Sit down, Kelp," Prosker offered. "We'll talk."

"We won't talk," Kelp said. "I'll talk to the Major."

Prosker's smile became saddened. "Do I have to ask the people behind you to force you to sit down? Wouldn't you rather we handled all this without violence?"

Kelp thought it over, then said, "All right, I'll listen. All it is is words so far." He sat down.

"Words is all you're going to get, I'm afraid," said Prosker, "so listen to them carefully. In the first place, you are going to turn the Balabomo Emerald over to me, and you are not going to get any more money for it. The Major has paid you all a total of over twenty-four thousand dollars, which he considers quite enough."

"For a half-million-dollar stone," Kelp said bitterly.

"Which really belongs to the Major's nation anyway," Prosker pointed out. "Twenty-four thousand dollars is a lot of money for a small emerging nation like Talabwo."

"Am I supposed to be feeling sorry for Talabwo?" Kelp asked. "I'm being hijacked, my partners and me are getting cheated out of two hundred thousand bucks, and you want me to feel sorry for some country in Africa?"

"I simply want you to understand the situation," Prosker said. "I will go on to the second point. Which is, the Major would prefer it if you and the others did not cause any trouble about this."

"Oh, would he?" Kelp smiled with half his mouth. "That's gonna be tough on the Major," he said.

"Not necessarily," said Prosker. "You recall the Major's passion for dossiers."

Kelp frowned. "Papers in folders," he said. "So what?"

"A lot depends," Prosker said, "on who opens those folders and reads those papers. The Manhattan District Attorney, for instance, would find the dossiers fascinating reading. It would solve five rather spectacular recent crimes for one thing, as well as giving him some broad hints about other unsolved crimes."

Kelp squinted at Prosker. "The Major's going to fink on us?"

"Only if you cause trouble," Prosker said. He sat back and spread his hands. "After all," he said, "you all made out rather well, considering how ineptly you handled the assignment."

"He intended this double cross from the beginning," Kelp said angrily.

"I have no opinion on that," Prosker said. "Please put the emerald on this desk now."

"You don't think I was crazy enough to bring it with me, do you?"

"Yes, I do," Prosker said, unruffled. "The question is, are you crazy enough to force those gentlemen behind you to force you to give it up."

Kelp thought it over angrily and bitterly, and decided there was no point bringing unnecessary lumps on oneself. One merely conceded the round, consoling oneself with the thought that the fight wasn't over. Kelp reached into his pocket, took out the black plush box, and put it on the desk.

"Very good," Prosker said, smiling at the box. He opened it, smiled at its contents, and looked past Kelp at the three silent enforcers. "One of you should take this to the Major," he said. The ebony man with the glasses came forward and took the box. Kelp watched him walk out of the room.

Prosker said, "Now, here is what is going to happen. Shortly, I am going to leave here and turn myself over to the police. I have a cock-and-bull story worked out about how I was kidnapped by a group that had the mistaken impression I knew where a former client's booty was hidden. It took them several days to accept their mistake, and then they let me go. I didn't recognize any of them, and I don't expect to see any of their pictures in the rogues' gallery. Neither the Major nor I, you see, are interested in causing you people any unnecessary difficulty."

"Get on with it," Kelp said. "What else?"

"Nothing else," Prosker said. "You have been paid all you will be paid. The Major and I will cover you for your crimes in regard to the emerald. If you all now go on about your own business, all five of you, that can be the end of it, but if any of you cause any trouble for either the Major or myself, we are in a position to make life very, very difficult for all of you."

"The Major can go back to Talabwo," Kelp pointed out. "But you'll still be around here."

"As a matter of fact, I won't," Prosker said, smiling amiably. "Talabwo has an opening for a legal adviser on matters concerning their new constitution. A well-paying job, actually, with a subsidy from the United States government. It should take about five years to get the new constitution ready for ratification. I'm looking forward to the change of scenery."

"I'd like to suggest a change of scenery for you," Kelp said.

"Undoubtedly," agreed Prosker. He glanced at his watch. "I hate to rush you," he said, "but I am a bit pressed for time. Do you have any questions?"

"None you'd like to answer," Kelp said. He got to his feet. "See you around, Prosker."

"I doubt it," Prosker said. "Those two gentlemen will see you to the door." They did, closing it firmly behind him once he was outside.

Murch's car was just around the corner. Kelp ran around and slid into the front seat. Murch said. "Everything okay?"

"Everything stinks," Kelp said quickly. "Pull up to where you can see around the corner."

Murch acted at once, starting the engine and pulling the car forward as he said, "What's the problem?"

"Double cross. I have to make a phone call. If anybody comes out of that mission before I get back, run him down."

"Right," said Murch, and Kelp jumped out of the car again.

Rollo walked into the back room and said, "The other bourbon's on the phone. He wants to talk to you."

"I knew it," Greenwood said. "Something had to go wrong."

"Maybe not," Dortmunder said, but his face showed he didn't believe it. He got up and followed Rollo out to the bar and hurried down to the phone booth. He slid in, shut the door, picked up the receiver, and said, "Yeah?"

"Cross," Kelp's voice said. "Come over quick."

"Done," Dortmunder said and hung up. He left the booth and hurried toward the back room, calling to Rollo on the way by, "We'll be back soon." He opened the back room door, stuck his head in, and said, "Come on."

"This is really irritating," Chefwick said, following Dortmunder and Greenwood out of the bar.

They got a cab right away, but it seemed forever before they got through Central Park and piled out at the corner half a block from the Talabwo mission. Murch came trotting over as the cab went away, and Dortmunder said, "What's going on?"

"Double cross," Murch said. "And Prosker and the Major are in it together."

"We should have buried him in the woods," Greenwood said. "I knew it at the time, I was just too softhearted."

"Shut up," Dortmunder said. He asked Murch, "Where's Kelp?"

Murch said, "About five minutes ago, the Major and Prosker and three others came out and took a cab. They had luggage. Kelp's after them in another cab."

"Damn," Dortmunder said. "It took us too long to get through the park."

Murch pointed at a glass-sided phone booth on the opposite corner. "He took that phone number," he said. "He'll call us when he gets the chance."

"Good thinking," Dortmunder said. "All right. Murch, you stay with the phone booth. Chefwick, you and me are going into the mission. Greenwood, you got your gun?"

"Sure."

"Pass it over." They stood close together briefly, and Dortmunder tucked the Smith & Wesson revolver into his jacket pocket. He said to Greenwood, "You stay outside and watch. Come on."

Murch went to the phone booth, and Dortmunder and Chefwick and Greenwood hurried up the block to the mission. Greenwood leaned against the ornamental iron railing and casually lit a cigarette while Dortmunder and Chefwick went up the stone stoop, Chefwick taking several small tools from his pockets as they went.

It was nearly four o'clock on a Friday afternoon, and Fifth Avenue was full of traffic, a sluggish stream heading downtown with the park on its right and the impressive old stone buildings on its left. The sidewalks were busy too, but Dortmunder and Chefwick kept their backs to it all, shielding Chefwick's busy hands. The door *ponged* open, and Dortmunder and Chefwick stepped quickly inside, Dortmunder drawing the revolver while Chefwick shut the door again.

The first two rooms they went through were empty, but the third contained typewriters and two black female typists. They were quickly tucked away in a closet with a bolt lock, and Dortmunder and Chefwick went on.

In Major Iko's office they found a notepad on the desk, with a pencil notation: "Kennedy—Flight 301—7:15." Chefwick said, "That must be where they're going."

"But what airline?"

Chefwick studied the note again. "It doesn't say."

"Phone book," Dortmunder said. "Yellow pages."

They both opened drawers and found the Manhattan yellow pages in the bottom desk drawer on the left. Chefwick said, "Are you going to call every airline?"

"I hope not. Let's try Pan Am." He looked up the number, dialed, and a pleasant but plastic female voice answered. Dortmunder said, "I have what may sound like a stupid question, but I'm trying to prevent an elopement."

"An elopement, sir?"

"I hate to stand in the way of young love," Dortmunder said, "but we've just found out the man is already married. We know they're taking a flight out of Kennedy tonight at seven-fifteen. It's flight three-o-one, but we don't know which airline, and we don't know where they're headed."

The office door opened and the ebony man walked in, white light glinting from his glasses. Dortmunder said into the phone, "Hold on a second." He put the mouthpiece against his chest and showed Greenwood's revolver to the ebony man. "Stand over there," he said, pointing to a bare stretch of wall far from the doorway. The ebony man put his hands up and walked over to the wall.

Dortmunder kept his eyes and gun on the ebony man, and spoke into the phone again. "I'm sorry. The girl's mother is hysterical."

"Sir, this may take a little while, but I'll be as fast as I can. Will you hold on?"

"Of course."

There was a click. Dortmunder said to Chefwick, "Search him."

"Certainly." Chefwick searched the ebony man, and came up with a Beretta .25-caliber automatic, a small nasty gun Kelp had already seen earlier in the day.

"Tie him up," Dortmunder said. "If he prefers to be shot, stick your gun in his belly to muffle the sound."

"Naturally," Chefwick said.

"I will cooperate," the ebony man said. "But it doesn't matter. You will fail."

Dortmunder held the phone to his ear and the gun pointed at the ebony man, who yielded his tie and shoelaces to Chefwick, who said, "Now remove your shoes and socks and lie face down on the floor."

The ebony man sat down on the floor and took off his shoes and socks, then turned to lie face down. Chefwick used one shoelace to tie his thumbs behind his back, the other to tie his big toes together, and stuffed the tie into his mouth.

Dortmunder heard another click, and the female voice said, "Phew. Well, I found it, sir."

"I really appreciate this," Dortmunder said.

"It's an Air France flight to Paris," she said. "That's the only flight with that number leaving at that time."

"Thank you very much," Dortmunder said.

"It's really very romantic, isn't it, sir?" she said. "Too bad he's already married."

"These things happen," Dortmunder said. "Thanks again." He hung up and said to Chefwick, "Air France to Paris. Now help me drag that bird out of sight behind the desk."

They toted the ebony man around behind the desk and left the mission without seeing anyone else. Greenwood was still loafing around out front. He fell in with them, and Dortmunder told him what they'd learned as they walked back to the corner and across to where Murch was sitting in the phone booth. There Dortmunder said, "Chefwick, you stay here. When Kelp calls, tell him we're on our way and he can leave a message for us at Air France. If they've gone someplace other than Kennedy, you wait here, and when we don't get any message at Air France we'll call you."

Chefwick nodded. "That's fine," he said.

"In case we get separated, we'll all meet at the O. J. when this is over," Dortmunder said.

"This may be a late night," Chefwick said. "I'd best call Maude."

"Don't tie up that phone."

"Oh, I won't. Good luck."

"Wouldn't that be nice," Dortmunder said. "Come on, Murch, let's see how fast you can get us to Kennedy airport."

"Well, from here," Murch said, as they trotted across the street toward his car, "I'm going to go straight up FDR Drive . . ."

THE GIRL AT THE Air France counter had a French accent. "Mister Dortmun-dair?" she said. "Yes, I have a message for you." She handed over a small envelope.

"Thank you," Dortmunder said, and he and Greenwood moved away from the counter. Murch was out parking the car. Dortmunder opened the envelope and inside was a small piece of paper containing the scrawled words GOLDEN DOOR.

Dortmunder turned the paper over, and the other side was blank. He turned it back and it still just said GOLDEN DOOR. "I needed this," Dortmunder said.

"Just a minute," Greenwood said and walked over to the nearest passing stewardess, a pretty shorthaired blonde in a dark blue uniform. "Excuse me," Greenwood said. "Will you marry me?"

"I'd love to," she said, "but my plane leaves in twenty minutes."

"When you come back," Greenwood said. "In the meantime, could you tell me what and where is the Golden Door?"

"Oh, that's the restaurant in the International Arrivals Building."

"Lovely. When can we have dinner there?"

"Oh, the next time you're in town," she said.

"Wonderful," he said. "When will that be?"

"Don't you know?"

"Not yet. When do you get back?"

"Monday," she said, smiling. "We come in at three-thirty in the afternoon."

"A perfect time for dinner. Shall we make it four?"

"Make it four-thirty."

"Four-thirty Monday, at the Golden Door. I'll reserve the table immediately. Under the name of Grofield," he said, giving his most recent name.

"I'll be there," she said. She had a lovely smile and lovely teeth.

"See you then," Greenwood said and went back over to Dortmunder. "It's a restaurant, in the International Arrivals Building."

"Come on."

They met Murch on his way in, brought him up to date, and took the bus over to the International Arrivals Building.

The Golden Door was upstairs, at the head of a long broad escalator. At the foot of it stood Kelp. They went over, and Kelp said, "They're up there feeding their faces."

"They're taking the seven-fifteen Air France flight to Paris," Dortmunder said.

Kelp blinked at him. "How do you know that?"

"Telepathy," Dortmunder said. "Let's go up."

"I'm not dressed to go up to a place like that," Murch said. He was in a leather jacket and work pants, while the other three were all in suits or sport jackets and ties.

Dortmunder said to Kelp, "Any other way down out of there?"

"Probably. But this is the only public way."

"Okay. Murch, you stay down here in case they get through us. If they do, follow them but don't try anything on your own. Kelp, is Chefwick still in the phone booth?"

"No, he said he was going to the O. J. We can leave messages there now."

"Fine. Murch, if somebody comes down and you follow him, leave us a message at the O. J. as soon as you can."

"Right."

The other three rode the escalator upstairs, emerging on a dark carpet in a dark open area. The headwaiter's lectern and a lot of artificial plants separated this area from the main dining room. The headwaiter himself approached and asked them how many they were. Dortmunder said, "We'll wait for the rest of our party before going in."

"Certainly, sir." The headwaiter bowed himself away.

Kelp said, "There they are."

Dortmunder looked through the plastic leaves. The dining room was large, and very nearly empty. At a table in the middle distance, beside a window, sat Major Iko and Prosker and three sturdy young black men. They were having a leisurely dinner, with over two hours left before their flight.

Kelp said, "I don't like jumping them here. Too public, and too boxed in."

"I agree," Dortmunder said. "All right, we'll wait for them downstairs." They turned and went down the escalator. They filled Murch in, and then the four of them spread out around the waiting room.

It was getting dark outside the terminal's windows when the Major's party finally came down from dinner. Dortmunder immediately got to his feet and walked toward them. Putting a big smile on his face, he stuck his hand out and advanced quickly, crying, "Major! What a surprise! It's great to see you again!"

He had reached the group by now, and he grasped the Major's limp hand and started to pump it. Keeping the big smile on his face, he said softly, "The others are all around. If you don't want shooting, just stand still."

"Dortmunder," the Major said, "I'm sure we can talk this over."

"You're damn right we can," Dortmunder said. "Just the two of us. No lawyers, no bodyguards."

"You wouldn't get—violent."

"Not me, Major," Dortmunder said. "But I don't know about the others. Greenwood would shoot Prosker first, that's only natural, but I think Kelp would go first for you."

Prosker said, "You wouldn't dare start anything like that in a crowded place like this."

"Perfect place for it," Dortmunder said. "Shooting. Panic. We mix in with everybody else. The easiest place in the world to hide is in a crowd."

The Major said, "Prosker, don't try to make him prove himself, it has the ring of truth."

"So it does, damn it," said Prosker. "All right, Dortmunder, what do you want? More money?"

"Major, I don't want to talk in front of all these people. Come on."

The Major was very reluctant, but Dortmunder was insistent, and finally the Major started to move. Dortmunder said to the others over his shoulder, "Just stay right here, and you won't start any posthumous panics."

Dortmunder and the Major strolled away down the long corridor overlooking the customs inspection area.

The Major said, "Dortmunder, Talabwo is a poor country. I can get you some more money, but not two hundred thousand dollars."

"So you figured this double cross from the beginning," Dortmunder said.

"I won't lie to you," the Major said.

Back in the main waiting room, Prosker was saying to the three black men, "If we take off in four different directions, they won't dare shoot."

"We don't want to die," one of the black men said, and the others nodded agreement.

"If you don't go help the Major," Prosker said, "and Dortmunder gets that emerald away from him, you'll get worse than shot and you know it."

The black men looked worried.

"I'll count three," Prosker said, "and on three we'll take off in different directions, then all circle around and go down that way after Dortmunder and the Major. I'll go back and to the left, you go straight ahead, you go at an angle to the left that way, and you go right. You all ready?"

They hated it, but the thought of the Major in a bad mood was even worse. Reluctantly they nodded.

"One," Prosker said. He could see Greenwood sitting behind a copy of the *Daily News* way over there. "Two," he said. In another direction he could see Kelp. "Three," he said, and started to run. The black men went on standing there a second or two longer, and then they began to run. Kelp and Greenwood and Murch looked after them, and then all of a sudden *they* started running, toward one another, for a quick conference.

In the meantime, Dortmunder and the Major were still walking down the corridor, Dortmunder trying to find an unpopulated corner in which to relieve the Major of the emerald and the Major talking on at great length about his regret at trying to dupe Dortmunder and his desire to make amends.

A distant voice cried, "Dortmunder!" Recognizing it as Kelp's, Dortmunder turned and saw two of the black men pelting his way. He closed a hand on the Major's elbow and locked it there. He looked around, and just ahead was a closed golden door marked No Admittance in black letters. Dortmunder pulled, the door opened, he shoved the Major through, and there they were at the top of a grimy gray staircase.

The Major said, "Dortmunder, I give you my word—"

"I don't want your word, I want that stone."

"Do you think I'd carry it?"

"That's exactly what you'd do with it, you wouldn't let it out of your sight till you were home free." Dortmunder pulled out Greenwood's revolver and shoved it into the Major's stomach. "It'll take longer if I have to search your body."

"Dortmunder—"

"Shut up and give me the emerald! I don't have time for lies!"

The Major looked in Dortmunder's face, inches from his own, and said, "All right, all right!" He was babbling now, caught up in Dortmunder's urgency. "You hold on to it," he said, pulling the black plush box from his pocket. "There won't be any other buyers. Hold on to it, I'll get in touch with you, I'll find the money to pay you."

Dortmunder snatched the box from his hand, stepped back, opened it and took a quick look inside. The emerald was there. He looked up, and the Major was jumping at him. The Major jumped into the barrel of the gun, then fell backward, dazed.

The door opened, and one of the black men started in. Dortmunder hit him in the stomach, remembering that they'd just eaten, and the black man said, "Phooff!" and bent over. But the other black man was behind him, and the third wouldn't be far away. Dortmunder turned and raced away down the stairs.

He heard them following him, heard the Major shouting. The first door he came to was locked, and the second one led him outside into the chill darkness of an October evening. But outside where? He stumbled through darkness, rounded a corner, and the night was full of airplanes.

He had gone through the looking glass, past that invisible barrier that closes half the world to unauthorized personnel. He was out where the planes are, in pockets of bright light, surrounded by darkness punctuated by strips of blue or amber runway lights.

And the black men were still after him. Dortmunder looked to his right, and there was darkness, and he ran into it.

For the next fifteen minutes Dortmunder kept running, and the three black men kept running in his wake. He was all over the territory reserved for airplanes, running now on grass, now on a taxiway, jumping over marker lights, and also trying not to get himself run down by a passing 707.

From time to time he saw the civilian part of the airport, with people walking and taxis driving along, but every time he headed that way the black men angled to head him off, and now he was getting farther and farther away from the passengers' part of the terminal. The runways were dead ahead, with the long lines of planes waiting their turns to take off, a pop singer's Lear jet followed by a Lufthansa 707, the monsters and the midgets one after another, obediently taking their turns.

One of the planes waiting to take off was a Waco Vela, a single-engine five-seater. At the controls was a computer salesman named Firgus, with his friend Bullock asleep across the backseat. Ahead of him was a TWA jet, which trundled up to the head of the runway, roared and vibrated a few seconds, and then began galumphing away like Sidney Greenstreet playing basketball, till it became airborne, at which point it also became graceful and beautiful.

Firgus drove his little plane out onto the runway and turned right. Now the runway stretched ahead of him. Firgus sat there waiting for the tower to give him the go-ahead, and all at once the right-hand door opened and a man with a gun got in.

Firgus stared at him in astonishment. "Havana?" he said.

"Just up in the sky will do," Dortmunder told him and looked out the side window at the three black men running his way.

"Okay, N733W," the tower said in Firgus's earphones. "Cleared for takeoff."

"Uh," said Firgus.

Dortmunder looked at him. "Don't do anything stupid," he said. "Just take off."

"Yes," Firgus said. Luckily he was an old hand with this plane and could fly it while his mind was doing flip-flops. He set the Vela going, they skeetered away down the runway, the black men came to a panting stop way back there, and the Vela climbed abruptly into the night sky.

"Good," Dortmunder said.

"We can't make it to Cuba," Firgus said. "With the gas I've got, we wouldn't make it much past Washington, D. C."

"I don't want to go to Cuba," Dortmunder said. "Where were you going?"

Firgus couldn't figure any of this out. "Well," he said, "Pittsburgh, actually."

"Head that way," Dortmunder said.

"You want to go to Pittsburgh?"

"Just do what you were going to do," Dortmunder said. "Don't mind me." He looked at the sleeping man in back, then out the window at the lights in the darkness below. They were away from the airport already. The Balabomo Emerald was in Dortmunder's jacket pocket. Things were more or less under control.

It took fifteen minutes to fly over New York and reach the darker, quieter New Jersey swamp. Firgus, more relaxed, now said, "Boy, I don't know what your problem is, but you sure scared the dickens out of me."

"Sorry," Dortmunder said. "I was in a hurry."

"I guess you must have been."

Another quarter hour went by, and then Dortmunder said, "What's that down there?"

"What's what?"

"That sort of pale strip."

Firgus looked down and said, "Oh, that's Route 287. That part isn't done yet."

"It looks done," Dortmunder said.

"Well, it isn't open yet."

"Land there," Dortmunder said.

Firgus stared at him. "Do what?"

"It's wide enough for a plane like this. Land there."

"Why?"

"So I can get out."

Firgus banked the plane and circled back over the pale strip on the dark ground below. "I don't know," he said dubiously. "There's no lights or anything."

"You can do it," Dortmunder told him. "You're a good pilot, I can tell you are." He didn't know a thing about flying.

Firgus preened. "Well, I suppose I could bring her in there," he said. "Be a little tricky, but not impossible."

"Good."

Firgus circled twice more before making the attempt. He was clearly nervous, and his nervousness communicated itself to Dortmunder, who almost told him to fly on, they'd find someplace better farther on. But there wouldn't be anyplace better. Dortmunder couldn't have Firgus land at a regular airport, so it had to be something irregular, and at least that was a straight ribbon of concrete down there and wide enough to land the plane on.

Which Firgus did very well, once he'd built his nerve up to it. He landed as light as a feather, brought the Vela to a stop in seven hundred feet, and turned a huge smile at Dortmunder. "That's what I call flying," he said.

"Me too," Dortmunder said.

Firgus looked back at Bullock and said testily, "I wish to hell he'd wake up." He poked Bullock's shoulder.

"Let him alone," Dortmunder said.

"If he doesn't see you," Firgus said, "he won't believe any of this. Hey, Bullock! Damn it, man, you're missing an adventure!" He punched Bullock's shoulder again, a little harder than before.

"Thanks for the lift," Dortmunder said. He got out of the plane and walked away into the darkness.

Bullock came up to consciousness amid a rain of blows, sat up, yawned, rubbed his face, looked around, blinked, frowned, and said, "Where the hell are we?"

"Route 287 in New Jersey," Firgus told him. "Look, do you see that guy? Look quick, will you, before he's out of sight!"

"What the hell you doin' on the *ground*? What are you doin' on Route 287?"

"He's out of sight," Firgus said, throwing up his hands in disgust. "I asked you to look, but no."

"You must be drunk or somethin'," Bullock said. "You're driving an *airplane* down Route 287!"

"I'm not driving an airplane down Route 287!"

"What the hell do you call it then?"

"We were hijacked, damn it! At Kennedy a guy jumped on the plane with a gun and hijacked us."

"Oh, sure he did," Bullock said. "And here we are in lovely Havana."

"He didn't want to go to Havana."

"No. He wanted to go to New Jersey. He hijacked an airplane to take him to New Jersey."

"Can I help it?" yelled Firgus. "It's what happened!"

"Yeah, well, one of us is having a bad dream," Bullock said, "and since you're at the wheel I hope it's me." He shook his head and lay down again. "Wake me up when we get to the Delaware Water Gap. I don't want to miss the expressions on their faces when we drive up to the tollbooth."

Firgus stayed half turned in the seat, glowering at him. "When we get to Pittsburgh," he said, "I am going to punch you in the mouth." And he faced front, turned the Vela around, took off, and flew in a bright fury all the way to Pittsburgh.

THE AKINZI AMBASSADOR to the United Nations was a large stout man named Nkolimi. One rainy October afternoon, Ambassador Nkolimi was sitting in his private dining room in the Akinzi mission, a narrow townhouse on East 63rd Street in Manhattan, when a member of the staff came in and said, "Ambassador, there is a man outside who wants to see you."

The ambassador was eating a Sara Lee Cinnamon Nut Coffee Cake. The whole thing, all by himself, as his midafternoon snack for today. With it he was drinking coffee with cream and sugar, enjoying himself hugely. He said, "What does he want to see me about?"

"He says it concerns the Balabomo Emerald."

The ambassador lifted an eyebrow. "Really. Bring him here."

Dortmunder was ushered into his presence, and the ambassador motioned for him to sit down across the table. Nkolimi, still chewing and swallowing, made hand motions suggestive of offering some coffee cake to Dortmunder, but Dortmunder said, "No, thank you." The ambassador drank some more coffee, swallowed hugely, patted his lips with his napkin, and said, "Ahh. Now. I understand you want to talk about the Balabomo Emerald."

"That's right," Dortmunder said, "but this is just between you and me. No police."

"Well, they're looking for it, of course."

"Sure." Dortmunder looked at the staff member standing alertly near the door, and back at the ambassador. "I don't like saying things in front of two witnesses, that's all," he said.

The ambassador smiled and shook his head. "You'll have to chance it, I'm afraid," he said. "I prefer not to be alone with strangers."

Dortmunder thought about it for a few seconds, then said, "All right. A little over four months ago, somebody stole the Balabomo Emerald."

"I know that," said the ambassador.

"It's very valuable," Dortmunder said.

The ambassador nodded. "I know that too," he said. "Are you building up to an offer to sell it back to me?"

"Not exactly," said Dortmunder. "Most valuable stones," he said, "have imitations made up by their owners, to put on display here and there. Are there any imitations of the Balabomo Emerald?"

"Several," said the ambassador. "And I dearly wish one of them had been on display at the Coliseum."

Dortmunder glanced mistrustfully at the staff member, then said, "I'm here to offer a trade."

"A trade?"

"The real emerald for one of the imitations."

The ambassador waited for Dortmunder to go on, then said with a puzzled smile, "I'm afraid I don't understand. The imitation, and what else?"

"Nothing else," Dortmunder said. "A straight trade, one stone for another."

"I don't follow that," the ambassador admitted.

"Oh, and one thing more," Dortmunder said. "You don't make any public announcement that you've got it back until I give you the all clear. Maybe a year or two, maybe less."

The ambassador pursed his lips. "It seems to me," he said, "you have a fascinating story to tell."

"Not in front of two witnesses," said Dortmunder.

"Very well," said the ambassador and turned to his staff member. "Wait out in the hall."

When they were alone, the ambassador said, "Now."

"Here's what happened," Dortmunder said, and told him the whole story, without names, except for Major Iko's. The ambassador listened, nodding, smiling, tut-tutting from time to time, and when Dortmunder was done he said, "Well. I suspected the Major might have something to do with the theft. All right, he tried to cheat you and you got the emerald back. Now what?"

"Someday," Dortmunder said, "the Major's going to come back with two hundred thousand dollars. It might be next month, next year, I don't know when, but I know it'll happen. He really wants that emerald."

"Talabwo does, yes," the ambassador said.

"So they'll raise the cash," Dortmunder said. "The last thing the Major shouted after me was that I should hold on to the emerald, he'd come pay me, and I know he will."

"But you don't want to give him the emerald anymore, is that it? Because he cheated you."

"Right. What I want to give him now is the business. And I will. That's why I want to work this trade. You get the real emerald, and keep it under wraps for a while. I take the imitation and hold on to it till the Major shows up. Then I sell it to him for two hundred thousand bucks, he takes it home to Africa on the plane, you break the story about having the real emerald back."

The ambassador gave a rueful smile. "They would not treat the Major well in Talabwo," he said, "if he paid two hundred thousand dollars for a piece of green glass."

"That's what I kind of thought."

Still smiling, the ambassador shook his head and said, "I must make a memo to myself never to try to cheat you."

Dortmunder said, "Is it a deal?"

"Of course it's a deal," said the ambassador. "Aside from having the emerald back, aside from anything else at all, it's a deal because I've waited years to give the Major one in the eye. I could tell some stories of my own, you know. Are you sure you won't have some coffee cake?"

"Maybe just a little slice," Dortmunder said.

"And some coffee. I insist." The ambassador glanced over at the rain-smeared window. "Isn't it a beautiful day?" he said.

"Beautiful," said Dortmunder.

ACKNOWLEDGMENTS
The condensations in this volume have been created by The Reader's Digest
Association, Inc., and are used by permission of and special arrangements with
the publishers and the holders of the respective copyrights.

Pioneer, Go Home!, copyright © 1959 by Richard Powell, is reprinted by permission of Curtis Brown, Ltd.
The Education of Hyman Kaplan by Leonard Q. Ross, copyright 1937 by Harcourt
Brace Jovanovich, Inc., renewed © 1965 by Leo Rosten, is reprinted by permission of Harcourt Brace Jovanovich, Inc., and Constable & Company, Ltd.
The Secret of Santa Vittoria, copyright © 1966 by Robert Crichton, is reprinted by
permission of Simon & Schuster, Inc., and Hodder & Stoughton, Ltd.
THE NIGHT THE GHOST GOT IN is taken from *My Life and Hard Times*, copyright
1933 by James Thurber, renewed © 1961 by Helen Thurber, reprinted by
special arrangement with the estate.
THE FAMILY THAT PLAYS TOGETHER GETS ON EACH OTHER'S NERVES is taken
from *Just Wait Till You Have Children of Your Own!*, copyright © 1971 by Erma
Bombeck and Bil Keane, reprinted by permission of Doubleday & Company,
Inc., and Methuen London, Ltd.
OUT OF THE NEST is taken from *At Wit's End* by Erma Bombeck, copyright ©
1965, 1966, 1967 by Newsday, Inc., reprinted by permission of Doubleday &
Company, Inc.
CARNIVAL WEEK IN SUNNY LAS LOS, copyright 1930 by Robert C. Benchley,
renewed © 1958 by Gertrude Benchley, is taken from *The Benchley Roundup*,
edited by Nathaniel Benchley, reprinted by permission of Harper & Row,
Publishers, Inc.
INSERT FLAP "A" AND THROW AWAY is taken from *Keep It Crisp*, copyright 1944,
renewed © 1972 by S. J. Perelman, reprinted by permission of Random House, Inc.
Mr. Blandings Builds His Dream House, copyright 1946 by Eric Hodgins, renewed
© 1974 by Frank G. Jennings, is reprinted by permission of Simon & Schuster, Inc.
The Hot Rock, copyright © 1970 by Donald E. Westlake, is reprinted by permission of Knox Burger Associates, Ltd.

ILLUSTRATION CREDITS
Pages 1–5: Sanford Kossin.
Original illustrations for *Mr. Blandings Builds His Dream House*, pages 413–504,
by William Steig for FORTUNE Magazine, copyright 1946 by Time, Inc.